Creating Links and Innovative Overviews for a New History Research Agenda
for the Citizens of a Growing Europe

THEMATIC WORK GROUP 5

Frontiers and Identities
III

CLIOHRES.net is a largescale research project, supported by the European Commission through the Sixth Framework Programme of its Directorate General for Research as a "Network of Excellence" for European History. It includes 180 researchers (90 staff and 90 doctoral students) from 45 universities in 31 countries. Working together in six thematic work groups, their aim is to achieve greater understanding of both the histories and the representations of the past current in Europe today, highlighting both diversities and connections.

The Consortium

Karl-Franzens-Universität Graz (Austria)
Universiteit Gent (Belgium)
Sofiyski Universitet "Sveti Kliment Ohridski" (Bulgaria)
Univerzita Karlova v Praze (Czech Republic)
Panepistimio Kyprou (Cyprus)
Roskilde Universitetscenter (Denmark)
Tartu Ülikool (Estonia)
Turun Yliopisto (Finland)
Université Pierre Mendès-France, Grenoble II (France)
Université de Toulouse II - Le Mirail (France)
Forschungszentrum Europäische Aufklärung (Germany)
Otto-Friedrich-Universität Bamberg (Germany)
University of Aberdeen (Great Britain)
Cardiff University (Great Britain)
University of Sussex (Great Britain)
Ethniko kai Kapodistriako Panepistimio Athinon (Greece)
Aristotelio Panepistimio Thessalonikis (Greece)
Debreceni Egyetem (Hungary)
Miskolci Egyetem (Hungary)
Háskóli Íslands (Iceland)
National University of Ireland, Galway/Ollscoil na hÉireann, Gaillimh (Ireland)
Università di Bologna (Italy)
Università degli Studi di Milano (Italy)
Università degli Studi di Padova (Italy)
Università di Pisa (Italy)
Latvijas Universitāte, Riga (Latvia)
L-Università ta' Malta (Malta)
Universiteit Utrecht (The Netherlands)
Universitetet i Oslo (Norway)
Uniwersytet Jagiellonski, Krakow (Poland)
Universidade de Coimbra (Portugal)
Universidade Aberta (Portugal)
Universitatea Babeş Bolyai din Cluj-Napoca (Romania)
Universitatea 'Stefan cel Mare', Suceava (Romania)
Moskowskij Gosudarstvennyj Oblastnoj Universitet (Russian Federation)
Univerzitet u Novom Sadu (Serbia)
Slovenskej Akademie Vied (Slovakia)
Univerza v Mariboru (Slovenia)
University of KwaZulu-Natal (South Africa)
Universidad de Alcalá de Henares (Spain)
Universidad de Deusto (Spain)
Universidad Autónoma de Madrid (Spain)
Universitat de Valencia (Spain)
Universität Basel (Switzerland)
Orta Dogu Teknik Üniversitesi (Turkey)

Frontiers and Identities
Cities in Regions and Nations

edited by
Luďa Klusáková and Laure Teulières

To Michele for a good memory
of her first visit to Prague.

Cordially from one of
the authors
Luďa

27.10.2011

EDIZIONI
plus
pisa university
press

Frontiers and identities : cities in regions and nations / edited by Lud'a Klusáková and Laure Teulières. - Pisa : Plus-Pisa university press, 2008. – (Thematic work group. 5, Frontiers and identities; 3)
302.5 (21.)

1. Individuo e società 2. Identità <psicologia sociale> I. Klusáková, Lud'a II. Teulières, Laure

CIP a cura del Sistema bibliotecario dell'Università di Pisa

This volume is published thanks to the support of the Directorate General for Research of the European Commission, by the Sixth Framework Network of Excellence CLIOHRES.net under the contract CIT3-CT-2005-006164.
The volume is solely the responsibility of the Network and the authors; the European Community cannot be held responsible for its contents or for any use which may be made of it.

Cover: Paul Klee (1879-1940), *Rocky Coast*, 1931, oil on plywood, Hamburg, Hamburger Kunsthalle.
Photo: Elke Walford. ©2005. Photo Scala, Florence/Bildarchiv Preussischer Kulturbesitz, Berlin

Published by Edizioni Plus – Pisa University Press
Lungarno Pacinotti, 43
56126 Pisa
Tel. 050 2212056 – Fax 050 2212945
info.plus@adm.unipi.it
www.edizioniplus.it - Section "Biblioteca"

Member of
Association of American University Presses

ISBN: 978-88-8492-556-5

Linguistic Revision
Kieran Hoare, Rhys Morgan, Gerald Power

Informatic editing
Răzvan Adrian Marinescu

Contents

Preface

Frontiers and Identities: Cities in Regions and Nations, edited by Professors Luďa Klusáková and Laure Teulières, is the third volume published by the Thematic Work Group 5 of the pan-European Network of Excellence for interdisciplinary historical research, CLIOHRES.net. The Work Group deals with "Frontiers and Identities". The present volume is particularly concerned with exploring approaches to the relationship between cities as places of creation, perception and representation of identities and political and territorial organisms, both within the city and outside of it.

Thanks to its particular multi-disciplinary approach – located between history, sociology and memory or culture studies – in this volume the Work Group has decided to focus on cities as optimal entrées for understanding how people give meanings to the physical places where they live and work. At the same time, by emphasizing the links between individuals' subjective experiences and their broader allegiances or belongings (political, ethnic, linguistic, religious, gender and so forth), the authors draw the city as a mirror that reflects the wider spaces and changing organisations that lie outside: hence the "regions" and the "nations" of the title.

In many of the cases considered, time – and the often dramatic events that take place in time, not least in recent centuries – is placed in correlation with the ways urban space is perceived and represented. Thus changes in cities (e.g. Kiev before, during and after the First World War; Thessaloniki from a multicultural to an ethnically divided city between the 19th and the early 20th century), and the perception of them by citizens, are read anew; at the same time, the ways citizens more or less consciously promote changes in the perceptions of cities (e.g. through city monuments or the writing of city histories) are also investigated. The theoretical underpinning of sociological and historiographical discourses on cities and the many boundaries that circle them, divide them and link them to broader regions and nations – producing multiple identities – is the central object of the volume, which continues the previous work of the Group, and prepares for the next step, the finalisation of its results on frontiers and borders as seen from regional and national perspective.

The cover illustration is Paul Klee's *Rocky Coast*, painted in 1931. A coast is a quintessential frontier, in that it has a clear spatial location and a lively border area while it indubitably demarcates territories that are truly and objectively diverse – the realm of the sea and the realm of the *terra firma*. It is everything that political frontiers usually purport to be but rarely are. The contradictory and conflictive aspect of this rugged coast with its sharp intersecting geometries seems appropriate for a volume that examines the changing frontiers in minds and perceptions of people who may even walk along the same streets and cross the same plazas while thinking quite different things.

The research group which has created this volume operates as part of the larger CLIOHRES Network, dedicated to exploring how better knowledge and more widespread understanding of the history of Europe can contribute to building European citizenship. For making this work possible we thank first of all the European Commission which supports the Network through its Sixth Framework Programme. We also thank the Rector Prof. Marco Pasquali, Pro-rector Paolo Miccoli and the Administration of the University of Pisa (in the persons of Dr Riccardo Grasso, Administrative Director, and Drs Vincenzo Tedesco and Cristiana Barghini) for their indispensable support for the complex tasks undertaken to coordinate the Network. And we thank the CLIOHRES team (Laura Burgisano, Laura Franciosi, Răzvan Adrian Marinescu and Giuseppe Bagnato) for their dedication and their intelligent and effective work in a variety of sectors, including those directly connected with publication.

We especially praise the Thematic Work Group 5, its members, its leaders and both the editors of this volume. They have been exemplary in their determination to debate and clarify the underlying issues and conceptual frameworks that distinguish different directions of research in the social sciences and the humanities. Cities – in regions and nations – are used as a testing ground and as an exemplification of the theoretical premises. The Work Group has taken seriously the opportunity and the challenge of using the human and intellectual resources of our Network to reach a better understanding of the conceptual and factual backgrounds of historical studies in different European contexts.

Our thanks also go to Professor Steven G. Ellis for organising the linguistic review and to Kieran Hoare, Rhys Morgan and Gerald Power for carrying it out.

Ann Katherine Isaacs
University of Pisa

Guðmundur Hálfdanarson
University of Iceland

The CLIOHRES Network of Excellence

CLIOHRES is a consortium of 45 universities and research institutions in 31 countries. Each institution is represented by two senior researchers and two doctoral students coming from various academic fields – primarily from history, but also from art history, archaeology, architecture, philology, political science, literary studies and geography. The 180 researchers in the network are divided into six "Thematic Work Groups", each of which deals with a broadly defined research area – 'States, Institutions and Legislation', 'Power and Culture', 'Religion and Philosophy', 'Work, Gender and Society', 'Frontiers and Identities', and 'Europe and the World'. Furthermore, the Network as a whole addresses 'transversal themes' of general relevance. These include 'Citizenship', 'Migration', 'Tolerance and Discrimination', 'Gender' and 'Identities'; one of these is targeted each year.

As a Network of Excellence, CLIOHRES is not an ordinary research project. It does not focus on a single research question or on a set of specific questions. Rather it is conceived as a forum where researchers representing various national and regional traditions can meet and elaborate their work in new ways thanks to structured interaction with their colleagues. The objective is not only to transcend the national boundaries that still largely define historical research agendas, opening new avenues for research, but also to use those very differences to become critically aware of how current research agendas have evolved. Thus, the goal is to examine basic and unquestioned attitudes about ourselves and others, which are rooted in the ways that the scientific community in each country looks at history. Historians create and cultivate selective views of the national or local past, which in turn underpin pervasive ideas about identities and stereotypes: national, religious, gender, political, etc. National historiographies today are still largely shaped by problems and preoccupations reflecting previous political and cultural contexts. CLIOHRES aims to create and promote a new structure and agenda for the community of historical research, redirecting its critical efforts along more fruitful lines.

The Network began its work in June 2005, thanks to a five-year contract with the European Commission through the Sixth Framework Programme of its Directorate General for Research, under Priority 7, dealing with "Citizenship". Its activities aim to contribute to the development of innovative approaches to history as regards both the European Research Area and European Higher Education Area. The Network works for a closer connection between research and learning/teaching, holding that this is essential in order to ensure that European citizens possess the necessary information, conceptual tools and more in general the vital critical and self-critical abilities which they will need in the future.

All the thematic groups have worked from the start according to a common research plan, beginning in the first year with reconnaissance or mapping, of how the questions perceived as important for the thematic area appear in the different national historiographies. During the second year they defined 'connecting' themes, which are relevant for research in a wider geographical and chronological context. The third phase has concentrated on comparing and reviewing sources and methodologies; the fourth will focus on cross-fertilisation, that is on showing how problems identified in the previous phases can be developed in new contexts. During the last phase, the groups will define new and relevant projects, in the broadest sense, for future research in the sector.

Each Thematic Work Group publishes one volume a year in order to share and discuss the results of their work with the broader academic community.

The volumes are not conceived as the final word on the issues that they deal with, but rather as work-in-progress. In addition to the six Thematic Work Group volumes, the Network publishes one common volume per year dealing with the transversal theme targeted. It also publishes abridged versions of the dissertations written by doctoral students who have participated in its work. Together the volumes already published form an invitation to discuss the results of the Network and the novel directions that are emerging from its work; they also constitute a unique patrimony of up-to-date studies on well-known and less well-known aspects of Europe and its history.

All publications are available in book form and on the www.cliohres.net website. Thei can be downloaded without charge. A list of publications to date can be found at the end of this volume.

Introduction: Urban Borders and Identities in Regional and National Contexts

This multi-authored volume emerged from discussions held by the members of the Thematic Work Group 5 of the CLIOHRES research Network of Excellence, and further discussions at one of the main sessions of the international conference of the European Association for Urban History at Stockholm at the end of August 2006. The session was organized both in and outside our group in collaboration with and among urban historians: Marjaana Niemi (Tampere), Richard Rodger (Edinburgh), Jaroslav Miller (Olomouc) and Luďa Klusáková (Prague), who co-chaired the session on borders and identities within cities. The theme proved very attractive and encouraged many others to present their papers and to attend the discussions. The idea for the format and structure of this collective volume concerning urban and regional spatial scales of borders and identities took shape in discussions following the Stockholm EAUH conference. Thus, the core chapters of the book originated in conference papers for the session in Stockholm given by Blanka Szeghyová (Bratislava), Iakovos Michailidis (Thessaloniki), Jaroslav Ira (Prague), Bram Vannieuwenhuyze (Ghent), Frédéric Moret (Paris), and Ruth Wallach (Los Angeles). The particular form of the chapters was then worked out by means of collaboration between the authors and through further discussions, particularly during the research meetings of the Thematic Work Group 5 during the year 2007 in Bratislava (February), Krakow (September) and Malta (December). The full team of authors was again drawn from the members of the Work Group, both its senior members and their doctoral students, and also from the larger circle of research collaborators in the Group who all helped to make the process of preparing this book so very stimulating and challenging. Although all the chapters are single-authored, they are result of lively team discussions and subsequently of a peer-reviewing procedure. Most typically, the interests of members of the Group lie predominantly in peripheral societies, in a comparative approach, in a clear formulation of familiar and established concepts, and in a symbolic attempt at least not to be exclusively Eurocentric.

The members of the Thematic Work Group are fully aware that the approaches, methods, analytical tools, and the types of sources used differ considerably, and particularly so given the very varied range of issues studied within the research field of frontiers and identities. A logical form of progression in the project leads us to focus in this book on problems of methods and sources, and to elaborate these problems by focusing on research outcomes in regard to such pertinent issues as intercultural communication, jurisdictions, the management of urban space from the middle ages to modernity, and the identification of urban communities both within and beyond the city's borders. One result of the debates was to highlight the need to address the linkage of the city's identity both with its hinterland, as well as with the wider region. Exploration of these issues pointed to the use of memory, heritage and art in constructing identity and in protecting identity by means of erecting various kinds of barriers. In this way, the principal issues of interest for research were gradually formulated, and the various chapters of our book put together.

At the meeting in particular of the Thematic Work Group in Bratislava entitled "Territorial Frontiers – Urban Identities" there was a lively brainstorming discussion which advanced considerably the conceptual debate surrounding the links between local and regional identities and the (de)construction of borders between the two. By way of an introduction to this volume, we should accordingly like to provide a foretaste of this very creative and stimulating collective work by reporting on some of the debates or controversies concerning the approach to problems discussed in the book[1]. At the Bratislava meeting a larger than normal group of external collaborators participated, and there was in particular an introductory contribution by Miroslav Hroch (Prague) which addressed the key issues of the definition and the concept of the region. This concept of a region is probably now the most frequently used term in this field of research, as it is linked to the study of problems both on national and transnational scales, and in their local dimensions. The term region is used in the context of place, town, country, state, and other names of spaces with regard to their particular dimensions. Our debates revolved in particular around definitions of urban and regional focus, and led to the formulation of the idea to organize our research discussions, and later the resultant volume, by focusing firstly on the problems of borders and identities in an urban context, so as to analyze the position of towns and urban society both within regions and in respect to national societies. The discussions highlighted a major need to clarify our understanding of how cities are currently approached as a legible text. Our discussions, moreover, also suggested the need to expand on and develop the contribution of the Chicago school as an inspiring approach for historians. By debating these points in a comparative context, it was possible to identify the varying usages of terms which express differences in size and also, in particular, in status in regard to towns and cities (*ville, bourg, bastide, město, městečko* and so on in other languages), which do not replicate the model of dichotomy between 'town' and 'city': in some parts of Europe the term 'city' historically denotes the seat of the cathedral, regardless of the city's size. Our discussions analysed in depth the shaping of identity by means of social frontiers, areas of exemption or interdiction, as for instance the gendered prohibition around medieval sanctuaries (William Aird). These processes highlight the constant struggle for space, and also indicate how traditions can establish boundaries. Nonetheless, these boundaries can be renegotiated as required.

Our discussion underlined the point that the development of the role of towns within a larger social context, and also the establishment of networks of towns, cannot be studied without taking into account the influence of the processes of state formation on the relationship between towns/cities and regions. As Steven Ellis suggested with reference to late medieval/early modern Europe, where there are city-states (as in Italy) or a cities with a significant hinterlands abutting a territorial frontier (the frontier between the United Provinces and Spanish Flanders, where control of the town determines the loyalty of its surrounding hinterland), relations between town and country are quite different from relations between town and country in a centralized kingdom (such as England – and also, in certain periods, France or Spain). In the former case tensions between town and country (and so senses of identity) are much less pronounced, because the countryside relies on the town for protection; whereas in a centralized kingdom town and country have less in common. The instrumental use and exploitation of the economic power of towns by the state and by royalty respectively calls for an in depth contents analysis of urban political strategies.

Our discussions also tackled the concept of "community": that is, religious and/or ethnic groups bonded by strong relations and a solidarity such as to be perceived as an entity by the surrounding society. In fact these frontiers appeared many times more fluid than fixed. Each community had a cultural heartland, but it often also had designated meeting points with the other communities in the city where they interacted while maintaining their own distinctive identity. It is thus important to analyse the everyday experience of inhabitants, the degree of closeness and direct contacts. The question of multi-ethnic relations needs therefore to be studied not only with statistical sources, but also linked to the relations between groups and individuals, as a complex social interplay. Our debates reminded us that historians have to be careful not to create communities artificially by using certain terms without a critical analysis.

Critical comments during debates at the following September meeting in Krakow were again offered in regard to the application of the theories of Immanuel Wallerstein. His ideas are still seen as both provocative and inspiring, and also offering both misleading and helpful insights in terms of core and periphery models of World System theory. The cores as well as peripheries are complex regions, which are hardly ever homogeneous. They may break into smaller regional units interlinked by hierarchically organized interdependences of core-periphery type within cores, semi-peripheries or peripheries. Thus a semi-peripheral region like Transylvania within the Hungarian kingdom or, during the time of its expansion, the Ottoman Empire, also had further internal subdivisions. For instance, the particular position of both Transylvania and of Transylvanian cities in a regional context displays this type of core-periphery relationship.

Very lively and even agitated debate continued about terms and concepts in relation to the contemporary situation in urban societies. First, there was the discussion about "ruralization/rurbanization" which is used for structural and social changes in the social space of Polish cities after World War II. Is this a modern concept for a modern phenomenon, caused by migrations, administrative changes and propaganda, or can it be used historically? Many members argued that it is only acceptable for the communist era when there was a programme of expelling urban elites and bringing in new people.

This is especially true of communist Poland which provides an example of ideological urbanisation: all towns were planned to be cities and peasants were disliked. In the Polish discourse, "rurbanisation" always refers to cities and towns: "agro-towns" were designed to be like cities (Barbara Klich). But other participants argued that it cannot be compared with other phenomena outside of its context. In France, in particular, rurbanisation has a different meaning in regard to rural areas that have become urbanised (Jean-Francois Berdah). There were also other terms used in this discussion, for example, the "crab-grass frontier", viz. a frontier which banishes the 'wild' rural attributes and expands the 'civil' urban space in the context of "rurbanisation" as studied by American urban historians – in other words, the expansion of contemporary cities to incorporate rural surroundings. According to Polish historians, "rurbanisation" means more than this: it was a plan to create a city lifestyle through reconstructing space and creating private space; it was a political strategy of the Polish communist state to transform modes of life. Thus "rurbanisation" produces borders in the city between old and new inhabitants (Ewelina Szpak). Some other commentators suggested that Poland was perhaps a specific case due to the state of rural society; but comparable processes in other European countries were also outlined. In the former Czechoslovakia the communist regime there also determined that rural life should be 'civilised' by the formal introduction of urban characteristics, such as the building of apartment houses for rural workers.

Finally, the discussion within the Group underlined the importance of defining such terms. Authors were asked to take into account a broader context – changes within the cities during the period considered, the gap caused by World War II, and consequently the fact that social norms have also changed. Another question is: how do the newcomers see the cities as compared to the natives? What values did the newcomers acquire in the city? The problem here is in some measure the lack of written sources from such people themselves.

The question of sources was also debated in regard to the historiography of towns, both as an indicator and as a factor in local identity. Many questions arose for historians. Who writes monographs? Who are the patrons? Who finances the books which are published? Were they successful? All these questions help us to understand the main theme of identity. At least in Czech case, those books published during the 19th century were written by a cultural elite, but the authors themselves were rarely locals. They were mostly mobile persons, often migrating teachers, sometimes clergy who themselves decided to write or were employed to do so by local elites. The audiences for these books were often very small; other readers included historians, visitors to the town, and even a patriotically-minded general public. These books usually included very different genres: not only a very historical narrative, but also geographical descriptions, practical information, a promotional discourse, and so on. They were much more important for small towns about which very little was written. Discussion then turned to local identity. Bearing in mind that they are created out of multiple identities, do small towns have an identity? Can one measure it? Or is this just propaganda? How do translocal and regional identities differ? Local identity contains a sense of belonging but not only that. Both identity and belonging have to be defined in a chronological perspective. Research has to reveal the historical content of a term and this will eventually help to create definitions which are more suitable for a particular period and/or an area of study.

The Group also tackled the problem of terminology used in various linguistic milieux in relation to the premodern socio-spatial collective identites. It was concluded that for the period before modern nationalism, the term "nationality" is not relevant; and the suggestion has been made to use the term "ethnic groups" as a more neutral descriptor. Quite often the term "nationality" is used to depict identification with a large collectivity with a shared history, language or territory in various historical conditions, but is this effective? It has been suggested that it is not relevant term before the modern period, and some participants think that it does not help to talk about "ethnic groups" (Steven Ellis). In Ireland, for instance, there is an established literature about English nationality in the later medieval lordship of Ireland, based on the fact that the population was conventionally divided into two nations, English and Irish. And these were the normal terms used in the records of the period, for instance "John Smith, of English blood and nation". However, the term "ethnic groups", in the period when modern nation building activities are about to take off, is thought to be appropriate by others (Elena Mannová).

Similar discussions were held about modern travel literature and the representation of urban space and places of memory. Does travel literature become part of the self-image of the city? Do 18th-century travel writings show that towns were attempting to improve their image or were (re)branding themselves? Bratislavan writers refer to travel writer accounts: often local books on Bratislava cite gossip in travel accounts as a reason for writing. Already at this date, there appears a tendency towards 'branding' towns in travel writings, even before the period when modern tourism began to emerge in the 19th century. Travel writing and travel as an instrument for the transfer of perceptions across different countries is obviously an attractive area for comparative research.

All these discussions, which also continued in late November in Malta, thus approached from different angles the question of the elaboration of a regional identity and the use of the region as a concept. What is at stake nowadays in the public usage of the historical and cultural heritage in regard to the building of collective identity? How are representations of history exploited for the branding of heritage towns and in regard to the heritage industry? We can observe this in comparative perspective in central Europe and in southwestern France in this book, but it is a much wider problem which might be observed and analysed from an extensive list of examples. Yet in establishing a heritage industry townspeople have developed national, regional and local identities. There is also a rural/urban border – towns which are viewed as rural from the capital, but as urban from their hinterlands. The development of a strategy for change and revival has opened up an important role for events in tourism. But what are people losing and gaining in this changed strategy? Sometimes the heritage industry strategy is imposed from outside. For example, many Polish towns are now copying Krakow, which has emphasised its multi-culturality and the blending of cultures. Many smaller towns have, for example, sought to rediscover their Jewish heritage, and they have highlighted some heritage identities over others. However, there is a need to develop other tools to link history, culture and economics. For example, how the heritage industry has branded itself says a lot about the forms of identity which it is trying to project. The debate demonstrated that historians wonder and ponder about the way history and the heritage industry interact with each other. The way history is manipulated to make it marketable is problematic – it often leads to a sanitised version of history – particularly when the role of the historian in this process is considered. A sociologist noted how the use of observation may differ in sociology, where it has a very specific meaning, and in regard to history, where it is used in a much looser manner. Does observation involve visiting sites? Does it consist of silent observation? And what is the role of informants? Observation was integrated as a point of departure and was only one of many sources used.

In response to the discussions reflected in the foregoing comments, the present volume is divided into four parts. It opens with a theoretical and methodological section, entitled "Concepts, Methods and Approaches", which comprises three chapters. These were designed with intention of deepening the thematic field of studies, being a part of the Group's work in identifying, defining and clarifying terms. The opening section outlines the discussion about what is meant by the city: often we are seemingly talking about the same thing, but this is not so. What is stressed here is the importance of the city-as-a-system-of-meanings approach and the need for adequate analytical tools, i.e. taken from anthropology or sociology. Walter Benjamin and Richard Sennett are held up as two key theoreticians of cities. Along with the social organisation of space, which has to be divided and labelled in order to be intelligible to those who use it, there is also the question of the types of urban spatial borders and their labels. One of most obvious, and at the same time constantly controversial, themes is the division between public and private, which has been restructured in the modern era. This concept is linked mainly to the work of Jürgen Habermas. Frontiers and identities refer also to sexuality, sexual norms and representations, in other words to a "moral territory" which pervades both urban and rural contexts. Thus the first three chapters develop tools to examine areas which were hitherto hidden in history and which offer fresh perspectives on how to examine history.

There then follow three large sections of the book which treat problems that the team of authors found essential for understanding and explaining problems of identification both within and between cities and also in linking cities within and between regions. The second section focuses on the topic "Internal administrative/physical borders creating identities". Using primary sources, the chapters underline changes in the way of conceiving and creating urban boundaries between medieval times and the early modern period. The names of territories often refer to morphological urban elements (town walls, places, buildings, streets, etc.) or administrative delimitations. Spatial terminology appears thus as a challenge in regard to a comparative historical perspective in Europe. The section presents some cases of such translation problems: *wijcken* in Brussels, *la zone* in Paris, etc. Taken as a whole, the chapters suggest a typology of urban areas: the delimitation of each type of territory and its social or political functions within urban society, varied in time and space. The authors think that internal administrative and physical borders were very important, and that they strongly influenced the self-identification of those who were enclosed within the spaces or excluded from them. We can observe these processes both in the middle ages and also in modernity. Another transversal theme links the urbanisation process to the formation and transformation of urban social groups set apart from their hinterlands.

From the perspective of urban communities which are composed of many variously defined groups, this process of identification is on the one hand accompanied by the spontaneous construction of borders and on the other by the policies of urban governments, religious hierarchies, and the politics of the state. These questions are explored across time in the section "Religions – Ethnicities – Mentalities – Politics", which demonstrates how important these problems were across Europe and in relation to the modernization of its societies. The chapters in this section provide in particular comparative insights about mutual relationships and coexistence between groups in modern and early modern Europe. The authors use a large spectrum of primary sources. Some research is based especially on ego-documents, affording space to testimonies, subjective experiences and popular voices, as for instance autobiographies or a specific genre of Rabbinic literature (*Responsa*). Cases of multicultural and multiconfessional neighbourhoods or local environments have been found in Ottoman society, Hungarian or Transylvanian cities, as well as in the northern Republic of Latvia. By contrast, strong inner frontiers created segregated cities where populations were politically, religiously and juridically divided. Authors insist on the role of influential stereotypes which contributed to deep and stable mental frontiers. The development of collective identities, of national consciousness, led to divisions amongst neighbours and the growth of nationalism, as we see between the Bulgarians and the Greeks in Thessaloniki. The formation of 'ethnic milieux' split Baltic Germans from Latvians during the interwar period, creating a gap which was visible in terms of segregated residential conditions and the relative rarity of personal inter-ethnic contacts. This is obvious in regard to the racial segregation policy and the enforced Germanisation of the Polish town of Krakow during World War II.

While the third section deals with social and political realities, and their perception, the last section, "Local and regional identities reflected and (re)created", focuses on the problem of reflections of place in the larger regional context and on the role of history and art in various creations and reconstructions of local and regional identities, mainly in modern and contemporary society.

If the chapters devoted to urban and regional spatial scales of borders and identities attract the attention of students and researchers interested in social history, they will demonstrate that the study of these problems through the optics of urban structures and their hinterlands and wider regions adds another perspective to social history. Urban history cannot be reduced to a mere city biography. We still see that urban studies are not equally strong in the different European historiographies. The chapters in this volume do not really reflect these differences, as they represent only the interests of members of the Thematic Work Group. Looking at the social history of Europe through the optics of urban societies in a wider European context is an effective way forward. This perspective demonstrates the strength of urban studies within social history. The chapters point to the interest of a young generation of historians who wish first to tie their research into the context of international methodological debates, and second to locate the urban issues of their respective national urban networks in the wider context of larger regions – or even in those wider European comparative perspectives which also view peripheral regions in comparative perspective with the core. Although Wallerstein's concept is viewed critically, the concepts of core, semi-periphery, periphery, internal periphery (Hans-Heinrich Nolte[2]) which it generated, or which were generated by the discussion initiated by Wallerstein, were used as terms which help effectively to place the phenomena or analysis of regions on the social and historical map of Europe. Research focused on the phenomena of urban life – like violence, or infiltrations of rural origin, and the export of urban modes of life – is all founded on inspiration either from ethnology or sociology. Precise terms are essential in this field of study, even though it is at the same time very hard to create precise terms for these concepts. Studies stemming from the interests of sociologists, geographers as well as historians start and end in terminological debates, controversies, and give rise to many questions. What are the features of European urban identity? How is it changing?

After many years of academic debates focused on the issue of identities and their spatial definitions, and with instrumental aid of borders, it is generally accepted that a self is composed of multiple identities and roles, and this same fact is valid also for social groups. Anthony D. Smith in his influential book *National Identity* enumerated as basic six identities: gender, as the essential one, and further familial, class, religious, ethnic, and last but not least, territorial. He also insisted that "each of these identities is based on social classifications that may be modified or even abolished"[3]. If Smith views gender cleavages as fundamental, in the second place he places the category of space. Territorial identities, be they local or regional are, according to Smith, "equally widespread, particularly in pre-modern eras"[4]. Also, he believes that localism and regionalism are more cohesive than gender identity. Further, regions often break into localities and even down to individual settlements. Despite this, he holds that regions rarely generate strong social movements, and regionalism is incapable of answering the particular needs of its population. Regions are geographically difficult to define, as "their boundaries are ragged" and "their centres are often multiple"[5]. As he is interested in national identity, it is only in this connection that he touches on territorial identities, as they are reflected in the nation state. Identities of cities and regions of various sizes and definitions are beyond the horizon of his interest.

The authors of this book hold that the identities of cities, their regions, and the borders they created, also influenced the history of European societies. Although it seems that they are particularly important in the integrated Europe of the present, they have a strong historical dimension. Smith is well aware of this: he chose as a paradigmatic text Sophocles and his *Oedipus Rex*. In this book, the authors do not venture back beyond the middle ages. On the other hand, beginning with the medieval city and continuing right through to the 21st century, they question the relations between space and identity, be it related to gender, religion, social status, ethnicity, or nationality. In the view of our contributors, territorial identity does not stand on its own. In modern societies the appropriation of territory is closely or even directly linked to the identification with the nation state. This connection of nation, territory and identity is one of the findings of Benedict Anderson in his *Imagined Communities*[6]. Imagined national communities have a common language, culture, history and territory. The permeable boundaries of Frederik Barth defined by ethnicity are most often nation-state boundaries, although they are also the symbolic borders transported by migrants in their cultural baggage[7]. For Larry Wolff, territorial identity is linked with culture or civilization of an imagined barbarous eastern Europe and a putative civilized west[8]. The team of authors in this book extends this questioning to smaller scales – towns and cities and their regions – in earlier periods, in modernity, as well as in the post-modern age. The inspiration for this can be seen not only in authors previously cited, but also in the work of Kevin Lynch and Michel de Certeau in reading the city as text, in understanding and identifying with it through using it[9]. Also motivating the discussion are the historiographical commentaries of Celia Applegate on the discussion of regionalism in Europe, and the concepts she has formulated in her monograph[10]. Here for readers find a common background in the chapters of the book.

The concept of borders and frontiers is, especially in public discourse, linked directly to variously defined territorial units. Inspired by geographers and sociologists in the multidisciplinary debates on the issues of the social organization of space, we propose to explore in the chapters of this book the spatial role of boundaries in the construction of socio-spatial identities, on the micro and mezzo level of spatial scales – in other words on local, urban and regional level[11]. But territories are not just about geographical or physical space. They may have many symbolic meanings, and extend to cultural, imaginary, gendered, fiscal, administrative, legal, and property boundaries, demarcated between private and public interests. Conveniently, these boundaries sometimes overlap precisely, but more often there are many layers of inexact overlap and conflicting jurisdictions, which forge alliances between interests, or generate tensions. At a theoretical level, urban polities were melting pots in which cultural, confessional and national diversities were mixed and homogenisation took place. In practice, however, such cohesion and unity proved unachievable and towns and cities were confronted with ongoing diversity – in religious, linguistic, political, cultural and ethnic forms. Amongst the consequences were a process of fragmentation and the rise of various frontiers within towns and cities. Thus inner frontiers developed through administrative procedures and local customs. Urban communities also sought to create an identity of their own which would underpin their role in the society of the region, state, or nation, and link them to, or identify them with any other larger unit.

Luďa Klusáková
Charles University in Prague
Laure Teulières
University of Toulouse II – Le Mirail

Notes

1 The fact that we were able to involve so many external collaborators in the discussions was in part due to the support provided by a research scheme of the Ministry of Education of the Czech Republic MSM 0021620827 *České země uprostřed Evropy v minulosti a dnes* [Czech Lands in the Middle of Europe, Past and Present], held by the Faculty of Philosophy and Arts of Charles University in Prague; which has thereby also contributed substantially to the genesis of the book.

2 See Nolte in his *Introduction* to H.-H. Nolte (ed.), *Internal Peripheries in European History,* Göttingen 1991.

3 A. D. Smith, *National Identity*, Reno 1991, p. 4.

4 *Ibid.*

5 *Ibid.*

6 B. Anderson, *Imagined communities: reflections on the origin and spread of nationalism*, London 1991.

7 F. Barth, *Introduction* in F. Barth (ed.), *Ethnic groups and boundaries. The Social Organization of Culture Diference*, Oslo 1969, pp. 9-38.

8 L.Wolff, *Inventing Eastern Europe: The Map of Civilization on the Mind of the Enlightenment*, Stanford 1994.

9 K. Lynch, *The Image of the City*, New York 1960; M. de Certeau, *The Practice of Everyday Life,* transl. by S. Rendall, Berkeley, Los Angeles 2002, particularly the chapter *Walking in the City*, pp. 91-110 (original edition: *L'invention du quotidien*, Paris 1974).

10 C. Applegate, *A Europe of Regions: Reflections on the Historiography of Sub-National Places in Modern Times*, "American Historical Review", 104, 1999, pp. 1157-1182; C. Applegate, *A Nation of Provincials. The German Idea of Heimat*, Berkeley - Los Angeles - Oxford 1990.

11 A. Paasi, *Region and place: regional identity in question*, "*Progress in Human Geography*", 28, 2003, 4, pp. 475-485.

Reading the City. Methodological Considerations on Urban History and Urban Studies

Dobrochna Kałwa
Jagiellonian University

Abstract

This chapter examines methodological concepts and theoretical implements used in urban studies and their impact on and development of historical research. Following a survey of debates on defining the city, the chapter presents three theoretical concepts that influenced the approach to the city in social science and opened up new prospects in urban history – the system of meanings, spatial terms of place, space, and borders, and the theory of liminality.

Historia miast nie jest wyłącznie domeną historyków, ale również przedstawicieli innych nauk społecznych – socjologii, antropologii, czy geografii humanistycznej. Ten zwrot ku historii jest przede wszystkim konsekwencją przyjęcia paradygmatu, który zakłada, że analiza fenomenu miasta wymaga spojrzenia z perspektywy międzykulturowej, jak i diachronicznej. Interdyscyplinarny wymiar historii miasta to również efekt braku większego zainteresowania nie tyle dziedziną, co teoriami i metodologicznymi koncepcjami stosowanymi przez badaczy miast, skutkiem czego wzajemna recepcja dorobku jest w dalszym ciągu utrudniona. Celem niniejszego tekstu jest prezentacja wybranych teorii z zakresu antropologii i socjologii i ich wykorzystania w badaniach nad historią miasta, która ma wskazać perspektywy dla dalszych badań, jakie powinny stać się udziałem także historyków.

Wśród kwestii tutaj analizowanych fundamentalne znaczenie ma ciągła debata antropologów i socjologów nad definicją miasta, dzięki której to dyskusji uwidacznia się zmienność zjawisk miejskich w czasie i przestrzeni. Szczególną pozycję zajmują koncepcje i terminy odnoszące się do przestrzeni, które są wykorzystywane do badania nie tylko fizykalnej struktury/planu miasta, ale także do badań zjawisk społecznych i kulturowych

Teoretyczna refleksja nad pojęciem miasta doprowadziła do poszerzenia obszaru badań o nowe, istotne kwestie dotyczące kulturowego wymiaru „życia miejskiego" – praktyk życia codziennego, form komunikacji i porozumiewania się mieszkańców, znaczenia systemu znaków wpisanego w przestrzeń i praktyki, form reprezentacji i historii wizji miasta, wreszczeie, systemu wartości i pamięci zbiorowej. Istotnym elementem współczesnych badań nad miastem jest jego semiotyczny system wszechobecnych znaków wpisanych w każdy wymiar miasta – od organizacji przestrzeni, poprzez symbole, po system praktyk życia codziennego. W tym ujęciu miasto jest tekstem kulturowym, pozwalającym na odczytanie i analizę wielowymiarowego fenomenu miejskiego, również jego historii.

Urban history is no longer the exclusive domain of historical research, but also of other social sciences, such as anthropology, sociology, social and human geography, semiotics, as well as cultural studies exploring the past[1]. This multidisciplinary interest in the history of cities has arisen due to two main factors. The first is connected with the comparative approach, both intercultural and diachronic, which is essential for urban studies. The quest for a universal definition of the city and models of urbanism has led social scientists to refer to knowledge of cities' past – their origins, transformations, developments and degenerations – since "an understanding of the origins and function of cities in the past will lead to an understanding of contemporary urbanisation"[2]. The second factor is intertwined directly with historiography. At the beginning of the 20th century, the dawn of urban studies, historians in general still adhered to a positivistic paradigm and mainly to political history; therefore they were hardly in a position to contribute to the development of urban studies, focused originally on the social and cultural aspects of the phenomenon of the city and "urbanism as a way of life"[3]. Although social and cultural history developed in the following decades, thus enabling historians to join urban studies, the past of cities remains a field of research which historians share with other social scientists.

Historians exploring urban history increasingly refer to theoretical and methodological concepts of social sciences, though not to the extent that they should. The main aim of this text is to focus on two main questions: whether anthropological and social concepts are useful implements and can provide fruitful inspirations for historians? And where the limits of interdisciplinary borrowings occur? Special attention will be paid here to three theoretical concepts present in contemporary urban studies: the semiotic system of meanings, urban borders, and liminality.

Conceptualising the City

A crucial issue in urban studies is the definition of the city. Social scientists have problems in reaching any consensus in this matter as the disparate approaches of the disciplines are concomitant with different theoretical criteria determining research interests and concepts of the city.

The Chicago School sociologists, such as Robert E. Park, William I. Thomas, Florian Znaniecki, Ernest Burgess, and Louis Wirth, who in the early 20th century carried out the first large-scale field research on urban society, referred directly to Chicago as the basis for their concepts of the city and the theory of urbanism. They undoubtedly followed the 19th-century European sociologists in perceiving the modern city, and urbanism in general, as a contemporary phenomenon arising from and integrally interwoven with the processes of modernisation, industrialisation and mass migration observed at that time. Strongly influenced by organicistic thinking, the sociologists from Chicago proposed to define the city "not only as a whole consisting of people, streets and buildings, but also as a 'state of mind', built up of traditions, customs, attitudes, and feelings, which were kept alive by these traditions"[4].

As a consequence of this integrative approach, the proposed model went beyond materialistic understanding of the city and urban space, though it remained extra-temporal and Western-centred. Similarly, the definition of urbanism proposed by Wirth was based on the terms of secularization, voluntary associations, segmented social roles, poorly defined norms, and an antithesis of rural community. Yet it did not take into consideration the historical and cultural diversification of cities and urban phenomena[5]. Other sociologists, such as Georg Simmel, associated the city with emancipation from traditional forms of social domination, and an increase of an individual's autonomy and self-identity. For the author of the segmentation theory, the city meant nothing but freedom, obviously a conclusion derived from the identification of the term "urban" with modernization[6].

It is no wonder that the anthropologists who studied very different urban societies of Latin America or Africa (e.g. the Manchester School) expressed doubts concerning sociological concepts excluding the cities which were irrelevant for the patterns of contemporary Western urban agglomerations. Sociologists' focusing on familiar "here and now" societies was concomitant with the dominating macro-level approach based on quantitative data – figures, statistics, and tables – ignoring an individual's experience. As a consequence of this perspective, as pointed out by Marc Blanchard, sociology constitutes an image of the city "as a reality of isolated facts and statistics" devoid of dwellers' emotions, thoughts and habits, and the dwellers themselves[7].

Anthropological reflection has been relevant in the development of urban studies. Focused on a human being rooted in culture, anthropologists put emphasis on an individual's experience and existence framed in urban culture. As culture is crucial for the anthropological approach, the city is defined as a cultural phenomenon combining space, time and social actors. Despite this difference, anthropologists retained some sociological criteria, such as transformation of social structure, fragmentation of social roles, and physical closeness of the dwellers. A good example of collaboration between anthropology and sociology is Ulf Hannerz's proposal to analyse urban culture according to segmented social roles performed by city dwellers[8]. There are mutual benefits between these two fields of social science, since sociologists doing micro-level research use anthropological implements for gathering and interpreting their data. Under the influence of anthropology, sociologists use the following criteria to outline the conditions essential for the city to function: socially constructed centre, functional and prestigious diversification of architecture, diversity of social space, and functions going beyond local environment[9].

Reciprocal development of the theoretical debate on the city broadens the spectrum of urban phenomena and makes urban scientists take into consideration historical issues also, these concerned with city origins and long-term changes within the city. Social scientists in urban studies tend to use history as a source of specific examples and data which they can analyse and use to create theoretical models. For example, the model of three urban types (i.e., the trade city, the city of power, and the industrial city) refers to the city-founding functions influencing spatial organisation, social diversification, and professional structure of dwellers. In his research on preindustrial cities, Gideon Sjøberg worked on the theoretical assumption that different types of societies, i.e. a preliterate society, a 'feudal' society and an industrial/urban society, correspond to different type of settlement. Sjøberg distinguished three models of societies in order to substantiate his comparative analysis of cities existing in different historical epochs and cultural areas[10]. This theoretical assumption blurs historical distinctions and ignores the range of diversification associated with the urban phenomena.

Such a use of history as the one mentioned above reveals sources of misunderstandings between a social scientist and a historian. The former perceives history as a collection of useful examples selected according to theoretical assumptions, even against the historical context[11]. On the other hand, theoretical debates on urbanism were rather beyond the field of interest of historians usually dealing with cities as unique, isolated objects always falling outside 'universal' definitions[12]. Instead of abstract theories, historians prefer to use general representations of the city derived from historical sources and based on physical, tangible or 'visible' elements. Historical reflection on urbanism takes on quite a different form:

> To understand the city, it is necessary to see it in its physical shape – city walls, streets, squares and symbolic buildings. They make the city excluded from rural landscape, and emphasize explicitly its distinctness from the countryside. Dense and walled-in, urban territory enabled the cities to gain independence[13].

This attitude is reflected also by those historians who refer to legal or administrative decisions in order to define the notion of a city. This practice has some limitations as it marginalizes the significance of other factors bound up directly with dwellers. It also omits the liminal aspects of urban life, such as history of towns deprived of city charter, the 19th-century industrial cities with a status of a village or towns that had more in common with villages than with the cities of the time[14].

The distance between social and historical approaches to the past based on a distinction between interpretation and reconstruction has been decreasing. History has become much more open to new paradigms from social sciences; therefore the mutual relations have been evolving into interdisciplinary collaboration. When in the 1970s and 1980s urban scientists became more interested in the mental sphere, imaginary and representative, as well as in the qualitative approach to investigation, micro-history turned out to be the relevant direction of research[15]. Since then, history has shared with anthropology and urban sciences an approach emphasizing the importance of anthropocentric, and most of all, cultural perspectives in research on the existential experience of a city dweller. These include, among others, community relations, identity building, the system of meanings or memory sites[16]. This leads, in turn, to a position where the central subject of urban history is not the city as such, but multidimensional civic life, which "is embedded in collective processes through which people living in the same urban space communicate, understand each other through familiar and distinctive signs, elaborate on the representations and visions of the city, cultivate certain values, appoint symbols of their affiliation and, simultaneously, preserve and adapt the memories of their experience"[17].

System of meanings

The anthropological approach to the city provides relevant implements for exploring multi-faceted aspects of urban history. One of the interesting and promising issues seems to be the system of meanings composed of objects [*significants*] and meanings attached to them (*signifiés*). To explore the semiotic dimensions of the city means to treat it as a (*cultural*) text on urban society. Reading the city does not concern recognizing signs attached to buildings, monuments, spatial structure and urbanistic plans only, but embraces other aspects of urban life:

> [Signs] are unconsciously repeated actions, characteristic of the habits understandable in our indigenous consciousness; other signs which constitute customs, are loaded with an axio-normative content. Such customs become norms enforced by social sanctions and group pressure. We read these signs and symbols of vernacularity in many cultural texts – in the landscape and architecture, in the profile of a church, in art, music and dance, in legends, local dialects and in the atmosphere prevailing at a Christmas Eve table[18].

The everyday life of city dwellers, norms determining social order and hierarchy, rituals, valorisation of spaces, conflicts, mobility and barriers – these all are elements of the system of meanings as well. The urban system of meanings is clear and obvious only to the dwellers, members of the cultural community; therefore reading the city requires interdisciplinary implements enabling researchers to decode messages inscribed directly and 'between the lines' rather than to interpret unfolded cultural/historical facts. In urban studies one might find all the variety of methods, for example a structuralistic net of dichotomous meanings[19], a thick description[20], an analysis of the city as a discourse or as a field for social play and rituals.

Sensitivity to tangible facts frees historians from the anthropological temptations of unfounded generalizations resulting from disregard to historical context. Anthropological tendencies to abstractive interpretation are criticized by anthropologists themselves. Clifford Geertz emphasizes the importance of taking into account a larger, I would here add, historical context in anthropological analyses of everyday life situations, rituals or other social events. In his opinion, both the lack of context and the preference for abstract models result in epistemological ambiguity, methodological vagueness[21] and, in consequence, unverifiable generalizations. On this account, semiotics pays special attention to describe and analyse specific manifestations of the system of meanings, including activity of social groups and institutions, historical context of analysed events, and dynamics of semiotic changes.

Urban historians provided with anthropological and semiotic implements usually recognize the historical city as a microcosm depicting visions and world outlook of the peoples of that time. Such an approach was represented by Walter Benjamin, one of the thinkers who exerted an influence on contemporary humanities, including urban history[22]. Benjamin had been analysing the semiotic dimension of the 19th-century city space, reflecting in his study the phenomena of modernisation, mass culture, ideology, social order and everyday life practices. In his work *The Arcade Project* (*Passagen-Werk*)[23], Benjamin explored the issue of structure, function and meanings of the Parisian Arcades as he reflected on the ambivalence of 19th-century modern society as a "landscape of consumption" and the egalitarian concepts encapsulated in the utopian phalanstere. According to Rollason, in Benjamin's interpretation, Arcades are:

> archetypal manifestations of the expanding market economy – creations of private enterprise and sources of profit, and most certainly not part of any public works project. The goods displayed are commodities – objects existing for profit above utility, manifestations of exchange value rather than use value: for Benjamin, they participate in the "fetishism of the commodity", the mystificatory conversion of human-made products into objects of irrational worship which Marx classically analyzed and denounced in the first volume of *Capital*[24].

The textual nature of the city emerges very clearly when Benjamin analyses and combines coherent elements: architecture, works by Baudelaire or Marx, or Fourier. Through reading the city, Benjamin reveals mental changes of 19th-century society personified in his works by a *flâneur* who experiences the city in a very new way:

> The streets become a dwelling for the *flâneur*; he is as much at home among the facades of houses as a citizen is in his four walls. To him the shiny, enamelled signs of businesses are at least as good a wall ornament as an oil painting to the bourgeois in his salon. The walls are the desk against which he presses his notebooks; newsstands are his libraries and the terraces of cafés are the balconies from which he looks down on his household after his work is done[25].

Benjamin was one of the very first researchers to consider the city as an *imago mundi*, a microcosm bound on other aspects of human existence and culture. Similarly, in his *Flesh and Stone*[26], Richard Sennett put emphasis on the anthropological, or more precisely anthropocentric approach to urban history. Sennett starts with an assumption that the city space is a mirror reflecting historically determined conceptualizations of a human body; thus, in consequence, he focuses on history of human experiences of physical dimensions. One by one he explores the meaning of nakedness for an ancient Athenian, visual sensitivity of citizens in the ancient Rome, the medieval concept of a sinful human body antithetic to the soul, and the impact of medical discourse on the conceptualization of both "flesh and stone" in modern times.

Obviously inspired by Michel Foucault, Sennett's reflection on the city concerns the history of discursive practices of power-knowledge that have been taking place on the levels of both dwellers' bodies and inhabited urban space. In his interpretation, the city is an arena where diversified social actors are constantly competing for control over creation, reproduction and change of the system of meanings. On the one hand, the city authorities strive to make the city space and the social order logical, rational, controllable and transparent with the purpose of governing the city efficiently. On the other hand, internally diversified and split, city dwellers tend to mould the city space according to their particular needs and interests. As Jacek Purchla noticed in his research on the development of cities of the Hapsburg Monarchy in the 19th century, "the natural process of urban development was always attended by a fundamental conflict between form and function. The changeability of function – as a dynamic element – forced the form of the cities to be altered, leading to the complete replacement of the fabric"[27]. However, such continuous rivalry and multifaceted tensions are the *sine qua non* of the existence and development of the city. When deprived of these, the city must die.

Anthropological interpretation based on the theories of either discourse or symbolic violence enables historians to bring new dimensions to their research and to expand their range of interests to include such issues as mechanisms of conflicts in urban society[28], disputes over collective memory, or the relevance of historical reality to utopian visions of a perfect social order embodied in a perfect city. The last case is especially relevant to urban history because it arises out of the comparison of the two faces of the city defined either as an artificial, self-contained project submitting to planning and controlling or as a field of dwellers' activity which is difficult to manage and falls beyond control. The first approach to the city corresponds to the history of utopia, while the second accounts for the history of everyday life, the history of customs or microhistory. Usually the two aspects are analysed separately as disparate and contradictory subjects, although they are complementary elements of the same city. Therefore when put together, they constitute a significant field of research opening up an insight into the history of civic life[29].

Between space and place

Space features prominently in urban studies. However, this is not only the matter of architectural structure of urban space (streets, squares, buildings, monuments, districts). Spatial terms, such as space, place, location, boundaries, are used for exploring cultural or social identities, which Henri Tajfel defined as "an individual's knowledge that he belongs to a certain group together with the emotional and value significance of this membership", visible at different levels in the practice of social roles[30]. Spatial terminology is also used to describe and interpret social phenomena of spatial sensitivity, processes of space construction, and dimensions of spatial practice "respectively as the realms of *the perceived*, *the conceived*, and *the lived*"[31]. Nowadays social sciences, especially geography, deprive space of the exclusively physical and objective dimension in favour of an anthropocentric perspective emphasizing the cultural determinants of spatial sensitivity, space organisation, and their historical change as well[32]. It is not without reason that one of Benjamin's most relevant thoughts concerns the historical nature of human senses:

> During long periods of history, the mode of human sense perception changes with humanity's entire mode of existence. The manner in which human sense perception is organised, the medium in which it is accomplished, is determined not only by nature but by historical circumstances as well[33].

The relations between space and history are dialogical and reciprocal. Each epoch, as Henri Lefebvre notices, produces its own space, imposing then a communality of use[34]. The main task of historians is to recognize the historical patterns of spatial sensitivity and its reflection in city forms and functions. In order to do that, historians assimilate an elaborate set of terms related to urban studies which reflect spatial dimensions.

Urban studies distinguish space from place according to dichotomy between the inner and the outer. Unlike space, place is different from an outer world, familiar and accustomed in order to guarantee psychological safety[35]. Dwellers convert space into place by means of the production of meanings embodied in the city and by associating their concept of self with the newly acquired civic area. Social signification of space produces not only places but also more important social identities and imaginary representation of the civic society[36]. In *City Sketches*, Benjamin analysed how motives of "the inside and outside" functioned and were used in culturally different cities (Naples, Marseille, and Moscow): this led him to the conclusion that only in bourgeois societies did separation of public and private spheres take place, while in proletarian cities or districts the two spaces were intermingled. Juxtaposed in social theories, private and public spaces, when explored empirically, co-exist, cross and merge with each other in manifold ways, depending on cultural background[37].

Borderlines between space and places resulting from everyday demarcation and signification are fluid and vague. What is sacral for some might be secular for others[38].

What is strange can be familiar. At the same time, clear and logical space is construed as uncontrollable and chaotic. These spatial paradoxes take place because of an incessant reinterpretation and modification of meanings organised according to different city dwellers' horizons, needs and interests[39].

The model of public-private dichotomy is the concept used most often with reference to mainly modern cities (and societies). In the beginning, urban scientists used it to distinguish the urban culture from the rural one, assuming that private space is intrinsic to urbanism. Soon the model raised doubts because it did not take into account either the multiplicity of cultural forms of dwelling or the complexity of spatial organisation of the city. Nonetheless, the private/public model remains a significant implement for analysing urban phenomena. The distinction into public and private space[40] is now used not to assign urban practices to two disparate spheres, but it also seems to be an intricate implement for the exploration other aspects of civic life and dwellers' identity. The model of the public/private-self corresponding to the social roles performed in the public/private order respectively applied to an analysis of the self-identity of dwellers led Peter Berger to conclusion about incompatibilities between the public self and the private self and significant for the process of self-identity[41]. Urban space is not a simple sum of isolated spatial units, the public as well as the private ones, but it is a new quality deriving from coexistence, reciprocity and combination of diverse elements. In consequence, the city can be defined as "both a site of public culture and association at the same time as preserving and even intensifying the 'closed world' of the family and the private household"[42].

The combination of the two models mentioned above, i.e., the space/place model and the public/private model is an up-and-coming method of exploring urban history. It is necessary, however, not to assume a simple attribution of the space to the public and place to the private; therefore the main task should remain answering the question of how the motives of the inside/outside, the public/private are related to each other, and what results derive from that.

Liminality of borders

Each dichotomy is concomitant with the question of the demarcation lines framing the spatial organisation of the city and separating juxtaposed areas. The concepts of borders and boundaries are very crucial for contemporary social sciences and urban studies. Borders, like space, concern a wide range of issues going beyond physical dimensions of the city, for they have not only spatial but also social, symbolic and institutional meanings. Borders in the sense of demarcation lines and zones take the forms of institutional actions (law, urbanizing policy), buildings and constructions (railways, cemeteries, streets, etc.), areas of deterioration[43] or everyday customs. Spatial borders, especially those visible on a micro-level of social practices (zones of danger, work, private life, leisure, etc.); designate areas of an individual's mobility within the city and within the society; they concern the way of recognizing and experiencing both space and place.

Social scientists attach great importance to institutional and symbolic borders[44]. Since they reflect a vast repertoire of factors determining urban phenomena, such as gender, religion, class, ethnicity, market mechanisms, policy planning, and law[45], borders are significant implements for research into social divisions, segmentation of roles or collective identity constructions. From the perspective of urban history, spatial concepts, however promising and worth introducing, tend to produce a rather static image of the city and civic life. To give proper weight to the dynamic character of historical processes, for instance that of border displacement (in every sense of the term), historians should pay attention to anthropological theories concerning the mechanisms of social and cultural transformation.

Here I would like to focus on Victor Turner's theory of liminality, as it considers aspects regarding borders and the temporal nature of social or symbolic changes. The concept of liminality refers to Van Gennep's theory of a "rite of passage" distinguishing three stages in the process of transition between social and cultural states: separation from ordinary social life, threshold between past and future modes, and re-aggregation, e.g. return to the society. For Turner, the crucial issue is the liminal phase with its reversal status because it reveals cultural patterns and a society in action[46].

According to Victor Turner, liminality is:

> a state or process which is betwixt-and-between the normal, day-to-day cultural and social states and processes of getting and spending, preserving law and order, and registering structural status. Since liminal time is not controlled by the clock, it is a time of enchantment when anything might, even should, happen. Another way of putting it would be to say that the liminal in socio-cultural process is similar to the subjunctive mood in verbs – just as mundane socio-structural activities resemble the indicative mood. Liminality is full of potency and potentiality. It may also be full of experiment and play. There may be a play of ideas, a play of words, a play of symbols, a play of metaphors[47].

Liminality is relevant to rituals and carnivals corresponding to either rural cultures or premodern urban communities, for it is based on the relationship between 'closed' social structure and liminal rituals. In modern cities, liminal rituals were replaced by stage dramas reflecting social structure. Although Turner attributes liminality to rural rather than urban culture, he admits the presence of liminal rituals (for example, a carnival or a stage drama) in civic life also. The city in this context is a stage for intermittent rituals celebrated by dwellers using urban space according to their needs. Squares and streets play different roles and determine the dynamic and repertoire of social actions and level of participation. Carnivals, one of the most significant examples of liminal rituals, take place on the streets, which is concomitant with active participation of the dwellers – observers looking at a procession could and did interact, comment, and in some cases join the march. The celebrations of stage dramas (social theatre of meetings, gatherings, etc.) take place on squares and open urban areas as well. However, unlike carnivals, stage dramas had a visible division of participants into actors (performers) and their audience. Richard Sennett, analysing scenarios of state celebration in Paris during the French Revolution, portrays the strict correlation between space and action[48]. Turner regards stage dramas as an essential genre of cultures recognizing the category of "the individual".

According to Turner, dramas

> involve actors, audience, producers, stagehands, often musicians and dancers, and, most of all, their plots and messages are communicated by various written and oral networks to a general public which varies in span and composition from society to society and epoch to epoch. It is a moot point whether plays derive from rituals - as carnivals clearly do - or whether they originated in the retelling of hunting and headhunting adventures, with pantomimic accompaniments. In either case they are liminal phenomena, with a good deal of reflexive commentary interwoven with the descriptive narrative[49].

The crucial aspects of liminal situations are subjectivity, temporality, symbolic reversal, subversive destruction of social distinctions, and escape classification. Liminality is a meta-language reflecting collective identity and the self-concept of a society. It is a way to react, re-work and transform stable social structures determining an individual life-course[50]. If we accept Andrew Abbot's suggestion to investigate relations between the boundaries and units of social structure in reversed order, for "boundaries come first, then entities"[51], a liminality approach enables historians to recognize factors determining acts of demarcating or displacing social or spatial boundaries, and to estimate their relevance for the history of the city.

Social scientists engaged in historical research use their own specific methodology, theoretical background and analytical tools with a set of key concepts broadening a spectrum of urban studies, such as city dwellers' identity, the systems of symbolic meanings, socio-spatial organisation of the city, urban rituals, acculturation and segregation, to mention a few. Urban studies offer more than just theoretical proposals or interpretations of empirical/historical data. The impact of social sciences consists also in casting doubts on and expressing reservations about universal theories of urbanism, and creating new issues for research in that way. Despite the never-ending debate on conceptualizing the city and the vagueness of definitions, urban studies have been a sphere of relevant methodological exchange and research inspirations.

This text does not present exhaustively all the aspects of interdisciplinary tools used in urban studies. The few mentioned theoretical concepts might open up possibilities to broaden the range of research. Indeed, an interdisciplinary approach in history has already become a fact as more and more researchers include new methods in their field of interests and take into account theoretical reflections on urban studies.

Notes

1 R. Traba, *Historia - przestrzeń dialogu*, Warsaw 2006.

2 W. A. Schwab, *Urban Sociology: A Human Ecological Perspective*, Reading 1982, p. 88.

3 The quotation refers to the title of the essay by Louis Wirth, published in 1939, which was a synthesis of the Chicago School's achievements. See W. A. Schwab, *Urban Sociology*, cit., pp. 18-23.

4 H. Jansen, *The Construction of an Urban Past: Narrative and System in Urban History*, Oxford 2001, p. 40.

5 G. Sjøberg, *The Preindustrial City. Past and Present*, New York 1965, p. 13.

6 S. Parker, *Urban Theory and the Urban Experience. Encountering the City*, New York 2004, p. 15.

7 M.E. Blanchard, *In Search of the City: Engels, Baudelaire, Rimbaud*, Saratoga 1985, pp. 4-5.

8 Hannerz distinguishes between the following five fields: house, kinship and relationship, supply, leisure and traffic. U. Hannerz, *Exploring the City. Inquiries toward an Urban Anthropology*, Krakow 2006, pp. 280-281.

9 E. Kaczyńska, *Pejzaż miejski z zaściankiem w tle,* Warsaw 1999, p. 120.

10 Sjøberg, *The Preindustrial City* cit., p. 7.

11 I leave aside the more general question of whether social scientists have an adequate understanding of the historical approach, which, in my opinion, they often do not.

12 Jansen, *The Construction* cit., p. 46.

13 Kaczyńska, *Pejzaż* cit., p. 120.

14 History of Polish cities provides examples for the two phenomena. In the 19th century, Sosnowiec was a village as defined by the applicable law, despite its dynamic industrial development and urbanisation. When garanted a city charter in 1902, the village of Sosnowiec had over 60 thousand inhabitants. Russian authorities in the 19th century revoked city charters of a number of small towns in the partitions.

15 P. Borsay, *New Approaches to Social History. Myth, Memory and Place: Monmouth and Bath 1750-1900,* in "Journal of Social History", 2006, 3, p. 867.

16 See D. Jędrzejczyk, *Geografia humanistyczna miasta,* Warsaw 2004.

17 A. Bélanger, *Urban Space and Collective Memory: Analysing the Various Dimensions of the Production of Memory*, in "Canadian Journal of Urban Research", 2002, 1, p. 81.

18 K. Krzysztofek, *Vernacular Cultures in the Face of Market Forces*, in J. Purchla (ed.), *From the World of Borders to the World of Horizons*, Krakow 2001, p. 128.

19 Dichotomous terms such as inner/outer, sacral/secular, local/stranger, centre/periphery are frequently used in urban studies, notwithstanding the ambivalence of structuralistic practices and the subjective nature of the distinctions.

20 Anthropologists focus their attention on social institutions perceived as places of creation of common meanings (for instance, a 19th-century salon, a coffee shop, a criminal gang, a religious community or a university). See Hannerz, *Exploring* cit., p. 325.

21 C. Geertz, *The Interpretation of Cultures. Selected Essays*, Krakow 2005, p. 45.

22 V. Schwartz, *Walter Benjamin for Historians*, in "American Historical Review", 2001, 5, p. 1722.

23 *The Arcade Project* was the last book by Walter Benjamin, published posthumously by Theodor Adorno, who made an effort to edit Benjamin's notes. See V. Schwartz, *Walter Benjamin* cit., pp. 1721-1743; C. Rollason, *The Passageways of Paris: Walter Benjamin's "Arcades Project" and Contemporary Cultural Debate in the West*, in C. Rollason, R. Mittapalli (eds.), *Modern Criticism*, New Delhi 2002, pp. 262-296; rev. version at http://www.wbenjamin.org/passageways.html [available at 30.06.2007]; S. Gunn,

City of Mirrors: The Arcade Project and Urban History, in "Journal of Victorian Culture", 2002, 2, pp. 263-275.

24 Rollason, *The Passageways* cit.

25 W. Benjamin, *Charles Baudelaire: A Lyric Poet in the Era of High Capitalism*, London 1977.

26 R. Sennett, *Flesh and Stone: The Body and the City in Western Civilization*, New York 1994.

27 J. Purchla, *Management of Historical Cities and Market Forces. The Central European Experience*, in J. Purchla (ed.), *From the World of Borders to the World of Horizons*, Krakow 2001, p. 99.

28 M. Perrot, *At home*, in P. Ariés, G. Duby (eds.), *A history of private life*, vol. 4, M. Perrot (ed.), *From the fires of Revolution to the Great War*, London 1990, pp. 341-357; N. Schindler, *Widerspenstige Leute. Studien zur Volkskultur in der frühen Neuzeit*, Warsaw 2002; Z. Bauman, *Urban Space Wars: On Destructive Order and Creative Chaos*, in "Citizenship Studies", 1999, 2, pp. 173-185; R. Sennett, *Flesh* cit., Kaczyńska, *Pejzaż miejski* cit.

29 Here I would like to mention only one illustration of this approach. In the essay dedicated to spatial organisation of the city, Zygmunt Bauman refers to the case of Brasilia, the laboratory created from scratch according to the concept of a perfect modern city. As a result, the city dwellers excluded from the process of creating the system of meanings suffer from anonymity, monotony, emptiness and lack of any unexpectedness in public places. According to Bauman, Brasilia "was certainly (at least in its intention) a space perfectly transparent for those charged with the task of administration and those who articulated such tasks. Granted, it could be a perfectly structured place also for those among the residents who identified happiness with life free of problems, because it was free of choice and adventure. For all the rest it proved to be a space denuded from everything truly human – everything that fills life with meaning and makes it worth living". Bauman, *Urban Space* cit., p. 183.

30 A.E. Echabe, J.L. Castro, *Social Knowledge, Identities and Social Practices*, in "Papers on Social Representations", 1993, p. 120.

31 Bélanger, *Urban* cit., p. 82.

32 Jędrzejczyk, *Geografia* cit., p. 207.

33 W. Benjamin, *The Work of Art in the Age of Mechanical Reproduction*, in H. Arendt (ed.), *Illuminations*, New York 1985, p. 222; quotation from: B. Gaucho, *Some Half-Baked Speculations on Benjamin, Privacy and Fascism*, in "Epoché. The University of California Journal for the Study of Religion", 2006, p. 104.

34 Parker, *Urban Theory* cit., p. 22.

35 C. Norberg-Schulz, *Meaning in Western Architecture*, Warsaw 1999, p. 224.

36 See M. Reisenleitner, *Tradition, Cultural Boundaries and the Construction of Spaces of Idenitity*, in "Spaces of Identities", 2001, 1, p. 9.

37 Parker, *Urban Theory* cit., p. 16.

38 E. Przybył, *Pałac Kultury i Nauki jako socjalistyczna sakralizacja przestrzeni*, in Grębecka, J. Sadowski (eds.), *Pałac Kultury* cit., p. 89.

39 It is not without significance either that the city is an object of authorities' endeavours to achieve specific (political, ideological or social) goals by organizing and adapting the space often against the dwellers. See T. Pisula, *Polis, utopia, inżynieria społeczna*, in D. Jędrzejczyk (ed.), *Humanistyczne oblicze miasta*, Warsaw 2004, p. 36; Bauman, *Urban Space* cit.

40 Similarly to the city, private and public space in an object of theoretical and historical debate. See P. Ariés, G. Duby (eds.), *A history of private life*, London 1990.

41 Hannerz, *Exploring* cit., p. 259.

42 Parker, *Urban Theory* cit., p. 140.

[43] This term derives from the concentric zone model developed by Ernest Burgess. The model, based on the research on Chicago in the 1920s, distinguishes five rings of space in the city: the central business district, the zone of transition, the zone of independent workers' homes, the better residential zone, and the zone of commuters. The second zone is especially interesting, because it is inhabited by lower classes or groups of exclusion and it is directly adjacent to the central districts.

[44] See also M. Lamont, M. Virag, *The Study of Boundaries in the Social Sciences*, in "Annual Review of Sociology", 2002, pp. 167-195; Echabe, Castro, *Social Knowledge* cit., pp. 177-125.

[45] H. Häussermann, W. Siebel, *Integration and Segregation – Thoughts on an Old Debate*, in "Zeitschrift für Kommunalwissenschaften", 2001, 40, available at: http://www.difu.de/publikationen/dfk/en/01_1/01_1_haeussermann.shtml [1 July 2007].

[46] V. Turner, *Frame, Flow and Reflection. Ritual and Drama as Public Liminality*, in "Japanese Journal of Religious Studies", 1979, 4, p. 476.

[47] *Ibid*., pp. 465-466.

[48] Sennett, *Flesh* cit., pp. 245-246.

[49] Turner, *Frame* cit., *Flow*, p. 486.

[50] This hypothesis was questioned by anthropologists emphasizing negative aspects of liminal existence. See M. Deflem, *Ritual, Anti-Structure, and Religion of Victor Turner's Processual Symbolic Analysis*, in "Journal of Scientific Study of Religion", 1991, 30, p. 14.

[51] A. Abbott, *Things of Boundaries. Defining the Boundaries of Social Inquiry*, in "Social Research", 1995, 4, pp. 857-882.

Bibliography

Abbott A., *Things of Boundaries – Defining the Boundaries of Social Inquiry*, in "Social Research", 1995, 4, pp. 857-882.

Bauman Z., *Urban Space Wars: On Destructive Order and Creative Chaos*, in "Citizenship Studies", 1999, 2, pp. 173-185.

Bélanger A., *Urban Space and Collective Memory: Analysing the Various Dimensions of the Production of Memory*, in "Canadian Journal of Urban Research", 2002, 1, pp. 69-92.

Benjamin W., *Charles Baudelaire: A Lyric Poet in the Era of High Capitalism*, London 1993.

Id., *Paris: A Capital of the Nineteenth Century*, in Benjamin W., *The Author as Producer*, Poznań 1975.

Blanchard M. E., *In Search of the City: Engels, Baudelaire, Rimbaud*, Saratoga 1985.

Borsay P., *New Approaches to Social History: Myth, Memory and Place: Monmouth and Bath 1750-1900*, in "Journal of Social History", 2006, 3, pp. 867-889.

Castells M., *Urban question*, Warsaw 1982.

Czyżewski A., *Kultura i myślenie obrazowe* [Culture and Imaginative Thinking], in Kowalski P., Libera Z. (eds.), *Poszukiwanie sensów. Lekcja z czytania kultury* [Looking for Meanings. A Lesson in Reading Culture], Krakow 2006, pp. 161-188.

Deflem M., *Ritual, Anti-Structure, and Religion of Victor Turner's Processual Symbolic Analysis*, in "Journal of Scientific Study of Religion" 1991, 30, pp. 1-25.

Echabe A. E., Castro J. L. G., *Social Knowledge, Identities and Social Practices*, in "Papers on Social Representations", 1993, 2, pp. 177-125.

Gaucho B., *Some Half-Baked Speculations on Benjamin, Privacy and Fascism*, in "Epoché. The University of California Journal for the Study of Religion", 2006, pp. 89-112.

Geertz C., *The Interpretation of Cultures. Selected Essays*, Krakow 2005.

Grębecka Z., Sadowski J. (eds.), *Pałac Kultury i Nauki. Między ideologią a masową wyobraźnią* [The Culture and Science Palace. Between an Ideology and Mass Imagination], Krakow 2007.

Gunn S., *City of Mirrors: The Arcade Project and Urban History*, in "Journal of Victorian Culture", 2002, 2, pp. 263-275.

Hannerz U., *Exploring the City. Inquiries toward an Urban Anthropology*, Krakow 2006.

Häußermann H., Siebel W., *Integration and Segregation – Thoughts on an Old Debate*, in "Zeitschrift für Kommunalwissenschaften", 2001, available at: http://www.difu.de/publikationen/dfk/en/01_1/01_1_haeussermann.shtml (7 January 2007).

Jansen H., *The Construction of an Urban Past: Narrative and System in Urban History*, Oxford 2001.

Jędrzejczyk D., *Geografia humanistyczna miasta* [Human Geography of the City], Warsaw 2004.

Kaczyńska E., *Pejzaż miejski z zaściankiem w tle* [Urban Landscape with a Backwater in the Background], Warsaw 1999.

Krämer-Badoni T., *Urbanity and Social Integration*, in "Zeitschrift für Kommunalwissenschaften", 2001, available at: http://www.difu.de/publikationen/dfk/en/01_1/01_1_kraemer-badoni.shtml [7 Jannuary 2007].

Krzysztofek K., *Vernacular Cultures in the Face of Market Forces*, in Purchla J. (ed.), *From the World of Borders to the World of Horizons*, Krakow 2001, pp. 127-142.

Kula M., *Wybór tradycji* [Choice of traditions], Warsaw 2003.

Lamont M., Virag M., *The Study of Boundaries in the Social Sciences*, in "Annual Review of Sociology", 2002, pp. 167-195.

Norberg-Schulz C., *Meaning in Western Architecture*, Warsaw 1999.

Parker S., *Urban Theory and the Urban Experience: Encountering the City*, New York 2004.

Perrot M., *At home*, in Ariés P., Duby G. (eds.), *A history of private life*, vol. 4, Perrot M. (ed.), *From the fires of Revolution to the Great War*, London 1990, pp. 341-357.

Pisula T., *Polis, utopia, inżynieria społeczna* [Polis, Utopia, Social engineering], in Jędrzejczyk D. (ed.), *Humanistyczne oblicze miasta* [A Humanistic Face of the City], Warsaw 2004, pp. 35-66.

Przybył E., *Pałac Kultury i Nauki jako socjalistyczna sakralizacja przestrzeni* [The Culture and Science Palace as a Socialist Sacralization of the Space], in Grębecka Z., Sadowski J. (eds.), *Pałac Kultury i Nauki. Między ideologią a masową wyobraźnią* [The Culture and Science Palace. Between an Ideology and Mass Imagination], Krakow 2007, pp. 89-124.

Purchla J., *Management of Historical Cities and Market Forces. The Central European Experience*, in Purchla J. (ed.), *From the World of Borders to the World of Horizons*, Krakow 2001, pp. 99-111.

Reisenleitner M., *Tradition, Cultural Boundaries and the Construction of Spaces of Idenitity*, in "Spaces of Identities", 2001, 1, pp. 7-13.

Rollason C., *The Passageways of Paris: Walter Benjamin's "Arcades Project" and Contemporary Cultural Debate in the West*, in Rollason C., Rajeshwar M. (eds.), *Modern Criticism*, New Delhi 2002, pp. 262-296; rev. version on http://www.wbenjamin.org/passageways.html [available at 31 June 2007].

Schindler N., *Widerspenstige Leute. Studien zur Volkskultur in der frühen Neuzeit*, Warsaw 2002.

Schwab W. A., *Urban Sociology: A Human Ecological Perspective*, Reading 1982.

Schwartz V. R., *Walter Benjamin for Historians*, in "American Historical Review", 2001, 5, pp. 1721-1743.

Sennett R., *Flesh and Stone: The Body and the City in Western Civilization*, New York 1994.

Sjøberg G, *The Preindustrial City. Past and Present*, New York 1965.

Stobiecki R., *Łódzkie "boje o historię"*, in Stobiecki R. , *Historiografia PRL. Ani dobra, ani mądra, ani piękna... ale skomplikowana. Studia i szkice*, Warsaw 2007.

Traba R., *Historia - przestrzeń dialogu* [History –Space of a Dialogue], Warsaw 2006.

Turner V., *Frame, Flow and Reflection: Ritual and Drama as Public Liminality*, in "Japanese Journal of Religious Studies", 1979 , 4, pp. 465-499.

Turner V., *Dramas, Fields and Metaphors. Symbolic Action in Human Society*, Ithaca 1974.

Public Space and Private Places within the City

BARBARA KLICH-KLUCZEWSKA
Jagiellonian University

ABSTRACT

The public/private dichotomy is commonly considered a distinctive feature of modern societies and as such frequently raises controversy among researchers. Although such controversies concern social development in general, this study will concentrate on the context of urban society and space. The chapter concerns the functioning of the notions of 'private' and 'public' in the field of social sciences and contains reflection, based on a case study of Krakow, on the possibilities of using this theory in historical practice.

Dychotomia prywatne/publiczne uważana jest powszechnie za zjawisko charakterystyczne dla społeczeństw nowoczesnych i jako taka wciąż wzbudza kontrowersje, stanowiąc jednocześnie punkt wyjścia krytyki rozwoju społecznego tak w sensie ogólnym jak i w kontekście szczególnie nas interesującego rozwoju przestrzeni miejskich.

Prywatność oraz sfera publiczna są definiowane oraz badane w rozmaitych kontekstach na polu filozofii, socjologii, antropologii kultury, nauk politycznych oraz psychologii społecznej. Z rozważań tych korzystają historycy, którzy śledzą przemiany wzajemnych relacji prywatne/ publiczne na przestrzeni dziejów.

Sfera publiczna jest najczęściej definiowana przez teoretyków w kategoriach metaforycznych, nie zaś terytorialnych. Urbaniści zwracają szczególną uwagę na zerwanie więzi między konkretną przestrzenią i jej znaczeniem. Z kolei najbardziej swoiste dla współczesnego definiowania prywatności jest przekonanie o "giętkości" jej granic, które są zależne od indywidualnych potrzeb jednostki.

Kategoria dychotomii prywatne/publiczne była z sukcesem stosowanym narzędziem analizy przemian społecznych w Europy Zachodniej. Jej zastosowanie w odniesieniu do krajów Europy Środkowo- Wschodniej doby realnego socjalizmu budzi jednak wciąż wątpliwości historyków, jako "sztuczne" przeniesienie na grunt badań tych państw kategorii charakterystycznej dla mieszczańskich społeczeństw dziewiętnastowiecznych. Faktycznie, przykładanie miary podziału publiczne/ prywatne w odniesieniu do funkcjonowania państwa i całego społeczeństwa "socjalistycznego" prowadzić może donikąd. Jednak zas-

tosowanie tego narzędzia jako pojęcia z obszaru badań społecznych w odniesieniu do mniejszych grup, szczególnie w obrębie miasta, wydaje się być uzasadnione metodologicznie i ciekawe, jako próba zastosowania w praktyce metod antropologii historycznej.

The private/public dichotomy[1]

> The public/private distinction is as pervasive as it is lacking in coherence. Rather than providing clear conceptual distinction the public/private division provides "a series of ways of thinking about public and private that are constantly undergoing revision, reformulation, and refinement"[2].

The words quoted above represent a typical example of contemporary thought concerning the public/private dichotomy. Despite extensive debate in the social sciences, beginning in the early 1960s, no consensus has been reached. Researchers are only unanimous on one point: the distinction between the private and the public has not yet been analyzed in a manner that takes into account sufficiently the multiple levels at which it operates. Some theorists even rule out the possibility of clarifying the two concepts and defining the spaces characterized by them. Nevertheless, the private/public dichotomy is still considered to be one of the most characteristic features of modern society and, in particular, the city.

The notion of 'public'

Usually, everything that happens outside the individual, in a realm accessible by others, is designated as "public". The term covers larger social structures in a given society, such as the state-run structures that organize defense, education, public health, and public order[3]. Other theorists, however, focus primarily on the nature of public interactions and differentiate them from the formal sphere of institutional relations[4].

In *The Fall of Public Man,* which is an attempt to trace the historical transformations of private and public life, the American researcher Richard Sennett emphasizes that the ideological struggle for individual identity and the craving for freedom caused a gradual division of the previously unified private and public spheres in the 18th century[5]. He paid special attention to how public life became a matter of formal obligation:

> Today (...) most citizens approach their dealings with the state in a spirit of resigned acquiescence. (...) Manners and ritual interchanges with strangers are looked on as at best formal and dry, at worst as phony. (...) It is the bond of a crowd, of a "people", of a polity, rather than the bond of family or friends[6].

Jürgen Habermas has attempted to reinterpret the concept of the public sphere by excluding the state and state administration. "Public" is thus defined as an intermediary sphere between the state and the private life of society. He restricts the "public" to areas, including political life, in which the entire society participates and expresses their "public opinion". In this case, the "public" means a sphere of life in which public opinion may develop freely through discussion and exchange of opinions facilitated by institutionalized freedom of assembly, association, and speech[7]. Public space has frequently been described as a "space of communication", of expressing one's opinion, of defining one's attitude towards the world in confrontation with other people's judgments[8].

Generally, the metaphorical approach toward public space prevails over the literal, topographic one. Changes in methods of communication have deepened the dissonance between the phenomenon of public space and the real topographic connotation. Jan Kajfasz asks:

> *Czy starożytna agora lub miejski rynek mogą wciąż odgrywać rolę prototypowego, najbardziej swoistego wcielenia sfery publicznej, którego materialne znaczenie harmonijnie przenika się ze znaczeniem funkcjonalnym?* [9]
>
> [Can the ancient agora or the urban market still play the role of the prototype, the most typical embodiment of the public sphere, when its material significance is harmoniously interpenetrating with its functional meaning?].

In this case, the public sphere is not simply the space beyond privacy, but a space that has special value and a certain privileged character, enabling people to identify with a specific place (i.e. the city). In the context of urban studies pessimists point to the rising significance of so-called "non-places", which are places which have appeared as a result of the disintegration of the public sphere. These places, such as airports, are seen to be deprived of values and the ability to create social bonds.

According to urban geographers and town-planners, public space should be described as a semi-autonomous structure, composed of various closely connected functional elements. This structure plays a vital role within urban space by integrating the urban tissue[10]. The public character of certain urban spaces does not lie in their formal description or through the methods of shaping or using it, but through the creation of a space in which it is possible to interact with strangers. Urban public space shapes the settings for unrestricted motility of any free human being, members and non-members of the urban community alike. The general rules of orderliness establish the only constriction in such an area. This attitude does not support the optimistic view of the public sphere as the space of the community created for the community.

To distinguish areas accessible only to members of a certain group, geographers, influenced by urban sociologists, make use of the notion of "group space". This half-public sphere is cared for by the group members, not, as in the case of public space, by the municipal authorities[11].

Studies of city dwellers show that in everyday social interactions (ranging from direct verbal communication to simple acknowledgement of others) strangers are evaluated by immediate observation of basic characteristics such as dress, demeanour and facial expression, related to the stereotypical images of for example dangerous people, and judged against existing knowledge about men's and women's patterns of behaviour in the city. According to the theory of urban overload, the practice of 'tuning others out' by selectiveness and non-involvement evolved as a cure for the stimulus overload in urban public space[12].

In contrast to this concept of avoidance and anonymity, Michael de Certeau emphasized the active side of city walkers as transformers of the spatial system:

> crossing, drifting away, or improvisation of walking privilege, transform or abandon spatial elements (...). The walker creates a discreteness, whether by making choices among the signifiers of the spatial 'language' or by displacing them through the use he makes of them. He condemns certain places to inertia or disappearance and composes with others spatial 'turns of phrase' that are 'rare', 'accidental' or 'illegitimate'[13].

Urbanites create a 'private path' within the setting of the urban public space simultaneously influencing its shape and significance.

Searching for 'private'

The narrowest meaning of privacy is "psychological privacy", *privacy of the mind*, consisting of the internal life of individuals, their experiences, thoughts and emotions. Researchers can access this form of private space through the process of interpreting the words and the actions of a person[14]. The concept exclusively covers what is individual and independent.

This concept appears most frequently in sociology, as it is used to describe social life. The analysis is further complicated by the fact that it is often ascribed a normative and evaluative nature, through which the condition of modern society is examined.

The oldest ideas concerning privacy, which originated in liberal philosophy, are the so-called "negative concepts", according to which the private sphere is perceived to be an ideal. It is the 'good' world, closest to a person, protected from intruders and interventions from the outside, and from the public. This definition of privacy implies a hostile opposition between the private and the public sphere[15]. Privacy is endangered by the state, mass democracy, schools, factories, hospitals, and the police[16]. It is difficult, however, to accept such a negative definition, as it indirectly encourages denying public institutions, and in particular the law, access to the sphere of private life[17]. The social transformations that followed World War II helped to discredit this definition. For example, the movements for children's rights and feminism attacked privacy as "a fig leaf covering up areas of unrestricted male domination over women and children". They advocated the necessity of public intervention and the invasion of privacy, if it is required in order to safeguard individual welfare. On the other hand, however, such far-reaching interventions bring to mind actions characteristic of totalitarian regimes[18].

Modern philosophical and sociological conceptions, based on the model of a human being as an active creator of the surrounding reality, strive for a positive and global definition. The borders of the private sphere are not considered to be fixed. Instead they are, to a certain extent, seen as flexible, shaped by the individual. This positive conception of privacy allows one to speak of "sharing one's privacy"[19] by demarcating its borders, for example by disclosing or withholding certain information, or by the choice of friends.

Thus, privacy, according to modern sociology, in material terms refers to a flat or a house and the property belonging to that household. In social terms it refers to the individual, their family and all so-called 'intimate groups'[20].

The sociological definition of privacy outlined above needs to be broadened, however. First of all, in terms of space, because scenes from entirely private life may take place in areas ascribed to the public sphere, which applies, for example, to spending free time, or religious practices. The private activity of an individual does not solely take place within the cohabiting community. According to some researchers such a perspective on the issue is still not sufficient as it exclusively concerns itself with social structures and human activity. It lacks elements of the concept of psychological privacy, such as personal attitudes and a value system[21].

The borders of privacy are also defined by means of philosophical and legal categories. For example, the right to privacy, which consists of levels of distance and isolation, which function in a specific cultural system, is usually regulated by the law and moral norms of a given society. This, especially in American scientific circles, is usually related to the issue of information being put into or prevented from public circulation[22]. The basis of such theories is the assumption that privacy is a natural requirement of human beings. Historical research suggests it is rather a need acquired in the course of evolution.

To sum up, the private sphere can be described as including psychological privacy and the sphere of private contacts with other people, including the family and "intimate groups" (friendly and social relationships). Whether someone belongs to the sphere of individual privacy depends on the emotional contact maintained with him/her. Each of the above areas may be associated with specific physical spaces, which are generally restricted to the home and selected spaces of community life which constitute the framework for friendly and social contacts.

When measuring the degree of privacy, sociologists suggest taking into account, apart from material facts and social conditions, factors such as population density, interaction rate (acceptable level of closeness), habitation patterns, the division of labor, and the nature of the family and other social contacts[23].

Privacy and public space within cities of the socialist era. The case of Krakow.

The public/private dichotomy has been successfully used as an instrument of historical analysis in the study of Western European societies, but its suitability for researching the socialist states of East Central Europe is still questionable. It can be argued that to use the dichotomy in this setting would be an 'artificial' transfer of a category that is much more typical of Western 19th-century societies. Use of the public/private division to study the functioning of the socialist state and society as a whole would lead to a simplified analysis. However, the application of this category to the analysis of specific groups, particularly within the city, seems to be methodologically well-grounded and would bring new and interesting conclusions about everyday life in a socialist state[24].

Krakow is a typical example of a large Polish city, but without the status of state capital. This makes it possible to analyze the public/private phenomenon, non-evident from the point of view of so-called "communist spaces", which have received much attention in studies of post-war communist cities in Poland. Krakow's urban space, consisting of the historical tenement houses, which in the postwar period was subjected to central directives issued by the state, has been dominated by modern multi-family housing construction of a block type, which surrounded the city with a ring of "vertical gardens" typical of the period. In spite of the illusion of uniformity, both the reality of the tenement houses and housing developments, often referred to in a contemptuous way, exhibit a large degree of variation.

In the second part of this chapter, three examples of wandering borders will be used to demonstrate the results of the transformation of the private/public division within the traditional urban tissue, which will present questions about the peculiarity of the socialist experience. These will include: how did the micro-level process of social transformation in Poland, resulting from the political process on the one hand and the late socialist urbanization on the other, differ from the effects of urbanization in general? Whether people used particular techniques to protect their privacy? Also, how did people transform the spatial system of their surroundings?

Meeting strangers: private made public

The historical tenement houses of Krakow, which were gradually acquired by the state during the socialist era, constituted a sort of closed world. They often resembled, in social terms, a 19th-century apartment house. During the late 1960s and 1970s, in the historic area of the Old Town, the majority of apartments were primitive one- or two-room units in back-premises, without any sanitary system, and only about 25% were high quality apartments with full facilities, including a bathroom[25]. The fate of the tenement houses in Krakow was largely decided by new legislation on the lease of premises, which determined housing standards per resident and paved the way to assigning new tenants to a house. One diarist wrote:

> *Kraków nie mógł pomieścić w swoich domach gwałtownego napływu nowych ludzi. Podjęta wówczas decyzja o dokwaterowywaniu we wspólnych mieszkaniach ludzi zupełnie sobie obcych i o różnych upodobaniach, zainteresowaniach i temperamencie wywołała wiele zła. Dało to okazję do nieuczciwych spekulacji (...) Powstawały ustawiczne konflikty i użeranie się o korzystanie ze wspólnych pomieszczeń i urządzeń sanitarnych, tym gorsze, że zwyciężał przeważnie ten silniejszy i bardziej brutalny* [26].

> [Krakow could never house the rapid inflow of new people. The decision to assign new tenants to an apartment, who were strangers to the people already occupying the apartment, had different inclinations, interests and temperament, caused a lot of harm. It created opportunities for unfair profiteering (...) there were constant conflicts and fighting over access to shared rooms and sanitary appliances, made even worse by the fact that the stronger and the more violent usually won.]

Over time the situation did not improve and the feeling of transience, typical of societies that experienced war, was part of life in 'old' Krakow. The problem of sharing apartments was caused by the lack of any significant extension of the housing tissue after the war in a city that received a considerable number of migrants, while existing resources were adapted for administrative and other purposes. As a result of the work of the Extraordinary Residential Committee in the years 1949-1950, comfortable four- or five-room apartments were used to house large numbers of migrants. This meant that a significant group of residents would share their kitchen and bathroom facilities with several households[27]. In 1960, almost one third of Krakow's residents led a forced community life among partition walls and tightly locked doors.

In subtenant apartments, the combination of excess and scarcity was striking. The excess of useless doors leading nowhere, which once indicated prestige but in post-War Krakow were more likely to symbolize poverty, was a source of much complaint. They shattered the natural order of the house, where the threshold and entrance play an essential role. In addition, the en suite doors, even when covered by wardrobes, beds, and tapestries, were little more than a membrane. The lack of sufficient access to the kitchen, bathroom, and toilet was also troubling. The situation caused the once stylish tenement houses to become run-down back-premises, where a lack of sanitation was not unusual. Using a shared toilet was a source of embarrassment to the subtenants and caused tension between the households.

The inhabitants developed tactics to avoid strangers by ignoring them, constructing plywood walls or fitting special systems of doorbells. Ignoring each other became one of the most important skills of inhabitants of the divided apartments, who usually never came to terms with their situation. This tactic, derived from the public space of the streets, played an extremely significant role in coping with the hardships of this form of accommodation and distinguishes the Polish situation from everyday life in common apartments in the Soviet Union of the 1930s, as analyzed by historians such as Sheila Fitzpatrick[28].

Home – the centre of privacy – described by anthropologists as a sacred area, a fixed point, and the centre of existence ordering human life into a reasonable system, was deprived of a part of its definitional substance in the urban space, and in many cases also its importance in terms of material space.

Due to the process of degradation, tenement houses ceased to form an integral whole. Staircases, which were the immediate entrance to the home, became gloomy and run-down. Caretakers, who used to be relentless guards of the world of tenement houses, were gradually disappearing from the urban landscape. The gate, one of the most significant symbolic borders between the private and the public world within the city, stayed wide open. The gate thus lost its protective nature and its ability to define the tenement house as autonomous and inaccessible to strangers[29]. Not surprisingly, the tenants found it increasingly difficult to identify with such 'half-public' rather than 'half-private' space.

Ritualization: private as compensation for public life

Stalinism deprived Krakow of that rich social life which could be considered one of the components that formed the special atmosphere of public life in the city before the Second World War. However, for the landed gentry, who were forced to leave the countryside and move to the city, and the intelligentsia this did not mean living in isolation. This group reestablished family and social contacts, which were necessarily limited during the occupation. It should be emphasized that these contacts were not confined to entertainment and leisure time. They were much more significant and thus, in this respect, the contacts resembled a form of private life.

In many cases, social life became a sort of compensation for public life (in Habermas' meaning of the term) for those who consciously rejected the political changes that were occurring in the country. This was particularly important as freedom of speech was only enjoyed in one's own apartment[30] and public life was clearly being pushed out of public places in Krakow. Certain traditional habits, which were normal before the war, were increasingly becoming unwelcome and ridiculed, an example of which may be the famous chairs in the Planty Park, close to the Main Market Square, where people would sit down for a while during a Sunday stroll.

A diverse range of customs emerged in the post-war period that regulated social contacts amongst the landed gentry and intelligentsia, all of which had something in common. This was the ritualization of social life, which was already widespread in the 19th century and cherished in certain circles during the inter-war period. This allowed the protection of family privacy. It was a very clear phenomenon in the second half of the

1940s. Meetings took place regularly at a specific time, on a specific day of the week or month.

On the basis of the notes made by the Krakow resident, Janina Turek, we can presume that domestic social life was thriving during the very period that Stalinization and the promotion of a collective public life was intensifying. We find that between 1950 and 1954 'bridge meetings' or 'poker meetings', which were often held two or three times a month during the 1940s, were being held up to two times a week, on Wednesdays and Saturdays or Sundays, and were often combined with a simple dinner.

One may agree with the opinion of Hanna Świda-Ziemba that during that time personal events were experienced much more deeply than normal:

> *Teren życia osobistego – nie zawłaszczony do końca przez świat stalinizmu – był terenem, na którym koncentrowały się przeżycia ludzi* [31].
>
> [The realm of personal life, which had not been completely dominated by the world of Stalinism, was an area where human experiences were concentrated.]

As for Krakow, it is worth pointing out that the above was also true beyond the family, and therefore it is difficult to speak of a successful "disruption of social bonds and groups (including those spontaneous ones, linked by bonds of liking)"[32].

In the first half of the 1950s, the political situation had a strong influence on the shape of social life in Krakow. On the one hand, as a result of the intensity of contacts, it caused gradual, yet not complete, breaking of the rituals which previously shaped them form, and on the other hand, it strengthened interpersonal bonds. The need to be part of a group and to surround oneself with relatives and friends was significant. The protective function of social life dominated over customs, which previously had constituted a framework for internal forms of private life, i.e. family and domestic life. This gave a greater feeling of safety and a sense of being rooted in a certain community during difficult times. This was true to such an extent that even personal family privacy was subordinated to that wider group by sharing part of its space and time.

> *Nieocenionym skarbem dla człowieka jest przyjaźń ludzka i życzliwość otoczenia (...) w okazywanej mi życzliwości kryły się jednak również nastroje społeczeństwa, w dalszym ciągu nieprzychylne dla reżimu*
>
> [An invaluable treasure for a man is human friendship and kindness of the environment (...) however also in the kindness the social mood, still hostile towards the regime, was hidden]

recalls Kochanowski about his release from prison. The information about his release spread fast, and friends sent flowers. Many of them visited him at home, staying for many days[33]. Moreover, social life created an order that was independent of and different from work, completely dependent on private desires. It was a kind of alternative life.

Cafés and clubs once again became alternative locations for social contacts after the Thaw of 1956. They were where birthdays were celebrated and boogie-woogie and the previously forbidden swing were danced. The most attractive places were concentrated primarily in the centre – the Old Town[34]. Both tourists and natives of the city were shocked by the number of clubs and cafés in the city[35], although in comparison with the inter-war period the number was remarkably meagre. It seems that, for the average inhabitant of Krakow, social life in cafés and restaurants was of a very intimate nature. An exception, which determined the atmosphere of many of these places, were writers, journalists, and artists, for whom the space was an extension of their workplace – the editor's office, publishing house, theatre, or drama school[36].

Backyard and Courtyard: public versus private

During the Stalinist era (1948-1956) backyards and courtyards were domesticated places, privatized mostly by children. They were seen to be in competition with public means of spending free time, such as youth centres, playgrounds or scout organizations. Therefore, that space was frequently discredited in official publications and unfavourably compared with places in which one could spend leisure time collectively, such as children's gardens. In the mid-1950s such places were perceived to be, in the ordered and hierarchized 'socialistic world' of a child, a transitional form between playgrounds and culture parks[37]*:*

> *W nich, w otoczeniu zieleni- drzew, krzewów, trawy i kwiatów-dziecko po pracy szkolnej znajduje możliwość kulturalnego wykorzystania czasu na swobodnej zabawie lub dowolnie wybranym zajęciu, zawsze pod okiem troskliwego przyjaciela –wychowawcy i instruktora.(...) W ZSRR oraz w krajach demokracji ludowej tworzy się dla młodzieży pałace i domy pionierów oraz parki kultury (...), w ustroju kapitalistycznym, miejscem "wypoczynku" dziecka w środowisku o wielkim skupieniu robotników jest ciasne i ciemne podwórko oraz ulic* [38].
>
> [In the gardens, surrounded by trees, bushes, grass, and flowers children find an opportunity to spend their time in a cultural way after school by playing freely or engaging in a chosen activity, always under the supervision of a caring friend – a counsellor and instructor. (...) In the USSR and in People's Republic's youth centres, Pioneer centres, and culture parks are created for the young (...). In the capitalist system, the place for children to spend their "leisure" time in an environment of high concentration of workers is a cramped and dark backyard, and the street.].

Roch Sulima emphasizes that it is the young (especially school and preschool children) who, apart from the elderly, set the essential parameters of localness and establish a discrete network of meanings within the urban space: "We can speak of a certain sort of ritualization of the local space connected with those two age groups"[39].

In the case of Krakow, the development of an emotional relationship between the surroundings and the child is very evident. It has a long tradition, which was reinforced during the occupation and continued through close relations with neighbours, from whom a child usually drew his or her first group of friends. The relationship with the backyard was further strengthened by the fact that until the mid-1960s the community of neighbours corresponded to the backyard community as elementary schools operated in the vicinity.

Irrespective of any actions undertaken by the state, the organization of a child's private space and time, which shall be construed as the area of their free activity and decisions, remained in the hands of the family, and thus belonged to the private sphere. Except for those families who were faithful to the tradition of confining the child's space to the domestic environment, the majority of the children of Krakow spent their time after school in the backyard or the street (or "on the pavement" as residents of detached housing developments would say).

The children, by wandering around Krakow, created the "discreetness" described by de Certeau, which still exists in the social memory of the time (and places).

There were significant differences between the urban and suburban backyards of Krakow. In the suburban zone, they were mostly forms of fenced gardens, depending on the sort of buildings. In the area of Aleja Trzech Wieszczów and the central part of the region of Podgórze, closed backyards, so-called wells, dominated, which were entered "under the close supervision of a caretaker, who did not always welcome the swarm of brats from the neighbouring tenement houses (...)"[40].

The tenement house backyard constituted a 'separate world', not only because of the urban nature of that type of building but because it was reinforced by a whole range of typical smells and everyday sounds:

> *Słychać było (...) odgłosy z mieszkań- mycia naczyń, prania na blaszanych tarkach, szycia, krzyki i rozmowy sąsiadek z okna do okna*"[41], *"pokrzykiwania specjalistów do ostrzenia, drutowania i zbierania starych szmat,[którzy] wyśpiewywali (...) różne melodie i rytmy"*[42], *"odgłosy stolarzy oraz dźwięki fortepianów"* czy wreszcie *"płynące z otwartych okien sprawozdania z Wyścigu Pokoju* [43].
>
> [(...)calls made by the experts on knife-sharpening, wiring, and collecting old rags, [who] sang (...) all sorts of melodies and rhythms", "the noises produced by carpenters and the sounds of grand pianos", or "the Peace Race commentary streaming out of the open windows.].

Familiar sound and smells, which as a rule "broaden and enrich the visual space"[44] reinforced the feeling of safety, which was given to the child by the backyard. However, it was not an oppressive safety, as the child's parents or grandparents, in spite of being very close, in an apartment whose windows often overlooked the backyard, were in fact absent from the intimate world of the backyard.

The development of housing estates brought about the domination of apartment block courtyards. The large-scale expansion of that type of housing in the 1960s was accompanied by the decline of the 'golden era' of closed backyards, which either decayed or were renovated. This was especially true within the area of the Planty city park, which experienced a complete change of tenants. Significant changes were also brought about by the increasing number of cars, which in turn resulted in an irreversible transformation of the backyard space.

In the case of the "group space" of the city courtyards (according to sociologists and urban geographers) or private/personal places (according to the witnesses and memoirists), the purposeful state policy of Stalinism suffered defeat. The fragile network of Krakow's urban spaces disappeared as a result of the total transformation of the urban space.

Conclusion

The examples of private/public tensions presented in this chapter demonstrate the metamorphosis of the everyday life of city dwellers in the triple context of political transformation, urbanization and industrialization.

Contrary to the current historical consensus, the experience of everyday life in Poland changed quite meaningfully due to the socialist/communist takeover and continued to alter over time. The cases described above represent only a small part of the everyday life of the people of Krakow. Further research is needed to create a fuller picture of public and private life in the city. Similarly, comparative studies looking at other Polish cities would shed light on whether the situation described above can be applied elsewhere, or if it is unique to Krakow. Comparative studies that have already been carried out suggest that the transformation of social bonds and mentality that occurred in Krakow did not happen to the same extent in Warsaw. This can, of course, be partly explained by the very different situations of the two cities after the Second World War.

One question has been left unanswered: are the private/public tensions that have been analyzed here part of the general European experience of the post-war era? The housing shortage caused by state policy and the political solutions employed to overcome it are not reflected in the situation outside the Communist Bloc. However, i.e. the attitudes and policies concerning children were, in general, the same on both sides of the Iron Curtain, even if they were expressed using extremely different tools.

Notes

1 The problem of the private/public dichotomy in post-war Krakow was analyzed in detail in the monograph titled *Przez dziurkę od klucza. Życie prywatne w Krakowie w latach 1945-1989*, Warsaw 2005.

2 G. Turkel, *Dividing Public and Private. Law. Politics, and Social Theory*, Westport 1992,

3 P. Herring, *Public interest,* in *The International Encyclopedia of the Social Sciences*, vol. 13, New York 1968, pp. 170-171.

4 S. Blackburn, *Social privacy*, in Id., *Oxford Dictionary of Philosophy*, Oxford 2005.

5 R. Sennett, *The Fall of Public Man,* New York 1974, p. 89.

6 *Ibid.*, pp. 3-4.

7 J. Turowski, *Dychotomia prywatnej i publicznej sfery życia (koncepcje i diagnozy)*, "Studia Socjologiczne" 1989, 3, pp. 68-70.

8 J. Kajfasz, *O przemianach przestrzeni publicznej* [The Transformation of Public Space], in I. Bukowska-Floreńska (ed.), *Studia Etnologiczne i Antropologiczne t.9: Problem ekologii kulturowej i społecznej w przestrzeni miejskiej i podmiejskiej* [Problem the of the Cultural and Social Ecology within the Urban Space and Suburban Area], Katowice 2006, p. 239.

9 *Ibid.*, p. 240.

10 P. Lorens, *Tematyzacja przestrzeni publicznej miasta*, Gdańsk 2006, p. 29.

11 *Ibid.*, pp. 29-30.

12 D. A. Karp, G. P Stone, W. C. Yoel, *Being Urban: A Sociology of City Life*, Westport 1991, pp. 84-86.

13 M. De Certeau, *L'invention du quotidien*, Paris 1980 [cited according to English translation, *The Practice of Everyday Life*, Berkeley 1984, pp. 98-99].

14 Blackburn, *Prywatność psychologiczna* cit., p. 320.

15 J. A. Beckford, *The Public, the Private, the Person: Elements of Ideologies of Privacy*, "Current Sociology", 1982, 30, p. 47.

16 B. S. Turner, *Privacy*, in *The Social Science Encyclopedia*, London 1985, pp. 646-647.

17 Blackburn, *Social privacy* cit., p. 321.

18 *Ibid.*, p. 321.

19 E. Shils, *Privacy in modern industrial society,* "Law and Contemporary Problems", 1966, 31, p. 22, cited in Beckford, *The Public* cit., p. 48.

20 "Intimate groups" are based on relationships of emotional closeness and in which the individual voluntarily participates. This concept was coined by Hans Paul Bahrdt; see Turowski, *Dychotomią prywatnej* cit., pp. 70-72.

21 *Ibid.*, pp. 76-78.

22 See, inter alia, A. F. Westin, *Privacy,* in *Encyclopedia Americana*, Connecticut 1993, pp. 626-627; A. Simmel, *Privacy*, in *The International Encyclopedia of Social Sciences*, vol. 12, New York 1968, pp. 480-487.

23 Simmel, *Privacy* cit., pp. 481.

24 See J. Musil, *Urbanizacja w krajach socjalistycznych*, Warsaw 1984, pp. 131-138.

25 According to the calculations of researchers, over half of the apartments within the Planty city park (58%) were artificially divided (in the case of 4-room apartments – over 74%; in the case of 5-room apartments – 92%). See A. Rębowska-Sowina, K. Z. Sowa, *Dzielnica Stare Miasto w Krakowie. Warunki i organizacja życia w starych budynkach*, Warsaw 1971, p. 6.

26 Cited in J. Mikułowski- Pomorski, *Kraków w naszej pamięci,* Krakow 1991, p. 209.

27 I. Paczyńska, *Gospodarka mieszkaniowa a polityka państwa w warunkach przekształceń ustrojowych w Polsce w latach 1945-1950 na przykładzie Krakowa*, Krakow 1994, pp. 201-203.

28 See S. Fitzpatrick, *Everyday Stalinism: Ordinary Life in Extraordinary Times: Soviet Russia in the 1930s*, Oxford 1999.

29 G. E. Karpińska, *Miejsca wyodrębnione ze świata. Przykład łódzkich kamienic czynszowych*, Łódzkie Studia Etnograficzne, vol. 38, Łódź 2000, pp. 170-171.

30 S. Kochanowski, *Zdarzenia, przygody, refleksje*, part 2, Jagiellonian Library, manuscript 102/72, pp. 9-10.

31 H. Świda- Ziemba, *Człowiek wewnętrznie zniewolony,* Warsaw 1998, p. 144.

32 *Ibid*., pp. 100-101.

33 Kochanowski, *Zdarzenia, przygody* cit., pp. 52-53.

34 J. Sulimski, *Kraków w procesie przemian. Współczesne przeobrażenia społeczności miejskiej*, Krakow 1977, pp. 225-226.

35 T. Binek, *Śląsk. Wojna. Śląsk. Wojna. Kresy. Wrocław. Nowa Huta. Wspomnienia 1930-1960,* Krakow 1997, p. 105.

36 Z. Niwińska, *Zapiski pamiętnikarskie 1961-1966*, Jagiellonian Library, manuscript 83/00.

37 K. Trześniowski, *Wychowanie fizyczne w ogródkach jordanowskich*, Warszawa 1954, p. 4.

38 *Ibid.*

39 R. Sulima, *Antropologia codzienności*, Krakow 2000, p. 63.

40 L. Lupa, *Muszę się tam znowu przejść*, "Gazeta Wyborcza. Kraków", 19 November 2001, p.10.

41 Z. Grzywacz, *Mój pierwszy kolor i zapach,* "Gazeta Wyborcza. Kraków", 10-11 November 2001, p. 5.

42 J. Bocheńska, Wspomnienie, "Gazeta Wyborcza. Kraków", 23 November 2001, p. 6.

43 W. Śniegowski, *Mój dobry nauczyciel Wawel*, "Gazeta Wyborcza. Kraków", 4 November 2001, p. 7.

44 Y.-F. Tuan, *Przestrzeń i miejsce*, Warsaw 1987, p. 87.

Bibliography

Aries P., Duby G. (eds.), *Histoire de la vie privée,* vol. I-V, Paris 1999.

Bailey J., *Some Meanings of "the Private" in Sociological Thought,* "Sociology", 2001, 34, pp. 381-401.

Beckford J.A., *The Public, the Private, the Person: Elements of Ideologies of Privacy,* "Current Sociology", 1982, 30, pp. 44-56.

Binek T., *Śląsk. Wojna. Kresy. Wrocław. Nowa Huta. Wspomnienia 1930-1960* [Silesia. The War. Kresy. Wrocław. NowaHuta. Memoire 1930-1960], Krakow 1997.

Blackburn S., Oxford Dictionary of Philosophy, Oxford 2005.

De Certeau M., *The Practice of Everyday Life*, Berkeley 1988 [orig. *L'invention du quotidien*, Paris 1960].

Dyczewski L., Krokowski J., McLean G. F. (eds.), *Prywatność i życie publiczne w nowoczesnym społeczeństwie USA- Polska* [Privacy and Public Life in Modern Societies (USA- Poland)], Lublin 1992.

Fitzpatrick S., *Everyday Stalinism: Ordinary Life in Extraordinary Times: Soviet Russia in the 1930s*, Oxford 1999.

Frysztacki K., *Miasta metropolitarne i ich przedmieścia. Z problematyki socjologii miasta oraz badań nad rzeczywistością krakowską* [The Metropolis and its Suburbs. Urban Sociology and Krakow's Reality], Krakow 1997.

Frysztacki K., *Organizacja życia społecznego zbiorowości wielkomiejskiej (Studium wybranych grup mieszkańców Krakowa)* [The Social System of the Urban Community (A Study of Selected Social Groups in Krakow)], Wroclaw 1982.

Goffman E., *Presentation of Self in Everyday Life,* New York 1959.

Herring P., *Public interest,* in *The International Encyclopedia of the Social Sciences*, vol. 13, New York 1968, pp. 170-175.

Jarosz D., *Polacy a stalinizm 1948-1956* [Poles and Stalinism 1948-1956], Warsaw 2000.

Kajfasz J., *O przemianach przestrzeni publicznej* [The Transformation of Public Space] in I. Bukowska - Floreńska (ed.), *Studia Etnologiczne i Antropologiczne t.9: Problem ekologii kulturowej i społecznej w przestrzeni miejskiej i podmiejskiej* [Problem the of the Cultural and Social Ecology within the Urban Space and Suburban Area], Katowice 2006.

Karp D. A., Stone G. P., Yoel W. C., *Being Urban: A Sociology of City Life*, Westport 1991.

Karpińska G. E., *Miejsca wyodrębnione ze świata. Przykład łódzkich kamienic czynszowych* [Isolated Places. The Case of the Tenement Houses in Lodz] , in "Łódzkie Studia Etnograficzne", 38, 2000.

Lorens P., *Tematyzacja przestrzeni publicznej miasta* [The Thematization of Urban Public Space], Gdańsk 2006.

Libura H., *Percepcja przestrzeni miejskiej* [The Perception of Urban Space], Warsaw 1990, pp. 187-188.

Mikułowski- Pomorski J., *Kraków w naszej pamięci* [Krakow in our memory], Krakow 1991.

Musil J., *Urbanizacje v socialistyckych zemich*, Prague 1977 [trad. pol. *Urbanizacja w krajach socjalistycznych*], Warsaw 1984; trad. eng. *Urbanization in Socialist Countries*, White Plains New York 1980].

Paczyńska I., *Gospodarka mieszkaniowa a polityka państwa w warunkach przekształceń ustrojowych w Polsce w latach 1945- 1950 na przykładzie Krakowa* [Housing Management and State Policy in the Era of the Political Transformation 1945- 1950. The case of Krakow], Krakow 1994.

Parker S., *Urban Theory and the Urban Experience: Encountering the City*, New York 2004.

Rębowska - Sowina A., Sowa K. Z., *Dzielnica Stare Miasto w Krakowie. Warunki i organizacja życia w starych budynkach* [Krakow Old Town. The Living Conditions and the System of Life in the Old Tenement Houses], Warsaw 1971.

Schildt A. (ed.), *European Cities, Youth and the Public Sphere in the Twentieth Century*, Aldershot 2005.

Schulze W. (ed.), *Sozialgeschichte, Alltagsgeschichte, Mikro-Historie, Eine Diskussion*, Gőttingen 1994.

Sennett R., *The Fall of Public Man*, New York 1974.

Simmel, *Privacy*, in *The International Encyclopedia of Social Sciences*, vol. 12, New York 1968, pp. 480-487.

Sulima R., *Antropologia codzienności* [The Anthropology of Everyday Life], Krakow 2000.

Suliński J., *Kraków w procesie przemian. Współczesne przeobrażenia społeczności miejskiej* [The Transformation Process of Krakow. The Metamorphosis of Contemporary Urban Society], Krakow 1977.

Szczepański M. S., *"Miasto socjalistyczne" i świat społeczny jego mieszkańców* ["The Socialist City" and Social World of Its Inhabitants], Warsaw 1991.

Świda-Ziemba H., *Człowiek wewnętrznie zniewolony* [The Internally Enslaved Man], Warsaw 1998.

Tuan Y.-F., *Space and place: the perspective of experience*, Minneapolis 1977, trad. pol. *Przestrzeń i miejsce*, Warsaw 1987.

Turkel G., *Dividing Public and Private. Law, Politics, and Social Theory*, Westport 1992.

Turowski J., *Dychotomia prywatnej i publicznej sfery życia (koncepcje i diagnozy)* [The Private – Public Dichotomy (Concepts and Diagnoses)], "Studia Socjologiczne", 1989, 3, pp. 11-21.

Wedel J., *The Private Poland*, New York 1987.

Westin A. F., *Privacy*, in *Encyclopedia Americana*, Danbury, Connecticut 1993, pp. 626-627.

The Moral Territory: Sexual Frontiers and Identities in Urban/Rural Historiography

LAURENT GAISSAD
University of Toulouse le Mirail (UTM- FRAMESPA – CNRS)
Free University of Brussels (ULB - FNRS)

ABSTRACT

This chapter attempts to present sexuality as a field of human experience which may help in conceptualizing frontiers and identities. Though written from a sociological perspective, the chapter is nevertheless interested in the contribution of historiography to the problem. It shows that historiography has frequently addressed sexual behaviour – including questions relating to designation and degrees of acceptability – in territorial terms, particularly urban or rural. Consequently, this study argues that sociological conceptions of (sexual) identities and frontiers may be seen as inspired by the diversity of historiographic and ethnographic evidence, rather than as simply sources of conceptual models disconnected from their specific historical and cultural contexts. Revisited from a sociological point of view, the considerable corpus of relevant historical research may be taken as representative 'data', and discussed without regard to customary chronological frameworks. The chapter will also assess the relevance of the concept of "moral territories" in the analysis of contrasted urban and rural living conditions, and to stimulate inventive empirical inquiry into the history of sexuality. Classic interpretations, particularly the Chicago School's conceptualization of the metropolis as a sociological laboratory, are also re-examined, showing how they continue to inspire socio-anthropological surveys as well as fieldwork. Overall, the study posits a sociologically-grounded historical explanation of sexual frontiers and identities, stressing in particular the scales and rhythms of mobility (or change) in spaces, times and norms revealed by the historiography in this specific field.

La sexualité, prise comme domaine de l'expérience humaine, constitue dans cet article une opportunité pour penser les notions de frontières et d'identité. S'appuyant sur le caractère historiquement construit des conduites sexuelles, il montre au combien l'historiographie s'est attachée à restituer leur désignation et leur degré d'acceptabilité en ville ou à la campagne. Il y est donc envisagé que les conceptions sociologiques de l'identité et des frontières (sexuelles) s'alimentent de la diversité des résultats historiographiques ou ethnographiques, plutôt que de faire office de boîtes à outils conceptuelles souvent universalisantes et deconnectées de leurs contextes historiques et culturels spécifiques. Pour autant, l'abondante bibliographie est revisitée d'un point de vue sociologique, en tant que "donnée" représentative, et abordée sans égard pour les conventions chronologiques. Le survol proposé entend démontrer la pertinence de la notion de "territoire moral" pour l'analyse comparée des modes de vie en milieu urbain et rural, et stimuler une recherche empirique innovante en histoire de la sexualité. Les définitions classiques de l'ordre moral, élaborées dans la métropole vue comme un laboratoire sociologique (École de Chicago), sont également ré-examinées, pour montrer comment s'en inspirent encore aujourd'hui les enquêtes socio-anthropologiques sur les réalités urbaines, rurales ou circulatoires. Surtout, l'article suggère une explication historique sociologiquement fondée des frontières et des identités sexuelles, en insistant plus particulièrement sur les échelles et les rythmes de la mobilité (ou du changement) dans l'espace, le temps et les normes tels que les révèle l'historiographie dans ce domaine précis.

Introduction

This chapter is written from a sociological point of view, and must therefore be understood as a transversal approach to the historiography of sexuality. Its objective is not to discuss interdisciplinary borders and definitions, though an essay which treated of the similarities and contrasts between history, sociology and anthropology with regard to urban spaces would be worthwhile[1]. The present discussion is based partly on ongoing interdisciplinary research on norms, gender and sexuality in Brussels[2]. Here, the spatial dimension of intimacy and sexuality throughout the 19th and 20th centuries in Europe and its colonies has emerged as particularly relevant, and has increasingly constituted a major axis on which to base our results. For instance, through the organisation of academic and cultural events such as conferences, exhibitions and film festivals on contemporary Western sexual practices and representations, attention has been drawn to various categories of sexual space, including public and intimate spaces, and what may be considered to be 'normative space'. While public spaces comprise urban areas traditionally associated with the sex industry (red light areas, public baths or brothels) or more implicitly sexualized social venues (cafés, dance halls, clubs), intimate spaces include the diverse range of domestic and matrimonial contexts, which may vary according to socio-economic and cultural influences. Of course, religious and educational spaces may also be analysed as normative spaces for the definition of sexuality, together with other more or less coercive institutions, such as those associated with health and medicine[3]. Besides this, social scientists have attempted to 'map' mental sexual space – for instance by locating the famous Freudian impulses, supposedly within every individual, on the frontier between the self and society, or between imagination and reality[4].

At first sight, this subdivision of sexual spaces may appear oversimplified, and the relation to differences in urban/rural lifestyles vague. However, it must be noted that one of Michel Foucault's early definitions of "other spaces"[5] as forms of *heterotopias* encouraged the conceptualizing of sexual experiences in territorial terms. Moreover, the so-called "crisis heterotopia" in traditional societies refers to privileged, sacred or forbidden spaces, generally reserved to individuals living in a state of crisis with society. Institutions like the 'Men's House', dedicated to initiation rites, are familiar concepts in classic anthropology[6], and their role in the production of gender or sexual frontiers and identities has been underlined by French[7] and American[8] ethnographers. Obviously, long-established same-sex institutions in religious, educational, martial and leisure spheres have constituted places for (first) sexual experiences too, but the role of an urban/rural dialectic in such processes has not attracted much scholarly attention, save for some controversial works on 'gay culture' in both history[9] and sociology[10], where the attraction for the urban world is sometimes evoked as a sexual form of rural exodus. In fact, mobility is mostly neglected when it comes to sexuality. It is nevertheless explicit in such well-established rites and rituals as the honeymoon, the locations of which Foucault characterised as "a place of nowhere", a "heterotopia without geographical markers". Other exceptions to the trend include recent French historiographers of sexuality and love during the First and Second World Wars[11], who have emphasised mobility as having had a major influence on the organisation of intimacy.

Therefore, it is clear that there has been considerable global interest in the *longue durée* history of sexuality as a spatial phenomenon. Foucault pioneered this with a celebrated three-volume essay; and continued with his collaboration with Arlette Farge on the *lettres de cachet* (royal writs which could be used to sanction a person's imprisonment) contained in the Bastille archives[12]. Here, the apparent breaching of norms governing spatial conducts was often the basis of the condemning *lettres*. Although the strategy of *lettres de cachet* lasted for a short period (1660-1760) and concerned only France, their study opened an important broader debate on the nature of judicial and penal archival material, and on the "lives of infamous men"[13] as evidence for everyday spatial and sexual conducts. A great deal of the historiography has concentrated on the margins of human sexual experience – which does not contradict the persistence of more or less implicit normative models both in the societies studied as well as the historical approaches themselves. However, the most 'visible' forms of sexual practices clearly appear to be the ones that have continuously fed the archives of control and sanction, precisely because they infringed established sexual orders and representations. Instead of considering them as mere peripheral deviations from the norm, current perspectives in the history of sexuality integrate the socio-anthropological idea that there is a continuity between normative and alternative (or subversive) expressions and practices, and that the latter may thoroughly document the former[14].

Suspicious spaces, conducts and creeds

Of course, many historians have shown that the archives constantly reveal the existence of 'suspicious spaces' for the expression of clandestine sexual activity. 18th-century Paris has provided copious examples, such as Rétif de la Bretonne's famous work on the territorial divisions of nocturnal Paris, and the diary of Jacques-Louis Ménétra, with its accounts of the Bois de Boulogne and Vicennes – wooded, marginal areas notoriously associated with sexuality[15].

One constant trend of historiography is to consider both sexual and religious conduct from a territorial perspective. In his famous book on homosexuality from the beginning of the Christian Era to the Renaissance, John Boswell[16] argues that most societies tolerating religious heterodoxies also accepted sexual deviance. Benassar's work on the Spanish Inquisition describes the opposite situation[17], showing the institution's tendency to associate religious and moral irregularity on a territorial base. For Benassar, this tendency does not simply concern the extreme peripheries of the empire, such as during the conquest of the New World, where native sexual behaviour was stigmatised as a sign of demonic influence[18]. His careful analysis of the Inquisition trials, and in particular their origins and evolution, demonstrates that during periods when rival religions were perceived as less threatening, the Inquisition focused on the moral (and sexual) crimes of the 'old Christians':

> As soon as it became interested in other goals, considered to be the priority, [the Inquisition's] rigour against 'the abominable sin' relaxed. Therefore, after the intense repression of the years 1570-1577, a rise in Moorish agitation diverted Aragon's Inquisition from sexual offences[19].

Religious uncertainty resulting from the European Reformation – in concert with the development of the nation state – has been related to the contemporaneous anti-witchcraft campaigns[20]. Moreover, it had been argued that witches were not only considered sexually suspicious members of the local community, but were represented as archetypes of the 'irrational female', whose ancient rural skills and knowledge was to be progressively destroyed in favour of 'rational male's' modern and urban science[21]. But such linkages between moral/sexual and religious misconduct are common in historiography – and may be used, for instance, by those interested in the etymology of sexual or religious designations. French historian Maurice Lever, for example, reveals the link between sodomy and heresy in the doctrinal struggles of the medieval Church, specifically in terms of the crusades against the Cathar heresy[22]. Lever shows how the French *boulgre* and *bougerie* derived between the 10th and 12th centuries in reference to migrating schismatics who became established in Bulgaria. Originally referring to foreign-based heretics, the words progressively came to signify sodomy. For Lever, such use of the word *bougre* to designate both the heretic and the homosexual until the 18th century illustrates clearly the conceptual confusion to be found in many other historical contexts. He cites the reputation of the court of King Henri III (1574-1589) as another example:

> The 'mignons' stand for starving the people; worse: they are enemies of France. Besides, don't they cultivate a foreign vice? Xenophobia becomes the rule, dominated by a hatred of the transalpine neighbour. The association is easy. Italian vice means Italian soul, breeding betrayal of the homeland. We are not far from the medieval confusion between heresy and sodomy[23].

A similar form of association is evoked by Guy Hocquenghem, whose work on official attitudes in France to sexual conduct during the Second World War argued that the French hatred of women and homosexuals was mainly expressed by the fear they might be in "communication of soul" with the enemy or the foreigner[24]. This fear of communication on sexual grounds has also been underlined in Alain Corbin's examinations of 19th-century metropolitan attitudes towards sexual conducts and migrants[25].

Times and spaces for moral (dis)order

Nevertheless, historians have also nuanced the concepts surrounding space and morality by emphasising the temporal dimension in the use of space, and the effects of mobility. This is exemplified by Jacques Rossiaud's study of prostitution in the Rhone valley in the 15th century. The importance of time is highlighted, showing how women gravitated towards markets and fairs, pilgrimages and seasonal agricultural events; certain locations saw increases in prostitution at specific times[26]. Within this framework Rossiaud identifies further temporal divisions – the periods before and after the organization of prostitution in the cities. He shows that between 1350 and 1450, many Rhone valley cities institutionalised prostitution, building their *prostibulum publicum*, if they did not already have one, at the central meeting point of public and political urban space[27]. In general these urban establishments practiced without common restrictions such as the interdiction of trade on the Sabbath. At times, however, regulations were introduced which forced prostitutes to wear special badges, or partitioned areas of prostitution from the rest of the city, such as the 'Lo Partit' area of Perpignan from 1380-1586[28]. But Rossiaud notes that, even in the restrictive context of such territorial confinement, the clandestine activity tended to mix with regular practices in the surrounding quarters, even at religious or public ceremonies, blending into the wider context.

Another interesting example is provided by David Stevenson's detailed study of the Beggar's Benison all male club in the small Scottish town of Fife (1732-1836). Vern L. Bullough reports that "The Benison (a term for benediction) was devoted to convivial and obscene celebration of the idea of free sex and free trade (read smuggling) with somewhat subversive political sentiments" and exposes the historian's speculation that "it grew out of a smugglers group (smuggling in eighteenth-century Scotland was a major industry) that expanded to include the custom official, mainly English, who, hated as outsiders, could be accepted by the power structure of the Benison club. Meetings could encourage the growth of male comradery and trust that crossed class and governmental barriers"[29].

But let us make another jump in time: there is of course a considerable amount of work on sexuality in antiquity, and some has addressed the issue of its territorial organisation. Catherine Salles' study of Greek and Roman underground sexual culture[30], for instance, shows the classical identification of sexual misconduct with foreign influence. Among its illustrative quotations is the following:

> I cannot abide, Quirites, a Rome of Greeks; and yet what fraction of our dregs comes from Greece? The Syrian Orontes has long since poured into the Tiber, bringing with it its lingo and its manners, its flutes and its slanting harp-strings; bringing too the timbrels of the breed, and the trulls [prostitutes] who are bidden ply their trade at the Circus[31].

It also underlines the specific role of big cities and, in particular, of the major ports of the Mediterranean. According to the correspondent Plautus, at these commercial hubs:

> The prostitutes usually send to the harbour their little slaves, their young servants. If a foreign ship enters the harbour, they ask what the country of origin is and who the owner is. They immediately hook the owner of the ship, sticking to him, and if they manage to trap him in their nets, they send him back completely broke. There is a real pirate vessel now in the harbour and I judge that we must be on our guard[32].

Some classical urban spaces developed protective areas for clandestine sexual and other activities. The sacred woods of Rome, for instance, sheltered the social outcasts – such as the lowest classes of prostitutes, minority religious groups, and hardened criminals – who all sought refuge beyond the reach of the civic authorities. Also, large portions of waste land outside the capital or along the avenues extending from it, and even in the Esquiline graveyard, constituted peripheral places for the development of marginal, and sometimes, secret sexual activities[33]. In fact, some scholars have established from Cicero's correspondence that urban space was defined by the existence of such 'frontier zones', particularly the vast peripheral zone of gardens which, delimited by the Tiber, formed a 'green belt' around the city[34].

The transformation of vast portions of the once wooded suburban landscape into public places dedicated to the leisure of city crowds has actually inspired recent European researchers in urban history focusing on more recent periods. Their particular taste for original archives thoroughly depicting the moral organisation of spaces and conducts (through legislation, autobiographies, drawings, police reports, court cases, etc.) does not simply reveal territorial conflicts in the central districts, nor those specific to established and visible 'milieux' – taverns, cabarets, brothels – as opposed to less official rendez-vous, prostitution[35], and men-to-men sexual settings scattered in streets, markets, railways, squares, public toilets and parks[36]. The direct outskirts of capitals newly converted into fashionable promenades are in their turn re-examined in detail, to show that they also inevitably favoured marginal, and of course, secret sexual activities. The Champs-Élysées, for example, which still constituted a frontier between the city and its countryside in late 18th-century Paris, are ambivalently portrayed throughout Swiss guard Ferdinand de Federici's meticulous daily reports (1777-1791): the tumultuous *tout Paris* not only gathered there in dangerous mobs, quarrels and duels; the peripheral public space concurrently happened to be the designated scene of gamblers, thieves, hawkers or hustlers, and of the continuous "schemes of pederasts" too[37].

For many historians, the role of local authorities and institutional control have been considered vital to understanding the presence of spaces associated with sexual deviance, and the demarcation of urban space according to sexual behaviour[38]. But some historiographical approaches insist on taking into account the collective and individual elaboration of moral frontiers and identities, not only speculating – as conceptual sociology or anthropology would – on the notions of law, norm or taboo, but building more complex evidence from a great diversity of sources. Examining prostitution in the French colonial world from multiple angles, Christelle Taraud describes the transition from male to colonial domination for women in Algeria, Tunisia and Morocco (1830-1962)[39]. Based on administrative, medical, judicial, and military sources, as well as perspectives offered by orientalist literature, the arts, city planning and architecture and the press, her arguments show how women involved in prostitution in the far margins of the French empire adapted 'sexual Taylorism' imposed by the occupying forces. In maintaining a strong link with their traditional society, while experiencing Europeanization, they assumed a very singular position in which they constantly connected the 'indigenous' and the European communities. While such an interpretation allows us to deconstruct stereotypes generally attached to colonial societies, it also defines the prostitute as a moral character standing at the frontier between different and antagonistic worlds and between contrasting social identities. Moreover, this example offers the possibility of considering moral frontiers on a larger geographical scale, in which the colony becomes a sort of hinterland of the metropolis, a place far away from home where sexual transgressions are not only permissible but implemented. In addition to this spatial organisation of sexual conducts, the colonial experience constitutes a specific period of time likely to breed exceptional forms of emancipation and constraints. Therefore, it is clear that vicissitudes in time and space should be considered when discussing sexuality.

In fact, many historians have considered temporal implications: some have examined the potential of the night as an agency in the development of clandestine activities in, for instance, urban and rural areas in the middle ages[40]; and recent studies of the introduction of public lighting to urban spaces reflects a growing interest in the differentiation between daily and nocturnal social life[41]. Yet sociology also considers night as a specific 'territory', and Murray Melbin's article, *Night as a frontier*[42], introduced useful data, which established similarities between geographic and temporal frontiers, and compared urban and rural circumstances. Melbin compared social activities observed in nocturnal Boston of the 1970s (namely, the gradual extension of nightlife into the nightly hours) to those described at the end of the 19th century on the North American frontier. According to his findings, the expansion of settlements into the time and space of the frontier relied on groups that were more isolated and more homogenous, especially in terms of gender: "The proportion of males in the population is higher on the frontier. Just as this part of the total is largest in Plains and Mountain States (71%), males comprise the largest part of the street population (89%) in the middle of the night"[43].

As a frontier, night also seemed to shelter stigmatized groups and promote new behavioural patterns. However, over time, it developed its own specific legitimacy, orders, and norms – as my own work on the ecology of male sexual locations in urban public space has shown[44]. Indeed, even very recently in France, some researchers have argued that night remains a territory for city planners to 'conquer'[45]. Nevertheless, other theorists maintain that city nights, just like days, create constraints and institutions that determine the spatial acceptability of behaviours[46].

The "moral region" revisited

Of course, such analysis inevitably leads us to consider the contribution to urban sociology developed by the Chicago School. Shaped in part by the German sociological heritage[47], it developed in the context of the tremendous urban growth of Chicago in the first decades of the 20th century, and the cultural changes brought about by a sudden influx of immigrants. The School was interested especially in the city's impact on its inhabitants, describing conflicts arising from the presence of cultures in close proximity; its founders also condemned the confusion between sociology and social morality in a period which experienced, for example, prohibition[48]. Among them was Robert Ezra Park, who had been a student of Georg Simmel, the German phenomenologist and theorist of modernity in sociology, whose articles *The Metropolis and Mental Life*[49] and *The Stranger*[50] constitute very useful methodological contributions to frontiers and identities. More particularly, Park's earliest studies on the urban moral order proposed the notion of "moral regions"[51], referring to districts notoriously dedicated to desire and emancipation that were simultaneously segregated and allowed by urban life. As a man of his times, he postulated that: "In order to understand the forces which in every large city tend to develop these detached milieus, in which vagrant and suppressed impulses, passions, and ideals emancipate themselves from the dominant moral order, it is necessary to refer to the fact or theory of latent impulses of men"[52].

Feminist historians later showed that Park was not the first to define neighbourhoods according to sexual behaviour. Meyerowitz[53], for example, in her study on the furnished room districts of Chicago argues that "evidence from newspapers, autobiographies, vice reports, and social surveys also suggests that the furnished room districts were indeed the centres of sexually unconventional subcultures". The "sexual subtext of several key concepts from the so-called Chicago School" was recently evoked to explain the erasure from historical memory of this field in the development of urban sociology[54]. However, the notion of the moral region deserves to be examined critically in order to understand the complex interactions which took place between the diverse populations of modern cities. As a matter of fact, the compartmentalized idea of the moral region was contradicted by the concept of the "marginal man", developed later by Park[55]. "Marginal man" is very close to the notion of liminality, since it refers to an individual condemned to stand at the threshold of two distinct social worlds. While the moral region necessarily conceived an individual as being from here or from there, "marginal man" implied that the individual might well be from neither here nor from there, and many contemporary sociological works – on migration for instance – have since established that one could be from here *and* from there at the same time, stressing the individual's ability to circulate between different social spheres (especially in urban contexts of intense social exchanges and mobility, but also in the exchange between urban and rural contexts)[56]. In fact, much ethnographic evidence has been put forward to demonstrate that the notion of the moral region itself could be in direct contradiction with the individual's ability to cross physical borders, and of course symbolic ones, since norms can be understood as social borders in the socio-anthropological tradition. Urban anthropologist Ulf Hannerz[57] has criticised further Park's propositions by arguing that: "To describe the separate 'moral regions' or 'social worlds' became one of the major tasks of the Chicago sociologists. But the fact of the coexistence of these worlds in the city could also lead to further questions about the relationships between them"[58].

Envisioning the city as a network of juxtaposed areas – a sort of mosaic, as Park would have put it – has been challenged seriously by the introduction of a temporal aspect to the analysis of contrasting sexual conducts, that often seem to be 'superimposed' onto daily life. The case of impersonal male sex on suburban highway rest areas, described by Humphreys[59], is one of the various examples of ethnographies that inspired my own observations of the scarcely visible sexual exchange in peri-urban woods during rush-hour, or discreet forms of prostitution in city market crowds and big railway stations. An even more serious remark concerning the notion of "moral region" and, in general, the Chicago ethnographic tradition, has come from David Mazra[60] who underlined the very little relevance it showed for the "ordinary facts of transiency" – in other words, *mobility* – declaring that "their approach of overlap was minimal. They exaggerated the separation between deviant and conventional worlds, building frontiers too firmly"[61]. Such a critique of the founding fathers of urban sociology encourages the examination of the nature, and of course, the scale of spatial and identity 'shifts' in human exchanges, not only in city contexts – where anonymity overcomes the dilemma of "multiple realities"[62] – but also in the narrow networks of acquaintances that characterise rural cultures, where secrecy and rumour are very likely to create an alternative relation to freedom and constraints.

Considering this dimension too, the methodological challenge may be confronted by returning to Foucault's advice regarding heterotopias: that they "always presuppose a system of opening and closing that both isolates them and makes them penetrable"[63], or to describe transitions, entry rites and, of course, the relation of such spaces to the rest of social life. Last but not least, the temporal dimension was not entirely excluded from Foucault's useful attempt to define alternative spaces, since: "Heterotopias are most often linked to slices in time, which is to say that they open onto what might be termed, for the sake of symmetry, heterochronies. The heterotopia begins to function at full capacity when men arrive at a sort of absolute break with their traditional time"[64].

Momentary emancipation can therefore be depicted following the extraordinary contingency of values experienced at, for instance, fairs, carnivals, holidays or migrations, and in the sudden meeting of normative uncertainty and self- or social conservation. It is very probably in this sense that Georges Gurvitch introduced the idea of "suspended" time as part of his general theory of the multiplicity of social times[65]. He wanted to indicate circumstances when the present conflicts with the past and future. This subjective conception of time has of course raised severe criticism from historians, who suggest that sociologists lack a real and objective sense of time[66]. The attention to scales and rhythms of mobility revealed by the historiography of sexuality must however be understood as a sociologically-grounded historical explanation of (sexual) frontiers and identities in time that is nevertheless likely to open promising perspectives for historical research.

Obviously, such historiography does not only establish the importance of real and potential spaces for the variety of sexual expressions (identities) and limits (frontiers), it also constitutes an opportunity to confront subjective and objective definitions of time[67]. Although marginal experiences are emphasized to an extent that objectively asserts a (historical) continuity of normative models, it also highlights at least two subjective yet contradictory temporal orientations. First, a strategic use of time – including the time of the unconscious postulated by Freud – made necessary by the constant constraints of social life or institutions; second, an eternal conception, mythically defining sexuality as 'natural' and unaltered by time.

Notes

1 The necessity for such epistemological developments is clearly illustrated by the cross-reading of this chapter with the contribution of D. Kalwa's to this volume.

2 The "Norms, gender and sexuality" project in the Université Libre de Bruxelles (ULB) is a collaboration between the Faculty of History and the Comparative and History of Law Centre supported by the Fonds National de la Recherche Scientifique (FNRS), bringing together researchers in History, Sociology, Anthropology and Law. Contact by e-mail: lgaissad@ulb.ac.be

[3] V. L. Bullough, *Science in the Bedroom: A History of Sex Research*, New York 1994, and more recently: S. Chaperon, *Les Origines de la Sexologie, 1850-1900* [The Origins of Sexology, 1850-1900], Paris 2007.

[4] D.W. Winnicott, *Playing and Reality*, New York 1971.

[5] M. Foucault, *Des Espaces Autres* [Of Other Spaces], in D. Defert, F. Ewald (eds.) *Dits et Écrits*, 4 vols., Paris 1994 IV, pp. 752-762. Reprinted from "Architecture, Mouvement, Continuité", 1984, 5, pp. 46-59, and from a conference paper delivered at the Cercle d'Études Architecturales, Tunis, March 1967. An English version is available on line at the following address: http://foucault.info/documents/heteroTopia/foucault.heteroTopia.en.html

[6] M. Mauss, *Manuel d'Ethnographie* [Manual of Ethnography], Paris 1926.

[7] M. Godelier, *La Production des Grands Hommes* [The Making of Great Men], Paris 1982.

[8] G. Herdt, *Guardians of the Flutes: Idioms of Masculinity*, Chicago 1981; G. Herdt, *Secrecy and Cultural Reality. Utopian Ideologies of the New Guinea Men's House*, Detroit 2002.

[9] The growing number of works in gay and lesbian historiography over the last thirty years include J. Boswell, *Christianity, Social Tolerance, and Homosexuality. Gay People in Western Europe from the Beginning of the Christian Era to the 14th Century*, Chicago - London 1980; G. Chauncey, *Gay New York: Gender, Urban Culture and the Making of Gay Male World, 1890-1940*, New York 1994; F. Tamagne, *Histoire de l'Homosexualité en Europe. Berlin, Londres, Paris. 1919-1939* [The History of Homosexuality in Europe. Berlin, London, Paris. 1919-1939], Paris 2000.

[10] M. Pollak, *Les Homosexuels et le Sida. Sociologie d'une Épidémie* [Gay Men and AIDS. Sociology of an Epidemic], Paris 1988; H. Bech, *When Men Meet: Homosexuality and Modernity*, Chicago 1997; W. L. Leap, *Public Sex/Gay Space*, New York 1999.

[11] L. Capdevila, F. Rouquet, F. Virgili, D. Voldman, *Hommes et Femmes dans la France en Guerre (1914-1945)* [Men and Women in France at War (1914-1945)], Paris 2003. A collective catalogue of the exhibition "Amours, Guerres et Sexualité" at the Hôtel National des Invalides in Paris (22 September – 31 December 2007) has recently been published for the occasion: F. Rouquet, F. Virgili, D. Voldman, *Amours, Guerres et Sexualité (1914-1945)* [Love, War and Sexuality (1914-1945)], Paris 2007.

[12] M. Foucault, A. Farge, *Le Désordre des Familles: Lettres de Cachet des Archives de la Bastille au 18ème Siècle* [The Disorder of Families. "Lettres de Cachets" from the 18th-century Bastille archives], Paris 1982.

[13] M. Foucault, *La Vie des Hommes Infâmes* [The Life of Infamous Men], in *Dits et Écrits* cit., III, pp. 237-256. Reprinted from "Les Cahiers du Chemin", 15 January 1977, pp. 12-29.

[14] This assumption was very clearly admitted in most of the works presented at a recent symposium organised in Brussels on the "History of Heterosexuality: Research Unthought?", Université Libre de Bruxelles, 12-13 October 2007.

[15] R. de la Bretonne, *Les Nuits de Paris* [Nights of Paris], Paris 1986; M. Lever, *Les Bûchers de Sodome* [Burning at the Stakes of Sodom], Paris 1985, pp. 255-265; D. Roche, *Journal de ma Vie. Jacques-Louis Ménétra, Compagnon Vitrier au 18ème Siècle* [The Diary of my Life. Jacques-Louis Menetra, Glaziers' guildsman in the 18th century], Paris 1982.

[16] Boswell, *Christianity*, cit. p. 15.

[17] B. Bennassar, *L'Inquisition Espagnole* [The Spanish Inquisition], Paris 1979.

[18] B. Bennassar's analysis has since been added to, in particular by the more complex approach suggested by J. Goldberg's article *Sodomy in the New world. Anthropology Old and New*, in "Social Text", 1991, 29, pp. 46-56, in which the usual paradigm of self and other, oppressor and oppressed, is revisited looking at the most violent episodes against sodomite Indians in the conquest of South America.

[19] Bennassar, *L'Inquisition* cit., pp. 337-338. My translation.

[20] G. Bechtel, *La Sorcière et l'Occident. La Destruction de la Sorcellerie en Europe, des Origines aux Grands Bûchers* [The Witch and the Western World. The Destruction of Witchcraft in Europe, from the Origins to the Great Burnings], Paris 1997.

[21] Muchembled R., *La Sorcière au Village. 15-18ème Siècles* [The Witch in the Village. 15th-18th Centuries], Paris 1979; and *Sorcières, Justice et Société au 16ème et 17ème Siècles* [Witches, Justice and Society in the 16th and 17th Centuries], Paris 1987.

[22] Lever, *Les Bûchers* cit., p. 44.

[23] *Ibid.*, p. 83. My translation.

[24] G. Hocquenghem, *La Beauté du Métis. Réflexion d'un Francophobe* [Beauty of the Metis. A Francophobe's Reflections], Paris 1979.

[25] He argues for an ethno-historical approach of social environment in the context of the (urban) industrial revolution: A. Corbin, *Le Temps, le Désir et l'Horreur. Essai sur le 19ème Siècle* [Time, Desire and Horror. Essay on the 19th century], Paris 1991.

[26] J. Rossiaud, *La Prostitution Médiévale* [Medieval Prostitution], Paris 1988.

[27] See the work of urban anthropologist F. Paul-Lévy in *La Ville en Croix* [The City in Cross], Paris 1984, correlating the 19th-century Haussmann 're-foundation' of Paris to the ancient territorial foundation of cities 'in cross' and to a quadripartite spatial organisation of traditional societies.

[28] É. Déplanque (archivist at Perpignan), *Les Infâmes dans le Perpignan du Moyen-Age* [The Infamous in Middle-Ages Perpignan], Narbonne 1998.

[29] D. Stevenson, *The Beggar's Benison: Sex Clubs of Enlightenment Scotland and their Rituals*, East Lothian 2001, reviewed by V. L. Bullough in "Albion: A Quarterly Journal Concerned with British Studies", 2003, 35, pp. 361-363.

[30] C. Salles, *Les Bas-Fonds de l'Antiquité* [Underworlds of Antiquity], Paris 1982.

[31] Salles, *Les Bas-Fonds* cit., p. 241. From Juvenal, *Satire III*, v. 62-65: http://en.wikisource.org/wiki/Satire_3

[32] Salles, *Les Bas-Fonds* cit., p. 88. From Plautus, *Menaechmi*, v. 338-344.

[33] Salles, *Les Bas-Fonds* cit., pp. 241-264.

[34] M. J. Kardos, *Lieux et Lumière de Rome chez Cicéron* [Sites and Lights of Cicero's Rome], Paris 1997.

[35] C. Huberty, L. Keunings, *La Prostitution à Bruxelles au dix-neuvième siècle* [Prostitution in Brussels in the 19th Century], in "Les Cahiers de la Fonderie", 1987, 2, pp 1-19, underlines the official distinction between *house* prostitutes and *scarce* (vagrant) girls.

[36] N. Chartier, *De Homoseksuele Subcultuur in Brussel in de negentiende eeuw* [Homosexual Subculture in Brussels in the 19th Century], MA dissertation, Leuven 2004.

[37] A. Farge, L. Turcot, *Flagrant délits sur les Champs-Élysées. Les dossiers de Police du Gardien Federici (1777-1791)* [Caught in the act on the Champs-Élysées. The Police Reports of the Guard Federici (1777-1791)], Paris 2008.

[38] The famous laws of Solon (around 640/558 BC) constitute an early attempt to organise prostitution for the preservation of Greek racial purity, diverting young people from married women, providing the Greeks with cheap pleasure without remorse or consequence as Salles, *Les Bas-Fonds* cit., pp. 20-21 puts it.

[39] C. Taraud, *La Prostitution Coloniale. Algérie, Tunisie, Maroc, 1830-1962* [Colonial Prostitution. Algeria, Tunisia, Morocco, 1830-1962], Paris 2003.

[40] J. Verdon, *La Nuit au Moyen-âge* [Night in the Middle-Ages], Paris 1994.

41 Brussels City Archives recently organized an exhibition dedicated to the historical uses of light in town: "Du halo au réseau. La lumière dans la ville" (7 September – 31 December 2007).

42 M. Melbin, *Night as Frontier*, in "American Sociological Review", 1978, 43, pp. 3-22.

43 *Ibid.*, p. 8.

44 L. Gaissad, *From Nightlife Conventions to Daytime Hidden Agendas: Dynamics of Urban Sexual Territories in the South of France*, in "Journal of Sex Research", 2005, 42, pp. 20-27.

45 L. Gwiazdzinski, *La Nuit, Dernière Frontière* [Night, the Last Frontier], in "Les Annales de la Recherche Urbaine", 2000, 87, pp. 81-88.

46 A. Cauquelin, *La Ville la Nuit* [The City at Night], Paris 1977.

47 In particular by the Weberian idea that city air sets you free: "Stadtluft macht frei" is in fact a German medieval proverb reminding us that moving to a city at that period was often an escape from serfdom.

48 In the 1960s and 1970s, a second generation of Chicago School social researchers would react to the behavioural functionalism trends notably at work in a sexual sociology of the family and of its "deviances", insisting on the fabric of norms themselves, and on the use of stigma in daily life.

49 G. Simmel, *Die Großstädte und das Geistesleben* [The Metropolis and Mental Life], in "Jahrbuch der Gehestiftung zu Dresden", 1903, 9, pp. 187-205.

50 Id., *Exkurs über den Fremden* [The Stranger], in Id. (ed.), *Soziologie. Untersuchungen über die Formen der Vergesellschaftung*, Berlin 1908, pp. 509-512.

51 R. E. Park, *The City. Suggestions for the Investigation of Human Behavior in the City Environment*, in "The American Journal of Sociology", 1915, 20, pp. 577-612.

52 *Ibid.*, p. 610.

53 J. Meyerowitz, *Sexual Geography and Gender Economy: The Furnished Room Districts of Chicago, 1890-1930*, in "Gender & History", 1990, 2, pp. 274–297.

54 C. Heap, *The City as a Sexual Laboratory: The Queer Heritage of the Chicago School*, in "Qualitative Sociology", 2003, 26, pp. 457-487.

55 R. E. Park, *Human Migration and the Marginal Man*, in "The American Journal of Sociology", 1928, 33, pp. 881-893.

56 See A. Tarrius, *Les Nouveaux Cosmopolitismes. Mobilités, Identités, Territoires* [New Cosmopolitisms. Mobility, Identity, Territory], Paris 2000, and Missaoui L., *Les Étrangers de l'Intérieur. Filières, Trafics et Xénophobie* [The Inside Outsiders. Networks, Traffics and Xenophobia], Paris 2003. The notion of "moral region" is also recently extended beyond its initial urban limits to describe vast European spaces of transnational migration in Andalucia and in the Balkans by A. Tarrius, *La Remontée des Sud. Afghans et Marocains en Europe Méridionale* [Southwards Rising. Afghans and Moroccans in Southern Europe], Paris 2007.

57 U. Hannertz, *Exploring the City. Inquiries Towards an Urban Anthropology*, New York 1980.

58 *Ibid.*, p. 26.

59 L. Humphreys, *Tea Room Trade. Impersonal Sex in Public Places*, Chicago 1970, inopportunely published in French under the title *Le Commerce des Pissotières. Pratiques Homosexuelles (sic) Anonymes dans l'Amérique des années 1960*, Paris 2007.

60 D. Matza, *Becoming Deviant*, New Jersey 1969.

61 *Ibid.*, p. 70.

62 A. Schütz, *On Multiple Realities*, in "Philosophy and Phenomenological Research", 1945, 5, pp. 533-576.

63 Foucault, *Des Espaces* cit., p. 760.

[64] *Ibid.*, p. 759.

[65] G. Gurvitch, *La Multiplicité des Temps Sociaux* [The Multiplicity of Social Times], Paris 1958.

[66] F. Braudel, *History and the Social Sciences*, in "American Behavioral Scientist", 1960, 3, pp. 3-13.

[67] J. R. Hall, *The Time of History and the History of Times*, in "History and Theory", 1980, 19, pp. 113-31 provides a complete overview of this general debate opposing historians and sociologists, far beyond what can possibly be discussed within the limits of this chapter.

Bibliography

Bech H., *When Men Meet: Homosexuality and Modernity*, Chicago 1997.

Bechtel G., *La Sorcière et l'Occident. La Destruction de la Sorcellerie en Europe, des Origines aux Grands Bûchers* [The Witch and the Western World. The Destruction of Witchcraft in Europe, from the Origins to the Great Burnings at the Stakes], Paris 1997.

Bennassar B., *L'Inquisition Espagnole* [The Spanish Inquisition], Paris 1979.

Boswell J., *Christianity, Social Tolerance, and Homosexuality. Gay People in Western Europe from the Beginning of the Christian Era to the 14th Century*, Chicago - London 1980.

Braudel F., *History and the Social Sciences*, in "American Behavioral Scientist", 1960, 3, pp. 3-13.

Bretonne R. de la, *Les Nuits de Paris* [Nights of Paris], Paris 1986.

Bullough V. L., *Science in the Bedroom: A History of Sex Research*, New York 1994.

Capdevila L., Rouquet F., Virgili F., Voldman D., *Hommes et Femmes dans la France en Guerre (1914-1945)* [Men and Women in war time France (1914-1945)], Paris 2003.

Cauquelin A., *La Ville la Nuit* [The City at Night], Paris 1977.

Chaperon S., *Les Origines de la Sexologie, 1850-1900* [The Origins of Sexology, 1850-1900], Paris 2007.

Chartier N., *De Homoseksuele Subcultuur in Brussel in de negentiende eeuw* [Homosexual Subculture in Brussels in the 19th Century], PhD thesis, Leuven 2004.

Chauncey G., *Gay New York: Gender, Urban Culture and the Making of Gay Male World, 1890-1940*, New York 1994.

Corbin A., *Le Temps, le Désir et l'Horreur. Essai sur le 19ème Siècle* [Time, Desire and Horror. Essay on the 19th century], Paris 1991.

Defert D., Ewald F. (eds.), *Dits et Écrits*, 4 vols., Paris 1994.

Déplanque É., *Les Infâmes dans le Perpignan du Moyen-Age* [The Infamous in Middle-Ages Perpignan], Narbonne 1998.

Farge A., Turcot L., *Flagrant délits sur les Champs-Élysées. Les dossiers de Police du Gardien Federici (1777-1791)* [Caught in the act on the Champs-Élysées. The Police Reports of the Guard Federici (1777-1791)], Paris 2008.

Foucault M., *Des Espaces Autres* [Of Other Spaces], in D. Defert, F. Ewald (eds.), *Dits et Écrits*, Paris 1994, IV, pp. 752-762. Reprinted from "Architecture, Mouvement, Continuité", 1984, 5, pp. 46-59, and from a conference paper delivered at the Cercle d'Études Architecturales, Tunis, March, 1967.

Id., *La Vie des Hommes Infâmes* [The Life of Infamous Men], in D. Defert, F. Ewald (eds.), *Dits et Écrits*, Paris 1994, III, pp. 237-256. Reprinted from "Les Cahiers du Chemin", 15 January 1977, pp. 12-29.

Foucault M., Farge A., *Le Désordre des Familles: Lettres de Cachet des Archives de la Bastille au 18ème Siècle* [The Disorder of Families. "Lettres de Cachets" from the 18th-century Bastille archives], Paris 1982.

Gaissad L., *From Nightlife Conventions to Daytime Hidden Agendas: Dynamics of Urban Sexual Territories in the South of France*, in "Journal of Sex Research", 2005, 42, pp. 20-27.

Goldberg J., *Sodomy in the New World. Anthropology Old and New*, in "Social Text", 1991, 29, pp. 46-56

Godelier M., *La Production des Grands Hommes* [The Making of Great Men], Paris 1982.

Gurvitch G., *La Multiplicité des Temps Sociaux* [The Multiplicity of Social Times], Paris 1958.

Gwiazdzinski L., *La Nuit, Dernière Frontière* [Night, the Last Frontier], in "Les Annales de la Recherche Urbaine", 2000, 87, pp. 81-88

Hall J. R., *The Time of History and the History of Times*, in "History and Theory", 1980, 19, pp. 113-131.

Hannertz U., *Exploring the City. Inquiries Towards an Urban Anthropology*, New York 1980.

Heap C., *The City as a Sexual Laboratory: The Queer Heritage of the Chicago School*, in "Qualitative Sociology", 2003, 26, pp. 457-87.

Herdt G., *Guardians of the Flutes: Idioms of Masculinity*, Chicago 1981.

Id., *Secrecy and Cultural Reality. Utopian Ideologies of the New Guinea Men's House*, Detroit 2002.

Hocquenghem G., *La Beauté du Métis. Réflexion d'un Francophobe* [Beauty of the Metis. A Francophobe's Reflections], Paris 1979.

Huberty C., Keunings L., *La Prostitution à Bruxelles au dix-neuvième siècle* [Prostitution in Brussels in the 19th Century], in "Les Cahiers de la Fonderie", 1987, 2, pp 1-19.

Humphreys L., *Tea Room Trade. Impersonal Sex in Public Places*, Chicago 1970.

Kardos M. J., *Lieux et Lumière de Rome chez Cicéron* [Sites and Lights of Cicero's Rome], Paris 1997.

Leap W. L., *Public Sex/Gay Space*, New York 1999.

Lever M., *Les Bûchers de Sodome* [Burning at the Stakes of Sodom], Paris 1985.

Matza D., *Becoming Deviant*, New Jersey 1969.

Mauss M., *Manuel d'Ethnographie* [Manual of Ethnography], Paris 1926.

Melbin M., *Night as Frontier*, in "American Sociological Review", 1978, 43, pp. 3-22.

Meyerowitz J., *Sexual Geography and Gender Economy: The Furnished Room Districts of Chicago, 1890-1930*, in "Gender & History", 1990, 2, pp. 274–297.

Missaoui L., *Les Étrangers de l'Intérieur. Filières, Trafics et Xénophobie* [The Inside Outsiders. Networks, Traffics and Xenophobia], Paris 2003.

Muchembled R., *La Sorcière au Village. 15-18ème Siècles* [The Witch in the Village. 15th-18th Centuries], Paris 1979.

Id., *Sorcières, Justice et Société au 16ème et 17ème Siècles* [Witches, Justice and Society in the 16th and 17th Centuries], Paris 1987.

Park R. E., *The City. Suggestions for the Investigation of Human Behavior in the City Environment*, in "The American Journal of Sociology", 1915, 20, pp. 577-612.

Id., *Human Migration and the Marginal Man*, in "The American Journal of Sociology", 1928, 33, pp. 881-893.

Paul-Lévy F., *La Ville en Croix. De la Révolution de 1848 à la Rénovation haussmannienne* [The City in Cross. From the 1848 Revolution to the Haussmannian Rehabilitation], Paris 1984.

Pollak M., *Les Homosexuels et le Sida. Sociologie d'une Épidémie* [Gay Men and AIDS. Sociology of an Epidemic], Paris 1988.

Roche D., *Journal de ma Vie. Jacques-Louis Ménétra, Compagnon Vitrier au 18ème Siècle* [The Diary of my Life. Jacques-Louis Menetra, Glaziers' guildsman in the 18th century], Paris 1982.

Rossiaud J., *La Prostitution Médiévale* [Medieval Prostitution], Paris 1988.

Rouquet F., Virgili F., Voldman D., *Amours, Guerres et Sexualité (1914-1945)* [Love, War and Sexuality (1914-1945)], Paris 2007.

Salles C., *Les Bas-Fonds de l'Antiquité* [Underworlds of Antiquity], Paris 1982.

Schütz A., *On Multiple Realities*, in "Philosophy and Phenomenological Research", 1945, 5, pp. 533-576.

Simmel G., *Die Großstädte und das Geistesleben* [The Metropolis and Mental Life], in "Jahrbuch der Gehestiftung zu Dresden", 1903, 9, pp. 187-205.

Stevenson D., *The Beggar's Benison: Sex Clubs of Enlightenment Scotland and their Rituals*, East Lothian 2001, reviewed by Bullough V. L. in "Albion: A Quarterly Journal Concerned with British Studies", 2003, 35, pp. 361-363.

Id., *Exkurs über den Fremden* [The Stranger], in Id. (ed.), *Soziologie. Untersuchungen über die Formen der Vergesellschaftung*, Berlin 1908, pp. 509-512.

Tamagne F., *Histoire de l'Homosexualité en Europe. Berlin, Londres, Paris. 1919-1939* [The History of Homosexuality in Europe. Berlin, London, Paris. 1919-1939], Paris 2000.

Taraud C., *La Prostitution Coloniale. Algérie, Tunisie, Maroc, 1830-1962* [Colonial Prostitution. Algeria, Tunisia, Morocco, 1830-1962], Paris 2003.

Tarrius A., *Territoires Circulatoires et Espaces Urbains* [Circulatory Territories and Urban Spaces], in "Les Annales de la Recherche Urbaine", 1993, 59-60, pp. 51-60.

Id., *Les Nouveaux Cosmopolitismes. Mobilités, Identités, Territoires* [New Cosmopolitisms. Mobility, Identity, Territory], Paris 2000.

Id., *La Remontée des Sud. Afghans et Marocains en Europe Méridionale* [Southwards Rising. Afghans and Moroccans in Southern Europe], Paris 2007.

Verdon J., *La Nuit au Moyen-âge* [Night in the Middle-Ages], Paris 1994.

Winnicott D.W., *Playing and Reality*, New York 1971.

The Boundaries of Medieval Misogyny: Gendered Urban Space in Medieval Durham

William M. Aird
Cardiff University

Abstract

This chapter examines the relationship between the medieval Church and an urban community in the North-East of England in the late 11th and early 12th centuries. It highlights the nature of the precincts that surrounded medieval churches through an investigation of the local tradition that St Cuthbert, the patron of the Cathedral of Durham, excluded women from a defined area surrounding his shrine. The chapter refers to the grant of an ecclesiastical immunity, namely the right of sanctuary, to the Church of St Cuthbert. In effect, this grant created a *sanctus locus* [sacred space] within the medieval city of Durham, which was also the foundation of the unusually strong local power wielded by the medieval bishops of Durham within their city and diocese. The exclusion of women from the cathedral-priory and its cemetery made the ecclesiastical precinct a "gendered" as well as a "sacred space". It is suggested that the two phenomena are related and demonstrate the importance of mental as well as physical boundaries in the medieval urban landscape. The origins of the misogynistic prohibition can be associated with the introduction in 1083 of the monastic Rule of St Benedict by Bishop William of Saint-Calais (1081-1096), but was most probably a response to problems encountered by the monastic community during the pontificate of Bishop Ranulf Flambard (1099-1128). Finally, the chapter questions whether this exclusion of women was rigidly enforced drawing on evidence that suggests that they were in fact welcomed at Cuthbert's shrine as circumstances changed. It concludes by pointing out that boundaries can be conceptual as well as physical and that tradition, however atavistic it may seem, can be invented and, like those boundaries, periodically renegotiated.

Countess Judith of Northumbria was a pious and inquisitive woman[1]. Her piety was expressed through gifts made jointly with her husband, Earl Tostig, to St Cuthbert, the greatest of the medieval saints of Northern England. The couple had made donations to the saint's church at Durham and promised more including landed estates. However, there was a condition: the Countess wanted to be able to enter the cathedral that housed Cuthbert's relics and worship at his tomb. There was also a problem: St Cuthbert had banned any woman from entering his church. Judith decided to test the saint's prohibition[2]. According to an early 12th-century history of the Church of St Cuthbert:

> She devised the plan of sending one of her servants ahead of her, so that if she were able to do this with impunity, the mistress would follow after her and would dare to enter the church with more confidence of her safety. So when the girl had learned her mistress's will, she undertook to approach the church at a very quiet time in order to attempt this. As she was about to place her foot inside the cemetery [*cimiterium*], she was suddenly repelled by a violent force as of the wind, her strength failed [*ueluti uentorum uiolentia repelli cepit et uiribus deficere*] and stricken with a grave infirmity, she was scarcely able to return to the hospice, where falling on to her bed, she was racked with terrible torment until at length she was deprived of both the pain and her life. The countess was absolutely terrified at what had happened and began to tremble all over[3].

The chastened Judith sought to make amends and with the proper humility she and Tostig arranged for an ornate crucifix to be made and presented at Cuthbert's shrine, together with images of the Blessed Virgin and John the Evangelist[4]. This account is interesting for a number of reasons, not the least of which is that it was associated with the gift of specific ornaments found in the Church of St Cuthbert. It is possible to imagine the elaborate gold and silver cross and the images of the Virgin and St John evoking memories of Tostig and Judith's rule in Northumbria, as well as a warning to observe the local prohibition on women approaching Cuthbert's shrine[5]. The story also makes it clear that the cemetery around the Church of St Cuthbert constituted a prohibited space within the medieval city of Durham and that the prohibited space was gendered, in that the ban applied only to women[6].

The miraculous punishment of Countess Judith's maid-servant was followed in the medieval narrative by a reference to another test of St Cuthbert's power[7]. Again, during Tostig's rule in Northumbria, a notorious bandit named Aldan-Hamal, the perpetrator of many heinous crimes for which offers of monetary compensation could not make amends, escaped the earl's justice and took refuge in St Cuthbert's Church in Durham[8]. Barcwith, one of the earl's men, pursued the fugitive to the threshold of the church. He advocated breaking through the doors in order to seize Aldan-Hamal, but as soon as he had finished saying that he had no regard for the "peace of a dead man", meaning the sanctuary offered by St Cuthbert, he was struck down "as if by an arrow from above [*quasi sagitta desuper veniens*][9]." The writer of the miracle account had heard the story from monks who had witnessed the events as well as from Aldan-Hamal himself. Barcwith expired three days after being struck down and for six months afterwards a fetid odour emanated from his grave[10]. Barcwith's death terrified Earl Tostig and his men to such an extent that they abandoned their pursuit of Aldan-Hamal and even accorded him some honour, presumably as one clearly favoured by St Cuthbert. In addition, many ornate and valuable gifts were made to the saint's shrine perhaps in expiation of the sin of attempting to break the sanctuary of the ecclesiastical precinct[11].

These narratives referring to events between 1055 and 1065, but written down in the early 12th century, highlight important aspects of the medieval Church's relationship with the community it served. In both accounts there are references to significant boundaries the transgression of which incurred uncompromising divine punishment. Therefore, this chapter examines the meaning of the spatial delineation of ecclesiastical power in the Middle Ages, focusing, in particular on the Church of St Cuthbert in its urban setting, the medieval city of Durham. The special status of urban "sacred space" and the social mechanisms deployed to preserve its status are discussed. The origins of the injunction against women are explored and related to the claims by St Cuthbert's Church to an ecclesiastical immunity and associated rights of sanctuary. Although it was claimed that both phenomena had their origins in the 7th century, it is argued here that they can be particularly associated with the aftermath of the reorganisation of the Church of Durham in 1083, when the rigour of the monastic *Rule of St Benedict* was imposed on the community serving the shrine of St Cuthbert. At the beginning of the 12th century the monks of Durham faced a threat from their own bishop and they responded by presenting a version of the past that served to reinforce the protected status of their abbey.

Durham is situated in the North-East of England. The city is dominated by its medieval cathedral and castle located on a plateau at the summit of a steep promontory surrounded on three sides by a loop of the River Wear. In the mid-12th century, the site of Durham was described in verse[12]:

The land
Is high, its foot is stone, its sides are rough.
On all sides steep and sheer it thwarts the foe;
By river girt, it laughs at hostile troops.
The rushing river, shaped like a horse's shoe,
Surrounds the lofty site with foaming gorge.
A hill, however, splits the river's horns,
To make the lofty site peninsular.

A wide and level surface crowns the top
Of solid Durham, flat, unbroken land.
Now at the northern end a hill stands up,
But all the rest is level as a plain.
So now you know how Nature guards the place[13].

Given Durham's proximity to a major Roman road, it seems unlikely that such an eminently defensible site was not occupied during the Roman governance of Britain[14]. However, the foundation of the city is usually associated with the arrival of the Community of St Cuthbert in 995[15]. Medieval Durham's identity was intimately connected with the presence of Cuthbert's relics and it became an important centre of pilgrimage rivalled in England only by the shrine of St Thomas of Canterbury[16]. The original church built at Durham by Bishop Ealdhun was eventually dismantled and replaced by the Romanesque cathedral which survives today[17].

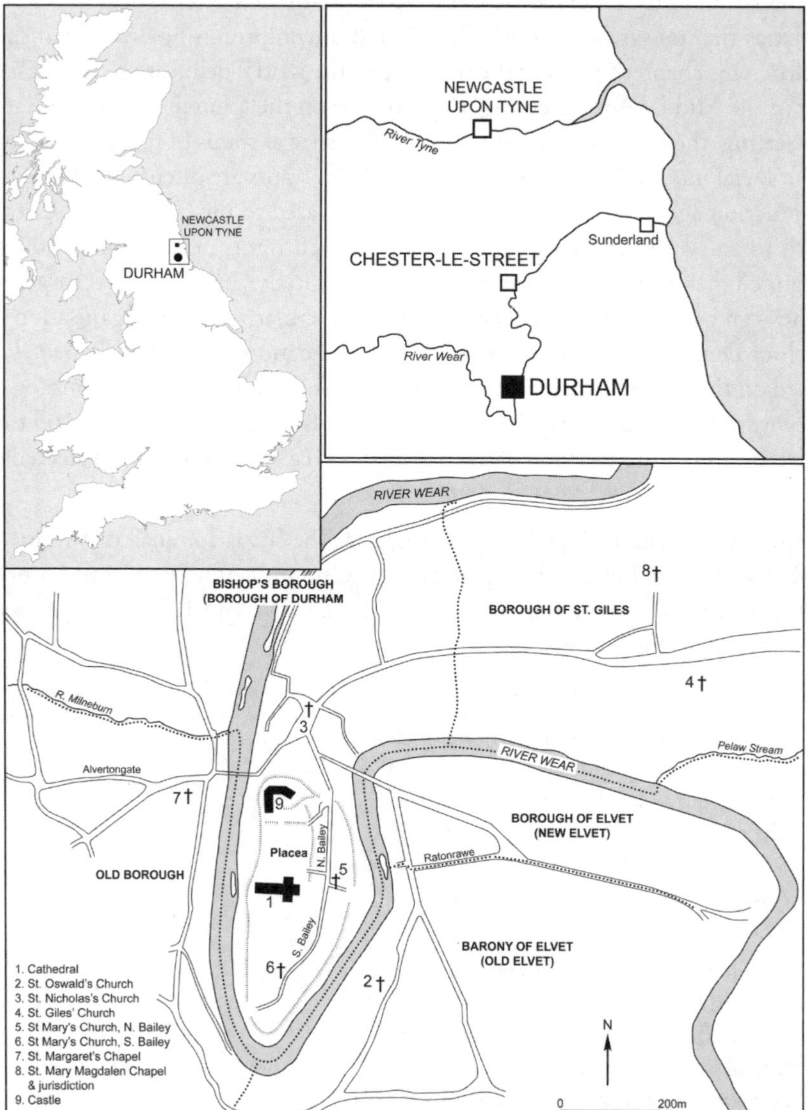

Map 1.
12th-century Durham.

Facing the cathedral and dominating the narrow isthmus of land giving access to the promontory is the castle. This was the bishop's residence until the building of the palace at Bishop Auckland in the late 13th century[18]. The cathedral and castle are emblematic of the twin lordships which dominated the medieval city of Durham. The constituent parts of Durham, the parishes and the boroughs, were thus in the lordship of either the bishop or the monks[19]. Throughout the Middle Ages the bishop of Durham enjoyed a great deal of local political autonomy and it was even suggested that within his bishopric he enjoyed a Palatine status not unlike that of the King of England in the rest of the kingdom[20].

The development of the urban settlement which today surrounds the cathedral-castle complex has been the subject of considerable research in recent decades[21]. The borough of Elvet, which lies across the River Wear from the promontory occupied by the Community, was the earliest urban settlement at Durham served by the parish church of St Oswald[22]. By the later medieval period the city had expanded and it is estimated that its population had reached perhaps 4000 or so by the 16th century, making it a medium-sized English town. The spiritual needs of this population were served by six parish churches in addition to the cathedral-priory[23].

A number of methodological approaches have been employed to study medieval urban topography[24]. For example, archaeological investigations and "plan analysis" are used to understand the growth, morphological changes, and internal divisions of medieval towns. Urban boundaries have been mapped and they are interpreted as marking stages in the development of the town and defining zones characterised by specific occupations or types of habitation[25]. Similarly, topographers have attempted to identify the original nucleus of urban settlements and from there tracing the history of the city's territorial expansion and contraction.

Methodologies adapted from social and cultural anthropology also inform interpretations of the significance of urban spatial arrangements. It has been recognised that divisions in the medieval urban landscape are symbolic vehicles resonating with social meaning. Urban space was, and is, one of the instruments through which social relations are produced, reproduced and expressed. It is culturally constructed and invested with meaning by those who occupy or otherwise utilise it[26]. An investigation of the boundaries organising the urban landscape reveals a great deal about the history, social relationships and cultural assumptions of the inhabitants, past and present, moving through, and interacting with, that environment.

Space in medieval towns was utilised in a number of ways. As well as the site of housing, commercial and industrial activities, it was also the stage for a variety of public and private rituals, through which religious beliefs and power relations of all kinds were enacted. The medieval church was particularly adept at utilising urban topography as a back-drop for its liturgical feasts, processions and ceremonies[27]. In medieval Durham, for example, the liturgical year was punctuated with a number of processions through the city, not only reinforcing religious belief, but also restating the urban lordship of the Church of St Cuthbert[28]. In a similar fashion, the built environment reflects the social assumptions and aspirations of the city's inhabitants. Buildings are as much expressions of different kinds of social power as they are shelters, dwelling places or ritual spaces[29]. For example, the great churches of medieval Europe with their variants on the cruciform ground plan literally marked the landscape, whether urban or rural, with crosses, the most potent symbols of Christianity[30]. Therefore urban space is socially and culturally meaningful operating through a combination of the symbolic and the functional.

Prominent among the topographical features identified in medieval towns is the ecclesiastical precinct, an urban space usually focused on a major church and removed from other jurisdictions, whether royal, seigneurial or civic. In some cases, as with many medieval monasteries, those excluded from the precinct might also include the local bishop[31]. These precincts usually comprised the church together with its ancillary buildings and cemetery[32]. In many cases the boundaries of these precincts were marked by walls or other physical barriers punctuated by gates regulating access and egress. In the case of cathedrals or monasteries located in urban centres, the ecclesiastical precinct might constitute a significant proportion of the urban area[33].

The exceptional nature of these "sacred spaces" might be recognised and marked by the urban population in ways other than through the use of purely physical boundaries such as walls and ditches. The limits of the ecclesiastical precinct marked the separation between the sacred and the profane, the pure and the dangerous[34]. Within the ecclesiastical precinct itself there were gradations of sacredness: some areas were more sacred than others. The church itself was the focus of concentric circles of numinous power. In most cases the high altar at the east end of the church, together with the shrine of the patron saint, was the most restricted area[35]. Access to these differentiated zones of sacred space within the precinct was regulated and before individuals were allowed to approach the more sacred areas, their social or spiritual status was assessed by members of the community in order to determine whether they were worthy of the privilege of access[36]. Unauthorised entry threatened to pollute the *sanctus locus* thereby compromising the religious practices carried out there.

In the later Middle Ages gatehouses and walls provided formidable physical boundaries, but the Church also made use of popular religious beliefs in order to erect mental boundaries and enforce and protect the ecclesiastical enclosure[37]. It was accepted that God and his saints took an active role in the protection of the holy places of medieval Europe. There are many narrative accounts of saints intervening in worldly affairs to protect those who served their shrines[38]. Within the ecclesiastical enclosure "Church Peace" operated theoretically protecting people and their property taking refuge there[39]. Related to this idea is that of the sanctuary of the church where fugitives might seek protection for a certain number of days. This respite allowed the parties involved to reach a settlement usually involving monetary compensation for the alleged crimes[40]. Fines were levied on those who breached the sanctuary and these increased the closer the intruder approached the most sacred space in the precinct, usually the saint's shrine[41]. Medieval narratives express horror at breaches of "Church Peace" or sanctuary, although the fact that such incidents were recorded suggests that not everyone was deterred by the threat of supernatural retribution[42].

However, the division between the sacred and profane should not be exaggerated. Like most frontiers or boundaries, that surrounding the ecclesiastical precinct was permeable. Medieval churches required the support of the laity and could not afford to exclude them completely even if that had been possible. Members of the laity were pilgrims and parishioners and provided food and drink, building materials, and other forms of non-clerical expertise to the Church. Even monastic houses, whose very ethos was founded on the principles of enclosure and separation, relied on a small army of seculars to supply their more mundane needs[43]. Those in monastic orders had families who visited the abbey and there are cases of the widowed mothers of monks joining their sons in retirement. Relatives might also seek burial in the abbey's churchyard, and, in a place of honour, benefiting from their proximity in death to the power of the *sanctus locus*[44]. Major churches were the economic foci of many towns and as well as providing employment, attracted markets and fairs. Many of the latter were held in the advantageous surroundings of the ecclesiastical precinct, where "Church Peace" and exemption from tolls and other taxes operated. In short, these enclosures were regularly visited by the laity and were used for a plethora of non-religious activities. With these general observations in mind, it is time to return to St Cuthbert's gynophobia.

The ban on women entering St Cuthbert's church was first recorded in Symeon of Durham's *Libellus de Exordio*[45]. None of the early medieval hagiographies or histories hints at any misogyny on Cuthbert's part[46]. In fact according to the earliest *Vitæ*, Cuthbert, who died in 687, seems have been on very good terms with women[47]. According to Symeon, Cuthbert's antipathy originated after a fire at the "double-monastery" of Coldingham (Berwickshire, Scotland):

> Everyone who was in a position to know, however, was aware that this had really happened because of the evil ways of the inhabitants. In that same place [i.e. Coldingham] indeed there were congregations of monks and nuns, albeit living separately in different dwellings, which had gradually fallen away from the discipline of the Rule and had, by their improper familiarity with each other, given the Enemy the opportunity of ensnaring them. For the cells which had been made for the purpose of prayer and reading they converted into dens of feasting, drinking, story-telling and other enticements[48].

Cuthbert "severed his monks from all female company" so that through "the indiscreet association of women with God's servants the monks should not endanger their resolve and so ruin them, thereby giving joy to the Enemy[49]." Symeon goes on say that with the agreement of all, "both men and women" Cuthbert "forbade to his monks then and in the future all female company and he completely removed from women the right of entry to his church[50]." Symeon ends his account by noting that:

> This custom is still meticulously observed today [i.e. early 12th century], to such an extent that women are not even given permission to enter the cemeteries [*cimiteria*] of those churches where his body rested for a time, unless they are forced to seek refuge there, either from fear of enemy attack, or because the place where they are living has been burned down[51].

Thus Symeon suggested that the exclusion of women applied to all those churches in which the saint's body had rested after his death in 687, a reference to relocations of Cuthbert's cult centre. During Scandinavian attacks on Northumbria in the 9th and tenth centuries, the community serving Cuthbert's shrine abandoned Lindisfarne in 876 and wandered about Northumbria until, in 883, it settled at Chester-le-Street[52]. It relocated to Durham in 995. No other evidence supports Symeon's assertions that the ban on women entering the church or its cemetery was enforced before the late 11th century. Indeed, as can be seen from the extract quoted above, Cuthbert had allowed that in certain circumstances of dire need, women might take refuge in his churches and their cemeteries. By the 11th century the *Haliwerfolc*, men and women, were accustomed to taking refuge in the cathedral at Durham, especially during attacks by the Scots[53].

In addition to the story of the fate of Countess Judith's maid servant, Symeon provided two other examples of women flouting St Cuthbert's ban. Immediately after the passages explaining the origins of the prohibition, Symeon tells us about Sungeova and her husband Gamel son of Bevo, who had attended a feast in the city and were making their way home one evening. Unfortunately, the street was a morass of muddy pot-holes so they decided to cross the cemetery. It is clear that Gamel and Sungeova were aware of the ban because they hoped to make amends to the saint by alms-giving at a later date. As the couple crossed the cemetery, Sungeova began to cry out that she was losing her mind. Her husband urged her on but as soon as she set foot outside the fence which surrounded the cemetery she collapsed. Gamel carried his wife home but she died that very night[54].

It is interesting to note that the denouement of Sungeova's punishment came as she stepped *out* of the cemetery across the boundary marked by a fence [*extra sepem que cimiterium ecclesie ambierat*]. As the sacred space was clearly marked by a fence there was no excuse for Sungeova's transgression. The couple were conscious of their sin and hoped that gifts to the Church might make amends. This last point about offering compensation for transgressing the boundaries of the church echoes similar demands for compensation from those, such as Barcwith, who challenged St Cuthbert's right of sanctuary.

Symeon's third example, involved the wife of a man who later joined the monastic community[55]. This woman developed an uncontrollable desire to see the beautiful ornaments that decorated the Church of Durham. There is no suggestion that she wanted to see inside the church for pious reasons, but rather out of her "womanly eagerness to see new things" [*femina auiditate uidendi noua*]. As her husband was an important man and she was used to getting her own way, she, too, set off across the cemetery but lost her mind and in her madness bit out her own tongue. Her husband tried to restrain her, but she took to wandering about until she was found one day under a tree with her throat cut, seemingly by her own hand[56]. Here, it was clearly the inquisitiveness and arrogance of the woman that brought about her demise. Before leaving the subject, Symeon assured his readers that "many other divine signs against similar audacity in other women could be related[57]."

It is noticeable in all three cases cited by Symeon that the women involved knew of the prohibition yet they chose to ignore it. It is also clear that the women entered the cemetery *without permission* and suffered the consequences[58]. In effect, the saint himself acted as a kind of supernatural gatekeeper patrolling the boundaries of the ecclesiastical precinct. That two of the women were driven mad suggests that the monks of Durham had successfully impressed on the minds of its parishioners the idea that Cuthbert himself guarded the privileges of his Church[59]. Only Countess Judith with her desire to enter Cuthbert's church to worship at his tomb could be construed as having a justifiable reason to test the prohibition, but even here punishment followed[60]. In the other cases, Symeon suggested that the sins of pride, avarice, and the "natural" female desire just to see "new things" lay at the heart of the transgression of the boundaries of Cuthbert's sacred space[61]. These stories do convey the idea that, at least for these women, an irresistible air of mystery and wonder surrounded the Church of St Cuthbert[62].

The tradition of St Cuthbert's misogyny was perpetuated by Reginald, another Durham monk, writing at the end of the 12th century[63]. One of Reginald's accounts concerning a little girl who wandered into the churchyard during a ball-game suggested that it did not matter whether women were unaware of the prohibition: even if they strayed into the churchyard by accident, they were still driven mad[64]. Here, as Victoria Tudor noted, Northumbria's greatest saint appears "vindictive and petty-minded"[65].

It seems strange that a monastic church, which relied so heavily on attracting pilgrims and their donations, should issue such a ban. To exclude more than half the number of potential visitors to the shrine was an odd decision by the monks and raises the question of how far Symeon's account of St Cuthbert's misogyny was an "invented tradition" designed to answer the needs of a specific set of circumstances. A closer look at the historical context of the production of Symeon's *Libellus de Exordio* suggests that the ban was devised for a particular reason and that, as the difficulties of the monks eased so arrangements were in fact made to cater for female visitors to the shrine of St Cuthbert. However, the tradition of Cuthbert's misogyny was never entirely forgotten and it was revived when similar threats to the monastic community materialised at later dates.

In 1083 Bishop William of Saint-Calais imposed the monastic Rule of St Benedict on the community of clerks serving the shrine of St Cuthbert at Durham[66]. Bishop William had been Abbot of Saint-Vincent in Le Mans and decided to regularise the constitution of the community at Durham by introducing the Rule of St Benedict[67]. Following the Norman victory at the Battle of Hastings in 1066 and the appointment of Lanfranc as Archbishop of Canterbury, there was an attempt to reform the English Church[68]. An aspect of English ecclesiastical organisation which the Norman bishops found particularly useful was the cathedral-priory because, as both diocesan and abbot, their authority over their cathedral chapters was boosted[69].

Symeon tells us that the pre-monastic community was made up of married priests who lived with their wives in close proximity to the cathedral[70]. Bishop William gave them a stark choice and insisted that "those who had previously dwelt in the church, and who had been canons only by name since they in no way followed the rule of canons, should henceforth lead their lives with the monks and according to the monastic vocation if they wished to remain in the church[71]." Symeon recalled that all except the dean left to be replaced by monks[72]. Thus, after 1083 the shrine of St Cuthbert was served by a cathedral-priory of Benedictine monks presided over by a prelate who was both bishop and abbot. As long as those appointed to the see of Durham were monks there was limited potential for disputes between the bishop and his monastic cathedral chapter. However, in 1099, a notorious royal "procurator" acquired the bishopric of Durham.

Ranulf Flambard was not in monastic orders. He had made a reputation as an effective, if rather unscrupulous, royal officer[73]. His appointment to Durham called into question the relationship between the bishop and his monastic cathedral chapter. According to the constitution established by Bishop William, Ranulf was nominal abbot as well as bishop, but his instincts were wholly secular and it was not long before the monks of the cathedral priory began to feel threatened[74]. Bishop Ranulf exploited the resources of his see in order to provide for members of his own family[75]. He also began to abstract property from the monks in order to reward his followers and finance his ambitious building projects[76]. It was said that he had also attempted to corrupt the monks with offers of forbidden foods and the company of women[77]. In addition, the bishop failed to respect another important aspect of the cathedral–priory's status, namely its right of sanctuary[78]. The response of the prior and monks to this threat was to set out clearly the boundaries of the relationship between the bishop and his monastic cathedral chapter in Symeon's *Libellus de Exordio* and other writings[79].

The misogyny attributed to St Cuthbert in the *Libellus de Exordio* was part of this defensive campaign against the new bishop. Clearly, the expulsion of the married clergy in 1083 and the establishment of a Benedictine cathedral chapter erected a new and strictly *monastic* enclosure around St Cuthbert's Church. Women and the temptations they represented were seen as a threat to the monastic vocations of those within the precinct and from then on their ability to approach the church had to be closely regulated. The women who had been living with members of the pre-monastic cathedral clergy were also symbolic of an older, corrupt state of affairs. Under William of Saint-Calais, bishop and monks had shared the same attitude to worldly affairs and there was no perceived threat to monastic interests. However, Symeon's work, composed during the early years of Ranulf's pontificate, suggests that the monks responded with some alarm to the changed circumstances that resulted from the appointment of this worldly cleric.

As there was no mention of St Cuthbert's prohibition on women before Symeon's *Libellus de exordio*, it looks as though this was an innovation of the early 12th century devised as a response to a new threat. The "misogyny of St Cuthbert" is, therefore, a medieval example of the familiar concept of the "invention of tradition"[80]. Through their misogyny, dramatised by the supposed actions of their patron saint, the monks emphasised their separation from their unsuitable bishop and his family connections. It was essential for the monks that the new bishop respected their legal and ecclesiastical immunity and so they also emphasised the right of sanctuary. The miracle story recounting Barcwith's demise reminded the bishop and his officers not to violate the sacred space around Cuthbert's shrine. It is also tempting to see another miracle story concerning the punishment of a certain tax collector named Ranulf as a not-so-subtle warning to the bishop not to take anything further from the saint or his monks[81]. An apt metaphor for the growing divide between bishop and cathedral-priory in the early twelfth century was the clearing of the urban space between the monastery and the castle during Ranulf's pontificate[82].

The prohibition against women entering the Church of St Cuthbert was also in accord with measures being taken by the Western Church as a whole to enforce clerical celibacy. One of the central policies of the papal reform movement, which began in the middle of the 11th century, was a prohibition against priests marrying or taking mistresses. It was argued that it was inappropriate for those who administered the sacraments to defile themselves and the Church through contact with women. In addition, there was the temptation for married priests to abstract ecclesiastical property to support their families. If this property then became hereditary it was lost to the Church. These prohibitions, promulgated through papal decrees, reinforced by the legislation of provincial synods, were not immediately effective, but they provided monastic writers with another opportunity to criticise their secular brethren[83].

Symeon's *Libellus de Exordio* contains passages expressing this antipathy towards clerical marriage. Women were intimately associated with the temptations of the flesh and the pollution of sexual intercourse, reminding us that for medieval monks the ecclesiastical precinct and the monastic enclosure separated pure, sacred space from the polluted and corrupt[84]. For example, when a priest named Feoccher presumed to celebrate Mass after sleeping with a woman the night before, the bread and wine took on the appearance of pitch[85]. In a more elaborate passage, Symeon recorded the vision of Boso, one of Bishop William's knights[86]. On recovering from a severe illness which rendered him unconscious for three days, Boso made a public confession before the prior of Durham[87]. He reported that he had had a vision of the Otherworld and had been taken by a spirit guide to a large plain where he had seen a procession of monks, most of whom had been admitted to a walled garden. Two monks were excluded because of their sins. Boso also saw the native English inhabitants of Northumbria "puffed up with arrogance", but they soon vanished to be followed by a group of even more arrogant Frenchmen. The French also seemed to be swallowed up by a sudden opening up of the earth. Finally, Boso reported that:

> Over several miles of the plain I saw an innumerable multitude of women, and while I was marvelling at such a crowd of them I learned from my guide that *these were the wives of priests*. "Eternal woe and the atrocious torment of the flames of hell," he said, "await these miserable women and those who were consecrated for offering service to God but yet were not afraid to involve themselves in the lascivious affairs of the flesh"[88].

This was a clear reference to the dreadful fate that awaited priests and the women with whom they cohabited.

Given that there was no specific injunction in the Rule of St Benedict denying women access to churches in the care of monastic communities beyond the requirement that inmates observe their vow of chastity, nor that early accounts of St Cuthbert's life provide any evidence of his misogyny, it is surprising that the Church of Durham would exclude so many worshippers and potential donors. There are, however, indications that the prohibition against women entering the ecclesiastical precinct at Durham might not have been as effectively enforced as Symeon suggested. Almost as soon as he instigated the prohibition, Cuthbert mitigated its effects. In order to cater for the spiritual needs of the excluded women, Cuthbert built a *Grene Cyrice* ["Green Church"] on the island of Lindisfarne where his episcopal church was based[89]. Other extant sources indicate that women were welcomed by the monastic community. In addition there are also clear signs that by the end of the 12th century, if not sooner, special arrangements were being made at Durham cathedral to accommodate the needs of pious women who wished to worship near Cuthbert's shrine.

From at least the beginning of the 11th century, women were allowed burial in the cemetery at Durham[90]. They may even have been allowed to reside in the ecclesiastical precinct as nuns or anchoresses under the protection of St Cuthbert[91]. Before 1083 the priests serving the shrine of St Cuthbert were married which also suggests that until the introduction of the *Rule of St Benedict* the local community saw nothing scandalous in the prevailing arrangements. In fact there were families in Durham who were proud to trace their descent from the 9th-century bearers of St Cuthbert's coffin during the period of wandering after leaving Lindisfarne[92]. Women had, therefore, a vital role in the transmission of the traditions of the community of the Church of St Cuthbert.

Ascelina, mother of the cathedral-priory's founder, Bishop William, was remembered, along with hundreds of other women, in the Durham *Liber Vitæ* ["Book of Life"], which recorded the names of those for whom the monks of Durham had pledged to pray[93]. The *Liber Vitæ* also included the text of an agreement [*conventio*] between the monks and King Malcolm III of Scotland and his wife, Margaret[94]. In addition, it is likely that a life of the saintly Queen Margaret was written by Prior Turgot[95]. There are also accounts of miraculous cures being granted to women through the intervention of St Cuthbert suggesting that the great Northumbrian thaumaturge did not neglect the prayers of his female suppliants[96]. Finally, towards the end of the 12th century another notorious bishop of Durham known for his contentious relationship with the monks of the cathedral priory began to build modify the West End of St Cuthbert's Church. Bishop Hugh du Puiset (1154-95) added the Galilee chapel specifically to cater for women visitors to the shrine[97]. Taken together these pieces of evidence hardly suggest that institutionalised misogyny operated in the Church of Durham and they warn us that we should be wary of taking Symeon's account too much at face value.

However, the memory of the tradition of St Cuthbert's antipathy towards women survived into the 16th century and there are indications that certain areas within the ecclesiastical precinct at Durham remained prohibited to female visitors[98]. The dissolution of the cathedral-priory at Durham after 1539 and the reintroduction of a secular dean and chapter marked the end of monastic rule in the Church of St Cuthbert[99]. Nevertheless, it seems that long before that date and despite the claims made by Symeon in the early twelfth century, it is to be doubted whether women were ever successfully excluded from the "sacred space" surrounding the shrine of the great Northumbrian saint.

Landscapes, whether urban or rural, are invested with meaning by those who interact with them[100]. Essential in these interactions are the physical and mental boundaries which human beings erect in order to make sense of their environment. Boundaries mark lines of friction and represent the point of contact between different interests. Boundaries might also represent the triumph of a particular party or indicate that a compromise has been reached. In either case they show where assumptions and rights have been challenged and defined. The presence of St Cuthbert's relics at Durham transformed the city into a sacred landscape. Within this landscape there were differing zones of sanctity, the boundaries of which had to be patrolled and enforced. This chapter has examined an aspect of the ecclesiastical precinct surrounding the Church of St Cuthbert in medieval Durham, namely the tradition of the exclusion of women. The boundary of this "sacred space" may have been marked by a fence but it was enforced by supernatural means. The actions of this medieval saint, acting as border guard and gatekeeper, remind us that frontiers and boundaries are as much phenomena created in the mind and patrolled by systems of belief, as they are physical barriers. Similarly, it is in the nature of tradition to seem fixed and immemorial, whereas, in fact, it is a constantly evolving phenomenon. This chapter has suggested that the tradition of the misogyny of St Cuthbert was invented in the early 12th century to meet specific needs and that it was continually re-negotiated, sometimes enforced and sometimes allowed to lapse. The urban boundaries of misogyny in Medieval Durham responded accordingly.

Notes

1 I am grateful to Peter Coss and Nicola Whyte, my colleagues at Cardiff University, for discussing aspects of this chapter and for providing valuable bibliographical references. My thanks also to Ian Dennis for preparing the map.

2 Tostig was Earl of Northumbria between 1055 and 1065. He was the brother of Harold Godwinson, who as King of England was defeated by Duke William of Normandy at the Battle of Hastings on 14 October 1066. For Tostig's career, see W. M. Aird, *Tostig, earl of Northumbria (c.1029-1066)*, in *Oxford Dictionary of National Biography*, Oxford 2004, [http://www.oxforddnb.com/view/article/27571, accessed 13 November 2007]. Judith, the daughter of Count Baldwin IV of Flanders (988-1035), had married Earl Tostig in the autumn of 1051 when he was in exile in Flanders. See Elisabeth van Houts, *Judith of Flanders, duchess of Bavaria (1030x35-1095), Oxford Dictionary of National Biography*, Oxford, 2004 [http://www.oxforddnb.com/view/article/54458, accessed 13 Nov 2007]. For Baldwin IV of Flanders, see D. Nicholas, *Medieval Flanders*, London 1992, pp. 45-9.

3 D. Rollason (ed. and trans.), *Symeon of Durham, Libellus de Exordio atque Procursu istius, hoc est Dunhelmensis Ecclesie. Tract on the Origins and Progress of this the Church of Durham*, Oxford 1998, pp. 176-7: *Puella ergo, domine sue uoluntate agnita, hora secretiori ad hoc temptandum conata est aggredi. Iam pedem intra cimiterium erat positura, cum subito ueluti uentorum uiolentia repelli cepit et uiribus deficere, et grauiter infirmata uix ad hospitium ualuit redire, decidensque in lectum, graui torquebatur cruciatu, tandem dolore cum uita caruit.*

4 Symeon, *Libellus de exordio*, pp. 176-7: *Hoc facto comitissa uehementer exterrita contremuit, atque humiliter satisfaciendo, imaginem crucifixi (que – sicut in sequentibus dicetur- a raptoribus suo fuerat spoliata ornatu) imaginem quoque sancta Dei genitricis Marie et Iohannis Euangeliste ipsa et eius coniunx fieri iusserunt et auro argentoque uestierunt, aliaque perplura ad decorum ecclesie obtulerunt.*

5 On memory and material objects, see Elisabeth M.C. van Houts, *Memory and Gender in Medieval Europe, 900-1200*, London 1999.

6 For St Cuthbert's prohibition on women entering his churches, see V. Tudor, *The Misogyny of Saint Cuthbert*, in "Archaeologia Aeliana", 5th Series, 1984, 12, pp. 157-67.

7 In some manuscript copies of Symeon, *Libellus de exordio*, the story of Barcwith was inserted at this point; see Symeon, *Libellus de Exordio*, pp. 176-7 and n. 52. Cf. B. Colgrave, *The Post-Bedan Miracles and Translations of St Cuthbert* in C. Fox, B. Dickins (eds.), *The Early Cultures of North-West Europe (H.M. Chadwick Memorial Studies)*, Cambridge 1950, pp. 307-332 and W.M. Aird, *The Making of a Medieval Miracle Collection: The Liber de Translationibus et Miraculis Sancti Cuthberti*, in "Northern History", 1992, XXVIII, pp. 1-24.

8 *Capitula de Miraculis et Translationibus Sancti Cuthberti*. Cap.V: *Quomodo miles comitis Tostii, nomine Barcwith, dum ianuas monasterii eius infringere cupit, subito percussus interierit*', in T. Arnold (ed.), *Symeonis Monachi Opera Omnia*, 2 vols., London 1882, I, p. 243: *Dum igitur Tostius, comes ille cunctis notissimus, in partibus Northanhumbranis comitatutm administraret, quidam pravæ actionis vir, nomine Aldan-Hamal, ab eo comprehensus, compedibus arctissime constringitur. Multa enim mala fecerat; furtis atque rapinis, homicidis atque incendiis comitem sæpe offenderat, nec unquam prius comprehendi poterat. Cuius parentes et amici, compassionis affectu permoti, multa pro eo ne capite plecteretur comiti offerebant, et plura promittebant. At ille, quia totiens tantisque malefactis eum irritaverat, nullum se pro vita ipsius auri vel argenti, aut cuiusquam alterius rei commodum vel respicere velle iuravit. Tunc ille animo consternates, solum sibi cogitabat esse remedium si, quoquomodo vinculis expeditus, beatissimi patris Cuthberti*

confugisset ad monasterium. In eadem quipped villa qua ipse corpore requiescit, hoc est in Dunelmo, tunc custodiebatur.

9 *Capitula de Miraculis*, p. 244: *"Quid," inquit, "moramur? Quare ianuas non infringimus? Neque enim huius hominis mortui pax a Deo est tenenda, ut fures, raptores, et homicidæ, huc si confugerint, nobis insultent quod impunity evaserint." Sic miser ille ore loquebatur contumelioso; furoris enim magnitude effecerat, ut quid loqueretur ipse ignoraret. Sed vix verba compleverat, ecce! Subito quasi sagitta desuper veniens, caputque sibi transverberans, ad cor usque suum pertingeret, sibi visum esse protestabatur.*

10 *Capitula de Miraculis*, p. 245: *Denique a suis ad hospitium deportatur, nec unum postea verbum proloquens, in eisdem tormentis ad diei tertii eandem usque horam supervixit. Sed et illo tandem ita defuncto atque sepulto, talis tantusque de tumulo ipsius fætor per dimidium spatium anni exhalavit, ut viæ transitum per id loci omnes fugerent.*

11 *Capitula de Miraculis*, p. 245.

12 See Map 1.

13 J. Raine (ed.), *Dialogi Laurentii Dunelmensis Monachi ac Prioris*, Surtees Society, LXX, Durham 1880, p. 8, lines 271-8 and p. 9, lines 297-301.

Consurgit in ardua tellus,
Et saxosa pedes, et salebrosa latus:
Undique declivis præruptaque summonet hostem,
Ludit et hostiles flumine cincta manus.
Flumen eam ferri præceps obit instar equini,
Circinat excelsum, vallis aquosa locum:
Quod tamen ille locus, locus arduus, insula non est,
Hoc dirimens fluvii cornua collis agit.

At solidi suprema loci prælarga serenat
Planities, æquum terra cacumen habet.
Collis vero plagam supereminet ad borealem,
Cætera planitie celsus amænat apex.
Ecce! quibus natura modis rem munit habetis.

The translation is from A.G. Rigg, *Lawrence of Durham: Dialogues and Easter Poem: A Verse Translation* in "Journal of Medieval Latin", 7, 1997, pp. 42-126 at 52. On the career of Prior Lawrence of Durham (1149-54), and his literary works, see A.G. Rigg, *A History of Anglo-Latin Literature, 1066-1422*, Cambridge 1992, pp. 54-61. Prior Lawrence's description followed the conventions of the *locus amoenus* ["pleasant place"] *topos* also found in a late 11th-century poem, *De Situ Dunelmi*: D. Howlett, *The shape and meaning of the Old English poem "Durham"* in D. Rollason, M. Harvey and M. Prestwich (eds.), *Anglo-Norman Durham, 1093-1193*, Woodbridge 1994, pp. 485-95, and H.S. Offler, *The date of Durham* (Carmen de situ Dunelmi), in "Journal of English and Germanic Philology", 61, 1962, pp. 591-4.

14 Before moving to Durham the Community of St Cuthbert occupied Chester-le-Street which had been a Roman fort; see E. Cambridge, *Why did the Community of St Cuthbert Settle at Chester-le-Street?* in G. Bonner, C. Stancliffe and D. Rollason (eds.), *St Cuthbert, His Cult and Community to AD 1200* Woodbridge 1989, pp. 367-86.

15 According to Symeon of Durham's *Libellus de exordio*, in 995 the community moved from Chester-le-Street to Ripon in order to escape renewed Viking attacks on the North of England; see Symeon, *Libellus de exordio*, pp. 144-7. See M.O.H. Carver, P.F. Gosling, *The Archaeology of Durham City* in P.A.G. Clack and P.F. Gosling (eds.), *Archaeology in the North: the report of the Northern Archaeological Society*, Her Majesty's Stationery Office, 1976, pp. 133-45; M. O. H. Carver, *Early Medieval Durham: the Archaeological Evidence*, in Nicola Coldstream, P. Draper (eds.), *Medieval Art and Architecture at*

Durham Cathedral. The British Archaeological Association Conference Transactions for the year 1977, Leeds 1980, pp. 11-19.

16 Symeon, *Libellus de exordio*, pp. 148-9: *Igitur prefatus antistes [Ealdhun] totius populi auxilio, et comitis Northanhymbrorum Vhtredi adiutorio totam extirpans siluam succidit, ipsumque locum in breui habitabilem fecit. Denique a flumine Coqued usque Tesam uniuersa populorum multitudo tam ad hoc opus quam ad construendam postmodum ecclesiam prompto animo accessit, et donec perficeretur deuota insistere no cessauit*. ["So the aforesaid bishop [Ealdhun], with the assistance of Uhtred, earl of the Northumbrians, cut down and uprooted the whole forest and soon made the place habitable. Later a multitude of people from the whole area between the river Coquet and the river Tees readily came to help not only with this task but also afterwards with the construction of the church, and they persevered devotedly until it was finished."] The boundaries of the catchment area that provided the work-force for the clearing of the site presumably reflect the extent of the Community's landholdings at this time; see W.M. Aird, *St Cuthbert and the Normans, The Church of Durham, 1071-1153*, Woodbridge 1998, pp. 46-7 and n. 137.

17 The foundation of the present cathedral church was marked in 1093 by a ceremony in which King Malcolm III of Scotland (1057-93) participated. See Symeon of Durham, *Libellus de exordio*, pp. 244-45 and M.G. Snape, *Documentary evidence for the building of Durham Cathedral and its monastic buildings*, in Coldstream, Draper, *Medieval Art and Architecture at Durham Cathedral* cit., pp. 20-36. M. Jarrett and H. Mason, *'Greater and More Splendid': Some Aspects of Romanesque Durham Cathedral*, "The Antiquaries Journal", 75, 1995, pp. 189-233.

18 Durham's castle has been greatly modified since its 11th-century foundation; see M. Leyland, *The Origins and Development of Durham Castle*, in Rollason, et al. (eds.), *Anglo-Norman Durham*, pp. 407-24. J. Raine, *A Brief Historical Account of the Episcopal Palace of Auckland*, Durham 1852.

19 The powerful Neville family were the patrons of the Church of St Mary in the South Bailey at Durham; see M. Harvey, *Lay Religious Life in Late Medieval Durham*, Woodbridge 2006, p. 16. For the division of lordship see M. Bonney, *Lordship and the Urban Community. Durham and Its Overlords, 1250-1540*, Cambridge 1990,

20 Jean Scammell, *The Origins and Limitations of the Liberty of Durham*, "English Historical Review", 81, 1966, pp. 449-73.

21 See references in n.19 above.

22 Harvey, *Lay Religious Life*, pp. 3-4; see Map 1.

23 *Ibid.*, p. 2.

24 For an introduction to this subject, see D.M. Palliser, T.R. Slater, E. Patricia Dennison, *The Topography of Towns, 600-1300* in D.M. Palliser (ed.), *The Cambridge Urban History of Britain*. Volume 1: *600-1300*, Cambridge 2000, pp. 153-86. On medieval urban centres more generally, see D. Nicholas, *The Growth of the Medieval City. From Late Antiquity to the Early Fourteenth Century*, London - New York 1997 and K.D. Lilley, *Urban Life in the Middle Ages, 1000-1450*, Basingstoke, 2002.

25 For the technique of plan analysis in an English context see M.R.G. Conzen, *Alnwick, Northumberland: a study of town plan analysis*, Transactions of the Institute of British Geographers, vol. 27, London 1960. See also, K.D. Lilley, *Mapping the medieval city: plan analysis and urban history*, in "Urban History", 27, 1, 2000, pp. 5-30 which looks at the development of medieval Coventry. On the occupational topography of late medieval Durham, see Bonney, *Lordship and the Urban Community* cit., pp. 161-8.

26 M. Parker Pearson, C. Richards, *Ordering the World: Perceptions of Architecture, Space and Time*, in M. Parker Pearson, C. Richards, *Architecture and Order. Approaches to Social Space*, London 1994, pp. 1-37. See also B. A. Hanawalt, M. Kobialka (eds.), *Medieval Practices of Space*, Minneapolis, London 2000.

27 For a discussion of the relationship between Christian liturgy and its urban setting in the late antique and early medieval context, see J.F. Baldovin, *The Urban Character of Christian Worship. The Origins,*

Development and Meaning of Stational Liturgy, Orientalia Christiana Analecta, 228, Rome 1987. See also B.A. Hanawalt, K.L. Reyerson (eds.), *City and Spectacle in Medieval Europe*, Minneapolis, London 1994 and J. Rahel Oesterle, *The Liturgical Dimension of Royal Representation* in P. Trio, M. De Smet (eds.), *The Use and Abuse of Sacred Places in Late Medieval Towns*, Leuven 2006, pp. 103-15. Marcia Kupfer has studied the interrelationship between religious practice and geographical space at the level of the parish in central France; see *eadem*, *Symbolic Cartography in a Medieval Parish: From Spatialized Body to Painted Church at Saint-Aignan-sur-Cher*, in "Speculum", 75, 3, 2000, pp. 615-67.

28 Harvey, *Lay Religious Life*, pp. 32, 35 and 38. Important as a guide to liturgical practices in late medieval Durham is J.T. Fowler (ed.), *Rites of Durham, being a description or brief declaration of all the ancient monuments, rites and customs belonging or being within the monastical church of Durham before the suppression. Written, 1593, Surtees Society*, 107, 1902. For processions, see *Ibid.*, p. 105.

29 R. Sennett, *Flesh and Stone. The Body and the City in Western Civilization*, London - Boston, MA, 1994.

30 M.T. Clanchy, *Reading the Signs at Durham Cathedral*, in Karen Schousboe and M.T. Larsen (eds.), *Literacy and Society*, Copenhagen 1989, pp. 171-82.

31 Some monasteries, for example the great Burgundian abbey of Cluny, succeeded in placing themselves directly under the protection of the papacy: see B.H. Rosenwein, *Negotiating Space. Power, Restraint, and Privileges of Immunity in Early Medieval Europe*, Ithaca, NY 1999, pp. 163-68, and Id., *To be the neighbour of Saint Peter: The Social Meaning of Cluny's Property, 909-1049*, Ithaca, NY 1989.

32 J. Barrow, *Urban cemetery location in the high Middle Ages*, in S. Bassett (ed.), *Death in Towns. Urban Responses to the Dying and the Dead, 100-1600*, Leicester - London - New York 1992, pp. 78-100. There were rituals devised for hallowing cemeteries: see Rosenwein, *Negotiating Space* cit., pp. 178 and 181.

33 Palliser, *et al.*, *The Topography of Towns* cit., pp. 127-45. Durham's medieval cathedral and its claustral buildings still dominate the plateau in the heart of the city.

34 The work of the anthropologist Mary Douglas has been influential on this characterisation of the boundaries between the ecclesiastical precinct and the secular world: M. Douglas, *Purity and Danger: An Analysis of Concepts of Pollution and Taboo*, London 1966.

35 R. Gilchrist, *Norwich Cathedral Close: the evolution of the English Cathedral Landscape*, Woodbridge 2005, p. 11. See also L.V. Hicks, *Religious Life in Normandy, 1050-1300. Space, gender and social pressure*, Woodbridge 2007, and D. M. Hayes, *Body and Sacred Place in Medieval Europe, 1100-1389*, New York - London 2003.

36 It is possible to apply the spatial technique of "access analysis" in order to trace the relative sacrality of different parts of these ecclesiastical precincts. See B. Hillier, J. Hanson, *The Social Logic of Space*, Cambridge 1984. For the technique in practice see R. Gilchrist, *Gender and Material Culture: The Archaeology of Religious Women*, London 1994.

37 Here anthropological concepts of *tapu* (taboo) have been influential: see Rosenwein, *Negotiating Space* cit., pp. 18-20.

38 See for example, P.J. Geary, *Living with the Dead in the Middle Ages*, Ithaca - London 1994.

39 In Old English this "Church Peace" was known as *ciric grið*: see D. Hall, *The Sanctuary of St Cuthbert*, in Bonner *et al.* (eds.), *St Cuthbert* cit., pp. 425-36 at 428. See Marjan De Smet, *Heavenly quiet and the din or war: Use and abuse of religious buildings for purposes of safety, defence and strategy* in Trio, De Smets, *The Use and Abuse of Sacred Places* cit., pp. 1-26.

40 G. Rosser, *Sanctuary and Social Negotiation in Medieval England*, in J. Blair - B. Golding (eds.), *The Cloister and the World: essays in medieval history in honour of Barbara Harvey*, Oxford 1996, pp. 57-79.

[41] On the legal development of sanctuary in medieval England see R.M. Helmholz, *The Law of Sanctuary* in Id., *The* Ius Commune *in England. Four Studies*, Oxford 2001, pp. 16-81.

[42] P. Draper, *Enclosures and entrances in medieval cathedrals: access and security*, in Janet Backhouse (ed.), *The Medieval English Cathedral: Papers in Honour of Pamela Tudor-Craig*, Harlaxton Medieval Studies, 10, Donington 2003, pp. 76-88.

[43] See Gilchrist, *Norwich Cathedral Close* cit., pp. 12-7. The great Benedictine abbeys tended to occupy urban sites, whereas those of the new orders of the 12th century such as the Cistercians were often located in rural areas away from centres of population: see J. Burton, *Monastic and Religious Orders in Britain, 1000-1300*, Cambridge 1994, pp. 63-84 and 131-58.

[44] Hicks, *Religious Life in Normandy* cit., pp. 127-52.

[45] The *Libellus de Exordio* appears to have been written between the opening of Cuthbert's tomb in August 1104 and 1107 or 1109, the date when Turgot relinquished the office of prior at Durham after his election as Bishop of St Andrews in Scotland. Therefore the completion of the text was before 1107, possibly 1109 or, at the latest 1115, the date of Turgot's death: see Symeon, *Libellus de Exordio* cit., pp. xx and xlii.

[46] B. Colgrave (ed. and trans.), *Two Lives of Saint Cuthbert*, Cambridge, 1940 and T. Johnson South, *Historia de Sancto Cuthberto. A History of Saint Cuthbert and a Record of his Patrimony*, Woodbridge 2002.

[47] Tudor, *The Misogyny of Saint Cuthbert* cit., pp.157-8, noting Cuthbert's positive relationship with two women, Kenswith his former nurse and a certain Abbess Verca.

[48] Symeon, *Libellus de Exordio* cit., pp.104-7: *Quod tamen a malitia inhabitantium in eo contigisse, omnes qui nouere facillime potuerunt aduertere. Erant siquidem in eodem loco diuersis tamen separate mansionibus monachorum sanctimonialiumque congregationes, qui paulatim a regularis discipline statu defluentes, inhonesta inuicem familiaritate decipiendi occasionem inimico prebuerant. Nam et domunculas que ad orandum uel legendum facte fuerant, in commessationum, potationum, confabulationum, et ceterarum cubilia illecebrarum conuertebant.* On the date of the fire which occurred before 687, see R. Bartlett, *The Miracles of St Æbbe of Coldingham and St Margaret of Scotland*, Oxford 2003, p. xiv

[49] Symeon, *Libellus de Exordio* cit., pp. 106-7.

[50] *Ibid.*

[51] Symeon, *Libellus de Exordio* cit., pp.108-9: *Que consuetudo usque hodie diligenter obseruatur, in tantum ut nisi metus hostilis uel concrematio loci compellat, nec in cimiteria quidem ipsarum ecclesiarum ubi ad tempus corpus eius requieuerat, mulieribus introire liceat.*

[52] On the significance of this episode, see D. Rollason, *The Wanderings of St Cuthbert* in Id. (ed.), *Cuthbert, Saint and Patron*, Durham 1987, pp. 45-59 and Aird, *St Cuthbert* cit., pp. 32-5.

[53] For example, the attack led by King Duncan I of Scotland in 1040: Symeon, *Libellus de Exordio* cit., pp. 168-9. *Haliwerfolc*, literally the "people (*folc*) of the saint (*halig wer*)", was a local name for the inhabitants of the lands of the Church of St Cuthbert, which came to refer to the land they inhabited.

[54] Symeon, *Libellus de Exordio* cit., pp. 108-9.

[55] Unfortunately Symeon does not name his source.

[56] Symeon, *Libellus de Exordio* cit., pp. 108-9.

[57] At this point in one of the manuscripts of the *Libellus* there is an erasure. Were other examples of Cuthbert's misogyny erased? Symeon, *Libellus de Exordio*, p. 110 and n. 60. See also D. Rollason, *The Making of the* Libellus de Exordio*: the evidence of erasures and alterations in the two earliest manuscripts*, in D. Rollason (ed.), *Symeon of Durham: Historian of Durham and the North,* Stamford 1998, pp. 140-56.

58 There is no sense that these stories were an attack on the morals of the Anglo-Saxons by their new Norman lords.

59 Medieval monks were also supposed to carry the idea of enclosure in their minds even when they left the physical boundaries of their cloisters: see Hicks, *Religious Life* cit., pp. 94-5.

60 It is also significant that the maid servant was punished rather than Countess Judith, a generous benefactress to the Church of St Cuthbert.

61 For a discussion of the attitudes of the 10th- and 11th-century Anglo-Saxon clergy towards women, see C. Cubitt, *Virginity and Misogyny in Tenth- and Eleventh-Century England* in "Gender and History", 12, 1, 2000, pp. 1-32.

62 C. W. Bynum, *Wonder*, "American Historical Review", 102:1, 1997, pp. 1-26.

63 J. Raine (ed.), *Reginaldi monachi Dunelmensis libellus de admirandis beati Cuthberti virtutibus quae novellis patratae sunt temporibus*, Surtees Society, 1, Durham, 1835. See Tudor, *The Misogyny of Saint Cuthbert* cit., pp. 157 and 160-1. For a brief account of Reginald of Durham (or Coldingham), see Rigg, *Anglo–Latin Literature* cit., pp. 97-8. See also Sally Crumplin, *Modernizing St Cuthbert: Reginald of Durham's miracle collection*, in K. Cooper, J. Gregory, *Signs, Wonders, Miracles: Representations of Divine Power in the Life of the Church*, "Studies in Church History", 41, 2005, pp. 179-91.

64 J. Stevenson (ed.), *Reginald of Durham, Libellus de vita et miraculis S. Godrici, heremitae de Finchale*, Surtees Society 20, Durham 1845, p. 403, cited in Tudor, *The Misogyny of Saint Cuthbert*, p. 157.

65 Tudor, *The Misogyny of Saint Cuthbert* cit., p. 157.

66 Symeon, *Libellus de Exordio* cit., pp. 224-35.

67 W.M. Aird, *An Absent Friend: The Career of Bishop William of Saint-Calais*, in Rollason (ed.), *Anglo-Norman Durham* cit., pp. 283-97.

68 Whether the Anglo-Saxon Church was in need of reform is a much-debated question. For a positive evaluation of the English church and its bishops before 1066, see M. F. Giandrea, *Episcopal Culture in Late Anglo-Saxon England*, Woodbridge 2007. For Lanfranc, see H.E.J. Cowdrey, *Lanfranc. Scholar, Monk, and Archbishop*, Oxford 2003, pp. 120-43.

69 This was a legacy of the 10th-century reformation of many English churches and was advocated by Archbishop Lanfranc and those of his episcopal colleagues who were also monks: see J. Blair, *The Church in Anglo-Saxon Society*, Oxford 2005, pp. 341-67 and Cowdrey, *Lanfranc* cit., pp. 149-74.

70 Symeon, *Libellus de Exordio* cit., pp. 260-61. An attempt by Bishop William's predecessor, Walcher, to reform the community appears to have failed: *Ibid.*, pp. 194-7.

71 Symeon, *Libellus de Exordio* cit., pp. 230-31: *Eos uero qui prius inibi habitauerant, nomen tantum canonicorum habentes, sed in nullo canonicorum regulam sequentes, precepit ut si in ipsa ecclesia residere uellent, deinceps in monachico proposito cum monachis uitam agerent.* There has been debate over the inconsistencies in Symeon's account especially concerning the fate of the members of the pre-monastic community: see Symeon, *Libellus de Exordio*, p. 230, note 20. The present author has argued that there was greater continuity in the personnel of Durham cathedral across 1083: see Aird, *St Cuthbert* cit., pp.100-41.

72 The monks were drawn from the nearby recently re-founded monasteries at Jarrow and Monkwearmouth: see Symeon, *Libellus de Exordio* cit., pp. 200-11 and A. Dawtry, *The Benedictine Revival in the North: the Last Bulwark of Anglo-Saxon Monasticism?* in "Studies in Church History", 18, 1982, pp. 87-98.

73 For Ranulf's career see Symeon, *Libellus de Exordio*, Appendix B: Continuation beginning 'Tribus dehinc annis', pp. 266-81 and R.W. Southern, *Rannulf Flambard and Early Anglo-Norman Administration*, in "Transactions of the Royal Historical Society", 4th series, 16, 1933, revised as *Ranulf Flambard*

in *idem.*, *Medieval Humanism and Other Essays*, Oxford 1970, pp. 183-205. Cf. H.S. Offler, *Ranulf Flambard as Bishop of Durham, 1099-1128*, "Durham University Journal", 64, 1971, pp. 14-25.

74 Ibid., p. 18: "Ranulf's was not a naturally Benedictine soul." Before Ranulf came to Durham, there had been a three-year vacancy in the bishopric during which the power of the prior, Turgot, had risen. In the absence of a bishop-abbot, the prior was the leading ecclesiastical figure in the diocese. According to Symeon of Durham, William of Saint–Calais had made the prior his archdeacon, that is his deputy in diocesan affairs: Symeon, *Libellus de Exordio*, pp. 244-7. See also H.S. Offler, *The early archdeacons in the diocese of Durham*, in "Transactions of the Architectural and Archaeological Society of Durham and Northumberland", 11, 1962, pp. 193-202.

75 For example, he granted land to his nephew Richard and a certain "William, son of Rannulf", perhaps the son of another nephew: H.S. Offler (ed.), *Durham Episcopal Charters*, 1071-1152, Surtees Society, 179, 1968, nos. 11 and 23, pp. 72-4 and 100-6; cf. Aird, *St Cuthbert* cit., pp. 203-7.

76 On his death bed Bishop Ranulf made formal restitution to the monks of the properties he had wrongfully taken from them [*omnia que eis uoluntate et cupiditate mea abstuleram*]: see Offler, *Durham Episcopal Charters*, no. 25, pp. 112-4. As well as continuing work on the cathedral, Bishop Ranulf built a border castle at Norham-on-Tweed and a hospital in Durham: see Symeon, *Libellus de Exordio*, pp. 276-7 and Offler, *Rannulf Flambard* cit., pp. 19-25.

77 N.E.S.A. Hamilton (ed.), *Willelmi Malmesbiriensis Monachi De Gestis Pontificum Anglorum Libri Quinque*, Rolls Series, London 1870, p. 274 n.5: *Et, ut magis religionem irritaret, puellas speciosissimas, quæ essent procatioris formæ et faciei, eis potum propinare iuberet, strictis ad corpus vestibus, solutis in terga crinibus. Ibi ergo erat videre ludibrium.* Cf. translation by D. Preest, *William of Malmesbury, The Deeds of the Bishops of England (Gesta Pontificum Anglorum)*, Woodbridge 2002, p. 184 and n.4.

78 According to William of Malmesbury, Bishop Ranulf "grew so bold that he did not hesitate to drag away guilty persons who sought sanctuary in the church of the saint, thus daring a crime unheard of in all the years of the past": Preest, *The Deeds of the Bishops* cit., p. 184; William of Malmesbury, *De Gestis Pontificum*, p. 274: *Sed uno et altero delicto commisso, nec vindicato, eo processit, ut reum, si quando ad ecclesiam Sancti confugeret, abstrahere non dubitaret, ausus scelus omnibus retro annis inauditum.*

79 W.M. Aird, *The Political Context of the Libellus de Exordio*, in Rollason (ed.), *Symeon of Durham* cit., pp. 32-45.

80 E. Hobsbawm, T. Ranger (eds.), *The Invention of Tradition*, Cambridge 1983.

81 Symeon, *Libellus de Exordio*, pp. 196-9: *Post tempus aliquot quendam uocabulo Rannulfum illo miserat, qui ipsius sancti populum regi tributum soluere compelleret. Quod illi grauiter ferentes (scilicet quod nouas consuetudines cogerentur subire), consuetum in aduersis sancti Cuthberti auxilium studebant inquirere. Nocte igitur qua finita tributum populo erat impositurus, beatus Cuthbertus ei per somnium assistens, baculo pastorali quem manu gestabat illum impulit, et auctoritate pontificali et uultu minaci increpauit, quod illuc ad populum suum affligendum ausus fuerit uenire, dicens quod non impune hoc presumpserit, et nisi cito recederet peiora passurus esset.* ["Some time later the king sent there (i.e. Durham) a certain man called Ranulf, who was to compel the people of St Cuthbert to pay tribute to the king. They took this badly, because it meant that they were being subjected to new customs, and they devoted their efforts to seeking the aid which St Cuthbert usually gave them in adversity. So during the night before the day on which the tribute was to be imposed on the people, St Cuthbert appeared to Ranulf in a dream, struck him with the pastoral staff which he held in his hand, rebuked him with episcopal authority and with a threatening countenance that he should have dared to have come there to afflict his people, and told him that he had not presumed to do this with impunity, and that he would suffer still worse if he did not go away quickly."] It is interesting to note that the boundaries of the bishopric were significant in that Ranulf's punishment only ceased when he crossed out of St Cuthbert's lands. The southern boundary was the River Tees and another tale recorded by Symeon describes a "terrible heat" visited upon

King William the Conqueror who had dared to threaten the Church of St Cuthbert: Symeon, *Libellus de Exordio* cit., pp. 196-7.

82 Symeon, *Libellus de Exordio* cit., pp. 276-7: *Locum inter ecclesiam et castellum, quem multa occupauerant habitacula in patentis campi redegit planitiem, ne uel sordibus contaminatio, uel ex ignibus ecclesiam attingerent pericula.* ["The space between the church and the castle, which had been occupied by many dwellings, he made as flat and open as a field, so that the church should be affected neither by the contamination of their filth, nor the danger of fires."]. This area is now known as Palace Green (marked as *placea* on Map 1): see Carver, *Early Medieval Durham* cit., pp. 15-6. It must be admitted that the continuator of Symeon's *Libellus de Exordio* found it difficult wholly to condemn Bishop Ranulf, probably due to the fact that much of what he abstracted from the monastic estate was reinvested in the diocese in the form of the extensive building works. He also presided over a splendid translation of the relics of the saint into the new cathedral in 1104: Arnold, *Symeonis Opera Omnia* cit., I, pp. 247-61. Cf. the praise for Ranulf in Prior Lawrence's *Dialogi* cit., p. 65, from line 231.

83 C.N.L. Brooke, *Gregorian reform in action: Clerical Marriage in England, 1050-1200*, in "Cambridge Historical Journal", 13, 1956, pp. 1-21.

84 On medieval theories about women's bodies see, for example, C.T. Wood, *The doctors' dilemma: sin, salvation, and the menstrual cycle in medieval thought*, in "Speculum", 56, 1981, pp. 701-727. Menstruating women were forbidden entry to the church. The medieval custom of "churching" women after childbirth was a ritual purification: see Harvey, *Lay Religious Life* cit., p. 48.

85 Symeon, *Libellus de Exordio* cit., pp. 172-3: *Hora uero qua sacrosancta mysteria sumere deberet, in calicem introspexit, et ecce particulam Dominici corporis que iuxta morem missa fuerat in calicem, ita cum sanguine in teterrimam speciem commutatam uidit, ut (sicut postea fatebatur) magis in calice picis colorem quam panis et uini conspiceret.*

86 *Ibid.*, pp. 246-51.

87 The fact that the confession was made to the prior who then imposed the penance might be seen as a challenge to the bishop's authority as these were usually his duties.

88 Symeon, *Libellus de Exordio* cit., pp. 250-1.

89 *Ibid.*, pp. 104-7.

90 Tudor, *Misogyny of St Cuthbert* cit., p. 164.

91 An 11th-century tract known as the *De obsessione Dunelmi* ["Concerning the siege of Durham"] tells us that Bishop Ealdhun's daughter took the veil and was buried in the cemetery at Durham. T. Arnold (ed.), *Symeonis Monachi Opera Omnia* cit., 2 vols., Rolls Series, London 1882 and 1885, I, p. 217: *...et postea uelamen accepit quod et bene seruauit usque ad extremum sui diem et sepulta in coemiterio Dunelmensi diem retributionis expectat.* ["...and afterwards she took the veil and served well until her last day and she was buried in the cemetery of Durham and awaits the Day of Judgement."].

92 Symeon, *Libellus de Exordio* cit., pp. 116-7: *Quorum quattuor qui tribus aliis maiores esse memorantur, hec fuerunt nomina: Hunred, Stitheard, Edmund, Franco, de quorum stirpe multi in Northanhymbrorum prouincia tam clerici quam laici se descendisse tanto magis gloriantur, quanto progenitores sui sancto Cuthberto fidelius deseruisse narrantur.* ["Four of these, who are remembered as being more important than the other three, had these names: Hunred, Stitheard, Edmund and Franco. Many of their descendants in the kingdom of the Northumbrians – clergy and laity – take pride that their ancestors are said to have St Cuthbert so faithfully."].

93 The Durham *Liber Vitæ* is preserved as British Library, Cotton Manuscript, Domitian vii. See D. Rollason, A.J. Piper, M. Harvey, L. Rollason (eds.), *The Durham Liber Vitæ and its Context*, Woodbridge 2004.

[94] British Library, Cotton Manuscript, Domitian vii, fol. 48v. For discussion see Aird, *St Cuthbert* cit., pp. 228-9 and references therein.

[95] *Vita sanctæ Margaretæ Scotorum reginæ* in J. Hodgson Hinde (ed.), *Symeonis Dunelmensis opera et collectanea*, Surtees Society, 51, 1868, I, pp. 234-54. Cf. Bartlett, *Miracles of St Æbbe and St Margaret* cit., pp. xxix-xxxi.

[96] Examples given by Tudor, *Misogyny of Saint Cuthbert* cit., pp. 160-1. Rival cults such as the local one of St Godric at Finchale near Durham and the powerful cult of St Thomas Becket at Canterbury probably also influenced the policy of St Cuthbert's monks towards women.

[97] R. Halsey, *The Galilee Chapel*, in Coldstream and Draper, *Medieval Art and Architecture at Durham Cathedral* cit., pp. 59-73. G.V. Scammell, *Hugh du Puiset. A Biography of the Twelfth-Century Bishop of Durham*, Cambridge 1956. Before the building of the Galilee chapel, it might be presumed that the majority of women worshipped in the city's six parish churches, four of which had female dedications (two to the Blessed Virgin, one to St Margaret and one to St Mary Magdalene).

[98] Fowler (ed.), *Rites of Durham*, pp. 34-7 and see Tudor, *Misogyny of Saint Cuthbert* cit., pp. 164-5.

[99] Harvey, *Lay Religious Life* cit., pp. 185-97.

[100] In another vision reported by Symeon, Ernan, a local man, was shown souls suffering the torments of Hell. Ernan's spirit guide led him to the southern side of the city of Durham where he "saw a valley of infinite depth full of the souls of men." For Ernan familiar landmarks provided recognition points in the geography of the Afterlife: Symeon, *Libellus de Exordio* cit., pp. 190-1.

Bibliography

Primary Sources

Arnold T. (ed.), *Symeonis Monachi Opera Omnia*, 2 vols., London 1882 and 1885.

Bartlett R. (ed. and trans.), *The Miracles of St Æbbe of Coldingham and St Margaret of Scotland*, Oxford 2003.

Colgrave B. (ed. and trans.), *Two Lives of Saint Cuthbert*, Cambridge 1940.

Fowler J.T. (ed.), *Rites of Durham, being a description or brief declaration of all the ancient monuments, rites and customs belonging or being within the monastical church of Durham before the suppression. Written, 1593, Surtees Society*, 107, 1902.

Hamilton N.E.S.A. (ed.), *Willelmi Malmesbiriensis Monachi De Gestis Pontificum Anglorum Libri Quinque*, Rolls Series, London 1870.

Hodgson Hinde J. (ed.), *Symeonis Dunelmensis opera et collectanea*, Surtees Society, 51, 1868.

Johnson South T. (ed.), *Historia de Sancto Cuthberto. A History of Saint Cuthbert and a Record of his Patrimony*, Woodbridge 2002.

Offler H.S. (ed.), *Durham Episcopal Charters*, 1071-1152, Surtees Society, 179, 1968.

Preest D. (trans.), *William of Malmesbury, The Deeds of the Bishops of England (Gesta Pontificum Anglorum)*, Woodbridge 2002.

Raine J. (ed.), *Reginaldi monachi Dunelmensis libellus de admirandis beati Cuthberti virtutibus quae novellis patratae sunt temporibus*, Surtees Society, 1, Durham 1835.

Id., *Dialogi Laurentii Dunelmensis Monachi ac Prioris*, Surtees Society, 70, Durham 1880.

Rigg A.G., *Lawrence of Durham: Dialogues and Easter Poem: A Verse Translation* in "Journal of Medieval Latin", 7, 1997, pp. 42-126.

Rollason D. (ed. and trans.), Symeon of Durham, *Libellus de Exordio atque Procursu istius, hoc est Dunhelmensis Ecclesie. Tract on the Origins and Progress of this the Church of Durham*, Oxford 1998.

Stevenson, J. (ed.), *Reginald of Durham, Libellus de vita et miraculis S. Godrici, heremitae de Finchale*, Surtees Society 20, Durham 1845.

Secondary references

Aird W.M., *The Making of a Medieval Miracle Collection: The Liber de Translationibus et Miraculis Sancti Cuthberti*, in "Northern History", 1992, XXVIII, pp. 1-24.

Id., *An Absent Friend: The Career of Bishop William of Saint-Calais*, in Rollason (ed.), *Anglo-Norman Durham*, pp. 283-97.

Id., *The Political Context of the Libellus de Exordio*, in Rollason (ed.), *Symeon of Durham*, pp. 32-45.

Id., *St Cuthbert and the Normans, The Church of Durham, 1071-1153*, Woodbridge 1998.

Id., *Tostig, earl of Northumbria (c.1029-1066)*, in *Oxford Dictionary of National Biography*, Oxford 2004, [http://www.oxforddnb.com/view/article/27571, accessed 13 Nov 2007].

Baldovin J.F., *The Urban Character of Christian Worship. The Origins, Development and Meaning of Stational Liturgy*, Orientalia Christiana Analecta, 228, Rome 1987.

Barrow J., *Urban cemetery location in the high Middle Ages*, in S. Bassett (ed.), *Death in Towns. Urban Responses to the Dying and the Dead, 100-1600*, Leicester, London – New York 1992, pp. 78-100.

Blair J., *The Church in Anglo-Saxon Society*, Oxford 2005.

Bonner G., Stancliffe, Claire, Rollason, D. (eds.), *St Cuthbert, His Cult and Community to AD 1200* Woodbridge 1989.

Cambridge E., *Why did the Community of St Cuthbert Settle at Chester-le-Street?* in Bonner G., Stancliffe C., D. Rollason (eds.), *St Cuthbert, His Cult and Community to AD 1200* Woodbridge 1989, pp. 367-86.

Bonney M., *Lordship and the Urban Community. Durham and Its Overlords, 1250-1540*, Cambridge 1990.

Brooke C.N.L., *Gregorian reform in action: Clerical Marriage in England, 1050-1200*, in "Cambridge Historical Journal", 13, 1956, pp. 1-21.

Burton J., *Monastic and Religious Orders in Britain, 1000-1300*, Cambridge 1994.

Bynum C.W., *Wonder*, "American Historical Review", 102, 1997, pp. 1-26.

Carver M.O.H., Gosling P.F., *The Archaeology of Durham City* in Clack P.A.G., Gosling P.F. (eds.), *Archaeology in the North: the report of the Northern Archaeological Society*, Her Majesty's Stationery Office 1976, pp. 133-45.

Carver M.O.H., *Early Medieval Durham: the Archaeological Evidence*, in Coldstream N., Draper P. (eds.), *Medieval Art and Architecture at Durham Cathedral. The British Archaeological Association Conference Transactions for the year 1977*, Leeds 1980, pp. 11-19.

Clanchy M.T., *Reading the Signs at Durham Cathedral*, in Schousboe K., Larsen M.T. (eds.), *Literacy and Society*, Copenhagen 1989, pp. 171-82.

Coldstream N., Draper, P. (eds.), *Medieval Art and Architecture at Durham Cathedral. The British Archaeological Association Conference Transactions for the year 1977*, Leeds 1980.

Colgrave B., *The Post-Bedan Miracles and Translations of St Cuthbert* in Fox C., . Dickins B (eds.), *The Early Cultures of North-West Europe (H.M. Chadwick Memorial Studies)*, Cambridge 1950, pp. 307-332.

Conzen M.R.G., *Alnwick, Northumberland: a study of town plan analysis*, Transactions of the Institute of British Geographers, vol. 27, London 1960.

Cowdrey H.E.J., *Lanfranc. Scholar, Monk, and Archbishop*, Oxford 2003.

Crumplin S., *Modernizing St Cuthbert: Reginald of Durham's miracle collection*, in Cooper K., Gregory J., *Signs, Wonders, Miracles: Representations of Divine Power in the Life of the Church*, "Studies in Church History", 41, 2005, pp. 179-91.

Cubitt, Catherine, *Virginity and Misogyny in Tenth- and Eleventh-Century England* in "Gender and History", 12, 1, 2000, pp. 1-32.

Dawtry A., *The Benedictine Revival in the North: the Last Bulwark of Anglo-Saxon Monasticism?* in "Studies in Church History", 18, 1982, pp. 87-98.

De Smet M., *Heavenly quiet and the din or war: Use and abuse of religious buildings for purposes of safety, defence and strategy* in Trio, De Smets, *The Use and Abuse of Sacred Places*, pp. 1-26.

Douglas M., *Purity and Danger: An Analysis of Concepts of Pollution and Taboo*, London 1966.

Draper P., *Enclosures and entrances in medieval cathedrals: access and security*, in Backhouse J. (ed.), *The Medieval English Cathedral: Papers in Honour of Pamela Tudor-Craig*, Harlaxton Medieval Studies, 10, Donington 2003, pp. 76-88.

Geary P.J., *Living with the Dead in the Middle Ages*, Ithaca and London 1994.

Giandrea M.F., *Episcopal Culture in Late Anglo-Saxon England*, Woodbridge 2007.

Gilchrist R., *Gender and Material Culture: The Archaeology of Religious Women*, London 1994.

Gilchrist R., *Norwich Cathedral Close: the evolution of the English Cathedral Landscape*, Woodbridge 2005.

Hall D., *The Sanctuary of St Cuthbert*, in Bonner *et al.* (eds.), *St Cuthbert*, pp. 425-36.

Halsey R., *The Galilee Chapel*, in Coldstream, Draper, *Medieval Art and Architecture at Durham Cathedral*, pp. 59-73.

Hanawalt B.A., Reyerson K.L. (eds.), *City and Spectacle in Medieval Europe*, Minneapolis and London 1994.

Hanawalt B.A. and Kobialka M. (eds.), *Medieval Practices of Space*, Minneapolis and London 2000.

Harvey M., *Lay Religious Life in Late Medieval Durham*, Woodbridge 2006.

Hayes, D.M., *Body and Sacred Place in Medieval Europe, 1100-1389*, New York - London 2003.

Helmholz R.M., *The* Ius Commune *in England. Four Studies*, Oxford 2001.

Hicks L.V., *Religious Life in Normandy, 1050-1300. Space, gender and social pressure*, Woodbridge 2007.

Hillier B., Hanson J., *The Social Logic of Space*, Cambridge 1984.

Hobsbawm E., Ranger T. (eds.), *The Invention of Tradition*, Cambridge 1983.

Houts Elisabeth M.C. van, *Memory and Gender in Medieval Europe, 900-1200*, London 1999.

Houts Elisabeth M.C. van, *Judith of Flanders, duchess of Bavaria (1030x35-1095), Oxford Dictionary of National Biography*, Oxford 2004 [http://www.oxforddnb.com/view/article/54458, accessed 13 Nov 2007].

Howlett D., *The shape and meaning of the Old English poem "Durham"* in Rollason *et al.* (eds.), *Anglo-Norman Durham*, pp. 485-95.

Jarrett M., Mason, H., *'Greater and More Splendid'. Some Aspects of Romanesque Durham Cathedral*, "The Antiquaries Journal", 75, 1995, pp. 189-233.

Kupfer M., *Symbolic Cartography in a Medieval Parish: From Spatialized Body to Painted Church at Saint-Aignan-sur-Cher*, in "Speculum", 75, 3, 2000, pp. 615-67.

Leyland M., *The Origins and Development of Durham Castle*, in D. Rollason, M. Harvey, M. Prestwich (eds.), *Anglo-Norman Durham, 1093-1193*, Woodbridge 1994, pp. 407-24.

Lilley K.D., *Mapping the medieval city: plan analysis and urban history*, in "Urban History", 27, 1, 2000, pp. 5-30.

Id., *Urban Life in the Middle Ages, 1000-1450*, Basingstoke 2002.

Nicholas D., *The Growth of the Medieval City. From Late Antiquity to the Early Fourteenth Century*, London - New York 1997.

Oesterle J.R., *The Liturgical Dimension of Royal Representation* in P. Trio, Marjan De Smet (eds.), *The Use and Abuse of Sacred Places in Late Medieval Towns*, Leuven 2006, pp. 103-15.

Offler H.S., *The early archdeacons in the diocese of Durham*, in "Transactions of the Architectural and Archaeological Society of Durham and Northumberland", 11, 1962, pp. 193-202.

Id., *The date of Durham* (Carmen de situ Dunelmi), in "Journal of English and Germanic Philology", 61, 1962, pp. 591-4.

Id., *Ranulf Flambard as Bishop of Durham, 1099-1128*, "Durham University Journal", 64, 1971, pp. 14-25.

Palliser D.M., Slater, T.R., Dennison, Patricia E., *The Topography of Towns, 600-1300* in Palliser D.M. (ed.), *The Cambridge Urban History of Britain. Volume 1: 600-1300*, Cambridge 2000, pp. 153-86.

Parker Pearson, M., Richards C., *Ordering the World: Perceptions of Architecture, Space and Time*, in Parker Pearson M., Richards C., *Architecture and Order. Approaches to Social Space*, London 1994, pp. 1-37.

Raine J., *A Brief Historical Account of the Episcopal Palace of Auckland*, Durham 1852.

Rigg A.G., *A History of Anglo-Latin Literature, 1066-1422*, Cambridge 1992.

Rollason D., *The Wanderings of St Cuthbert* in *idem*. (ed.), *Cuthbert, Saint and Patron*, Durham 1987, pp. 45-59.

Rollason, D., *The Making of the* Libellus de Exordio*: the evidence of erasures and alterations in the two earliest manuscripts*, in D. Rollason (ed.), *Symeon of Durham: Historian of Durham and the North*, Stamford 1998, pp. 140-56.

Rollason D., Piper A.J., Harvey M., Rollason L. (eds.), *The Durham Liber Vitæ and its Context*, Woodbridge 2004.

Rosenwein B.H., *To be the neighbour of Saint Peter: The Social Meaning of Cluny's Property, 909-1049*, Ithaca, NY 1989.

Id., *Negotiating Space. Power, Restraint, and Privileges of Immunity in Early Medieval Europe*, Ithaca, NY 1999.

Rosser G., *Sanctuary and Social Negotiation in Medieval England*, in Blair J., Golding B. (eds.), *The Cloister and the World: essays in medieval history in honour of Barbara Harvey*, Oxford 1996, pp. 57-79.

Scammell G.V., *Hugh du Puiset. A Biography of the Twelfth-Century Bishop of Durham*, Cambridge 1956.

Scammell J., *The Origins and Limitations of the Liberty of Durham*, "English Historical Review", 81, 1966, pp. 449-73.

Sennett R., *Flesh and Stone. The Body and the City in Western Civilization*, London - Boston 1994.

Snape M.G., *Documentary evidence for the building of Durham Cathedral and its monastic buildings*, in Coldstream and Draper, *Medieval Art and Architecture at Durham Cathedral*, pp. 20-36.

Southern R.W., *Rannulf Flambard and Early Anglo-Norman Administration*, in "Transactions of the Royal Historical Society", 4th series, 16 (1933), revised as *Ranulf Flambard* in Id., *Medieval Humanism and Other Essays*, Oxford 1970, pp. 183-205.

Trio P., De Smet M. (eds.), *The Use and Abuse of Sacred Places in Late Medieval Towns*, Leuven 2006.

Tudor V., *The Misogyny of Saint Cuthbert*, in "Archaeologia Aeliana", 5th Series, 1984, 12, pp. 157-67.

Wood C.T., *The doctors' dilemma: sin, salvation, and the menstrual cycle in medieval thought*, in "Speculum", 56, 1981, pp. 701-727.

Urban Territories in Late Medieval Brussels. Imagined Frontiers and Responsible Institutions

Bram Vannieuwenhuyze
University of Ghent

Abstract

This chapter[1] focuses on the spatial analysis of intra-urban territories which existed in late medieval and early modern Brussels (Belgium). By studying their morphological characteristics and origins, I seek to understand their functions within urban society. These intra-urban territories did not have clear or stable frontiers, unless they were demarcated by town walls. The territories were defined by a chain of loose spatial elements. The town council used them to organise urban defence and to apply fiscal and commercial rules. Therefore, they were created *ex nihilo*, revealing the *divide et impera* policy of the town council.

In deze bijdrage wordt een ruimtelijke analyse van een aantal specifieke binnenstedelijke territoria in het laatmiddeleeuwse Brussel uitgevoerd. Hierbij gaat de aandacht vooral uit naar de morfologische eigenschappen van deze territoria, hun ontstaanscontext, hun ruimtelijke begrenzing en hun maatschappelijke rol. Uit het onderzoek blijkt dat deze territoria geen duidelijke en vaste grenzen bezaten. Enkel de beide stadsomwallingen fungeerden als dusdanig. Voor het overige werden ze beschreven door middel van een keten van losse ruimtelijke elementen. De verschillende territoria werden vermoedelijk gecreëerd in het kader van een divide et impera*-beleid vanwege de Brusselse stadsoverheid. Ze werden gebruikt om de stedelijke defensie te organiseren en om fiscale en commerciële reglementen op te leggen.*

Introduction

Throughout history, cities have been described in many ways. Some authors enumerate the most striking properties and qualities of the city. Other writers conceive of cities as conglomerations of significant buildings and structures (e.g. city halls, churches, town walls, palaces, important roads and markets). In both approaches the city is reduced to its most characteristic elements. Other aspects of the urban experience remained unstudied although they were certainly characterized by specific particularities.

During the 18th century, some guides and chronicles of Brussels tried to fill this gap by describing the different parts of the city one by one[2]. The 'advertisement' for the readers of such an edition clearly indicated that the inhabitants of large cities often ignored the things that made their city famous[3]. Because of improvements in statistical methods and administrative practice, the entire urban surface could more easily be grasped in one single approach. Yet, this kind of description and analysis often risks being static and colourless.

Nowadays, historians also need to elaborate appropriate ways of describing and – more importantly – understanding historic urban space. This chapter focuses on a specific method for describing and understanding the space of late medieval and early modern Brussels, examining the intra-urban territories that existed in the 15th and 16th centuries using a particular approach.

Intra-urban territories

From the 15th century, Brussels town council edicts mentioned specific territories. Some territories were demarcated outside of the town walls and enclosed city and hinterland, e.g. the so-called *Ammanie*, *Vrijheid* (Liberty) and *Kwartier* (Quarter) of Brussels. They have already been studied thoroughly and will not be dealt with here[4].

However other small territories existed within the city walls and are therefore defined as strictly intra-urban and have not been studied by historians. Generally they were mentioned in the records that were issued by the Brussels town council, indicating that there was a close relationship between these territories and the town council[5]. They can be classified typologically by using the terminology of the day (*wijcken*, circles and quarters). The *wijcken* are the best supported with evidence from the records and seem the most important and developed intra-urban territories in late medieval times. These territories will be treated in detail, the others will be discussed more briefly.

Beside their morphological properties and date of creation or first mention in the records, special attention is paid to the delimiting of each type of territory as well as to its social and political functions within society. Since they were created artificially, studying these territories is bound to reveal the policy of the creators and users. The conclusions will consider whether the configuration of these territories has evoked a corresponding identity.

The *wijcken*

The medieval Dutch word *wijck* is difficult to translate into English or French. French historians generally used the word *quartier* (quarter), but that would make it complicated to distinguish between the *wijcken* and the *quartieren* (see below). The use of the Latin word *vicus* is not a solution either, since *vicus* was the common translation for 'street' in medieval Brussels (at least in Latin records). In other regions the word *vicus* referred to medieval settlements as a whole, some of which dated as far back as Antiquity or Carolingian times (Quentovic for instance). The English word *district* largely covers the meaning of *wijck*, but could also be used to translate *quartier* and *singel*. To eliminate any confusion, I prefer to use the medieval Dutch word *wijck*.

The medieval *wijcken* of Brussels appeared in the sources in the middle of the 15th century. An urban edict of 10 January 1453 enumerated and described 21 *wijcken* within the city. R. Laurent edited this edict, yet commented little on the term[6]. The *wijcken* were divided in two groups: 11 *wijcken* were located "outside of the old town walls", while the other 10 *wijcken* were placed "within the old town walls". These "old town walls" are now called the "first town wall of Brussels" and were constructed during the 13th century[7]. The construction of the "second town wall of Brussels" began a century later[8], and greatly increased the area of the city. All of the 11 *wijcken* "outside of the old town walls" were incorporated within the second town wall and were therefore present between both town walls. This clearly shows that the town walls functioned as frontiers, although only the first town wall was explicitly mentioned as such.

Both groups of *wijcken* are mentioned again in a list dating from 1496[9], although the number of *wijcken* listed is higher. In this year, the city of Brussels was divided into 41 *wijcken*: 19 were located between both town walls (though this is not explicitly mentioned) and 22 within the old town wall. Except for the different number of *wijcken*, the same conclusions can be drawn. The town walls functioned as frontiers and only the oldest walls were explicitly mentioned as such. Nevertheless, some parts of this wall fell into disrepair, while other parts were absorbed by the building plots, hollowing out its demarcating power[10].

The *wijcken* are presented in both records in a largely similar way. This is a translation of a representative text extract describing the tenth *wijck* of Brussels in 1453:

> The tenth wijck, outside of the Wolfsgate, along the ditch, with the Silverstreet, continuing through the Vegetable Marsh up to Orsendal and Cabbage Gate and behind Saint Laurens along the within of the ditches up to the church of the monastery[11].

As can be concluded from this extract, a description rather than a demarcation of the *wijck* is given. By reading these words, it is nearly possible to walk along the track through the city. Indeed, the people who were responsible for the descriptions of the *wijcken* simply communicated the tracks they followed. They did not measure the surface of the entire *wijck*, nor did they determine precise and visible boundaries by using border lines or stakes.

The crucial components of the description of the *wijck* are material orientation points such as well-known places, public buildings, streets and infrastructures. In other words, the *wijck* is defined by a chain of these elements. In the example given above, a pedestrian gate (*Wolfsgate*), the ditches of the first town wall, a street (*Silverstreet*), a gate of the second town wall (*Cabbage Gate*) and a monastery with a church (*Saint Laurens*) are the crucial components. To estimate the exact location and surface of the *wijcken* a good comprehension of the urban topography is absolutely required. Unfortunately, Brussels historiography has not reached that level yet.

Although the descriptions of the *wijcken* in 1453 and 1496 were very much alike, they were not compiled for the same purpose. The list with the 21 *wijcken* of 1453 is an appendix belonging to an urban edict stipulating specific rules and measures for fire prevention in the city. Every year the town council charged two 'good, honourable and peaceful' men in each *wijck* with the duty to assist their neighbours in preventing fire[12]. These masters of the *wijcken* (*wijckmeesters*) also had to report every kind of trouble or irregularity within their *wijck*. Apart from the recording of their oath in the 1470s, the masters of the *wijcken* did not appear in the sources again. Their duties were taken over by other public officers known as the centurions (*honderste mannen*). This change occured during the time the number of *wijcken* increased (between 1453 and 1496).

In the list dating from 1496, the names of the centurions responsible for the *wijck* are written above the description. However their role and functions within the city of Brussels remain unclear until now it is very likely that they were officially responsible for their *wijck*. Indeed, their duties belonged to the domain of public order: the mobilisation of fighting men, fire prevention, the proclamation of urban edicts and the collection of taxes[13].

The second list of the *wijcken* was intended for the collection of taxes. The descriptions of the *wijcken* are part of a so-called hearth counting (*herttellinghe*)[14] in the duchy of Brabant which was set up to collect new taxes from the population[15]. This list includes the number of inhabited, uninhabited and poor hearths for each Brussels *wijck*. Therefore, tax purposes stimulated the description of the *wijcken* in this way. In 1526 a new hearth counting took place in the city of Brussels and the *wijcken* were described again in a similar list[16]. The number of wijcken in 1526 was the same as in 1496.

In addition to the lists of the *wijcken* dating from 1453, 1496 and 1526, the Brussels archives contain another interesting text with a partition scheme of the different *wijcken*. It is included in a partly conserved register containing defensive and preventive measures to protect the city in the year 1542 ("done and passed on the 2nd of August 1542 to know the number of fighting men within the city")[17]. This document consisted in a division of the city in three quarters (see below), each of them subdivided in a certain number of *wijcken*, all together resulting in 41 *wijcken* (as before). The *wijcken* are listed without a description of their content, but rather with the inclusion of the number of fighting men, divided under several banners (*vaenkens*).

In 1453 the *wijcken* of Brussels did not have specific names. They were listed numerically 1 to 11 (outside of the old walls) or from 1 to 10 (within the old walls). This changed over time: in the lists of 1496, 1526 and 1542, each *wijck* was designated by its own name. By evaluating these names, it is possible to understand the structure and meaning of these territories. The list below shows the typology of the identifying elements in the nomenclature of the *wijcken* in 1542[18]:

streets (including vaulted streams): 16

buildings: 10

public spaces or markets: 7

place names: 5

fountains: 3

Although a *wijck* was a territory – which means that it covered several urban elements – it was always named after a single morphological or spatial element. Not one single name referred to a person or to a social group, which sharply distinguished *wijck* names from medieval street names. Neither a "Butchers' *wijck*", an "*Ophem wijck*" or a "Monks' *wijck*" existed, whereas the "Butchers' street" (*Vleeschouwerstrate*), the *Ophemstrate* (named after the well-known Brussels family *van Ophem*) and the "Monks' ditch" (*Papenvest*) are examples of personified street names.

Hence, all *wijcken* were named after one of their morphological elements, public spaces (streets and markets) in particular. These spaces structured the territory of the corresponding *wijck*, either as important arteries or as central market squares. Yet, ten *wijcken* bore a name referring to a public building, and three to a fountain. Most of these buildings were (semi-)ecclesiastical, except for the court of the duke of Brabant, the Corn Hall and a city gate (*Sint Jacops poorte*). Both these buildings and fountains were commonly used as orientation points within the late medieval city.

The names reveal a high degree of centrality inside the *wijcken*. Most of them included a central space – artery, market or building – around which the *wijck* was structured. Only a few *wijcken* bore a name referring to a wider zone – called "place names" in the list above – but this resulted from the lack of a central space inside these *wijcken*. The central spaces played a very important political and social role. They were undoubtedly the areas where the fighting men gathered and the places designated for organising a response to such problems as fire, crime or street fights. The centurions (and previously the masters of the *wijcken*) assumed their public tasks within these spaces.

In conclusion, during the 15th and first part of the 16th century the *wijcken* were administrative concepts rather than spatial realities. Their names, their undefined boundaries, their functions and associated public servants point to that conclusion. Instead of the *wijcken*, the central spaces figured as the most important spatial structures, while the *wijcken* themselves were artificially created around them.

The quarters

In the document dating from 1542 all the *wijcken* are classified in one of the three large quarters (*quartieren*): the Cattle Market (*Veedemerct*), the Grand-Place (*Grooten Merct*) and the Horse Market (*Peerdemerckt aenden Savel*)[19]. Unfortunately, this is the only contemporary record using this classification. Similar to the nomenclature of the *wijcken*, the names of the quarters neither covered nor described the whole territory, but referred to a public space – a market place – within the quarter. The three quarters were more or less equal in size and number of *wijcken*. They respectively contained 14, 13 and 14 *wijcken*. The document also indicated that each quarter counted approximately 1650 fighting men.

In contrast to the *wijcken*, the three central market places of the quarters did not have a central location. The Grand-Place, for instance, was situated on the right bank of the Zenne river, while its quarter scarcely covered the left bank. However, the names were not chosen by accident. Within the dense street network of late medieval Brussels, the three market places were the sole wide public spaces. Therefore, these spaces served as perfectly gathering places for the fighting men in times of trouble.

It appears that the division of the city in three quarters was not based on topographical or geographical imperatives. Demographical, military and administrative parameters determined the extension of these territories and explain why each quarter contained an equal amount of *wijcken* and fighting men, in addition to one of the three wide market places where they could be gathered.

The circles

Besides the *wijcken* and *quarters*, the urban edicts reveal another type of intra-urban territories. They are indicated by using the medieval Dutch word *cingule*, which can be translated as "circle". This word suggests the idea of a territory with a round perimeter. The records however do not confirm this hypothesis. The descriptions of the circles are an enumeration of loose spatial elements (just as in the case of the *wijcken* and quarters). Clear boundaries are not mentioned, which contrast with the idea of a round perimeter.

The oldest known circle, which appeared in the records in 1409, did not bear a specific name[20]. It can be called the "wine circle". This circle was located between two houses in the city, probably two taverns. Unfortunately, their exact location is unknown. The circle led upwards from the house known as "the Bellows" (*den Blaesbalge*), located on the so-called *Steenwech*, one of the most important arteries which led through the heart of the medieval city of Brussels. Similarly for the second house: the circle led upwards starting from the house called "the Golden Spike" (*den Guldenen Aer*). At the end of the record, reference is made to older rights, implying that the wine circle already existed before 1409.

A later mention of the wine circle, dating from 1430, specifies a third house that functioned as frontier: the house known as "the Mirror" (*den Spiegel*), located in Mountain-street (*Bergstrate*)[21]. Despite the quite precise localisation of this building, it remains difficult to reconstruct the area of the wine circle.

The same localisation problems occur in reconstructing the territory of the second circle, of which only one mention is known (1449)[22]. The circle extended from the lowest forge in the Vegetable Marsh (the forge of Janne Robbijns, called the *Hootstal*), located opposite the Sandstreet, up to the town wall and also alongside this same Sandstreet in the direction of the previously mentioned wall up to the Orsendalpool (*Orssendalpoele*) and from there to the Cabbage Gate. In fact, this territory was situated in the same neighbourhood of the tenth *wijck* in 1453 (see above). It can be called the "thatched roofs circle".

The third circle was called the "circle (or freedom) of the Corn Hall" and appeared several times in the sources around 1460[23], when the town council temporarily received this Corn Hall from the duke of Brabant. The circle was located between the Hall itself, the Stone Gate, the church of the Saint-John's hospital and the fountain near the monastery of the Carmelites. Although these frontier markers are easier to locate, the area of this circle cannot be identified exactly.

The functions of the three circles were different from those of the *wijcken* and quarters. The "wine circle" and the "circle of the Corn Hall" demarcated fiscal zones. The urban edicts stipulated taxes on wines that entered into the "wine circle". These taxes were lower than the taxes paid for wines that did not enter the circle. Furthermore, the "circle of the Corn Hall" was the only place in which the wholesale trade of grain was allowed. The ducal taxes also had to be paid within this circle.

The "thatched roofs circle" demarcated a zone of exemption within the late medieval city. The inhabitants of this territory were not officially ordered to cover the roofs of their houses and farms with hard materials (especially roofing tiles). This part of the city was a marked agricultural zone with many farms, vegetable gardens, granges and stables where thatched roofs remained.

Territories demarcated by the town walls

The last type of territories did not have a name either. As stated above, late medieval Brussels was characterized by at least two town walls, which the historians call the first and the second town wall. The so-called "old wall" dated from the 13th century, the "new wall" from the second half of the 14th century. The territories that were demarcated by both or one of both town walls were simply indicated by the words "within/outside of the old walls" (*bynnen der ouder mueren, buten der ouder mueren*), "in between both walls" (*tusschen beide de mueren van Bruessele*) or "within the new walls" (*binnen den nuwen mueren vander stad van Bruessel*).

These kinds of territories appeared many times in the late medieval urban records, which can undoubtedly be explained by the strongly demarcating role of the walls. The oldest trace of this type of territory dated back to 1306, when it was forbidden to the weavers and fullers to stay the night within the walls of Brussels[24].

Generally, the town council used these territories for the application of rules derived from urban law. Examples are plentiful: certain city officials were allowed to acquire a domicile within the new walls; it was forbidden to play dice within the old walls; it was forbidden to keep geese within these walls; people bearing weapons within the walls received penalties, *et cetera*. As a final example, I refer to the repartition of the *wijcken* according to the position of the town walls: no *wijck* extended over both town walls.

Conclusions

The medieval intra-urban territories of Brussels did not have precise and fixed frontiers, except from those demarcated by the town walls. Although the contemporaries disposed of some embryonic instruments of surveying, they did not use them for setting down the frontiers of the *wijcken*, quarters or circles. Only a few examples report on the use of such instruments, for instance placing stakes to measure small parcels. The position and location of nearly all intra-urban territories – from little, individual parcels to greater surfaces as the *wijcken* – was described instead of precisely measured.

The descriptions located the territory with respect to loose spatial elements. These elements were either located outside or inside the territory. Natural elements and structures were sometimes used (for instance streams, mountains, valleys, marches, etc.), but most of the times artificial elements like streets, public spaces and buildings were used.

Only one kind of spatial element functioned as a true frontier (meaning a continuous, stable and visual borderline): the town walls. Especially the first town wall of Brussels was explicitly mentioned as such, even in the period after the construction of the second town wall (emptying the old one of its former military functions). All the other topographical and spatial elements that were used in the descriptions did not function as true frontiers, although some of them did indicate the limits of certain territories (for instance the buildings that limited the circles). To estimate the territorial surface, it is necessary to draw an imaginary line between several spatial elements. Due to the lack of clear and stable frontiers, these can be considered as porous territories which existed especially (if not only) in the mind of their creator, the town council (at least, during the late medieval period).

The creation of all these territories was a result of a kind of *divide et impera* policy of the Brussels town council. The intra-urban territories were used for many purposes. Some served for the military organisation of the city, while others for the application of fiscal and commercial measures. The circles and the town walls demarcated zones of exemption and interdiction, while the creation of the *wijcken* and quarters was due to demographic, defensive and fiscal imperatives. In this latter case the town council assigned public servants (the masters of the *wijcken*, later on the centurions) who accomplished the civil tasks within their territory.

It is difficult to correlate the intra-urban territories with the existence of specific social identities. First of all, the porous character and the unclear visibility of their frontiers caused an identification problem. Passing from one to another territory did not matter or cause trouble. This was not the case with the parishes: moving from one parish to another could lead to intensive discussions between the ecclesiastical authorities (because it implied loss or gain of revenues from processions, baptisms, weddings, funerals, *et cetera*).

Secondly, the creation of the intra-urban territories took place 'from above'. The town council tried to control and order urban society by creating a kind of superstructure which consisted in dividing the territory into pieces. The repartition, form and structures of the intra-urban territories thus only reflected the purposes and desires of the governors, not of their inhabitants. However, it is probable that in case of emergencies – war, street riots, fire – the inhabitants of a given *wijck* collaborated very closely and acted more or less as a group. Unfortunately, to prove this with reference to late medieval records is virtually impossible.

Notes

1 This chapter began as a communication in the session on 'Frontiers and Identities within Cities' at the EAUH Conference in Stockholm, 2006. I wish to thank participants at the session and the members of the CLIOHRES network for their remarks and encouragements to publish the study in its present form. I am also very grateful to Elisabeth Vercammen and Annelies Puype for the correction of my English.

2 *Description de la ville de Bruxelles d'après Bruxelles, G. Fricx, 1743*, Brussels 1996; *Description de la ville de Bruxelles [1782]*, Brussels, 1996; J. Rombaut, *Bruxelles illustrée. Tome Second*, Brussels 1996; T. Mann, *Description de Bruxelles*[1785], Brussels 1996.

3 *Il n'est pas rare que les habitans d'une grande ville ignorent une partie des choses qui rendent leur ville célèbre; moins rare encore de les voir considérer ces mêmes choses avec une forte indifférence* (*Description G. Fricx, 1743* cit., p. I).

4 P. Bonenfant, *Quelques cadres territoriaux de l'histoire de Bruxelles. (comté, ammannie, quartier, arrondissement)*, in "Annales de la Société Royale d'Archéologie de Bruxelles", 1934, 38, pp. 5-45; Ph. Godding, *Impérialisme urbain ou auto-défense : Le cas de Bruxelles (12e-18e siècles)*, in "Bijdragen tot de Geschiedenis. De Brabantse stad. Vierde Colloquium, Brussel 29-30 maart 1974", 1975, 58, 1-2, pp. 117-138; Ph. Godding, *Juridische betrekkingen tussen de stad en haar omgeving*, in A. Smolar-Meynart,

J. Stengers (eds.), *Het Gewest Brussel. Van de oude dorpen tot de stad van nu*, Brussels 1989, pp. 110-117.

5 Other powers that were present within the city, such as the Church or the duke of Brabant (the local sovereign), can also be linked to specific intra- and extra-urban territories (for instance the parishes), but these will not be treated. See for instance R. Laurent, *Les limites des paroisses à Bruxelles aux XIVe et XVe siècles*, in "Cahiers bruxellois", 1963, 8, 3-4, pp. 161-234; P. Lefèvre, *Le problème de la paroisse primitive de Bruxelles*, in "Annales de la Société Royale d'Archéologie de Bruxelles", 1934, 38, pp. 106-116; J. Verbesselt, *Het ontstaan van de Sint-Michielsparochie*, in « *Sint-Michielskathedraal – Kunst en Geschiedenis* » *Tentoonstelling ingericht in de Sint-Michielskathedraal te Brussel*, Tielt 1975, pp. 19-30.

6 R. Laurent, *L'acte de 1453 concernant les limites des quartiers à Bruxelles*, in *Hommage au professeur Paul Bonenfant (1899-1965). Etudes d'histoire médiévale dédiées à sa mémoire par les anciens élèves de son séminaire à l'Université Libre de Bruxelles*, Wetteren 1965, pp. 471-478.

7 S. Demeter, *La première enceinte, un patrimoine majeur pour Bruxelles*, in P. Blanquart, S. Demeter, A. De Poorter, C. Maasart, S. Modrie, I. Nachtergael, M. Siebrand (eds.), *Autour de la première enceinte. Rond de eerste stadsomwalling*, Brussels 2001, pp. 18-20.

8 C. Dickstein-Bernard, *La construction de l'enceinte bruxelloise de 1357, essai de chronologie des travaux*, in "Cahiers bruxellois", 1995-1996, 35, pp. 91-128.

9 J. Cuvelier, *Les dénombrements de foyers en Brabant (XIVe – XVIe siècles)*, Brussels 1912, pp. 219-292.

10 M. Martens, *De gebruiksrechten en renten op de eerste vestingmuur van Brussel onder het Ancien Régime*, in "Tijdschrift van het Gemeentekrediet van België", 1968, 22, 86, pp. 203-213; Demeter, *Première enceinte* cit., pp. 20-21.

11 *Den thiensten wijck, buten tsWolfs wyket langhs der grecht mitter Silverstrate vervolgende int Warmoesbroeck tot den Orsendal ende ter Coelscher poirten toe ende achter Sinte Laureys langs binnen vesten totter kerken van der cloestere* (Laurent, *Acte* cit., pp. 474-475).

12 *Ibid.*, p. 471.

13 B. Vannieuwenhuyze, *"Allen dengenen die in der stad dienste sijn." Een overzicht van de stedelijke openbare ambten en diensten in het laatmiddeleeuwse Brussel 1229-1477*, Ghent, 2002, pp. 138-139.

14 A general overview of this kind of sources is given by M. Arnould, *Les relevés de feux*, Turnhout 1976.

15 Cuvelier, *Dénombrements* cit., pp. CCXIX-CCXLV.

16 *Ibid.*, pp. CCXLVIII-CCCII.

17 *Monstren gedaen ende gepasseert opten 2e dach augusti 1542 om te weten wat volck van weeren hier inder stadt waeren* [...] (Archives of the City of Brussels, Archives anciennes, n° 1223, f° 46 v°).

18 Streets : *Loevenen wech, Berchstrate, Schoenbeke, Cruepelstrate, Ridderstraete, Spiegelbeke, Putterie, Vleeschouwers strate, Ruijsbroeck, Stoofstraete, Smaelbeke, Guldestraete, Steenstraete, Verwers straete, Vleemschen steenwech* and *Ste Cathelijnen straten;* buildings : *wijck opt Hoff, Sinte Laureijs wijck, Sinte Marie Magdaleenen, Capellewijck, Ste Peeters ten Sieckelieden, Ste Juliaens, tCorenhuijs, Sint Jacops poorte, tHerico, dBegijnhoff*; public spaces/markets : *Veedemerckt, Houtmarckt, Savel, Waelsche plaetse, Coolmerckt, Verff, Melckmerckt*; place names : *dWermoesbroeck oft Orssendael, Bavendal, Blijckerie, Overmolen, Cruijskenen;* fountains : *Gelaeskens borre, Sinter Claes borreput* and *St Thoensborre.*

19 Record already mentioned in note 16.

20 Archives of the City of Brussels, Archives anciennes, IX, f° 55.

21 *Ibid.*, f° 53 and v°.

22 Archives of the City of Brussels, Archives anciennes, IV, f° 159 v°.

[23] For instance on 3 March 1460 (*Ibid.*, f° 217); on 17 May 1462 (Archives of the City of Brussels, Archives anciennes, IX, f° 203 v°); in an undated record dating from the 15th century (Archives of the City of Brussels, Archives anciennes, IV, f° 139).

[24] *Voert es onse seggen dat en geen wevere noch volre binnen den mure van Brussel bliven en sal noch en mach over nacht, wat wevere ofte wat volre daer binnen bleven over nacht, si waren tonsen wille van live ende van goede.* (ducal privilege from 12 June 1306, edited in P. De Ridder, *De oorkonden verleend door hertog Jan II van Lotharingen, van Brabant en van Limburg (1294-1312) aan de stad Brussel (1303-1312)*, in "Eigen Schoon en de Brabander", 1974, 57, 8-9-10, pp. 307-313. See also H. Vandecandelaere, Een opstand in 'zeven aktes': Brussel 1303-1306, in "Cahier bruxellois", 2008 (in press).

Bibliography

Arnould M.A., *Les relevés de feux*, Turnhout 1976. (=Typologie des Sources du Moyen Âge Occidental, 18)

Bonenfant P., *Quelques cadres territoriaux de l'histoire de Bruxelles. (comté, ammannie, quartier, arrondissement)*, in"Annales de la Société Royale d'Archéologie de Bruxelles", 1934, 38, pp. 5-45.

Cuvelier J., *Les dénombrements de foyers en Brabant (XIVe – XVIe siècles)*, Brussels 1912.

Demeter S., *La première enceinte, un patrimoine majeur pour Bruxelles*, in Blanquart P., Demeter S., De Poorter A., Maasart C., Modrie S., Nachtergael I., Siebrand M. (eds.), *Autour de la première enceinte*, Brussels, 2001, pp. 12-28. (=Archéologie à Bruxelles, 4)

Dickstein-Bernard C., *La construction de l'enceinte bruxelloise de 1357, essai de chronologie des travaux*, in "Cahiers bruxellois", 1995-1996, 35, pp. 91-128.

De Ridder P., *De oorkonden verleend door hertog Jan II van Lotharingen, van Brabant en van Limburg (1294-1312) aan de stad Brussel (1303-1312)*, in "Eigen Schoon en de Brabander", 1974, 57, 8-9-10, pp. 289-321.

Description de la ville de Bruxelles [1782], Brussels 1996. (=Algemeen Rijksarchief en Rijksarchief in de Provinciën. Reprints, 60)

Description de la ville de Bruxelles d'après Bruxelles, G. Fricx, 1743, Brussels 1996. (=Algemeen Rijksarchief en Rijksarchief in de Provinciën. Reprints, 59)

Godding Ph., *Impérialisme urbain ou auto-défense: Le cas de Bruxelles (12e-18e siècles)*, in "Bijdragen tot de Geschiedenis. De Brabantse stad. Vierde Colloquium, Brussel 29-30 maart 1974", 1975, 58, 1-2, pp. 117-138.

Id., *Juridische betrekkingen tussen de stad en haar omgeving*, in Smolar-Meynart A., Stengers J. (eds.), *Het Gewest Brussel. Van de oude dorpen tot de stad van nu*, Brussels 1989, pp. 110-117.

Laurent R., *Les limites des paroisses à Bruxelles aux XIVe et XVe siècles*, in "Cahiers bruxellois", 1963, 8, 3-4, pp. 161-234.

Id., *L'acte de 1453 concernant les limites des quartiers à Bruxelles*, in *Hommage au professeur Paul Bonenfant (1899-1965). Etudes d'histoire médiévale dédiées à sa mémoire par les anciens élèves de son séminaire à l'Université Libre de Bruxelles*, Wetteren 1965, pp. 467-478.

Lefèvre P., *Le problème de la paroisse primitive de Bruxelles*, in "Annales de la Société Royale d'Archéologie de Bruxelles", 1934, 38, pp. 106-116.

Mann T., *Description de Bruxelles*, Brussels 1996. (=Algemeen Rijksarchief en Rijksarchief in de Provinciën. Reprints, 62)

Martens M., *De gebruiksrechten en renten op de eerste vestingmuur van Brussel onder het Ancien Régime*, in "Tijdschrift van het Gemeentekrediet van België", 1968, 22, 86, pp. 203-213.

Rombaut J., *Bruxelles illustrée. Tome Second*, Brussels 1996. (=Algemeen Rijksarchief en Rijksarchief in de Provinciën. Reprints, 65)

Vandecandelaere H., *Een opstand in 'zeven aktes': Brussel 1303-1306*, in "Cahier bruxellois", 2008 (in press).

Vannieuwenhuyze B., *"Allen dengenen die in der stad dienste sijn." Een overzicht van de stedelijke openbare ambten en diensten in het laatmiddeleeuwse Brussel 1229-1477*, Ghent (unpublished master dissertation) 2002.

Verbesselt J., *Het ontstaan van de Sint-Michielsparochie*, in "Sint-Michielskathedraal – Kunst en Geschiedenis "Tentoonstelling ingericht in de Sint-Michielskathedraal te Brussel", Tielt 1975, pp. 19-30.

The Evolution of Urban Oligarchies in Irish Towns, 1350-1534

Kieran Hoare
National University of Ireland, Galway

Abstract

This chapter begins with the historiographical setting for the study of Irish towns in the later middle ages, which emphasises the pre-colonial urban centres, topographical and morphological models and the European context in an agenda primarily driven by historical geographers. This chapter will argue for the development of a self-confident ruling class within the major towns of Ireland which had the wealth and status to control these towns and which interacted both with royal government and with the new lordships rising to pre-eminence at this time in the towns' hinterlands.

Glactar i gcoitinne go raibh tiarnas Sasanach na hÉireann ag dul i leig i rith na mean-aoise deireannaí, go háirithe an gréasán cathracha agus bailte móra a tháinig chun cinn i ndeisceart agus in oirthear an oiléain sa 13ú haois. D'éirigh saol na gcathróirí níos deacra i gcónaí, chomh maith, mar gheall ar mheath údarás an rí, forbairt tiarnaisí (leath-)neamhspleácha i measc Ghaeil agus Gaill, agus an t-ollmheath éacnamaíochta ar fud na hEorpa. Taobh istigh de gach baile mór, áfach, tháinig teaghlaigh áirithe chun cinn a chuaigh i gceannas ar shaol polaitíochta agus eacnamaíochta na mbailte móra. Tháinig na teaghlaigh seo le chéile in olagarcachtaí na gceannaithe; agus i gcaitheamh na 15ú haoise bhain siad sochar as a gcumhacht agus a dtionchar sna bailte lena stádas agus a saibhreas a mhéadú. Mar an gcéanna, chomhoibrigh siad leis an rialtas ríoga agus le tiarnaí móra a gcúlchríocha faoi seach. Bhain said sochar as tionscnaimh eile taobh istigh den bhaile mhór, idir an eaglais, rialtas bardasach, agus struchtúirí na ngildeanna, le cathróirí eile na mbailte móra a smachtú. Dá bharr seo, le hathbheochan agus leathnú údarás an rí ó 1534 i leith, bhí na teaghlaigh ceannaithe seo i riocht sochair a bhaint as na deiseanna agus failleanna a bhí ar fáil sna cúinsí polaitíochta nua. Tháinig na teaghlaigh ceannaithe chun cinn mar aicme mhuiníneach fhorásach i ríocht nua na hÉireann.

It is generally accepted that later medieval Ireland was a period of decline for the modest urban network which had developed in the south and east of the island in the

13th century. Receding royal authority, the development of a number of Gaelic and Gaelicised lordships, and the general European economic decline combined to make life difficult for most citizens in Irish towns. However, within each town or corporate borough a small numbers of families came to dominate political and economic life. These families formed merchant oligarchies, and used their positions of pre-eminence to build up wealth and status in the course of the 15th century. They used their relations with royal government and neighbouring lords in their respective hinterlands to build up their authority. They also used institutions within the town such as the Church, municipal government and guild structures to control other citizens of these towns. With the restoration and expansion of royal authority – beginning in 1534 – these merchant families were well-placed to take advantage of the opportunities which arose, allowing them to form an articulate and confident class within Ireland.

The study of later medieval/early modern urban history in Ireland has evolved rapidly since the 1970s. Historians, archaeologists and – in particular – historical geographers have produced numerous articles and books on particular towns as well as working on a model of urban development for Ireland. However, the period under consideration has been rather neglected by historians, as it comprises, or is thought to coincide with, the decline from the zenith of the English lordship in 1300 through to the major Tudor reforms from the mid-1530s on. Very little has been done, for example, to move beyond the localism of individual town histories into a comparative history of towns and their relationship to one another. The appropriate paradigm is simply not there. Similarly, while attempts at putting Ireland's overseas trade within the context of the north-western European network have been successful, this work has not found its way into the mainstream of Irish history. The most recent work on the subject has stated that the towns were in decline – to adopt that into a more sophisticated model – it was "a manifestation of a new and possibly more dynamic form of economic organisation"[1]. A number of recent works, examining such topics as the later medieval British economy, towns, and pre-modern urban decline, have drawn tentative conclusions on Ireland based on the most recent Irish research. In particular, an important article by H.B. Clarke has synthesised his work over the past three decades on the subject, along with that of Brian Graham and John Bradley[2].

The model postulated by these and other historical geographers has become the orthodox view of urbanisation in Ireland. In 1970 A.R. Orme produced a map of land quality in Ireland, showing the best land to the south and east, with the physically harsher country to the west and north[3]. Also, in terms of international trade, the south and east were closer to Britain and France, enjoying shorter lines of communication and, relatively speaking, less treacherous seas. It is not surprising therefore, that the earliest and most embedded towns should be in this part of the country. This orthodox view emphasises three strands of enquiry, each of which we will examine in turn. Firstly, it emphasises the continuity between the early medieval urban framework, and the later framework evolved under the English lordship of Ireland in the 13th century. Secondly, it provides a model of the urban network based on topography and morphology, giving lists of functions associated with towns and grading each site on the basis of the range of functions associated with it. Finally, it seeks to place the expansion of the manorial economy and urbanisation in 13th-century Ireland within the context of a similar expansion in other parts of Europe.

Indeed, within the context of the British Isles in the 10th and 11th centuries, the five Viking ports of Limerick, Cork, Waterford, Wexford and Dublin were the only examples of urbanisation outside of the south of England[4]. Initially used as staging ports for Scandinavian raiders in the later 9th century these *longphuirt* evolved into towns over time, with permanent settlements, economic and political interaction with the Irish in their hinterlands, and integration into the overseas trading network[5]. In Clarke's view:

> The phrase "minimal trend towards urbanization" would seem therefore to characterize the whole north Atlantic seaboard in the early Middle Ages. Norwegian raiders, traders and settlers came from, and contributed to, an essentially non-urban culture[6].

Another aspect of continuity has focused on the role of the "monastic town". Traditionally, our understanding of town life in Ireland was based on what has been termed "invasion hypotheses", with the Vikings and Anglo-Normans bringing urbanisation to Ireland. Towns were viewed as civilising and modernising agents, dragging Ireland out of barbarism. Taking their lead from the work of Hilton, Abrams and other British historians, Irish urban geographers stressed the concept of indigenous origin and rejected the idea that colonization by more advanced cultures brought urbanisation[7]. The work of Charles Doherty in particular has highlighted proto-urban centres in Gaelic society, focusing on the "monastic town"[8]. If the Irish "monastic town" did exist, it had primitive urban characteristics, perhaps involved in trade and manufacturing in a limited way, but they did not constitute an urban network[9]. While it is true to say that urban centres existed prior to the Anglo-Norman invasion of 1169, they were a mixture of secular, religious and market centres, but they certainly did not constitute a cohesive urban network. Nevertheless the idea that there was continuity into the 13th century has found its way into the historiography of the subject[10], and – as we shall see – the people populating and running Irish towns changed dramatically in the 13th century, making this strand somewhat misleading.

A second strand from the historiography centres on the work of historical geographers on the modelling of the Irish urban network in the High Middle Ages (*c.* 1150 to *c.* 1350). The work of B.J. Graham from 1975-1985 was synthesised into a model for colonial towns in Ireland, where the distribution of power within the hierarchical feudal society decided the importance of the town. Simply put, the more important the lord the more favourable the chances for the urban foundation to flourish. At the top of the network were the royal ports and major seigniorial boroughs involved in the overseas trade, which provided a means for the commercialisation of Irish society in the 13th century. Below that there are lesser seigneurial boroughs, followed by manorial boroughs, and finally manorial villages[11]. In all over 250 centres were identified by Graham. In 1985 John Bradley indicated the interacting criteria which would help define the medieval Irish town. He highlighted a strong emphasis on commerce, legal independence, communal organisation, social hierarchy and specialist activity. Bradley also proposed that a *Kriterienbündel* [bundle of criteria] of morphological features be used to identify real urban centres. These features included street layout, town walls, castles, bridges, religious foundations, quays and suburbs. In searching for physical remains of urban activity in this way Bradley was attempting to short-circuit the need for documentary evidence (often absent), and shifted the focus away from the legal (i.e. if a centre had borough status) to the topographical. Only centres which had three of the five criteria could be considered urban. In this way the number of urban centres was whittled down to 56 towns. There are problems with this methodology. It does not take into account whether criteria were present at the same time. Also, it fails to take into account the connection between town and country, which was particularly vital in an Irish setting given the role of towns in the commercialisation of Irish society. Indeed, the most recent attempt at classification of towns involves a functional analysis, involving an analysis of the market within each town, and the role merchants played in society[12]. This classification identified 25 mercantile towns (with 12 major and 13 lesser centres, 80 small peasant towns and 171 rural-boroughs).

The final strand in the historiography of Irish towns has been to place it within a European context. The colonisation of Ireland was one of several colonial movements in 12th-century Europe. There was also a move into the Iberian Emirates, the crusades and German eastward colonisation into Pomerania and Hungary. While portrayed as a great success story, with feudal society expanding into the peripheries of Europe, the downside of this expansion was the treatment meted out to the 'barbarians' already in these peripheries. Angret Simms assesses the views of the colonists as follows:

> Medieval chronicles show that the image of the 'barbarian' was that of a heathen or a bad Christian, a pastoralist rather than a cultivator of fields, a rural dweller rather than a town dweller and a follower of a barter economy rather than a user of coins[13].

The views of Otto of Freising writing on the Maygars, or Helmold of Bosau on the Wendish Slavs highlighted these points. Furthermore, their portrayal of these peoples as heathen emphasised the crusading nature of the conquests, and salved their consciences somewhat. It was easier to take land from and enslave heathens rather than Christians.

That the Welsh and Irish were viewed in the same manner is clear. Gerald of Wales wrote of the Irish:

> They were a wild and inhospitable people. They lived on beasts ... while man usually progresses from the woods to the fields, and from the fields to towns and communities of citizens, this people despises agriculture, had little use for the money making of towns

> and condemns the rights and privileges of citizenship ... cultivated fields are indeed few in number through the neglect of the cultivators; nevertheless the land is naturally fertile and fruitful[14].

William of Malmsbury in his *Gesta Regum Anglorum* poses a rhetorical question to himself. What would Ireland be worth without the foods that come in by sea from England? William's response again reflects an ethnographic bias:

> The soil lacks all advantages, and so poor, or unskilled, are its cultivators that it can produce only a ragged mob of rustic Irishmen outside the towns: the English and French, with their more civilised way of life, live in the towns, and carry on trade and commerce[15].

In the early 13th century Stephen of Lexington, who was inspecting the Cistercian houses in Ireland, gave strict instruction that only Latin or French speaking monks be accepted into the order. And the same order is reputed to have preached that the killing of an Irishman was not a sin[16]. It is clear, therefore, that the town was seen as the epitome of civilisation. Writers such as Orderic Vitalis and William fitzStephen in the 12th century extolled the nobility and beauty of cities such as Chester, London and Rouen because of their Roman heritage. The *civitates* were thus placed on a higher level than the Welsh or Irish towns. The Anglo-Norman chroniclers were thus able to justify the occupation and settlement of Wales and Ireland in order to, as they saw it, improve and civilise them[17].

In the view of historical geographers, Irish colonisation can be viewed within its European context in three interconnected ways. Firstly, in terms of the settlement patterns established; secondly, through the extension of settler law, and, finally through urbanisation. In the German eastward colonisation we find references again and again to the *locator*, who organised life for the initial settlers, measured out their farms in equal shares, and became the village mayor (*seultetus*). Reference to surveyors (e.g. *mensurator noster* appears in a text) and a unitary measure (known as the *Hufe*) implies that there were regularly planned settlement forms[18]. Such clear rural settlement forms are absent in an Irish setting, where pre-existing land-divisions (which recognised geographical constraints) were used. There was no one comparable to the *locator* in an Irish setting, and while land-divisions called town-lands, plough-lands and burgage plots evolved, there was no unified or distinct settlement pattern. Furthermore, the piecemeal nature of the conquest meant that different aims and resources were applied to the settlement of particular areas. Yet in an Irish setting the manor became the key institution in attracting settlers and – as in other medieval colonisations – the organisation of the manor was essentially an exercise in lordship. Time and again in an Irish setting we find a lord establishing his *caput* or chief manor, and quickly sub-infeudating his lands with the appointment of sub-tenants, who in turn built lesser manors[19]. The resultant settlement patterns of this manorial economy, the commercialisation of Irish society over the 13th century, and the influx of large numbers of settlers, gave the English lordship in Ireland a distinct identity. As C.A. Empey notes when comparing the conquests of England and Ireland:

> Nowhere is the difference between the conquests more evident: though less complete in its military and political consequences, the invasion of Ireland resulted in a significant inflow of the non-military classes – particularly in the south and east – of a kind scarcely visible in England a century earlier[20].

Another cornerstone of medieval European colonisation was the imposition of a new legal system. In the instance of German eastward colonisation we find German law (*ius teutonicum*) which provided the colonists with immunities, and was applied to new settlements rather than individuals. Under this arrangement the lord still owned the land, but the settler had the right to make free use of the land, hand on his holding to his heirs and also to have a certain degree of self-administration. Another interesting aspect was that *ius teutonicum* could be acquired by Slavic peoples through payment. This brought structural changes to rural societies there, and gave people a much greater degree of freedom. At least one-third of the *c.* 1,200 villages established in Silesia, for example, were as a result of this re-organisation rather than by settlement[21]. In Ireland the Anglo-Normans introduced English common law into the country. There are also interesting parallels between the application of *ius teutonicum* to settle villages, and the application of the Law of Breteuil which conferred legal privileges and responsibilities on burgage holders in a lord's borough. First formulated at the town of Breteuil in Normandy, transferred to Hereford in the late 11th century, the rights were granted to a number of towns in south Wales in the 12th century. Subsequently the laws found their way into the Irish colony. Their importance has been summarized by K.D. Lilley:

> In effect, urban laws such as the law of Breteuil were used by Norman lords to enfranchise towns with Norman borough customs. It was the means by which lords established new communities of burgesses who received particular legal and economic privileges from the lord, including the right to buy or sell their property in a town, as well as the freedom to engage and profit from trade on a given market day. Most importantly, the townspeople lived under the protection of the town's lord who, through granting a borough charter outlining the townspeople's legal and economic privileges, acts as a guarantor[22].

The extension of the laws of Breteuil to over 220 rural boroughs in the Anglo-Norman colony meant that a sizable proportion of the settler population had access to these laws and they would have been part of the set of incentives used to bring in settlers. Also, Gaelic Irish were, apart from those functioning within the colony such as clergy or merchants, excluded from English law, having to purchase English law when it was required. Thus, two systems of law co-existed. Where Irish tenants were incorporated into English manors, they were called *betagii* and operated essentially as pastoralists in wooded and upland areas[23].

The historiographical tradition, in an Irish setting, has therefore emphasised pre-colonial urban centres, topographical and morphological models and the European context.

This chapter will emphasise the role of the commercialisation of Irish society, bringing the focus firmly back on the people who lived in Irish towns in the later middle ages and will seek to address the questions raised in three important essays which have examined the identity of the ruling elite in these towns[24]. Gearóid Mac Niocaill posed three questions to historians, which still await adequate answers. Firstly, can Irish towns be studied together, were the problems of Dublin, Drogheda and Waterford similar to those of Cork, Limerick and Galway? Secondly, one gets the impression there was a concentration of wealth into the hands of a few burgesses in the later 15th century. Is this impression correct, and if it is to what extent was it a new development? Mac Niocaill then poses a challenge, calling for a study "into the problems of agricultural progression or regression in the late medieval period". Brian Graham has argued for a more complex division of settlement types, which has important implications for the major mercantile towns which are the subject of this study. Finally Howard Clarke has assessed in broad terms the role of colonial retreat in the 14th and 15th centuries. Clarke has identified forty urban "survivals", walled towns which had retained their urban characteristics into the 16th century. He also pointed to a new economic dynamic being created in the wake of 14th-century decolonization:

> The most dynamic urban centres were probably ports for the most part, suggesting that the economy had moved away from grain-based marketing and toward international trade in other products[25].

This new economic dynamic created opportunities for the occasional merchant prince to emerge, questioning the concept of urban decline, arguing that varying degrees of actual decline can be distinguished. The remainder of this chapter will be devoted to the question of whether Clarke is correct. If there was urban decline or the period 1350-1550 in Ireland, then the townspeople are indeed the battered remnants of an English urban network, sheltered behind stout town walls until their fortunes changed in the 16th century with the gradual re-conquest of Ireland by the English. If, however, Clarke is not correct, then we are looking at the evolution of something different, the rise of a self confident ruling class within the major towns of Ireland, able to interact with royal government, the newly evolving, politically independent lordships which rise to pre-eminence within their hinterlands, as well as the links between the towns themselves. Utilising their wealth and status, urban elites create a corporate identity that differentiates them from other local ruling elites, as well as from the bulk of the population within the towns.

In the 13th century, five economic regions emerge and they are closely connected to the manorial economy which developed at this time. One region, centred on the ports of Dublin and Drogheda on the east coast, developed into an important tillage based economy, also servicing the major town of Dublin as the seat of royal government in Ireland, and closely connected in terms of trade and administration with the ports of Chester and Bristol on England's west coast[26]. A second region, based on the south-east of the country and centred at Waterford, serviced the important river network of the Suir, Nore and Barrow. This remained, economically, the most important region into the 15th century, when it became increasingly depopulated due to disorder, as well as the migration of large numbers back to the West of England and South Wales, where the demand for labourers in a more stable society attracted many people back across the Irish Sea[27]. Smaller economic regions were centred on the important ports of Cork[28], Limerick[29] and Galway[30], roughly equated to the south, mid-west and west regions of the country.

In reality then, Irish merchant families were in a good economic position at the end of the 13th century, a manorial economy was firmly established in the south and east of the country and Ireland had been integrated fully as a regional economy, focused primarily on southern Britain, but with well-established links with Gascony, Flanders and elsewhere. It would appear, therefore, that long-distance trade (overseas trade) would have been sufficient to generate wealth for the merchant families in these ports. However, the period between 1350 and 1460 did see a general downturn in the European economy and two periods in particular stand out. Between 1390 and 1415 Europe experienced a major crisis in liquidity or bullion famine. This was associated in particular with reduced currency circulation and declining mint output. The effects of this bullion famine have been the subject of intense debate among economic historians but its effects were clearly felt in Ireland. It would have been offset to some degree by an increase in currency velocity or the rate of circulation, and the constant complaints of worn or clipped coinage in the Irish parliament attest to this. A change in the character of English rule in Ireland can be dated to this time, where English subventions of the later 14th century were stopped, and a cash-starved Dublin administration saw its revenue decline from £2,000 p.a. in the 1390s to under £1400 in the 1420s, and less again in the 1430s and 1440s[31]. While historians have correctly highlighted the mismanagement of Henry VI of England as a reason for this decline, it is clear that the developing dependence on magnate rule and 'coign and livery' by the Dublin administration owed something to this scarcity of coinage. Finally, when the government belatedly addressed the availability of coinage with an Irish mint in the 1460s it did seem to have a beneficial effect on the Irish economy. A second depression between 1445 and 1465 was more directly attributable to Lancastrian mismanagement and a fall off in demand across Europe.

There were, however, particular constraints to Irish overseas trade which meant that it did not have a huge role to play in wealth generation for merchants. As with the north of England, Scotland and Wales, local conditions such as weather, warfare and disease played an important role in slowing the economy. In the Palatinate of Durham in northern England, for example, agrarian expansion was noticeable up to the second decade of the 14th century only to take a rapid downturn due to the collapse of border defences in 1314 and the famine of 1315-8[32]. A similar downturn is evident on manors throughout Ireland. By 1307 the Bigod manors in south-eastern Ireland were showing a decline in arable farming from the 1280s[33], there was a noticeable decline around Dublin by 1326[34] and, on the demesne farm at Carrick-on-Suir in 1358, only 20 out of 216 acres were under arable[35]. Local raiding and warfare took its toll on trade, as did piracy off the coast[36].

Irish merchants also faced increasing regulation of their trade through the later 14th century, particularly with the establishment of the wool staple at Calais, and the more determined enforcement of customs collection. Towns in England responded to this downturn by diversifying into cloth production in the 14th century to offset the decline in raw wool exports. There was some manufacture of rough cloth called frieze or serge around Dublin and Waterford in the later middle ages, and some friezes in Coventry were made of Irish wool, but there was no sustained growth in the export of Irish cloth. Indeed, as the many references to English cloth in the later 15th-century Pale suggest, the ready availability of better quality cloth from centres like Coventry militated against an indigenous cloth industry.

Fisheries were important to certain towns, and the trade in wine remained fairly constant throughout this time, but the real commodity of 14th- and 15th-century Ireland were hides. Even in regional economies such as the south-east, wool and grain were supplanted to a large extent by hides. This reflects the decline of grain production outside of the Pale but also the decline of sheep-rearing in the south and south-east. However the Gaelic and increasingly Gaelicised lordship society focused primarily on hides, and this became the chief export in Ireland.

And it is clear when one turns to the internal trading network that the merchants who could reach into their hinterland and acquire the hides at source were those most likely to find their way onto town oligarchies. In 1426 Thomas Arthur of Limerick owed 14 people for hides, ten of whom were clearly of Gaelic origin, many of those identifiable with the Uí Bhriain, Mhic Conmara and Mac Mhathghamhna families of south Clare. In a 1468 inventory of hides held from people by John Blake of Galway at his death, one was English and 16 were from Gaelic families in northern and eastern county Galway. In Cork the Lumbard family retained links with the inland town of Buttavant, the Tirrys with Rathcormack and Castlelyons[37], and the Sarsfields with Glanmire[38]. Originally from these areas where they would have been free tenants of the manor, and moving into the nearest city to improve their economic prospects, these merchant families used their regular supply of hides to gain a foothold in the town. Similarly in the Pale, the snapshot of debts owned by tenant farmers from the Register of Wills from the Diocese of Dublin between 1457 and 1483 confirms this[39]. For example, Margaret Brownaysyn of Killadoon, on 12 January 1467 owed John Rossele, merchant, 8 *s.* [shillings], and 4*s.* to John Shynnagh, merchant. John Gogh, citizen of Dublin with lands in the south-east, owed various sums, 5*s.* to Nicholas Brown, 3*s.*8*d.* [pence] to John West, 14*d.* to

Thomas Collier, as well as sums to bakers, millers, tutors and a number of English merchants, as well as a number of landowners of Kilkenny and Waterford for hides.

What all this shows is that there was a substantial body of traders operating within Irish society at this time, trading in the countryside and small towns. Some of these traders, such as the Kirwans of Galway or the Sextons of Clare, found their way into larger towns where they could operate in the overseas market. What is equally clear from the large number of small traders operating at this time was that wealth generation from trade alone was not enough to get onto a town's oligarchy. For example, between 1467 and 1485 165 merchants were admitted to the freedom of Dublin, so why were the same fifteen families in control of municipal government?

The role of property holding as a source of wealth generation has not been examined in great detail, but there can be little doubt the rents generated from properties either controlled or owned by merchants in or near port-towns would have been a regular source of income, unlike the risky business of trading. In 1306 John de Wynchedon (Nugent) of Cork bequeathed a stone house near the Church of the Holy Trinity to his son William and the one beside it to his son Nicholas. The holding at Dungarvan (a suburb of Cork) which he bought from Helena de Stackpol was given to his son Walter once the sum of £27 was raised from it. To his son Thomas a house he purchased on the street of St John the Evangalist and to his son Richard the holding of Robert Coffyn and his part holding of the property[40]. In a Landgable Roll of Cork City dated to 1453, John Skiddy had ten burgage plots including Skiddy's Castle on North Main Street, begun in 1445. The de Wynchedon family, mentioned earlier and which provided Cork with a provost (a precursor of the mayor) in 1254, had twenty six holdings in the suburb of Dungarvan as well as other parts of the city. The Gould, Coppinger, Lumbard and Tirry families also had multiple holdings. Indeed 53% of holdings in the roll were held by nine families. Many of these families would have agricultural land around the city. There were constant processes at work to accumulate wealth and property. For example, between 1385 and 1387 William Tanner of Dundalk received a messuage in the New Town of Dundalk from William Rowe, the manor of Faghard by Robert Kerdyff, a half messauge again in the New Town of Dundalk by Andrew Houchon and Alice Scheroysberi. Roger Clynton granted Adam Manley, burgess of Drogheda and Matthew Tanner 54 *s.* of rent from his tenements in Dundalk for a year, and Walter Loyde of Drumeskyn released a messauge in the New Town of Dundalk to him[41]. A similar process of property accumulation can be seen for the Blakes of Galway. Thomas O'Grade, on 23 June 1380 granted a castle in the market-place in Athenry and extending to the tenement of Thomas Lange, to Geoffrey Black, burgess of Galway[42]. In 1391 the same Geoffrey was granted all the property of Robert Steven in the town and franchises of Athenry. Another scion of the family, John, son of Walter, Blake, between 1392 and 1407 in seven different grants received extensive property and fishery rights in the towns of Galway, Athenry and Clare (present day Claregalway). On his death in

1420 is possessions included 2 gallies, 42 crannoges of salt, and tin vessels for salting (showing his involvement in fishing) and his extensive list of debtors were 80% Gaelic, owing him for loans of money, salt and "white English clothe". This John, styled 'John Oge' used money generated from fishing and trade to mortgage property from people leaving the area, and acquired enough property in this way to make his son Henry the leading member of the family in the 1420s and 1430s. There is archaeological evidence that burgage plots in Galway were sub-divided into holdings and these would have generated more income in rent then. Similarly, in Dublin in the 1350s, certain citizens seem to have benefited from property grants. William Foil, Geoffry Crompe, John de Grauyntset and Roger Hegreve received extensive properties both within the city and in lands near the city. All four served as mayors and they were among those who leased lands from the extensive estate of Elias de Asshebourn on very favourable terms[43].

What all this shows is that trade alone was not the key aspect of wealth generation for leading families in the late medieval Irish town. Surviving wills do not show large amounts of coinage or silver in their possession. It shows rather modest amounts of commodities passing through their shops and stores into the hinterland, as well as the agricultural produce garnered from lands they controlled near the towns. Unlike many English merchants they did not invest their money in fulling mills and other enterprises. They sought, rather, to acquire property (both tenements and land) and it was this control of property and the cash rents from it which propelled them into positions of power within their towns.

Control of wealth generation allowed these merchant oligarchies access status in a number of ways. Most obviously they controlled municipal government. This meant not only holding positions (such as mayor, provost or sovereign) or attendance at the Common Council of the town, but also control of market regulation, town courts and the disposition of the common property of the town. Where towns were by the sea, admiralty rights over the harbour and beyond were also granted. Cash-strapped royal administrations were more than happy to hand the running of Irish towns to these oligarchies. The fee farm of the town (the annual rent paid for the royal grant of town privileges) and the administration of customs were handed over to town councils in the course of the later 14th century, when the crown abjured its responsibilities on defence to the town councils. There is ample evidence that towns took these rights seriously. In 1480, for example, a meeting of the Dublin City Council was postponed as the Council was campaigning with the Lord Deputy in O'Byrne country, to the south of the town[44]. In 1480 several of the younger men of the leading families of Cork were killed when they went to confront a raiding party from McCarthy Muskerry to the west of the city.

The very real danger posed by Irish enemies and English rebels (as they were often termed in the ordinances and petitions of the townspeople) meant that townspeople often had to act in unison to protect their interests, both against the depredations of local pirates and those raids emanating from neighbouring lordships. The long-running feud between the O'Driscoll lordship in the south-west and the citizens of Waterford was well-known,[45] while the seas around Kinsale were noted for lawlessness at this time, with both Irish and Breton pirates noted. Perhaps the clearest indication for the defensive needs of towns is the strengthening of town walls and defences at a time when, elsewhere in the British Isles, they were left to fall into decay[46]. To take one example, in 1419 work began on walling the 'Irish town' of Limerick, the suburbs to the south of the town. Work began on Tower na Clouna, and in 1428 work began on the eastern side of the suburb with Cahan's and Cogan's towers, and by 1441 William Arthur, then mayor, furnished an account for the completion of the walls in the southern suburbs[47]. Behind the colourful stories of raids and pirates we find merchant oligarchies applying for grants, gathering monies and organising both expeditions and building projects to counter the threat posed by lawlessness from lordship society. It should noted also that local warfare afforded opportunities to gather booty and conferred status on town leaders.

The Church also conferred status on leading townspeople, both by allowing them to be buried in the prestigious precincts of town churches, and through the funding of building projects, masses and charitable work. Space does not permit listing the benefactors for every urban medieval church, chantry or religious order, but the evidence is impressive. In this way the prominent standing of merchant families within their towns was reflected and reinforced. Pride of place was given to the Merchant Guild during the Corpus Christi procession and other civic ceremonial occasions. The consequent opportunity to extend largess through feasting served to cement the status of prominent families. Unlike other towns in the British Isles such as York or Norwich there was no attempt to oust the ruling elite from any Irish town. Their right to rule was never openly questioned either by other townspeople or royal officials. Only the strongmen operating in their hinterlands seriously threatened these merchant oligarchies, and more often than not these could be bought off.

The final aspect of the status I would like to touch on briefly is the connection between urban oligarchies and royal administration. Although royal government did step back from direct intervention in local government in the later 14th century, it did maintain an overseeing role, and when crises developed royal officials looked to the towns for support. Towns also had strong representation in the Irish parliament, and while the attendance of towns from outside the east and south-east of the country was intermittent to say the least, we can say that townspeople were able and willing to use the Irish parliament as a higher court of appeal and as a means of getting acts which served their interests adopted. Examples include the 1380 statute opening trade with Portugal and Spain and the 1464 act allowing trade with the Irish. Positions in local government which needed local personnel were often filled from the towns. Royal commissions, inquiries, courts, sheriffs and customs collectors were often populated with prominent townspeople. We also find examples of magnate families such as Desmond and Ormond employing townspeople to expedite dealings with royal government when required. In general then, the placing of local government and defence in the hands of merchant oligarchies, as well as their close association with clerical elites, royal officials and lordship elites ensured that the status of these oligarchies within towns was secure, and their authority to govern unchallenged.

It is within this complex framework of wealth creation, augmented by the various means of conferring status, that we come to the final question in this chapter, to what extent was race a factor in the identity of these urban oligarchies. On the face of it, it would appear that race was indeed a factor, very few Gaelic names appear in surviving municipal records. The O'Neonen family in Limerick held the office of bailiff of Limerick Corporation on a number of occasions between 1380 and 1461. Thomas O'Kabrane was mayor of Waterford in 1422 and 1425. Certainly Gaelic families such as the Kirwans and Darcys of Galway, the Sextons of Limerick and Roynaynes of Cork found their way into the heart of the merchant oligarchies of their respective towns. This involved a process of divesting themselves of their Gaelic identities over two or three generations. At a time when we speak of the "Gaelicisation" of Irish society generally why do urban oligarchies appear to buck the trend or what impact did this have on identity formation within the towns?

The Statutes of Kilkenny in 1366 had established a legal framework for the exclusion of Irishmen from governmental office and ecclesiastical benefices in English districts generally. Other provisions sought to introduce good government, keep down the price of merchandise, control wages and the movement of labour. While the stepping back of royal administration from local government in the later 14th century may have blunted the effectiveness of the Statutes somewhat, it is clear that – where practical and in the interests of the local ruling elites – they were enforced.

In looking at their enforcement within municipal jurisdictions, the Statutes themselves did not provide the impetus. However, when the urban ruling class sought to control the admission of freemen into their towns they proved adept at using crown ordinances to suit their needs. The enforcement of municipal statutes against the Irish must be viewed in the content of the decline in people deemed suitable to serve on the Corporation. Gearóid Mac Niocaill summarised the situation as follows:

> What is being suggested is that towards the end of the middle ages, the Irish town was suffering from a population crisis, not necessarily in the form of falling population at this period, but perhaps stagnation after a fall at an earlier period, which rendered difficult the recruitment of a governing class within the town...[48].

On 24 June 1448 Dublin Corporation ordained that no man with the right to the liberties of Dublin should be refused admission to the Corporation "provided he be of free condition and not of the Irish nation"[49]. This ordinance was followed up by a much sterner decree of 1454 which ordered the expulsion of all people of Irish blood from the city. This ordinance also included an order that no Irish apprentices or servants could be taken on by any freeman of Dublin. There was a fine of 40*s.* for each infringement[50]. In Waterford in 1459-60 it was ordered that no man of Irish blood be given the freedom of the city unless he first had the freedom and liberty of the King[51]. While there was no express order in the Galway Corporation records against the admission of Irishmen, there were prohibitions against the sale of boats to Irishmen, or the material to make boats and weapons in 1516-17. There was also, in 1500, a very detailed explanation as to why goldsmith Donill Ovolloghan was allowed to practice his trade and be a freeman of Galway so that he could look after his infirm father-in-law, also a freeman[52]. It can be inferred that the detailed explanation of this case was necessary to counter any complaint that the Corporation allowed someone of Irish blood into the freedom of the town.

One of the ways that one could acquire the freedom of an Irish town in the later 15th and early 16th centuries was through serving as an apprentice. An examination of the roll of freemen admitted to the franchise of Dublin between 1468 and 1485, for example, shows that there were 635 admissions, of which thirty-two were by marriage, 67 were by birth, 237 were by special grace and 301 were through service as apprentices to freemen[53]. 59% had a trade. It was therefore important that the rules governing admission of apprentices was closely supervised. The charter granted to the Guild of Barbers in 1470 allowed them to "received as brethren or sisters any honest and fitting persons willing freely to join them"[54]. Similarly, the Guild of Carpenters, Millers, Masons and Heliers would only take on apprentices who were free, of the English nation and of good conversation, to be bound for seven years under indenture and at the end presented by the guild to the corporation to be enrolled as freemen of the town. A bye-law for 1438 for the Merchant Guild of Dublin noted that admission of new brethren into the Guild could only take place at the 'grete quarter semblies' of the Guild before all the brethren[55]. In Waterford it was ordered in 1458-9 that no man should be admitted into the city freedom unless he practiced the one craft he stated at the time he received his freedom[56]. It is clear, therefore, that municipal authorities expected the craft guilds to control admittance to their craft, and to ensure that none of the Irish nation or unfree persons could claim the freedom of the town through apprenticeship at a later date[57].

That said, there were people of the Irish race living in later medieval Irish towns, and not just the few who were dubbed knights, that become privileged merchants or respected clergy. In 1463, for example, we find a fisherman, Philipus McDonnell, renting a tenement in Straid na Gabhair in Kinsale from James Roche[58], or the O'Toole stonemasons in Dublin in the 1480s[59], and the many Irish people renting tenements in the town. The use of the Irish language is well attested to in the towns, and would have been required to do business in the hinterlands of most towns. However, there was a conscious effort made to exclude Irish people from any representation in local government, the freedom of the town or any role in overseas trade. It could, of course, be argued that those Englishmen not of the town were also excluded, but race was certainly used as a factor in deciding if one was allowed into a town oligarchy. Those of Irish race were not allowed to acquire property to any great extent in Irish towns, unlike their Welsh counterparts in towns such as Ruthlin in Wales, where Welsh merchants found their way onto municipal government, albeit in smaller numbers than their English counterparts[60]. This exclusion allowed members of town oligarchies to acquire property more easily than if they had to compete with those of Irish descent.

In conclusion therefore, we have examined the historiographical framework within which the formation of ruling urban elites has been studied in detail, before examining the role of wealth, status and race in the formation of identity for this class within later medieval Irish society. Traditional views, lacking primary records and a meaningful comparative perspective, have focused on overseas trade as the basis for their power. This chapter has sought to show that internal trading networks and the control of properties within the towns were more important than overseas trade in terms of wealth generation. Furthermore, the utilisation of status-enhancing mechanisms such as control of local government and defence, royal patronage, and a close working relationship with ecclesiastical elites all served to confirm a handful of families in each town as a ruling elite. Finally, the effective exclusion of those of Irish race from urban elites (apart from the few Irish merchants who adopted English ways), and the control of the quantity and type of freemen entering towns, saw urban elites make a conscious decision to maintain and enhance their 'Englishness'. This set them apart from their hinterlands and indeed from the non-freemen in their own towns, and reversed the trend of 'Gaelicisation' evident elsewhere in Irish society. Ultimately, it was the self-confidence of two hundred years of self-government underpinned with their control of wealth and status which saw these urban elites play a pivotal role in the formation of an old English elite in the later 16th and early 17th century and assert their right to remain Catholic under a Protestant monarch.

Notes

1 H. Swanson, *Medieval British Towns*, Basingstoke 1999, p. 20.

2 R. Britnell, *Britain and Ireland, 1050 1530: Economy and Society*, Oxford 2004; B. Graham, *Urbanisation in Ireland during the High Middle Ages, c.1100 to c. 1300*, in T.B. Barry (ed.), *A History of Settlement in Ireland*, London 2000, pp. 124 - 139; B. Graham, *Town in Medieval Ireland* in *Medieval Ireland* in *The Barryscourt Lectures*, Kinsale 2004, pp. 289-310; H.B. Clarke, *Decolonization and the dynamics of urban decline in Ireland, 1200-1550*, in T.R. Slater (ed.), *Towns in Decline AD100-1600*, Ashgate 2000, pp. 157-192.

3 A.R. Orme, *Ireland*, London 1970.

4 R.H. Britnell, *Britain and Ireland, 1050 - 1530*, p. 107.

5 J. Bradley, *The Interpretation of Scandinavian Settlement in Ireland*, in J. Bradley (ed.), *Settlement and Society in Medieval Ireland: Studies presented to F.X. Martin*, Kilkenny 1988, pp. 49-78; H.B. Clarke,

Proto-Towns and Towns in Ireland and Britain in the Ninth and Tenth centuries, in H.B. Clarke, M. Ní Mhaonaigh, R.Ó Floinn (eds.), *Ireland and Scandinavia in the Early Viking Age*, Dublin 1998, pp. 331-380; B.T. Hudson, *The Changing Economy of the Irish Sea Province*, in B. Smith (ed.), *Britain and Ireland 900-1300*, Cambridge 1999, pp. 39-68.

6 H.B. Clarke, *Proto-Towns and Towns in Ireland and Britain*, p. 341.

7 R.A. Butlin, *Urban and proto-urban settlements in pre-Norman Ireland* in Id. (ed.), *The Development of the Irish Town*, London 1983, pp. 1-17; R.H. Hilton, *Towns in English feudal society* in "Review", 3, 1979, pp. 3-20; P. Abrams, *Towns and economic growth: some theories and problems*, in P. Abrams & E.A. Wrigley (eds.), *Towns in Societies*, Cambridge 1978, pp. 9-34.

8 C. Doherty, *Exchange and Trade in early medieval Ireland*, "Journal of the Royal Society of Antiquaries of Ireland", 110, 1980, pp. 67-89; C. Doherty, *Some Aspects of hagiography as a source for Irish economic history* in "Peritia", 1, 1982, pp. 300-328; id., *The Monastic Town in Ireland*, in H.B. Clarke, A. Simms (eds.), *The comparative history of urban origins in non-Roman Europe*, BAR International Series 255. Oxford 1985, pp. 45-76.

9 B.J. Graham, *Urban genesis in early medieval Ireland*, in "Journal of Historical Geography", 13, 1987, pp. 3-16; M. Valante, *re-assessing the Irish 'monastic town'*, in "Irish Historical Studies", 31, 1998, pp. 1-18.

10 B.J. Graham, *The High Middle Ages: c. 1100 to c. 1350*, in T. Barry (ed.), *A History of Settlement in Ireland*, London 2000, pp. 66- 68; B.J. Graham, *The Anglo-Norman Colonisation of Ireland*, in *Medieval Ireland: The Barryscourt Lectures I - X*, Kinsale 2004, pp. 292-294.

11 B.J. Graham, *The evolution of the settlement pattern of Anglo-Norman Eastmeath*, in R.H. Buchanan, R.A. Butlin and D. McCourt (eds.), *Fields, Farms and Settlements in Europe*, Belfast 1976, pp. 38-47; B.J. Graham, *The towns of medieval Ireland*, R.A. Butlin (ed.), *The Development of the Irish Town*, London 1977, pp. 28-66; B. Graham, *Anglo-Norman Colonisation and the size and spread of the colonial town in medieval Ireland* in H.B. Clarke, A. Simms, *The Comparative History of Urban Origins in Non-Roman Europe*, BAR International Series 255, Oxford 1985 (ii), pp. 355-372.

12 B.J. Graham, *The Definition and Classification of Medieval Irish Towns* in "Irish Geography", 21, 1988, pp. 20-32.

13 A. Simms, *Core and Periphery in Medieval Europe: The Irish experience in a Wider Context*, in W.J. Smyth, K. Whelan (eds.), *Common Ground: Essays on the Historical Geography of Ireland*, p. 22; R.J. Bartlett, *Gerald of Wales, 1146 - 1223*, Oxford 1982, pp. 158-177.

14 Giraldus Cambrensis, *Topographica Hiberniae*, in J.J. O'Mara (ed.), Dundalk 1951, pp. 85-6.

15 William of Malmsbury, *Gesta Regum Anglorum*, Oxford 1998, p. 739.

16 J. Watt, *The Church in Medieval Ireland*, Dublin 1972, pp. 57-8; R.R. Davies, *Lordship or Colony?* in J. Lydon (ed.), *The English in Medieval Ireland*, Dublin 1984, p. 158.

17 K.D. Lilley, '*Non urbe, non vico, non castris*', *territorial control and the colonization and urbanization of Wales and Ireland under Anglo-Norman lordship*, in "Journal of Historical Geography", 26, 2000, p. 519.

18 Simms, *Core and Periphery* cit., p. 26.

19 See, for example, the case of counties Tipperary and Kilkenny, C.A. Empey, in *Conquest and Settlement: Patterns of Anglo-Norman Settlement in North Munster and South Leinster*, "Journal of the Irish Economic and Social History Society", 13, 1986, pp. 5-31; for county Limerick see C.A. Empey, *The Settlement of the Kingdom of Limerick*, in J. Lydon (ed.), *England and Ireland in the Later Middle Ages*, Dublin 1981, pp. 1-25; for Cork see K.W. Nicholls, *The Development of Lordship in County Cork, 1300 - 1600*, in P. O'Flanagan, C.G. Buttimer (eds.), *Cork: History and Society*, Dublin 1993, pp. 157-212; P. McCotter, *The sub-infeudation and descent of the Fitzstephen/Carew moiety of Desmond* (Part 1),

in "Journal of the Cork Historical and Archaeological Society", 101, 1996, pp. 64-80 and (Part 2), "Journal of the Cork Historical and Archaeological Society", 102, 1997, pp. 89-106; for Galway see P. Holland, *The Anglo-Normans in County Galway: the Process of Colonisation*, in "Journal of the Galway Archaeological and Historical Society", 41, 1997, pp. 73-89; P. Holland, *The Anglo-Normans and their Castles in County Galway*, in G. Moran (ed.), *Galway: History and Society*, Dublin 1996, pp. 1-25.

20 Empey, *Conquest and Settlement* cit., p. 7.

21 S. Trowkowski, *Die Rolle der deutschen Dorfkolonisation und des deutschen Rechtes in Polen im 13. Jahrhundert* in W. Schlesinger (ed.), *Die deutsche Ostsiedlung des Mittelalters als Problem der Europäischen Geschichte*, Sigmaringen 1975, pp. 349-368; A Simms, *Core and Periphery* cit., pp. 26-27; for a more recent assessment of our understanding of *ius teutonicum* see J.M. Piskorski, *The Medieval Colonization of Central Europe as a Problem of World History and Historiography*, in "German History", 22, 2004, pp. 323-343.

22 Lilley, *'Non urbe, non vico, non castris'* cit., pp. 520-1.

23 G.J. Hand, *The Status of the Native Irish in the Lordship of Ireland*, in "Irish Jurist", new series, 1, 1966, pp. 93-115; G.J. Hand, *English Law in Ireland, 1290-1324*, Cambridge 1967; K.W. Nicholls, *Land, Law and Society in Sixteenth Century Ireland*, Cork 1976.

24 G. MacNiocaill, *Socio-Economic problems of the Late Medieval Irish Town*, D. Harkness, M. O'Dowd (eds.), *The Town in Ireland*, Belfast 1981, pp. 26-49; B.J. Graham, *The Definition and Clarification of Medieval Irish Towns*, "Irish Geography", 21, 1988, pp. 20-32; H.B. Clarke, *Decolonization and the dynamics of urban decline in Ireland, 1300-1550*, pp. 157-192.

25 H.B. Clarke, *Decolonization and the dynamics of urban decline in Ireland, 1300-1550*, p. 179.

26 Id., *Medieval Dublin: the making of a metropolis*, Dublin 1990; J. Bradley, *A Tale of Three Cities: Bristol, Chester and Dublin and the Coming of the Normans*, in H.B. Clarke, J.R.S. Philips (eds.), *Ireland, England and the Continent in the Middle Ages and Beyond*, Dublin 2006, pp. 51-66.

27 E. McEneaney, *Mayors and merchants in Medieval Waterford City, 1169-1495* in W. Nolan, T.P. Power (eds.), *Waterford: History and Society*, pp. 147-176; J. Bradley, *The Early Development of the medieval Town of Kilkenny*, in J. Bradley (ed.), *Kilkenny, History and Society*, Dublin 1990, pp. 63-74; B. Colfer, *Anglo-Norman Settlement in County Wexford*, in K. Whelan (ed.), *Wexford: History and Society*, Dublin 1987, pp. 65-99; J. Bradley, *The medieval towns of Tipperary*, in W. Nolan (ed.), *Tipperary: History and Society*, Dublin 1985, pp. 34-59.

28 A.F. O'Brien, *Politics, Economy and Society: The Development of Cork and the Irish south-coast region c. 1170 to c. 1583* in P. O'Flanagan, C.G. Buttimer (eds.) *Cork: History and Society*, Dublin 1993, pp. 83-156.

29 C. Lennon, *Archbishop Richard Creagh of Armagh, 1523-86*, Dublin 2000, pp. 17-31; M. Potter, *The Government and the People of Limerick*, Limerick 2006, pp. 19-96.

30 G. Mac Niocaill, *Medieval Galway: It's Origins and Charter*, in D. Ó Cearbhaill (ed.), *Galway: Town and Gown*, Galway 1984, pp. 1-9; P. Walsh, *The Topography of Medieval and Early Modern Galway City*, in G. Moran (ed.), *Galway: History and Society*, Dublin 1994, pp. 27-96.

31 P. Spufford, *Money and Its Uses*, Cambridge, 1988; S.G. Ellis, *Ireland in the Age of the Tudors, 1447-1603*, Harlow repr. 1998, pp. 24-28; Id., *Ioncam na hÉireann, 1384-1534*, in "Studia Hibernica", 22 1982-3, pp. 39-49; Id., *The Struggle for Control of the Irish Mint, 1460-1506*, in "Proceedings of the Royal Irish Academy", C 78 1978, pp. 17-36; M. Dolley, *Coinage to 1534: The Sign of the Times*, in A. Cosgrove (ed.), *A New History of Ireland*, ii (*hereafter, NHI*) Oxford 1987, pp. 816-826.

32 R. Britnell, *Britain and Ireland 1050-1530* cit., p. 315.

33 London: Public Record Office, S.C. 6/1237/51,53, 55; P.H. Hore, *History of the town and county of Wexford*, London 1900-11, i, p. 30; K. Down, *Colonial Society and Economy in the High Middle Ages*, *NHI*, ii, pp. 477-480.

34 J. Lydon, *The Impact of the Bruce Invasion, 1215-27*, in *NHI*, ii, pp. 275-302; B. Smith, *Colonisation and Conquest in Medieval Ireland: The English in Louth, 1170-1330*, Cambridge 1999, pp. 105-109.

35 *Calendar of Ormond Deeds*, ii, E. Curtis (ed.), Dublin 1934, p. 42.

36 T. O'Neill, *Merchants and Mariners in Medieval Ireland*, Dublin, 1987, pp. 119-129; W. Childs, T. O'Neill, *Overseas Trade*, *NHI*, ii, pp. 522-524.

37 W. Coppinger, *Additional Historical Notes*, in "Journal of the Cork Archaeological and Historical Society", 1 1892, pp. 117-8

38 Dublin: Marsh's Library: *Sarsfield Mss.*; K.W. Nicholls, *Anglo-French Ireland and After*, in "Peritia", 1, 1982, p. 396.

39 *Register of Wills and Inventories of the Diocese of Dublin in the time of Archbishops Tregury and Walton 1457-1483 from the original manuscript in the library of Trinity College, Dublin*, Dublin 1898.

40 D. O'Sullivan, *The Testament of John de Wynchedon of Cork Anno 1306*, "Journal of the Cork Historical and Archaeological Society", 61, 1956, pp. 75-88.

41 C. MacNeill, A.J. Otway Ruthven (eds.), *Dowdall Deeds*, Dublin 1961, pp. 120-2.

42 M.J. Blake, *Blake Family Records*, London 1902, p. 6.

43 *Christ Church Deeds*, M.J. McEreny, R. Refaussé (eds.), Dublin 1999, pp. 160-166.

44 J.T. Gilbert (ed.), *Calendar of ancient records of Dublin, in the possession of the municipal corporation*, [hereafter *Cal Anc Rec Dub*] Dublin 1889-1944, i, p. 357.

45 J. Lydon, *The City of Waterford in the Later Middle Ages*, in "Decies", 12, 1979, pp. 12-20.

46 A. Thomas, *Walled Towns of Ireland*, Dublin 1990; J. Bradley, *Walled towns in Ireland*, Dublin 1995.

47 Dublin: National Library of Ireland, *White Mss.*; London, British Museum, Add. Ms. 14331 (*Arthur Manuscripts*)

48 G. Mac Niocaill, *Socio-economic problems of the medieval Irish town* in D. Harkness, M. O'Dowd (eds.), *The Town in Ireland*, Dublin 1981, pp. 20-1.

49 *Cal Anc Rec Dub* cit., p. 272.

50 *Ibid.*, cit., pp. 280-1. The effectiveness of these ordinances may be questioned when one notes O'Tooles and O'Byrnes working as masons in the city.

51 J.T. Gilbert, *Archives of the Municipal Archives of Waterford*, in Historical Manuscripts Commission [hereafter HMC], *10th Report*, London 1885, pp. 299-300.

52 J.T. Gilbert, *Archives of the town of Galway* cit., pp. 390-1, 397.

53 Dublin: National Archives of Ireland, TA 1416.

54 H.F. Berry, *The Ancient Corporation of Barber-Surgeons, or the Gild of Mary Magdalene, Dublin*, in "Journal of the Royal Society of Antiquaries of Ireland", 33, 1903, p. 218.

55 Dublin: City Library and Archives: Gilbert Library MS 78.

56 J.T. Gilbert, *Municipal Archives of Waterford*, p. 299.

57 K. Hoare, *Guilds in Irish Towns*, "Historical Studies", 7, Limerick 2006, pp. 53-65.

58 R. Caulfield, *Council Book of the Corporation of Kinsale*, Guildford 1878, p. 412.

59 Dublin, National Archives of Ireland cit., TA 1435.

60 M. Stevens, *Wealth, status and 'race' in the Ruthin of Edward II*, "Urban History", 32, 2005, pp. 17-32.

Bibliography

Abrams P., *Towns and economic growth: some theories and problems*, in Abrams P., Wrigley E.A. (eds.), *Towns in Societies*, Cambridge 1978, pp. 9-34.

Bartlett R.J., *Gerald of Wales, 1146-1223*, Oxford 1982.

Blake M.J., *Blake Family Records*, London 1902.

Bradley J., *The medieval towns of Tipperary*, in Nolan W. (ed.), *Tipperary: History and Society*, Dublin 1985, pp. 34-59.

Id., *The Interpretation of Scandinavian Settlement in Ireland*, in Bradley J. (ed.), *Settlement and Society in Medieval Ireland: Studies presented to F.X. Martin*, Kilkenny 1988, pp. 49-78.

Id., *The Early Development of the medieval Town of Kilkenny*, in Bradley J. (ed.), *Kilkenny, History and Society*, Dublin 1990, pp. 63-74.

Id., *Walled towns in Ireland*, Dublin 1995.

Id., *A Tale of Three Cities: Bristol, Chester and Dublin and the Coming of the Normans* in Clarke H.B., Philips J.R.S. (eds.), *Ireland, England and the Continent in the Middle Ages and Beyond*, Dublin 2006, pp. 51-66.

Britnell R., *Britain and Ireland, 1050-1530: Economy and Society*, Oxford 2004.

Butlin R.A., *Urban and proto-urban settlements in pre-Norman Ireland*, in Butlin R.A. (ed.), *The Development of the Irish Town*, London 1983, pp. 1-17.

Caulfield R., *Council Book of the Corporation of Kinsale*, Guildford 1878.

Clarke H.B., *Medieval Dublin: the making of a metropolis*, Dublin 1990.

Id., *Proto-Towns and Towns in Ireland and Britain in the Ninth and Tenth centuries*, in Clarke H.B., Ní Mhaonaigh M., Ó Floinn R. (eds.), *Ireland and Scandinavia in the Early Viking Age*, Dublin 1998, pp. 331-380.

Id., *Decolonization and the dynamics of urban decline in Ireland, 1200-1550*, in Slater T.R. (ed.), *Towns in Decline AD100-1600*, Ashgate 2000, pp. 157-192.

Colfer B., *Anglo-Norman Settlement in County Wexford*, in Whelan K. (ed.), *Wexford: History and Society*, Dublin 1987, pp. 65-99.

Davies R.R., *Lordship or Colony?* in Lydon J. (ed.), *The English in Medieval Ireland*, Dublin 1984, pp. 142-160.

Doherty C., *Exchange and Trade in early medieval Ireland*, in "Journal of the Royal Society of Antiquaries of Ireland", 110, 1980, pp. 67-89.

Id., *Some Aspects of hagiography as a source for Irish economic history*, in "Peritia", 1, 1982, pp. 300-328.

Id., *The Monastic Town in Ireland*, in Clarke H.B., Simms A. (eds.), *The comparative history of urban origins in non-Roman Europe*, BAR International Series 255, Oxford 1985, pp. 45-76.

Dolley M., *Coinage to 1534: The Sign of the Times*, in Cosgrove A. (ed.), *A New History of Ireland*, ii, Oxford 1987, pp. 816-826.

Down K., *Colonial Society and Economy in the High Middle Ages*, in Cosgrove A. (ed.), *A New History of Ireland*, ii, Oxford 1987, pp. 439-491.

Ellis S.G., *The Struggle for Control of the Irish Mint, 1460-1506*, in "Proceedings of the Royal Irish Academy", C 78 1978, pp. 17-36.

Id., *Ioncam na hÉireann, 1384-1534*, in "Studia Hibernica", 22 1982-3, pp. 39-49.

Id., *Ireland in the Age of the Tudors, 1447-1603*, Harlow repr. 1998.

Empey C.A., *The Settlement of the Kingdom of Limerick*, in Lydon J. (ed.), *England and Ireland in the Later Middle Ages*, Dublin 1981, pp. 1-25.

Id., *Conquest and Settlement: Patterns of Anglo-Norman Settlement in North Munster and South Leinster*, in "Journal of the Irish Economic and Social History Society", 13, 1986, pp. 5-31.

Gilbert J.T. (ed.), *Calendar of ancient records of Dublin, in the possession of the municipal corporation*, Dublin 1889-1944.

Graham B.J., *The evolution of the settlement pattern of Anglo-Norman Eastmeath*, in Buchanan R.H., Butlin R.A., McCourt D. (eds.), *Fields, Farms and Settlements in Europe*, Belfast 1976, pp. 38-47.

Id., *The towns of medieval Ireland*, Butlin R.A. (ed.), *The Development of the Irish Town*, London 1977, pp. 28-66.

Id., *Anglo-Norman Colonisation and the size and spread of the colonial town in medieval Ireland* in Clarke H.B., Simms A., *The Comparative History of Urban Origins in Non-Roman Europe*, BAR International Series 255, Oxford 1985, (ii), pp. 355-372.

Id., *Urban genesis in early medieval Ireland*, in "Journal of Historical Geography", 13, 1987, pp. 3-16.

Id., *The Definition and Classification of Medieval Irish Towns*, in "Irish Geography", 21, 1988, pp. 20-32.

Id., *Urbanisation in Ireland during the High Middle Ages, c.1100 to c.1300*, in Barry T.B. (ed.), *A History of Settlement in Ireland*, London 2000, pp. 124-139.

Id., *Town in Medieval Ireland* in *Medieval Ireland* in *The Barryscourt Lectures*, Kinsale 2004, pp. 289-310.

Hand G.J., *The Status of the Native Irish in the Lordship of Ireland*, in "Irish Jurist", new series, 1, 1966, pp. 93-115.

Id., *English Law in Ireland, 1290-1324*, Cambridge 1967.

Hilton R.H., *Towns in English feudal society*, in "Review", 3, 1979, pp. 3-20.

Hoare K., *Guilds in Irish Towns*, in "Historical Studies", 7, Limerick 2006, pp. 53-65.

Holland P., *The Anglo-Normans and their Castles in County Galway* in Moran G. (ed.), *Galway: History and Society*, Dublin 1996, pp. 1-25.

Id., *The Anglo-Normans in County Galway: the Process of Colonisation*, in "Journal of the Galway Archaeological and Historical Society", 41, 1997, pp. 73-89.

Hore P.H., *History of the town and county of Wexford*, London 1900-11.

Hudson B.T., *The Changing Economy of the Irish Sea Province*, in Smith B. (ed.), *Britain and Ireland 900-1300*, Cambridge 1999, pp. 39-68.

Lennon C., *Archbishop Richard Creagh of Armagh, 1523-86*, Dublin 2000.

Lilley K.D., *'Non urbe, non vico, non castris', territorial control and the colonization and urbanization of Wales and Ireland under Anglo-Norman lordship*, in "Journal of Historical Geography", 26, 2000, pp. 517-531.

Lydon J., *The City of Waterford in the Later Middle Ages*, in "Decies", 12, 1979, pp. 12-20.

Id., *The Impact of the Bruce Invasion, 1215-27* in Cosgrove A. (ed.), *A New History of Ireland*, ii, Oxford, 1987, pp. 275-302.

MacNeill C., Otway Ruthven A.J. (eds.), *Dowdall Deeds*, Dublin 1961.

MacNiocaill G., *Socio-Economic problems of the Late Medieval Irish Town*, Harkness D., O'Dowd M. (eds.), *The Town in Ireland*, Belfast 1981, pp. 26-49.

Id., *Medieval Galway: Its Origins and Charter*, in Ó Cearbhaill D. (ed.), *Galway: Town and Gown*, Galway 1984, pp. 1-9.

McCotter P., *The sub-infeudation and descent of the Fitzstephen/Carew moiety of Desmond* (Part 1), in "Journal of the Cork Historical and Archaeological Society", 101, 1996, pp. 64-80 and (Part 2), in "Journal of the Cork Historical and Archaeological Society", 102, 1997, pp. 89-106.

McEneaney E., *Mayors and merchants in Medieval Waterford City, 1169-1495* in Nolan W., Power T.P. (eds.), *Waterford: History and Society*, Dublin 1992, pp. 147-176

Nicholls K.W., *Land, Law and Society in Sixteenth Century Ireland*, Cork 1976.

Id., *The Development of Lordship in County Cork, 1300-1600*, in O'Flanagan P., Buttimer C.G. (eds.), *Cork: History and Society*, Dublin 1993, pp. 157-212.

O'Brien A.F., *Politics, Economy and Society: The Development of Cork and the Irish south-coast region c. 1170 to c. 1583* in O'Flanagan P., Buttimer C.G. (eds.) *Cork: History and Society*, Dublin 1993, pp. 83-156.

O'Neill T., *Merchants and Mariners in Medieval Ireland*, Dublin 1987.

O'Sullivan D., *The Testament of John de Wynchedon of Cork Anno 1306*, in "Journal of the Cork Historical and Archaeological Society", 61 1956, pp. 75-88.

Orme A.R., *Ireland*, London 1970.

Piskorski J.M., *The Medieval Colonization of Central Europe as a Problem of World History and Historiography*, in "German History", 22, 2004, pp. 323-343.

Potter M., *The Government and the People of Limerick*, Limerick 2006.

Simms A., *Core and Periphery in Medieval Europe: The Irish experience in a Wider Context*, in Smyth W.J., Whelan K. (eds.), *Common Ground: Essays on the Historical Geography of Ireland*, Cork, 1988pp. 22-40.

Swanson H., *Medieval British Towns*, Basingstoke 1999.

Trowkowski S., *Die Rolle des deutchen Dorfkolonisation und des deutchen Rechtes in Polen im 13. Jahrhundert* in Schlesinger W. (ed.), *Die deutsche Ostsiedlung des Mittelaltums als Problem der Europaischen Geschichte*, Sigmaringen 1975, pp. 349-368.

Smith B., *Colonisation and Conquest in Medieval Ireland: The English in Louth, 1170-1330*, Cambridge 1999.

Spufford P., *Money and Its Uses*, Cambridge 1988.

Stevens M., *Wealth, status and 'race' in the Ruthin of Edward II*, in "Urban History", 32, 2005, pp. 17-32.

Thomas A., *Walled Towns of Ireland*, Dublin 1990.

Valante M., *re-assessing the Irish 'monastic town'*, in "Irish Historical Studies", 31, 1998, pp. 1-18.

Walsh P., *The Topography of Medieval and Early Modern Galway City*, in Moran G. (ed.), *Galway: History and Society*, Dublin 1994, pp. 27-96.

Watt J., *The Church in Medieval Ireland*, Dublin 1972.

Fortification Territories: Fragmentation and Hierarchisation of Parisian Spaces in the 19th Century

Frédéric Moret
Université Paris-Est, Laboratoire Analyse Comparée des Pouvoirs

Abstract

The building, during the July Monarchy, of the fortifications of Paris caused a lasting segmentation of the Parisian space. In opposition to the 18th-century conception of an "open city", the French Government chose to enclose Paris and a part of its *faubourgs* within a double belt of fortifications: an *enceinte continue* (curtain wall), itself surrounded with detached forts. The fortifications went through overlapping Parisian boundaries, including all or part of the suburban municipalities. This defines a range of complex and different juridical states. From the centre of Paris to the outside, no less than six different territories can be defined. This led to a real intermeshing of administrative divisions and regimes, which affected largely the urban expansion of the Parisian metropolis, all the more since population growth changed semi-rural spaces into urban space. Conflicting interests came into play in determining the status of the various territories formed by the fortifications. In fact, the laws and regulations on the building of the fortifications did not provide for a clear sharing of responsibilities between political and administrative, civil and military, national, regional and local powers.

In 1860, Napoléon III and his prefect Haussmann decided that Paris would annex the suburbs inside the fortifications. This decision simplified the situation, even if a real difference remained between centre and peripheral areas. This reform drew a permanent frontier – still central for urban and political matters – between "Paris *intra muros*" and its "banlieue". Banlieue municipalities lost a large part of their territories, or were (like Belleville, Montmartre or Bercy) fully absorbed by Paris. The new municipalities had to reorganize their space and build new polarities. Conflicts over use and jurisdiction focused specially on a space in front of the fortifications, the *non aedificandi* zone. In theory, no building was allowed on this space, but this was never to be defined legally. Urban pressure and deficiencies in public authorities changed what is now called "la Zone" into an 'outlaw space', illegally occupied by industrial and entertainment establishments.

La construction, sous la Monarchie de Juillet, des Fortifications de Paris est à l'origine d'une segmentation durable de l'espace parisien. Tournant le dos aux conceptions urbanistiques héritées du XVIIIe siècle qui valorisaient la "ville ouverte", le gouvernement français fit le choix d'enfermer Paris et une partie de ses faubourgs dans une double ceinture de fortifications : une enceinte continue, elle même entourée d'une ligne de forts détachés.

Projet d'origine étatique, la construction des Fortifications vient bouleverser les frontières locales héritées de l'Ancien Régime et de la Révolution française. De part et d'autre des barrières de l'octroi, l'espace parisien et celui des communes de la périphérie étaient alors nettement distincts. La ligne des Fortifications, qui déborde les limites parisiennes, englobe donc tout ou partie du territoire des communes suburbaines, et définit ainsi toute une série d'espaces obéissant à des statuts juridiques complexes et différents. Du centre de Paris vers l'extérieur, se succèdent ainsi:

- *un territoire parisien soumis à un droit d'octroi pour l'entrée et la sortie des marchandises aux barrières*
- *une partie du territoire des communes suburbaines qui se trouve enfermée dans le double anneau que constituent la ligne des barrières de l'octroi et les fortifications*
- *l'enceinte militaire elle-même, dotée d'un statut spécial*
- *une bande de terrain, de 250 mètres de large, devant les fortifications, est grevée de servitudes militaires, et constitue la «zone non aedificandi»*
- *le reste du territoire des communes suburbaines, sous le régime normal, à l'exception des portions de territoire occupées par les forts détachés et leurs glacis.*

L'enchevêtrement des circonscriptions et des régimes administratifs qui en découle conditionne très largement l'expansion urbaine de l'agglomération parisienne, d'autant plus que la croissance de la population parisienne transforme les espaces semi-ruraux de la périphérie en un espace urbain, de plus en plus peuplé. Il s'exerce donc sur ces différents territoires, et sur leurs frontières, une forte concurrence entre différents pouvoirs, d'autant plus que la législation à l'origine de la construction des fortifications n'a pas prévu clairement une répartition des responsabilités entre pouvoirs politiques et administratifs, civils et militaires, nationaux, départementaux et municipaux...

L'annexion par Paris, en 1860, des faubourgs à l'intérieur des fortifications simplifie la situation, même si persiste une différenciation entre les arrondissements du centre et les arrondissements périphériques. Cette réforme dessine durablement la frontière – aujourd'hui encore au centre des préoccupations urbanistiques et politiques – entre « Paris intra-muros » et sa banlieue. Largement amputées, quand elles ne sont pas totalement absorbées par Paris, les communes de banlieue doivent bien souvent totalement restructurer leurs territoires et construire de nouvelles polarités. D'autre part, l'intégration des quartiers périphériques de Paris, qu'Haussmann ne mit pas réellement en œuvre constitue un très long processus. Un espace en particulier concentre les conflits de juridictions et d'usage : la zone non aedificandi, en principe interdite à toute construction, n'a jamais reçu de définition juridique précise. La pression urbaine, l'absence d'autorités publiques et d'aménagements ont fait de ce qui est devenu "la Zone", un espace de non-droit, occupé illégalement par des établissements industriels ou de récréation, qui nourrit l'imaginaire de la délinquance parisienne, des "Apaches", ces bandes de jeunes à la mythique "Casque d'Or", immortalisée par Simone Signoret.

Since July 2007, Parisians – and foreigners – can rent bicycles everywhere inside the territory of the French capital at a very reasonable price. These "*Vélibs*" have been a great success and the authorities decided to extend the system beyond the "*boulevard périphérique*" (the large ring road between the city of Paris and the suburban towns). An administrative court refused this extension in December 2007, in accordance with the defence of free competition. This anecdote gives a good illustration of the sharp divide that still exists between Paris and its suburbs, called *la Banlieue*. The boundaries of the French capital restrict the city to a small area. As opposed to London or Berlin, the importance of Paris in the metropolitan area that surrounds it is weak. Only two million out of the ten million inhabitants of the agglomeration live within Paris. This phenomenon creates numerous problems when it comes to the urban and economic development of the French capital. For a century, Paris and its suburban neighbours have been competing with each other, to the detriment of urban growth and development. For the first time, in 2001 the current leftwing mayor of Paris Bertrand Delanoë decided to appoint a deputy-mayor in charge of relations between Paris and the *Banlieue*. But the question of *Grand Paris* [greater Paris] is still a taboo: on one hand Paris is afraid of being submerged by the larger suburban population whereas, on the other hand, suburban towns are proud of their autonomy[1]. This chapter focuses on the origins of this division. The building of the fortifications of Paris during the July Monarchy (1830-1848) has created a long-lasting segmentation of the Parisian area. In opposition to the concepts of urban development of the 18th century – when the 'open city' was promoted – the French government chose to hem in Paris and a part of its suburbs with a double belt of fortifications: an enclosing wall surrounded by detached forts. In the beginning, the project of the government only focused on the detached forts, some distance away from the limits of the city. This solution would have had a minor impact on the future development of the metropolis from an urban point of view, but the Republican party and a part of the liberal opposition struggled against this project, which was proposed by the Thiers and Guizot governments. These opponents were afraid of the possibility of the government using these detached forts to repress the Parisian people. They consequently advocated an enclosing wall around the capital, defended by the Parisian people themselves[2]. Thus, the construction work which began in 1841 and lasted four years, combined both systems – without any military advice. Consequently, Paris was surrounded by both a wall 34 kilometres long and a range of detached forts, in front of the wall. This new urban reality had an important influence not only on the development of the metropolis for the rest of the 19th century, but also after the demolition of the fortifications, initiated shortly after World War I. This reality still influences the Parisian region today, and explains to a large extent the division between Paris and its suburbs.

This chapter focuses on the way in which the building of internal boundaries in urban areas results from different factors: including legal, urban and demographic developments as well as political-administrative decisions.

The legal context

The juridical status of the different spaces is tremendously important, to the extent that it creates different legal frontiers of competence, with a direct influence on spatial realities. Before the French Revolution, the Ancien Régime distinguished the different spaces quite clearly. The urban territory was defined by privileges (also called liberties): municipal authorities (or a central government subdivision as in Paris) exerted their power in a specific area and could impose tariffs or tolls on products crossing the borders. Those privileges were usually based on a charter granted by the King. Those localities, towns or villages without any chartered status were organized only as civil parishes, without any privileges. The Law inherited from the French Revolution defined the *commune* as the basic unit in the organization of the national territory. Two superior levels of organization were created: the *canton* (which included around ten or fifteen *communes*) and the *département* (which included about thirty *cantons*). The legislators' objective was to break away from the liberties and privileges of the Ancien Régime. As a consequence they rejected any legal distinction between urban and rural *communes*. Paris or Bordeaux had to be *communes* in the same way as little villages of a rural district were, as did the suburban boroughs surrounding them. The only legal definition was a fiscal one specified during the Napoleonic era: only urban localities could collect town dues (*octroi*). The concept of communes proved ineffective when it came to controlling urban development of the semi-rural spaces between Paris and its suburbs. It did not allow Paris to evolve regional policies. Also, the policy of centralization in France (existing since the Ancien Régime and reinforced by the French Revolution and Empire) forbade the right of enlarging boundaries of towns: enlargement depended on political decisions, taken by the central government. The municipal council (in every *commune* except Paris, that was under government authority) had little power; it was largely seen as an administrative level of the central executive power, under the authority of the *préfet*, the representative of the government in each *département*. The municipal council – whose members are managed by the mayor (elected in the little villages, but chosen by the *préfet* in *communes* of over 2000 inhabitants) – attempted to express the local opinion with difficulty.

This legal context had significant consequences on expanding towns, limiting their development within existing political and administrative structures. Relations between large towns and suburban villages or boroughs were often fraught. It is significant that the most commonly used word to describe suburban space in French is *banlieue*. It is made of two medieval terms: *ban*, which expresses the power exercised on particular places or people (e.g. the royal army is made using the *ban* and the *arrière-ban*, gathering the king's vassals and their own vassals); and *lieue* [league], which indicates a 4-kilometre distance. In accordance with this definition, the *banlieue* is a space outside the city territory, but under its power. This traditional concept is still present in the French representation of urbanity, establishing an unflattering image of the *banlieue* described by French novelist Louis-Ferdinand Céline as a "doormat in front of the city where each and everyone wipes their feet"[3].

Mental representations of the Parisian territory

The fortifications radically changed the representations of the Parisian territory. The original village was built on a small island situated on river Seine – the *Ile de la Cité* [Isle of the City] and Paris has subsequently grown on both sides of the river; on the north bank mainly (the *Rive Droite*), but also on the south bank (the *Rive Gauche* or the Latin Quarter, in reference to the University of the Sorbonne). The traditional conception of internal frontiers in Paris dates back from the end of the Ancien Régime and can be seen on maps of Paris of that time. The famous map by Ambroise Tardieu[4], published in 1839, made a clear distinction between the historic heart of the city and its *faubourgs*. The *faubourgs* formed a part of Paris, but were considered peripheral. In earlier times this area was occupied by fields, gardens and residential estates. Its boundary was determined by the line formed by the *Boulevards*, the large avenues that replaced the old fortifications from the early 18th century. After 1785, the external limits of the city were fixed by the "Wall of the Farmers General", which defined the space within which toll was due on goods entering Paris. The development of the suburban townships mostly resulted from the attractiveness of the different establishments offering liquors, placed outside of the *Barrières* and exempted from taxes on consumption. For this reason, the ballrooms, *guinguettes* [open-air cafés] and theatres of Belleville, Montmartre or Montrouge were very attractive to the Parisian population. Their growth during the first half of the 19th century changed those villages and gave them an urban aspect. The building of the fortifications of Paris seriously affected this traditional division of space; the wall gave a new meaning to the spatial organization of the metropolis. An important area (only annexed in 1860, twenty years after the works, and which corresponds to the current twelfth to twentieth *arrondissements*) happened to be doubly enclosed. With the new fortifications forming two rings around the capital, this area was surrounded by the toll limits on one side, and by the boundaries of the suburbs on the other. Some localities such as Bercy, La Villette, or Belleville became almost completely incorporated within the fortification line. Others, such as Ivry, Montrouge, or Le Pré Saint-Gervais were divided by the fortifications, resulting in the fragmentation of these boroughs.

The juridical situation of those territories was particularly complex. For example, Le Pré Saint-Gervais was a little village in the north-east of Paris which did not have a large territorial extension.

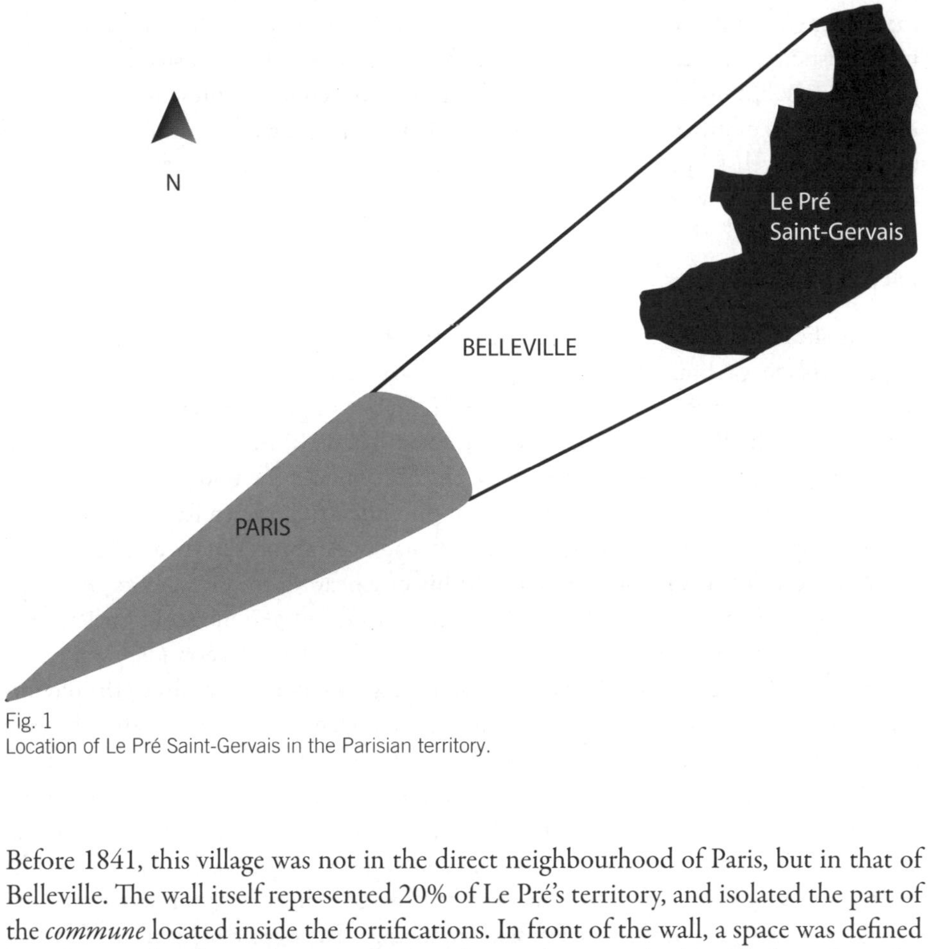

Fig. 1
Location of Le Pré Saint-Gervais in the Parisian territory.

Before 1841, this village was not in the direct neighbourhood of Paris, but in that of Belleville. The wall itself represented 20% of Le Pré's territory, and isolated the part of the *commune* located inside the fortifications. In front of the wall, a space was defined by military rules; due to the special status of Paris, the normal rules of military boundaries were modified, and the law defined a 250 metre zone, called the "Non-aedificandi zone", inside of which no construction could take place.

In Le Pré Saint-Gervais, the *Zone* (a designation that soon became generic) represented almost a third of the territory, now divided into four spaces with different juridical and governmental status. Within the internal boundaries of Paris, five types of social and juridical spaces succeeded one another and defined a range of inner frontiers. This situation unfolded against a backdrop of population growth with the development of the Parisian population, creating a real metropolitan agglomeration whose population grew from one to two millions between 1836 and 1866. Paradoxically the urbanization of rural or semi-rural spaces placed between Paris and the towns or boroughs of the *banlieue* was thwarted in order to build a homogeneous territory. Each juridical boundary had an influence on urban development but also on the day-to-day business of its citizens.

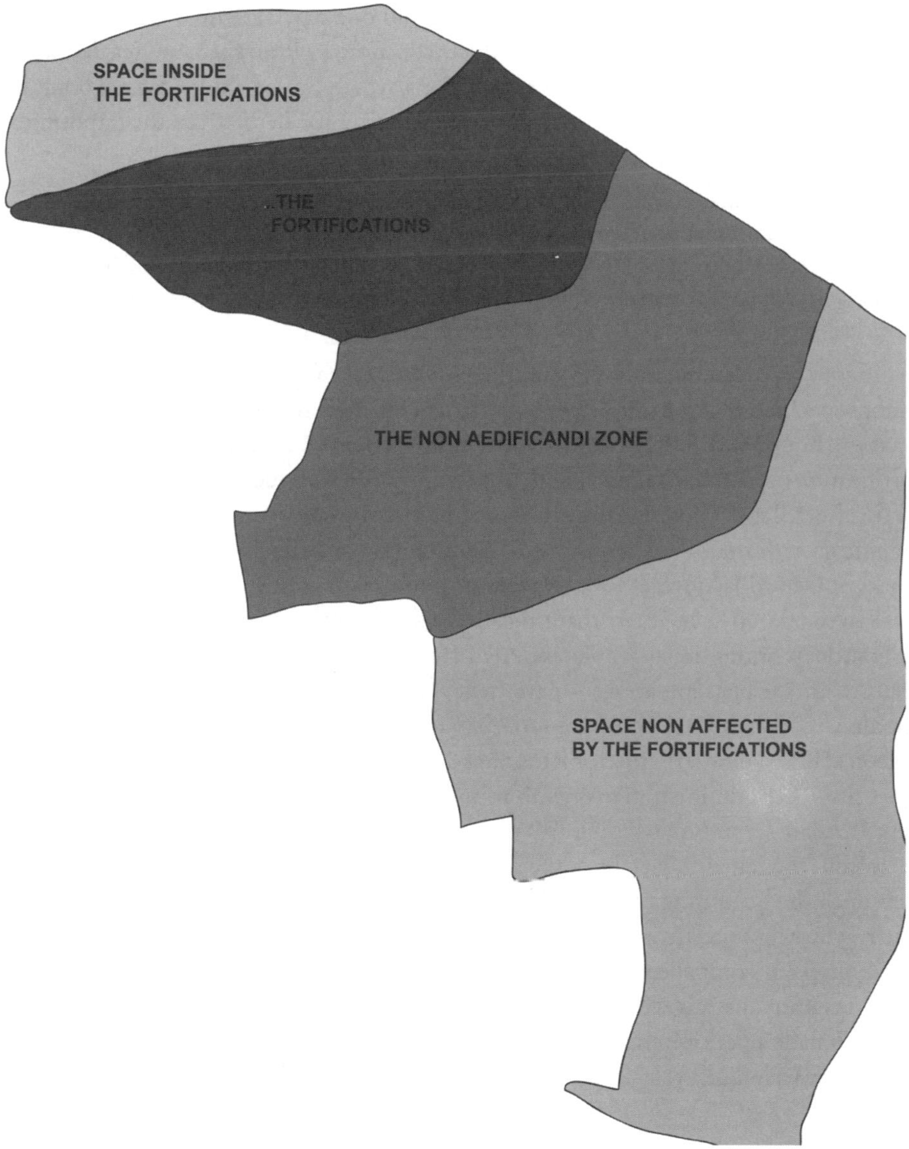

Fig. 2
The divisions of the municipal territory of Le Pré Saint-Gervais.

PARIS'S BOUNDARIES AND THE QUESTION OF THE TOWN *DUES*

Even before the construction of the fortifications, the future of the space placed between the legal boundaries of Paris and the wall was the cause of huge debate, with numerous public interventions. In November 1840, the municipal council of Bercy voted to print a letter to the government, focusing on the consequences of the expected fortifications[5]. More than the material loss due to the fortifications themselves, the municipal officials feared that "the city of Paris could one day take those fortifications as boundaries and collect duties on the products consumed within the new area delimited by the wall"[6]. The annexation of this area by Paris, which caused a shift in fiscal boundaries, was seen as an economic and demographic disaster for Bercy given the importance of public houses in the area:

> Such an exorbitant decision cannot be taken thoughtlessly; and Paris has never to gain from it, because the prosperity of the most populous localities such as Belleville, La Villette, Bercy, Vaugirard, Montrouge, only results from beverage trading. This trading would be impossible, and would move outside of those boundaries; those localities, booming today, would be changed into deserts[7].

In order to give guarantees to the suburban *communes*, the law of April 1841 on fortifications specified that the municipal boundaries could not be changed by administrative decision, but only through a new law. For almost twenty years, the territory inside the fortifications remained independent from Paris and continued to develop thanks to its fiscal privilege. Those localities adopted an urban aspect, and had stronger demographic growth than Paris *intra-muros*. The example of Belleville, made famous in the works of Gérard Jacquemet[8], was typical. Its population grew from 10,000 inhabitants in 1836 to 60,000 in 1856. At that time, Belleville was one of the most populous towns in France. Working class people excluded from the centre of Paris – particularly by Haussmann's urban operations – gave Belleville a typical popular style, which would remain after the annexation of the suburban localities decided by Haussmann and Napoléon III. The new structure of Paris after 1860 kept the earlier inner borders for the most part. The administrative organization highlighted those differences: the twenty new Parisian *arrondissements* clearly separated the eleven central districts of ancient Paris from the remaining eight in the surrounding area. Those peripheral spaces had to wait until the beginning of the 20th century to be truly integrated in the metropolis. The towns, whose territory extended on both side of the fortifications before the annexation, were compelled to completely reorganize their municipal space, and their most dynamic districts were often disconnected. In 1859 for instance, the Municipal Council made a petition that demanded the annexation of the entire territory of Le Pré Saint-Gervais in Paris.

The Fortifications, a physical barrier

The reality of the fortifications, as an element of landscape, must be emphasized. The wall was massive; the belt consisted of an inner military road, a 6-metre wide parapet, a 10-metre high *mur d'escarpe* ([escarp] a 3.5-metre thick military wall), a 40-metre wide *fosse*, a *contrescarpe* and, of course, the Zone. The belt was under military authority, largely autonomous from civilian power, both administrative (the *Prefecture de la Seine*) or political (municipal councils). The history of the fortifications includes many complaints by civilian authorities or local inhabitants against military activity. In 1846, the municipal council of Le Pré Saint-Gervais protested against "the surprising and unpleasant decision to block two sewer outlets"[9], which made a whole district unsanitary. For military reasons, the entire structure of some localities was changed, in a radical way. For instance, the line of fortifications cut ancient roads and put a halt to the formerly established circulation of people and goods. During the big debate that preceded the 1841 law, several alternative solutions were proposed. César Daly, an architect influenced by Saint-Simon's ideas, editor of the "Revue de l'Architecture et des travaux publics", advocated the structuring of a Parisian defence based on a large canal, useful for both protection and trading. Le Pré Saint-Gervais, already mentioned above, was almost totally isolated, having no new roads leading to Paris within its territory. Municipal officials protested when the crisis hit their trading and economic activities. In the second half of the 19th century, the growth of population on both sides of the fortifications emphasized these problems. As of 1880, many demands from municipal councils or inhabitants concerning the opening of new gates or the enlargement of previous ones were issued to promote the traffic between Paris and its suburbs[10].

"La Zone", margin and barrier of Parisian urbanity

The area on which military easement was effective evidently sustained the biggest change in term of definition and boundaries. The *zone de servitude* [servitude zone], also called *zone non aedificandi*, delineated an entirely new urban and juridical problem. This area was already largely occupied when the building of the fortification began, essentially by agricultural fields and stone pits. Some recreational establishments also offered a country haven to city men. The future of the *Zone* had been hard-fought over since the origin of the project. The principle of private ownership was the very basis of the French social system since it had been sanctified by the Napoleonic Civil Code. From 1841, in this context, the landowners of the *Zone* – soon called *Zoniers* – asked for indemnities in compensation for the loss that their properties underwent[11]. The Law characterizing the fortifications created a special dispensation from the standard definition of a fortified town: the change of Paris into a *place de guerre* could not be achieved without a special law. This decision made numerous land owners of the *Zone* assume that they were not concerned with military obligations on the grounds that Paris was not officially classified as a fortified town. As a result, this decision to build fortifications created a specific type of development: the *Zone* became a territory on its own within the Parisian area, generating a lot of debates concerning its status. Many owners and tenants took advantage of this situation to occupy the *Zone* in a more permanent way, creating numerous conflicts with civilian administrations and military powers. When demanding some compensation for the *Zoniers* in 1848, the municipal council of Le Pré Saint-Gervais criticised how the administration agents had tried to persuade the owners that the fortifications would be profitable for them. "Messrs. the administration agents have explained to the deprived owners that the creation of new roads and streets could be of great advantage to their business"[12]. The municipal council stated that the same promise had been made when it came to compensation for the destruction generated by the recent construction. The problem was that the army refused the building of new houses along the new roads. The fact that municipal councils were compelled to reiterate those complaints proved the ineffectiveness of these protests. The specific ways of creating boundaries with the help of the *Zone* gave a good illustration of the conflicts between powers, owners and inhabitants. In 1849, a *Lieutenant-colonel du Génie* had to write to the mayors on this subject: "I have the honour to pray you to inform the inhabitants of your *commune* that it is forbidden to dig up the pickets hammered in their estates"[13]. The definition of the *Zone* itself and that of its easements constituted a real issue of power. At the beginning, the civilian and military authorities were largely tolerant, but became more interventionist from the 1850s onwards, by forbidding some of the works of settlement and construction. The history of this border area known as the *Zone* was shaped by the many persistent conflicts that opposed the those who tried to inhabit it, and the authorities who tried to keep it clear. The ill-managed development of the capital, associated with the general absence of public powers that resulted from the competition of diverse authorities in this area, turned the *Zone* into a lawless territory occupied by illegitimate industries and recreational establishments. The legend was born: the *Zone*, became the land of the "Apaches"[14], juvenile delinquents immortalized in Jacques Becker's movie *Casque d'Or* and whose eponymous heroin-addict was played by Simone Signoret. Only in 1919 did the area acquire normal legal status, when the decision to destroy the fortifications was taken.

At the end of the 19th century, the Parisian area was composed of three concentric belts: two well integrated and densely populated urban areas managed by a more and more interventionist administration, enclosing a nearly abandoned part of the territory only used as a refuge by a portion of the population excluded from the development of Paris and that of the suburban towns. Between Paris and its *banlieue* stood this *Zone*, a depreciated area that housed the most degrading works (notably that of rag-and-bone men) and formed a permeable yet fundamentally different buffer zone, preventing any organization or future development of the metropolis on it. Patrick Gervaise studied the district of *les Passages* in Levallois-Perret, stuck between the 17th *arrondissement* of

Paris organised by Haussmann on one side, and the new town based on a very meticulous plan by Nicolas Levallois on the other. The district of *les Passages* was occupied by an extremely poor population of rag-and-bone men who formed a very specific community, characterized for instance by a high degree of endogamy: from 1867 to 1912, 75% of the inhabitants chose their spouses in the five alleys of the district[15].

The later demilitarization and demolition of the fortifications did not resolve the problem of these Parisian areas disconnected from the rest of the capital. In accordance with the triumphant ideology of "hygienism" of that time, the authorities promoted large greenways and built large social buildings in response to the housing shortage.

The territory of the *Zone* was ultimately used to install the wide ring road (in the early 1970s) that still today constitutes a hermetic barrier between Paris and its suburbs. It is a good illustration of how a political and military decision made in the early 19th century under the pressure of the urban development and without any preoccupation for subsequent city planning, still represents an open wound for the capital.

Notes

1 The political aspect of this problem adds more complexity. Those questions were discussed in a seminar, co-organized by the Municipality of Paris and Pr. Annie Fourcaut, director of the centre for 20th-century Social History (University Paris 1; http://histoire-sociale.univ-paris1.fr/Gouvernance.htm) on "The history of the relationships between Paris and the Banlieue".

2 P. O'Brien, *L'Embastillement de Paris: The Fortification of Paris during the July Monarchy*, "French Historical Studies", 9, 1975, pp. 63-82; J.-L. Cohen, A. Lortie, *Des fortifs au périf. Paris, les seuils de la ville*, Paris 1991; F. Moret, *Chronique d'un espace communal disputé et amputé* in V. Perlès (ed.), *Le Pré entre Paris et banlieue. Histoire du Pré Saint-Gervais*, Paris 2004; Id., *Enjeux sociopolitiques et conflits territoriaux à propos de la construction des fortifications de Paris : oppositions, négociations, décisions* in J.-C. Caron (ed.), *Violence et conciliation. La résolution des conflits socio-politiques en Europe au XIXe siècle*, Paris 2008.

3 L.-F. Céline, *Voyage au bout de la nuit*, Paris 1932.

4 This map can be seen, and downloaded, from the site http://photostereo.org/pages/paris1.html.

5 *Département de la Seine. Commune de Bercy (arrondissement de Sceaux). Fortifications de Paris. Conseil Municipal, séance du 3 novembre 1840*, Bercy 1840.

6 *Ibid*, p. 2. "la ville de Paris ne vienne un jour prendre ces fortifications pour limites, afin de frapper du droit d'octroi la consommation qui se ferait dans cette enceinte".

7 "Une mesure aussi exorbitante ne peut être prise légèrement, et ce serait à tort que la ville de Paris penserait y trouver quelque avantage; car les communes les plus populeuses, telles que Belleville, La Villette, Bercy, Vaugirard, Montrouge, ne doivent leur prospérité qu'au commerce des fluides: or ce commerce, une fois rendu impossible, se déplacerait aussitôt, et ces communes, florissantes aujourd'hui, ne seraient bientôt plus qu'un désert qui viendrait s'ajouter aux terrains encore en culture situés dans l'intérieur de l'enceinte actuelle".

8 G. Jacquemet, *Belleville au XIXe siècle, du faubourg à la ville*, Paris 1984.

9 Conseil municipal du Pré Saint-Gervais, *Délibération du Conseil du 9 août 1846*, Archives municipales du Pré Saint-Gervais (AMPSG).

[10] C. Charvet, *Les fortifications de Paris. De l'hygiénisme à l'urbanisme, 1880-1919*, Rennes 2005.

[11] Cf. for instance the publications of Vatimesnil, *Mémoire à l'appui des observations présentées par les communes de la Banlieue de Paris, sur le projet de loi relatif aux Fortifications de la Capitale*, Vaugirard 1841; or by d'Augé de Fleury, *Banlieue de Paris. Servitudes militaires. Etat actuel (en novembre 1846) de la question sur les servitudes militaires dans la banlieue de Paris*, Paris 1846.

[12] "Messieurs les agents du domaine n'ont pas manqué de faire valoir aux propriétaires dépossédés l'immense avantage qu'ils retireraient de tous ces chemins qui ouvriraient des communications faciles et pour la plupart préférables à celles qui se trouveraient supprimées". *Délibération du conseil municipal du Pré Saint-Gervais du 6 février 1846*, AMPSG.

[13] *Lettre du Lt-colonel du Génie en chef, 5 novembre 1849*, AMPSG. "J'ai l'honneur de vous prier d'informer officiellement les habitants de votre commune de ne pas arracher les piquets d'alignement qui seraient plantés dans leurs propriétés".

[14] M. Perrot, *Dans le Paris de la Belle Epoque : les 'Apaches', premières bandes de jeunes*, in B. Vincent (ed.) *Les Marginaux et les exclus dans l'histoire*, "Cahiers Jussieu", 1979; printed in M. Perrot, *Les ombres de l'histoire. Crime et châtiment au XIXe siècle*, Paris 2001, pp. 351-364.

[15] P. Gervaise, *Les 'Passages' à Levallois-Perret: ruelles pauvres en banlieue* in Faure A. (ed.), *Les premiers banlieusards. Aux origines des banlieues de Paris 1860-1940*, Paris 1991, pp. 121-163.

Bibliography

Charvet C., *Les fortifications de Paris. De l'hygiénisme à l'urbanisme, 1880-1919*, Rennes 2005.

Cohen J.-L., Lortie A., *Des fortifs au périf. Paris, les seuils de la ville*, Paris 1991.

Gervaise P., *Les 'Passages' à Levallois-Perret : ruelles pauvres en banlieue* in Faure A. (ed.), *Les premiers banlieusards. Aux origines des banlieues de Paris 1860-1940*, Paris 1991, pp. 121-163.

Jacquemet G., *Belleville au XIXe siècle, du faubourg à la ville*, Paris 1984.

Moret F., *Chronique d'un espace communal disputé et amputé* in Perlès V. (ed.), *Le Pré entre Paris et banlieue. Histoire du Pré Saint-Gervais*, Paris, 2004.

Moret F., *Enjeux sociopolitiques et conflits territoriaux à propos de la construction des fortifications de Paris: oppositions, négociations, décisions* in Caron J.-C. (ed.), *Entre violence et conciliation. La résolution des conflits socio-politiques en Europe au XIXe siècle*, Rennes 2008.

O'Brien P., *L'Embastillement de Paris: The Fortification of Paris during the July Monarchy*, "French Historical Studies", 9, 1975, pp. 63-82.

Perrot M., *Dans le Paris de la Belle Epoque : les 'Apaches', premières bandes de jeunes*, in Vincent B. (ed.) *Les Marginaux et les exclus dans l'histoire*, "Cahiers Jussieu", 1979; re-printed in Perrot M., *Les ombres de l'histoire. Crime et châtiment au XIXe siècle*, Paris 2001, pp. 351-364.

Coexistence of Diversities: Social, Ethnic and Religious Frontiers and Identities in Early Modern Hungarian Towns

Blanka Szeghyová
Institute of History, Slovak Academy of Sciences, Bratislava

Abstract

This chapter deals with factors that promoted the emergence of various forms of identities and boundaries in the towns of the late medieval and early modern Hungarian kingdom. Hungary was a multi-ethnic kingdom, and the role of ethnicity as an agent of identity and frontier formation is treated here. However, there is no doubt that social and – later – religious factors were also of great importance: frequently the impulse to maintain social and economic hierarchies or the promotion of one confession rather than its rival transcended ethnic divisions. In addition, external events, such as the Hussite Wars and the Ottoman advance, had profound effects on life in Hungarian towns. Drawing from a wide range of primary material, including judicial records, guild statutes, municipal petitions and royal edicts, this chapter draws general conclusions on the diverse and complex patterns surrounding urban communities and the formation and transformation of identities and boundaries.

Štúdia je stručným prehľadom tých faktorov a javov, ktoré formovali a menili identitu obyvateľov miest a súčasne vytvárali rôznorodé hranice v uhorských mestách, či už súviseli so spoločenskými, stavovskými, etnickými, náboženskými a inými rozdielmi, a to v období neskorého stredoveku a raného novoveku. Zásadný význam na rovnováhu týchto faktorov mali často externé udalosti, ako vojny a s ňou spojené presuny obyvateľstva, náboženské reformačné hnutia či nestála politická situácia. Väčší dôraz sa kladie na prepojenie etnického aspektu s inými faktormi, keďže v mnohých sporoch, ktoré sa odohrávali vo vnútri jednotlivých miest hrala etnicita neraz dôležitú úlohu. Aj keď konflikty v mestách sa často odohrávali medzi dvoma etnickými komunitami (najmä nemeckej voči ostatným nenemeckým), vo väčšine prípadov nešlo o čisto etnický problém ako taký, ako skôr o zrovnoprávnenie znevýhodneného etnika, či už vo forme zapojenia sa do mestskej samosprávy, alebo získania rovnocenných možností v hospodárskej, náboženskej či politickej sfére.

Problémy identity obyvateľov miest sa nedajú jednoznačne zovšeobecniť. Do úvahy treba brať viacero faktorov, silu ich vplyvu a vzájomnú rovnováhu, keďže aj menší individuálny rozdiel mohol do značnej miery ovplyvniť situáciu a vývoj v jednotlivých mestách. V 16. storočí v dôsledku zmenenej spoločenskej a politickej situácie, spory medzi jednotlivými pôvodne nepriateľskými etnikami postupne ustupujú a nahrádzajú ich nezhody náboženského charakteru. Turecká okupácia Uhorska spôsobila väčšie presuny obyvateľstva a s nimi súvisiace sa problémy spolužitia 'starých' obyvateľov miest s novoprisťahovalcami vo všeobecnosti a jednak aj špecificky zosilnila konflikty meštianstva so šľachtou.

Introduction: characteristics of Hungarian towns

The aim of this chapter is to provide an overview, based on the analysis of contemporary archival material, of the creation of urban frontiers and identities in the medieval and early modern Hungarian kingdom. I hope to address three issues. First, the methods used to form various identities and boundaries; second, how, once established, these identities and boundaries altered according to changing external circumstances; and third, how this diversity functioned in ethnically- and socially-mixed urban milieux. Towns in the Hungarian kingdom in the late medieval and early modern periods were not large by contemporary Western European standards[1]. Moreover, the capital Buda, the largest town with a population of almost 10,000, fell to the Ottomans in 1526[2]. Consequently, in 1536 Bratislava (previously Prešporok, Pressburg or Pozsony) was officially proclaimed the new capital, thereby becoming the main political, economic and cultural centre of Habsburg Hungary. Yet, irrespective of their size and prevailing agricultural character, the rights granted to the Hungarian towns – especially to the free royal towns – were very wide-ranging. From the 15th century they constituted the fourth estate of the country, with the right to attend the Diet[3]. The status of each town was enshrined in its royal charter, which granted the town a set of privileges including judicial autonomy and independence from local magnates. Generally, administrative and judicial powers were not divided. Therefore, the mayor of the city was called the *iudex* (judge) and together with the town council and with the larger or common council – which also spoke for the broader group of burghers – governed town affairs.

Social factors and implications

Family, office, and wealth: all were crucial determinates of social status in Hungarian urban society. The acquisition of burgher status was dependent on lineage, reputation and wealth: only the wealthier inhabitants could buy property, establish a workshop and join a guild. In turn, possession of burgher rights was a prerequisite if one wanted to become a mayor or a member of a town or common council. In the late medieval period, then, urban society was dominated by a small oligarchy. Meanwhile the 'middle class' constituted a larger group of lesser merchants, innkeepers, retailers, and artisans, ranging from the more prestigious craftsmen down to the least profitable and honourable trades. Unskilled labourers, servants and the unemployed or unemployable occupied the lowest ranks. Typically, they lived in the poorest parts of a town, near or beyond the town walls. The larger the town or city, the more heterogeneous was its population both in terms of occupation and social class.

Social, economic, and other distinctions were also reflected in the administration of justice[4]. The social position and wealth of the defendant, as well as the plaintiff, played an important role in deciding the outcome of a trial. Different weight was placed on the testimony of a noble, burgher, peasant or vagrant, and their credibility depended on their status and reputation, with priority being given to a character witness over an eye-witness. Punishments were designed to maintain social stratification. Often members of the elite found guilty would pay financial penalties; poorer classes were more likely to be subject to corporal punishment. When custodial sentences were imposed, conditions of imprisonment and terms varied according to the social status of the criminal rather than the offence committed. Judicial practices also discriminated between genders. Women, for instance, were more likely to be punished for sexual offences, and women had different forms of punishment.

As elsewhere in Europe, the lower orders' discontent with the authorities sometimes manifested itself in vigorous protest. Konrad Streun led a protest of Bratislava vineyard workers in 1373, while one Jensel Sulzrübel had his property forfeited for his frequent railings against the town magistrate. Poor migrant workers demanded higher wages and better working conditions in the 1440s and in 1516[5]. On one occasion, such protest was fomented by the mayor, when in 1410 Ulrich Rauchenwarter distributed 13,000 guldens from the town treasury to the poor, and encouraged them to revolt. It seems that Rauchenwarter's motives were populist, connected to his wish that the oligarchy pay the town's debts; but, in any case, the town council dismissed Rauchenwarter and deprived him of his burgher status[6]. Protest also emerged from the abundant middle classes, who were dissatisfied with being excluded from the oligarchy. Disturbances broke out in 1567, and, despite the establishment of a royal commission to resolve the conflict, re-emerged in 1578 and 1596[7].

Northern mining towns also witnessed social turbulence. The ill-effects of inflation provoked the miners to demand wage increases, leading in turn to a miners' revolt against the foremen and town councils in 1525-26[8]. Inter-elite conflict emerged in Buda, when in 1402 members of prominent guilds assailed the town council of twelve. The assembled protesters dismissed the council and created a new body consisting of 36 members, including representatives from the poorer people. While the unrest had a social dimension, it may also be seen as a manifestation of ethnic rivalry between the Italian merchants and the German elite[9]. Ethnic rivalry in Buda became violent once more, in 1439, this time between Hungarians and Germans. It began with demands from Hungarian artisans for more participation in the German-dominated civic government. Protests turned into mob violence, and the houses of the rich were pillaged, regardless of their owner's ethnicity[10]. The ethnic dimension, then, was a significant factor in the origins of civic rivalry and conflict, and will be discussed in more detail in the following section.

Ethnic structures and economic and political privileges

The term *ethnicity* is deliberately used in this chapter to avoid using terms such as *nationality*, which, loaded with meaning derived from 18th- and 19th-century political ideology, have been rejected by many historians of the pre-modern era as anachronistic and unhelpful. Even though the Latin sources of medieval and early modern refer to *natio* and *nationes,* the term was ambiguous:[11] an individual could be a member of several *natione*s, according to their lingual, territorial or social identities[12]. Here, unless stated otherwise, the terms like ethnic and ethnicity may best be understood in a lingual sense: an individual's everyday language or 'mother tongue' denoted their ethnicity. In the same sense, terms like 'Hungarization' or 'Slovakization' describe the rising influence of these communities and the spread of their languages and cultures in the towns.

Hungary was a multi-ethnic kingdom. There were large contingents of Hungarians, Germans, Slovaks in the north; Ruthenians/Ukrainians in the northeast; Romanians in the east; Serbians and Croatians in the south; Austrian Germans in the west; some Polish in towns in the north; and, in smaller minorities, Italians[13], Jews[14] and Gypsies[15]. The lack of sources makes it difficult to establish more precisely the populations and proportions of the various ethnic groups in the kingdom[16]. During the Hussite period, migrating Czechs and Moravians strengthened the Slavic element in the Hungarian kingdom. After 1526, due to the occupation of the Danube basin by the Ottomans, refugees mainly of Hungarian decent, and to a lesser degree of Croatian and German origin, moved from the southern and central parts of the kingdom into the safer northern parts inhabited mainly by Germans and Slovaks, or into Transylvania in the east, causing yet more change to the already mixed ethnic makeup of the region[17].

Germans had an important position in the Hungarian kingdom. Urban development in Hungary was primarily due to German colonization in the 12th and 13th centuries; and subsequently Germans were predominant in town oligarchies[18]. (Walloons and Flemings had played a similar role, but were largely displaced by the 15th century[19].) The German urban elite – surrounded by other ethnic groups in generally inferior social positions – guarded jealously their social and political ascendancy in the towns, and tried to prevent non-Germans from participation in civic administration, commerce and guilds. According to the law code of Buda (based on the Nuremberg law) judges had to be German, with all four grandparents of German origin. No more than two Hungarians were to be elected aldermen[20]. The law custom of Krupina (based on the Magdeburg law) stated that the testimonies of Hungarians could only be accepted when corroborated by German witnesses[21]. Unequal status was reflected also in some guild statutes. The butcher's guild of Banská Štiavnica stated in 1487 that no Slav or Hungarian could be admitted to its ranks or serve as a burgher[22]. Similarly, in 1508 the statutes of the cobblers' guild of Kremnica asserted that nobody of Slovak origin or custom could be accepted into the guild, and German craftsmen were not to take on Slovak or Hungarian apprentices[23]. Less formal examples of discrimination are plentiful. For example, the mid-15th-century Slavic merchant Stanko Vilhelmovič attempted to buy a house in the main square of Kremnica, but was frustrated by the obstacles engineered by the German burghers[24]; later in Kremnica, a widow complained to the king that the town council prevented her from selling her house to a non-German[25].

The German elite, however, was unable to prevent the slow but steady infiltration of non-Germans ethnic groups[26]. The first gains were made in the ecclesiastical sphere. In the 15th century, though parish priests and school rectors were usually Germans, many town magistrates also retained Hungarian or Slovak preachers, teachers, cantors or chaplains who delivered sermons and taught in their vernacular. In the towns, more non-German merchants, rich artisans, educated professionals, and other town dwellers of Hungarian and Slavic origin, began to obtain urban privileges equal to those enjoyed by Germans, and thereby gradually succeeding in penetrating the governing class. In the 16th century this alteration was met with resistance by the Germans, leading to inter-ethnic conflict.

The pattern was not universal or consistent, but depended on the ethnic composition of the towns. In some towns Germans lost their dominant position rather early, but some two centuries later they were still strong enough to avert the participation of the influential Hungarian nobility in town economics and government[27]. As early as the 14th century, so-called 'Slovakization' took place in the northern town of Žilina. In 1381, after petitioning the king, Slovaks there gained an official privilege to form half of the city council[28]. From the middle of the 15th century, the town council had begun using the Slovak language orally, and writing in Czech (though based on Czech – a language with a strong literary tradition and close to Slovak – it was in fact a hybrid language that used numerous Slovak words)[29]. Similar events took place in other, usually small, towns[30]; on the other hand, towns such as Bratislava and Levoča (the centre of the German enclave of Spiš) maintained their German character longer. By the 15th century Hungarians came to dominate the towns of Szeged, Pest, Esztergom and Székesfehérvár[31]. In 1439, after violent struggle, the Hungarians of Buda secured a ruling which stipulated that the mayoralty alternate between a German and a Hungarian[32]. Similarly, Hungarians in the town of Cluj in Transylvania gained in prominence from the second half of the century, achieving equality with Germans in the town council[33].

External factors had a great impact on the balance of power of the ethnic communities. The Hussite movement (1419 - 1485)[34] acquired national, anti-imperial and anti-German manifestations, resulting from long-term Czech-German conflict. In the years

1428-33 Taborite Hussite armies made several inroads into Hungary. From 1440 to 1452, the Czech noble warlord, Jan Jiskra of Brandýs, occupied much of present-day Slovakia in support of Elizabeth, widow of Albrecht Habsburg, and their son, future king, Ladislas V Posthumus. The presence of Hussites in Hungary strengthened the position of Slovaks in the towns[35]. For example, Hussites occupied the town of Trnava for three years, leading to an exodus of Germans, many of whom did not return[36]. The German majority in the town was undermined and by the 1460s the Slovaks sent petitions for a Slovak preacher. Soon, bitter feuding took place between Germans and Slovaks over the election of mayor and priest, requiring the intervention of King Matthias I Corvinus. Twenty years later royal letters to the town were being written in Czech[37]. While the extent of the influence of Hussite ideas on the Slovak population is doubtful, the movement stimulated the challenge to German hegemony and helped establish Czech as an alternative bureaucratic language. Of greater import was the westward advance and occupation of the Danube basin by the Ottoman Turks during the 16th century. In 1541 the country was divided into three parts: the north and western areas remaining under Habsburg control (Royal Hungary), Transylvania to the east was a formally independent principality, while much of the south and centre was under Ottoman rule. These events triggered large-scale migration from the southern and central parts into the safer northern parts of the realm.

The population movements into Upper Hungary influenced considerably the balance and character of urban ethnic relations and conflicts. The influxes of new settlers, mainly of Hungarian origin, diluted the majorities of Germans in Upper Hungarian towns and both ethnic groups jostled for commercial and administrative supremacy. Again, the situation differed from town to town. Some towns attempted to forestall the infiltration of the elite by barring Hungarians or Slovaks from joining guilds or serving apprenticeship – even when no such legislation had previously been enacted[38]. In Banská Štiavnica, where Germans were well represented, the town council instructed the school rector in 1594, and again in 1660, that no student, especially Slovak, be accepted for a stipend without their approval, and that German students were to be preferred above others[39]. However, other towns, such as Prešov, abandoned discriminatory legislation previously in place[40], while others asserted the rights of all ethnic groups to equal rights within the guild system[41].

However, it would be a mistake to interpret these conflicts as purely Germans against non-Germans; in many ways, people were concerned about maintaining traditional privileges. When Slovaks secured a stable position in the town administration, they proved as keen as Germans had been to exclude newcomers. That ethnicity was not always paramount can be seen from the case of Trnava. In 1551, Slovaks, who had previously won a share of civic privileges, joined the once antagonistic Germans in excluding Hungarians from the town[42]. The case was discussed in the Diet and was eventually resolved by the king. In his decree, he ordered that the burghers and alderman had to consist of equal numbers of Germans, Slovaks and Hungarians, *comunitas trium nationum*, with the mayoralty shared among the groups on a triennial basis[43]. Even later conflicts showed the primacy of social and economic considerations. In 1611 German merchant Erhard Freudenreich from Eisenstadt complained that as a newcomer to Banská Bystrica he was denied commercial opportunities. Though Freudenreich drew support from the lower orders, the town council – dominated by Germans but with some Slovak representation – opposed the newcomer[44].

Political loyalties and ethnicity

In general, rulers tried to compromise with the ethnic communities whenever conflicts arose. This pattern altered, and ethnic quarrels assumed greater political importance, after the death of King Louis II in 1526, and a period of struggle for the Hungarian crown began between the Habsburg archduke and Bohemian King Ferdinand I and the native aristocrat of Transylvania, John Zápolya. Zápolya was openly anti-German, so it was natural that Germans preferred the Habsburg candidate. Zápolya divided Slovak and German miners in the mining towns, who previously fought together against the oppressive foremen and town councils.

It was in this period that ethnic conflicts among urban communities began to be discussed in the Diet, a trend that undoubtedly enhanced the awareness of ethnic identity on a larger scale. At the same time, opposition to Habsburg centralism by the Hungarian nobility strengthened their sense of belonging to the *natio hungarica* – meaning the privileged class of the realm, regardless of the ethnic origin of its members[45]. Political tensions between the Habsburg rulers and the Hungarian nobility encouraged the identification with ethnicity; in Hungarian aristocratic ideology a polarity emerged between 'Habsburg – foreign – German' and 'Hungarian (in the territorial sense) – native – non-German'. The decision of Ferdinand I in the case of Trnava in 1551, alluded to above, was the last royal intercession in support of non-German urban ethnicities. From then on the main promoters of non-Germans in towns became the Palatine – the highest officer in the kingdom – and the nobility. At that time, the relationship between Hungarians and Slovaks, and other Slavic ethnicities, was relatively harmonious and the Hungarian nobility supported all the non-German town inhabitants in their attempts to gain equal status with the German burghers[46].

Tensions between nobility and townspeople

Another factor influencing relations in Royal Hungarian towns was the large influx of nobles, who often preferred to reside in towns than in countryside residences more exposed to Ottoman attack. Though Hungarian towns had experienced tension between nobles and townsmen in the past[47], the scale and import of the problem became much greater from 1526[48]. Conflict between incoming nobles and the established oligarchy stemmed from the formers' reluctance to yield traditional privileges, such as exemption from taxation, and accept internal rules and customs of the town. Burghers, on the other hand, reasoned that any newcomer who wished to avail himself of the advantages of life in fortified towns should adhere to the same conditions which governed the rest of the elite. The conflicts became aggravated, so much so that Bratislava, together with other towns, sent envoys to the Diet with complaints against the nobility living in their territory. In 1546 a law was passed exempting those nobles who had lost their property to the Turks from paying civic taxes[49]. Nevertheless, problems persisted and in several cases town authorities refused or were unwilling to allow houses in towns to fall into aristocratic hands. However, the state took the side of the nobility when in 1563 a law was passed which cited the Turkish threat as justification for granting aristocrats the right to purchase urban property[50].

However, the legislation proved difficult to implement and the nobles complained that it was not sufficiently comprehensive. The Hungarian estates had to wait until the beginning of the 17th century to reform the law, when they exploited the discord between King Rudolph II and his brother Matthias, to take the initiative. The 1608 law (act 13) acknowledged the equal rights of Germans, Hungarians, Czechs and Slovaks to participate in town government and to buy or build houses in free royal towns, under the condition that they share public duties with the other burghers[51]. While the law formally emancipated the non-German ethnicities within towns, it was more of a triumph of incoming nobility over the burghers than a victory for non-German ethnic communities over German urban elites[52]. Implementation of the law required further struggles, especially in the mining towns of Upper Hungary, where the German element was particularly strong[53].

At the same time the law of 1608 forbade the king to create new royal towns without the consent of the Diet. The law of 1608 and subsequent laws strengthened the position of nobility and at the same time curtailed the privileges of the towns[54]. All in all the early 17th century marked the beginning of a decline in independence and power of towns and municipal governments in the Hungarian kingdom.

The Reformation and ethnicities

The role of towns in spreading the ideas of Martin Luther was crucial for the development of the Reformation in Hungary. Luther's first adherents in Hungary were German communities through their contact with Germany, but before long Lutheran teachings found their way into other ethnic communities. It is estimated that between the second half of the 16th century and the beginning of a strong Counter-Reformation movement in Hungary by the 1620s about three quarters of the population became adherents of one of the various forms of Protestantism, though none of the Protestant denominations received the status of a state religion[55]. The spread of the Reformation produced new identities and religious controversies which often overshadowed older ethnic conflicts. In the Protestant town of Banská Bystrica, where previously ethnic conflicts had dominated, the townsmen rebelled in 1617 against the decision of the king to appoint a Catholic rector to the Hospital of St Elizabeth[56]. Furthermore, schools could act as agents of cohesion between ethnic groups: in some schools shared adherence to Catholicism or Protestantism became more important than traditional ethnic divisions[57].

Once again, Trnava provides an illuminating case study. It was this town that the king intervened in 1551 to resolve ethnic tensions. In the second half of the 16th century religious differences became entrenched. Trnava became the seat of the archbishop of Esztergom, with his chapter, from 1543; it marked a new phase of ecclesiastical importance for the town, with the chapter remaining there for over 300 years. From the 1540s, the city vicarage was taken over by the chapter, and consequently parish priests were chosen from amongst the canons of the chapter. To the annoyance of the town council, the influence of the chapter extended into other spheres. This was bound to be provocative: Lutheranism and Calvinism were widespread in the town, the latter especially so among the Hungarian population. Protestant preachers of one or other denomination were often invited to the town, but attempts to render Protestantism the official religion of the town, as was the case in many other Hungarian towns, failed. Failure was due to the resistance of the archbishop. The prelate enjoyed the full support of the Habsburgs, who were keen to implement the Counter Reformation in Hungary. Protestant preachers had to leave the town together with their most ardent supporters[58]. The Habsburgs' emphatic endorsement of the Counter-Reformation in Hungary encouraged a major shift in urban identity to begin, as townsmen came to perceive a dichotomy between 'Hungarian (in a territorial sense) – Protestant' and 'Habsburg – Catholic'.

Conclusion

Identities and frontiers in urban communities are based on complex phenomena that often evade unequivocal generalisations. Social position, wealth, ethnicity, religion and education were major, though not the only, factors that shaped identity and created boundaries. Ethnic conflicts, though similar in nature in different Hungarian towns usually functioned only on the small-scale intra-urban level[59]. Though these confrontations were often between rival ethnic groups, the issues of contention were for the most part not connected to ethnicity at all. Apart from demands for clergy competent in vernaculars, the majority of controversies were focused on economic and administrative issues.

External agencies, such as wars, population movements, volatile political situations or religious movements, impacted upon urban communities. New problems, such as the coexistence of burghers and nobility, coincided with tensions between the nobility and the Habsburg absolutist government. Together with the spread of the Reformation, these factors created new identities and dichotomies (natives versus newcomers, Catholics versus Protestants), which sometimes cut across traditional divisions. It seems that these identities were fluid concepts. Depending on circumstances, identity could be transformed, and different aspects stressed according to need.

Notes

1 Among the most important royal towns of the realm were Buda, Bratislava, Košice, Sopron, Trnava, Pest, Bardejov, Prešov, Zagreb, Székesfehérvár, Esztergom, Levoča, Krupina, Sabinov, Szeged and the Saxon towns in Transylvania - Cluj, Sibiu, Braşov and Bistriţa. Also, the eastern mining town of Baia Mare was granted royal liberties and the mining towns of the north (Kremnica, Banská Štiavnica, Banská Bystrica, Pukanec, Ľubietová, Nová Baňa and Banská Belá) were given corporate autonomy. V. Bácskai, *Small towns in Eastern Central Europe*, in P. Clark (ed.), *Small towns in Early Modern Europe*, Cambridge 1995, pp. 77-79. M. Bogucka, *The Towns of Eastern Europe from the Fourteenth to the Seventeenth Century* in A. Maczak, H. Samsonowicz, P. Burke (eds.), *East-Central Europe in Transition. From the 14th to the 17th Century*, Cambridge 1985, p. 98.

2 Together with some other towns of the central part of the realm, such as Pest, Székesfehérvár, Esztergom and Szeged.

3 The other three estates of the realm were the highest aristocracy, prelates and the lower ranking nobility.

4 The following remarks are based on the author's *Súdnictvo a súdna prax v mestách Pentapolitany v 16. storočí* [The Judiciary and Judicial Practice in the Pentapolitana Towns in the 16th Century]. PhD. Dissertation, Bratislava 2003.

5 D. Lehotská, *Dejiny Bratislavy* [History of Bratislava], Bratislava 1966, pp. 61-62.

6 B. Varsík, *K sociálnym a národnostným bojom v mestách na Slovensku v stredoveku* [On the Social and Ethnic Struggles in the Towns of Medieval Slovakia], in *Zo slovenského stredoveku* [From the Medieval Slovakia], Bratislava 1972, p. 332; Lehotská, *Dejiny* cit., p. 86.

7 Lehotská, *Dejiny* cit., pp. 129-130.

8 P. Ratkoš, *Povstanie baníkov na Slovensku 1525-1526* [The Miners' Revolt in Slovakia 1525-1526], Bratislava 1963, 103-275.

9 M. Rady, *Medieval Buda: A study of Municipal Government and Jurisdiction in the Kingdom of Hungary*, New York 1985, pp. 106-109; A. Kubinyi, *Budapest története II* [History of Budapest II], Budapest 1973, pp. 68-69.

10 Kubinyi, *Budapest* cit., pp. 149-150.

11 Roughly until the end of the 17th century, although the meanings were gradually changing and developing during the period. J. Szűcs, *'Národnosť' a 'národné povedomie' v stredoveku. K vytváraniu jednotnej terminológie* ['Nationality'and 'National Consciousness' in the Middle Ages. On the Creation of Universal Terminology] in "Historický časopis", 1971, 4, pp. 495-546.

12 *Ibid.*, pp. 513, 536, 545.

13 In the medieval period Italians in Hungary were mostly rich merchants in Buda, later they were popular as architects and masons and therefore invited to work in towns by town councils, nobles and rich burghers.

14 There are records of Jewish communities in Hungarian towns as early as the 11th century. However, there were pogroms. The attitudes of Hungarian rulers towards Jews changed from welcome to discri-

mination and expulsion. Those that stayed in Buda were distributed later by decree of Sultan Suleiman among the cities of the Ottoman Empire. Those who stayed in Hungarian towns that did not fall to the Ottomans were soon expelled: from Bratislava and Sopron (1526); from Trnava (1539); in 1529 the Jews of Pezinok were accused of blood-libel and burnt at the stake. It was probably not until the second half of the 17th century that sizeable Jewish communities began to re-establish themselves in the towns. E. Bárkány, Ľ. Dojč, *Židovské náboženské obce na Slovensku* [Jewish Religious Communities in Slovakia], Bratislava 1991; Ľ. Chorváthová, *Židia v Prešporku a Benyovszkého Obrázky z prešporského geta* [Jews in Prešporok and Benyovszký. Pictures from the Prešporok ghetto] in K. Benyovszky, J. Grünsfeld junior (eds.), *Obrázky z prešporského geta*, Bratislava 1993, pp. 165-185; F. Grünvald, S. Schreiber, (eds.), *Monumenta Hungariae Judaica V/1*, Budapest 1959, pp. 392-399.

15 Gypsies in Hungary were first recorded in the early 14th century. They immigrated in greater numbers in the 16th and 17th centuries. E. Horváthová, *Nachwort,* in V. Urbancová (ed.), *Samuel Augustini ab Hortis: Zigeuner in Ungarn 1775*, Bratislava 1995, pp. 192-194; Z. Kollárová, *K vývoju rómskej society na Spiši do roku 1945* [The Development of Roma Society in the Spiš Region before 1945] in A. Mann (ed.), *Neznámi Rómovia* [Unknown Roma], Bratislava 1992, p. 61.

16 Historians have therefore in the past resorted to such unreliable methods as assessing the ethnicity of inhabitants from their names.

17 Croats settled in the Sopron County and the southwest territory of present-day Slovakia, where they later often assimilated with the linguistically related Slovaks. Several Hungarian nobles resettled their subjects from southern areas into northern parts. Large numbers of people moved into towns, especially to Bratislava, Trnava and Košice. To a lesser extent other towns also experienced immigration from the southern parts of Hungary according to their size and ability to absorb new inhabitants (Nitra, Hlohovec, Banská Štiavnica, Krupina). B. Varsik, *Slováci a ich etnický priestor v minulosti* [Slovaks and their Ethnic Space in the Past], in "Slovenská liga", 1948, 9-10, pp. 11-12.

18 This trend was enhanced after the devastation of the country by the Mongolian invasion in 1241, when Hungarian kings started to invite Germans, known for their more advanced economic and technical skills, to settle. As an incentive they were given economic and political privileges, among those was the right to self-rule.

19 E. Fügedi, *Die Enstehung des Städtewesens in Ungarn* in "Alba Regia. Annales Musei Stephani Regis", 1969, 10, pp. 101-118; A. Kubinyi, *Národnostné pomery stredovekých miest v ústrednej časti Uhorska* [Nationalities in the Medieval Towns of Central Hungary], in "*Historický časopis*", 1982, 6, pp. 847-858.

20 E. Michnay, P. Lichner, *Buda városának törvénykönyve. Ofner Stadtrecht von MCCXLIV-MCCCCXXI*, Pressburg 1845.

21 G. Fejér, *Codex diplomaticus Hungariae ecclesiasticus ac civilis* (CDH) XI, Buda 1829–1844, p. 522; D. Lehotská, *Vývoj mestského práva na Slovensku* [The Development of Urban Law in Slovakia] in "Sborník Filozofickej fakulty Univerzity Komesnkého", 1959, 10, pp. 82-86.

22 B. Varsik, *Zo slovenského stredoveku* [From Medieval Slovakia], Bratislava 1972, p. 341.

23 A. Špiesz, *Remeslo na Slovensku v období existencie cechov* [Crafts in Slovakia in the era of the Guild System], Bratislava 1972, p. 53.

24 Vilhelmovič bought it when the town was under the influence of the Czech military leader Jan Jiskra and it is likely that the Germans waited until their situation improved before acting. Varsik, *Zo slovenského* cit., pp. 339-340.

25 *Ibid.*, p. 340-341.

26 I use terms 'Slovak' and 'Slovakization' even though there has been a controversy over translating and interpreting Latin term *Sclavus* or *Slavus* as Slovak. The problem stems from the fact that there had been special names for other Slavic ethnic groups, but there was no exclusive term for Slovaks. Never-

theless, there are historians who have shown convincingly that *Sclavus/Slavus* could mean both general term Slav or specifically Slovak and it should be interpreted according to the context of the sources. P. Ratkoš, *Otázky slovenskej národnosti do začiatku 17. storočia* [Questions of Slovak Nationality until the Beginning of the 17th Century] in "Historický časopis", 1972, 1, pp. 34-59.

27 J. Vozár, *Národnostné pomery v stredoslovenských banských mestách v období neskorého feudalizmu* [Nationalities in the Mining Towns of Central Slovakia in the Late Medieval Period] in R. Marsina (ed.), *Národnostný vývoj miest na Slovensku do roku 1918* [Development of Nationalities in Towns of Slovakia to 1918], Martin 1984, pp. 190-191, 194-195.

28 R. Marsina, *Výsady pre žilinských Slovákov z roku 1381* [Privileges for the Slovaks of Žilina from 1381] in Id. (ed.), *Národnostný vývoj miest na Slovensku do roku 1918* cit., pp. 33-34.

29 V. Chaloupecký, *Kniha žilinská* [Žilina Town Book], Bratislava 1934, p. 16.

30 Such as Trenčín, Ružomberok, Topoľčany, Hlohovec, Nové Mesto nad Váhom, Martin, Prievidza, Bytča, Ilava, Zvolen and Skalica. Marsina, *Výsady* cit., p. 20. Varsik, *Slováci* cit., p. 10.

31 Kubinyi, *Národnostné* cit., pp. 847-858.

32 Kubinyi, *Budapest* cit., pp. 149-150.

33 G. Lang, *Die Nationalitätenkämpfe in Klausenburg im ausgehenden Mittelalter. Die Entdeutschung einer mittelalterlichen Stadt des Südostens*, München 1941, pp. 7-9. Later the status had to be reconfirmed by king Matthias I Corvinus in 1486 and 1488.

34 The Hussite War era is usually dated from 1419 to 1436, but Šmahel argues for 1485 as a terminal date, the year when Czech Catholics accepted the Compact of Basel and were reconciled with the Utraquists. F. Šmahel, *Husitské Čechy. Struktury, procesy, ideje* [Hussite Bohemia. Structures, processes, ideas], Prague 2001.

35 Varsik, *Zo slovenského* cit., pp. 241-243. In 1439 Bratislava accepted thirty Czech mercenaries. Lehotská, *Dejiny* cit., p. 89.

36 B. Varsik, *Husiti a reformácia na Slovensku do Žilinskej synody* [Hussites and the Reformation in Slovakia until the Synod in Žilina], Bratislava 1932, p. 38.

37 Varsik, *Zo slovenského* cit., pp. 328-332.

38 For example, in Levoča the guilds of tailors (1570), ropemakers (1579), clothmakers (1590), beltmakers (1606), shoemakers and weavers (1643), butchers (1660), potters (1699) all enacted statutes restricting membership to Germans. In Kremnica guild statutes denying Slovaks and Hungarians the right to join were of older origin: butchers (1478) and tailors (1508). M. Suchý, *Dejiny Levoče* I. [History of Levoča I], Košice 1974, pp. 286-287; Špiesz, *Remeslo* cit., p. 53.

39 P. Vajcik, *Školstvo, študijné a školské poriadky na Slovensku v XVI. storočí*, [Education, Curricula and School Orders in Slovakia in the 16th Century], Bratislava 1955, p. 110.

40 J. Vozár, *Národnostné zápasy v stredoslovenských mestách a slovenské národné povedomie od 16. do polovice 18. storočia* [Ethnic Conflicts in the Towns of Central Slovakia and Slovak National Consciousness, 1500-1750] in "Historický časopis", 1980, 4, p. 559; I. Sedlák (ed.), *Dejiny Prešova I.* [History of Prešov I], Košice 1965, pp. 170-171.

41 Varsik, *Husiti* cit., p.195.

42 According to Varsik, *Slováci* cit., pp. 11-12, there were no Hungarians in Trnava until the middle of the 16th century.

43 J. Vlachovič, *Národnostné boje v mestách na Slovensku v 16. a 17. storočí* [Struggles between Nationalities in the Towns of Slovakia in the 16th and 17th Centuries] in *Slováci a ich národný vývin* [Slovaks and their National Development], Book of Conference Proceedings, Bratislava 1966, pp. 76-7; E. Vrab-

ková, *Štatúty Trnavy ako historický prameň*, [Statutes of Trnava as a Historical Source], in J. Šimončič (ed.), *Trnava okres a mesto* [The town of Trnava and its region], Bratislava 1980, pp. 191-215.

44 Vlachovič, *Národnostné* cit., pp. 84-86.

45 A similar effort was the *Unio Trium Nationum* of 1438 between three Estates of Transylvania: the nobility (mainly of Hungarian origin), the German burghers, and the free Szeklers; the pact secured their political rights while excluding Romanian peasants from political life.

46 J. Tibenský, *Problémy výskumu vzniku a vývoja slovenskej feudálnej národnosti* [Research Problems, Origin and Development of Slovak Feudal Nationality] in "Historický časopis", 1961, 3, p. 413. 397-419.

47 Sedlák, *Dejiny* cit., pp.88-89; in Buda nobles were exempt from taxation: D. Márkus, G. Nagy, S. Kolosvári, K. Óvári (eds.), *Corpus Juris Hungarici. Magyar Törvénytár I. 1000-1526* (CJH I), Budapest 1899, p. 616.

48 M. Suchý, *Z politických zápasov miest so šľachtou od 16. do začiatku 18. storočia* [Political Struggles of Towns with Nobles between the 16th and the early 18th Century] in "Historické Štúdie" 1974, 19, pp. 112-131.

49 D. Márkus, G. Nagy, S. Kolosvári, K. Óvári (eds.), *Corpus Juris Hungarici. Magyar Törvénytár II. 1526-1608* (CIH II), Budapest 1899, no. /1546.

50 *Ibid*., no. 62/1563, p. 518.

51 *Ibid*., no. 13/1608.

52 Suchý, *Z politických* cit., pp. 116-118.

53 In Banská Štiavnica and Kremnica Germans elite maintained their political and economic dominance until the early 18th century; in the other mining towns it was lost in the 17th century. Vlachovič, *Národnostné* cit., pp. 80-90.

54 D. Márkus, G. Nagy, S. Kolosvári, K. Óvári (eds.), *Corpus Juris Hungarici. Magyar Törvénytár III. 1608-1657*, Budapest 1900, laws no. 4/1608, 23/1613, 87/1647, 78/1647.

55 Calvinism prevailed mainly in Transdanubia between the Danube and Tisza and in the east, while Lutheranism predominated in northern royal Hungary, where also some Catholic strongholds remained such as Bratislava, Trnava, Nitra and Skalica. P. F. Sugar, P. Hanák, T. Frank, *A History of Hungary*, London 1990, p. 93.

56 Vlachovič, *Národnostné* cit., p. 87.

57 See Levoča school order. Vajcik, *Školstvo* cit., pp. 77, 125.

58 V. Jankovič, *Ideové a spoločenské pomery v Trnave za sto rokov pred založením Univerzity* [Ideology and Society in Trnava a century before the foundation of the University] in J. Šimončič (ed.), *Trnava 1238-1988*, Conference proceedings, Bratislava 1991, pp. 44-88.

59 This corresponds to the theory that identities in pre-modern times tended to be small-scale and conflicts local. A. Varshney, *Ethnic Conflicts and Ancient Hatreds: Cultural Concerns* in N.J. Smelser, P.B. Baltes (eds.), *International Encyclopedia of the Social & Behavioral Sciences*, vol. 7, 2001, p. 4811.

Bibliography

Primary Printed Sources

Fejér G., *Codex diplomaticus Hungariae ecclesiasticus ac civilis* XI, Buda 1829–1844.

Grünvald F., Schreiber S. (eds.) *Monumenta Hungariae Judaica V/1*, Budapest 1959.

Márkus D., Nagy G., Kolosvári S., Óvári K. (eds.), *Corpus Juris Hungarici. Magyar Törvénytár I. 1000-1526, II. 1526-1608*, III. *1608-1657*, Budapest 1899, 1900.

Michnay E., Lichner P., *Buda városának törvénykönyve. Ofner Stadtrecht von MCCXLIV-MCCCCXXI*, Bratislava 1845.

Secondary Works

Bácskai V., *Small towns in Eastern Central Europe*, in Clark P. (ed.), *Small towns in Early Modern Europe*, Cambridge 1995, pp. 77-89.

Bárkány E., Dojč Ľ., *Židovské náboženské obce na Slovensku* [Jewish Religious Communities in Slovakia], Bratislava 1991.

M. Bogucka, *The Towns of Eastern Europe from the Fourteenth to the Seventeenth Century* in A. Maczak, H. Samsonowicz, P. Burke (eds.), *East-Central Europe in Transition. From the 14th to the 17th Century*, Cambridge 1985, pp. 97-108.

Chaloupecký V., *Kniha žilinská* [Žilina Town Book], Bratislava 1934.

Chorváthová Ľ. *Židia v Prešporku a Benyovszkého Obrázky z prešporského geta* [Jews in Prešporok and Benyovszký. Pictures from the Prešporok ghetto] in Benyovszky K., Grünsfeld J. junior (eds.), *Obrázky z prešporského geta*, Bratislava 1993, pp. 165-185.

Fügedi E., *Die Enstehung des Städtewesens in Ungarn* in "Alba Regia. Annales Musei Stephani Regis", 1969, X, pp. 101-118.

Horváthová E., *Nachwort,* in Urbancová V. (ed.), *Samuel Augustini ab Hortis: Zigeuner in Ungarn 1775*, Bratislava 1995, p. 189-199.

Jankovič V., *Ideové a spoločenské pomery v Trnave za sto rokov pred založením Univerzity* [Ideology and Society in Trnava a century before the foundation of the university] in Šimončič J. (ed.), *Trnava 1238-1988*, Conference proceedings, Bratislava 1991, pp. 44-88.

Janota E., *Bardyjów* [Bardejov], Krakow 1862.

Kollárová Z., *K vývoju rómskej society na Spiši do roku 1945* [Development of Roma Society in the Spiš Region to 1945] in A. Mann (ed.), *Neznámi Rómovia* [Unknown Roma], Bratislava 1992, p. 61.

Križko P., *Stanislav Vilhelmovič* in "Slovenské pohľady", 1885, 5, pp. 255-264.

Kubinyi A., *Budapest története II* [History of Budapest II], Budapest 1973.

Id., *Národnostné pomery stredovekých miest v ústrednej časti Uhorska* [Nationalities in the Medieval Towns of central Hungary] in "*Historický časopis*", 1982, 6, pp. 847-858.

Lang G., *Die Nationalitätenkämpfe in Klausenburg im ausgehenden Mittelalter. Die Entdeutschung einer mittelalterlichen Stadt des Südostens*, Munich 1941.

Lehotská D., *Dejiny Bratislavy* [History of Bratislava], Bratislava 1966.

Id., *Vývoj mestského práva na Slovensku* [Development of Urban Law in Slovakia] in "Sborník Filozofickej fakulty Univerzity Komenského", 1959, X, pp. 65-114.

Marsina R., *Výsady pre žiliských Slovákov z roku 1381* [Privileges for the Slovaks from Žilina from 1381] in Marsina R. (ed.), *Národnostný vývoj miest na Slovensku do roku 1918,* [Development of Nationalities in Towns of Slovakia before 1918], Martin 1984, pp. 13-40.

Rady M., *Medieval Buda: A study of Municipal Government and Jurisdiction in the Kingdom of Hungary*, New York 1985.

Ratkoš P., *Otázky slovenskej národnosti do začiatku 17. storočia* [Questions of Slovak Nationality before the early 17th Century] in "Historický časopis", 1972, 1, pp. 19-59.

Id., *Povstanie baníkov na Slovensku 1525-1526* [The Miners Revolt in Slovakia 1525-1526], Bratislava 1963.

Sedlák I. (ed.), *Dejiny Prešova I.* [History of Prešov I], Košice 1965.

Šmahel F., *Husitské Čechy. Struktury, procesy, ideje* [Hussite Bohemia. Structures, processes, ideas], Prague 2001.

Špiesz A., *Remeslo na Slovensku v období existencie cechov* [Crafts in Slovakia in the era of the Guild System], Bratislava 1972.

Suchý M., *Dejiny Levoče* I. [History of Levoča I], Košice 1974.

Id., *Z politických zápasov miest so šľachtou od 16. do začiatku 18. storočia* [Political Struggles of Towns with Nobles between the 16th and the early 18th Century] in "Historické Štúdie" 1974, XIX, pp. 109-132.

Sugar P. F., Hanák P., Frank T., *A History of Hungary*, London 1990.

Szeghyová B., *Súdnictvo a súdna prax v mestách Pentapolitany v 16. storočí* [The Judiciary and Judicial Practice in the Pentapolitana Towns in the 16th Century]. PhD. Dissertation, Bratislava 2003.

Szűcs J., *'Národnosť' a 'národné povedomie' v stredoveku. K vytváraniu jednotnej terminológie* ['Nationality' and 'National Consciousness' in the Middle Ages. On the Creation of Universal Terminology] in "Historický časopis", 1971, 4, pp. 495-546.

Tibenský J., *Problémy výskumu vzniku a vývoja slovenskej feudálnej národnosti* [Research Problems: Origins and Development of Slovak Feudal Nationality] in "Historický časopis", 1961, 3, pp. 397-419.

Uličný F., *The Nationality of Townspeople in Slovakia from the 13th to the 16th Centuries* in Kováč D. (ed.), *Slovak Contributions to the 19th International Congress of Historical Sciences*, pp. 168-176.

Vajcik P., *Školstvo, študijné a školské poriadky na Slovensku v XVI. storočí* [Education, Curricula and School Orders in Slovakia in the 16th Century], Bratislava 1955.

Varshney A., *Ethnic Conflicts and Ancient Hatreds: Cultural Concerns* in Smelser N. J., Baltes P. B. (eds.), *International Encyclopedia of the Social & Behavioral Sciences*, vol. 7, 2001, pp. 4810-13.

Varsik B., *Husiti a reformácia na Slovensku do Žilinskej synody* [Hussites and the Reformation in Slovakia until the Synod in Žilina], Bratislava 1932.

Id., *Slováci a ich etnický priestor v minulosti* [Slovaks and their Ethnic Space in the Past], "Slovenská liga", 1948, 9-10, pp. 11-12.

Id., *Zo slovenského stredoveku* [From the Medieval Slovakia], Bratislava 1972.

Vlachovič J., *Národnostné boje v mestách na Slovensku v 16. a 17. storočí* [Struggles between Nationalities in the Towns of Slovakia in the 16th and 17th Centuries] in *Slováci a ich národný vývin* [Slovaks and their National Development], Book of Conference Proceedings, Bratislava 1966.

Vozár J., *Národnostné pomery v stredoslovenských banských mestách v období neskorého feudalizmu* [Nationalities in the Mining Towns of Central Slovakia in the Late Medieval Period] in Marsina R. (ed.), *Národnostný vývoj miest na Slovensku do roku 1918* [Development of Nationalities in Towns of Slovakia till 1918], Martin 1984, pp. 188-206.

Id., *Národnostné zápasy v stredoslovenských mestách a slovenské národné povedomie od 16. do polovice 18. storočia* [Ethnic Conflicts in the Towns of Central Slovakia and Slovak National Consciousness from the 1500 till 1750] in "Historický časopis", 1980, 4, p. 554-577.

Vrabcová E., *Štatúty Trnavy ako historický prameň*, [Statutes of Trnava as a Historical Source] in Šimončič J. (ed.), *Trnava okres a mesto* [The Town of Trnava and its Region], Bratislava 1980, pp. 191-215.

Living in a Multicultural Neighbourhood: Ottoman Society Reflected in Rabbinic *Responsa* of the 16th and 17th Centuries

Markéta P. Rubešová
Charles University, Prague

Abstract

This chapter contributes to the current discussion on how concepts related to frontiers and identities may be useful for research on early modern urban societies. It focuses on a specific type of space – "Ottoman urban space" – and shows how this was perceived and represented by its Jewish inhabitants in the 16th and 17th centuries. The principal primary source used is the so-called *Responsa* literature, a special genre of rabbinic literature, based on a question-and-answer format. Responsa texts dealt with various situations and problems that confronted Jews and which were too complicated to be resolved by one individual. The issue of language has meant that for some time this source has not been used by historians. The present study sees Ottoman society as heterogeneous, comprising multiple individual and collective identities, and divided by mental boundaries which were dynamic, fluid and often permeable. The aim here is to illustrate different types of identity from the Jewish perspective, with a special emphasis on the fact that Jewishness (which may be understood in religious, ethnic, and cultural terms) was only one way of self-identification. Specifically, three types of border are explored: administrative, cultural and religious – thematic fields which are richly documented in the Responsa literature.

Osmanské město raného novověku lze chápat jako specifický typ prostředí, v němž docházelo k setkávání mnoha kulturních, náboženských a etnických skupin. Mluvíme-li o setkávání jednotlivců a skupin, nevyhnutelně se dostaneme k otázce existence hranic mezi nimi a také k otázce kolektivních identit. Referenční rámec tohoto příspěvku tvoří každodenní zkušenost příslušníků osmanských židovských komunit v multikulturním prostředí osmanského města v centrálních oblastech říše (Istanbul, Soluň) a druhotně i názory a interpretace židovských učenců, tak jak jsou zachyceny a prezentovány v rabínské responsivní literatuře. Tato literatura má podobu otázek a odpovědí, které se dotýkají všech životních situací a které řeší aktuální problémy, se kterými si tazatel sám nevěděl rady. Problém (jádro dotazu) je vždy vylíčen v širších souvislostech, podává detailní popis vzniklé situace, chování aktérů, někdy dokonce cituje či parafrázuje jejich přímé výpovědi. Na poli responsivní literatury se tak střetávají dva světy – svět učenců a svět „lidových" vrstev. Přestože je tento pramen mimořádným zdrojem informací, jeho využití zůstává v celosvětovém měřítku stále marginální, především vinou jazykové bariéry.

V příspěvku jsou pojednány tři tématické okruhy, v nichž problematika hranic a identit zaujímá centrální místo. Osmanská vláda explicitně nezakazovala (ale ani nepovolovala) činnost křesťanských a židovských soudních dvorů a autorit, pokud v případu nefiguroval muslim. Tato tichá tolerance administrativní a soudní činnosti náboženských minorit se omezovala pouze na sféru rodinného a občanského práva (sňatky, rozvody, dědictví) a nikoli na trestně-právní oblast. Rabíni jakožto představitelé soudní moci židovských komunit apelovali na důsledné využívání této tolerance a ostře kritizovali jedince, kteří vyhledávali osmanské soudy a úřady v interních záležitostech komunity. Administrativní hranice a její překračování je tedy jednou dělící čarou mezi židovským společenstvím a okolím, její legitimita i reálná účinnost však zůstávala diskutabilní a proto neustále zdůrazňovaná.

Prostor osmanského města nabízel jeho obyvatelům množství příležitostí k vzájemné komunikaci. Přestože příslušníci jednotlivých náboženských skupin projevovali tendenci usazovat se v blízkosti svých souvěrců, nevznikaly uzavřené čtvrti s obyvatelstvem pouze jedné denominace. Bezprostřední styk Židů s muslimy a křesťany se tedy neodehrával pouze v místech obchodních aktivit, ale také neformálně „na ulici", v nejbližším sousedství nebo i v soukromé sféře, a jeho charakter určovalo leckdy spíše sociální postavení než náboženská příslušnost. Nežidovští obyvatelé osmanského města nebyli vnímáni jednotně formou obecně přijímaného stereotypu. Mezi Židy a nežidy byla navazována přátelství, jindy ale slyšíme o nebezpečí, které číhá na každého, kdo udržuje neformální styky s nežidovským okolím.

Představa, že mezi židovskou komunitou a okolní splečností existovala tlustá zeď znemožňující vzájemný kontakt, je stejně neudržitelná jako představa o kompaktnosti osmanské židovské komunity. I v ní byly přítomné různé rozdělující momenty, které jedince nebo určitou skupinu mohly odsunout na okraj židovské společnosti nebo dokonce z jejího středu vyloučit.

Conventionally, scholars have viewed the 16th-century as the zenith of the Ottoman Empire: as it expanded from Buda in the west to the Persian Gulf in the east, its political and economic power increased. The presence of an expansive Ottoman empire had a profound effect on Europe's Jewish population. In the 1490s Jews in the Iberian Peninsula were both expelled and forcibly baptised, and many left for other Christian European countries, the Americas, and the Ottoman Empire. In many cases, the latter destination proved to be the best option, and up to the 19th century Ottoman territory retained a positive image among Jews. Among the factors which made the Empire more favourable to the Jews than Christian Europe included an already significant Jewish presence, less state interference in religion, and relative security of person and property. One of the chief sources for this chapter – the writings of Rabbi Shemuel di Medina – observed the more favourable conditions in the Ottoman Empire compared to Italy, concluding that Ottoman cities such as Salonica (today Thessaloniki) had Jewish majorities and protected Jewish culture, religion and property[1].

The Jewish influx to the regions under Ottoman rule did not abate throughout the 16th century, and the Sephardim (Spanish Jews) were by no means the only newcomers that relocated to the Empire. Ottoman urban space offered safety, commercial opportunities, and freedom to associate with co-religionists. Consequently, Jewish migration to the countryside was rarer, and the overall character of Jewish settlement remained firmly urban. Moreover, the rabbinic establishment was urban-based in its perception of the world – though it claimed a general validity and aimed to influence lives of the Jewish people in rural as well as urban areas.

'Ottoman urban space' was simultaneously strictly segregated and integrated. Generally speaking influences 'from above' – the secular and religious authorities – endeavoured to maintain firm boundaries between Muslims and non-Muslims. Institutions such as Mosques and Koranic schools were clustered together and non-Muslims were debarred from entering them. On the other hand, spontaneous impulses 'from below' attempted to promote a fluid and less constrained everyday life. Coffee houses, for instance, were accessible to all. Unconsciously, 'survival strategies' were developed by citizens of a multicultural society, in an environment where strict application of Shariah law would be inconvenient for Muslims as well as others. In terms of residential structure Ottoman towns were truly multicultural neighbourhoods, and there was no institution parallel to that of the ghetto, found in Christian cities. The only restrictions that were enforced prevented non-Muslims from residing in the proximity of Muslim religious buildings. Otherwise, non-Muslims and Muslims could live side-by-side. Thus many neighbourhoods were actually multicultural, comprising Muslim, Jewish, as well as Christian elements.

One of the features of early modern European cities was the regulation of trade by the city within its borders. Town officials controlled the buying and selling of goods. The economic restrictions found echoes in the fortified character of many towns: enclosed spaces with restricted access. However, the situation in the Ottoman realm was rather different. The Jewish sources attest to considerable freedom. Of the Greek city of Ioannina it was written that:

> the city [remains] open without walls, its gates opened day and night; who wants to enter enters, who wants to leave does so; it stands to reason and to sense, that the Jewish inhabitants of a certain city have no power to keep the Jews from different a city, or from this or another kingdom, from coming; on the contrary, who needs to come and trade is allowed to do so, according to his will[2].

The author portrays the city-borders as permeable, although their existence is not denied. It is assumed that the potential reader is familiar with the limits of the town space, and no additional clarification is found necessary. Moreover, in the eyes of the author, the Ottoman city does not constitute an autonomous and independent unit: quite the contrary.

It seems that common 'secular' interest was a prime reason for Jewish merchants of Ottoman cities to stick together, and this interest could have been shared with merchants of another religion as well. This leads us to another complex issue: the question of multiple identities. An analytical tool developed by sociologist Norbert Elias, so-called "figurations", may help us to understand various identities within larger groups[3]. Figurations are evolving networks of interdependent individuals, which the individual enters and leaves in the course of his lifetime. The more diverse the societies the more complex were the chains of figurations they contained. Using the concept of figurations allows us to treat the individual, with his or her multiple identities, as an active factor in society, while at the same time retaining the idea of social structure. We can imagine the multiple identities of an individual – usually linked to different kinds of collective identities – as chains of figurations.

Primary sources

The empirical part of this chapter is based on *Responsa* literature. The books of Responsa constitute a special genre of rabbinic literature. Originally these works, which take the form of a set of questions and answers, aimed to resolve specific problems and to regulate and preserve legal, religious, and social norms within the Jewish society; they also attempted to reconcile the Jewish lifestyle in a non-Jewish setting. Thus, we can classify them as religious-legal treatises – and they constitute a useful source for historians. The enquirers asked their questions either in a written or an oral form (by themselves, but frequently also through another rabbi or some literate member of the community). Although the authentic formulations might not have been preserved in the text, the key information remains traceable and enables the reader to investigate everyday life in the Ottoman realm over several centuries. Regarding authorship, it may initially appear that the Responsa are the product of the learned elite, but in fact, we hear also the voices of the ordinary, often illiterate and uneducated, people. Their experiences are documented and we may therefore acknowledge their 'co-authorship'. The Responsa texts may be viewed as a document of a meeting of worlds – the scholars and the ordinary people.

Despite their richness and detail one has to bear in mind the limits of this type of source. Some emendations by the original scribe or later editors may be detected. They also present some interpretive challenges. To help resolve these, we may divide the text (the questions, as well as the answers) into two levels of attainable 'testimony'. The core of the text relates to the legal, or *halachic*, dimension: the presentation of the problem to which a solution was sought. A second layer is the 'embellishment' of the problem – including detailed accounts of incidents, and sometimes speech. While the core usually presents a deviation from social or legal norm, or records complicated and extraordinary situations (otherwise no question would have been posed), the narrative 'embellishment' provides a window onto the everyday life of the actors.

The Responsa volumes used in this chapter originate from the central parts of the Ottoman Empire (Istanbul, Thessaloniki) and Jerusalem. However, questions were also submitted from other cities (such as Bitola and Ioannina), and in a number of cases the location remains unknown. As mentioned earlier, the urban-orientated range of perceptions, ideas, and opinions of the Jewish scholars deeply influenced and shaped the texts of the Responsa. Therefore, we can read the texts and interpret them as an outcome of the urban life experience, even if some of them deal with events beyond the town walls.

Jewish and non-Jewish authorities in the Ottoman city

Ottoman law acknowledged *de iure* only Ottoman public administration and courts. Yet, in reality, non-Muslim official bodies also functioned in the city, and, though not explicitly licensed by the government, were tolerated. The state allowed non-Muslims to deal with personal and religious matters that did not involve a Muslim subject, within their own legal system; but Muslim legal authorities were superior to Jewish or Christian courts and could override their judgements. Still, some historians have argued that the Jewish population had considerable economic, social and administrative and judicial self-sufficiency[4]. But to clarify further these legal observations, we need to look at the role and powers of the Kadi, or Ottoman civil judge.

The Kadi's daily agenda encompassed a wide range of activities: he worked as a local judge, as a public notary, he dealt with various fiscal issues, and registered marriages, divorces, collective agreements of professional groups, and real estate transactions. The Kadi also represented the state authority in the town or district. All the imperial decrees sent from the capital were directed to the local Kadi, who was responsible for their local implementation.

Many Jews and Christians appealed to the Shariah court even in internal matters, which could have been very well resolved in the framework of the Jewish or Christian legislative. At a first glance, this behaviour may seem strange. The picture becomes clearer when we consider the diverse motivations of those who appealed to the Ottoman court or authority rather than to the rabbinic court. Sometimes the need for official and generally accepted approval proved stronger than the appeal of a purely Jewish settlement. On other occasions, however, the motivation was simple pragmatism, as one litigant shows:

> You also know what my dear father-in-law Yakob Katalani did to me. He emptied my house and took all my belongings and goods away in containers. And also what my wife Rachama did, that is she escaped our house and went to the house of her father on the 9th of Av, when

I was praying in the synagogue. They want me to divorce her and to abandon my firstborn son, who had been born to us, and not to see him any more. What is more, they menace me and threaten me saying that they will hand me over to the non-Jews with the help of the Lady, who has a good name before the King and before the notables[5].

The view of the greater Jewish population seems to have been an influence on rabbis. In one example a rabbi refused to perform a divorce ceremony in the presence of Muslims merely out of fear that the ordinary people would regard the ceremony as forced:

This wicked initiator [of the divorce ceremony] wanted to disregard deliberately the simple people and he enabled [the girl to undergo] *halitzah*[6] and gave her a *get*[7] in front of three or two messengers of the non-Jewish judge, even though I had said to those people before they came to my house: "remember, that I won't do anything unless you send the men of the white turban [i.e., Muslims] away, for I don't want people to think this divorce ceremony was performed unwillingly, under pressure and with a help of the non-Jews"[8]. But he paid no attention to this[9].

Such a cautious approach to the affair indicates not only what people might have thought of this procedure, but also that the community could refuse to accept a forced divorce. Thus, the limits of rabbinic jurisdiction were set by the rabbinic discourse and the state regulation on the one hand, but on the other, by the consent of the greater Jewish community.

The Responsa texts clearly define the status of non-Jewish authorities within Jewish law: it supported the law of the secular state, unless it directly contradicted the Torah. In the Ottoman Empire, however, the legal system was a complex of several parallel institutions. In the eyes of the Jewish legal system, the Kanun – a collection of the laws issued by the Sultan – represented state law. However, the Ottoman courts and administrative bodies also upheld the religious Shariah law and custom. This created a dilemma for the Jewish authorities, which they attempted to resolve in the Responsa. In one case regarding a widow's property, a Jewish judge wrote:

There is no need to take into account the decree of a royal judge [Kadi]; that is to hand the said house over to the brother of the deceased, for the royal law [i.e. the state laws], about which we say "the state law is valid law" [*dina de'malchuta dina*] does not apply here. These authorities administrate justice in compliance with the books of their own law [...] The rules of the authorities cannot invalidate just laws and decrees held by the holy Jewish nation, and these authorities have no power to invalidate the Christian religious law, for according to the Christian law a Christian widow is the property-owner [...] And it follows that Reuven has a right to hold this house.

The Istanbul rabbi, Moshe Benvenisti, came to a similar conclusion: "Although the King insists consistently on strict observance of the law [...] the rules applied by the authorities are not of a royal origin, but in fact these authorities decide according to their own [system of rules]"[10]. Although an appeal to an Ottoman court could have been justified on the grounds of the rule of *dina de'malchuta dina*, many rabbis urged members of the community to follow and rely on rabbinic verdicts when possible. It was rare for Jewish courts to transfer litigants to Ottoman authorities. Such cases involved notorious and intractable individuals: "I dare say that one who is cruel and relentless should be handed over to the non-Jews, in order to protect the oppressed from his oppressor [...] Moreover, we are entitled to act for the sake of the oppressed, and it is stated that this is indeed our duty"[11]. The demand for communal solidarity dictated the exclusion of elements who were considered threats to the well-being of the wider community. In general, no definitive and consistent attitude prevailed among rabbis regarding the right of a Jew to appeal to a non-Jewish authority, and this made the task of delineating a clear border between the Jewish and non-Jewish administration and jurisdiction even more complicated. Moreover, Jewish official bodies lacked effective tools for the complete consolidation of their legal proceedings, and relied to some degree on cooperation with the local authorities (for example, the imprisonment of Jewish convicts in state gaols). It was not exceptional for Ottoman judges to favour rabbinic law over royal law. One judge rejected the Kadi's decision:

> [I have] rejected [the legal decision of the Kadi] and forbade the division [of the inheritance] among the family members in the above mentioned manner [according to Shariah law], and this [manner] would be acceptable only if they asked [the Kadi] to divide [the inheritance] among them according to the glorious Shariah, [demonstrating that] they abandon [a religion], which is their confession[12].

A more surprising example of Muslim use of rabbinic law was the case of the man who looked to the Jewish legal system in order to avoid future controversies over property acquired:

> Reuven owned a shop according to the law of *hazakah* and pledged it to a Turk for a certain sum of money, because a purchase was impossible according to their [Ottoman] law. The Turk told Reuven "what shall I do in case you default on payments? No Jew will come to settle in the house and no Turk will buy it". Therefore, the Turk asked a Jew for advice and was told "Provide yourself with a contract issued according to our laws"; and so he did, and Reuven gave the purchase contract to the Turk in accordance with Jewish law[13].

Besides the mutual agreement between the Muslim and the Jew based on Jewish law, the concern of the Muslim for finding Jewish or Muslim tenants deserves our attention. The Muslim obviously had a broad knowledge of Jewish commercial habits. This familiarity could only be attained by consistent exposure to Jewish society. This leads us in return to the notion of the multicultural character of the Ottoman urban space, which encouraged mutual knowledge of the norms of other societies.

Everyday encounters of Ottoman subjects

Jews, then, were not completely isolated within the greater Ottoman urban environment. Yet the inclination to concentrate into co-religious groupings of various sizes was understandable. The Responsa evidence is illustrative of everyday interaction between societies. First, let us clarify our pre-suppositions regarding a 'typical' Jewish individual in a 16th-century Ottoman city. Certainly, he is a member of a nuclear and a wider family, a town dweller and a subject of the Sultan (and as such shares this quality with all the subjects under the Sultan's rule). Undoubtedly, he belongs to some social stratum, and at the same time, he must be a member of one of the Jewish congregations[14]. Very likely, he has a trade or profession, and enters the local market. Perhaps he is a member of one of the Jewish or mixed professional corporations (*esnaf*). His mother tongue can be Ladino or Greek, or another language that was spoken among the Jews (and he thus also belongs to a group marked by language), but there is a great chance that he speaks also Ottoman Turkish and maintains contacts with his non-Jewish neighbours or co-workers. There are plenty of coffee houses in which to socialize, and the streets are always crowded during the day. If he is a merchant, he has many contacts throughout the Ottoman Empire and beyond. If he is a shopkeeper, he will have strong ties to the local market and to 'his' city. This 'profession-based solidarity' of shopkeepers would be outwardly manifested when they felt jeopardized by economic rivals that entered without permission into 'their' domain demarcated by the borders of the town. If we carried on, we would possibly find many other links between the individual and his surroundings. Each of these affiliations implies a wide range of experiences, sometimes of a different or even conflicting nature.

There was no single experience which characterised Jewish life in Ottoman cities. This is one reason why no single stereotype related to the 'Turk' – which we encounter in contemporary Christian European civilization – emerged in Jewish communities in Ottoman cities. In fact, Jewish perceptions of the Sultan as both institution and personality were generally positive. Rather like the European idea of 'evil council', Jews blamed officials and servants for misconduct, corruption or injustice, but not the sovereign. The Responsa literature affirmed the supremacy of the Sultan as divinely-authorised and with Scriptural legitimacy:

> Those who do not hold our King, a great and merciful King (may his majesty be exalted and Kingdom elevated) in high regard are not worthy to come into this world. For everyone who claims for himself the name Israel[15] is obliged to follow with a great awe his ordinances and fulfil his orders and decrees in the same manner as he fulfils the commandments of the Lord of the World. As [King] Solomon (may he rest in peace) wrote: "Fear God, my son, and the king, too", and this is even more true for such great and merciful King like this, under whom we find our haven, which is the will of the Lord of the World[16].

In the Responsa literature, non-Jews are often identified as friends and beloved ones. Friendships may have been genuine. An interesting example came from an observer of a pilgrimage to Jerusalem (though the story may have taken place in another Ottoman city):

> One of the guest pilgrims asked me about Reuven, who was a passionate smoker of what was called in all the languages *tutun*[17], all the weekdays including the nights, until he fell asleep.

> He was deeply troubled on the Holy Shabbath, when the evil inclination tempted him to visit a non-Jew who smoked, to enjoy the fragrance of the smoke coming out of his mouth, and so he did and he was calmed. It followed that Reuven became his friend[18], and he noticed Reuven's pleasure from the fragrance. Moreover, the non-Jew himself told Reuven on the Holy Shabbath to open his mouth and inhale the smoke, and to fill his mouth with smoke, and to emit it slowly afterwards. And this is what Reuven did every Holy Shabbath. It came to such a point that when the non-Jew saw Reuven approaching on Shabbath, he made an effort to light the smoking-machine[19] in order to please Reuven, who came and sat down next to him and carried out the above-mentioned action, even though the non-Jew originally did not intend to smoke. He did so only to pay honour to his friend Reuven[20].

What is of great importance is that a rabbi did not see anything wrong with socializing with non-Jews, or even becoming firm friends. And given the significance attached to concepts of honour in Muslim society, the relationship between Reuven and his Muslim friend must be evidence of mutual regard and acceptance of 'the other'. Alternatively we may say that different aspects of one's identity are stressed in different situations – or different social figurations, to utilize Norbert Elias' term – according to the nature of the situation and the character of the participants in the figuration. In this particular case, the social identity outweighed the religious identity, even though the latter does not lose its significance: after all, Reuven's adherence to Jewish religious observance brought him closer to a non-Jewish neighbour.

Quite often Muslims figured as eyewitnesses in cases related to so-called *agunot* (deserted wives); such cases are especially valuable as evidence for interaction between Jews and non-Jews in everyday life. Any married woman could fall into the category of 'deserted wife', if her husband had been missing for a long period. Even if there was a valid reason to assume he had died, his wife could not be proclaimed a widow unless two Jewish witnesses confirmed the identity of a corpse as the husband. If no such testimony was available, Jewish courts were prepared to accept, under clearly defined conditions, a testimony of a non-Jew. The non-Jewish witness had to describe the situation in detail, and he had to narrate the event in front of Jews without having been influenced in favour of the woman. The very fact that non-Jews exercised readiness and capability to testify, and that a Jewish jurisdiction relied on their testimony, indicates close ties between the societies. The following story shows the initiative of a non-Jew who reported the death of his Jewish friend to his community:

> It happened once that a non-Jew came to a Maskalor market [...] and told a couple of the Jews standing at the market place, that, on his way from Platamona, he encountered the body of Yakob Ezrah, who was lying in a field dead, and he was obviously dead for a long time, may God avenge the blood of his friend and colleague [...] And the dead Yakob was a very good and old friend of his[21].

Here, we can see the multiculturalism of the market place: apart from its commercial function, it was a locus of informal social interaction. The non-Jew knew exactly where to seek out someone who would listen to his news. A similar incident recorded in the Responsa literature ran:

> A certain Jew came and said "I have been in the *bedestan*[22] and encountered one Turk, whom I know, and he said to me 'Avraham, don't you know Avraham's son-in-law, who had a blotched face? One *emir* said to me: "I was on the same boat like him and there was no other Jew there. And the boat sank and I escaped with other few Ishmaelites. He was thrown out from the sea at one of the islands and I have recognized him and buried him"'[23].

For a non-Jew's evidence to be acceptable it would have to be clear that the deponent was offering evidence of his own volition, that he named the victim and his father, that he referred to distinguishing marks by which the body's identity could be confirmed, and that the deponent had buried the corpse. In the case cited, the non-Jewish deponent fulfilled all the above criteria, except mentioning the father's name. It is therefore likely that the non-Jew was aware that his information could be crucial with regard to the future of the widow. Everyday contact meant that various groups were familiar with the norms and laws of other groups, especially if friendly relations between them existed.

The following extract from the Responsa offers insights into the life of inter-city merchants, the relations between Jews and Christians and between urban and rural dwellers:

> And we also ask you to explain, whether [this woman] can remarry on the grounds of these testimonies; the above mentioned Reuven was actually killed on his trade journey in the countryside. The incident happened as follows. The above mentioned Reuven travelled together with his friend, and since the day was Thursday, he slaughtered five or six hens with the intention to enter the city and spend there the Holy Shabbath. He said to his friend "Go ahead [...] and we will meet in such and such village and we will spend the Shabbath in the city"; and the friend proceeded to that village and waited for him. When he saw that he was not coming, he turned back and searched for him in all the villages, but he did not find him. So he went to the city to report that bad affair to the brother [of his friend], who started to look for him. He did not find him, and so he went to a village called Istoriplis, from where his brother departed, and walked in the house of certain non-Jewess, who knew the murdered Reuven. He asked her in a roundabout way if she had some wax or almonds to sell as always in the past and the non-Jewess replied: "I know you didn't come to buy either wax nor almonds, but you came to look for your brother Reuven. Right now eight days have passed since my husband saw him dead on the hill called Kinoliri, his cattle grazing around him. And the *veyvoda*[24] saw him too, when he passed by and collected almost 3000 *levanim* in the villages". Therefore, his brother climbed the hill, but he could not find him [...] Another time two of us went there, with a judge and with a couple of Jews, who testified that the judge's auxiliaries caught a Greek and wanted him to say what had happened to the Jew. The Greek replied: "I know nothing, I just went once to tend the cattle, and a Greek called Jorgo Lionei came up and warned us against climbing the hill called Kinoliri and against tending the cattle there, for he saw there a murdered Jew, and cattle grazing around him. Do not pass through that place, so that no harm and no loss may happen to you from the *veyvoda*". And this Greek Jorgo Lionei is a husband of the above mentioned non-Jewess, who testified on his behalf to the brother of the victim[25].

It appears that the villagers knew the fate of the Jew, but refrained from reporting it to the authorities, since they could have been interrogated in the connection with a murder. Note that the victim's brother, after an unsuccessful search for his sibling, decided to visit a very specific Greek woman who worked as a local shopkeeper, expecting to receive useful information on passers-by. The remark made about the local official and tax collector is of high importance. Since the corpse disappeared, there was no tangible evidence of Reuven's death. Therefore, the more reliable eyewitnesses were available, the more likely it was that the victim's wife would be proclaimed a widow. In this respect, a testimony passed by a local authority representative, whose presence in the locality at a given time was held indubitable, was extremely valuable.

Jew as 'the Other': strategies of social exclusion/inclusion

Up to now, we have explored aspects of Jewish experience in a largely non-Jewish environment. There were, however, internal borders within the Jewish community; there were cases in which the Jewish community saw some of its members as 'others'. This usually occurred in cases of apostasy, or a transgressing of the secular rules, which was punishable by excommunication. The implications of excommunication, apart from social degradation inherent in the denial of public services and membership of the synagogue, also included economic sanctions. Members of a congregation, and sometimes even the Jewish population in the city or region, were forbidden to purchase products which were subject to *halachic* regulations, such as wine, diary products, or bread, from an excommunicated person. He was an outcast from Jewish society, and his word was devalued in the eyes of the Jewish judiciary. Yet, theory aside, the wishes of the congregation were crucial: if a local rabbi decided to excommunicate a certain transgressor of social or legal norms and the congregation itself refused to follow his decision, the individual in fact remained within the borders of the congregation as a full member.

An extreme case of religious deviation was conversion – mainly to Islam, but sometimes also to Christianity. Although we would expect an individual, who abandoned Judaism, to leave the Jewish congregation, it was not uncommon for converts to stay in the community, maintaining contacts with their Jewish families. Paradoxically, in some cases the representatives of the Jewish congregation appealed to the local Ottoman authority, asking them to persuade converts to move[26]. The individual stories contained in the Responsa texts suggest that social and economic factors were most important in cases of conversion. Apostates, for instance, were sometimes held in higher regard by the Ottoman authorities than practising Jews:

> An apostate frightened Reuven and denounced him [to the authorities]. He told him that unless he gave him 500 florins, he would inform on him to the Muslims, and say he had cursed the King and his religion [...] When Reuven saw the catastrophe falling upon him, he went to the friends and begged them to pacify and bribe the apostate [...] they went as Reuven wished, and succeeded in pacifying him with a bribe of 4000 *levanim*[27].

With a new religious status, a convert gained a higher social position, which accorded him an advantage over the members of Jewish community. However, despite the fact that the Ottoman authorities considered conversion to Islam to be irreversible, there were opportunities for former Jews to return to the old faith. Jewish law enabled this; moreover, the expansion of the Ottoman Empire made in easy for former Jews to relocate and reintegrate themselves into the Jewish community:

> A year after the great plague [Mordechai Gim'ah] went to the city of Safed (may God soon rebuild and renew it in our days) and he embarked the ship together with Yehoshua de Yanko, and he found there also Yosef Amigo, who was in these days a Turk. When he got to Safed, Dona Sol la Galdita, mother of the above mentioned Yosef, came over and when she came near to the city, her son Yosef met her halfway, and she wailed, breaking her head with two stones, [saying] she had no children any longer and remained childless. Her son Yosef tried to comfort her, asking her to stop crying, [promising] he would become a Jew, but she replied, better he would die because of the apostasy like his brother Yakob. She came to the house of her two daughters, where all these mourned for her son Yakob, who had died here in Thessaloniki[28].

While we do not know if the apostate returned to his former religion, it is significant that it was considered to be a viable option.

The Responsa texts also refer to conversion to Judaism. In most cases, the converts were servants (mostly Muslim) in Jewish households. Ottoman law, of course, forbade this practice, but even the most severe sanctions could not eradicate it completely. Less frequently, we also encounter sincere converts to Judaism, who reportedly abandoned their possessions and families in order to become members of the Jewish community: "[t]his man was a righteous convert [to Judaism], and he had given up all the wealth, property, and pleasures in order to hide under the wings of the Divine presence, and those who mock him deserve a severe punishment"[29]. Unfortunately, the sources remain silent about the background of such individuals and about the details of their conversion. What seems clear, however, is a resolute rabbinic order to accept the convert without hesitation; nevertheless, once again successful integration into the community depended on the nature of each congregation and the elasticity of its symbolic borders.

Sometimes a Jewish congregation consciously built its collective identity on a common history, language and family relations that could not have been shared by the rest of the city's Jewish population. This is especially true for the Iberian Peninsula Diaspora and their descendants, who portrayed themselves as a unique 'Spanish nation', in opposition to other Jewish ethnic and cultural groups (Ashkenazic Jews, Romaniots, and Jews from the Arab provinces)[30]. The "Spanish nation" was, admittedly, far from homogeneous. It embraced those Jews who left Spain in 1492 for other European countries as well as Portugal, where Jews were tolerated until the late 1490s when forced baptism was introduced. Many of the "New Christians"[31] consequently left Portugal. Some of the expellees headed directly to the Ottoman Empire; some reached the Ottoman realm only after a period in the European Christian countries. What made the choice of the Ottoman Empire even more attractive was the fact that the *anusim* (those forcibly baptised) could freely return to Judaism there. The position of the *anusim* in the Jewish community was, however, ambivalent. Sometimes they were denigrated by other Jews; at other times they were recognised as full members of the Spanish nation. A legal case brought before Rabbi Shemuel di Medina forced him to draw a distinction between Jews and their former co-religionists:

> Reuven has died and left behind all his property in the hands of the Jewish court, until his heir comes to claim it. But the heir lives in Portugal as a non-Jew, and there is a Jewess called Leah standing in front of us, who is a sister of the above-mentioned heir, whose father was a non-Jew, and she raises a legal claim upon the inheritance left by the above mentioned Reuven. She maintains that her brother and a relative of the deceased should be considered dead, since he lives as a non-Jew, and that she is the only legal inheritor, and all the rights and issues related to her brother are to be transferred to her [...] The answer: I believe the case is clear, for the heir had an opportunity in the past few years to return to the Jewish law [...] Apparently, the legal decision stands as follows: the inheritance passes to his sister for the above-mentioned reason, that is, as if the heir had died [...] The inheritance [...] passes to this woman called Leah, who is a Jewess and stands in front of us, and maintains a truly Jewish lifestyle. And we do not need to wait for a removed relative, for such relative could have come during the past couple of years, but this did not happen, and as such he lost all the rights as an heir [...] Even though in the case of levirate marriage we recognize those *anusim* as Jews [...] in property issues they are not to be taken into account [...] and in our case [...] since they could have come, but they did not, he is not to be called a Jew or brother in the question of property[32].

Here Rabbi di Medina was clearly cautious in declaring *anusim* separate from the Jewish community. Only when he had to solve a question of property ownership, did he deny the Christian relatives of the deceased their inheritance rights.

Conclusion

Borders existed within the Jewish community, but at any moment these borders were liable to alter, or even disappear, when such action was considered to be essential for the wider community. These alterations to inner and exterior frontiers decided by Jewish congregations could be formal or informal. Meanwhile, relations with the wider Ottoman urban population ranged from cordial to hostile, depending on specific circumstances and personal experiences. As a result, we encounter multiple images that correspond to multiple experiences and to the heterogeneity of the Ottoman urban population. In this respect, we should consider also the role of the individual's own experiences and the way this helped to shape his perceptions of the environment. Ultimately, individuals were able to select the most suitable image or conception, and apply it to the appropriate circumstance: this characterised Jewish life in the 'multicultural neighbourhood' that was the Ottoman city.

Notes

1 R. Shemuel di Medina, *Shu"t Maharashdam*, IV, 434, a reprint of the Lvov edition from 1862, undated. Rabbi Shemuel di Medina (Maharashdam, 1506/7- 1589) worked in Thessaloniki. He was an outstanding Torah scholar and his legal decisions have had far-reaching impacts on Ottoman Jewry and beyond.

2 R. Shemuel di Medina, *Shu"t* cit., IV, 407.

3 N. Elias, *The Court Society*, Oxford 1983, p.18.

4 H. Gerber, *On the History of the Jews in Istanbul in the 17th and the 18th centuries*, in "Pe'amim", 1972, 12, pp. 27-46.

5 R. Shemuel di Medina, *Shu"t* cit., III, 214. The lady mentioned here is probably Dona Gracia Mendez, a very rich and influential Jewess with access to the royal harem and to the Palace.

6 *Halitzah* is a name for a ceremony connected to the levirate marriage, in which the brother of the deceased husband refuses to marry the childless widow, and thus enables her to marry somebody else.

7 *Get* is a divorce document presented by a husband to his wife during the divorce ceremony.

8 Literally *umot ha-olam,* the nations of the world.

9 R. Shemuel di Medina, *Shu"t* cit., III, 93.

10 R. Moshe Benvenisti, *Sefer Penei Moshe* (reprint of the Istanbul edition from 1669-1713), II, 116.

11 R. Shemuel di Medina, *Shu"t* cit., IV, 378.

12 A. Cohen, *Jews in the Moslem Religious Courts. Society, Economy and Communal Organization in the XVIth Century Documents from Ottoman Jerusalem*, Jerusalem 1993, document no. 424. This legal decision was issued by Ebu's Su'ud Efendi, who worked as a royal judge during the reign of Süleyman I and Selim II.

13 R. Shemuel di Medina, *Shu"t* cit., IV, 352.

14 Some confusion may arise over terminology. Herein *Congregation* relates to a religious and administrative unit with a rabbi, synagogue, and secular leadership at its centre, often congruent with a certain fiscal unit. The aim of achieving fiscal control meant that congregations were well-defined and autonomous collectives. *Community* is taken to mean the overall Jewish population of the town, irrespectively their belonging to one or another congregation. In some Ottoman towns there was an official Jewish community encompassing all the congregations, in head of which was a supra-congregational court.

15 i.e. a Jew.

16 *Ibid..*, II, 124.

17 i.e. *tütün*, tobacco.

18 Literally "beloved".

19 i.e. a pipe.

20 R. Nisim Haim Moshe Mizrahi, *Admat kodesh*, Bar Ilan Responsa Project version 11 on CD-ROM, I 4.

21 R. Shemuel di Medina, *Shu"t* cit., III, 35, the text does not allude to the non-Jew's religious affiliation.

22 *Bedestan,* or bazaar, was a covered marketplace in the city-centre, typical of Oriental urban architecture.

23 *Ibid.*, p. 70. In Hebrew sources, the term *emir* indicates an upper class Ottoman Muslim.

24 *Veyvoda* was lower-ranking governor appointed by the central government.

[25] *Ibid.*, III, 75.

[26] A. Cohen, *Jews* cit., document no. 119.

[27] R. Shemuel di Medina, *Shu"t* cit., IV, 359.

[28] *Ibid.*, III, 59. The Responsa literature has no data on conversions to Christianity within the Ottoman Empire.

[29] *Ibid.*, IV, 354. The said Avraham Mindo became a tax collector and another Jew aimed to deprive him of this function. This behaviour was condemned unreservedly by the rabbi.

[30] The term *uma* (nation), which was used to designate the Spanish nation, differs from the term used to designate the Jewish nation as a whole, i.e. *am Jisra'el* (the People of Israel). This linguistic distinction deserves a broader elaboration, but this is not our aim here.

[31] Sometimes the derogatory term *marranos* (swine) was, and still is, used. In Jewish sources, they are called *anusim* (those, who were forced to do something against their will).

[32] *Ibid.*, 315.

Bibliography

Al-Khowli R., *Observations on the Use of Shari'a Court Records as a Source of Social History*, in Sonbol A. E. (ed.), *Beyond the Exotic. Women's Histories in Islamic Societies*, New York 2005, pp. 139-151.

Barnai J, *Jewish Guilds in Turkey in the 16th-19th Centuries*, in Gross N. (ed.), *Jews in Economic Life. Collected Essays*, Jerusalem 1985, pp. 133-147.

Bornstein-Makovetsky L., *Social Relations between the Jews and the non-Jews in the Ottoman City*, in "Mikedem umi-yam", 1995, 4, pp. 13-33.

Cohen A., *Jews in the Moslem Religious Courts. Society, Economy and Communal Organization in the XVIth-Century Documents from Ottoman Jerusalem*, Jerusalem 1993.

Elias N., *The Court Society*, Oxford 1983.

Faroqhi S., *Subjects of the Sultan: Culture and Daily Life in the Ottoman Empire*, London 2000.

Freehof S. B., *The Responsa Literature*, Philadelphia 1955.

Gerber H., *On the History of the Jews in Istanbul in the 17th and the 18th centuries*, in "Pe'amim", 1982, 12, pp. 27-46.

Gerber H., *Ottoman Jews in the 16th and 17th Centuries. Economy and Socitey*, Jerusalem 1983.

Goodblatt M., *Jewish Life in Turkey in the 16th Century as Reflected in Legal Writings of Samuel de Medina*, New York 1952.

Goffman D., *The Ottoman Empire and Early Modern Europe*, Cambridge 2002.

Hacker J. R., *Jewish Autonomy in the Ottoman Empire: Its Scope and Limits. Jewish Courts from the 16th to the 18th Centuries*, in Levy A. (ed.), *The Jews of the Ottoman Empire*, New Jersey 1994, pp. 153-202.

Quataert D., *The Ottoman Empire 1700-1922*, Cambridge 2004 [1st edition 2000].

Rozen M., *A History of the Jewish Community in Istanbul. The Formative Years, 1453-1566*, Boston 2002.

Rozen M., *Individual and Community in the Jewish Society of the Ottoman Empire: Salonica in the XVIth Century*, in Levy A. (ed.), *The Jews of the Ottoman Empire*, New Jersey 1994, pp. 215-273.

Sources

R. Nisim Haim Moshe Mizrahi, *Admat kodesh*, Bar Ilan Responsa Project version 11 on CD-ROM.

R. Moshe Benvenisti, *Sefer Penei Moshe*, reprint of the Istanbul edition from 1669-1713, Jerusalem 1988-1991.

R. Shemuel di Medina, *Shu"t Maharashdam*, reprint of the Lvov edition from 1862, undated.

Ethnic and Professional Frontiers in Transylvanian Cities from the 16th to the 18th Centuries

FLORIN PINTESCU
"Ştefan cel Mare" University of Suceava

"Stadtluft macht frei"[1]

ABSTRACT

This study attempts to demonstrate the influence of the dynamic sense of the 'frontier' phenomenon on the history of Romanians living in Transylvania between 1500 and 1800. It will be argued, drawing on primary source material, that Romanians in Transylvanian cities were socially and professionally discriminated against. Due to this, Romanians could not officially settle in Transylvanian cities (except in the suburbs of some cities or small boroughs) until the 18th century. Also, they could not officially establish Romanian professional guilds until the 17th century. It will be argued here that this demonstrates that ethnic and professional 'frontiers' operated in Transylvanian cities in this period, which were favorable to the Hungarians, Saxons and Szeklers, but unfavorable to the Romanians.

Studiul intenţionează să demonstreze că istoria românilor din oraşele Transilvaniei secolelor XVI-XVIII a fost negativ influenţată de acţiunea a două tipuri de "frontieră": frontiera etnică şi cea profesională.

Analiza teoretică a acestui articol pleacă de la înţelesul dinamic al noţiunii de "frontieră", lansată în câmpul sociologiei de către Frederick Jackson Turner (1893), cu aplicaţii ulterioare largi în istorie, geopolitică şi geostrategie. Înţelesul dinamic al fenomenului de frontieră cuantifică fenomenul expansiunii unei naţiuni, civilizaţii, religii, ideologii sau imperiu.

În introducere, articolul analizează importanţa fenomenului de frontieră în istoria medievală a Europei, punând totodată în evidenţă condiţiile istorice speciale care au influenţat evoluţia Transilvaniei medievale. Ulterior este descrisă succint situaţia religioasă şi politică a românilor din Transilvania, care explică statusul lor social-urban şi profesional precar.

Partea cea mai consistentă a articolului conţine o serie de informaţii despre evoluţia oraşelor transilvănene din secolele XVI-XVIII, cu referire specială la situaţia socială şi profesională a românilor ardeleni din suburbiile ("măierişti") unor oraşe şi din târgurile acestui stat.

Articolul subliniază, pe baza unor izvoare şi mărturii de epocă, că românii nu s-au putut stabili în mod oficial în oraşele transilvănene (nu le-a fost permis accesul) – cu excepţia notabilă a unor suburbii şi a unor mici târguri, până în secolul XVIII. De asemenea, ei nu şi-au putut constitui bresle profesionale până în secolul XVII.

Concluzia finală a articolului este că oraşele transilvănene din secolele XVI-XVIII au îndeplinit rolul unor frontiere etnice şi profesionale, care au fost favorabile maghiarilor, saşilor şi secuilor, însă au fost nefavorabile românilor.

Having complex sociological and geopolitical connotations, the word "frontier", as a collective experience, represents "a true anthropologic, spiritual, ethnologic and even religious laboratory"[2]. This study seeks to demonstrate that the history of Romanians[3] in Transylvanian cities, between the 16th and 18th centuries, was negatively influenced by the effects of two types of 'frontiers': ethnic and professional.

This chapter will be presented in three parts. The various meanings of the concept of "frontier" and its historical significance for the history of Europe will be discussed. This analysis will emphasize the peculiar historical conditions which influenced the evolution of mediaeval Transylvania. Secondly, the chapter will analyze the political and religious situation of the Romanians in Transylvania and how this explains their special social and professional status in the urban context. Finally, the evolution of Transylvanian cities between the 16th and 18th centuries will be explored and the status of Romanians in these cities will be assessed.

The term "frontier" arose in the field of sociology after the printing of Frederick Jackson Turner's 1893 essay, *The Significance of the Frontier in American History*. The concept has acquired a double meaning, simultaneously static and dynamic. If we concern ourselves with the static meaning, "the frontier evokes the point where the territorial competence [of a state] ends"[4]. If we refer to the dynamic sense, "the phenomenon of the frontier expresses all processes by which historical expansion, either of a nation, civilization, religion, ideology or empire manifests itself"[5].

Historically speaking, the dynamic meaning of "frontier" is very important for understanding European civilization's expansion, due to the creation of the so-called European world economy[6] around the turn of the 16th century. This process was accompanied by the expansion of the 'frontier' of Western civilization in such a manner that, during the following four centuries, "intercivilizational relations consisted in subordinating other societies to Western civilization"[7].

Among the elements that favoured the "dramatic development" of Western civilization, an important role was played by the emergence of cities[8]. These entities contributed to the rise of the bourgeoisie, the enrichment of culture in the Middle Ages and the use of vernacular languages in the administration. Also, cities promoted the secularization of medieval society[9].

Between the 16th and 18th centuries, due to the historical circumstances outlined below, Transylvanian cities were only able to carry out part of the role assumed in the same period by cities in Central and Western Europe.

The reasons for this have been outlined by I. Wallerstein as part of his core-periphery theory. Wallerstein argues that the foundation of the "European world system" helped to divide the world into "central states", "semi-peripheral zones" and "peripheral zones". This global division led to the shift of the commercial centre of Europe from the Mediterranean Sea to the Atlantic Ocean. Also, it determined the impoverishment of the states of Eastern Europe (including Transylvania). Therefore, these states were, for centuries, reduced to the role of an agrarian area exploited by Western European states[10]. Also, in 1541, Transylvania was subdued by an economically regressive Great Power, the Ottoman Empire[11]. All these factors prevented Transylvanian cities from developing in a West-European fashion.

Today, Transylvania is a large geographical unit (approximately 102,000 km^2), which includes 42.2% of the area and 33.8% of the population of Romania[12]. This term is also applied to the provinces of Banat, Crişana and Maramureş, which were, at times during the Middle Ages, under the control of different states. Thus, using the generic term Transylvania for all these provinces could be considered to be inaccurate. However, in this study, the term Transylvania is extended to include the above mentioned provinces for two reasons. Firstly, to simplify the text and, secondly, because the data used for analysis is drawn from all four provinces.

Transylvania was a part of the Kingdom of Hungary until early in the 16th century. During the period of Hungarian rule Romanians in Transylvania were politically, religiously and judicially discriminated against[13]. In 1366, King Ludovic I (Lajos) of Hungary (1342-1382) proclaimed several anti-Romanian measures by royal decree. The new laws stipulated that no person could be considered a noble if they did not have a royal diploma, which rewarded them with this title. This decision automatically excluded the majority of Romanian nobles from the ranks of the nobility because they possessed their lands by virtue of an unwritten ancestral law (i.e. *jus valachicum, jus keneziale*). It was also stipulated that no person in Transylvania, including Romanian nobles (Lat. *Kenezi*), could possess estates, if he was not of the Catholic religion[14]. This royal decision represented a great danger for the interests of the majority of the Romanian nobles, who were Orthodox Christians. Therefore, these measures encouraged "the exclusion of the Romanian elite as an entity from among the social orders [i.e. in the mediaeval meaning] and outlawing of their orthodox confession"[15].

Later, after 1437[16], Romanians were denied the status of a political 'nation' (*natio* in mediaeval Latin) in the Diets or Assemblies of Estates (i.e. *congregationes*, *universitates*) of Transylvania. It is important to note that, after 1437, those Assemblies were made up only of Nobles (whose ethnic descent did not matter), Saxons and Szeklers (*Nobiles, Saxones et Siculi*).

After 1437, the notion of *nobiles* gradually attained a stronger ethnic connotation. Nobles of non-Hungarian descent converted, in different periods, to Catholicism and Calvinism. Over time, these nobles began to Magyarize themselves. Therefore, the ethnic evolution of the nation was encouraged by the overwhelming Magyar character of the nobility, by their preponderance in the political life of the Principality and by the influence of the Reformation, which supported the mother-tongue in the Church and culture. As the nation progressed towards modernity, the expression *natio nobilium* or *nemes nemzet* became unsuitable, being replaced by general terms such as nobles or nobility, counties (Rom. *comitate*) or noble counties (Rom. *nobile comitate*) and finally by the Magyar nation (*natio hungarica, magyar natio, magyar nemzet*)"[17].

After the triumph of the Reformation and Counter-Reformation in Transylvania, the Orthodox religion of the Romanians was not accepted as a formal religion in the country, unlike Catholicism, Calvinism, Lutheranism and Unitarianism. Orthodox Christianity was refered to as "tolerated" in Transylvanian judicial texts[18].

Generally, at the end of the 16th century, neither their countrymen (i.e. Magyars, Saxons and Szeklers) nor foreign observers considered Transylvanian Romanians to be strongly discriminated against. They considered Romanians to be rude, uncivilized, without an elite, rustic and backward. They characterized them as paupers, vigilantes, thieves and bandits[19]. Naturally, this mind set did not stimulate cooperation between Romanians and the other Transylvanian peoples (i.e. Hungarians, Saxons and Szeklers).

Due to the factors mentioned above, between the 16th and 18th centuries Romanians from Transylvania had "a peripheral status in relation to the urban life, which was almost inaccessible to them"[20].

During the period of Transylvanian 'Voivodship' (between the 12th century and 1541), the cities in the country were partially influenced by western culture and civilization. The administration of the cities was divided between their representatives and the representatives of the voivod (prince) or bishop (when the city was a bishop's residence)[21]. All the same, in the Transylvanian cities Assemblies of Estates functioned in a similar manner to those in Western Europe. Thus, from the 13th century, the Transylvanian cities sent their representatives to the General Assembly (*congregatio generalis*) of the Voivodship[22].

Between 1300 and 1600, the most important Transylvanian cities were given the status of "royal free cities" (i.e. *civitas libera ac regia*)[23]. In mediaeval documents, the leaders of these cities were called *providi viri, circumspecti et prudentes*[24], *probo set notabiles viros, sapientiores et intellectiores*[25] etc.

From the 16th century until the end of the 18th, Transylvanian cities were divided, depending on their importance, into three categories: "royal free cities" (i.e., *civitas libera ac regia*), "noble cities" or "noble boroughs" (i.e., *civitas, oppidum nobilium*) and 'boroughs' (i.e., *oppidum*). The main 'royal free cities' were Cluj (until 1660, when it became a 'noble' city), Târgu Mureş (from 1616), Sibiu, Braşov, Sighişoara, Mediaş, Bistriţa and Sebeş. The main "noble" cities or boroughs were Dej (1668), Turda Nouă (1619) and Turda Veche (1668). The most important Transylvanian boroughs were Alba Iulia, Ocna Sibiului, Târgu Secuiesc, Sfântu Gheorghe, Hunedoara, Ilieni, Breţcu, Abrud, Haţeg, Zalău, Sic, and Cojocna[26].

Cities in mediaeval Transylvanian imposed judicial measures in order to hinder outsiders from staying for long periods or settling inside of the cities' walls (i.e. *intra muros*). For example, nobles were forbidden from settling in the royal free cities of Cluj in 1537 and Braşov in 1544[27]. Even the king of the country had a limited right to stay in Sibiu: he could only remain for three days accompanied by a small escort[28]. In a section on Sibiu in his 1564 description of Transylvania, the Italian Giovan Andrea Gromo (1518 - after 1567) wrote: "and neither can the other nations get work in these Saxon cities or have the right to live here except for a very skilled or necessary person. Not even the king can stay here for more than three days or enter the city unless with an escort which is so small that it cannot raise any fear"[29].

Speaking about Braşov, the same author emphasized that "the leading functions of the cities belong to the learned people, wise and old people most of whom can speak several languages. *They will not permit others than their citizens to get work there or anybody who is not a Saxon to work in the city*" (our italics)[30].

Naturally, the Romanians insisted, both during the Principality and afterwards, on their right to live in the cities. But the authorities only "allowed them in as long as they were shepherds, because the Hungarians would not accept this trade"[31]. The council of the city of Turda even decided, though later, between 1711-1712:

> We are learning that the Walachians are breeding among us and against us at a high rate. The beautiful old villages and towns inhabited before by Hungarians and Saxons are so deserted because of the Walachians' breeding that we cannot even hear about them. For this reason we decide that every man or widow in the town has the duty to chase away, within eight days, all the Walachians from their houses and lands or be fined with three florins[32].

Due to these restrictive measures, during the 16th century, Romanians only managed to settle in some of the smaller Transylvanian boroughs or in the suburbs (in Romanian: *maieri, măierişti*)[33] of some larger cities. Around 1572 Romanians were living in the borough of Caransebeş and were represented in the local Senate[34], and in the borough Zlatna, where they worked in the mines near the city[35]. Between 1452 and 1536, the representatives of the Olahus family, natives of Walachia, established, with interruptions, a veritable dynasty of administrative rulers (in Romanian *juzi scăunali*) in the borough Orăştie, a citadel of Transylvanian Germanism[36].

During the 16th century, a series of scholars, both military men and clergymen wrote accounts of Romanian residents in the suburbs of some Transylvanian cities and several boroughs. The Saxon scholar Georg Reicherstorffer (*c.*1500 - *c.*1550) depicts Romanians living in the suburbs of Braşov (Şcheii Braşovului), Zlatna, Hatzeg and Baia de Criş[37]. The Italian officer Giovan Andrea Gromo also states that Romanians lived in a "suburb" of Cluj (Cluj-Mănăştur)[38]. The same soldier notes that Romanians "provide the cities with cheese, milk and fruits daily"[39]. Similarly, on 24 July 1586, the clergyman Valentin Ladó wrote in a letter to the priest Campani that at Caransebeş there was a numerous Romanian population, to which he "often" preached the Catholic liturgy[40]. The Venetian Giorgio Tomasi (? – *c.* 1621), Prince Sigismund Báthory's secretary, writes that the suburbs of the city of Alba Iulia were "mainly inhabited by the Greeks and Romanians"[41]. Finally, the mathematician, geographer and traveler David Frölich (1595-1648) visited Transylvania in 1630 and recorded his impressions of his travels in a famous work, printed in 1639 *(Medulla Geographiae practicae, Peregrinantium imprimis usui deinde Historiarum et rerum hoc tempore belicossisimo gestarum gerendarumque cognitioni accomodata...*). In his book Frölich states that the Romanians lived in the boroughs of Abrud, Baia de Criş, Zlatna Mare, Zlatna Mică and Haţeg[42]. The names of the regions or places mentioned in these documents can be found on many of the maps printed in the 16th century[43].

The following table contains the places (boroughs) in Transylvania that were inhabited by Romanians, as they appear on a map of Hungary drawn in 1528 by 'Lazarus Secretarius' and Georg Tannstetter (1482-1535), a map of Transylvania created by J. Honterus and a map of Hungary, drawn by Wolfgang Lazius[44].

PLACE NAME (in Romanian)	LAZARUS/ TANNSTETTER	HONTERUS	LAZIUS
Abrud	Abrotania	Schlotten	Abrukbanya
Baia de Criş	Keresbama	Altemburg	Kerezbanya
Caransebeş	Karansebes	-	-
Grădişte	-	-	Varhel
Orăştie	Zazuaros	Bros	Zazuara(s)
Zlatna	-	-	Zaladna

The next section of this chapter will analyze the fascinating example of the struggle by the Romanians in the suburbs of Şcheii Braşovului to be accepted as full citizens by the Braşov authorities. This example illustrates the effect of a 'frontier' of the locative urban type on the social, economic and cultural development of Romanians in Transylvania. Although the presence of Romanians in the suburb of Şcheii Braşovului has been documented since the end of the 14th century[45], the Romanians did not officially have the right to live in Braşov. Throughout the 18th century, the Romanians in this suburb tried to create a city administration of their own, independent of Braşov Saxon government. They won an indirect victory when, on 4 July 1781, the emperor Joseph II permitted the "recognized nations" (i.e. *Nobiles, Saxones et Siculi*) from Transylvania to obtain citizen rights and estates in the territory of the 'Saxon University' an organization of Saxons in Medieval Transylvania[46]. This decision allowed Romanians to obtain citizen rights and buy houses in the city of Braşov. The first to do so were the trader Ioan Boghici, who bought a house in 1781, and the butcher Dumitru Orghidan[47].

In 1790, however, Joseph II's reform was revoked and the authorities of Braşov refused to give Romanians the rights to which it had entitled them. It was not until the first decades of the 19th century that the Romanians of Şcheii Braşovului began seriously to campaign for the acknowledgment of their rights. Their movement consisted mostly of petitions addressed to the central authorities of Transylvania, as well as to the Aulic Committee for reorganizing Royal Land (*Fundus Regium*, the land held by the Saxons in Medieval Transylvania). In these petitions, the Romanians from Şcheii Braşovului mainly requested the elimination of restrictions on their economic activities, their acceptance to the guilds, the unbiased assignment of public tasks and a role in the government of the city of Braşov[48].

The Transylvanian guilds date back to the 14th century[49] and continued to be active until the 19th century. The first statutes of these organizations date back to the year 1376 and originally established nineteen guilds in Sibiu, Sighişoara, Sebeş and Orăştie. In Transylvanian documents from the 14th and 15th centuries the guilds are referred to as brotherhoods (*fraternitates*), societies (*societates*), associations (*confederationes*), communities (*communitates*) and guilds (*cehae, Zünfte*)[50].

As a historical curiosity, the official decree of abolishment of the Transylvanian guilds was passed in 1872[51]. In Western Europe, the golden age of these professional organizations had come to an end in the 15th century. As has been emphasized by Fernand Braudel, by this time western cities already had forms of market economy[52].

Transylvanian handicrafts had also failed to rise to the qualitative and quantitative standards of those practiced in Central or Western Europe. The Transylvanian guilds kept the mediaeval system, a system which drastically limited the possibility of any interference from external institutions. The transition to Western manufacturing standards was also excessively drawn out.

Although Romanians were partially successful in gaining the right to settle in the cities, they were not able, in the 15th and 16th centuries, to overcome the restrictions against them being received into the Saxonian, Hungarian or Szeklerian guilds. For example, the 1484 statute of the furrier guilds in Bistrița and Sighişoara threatened that any Romanian or other foreigner transporting merchandise would be punished with a fine equal to the value of the goods[53]. The statutes of 1586 issued by the leather dressers guild of Orăştie explicitly stated that its members were not allowed to sell products to Romanians or any other foreigners[54]. The statutes of 1589 for the same guild explicitly stated that Romanians were not to be accepted into the guild[55].

All the guild statutes of Baia Mare and Cluj declared that no one but he who is "born of honest marriage", not a serf, and is of Hungarian or German nationality can be accepted as an apprentice[56]. Article IV of the Statute of 1652 issued by the butchers' guild in Baia Mare explicitly stated that the apprentice must present, when entering the guild, along with his apprenticeship document, a letter regarding his nationality and proof that he is a freeman[57].

Transylvanian Romanians did not manage to establish their own guilds in the 16th century, and were not granted access to the Hungarian, Saxonian or Szeklerian guilds. Due to this, Romanians established their own guilds in villages[58]. There were, nevertheless, some Romanians who managed to break the guild monopoly. The first was Philippus Pictor (i.e. Philip the Moldavian)[59], who wrote a Slavonic gospel at Sibiu in 1546. In 1552-3, the same man wrote a bilingual Slavonic-Romanian gospel, which is considered to be the oldest surviving writing in Romanian[60].

The first Romanian guild, or at least a guild that contained Romanians, appeared at the end of the 16th century. This was the guild of the shoemakers in Făgăraş (a borough largely populated by Romanians), which had been given a privilege in 1598 by Princess Maria Christina. The same guild was also given a privilege in 1622 by Prince Gabriel Bethlen[61].

On 15 July 1635, Gh. I Rakoczi approved the statutes of the guilds of shoemakers and leather dressers in Hunedoara. These guilds incorporated Hungarian and Romanian craftsmen. According to the statutes, the Romanians Teodor Vlad and Nicolae Cizmăşia represented the shoemakers' guild, requesting the approval of the statute from the Transylvanian prince. The Romanian Mihail Oprea performed the same role in the leather dressers' guild[62].

The guild of the Romanian tanners in Făgăraş was established in 1643, and by 1672 the guild of Romanian shoemakers and "solemakers" (makers of boot soles) had already been established in Hațeg[63]. It is also worth mentioning that the Romanian potters' guild of Hațeg obtained a privilege in 1708[64].

The Romanians who settled in the suburbs of Şcheii Braşovului (Braşov) and earned a living through handicrafts and commerce had a remarkable impact on Transylvania between the 14th and 18th centuries. The Saxon chronicles offer us interesting information about the Romanians who lived in the vicinity of the cities of Sibiu and Braşov. The Romanians in those regions are thought to have possessed a large number of animals, while the ones in Şcheii Braşovului were described as rich and involved in various economic activities. Some escorted young Saxon students from Braşov and Sibiu to German universities, especially to that of Leipzig, and also lent them money and brought back letters to their parents[65].

The involvement of Romanians living in the regions surrounding Sibiu and Şcheii Braşovului in Transylvanian commerce is well documented from as early as the 16th century. In 1503, sixty Romanian traders from Şcheii Braşovului participated in trade with Walachia[66]. Of the traders operating between Braşov and Walachia and Moldavia in 1530, the Romanians made up 46.12%, the Saxons 13.99%, the Hungarians 8.77% and the Greeks 5.56%, while the rest were Armenians and other ethnicities[67].

During the 17th and 18th centuries a significant number of Romanians from Transylvania were involved in the commercial activities of the so-called 'Greek' companies in Sibiu (founded in 1636) and Braşov (founded in 1678)[68].

Saxon chroniclers describe the Romanians around Sibiu and Braşov as shepherds, servants, chefs, fishermen, fish salesmen or carters[69]. In addition, especially in the 18th century, Romanians from Şcheii Braşovului were furriers, dressmakers, carpenters, blacksmiths, silversmiths, barbers, shoemakers etc., and intended to open a string factory in 1773. Despite all this, most of their income came from commercial activities and transportation[70].

Romanian butchers from Şcheii Braşovului, mentioned in a document of 1634, fought an interesting judicial battle for about two centuries, to gain acknowledgement of their professional rights from the authorities of Braşov[71]. In 1791 the Association of Romanian butchers was established in Brasov (*Compagnia Laniorum Vallachorum Bolgarszegiensium*), although this did not have all the elements of a guild (functional status, right to monopoly, measures of protection against external competition, management organisms, the professional hierarchic steps, regular member subscription, its own treasury, etc.)[72]. The Romanian butchers in Şcheii Braşovului were only successful in 1872, when they managed to establish *The Industrial Society of Romanian Butchers in Braşov*[73].

At the end of this study, some conclusions must be drawn. The history of Transylvanian Romanians between the 16th and 18th centuries was negatively influenced by the effects of two types of "frontiers": the ethnic and the professional. Due to this, their social, economic and cultural development was hindered, especially when it is compared to that of the Hungarians, Saxons and Szeklers in Transylvania. Romanians could not officially settle in the Transylvanian cities (except in some cities' suburbs or small boroughs) until the 18th century. Also, they could not officially build their Romanian professional guilds until the 17th century. In this context, it can be seen that Transylvanian cities, between the 16th and 18th centuries, acted as ethnic and professional frontiers, which were favorable to the Hungarians, Saxons and Szeklers, but unfavorable to the Romanians.

All the same, especially because of their ethnic and religious conservativeness, the Romanians in Transylvania had, until the 20th century, a fundamental role in the process of consolidating the Transylvanian rural 'frontier' against the expansion of the urban 'frontier'.

Notes

1 "The city air makes you free" – German mediaeval saying.

2 I. Bădescu, D. Dungaciu, *Sociologia şi geopolitica frontierei* [The Sociology and Geopolitics of the Frontier], vol. 1, Bucharest 1995, p. 31.

3 In Transylvanian mediaeval documents Romanians were designated by the ethnonyms *Olachi, Olaci, Valachi* (See, for instance, Ş. Pascu, Ş. Ştefănescu et al. (eds.), *Documenta Romaniae Historica,* series C, *Transilvania (1366-1370),* vol. 13, Bucharest 1994, p. 915 – Index. According to the opinions of different experts, these ethnonyms originated from *Volcae,* the name given by C.I. Caesar and Titus Livy to a population from Gaul (A. Armbruster, *La romanité des roumains. Histoire d'une idée*, Bucharest 1979, *passim*).

4 J. Soppelsa, M. Battesti, J.-Ch. Romer, *Lexique de géopolitique*, Paris 1988, p. 124.

5 Bădescu, Dungaciu, *Sociologia* cit., p. 1.

6 I. Wallerstein, *The Modern World System: Capitalist Agriculture and the Origins of the European World-Economy in the Sixteenth Century*, New York 1974, *passim.*

7 S. P. Huntington, *The Clash of Civilizations and the Remaking of World Order*, London 1998, p. 51.

8 *Ibid.*

9 H. Pirenne, *Medieval cities. Their origins and the revival of trade*, Princeton 1946, pp. 222, 224, 231-232, 233.

10 D. Prodan, *Iobăgia în Transilvania în sec. XVI* [Serfdom in Transylvania in the 16th Century], vol. 1, Bucharest 1967, p. 577.

11 See the arguments concerning the affiliation of Transylvania to a marginal zone of the European economy in F. Pintescu, *Românii din Transilvania la sfârşitul secolului XVI şi începutul secolului XVII* [Romanians from Transylvania at the end of the 16th Century and the Beginning of the 17th Century], Suceava 2004, pp. 63-66.

12 G. Pop, *Introducere* [Introduction], in A. Drăgoescu (ed.), *Istoria României. Transilvania* [History of Romania. Transylvania], vol. I, Cluj-Napoca 1997, p. 14.

13 F. Pintescu, *Românii* cit., pp. 86-90.

14 "*ut in tota provincia* (i.e. Transylvania, our note) *seu toto districtu de Sebes nullus alter nisi vere catholicus et fidem quam Romana tenet et profitetur ecclesia fideliter colens, possessiones aliquas sub titulo nobilitatis aut sub titulo keneziali tenere posset et conservare*" – *Documenta* cit., p. 2.

15 I. Aurel Pop, *Voievodatul Transilvaniei şi părţile vestice în sec. XII-1541* [The Voivodship of Transylvania and the Western Parts in the 12th Century - 1541], in A. Drăgoescu, *Istoria* cit., pp. 478-479.

16 I. Aurel Pop, *Instituții medievale românești. Adunările cneziale și nobiliare (boierești) în secolele XIV-XVI* [Romanian Medieval Institutions. The Assemblies of "Cnezi" and Nobles (boyars) from the 14th to the 16th Century], Cluj Napoca 1991, p. 18.

17 A. Andea, S. Andea, *Principatul Transilvaniei sub suzeranitate otomană (1541-1691)* [The Principality of Transylvania under Ottoman Rule (1541-1691)], in A. Drăgoescu, *Istoria* cit., p. 556.

18 In *Approbatae Constitutiones Transilvaniae* (1653), a synthesis of the resolutions of the Transylvania General Assembly (i.e. *Dieta*) between 1540-1653, is mentioned: "Because the religion of the Walachian nation is not included among those four recognized (i.e. legal, our note) religions, the guild whose members were called 'călugări' (i.e. Walachian [Romanian] monks, our note), was not accepted, in fact, it was forbidden. Therefore, even now it is up to the country and princes whether or not to completely eliminate it according to their best judgement". This text is taken from L. Marcu (ed.), *Constituțiile Aprobate ale Transilvaniei (1653)* [The Sanctioned Constitutions of Transylvania (1653)], Cluj-Napoca 1997, p. 155.

19 I. Aurel Pop, *Națiunea românească medievală* [The Mediaeval Romanian Nation], Bucharest 1998, p. 119.

20 Aurel Pop, *Voievodatul* cit., p. 496.

21 *Ibid.*, p. 494.

22 G. Bichicean, *Contextul european și reprezentarea orașelor în congregațiile generale din Transilvania voievodală – secolele XIII-XVI* [The European Context and the Cities' Representations in the General "Congregations" from the Transylvanian Voivodship], in "Historia Urbana", tom IV, 1996, nr. 1-2, pp. 30-36, *passim*, with the bibliography of this problem.

23 Aurel Pop, *Voievodatul* cit., pp. 494-495.

24 Ș. Ștefănescu, *Economie și societate* [Economy and Society], in Ș. Ștefănescu, C. Mureșanu (eds.), *Istoria Românilor* [The History of Romanians], vol. IV, Bucharest 2001, p. 81.

25 G. Bichicean, *Contextul* cit., p. 35.

26 S. Andea, *Instituțiile centrale și locale în Transilvania* [The Central and Local Institutions in Transylvania], in V. Cândea (ed.), *Istoria românilor* [The History of Romanians], vol. V, Bucharest 2003 pp. 738-739.

27 Ștefănescu, *Economie* cit., p. 79.

28 I. Lupaș, *Sibiul ca centru al vieții românești din Ardeal* [Sibiu as the Center of the Romanian Life in Transylvania], in "Anuarul Institutului de istorie națională din Cluj" [The Yearbook of the Institute of National History in Cluj], nr. 4-5, 1926-1927, p. 41.

29 M. Holban (ed.), *Călători străini despre țările române* [Foreign Travelers about the Romanian Countries], vol. II, Bucharest 1970, p. 352.

30 *Ibid.*, p. 357.

31 K. Viski, *Volksleben im Siebenbürgen*, in *Siebenbürgen*, Budapest 1940, p. 133.

32 V. Jinga, *Probleme fundamentale ale Transilvaniei* [Transylvania's Fundamental Problems], 2nd edition, Brașov 1995, p. 263.

33 O. Sachelarie, N. Stoicescu (eds.), *Instituții feudale din Țările Române. Dicționar* [Feudal Institutions in the Romanian Countries. Dictionary], Bucharest 1988, p. 281.

34 S. Goldenberg, *Caransebeșul în comerțul sud-est european din secolul al XVI-lea* [Caransebeș in South-Eastern European Trade in the 16th Century], in "Banatica", nr. 1, 1971, pp. 166-167.

35 Holban, *Călători* cit., pp. 345 and 351.

36 A. E. Dörner, *Elita administrativă a scaunului Orăştie în veacurile XIV-XV* [The Administrative Elite of the 'scaun' of Orăştia in the 14th and 15th Century], in "Yearbook of the Institute of History in Cluj", 32, 1993, pp. 23-27.

37 Holban, *Călători* cit., vol. I, Bucharest 1968, pp. 217, 223, 224.

38 *Ibid.*, vol. II, pp. 345, 346, 357.

39 *Ibid.*, p. 337. Also see L. Vasile, *Achiziţii de produse agricole şi meşteşugăreşti ale municipalităţii clujene de la ţăranii români. Secolul al XVI-lea* [Cluj Municipalities' Acquisitions of Agricultural Products and of Handicrafts from Romanian Peasants. The 16th Century], in "Acta Musei Porolissensis", (AMP), XVIII, 1994, pp. 271-320.

40 Holban, *Călători* cit., vol. III, Bucharest 1971, pp. 120-121.

41 *Ibid.*, p. 671.

42 *Ibid.*, vol. V, Bucharest 1973, p. 53.

43 For a general presentation of maps from the fifteenth and sixteenth centuries which depict the Romanian countries (including Transylvania), see M. Popescu-Spineni, *Românii în izvoare geografice şi cartografice. Din antichitate pînă în pragul veacului nostru* [Romanians in Geographic and Cartographic Sources. From Antiquity to the Beginning of Our Century], Bucharest 1978, pp. 114-152.

44 H. Meschendörfer, O. Mittelstrass (eds.), *Siebenbürgen auf Alten Karten. Lazarus/Tannstetter 1528, Johannes Honterus 1532, Wolfgang Lazius 1552/1556*, Heidelberg 1996, pp. 110-133 and maps from the end of the book.

45 A. Răduţiu, L. Gyémant, *Autonomie şi integrare. Şcheii Braşovului între suburbiu şi oraş* [Autonomy and Integration. Şcheii Braşovului between Suburb and City], in "Historia Urbana", tome I, 1993, no. 2, p. 196.

46 Gernot Nussbächer, *Contribuţii la istoria administraţiei oraşului Braşov în perioada medievală (secolele XVII-XVIII)* [Contributions to the History of the City of Braşov's Administration in Medieval Times (17th / 18th centuries)], 2nd part, in "Historia Urbana", tom IV, 1996, nr. 1-2, p. 60.

47 *Ibid.*

48 Răduţiu, Gyémant, *Autonomie* cit., p. 201.

49 Ş. Pascu, *Meşteşugurile din Transilvania până în secolul al XVI-lea* [Handicrafts from Transylvania up until the 16th Century], Bucharest 1954, p. 82.

50 Ştefănescu, *Economie* cit., p. 86.

51 D. Nägler, *Breasla blănarilor din Sibiu în cursul secolelor XIV-XVIII* [The Furriers' Guild of Sibiu from the 14th to the 18th Century], in "Studii şi comunicări. Muzeul Brukenthal Sibiu. Arheologie Istorie", [Studies and Communications. The Brukenthal Muzeum Sibiu. Archaeology History] 14, 1969, p. 250.

52 "... à ce moment-là (15th century, our note), le rôle moteur est celui des boutiques d'artisans ou, mieux encore, des marchés urbains. Ce sont ces marchés qui dictent leur loi", F. Braudel, *La dynamique du capitalisme*, Paris 1989, pp. 28-29.

53 Pascu, *Meşteşugurile* cit., pp. 316-317.

54 *Ibid.*, p. 316.

55 *Ibid.*, p. 283.

56 E. Anton, *Organizarea breslelor din Baia Mare şi Cluj în secolul al XVII-lea* [The Organization of the Guilds in Baia Mare and Cluj in the 17th Century], in "Hrisovul, Bulletin of the Faculty of Archivistics" (Bucharest), new series, tom III, Bucharest 1998, p. 56.

[57] E. Anton, *Statutul breslei măcelarilor din Baia Mare (1652)* [The Statute of the Butchers' Guild in Baia Mare], in "Hrisovul", new series, tom VI-VII, 2001, p. 198.

[58] D. Prodan, *Supplex Libellus Valachorum*, Bucharest 1984, p. 102.

[59] Moldavia is today a province located in the north-eastern part of Romania.

[60] F. Pap, *Contribuţii noi cu privire la biografia primului tipograf român* [New Contributions to the Biography of the First Romanian Printing Worker], in "Acta Musei Napocensis", 22-23, 1985-1986, p. 599.

[61] N. Edroiu, *Populaţie şi economie în Transilvania* [Population and Economy in Transylvania], in Cândea, *Istoria* cit., p. 507.

[62] C. Feneşan, I. Lazăr, *Trei statute de breaslă de la Hunedoara din prima jumătate a secolului al XVII-lea* [Three Guild Statutes in Hunedoara in the First Half of the 17th Century], in "Sargetia", 14, 1979, p. 244.

[63] Jinga, *Probleme* cit., p. 180.

[64] Edroiu, *Populaţie* cit., p. 507.

[65] A. Armbruster, *The Portrayal of the Transylvanian Romanian in Saxon Historical Writings between the Fifteenth and the Eighteenth Centuries*, in L. Péter (Ed.), *Historians and the History of Transylvania*, New York 1992, p. 106.

[66] Răduţiu, Gyémant, *Autonomie* cit., p. 198.

[67] Jinga, *Probleme* cit., p. 176.

[68] O. Cicanci, *Structura etnică a companiilor comerciale din Transilvania* [The Ethnical Structure of Commercial Companies in Transylvania], in "Academia Română. Memoriile Secţiei de Ştiinţe Istorice" [The Romanian Academy. Memoirs of the Section of Historical Sciences], tome IV, 1979, p. 40.

[69] Armbruster, *The Portrayal* cit., p. 106.

[70] Răduţiu, Gyémant, *Autonomie* cit., p. 198.

[71] I-G. Andron, *Măcelarii români din Şcheii Braşovului în secolul al XVIII-lea* [Romanian Butchers in Şcheii Braşovului in the 18th Century], in D. Nazare et al. (eds.), *In honorem Gernot Nussbächer*, Braşov 2004, pp. 299-308, *passim*.

[72] *Ibid.*, p. 299.

[73] *Ibid.*, p. 308.

Bibliography

Andron I.-G., *Măcelarii români din Şcheii Braşovului în secolul al XVIII-lea* [Romanian Butchers in Şcheii Braşovului in the 18th Century], in Daniel Nazare et al. (eds.), *In honorem Gernot Nussbächer*, Braşov 2004.

Anton E., *Organizarea breslelor din Baia Mare şi Cluj în secolul al XVII-lea* [The Organization of the Guilds in Baia Mare and Cluj in the 17th Century], in "Hrisovul, Bulletin of the Faculty of Archivistics" (Bucharest), new series, tom III, Bucharest 1998.

Id., *Statutul breslei măcelarilor din Baia Mare (1652)* [The Statute of the Butchers' Guild in Baia Mare], in "Hrisovul", new series, tom VI-VII, Bucharest 2001.

Armbruster A., *The Portrayal of the Transylvanian Romanian in Saxon Historical Writings between the Fifteenth and the Eighteenth Centuries*, in Lászlo Péter (ed.), *Historians and the History of Transylvania*, New York 1992.

Aurel Pop I., *Instituții medievale românești. Adunările cneziale și nobiliare (boierești) în secolele XIV-XVI* [Romanian Medieval Institutions. The Assemblies of 'Cnezi' and Nobles (boyars) from the 14th to the 16th Century], Cluj Napoca 1991.

Id., *Națiunea românească medievală* [The Mediaeval Romanian Nation], Bucharest 1998.

Bădescu I., Dungaciu D., *Sociologia și geopolitica frontierei* [The Sociology and Geopolitics of the Frontier], vol. 1, Bucharest 1995.

Bichicean Gh., *Contextul european și reprezentarea orașelor în congregațiile generale din Transilvania voievodală – secolele XIII-XVI* [The European Context and the Cities' Representations in the General "Congregations" from the Transylvanian Voivodship], in "Historia Urbana", tome IV, 1996, no. 1-2.

Cândea V. (ed.), *Istoria românilor* [The History of Romanians], vol. V, Bucharest 2003.

Cicanci O., *Structura etnică a companiilor comerciale din Transilvania* [The Ethnical Structure of Commercial Companies in Transylvania], in "Academia Română. Memoriile Secției de Științe Istorice" [The Romanian Academy. Memoirs of the Section of Historical Sciences], tom IV, 1979.

Dörner A. E., *Elita administrativă a scaunului Orăștie în veacurile XIV-XV* [The Administrative Elite of the "scaun" of Orăştia in the 14th and 15th Century], in "Yearbook of the Institute of History in Cluj", 32, 1993.

Drăgoescu A. (ed.), *Istoria României. Transilvania* [History of Romania. Transylvania], vol. I, Cluj-Napoca 1997.

Feneşan C., Lazăr I., *Trei statute de breaslă de la Hunedoara din prima jumătate a secolului al XVII-lea* [Three Guild Statutes in Hunedoara in the First Half of the 17th Century], in "Sargetia", 14, 1979.

Holban M. (ed.), *Călători străini despre țările române* [Foreign Travelers about the Romanian Countries], vol. I-V, Bucharest 1968-1973.

Jinga, V., *Probleme fundamentale ale Transilvaniei* [Transylvania's Fundamental Problems], 2nd edition, Braşov 1995, p. 263.

Lechințan V., *Achiziții de produse agricole și meșteșugărești ale municipalității clujene de la țăranii români. Secolul al XVI-lea* [Cluj Municipalities' Acquisitions of Agricultural Products and of Handicrafts from Romanian Peasants. The 16th Century], in "Acta Musei Porolissensis", (AMP) XVIII, 1994.

Lupaş I.., *Sibiul ca centru al vieții românești din Ardeal* [Sibiu as the Center of the Romanian Life in Transylvania], in „Anuarul Institutului de istorie națională din Cluj" [The Yearbook of the Institute of National History in Cluj], nr. 4-5, 1926-1927.

Marcu L. (ed.), *Constituțiile Aprobate ale Transilvaniei (1653)* [The Sanctioned Constitutions of Transylvania (1653)], Cluj-Napoca 1997.

Meschendörfer H., Mittelstrass O. (eds.), *Siebenbürgen auf Alten Karten. Lazarus/Tannstetter1528, Johannes Honterus 1532, Wolfgang Lazius 1552/1556*, Heidelberg 1996.

Nägler D., *Breasla blănarilor din Sibiu în cursul secolelor XIV-XVIII* [The Furriers' Guild of Sibiu from the 14th to the 18th Century], in "Studii şi comunicări. Muzeul Brukenthal Sibiu. Arheologie Istorie", [Studies and Communications. The Brukenthal Muzeum Sibiu. Archaeology History], 14, 1969.

Nussbächer G., *Contribuții la istoria administrației orașului Brașov în perioada medievală (secolele XVII-XVIII)* [Contributions to the History of the City of Braşov's Administration in Medieval Times (17th / 18th centuries)], 2nd part, in "Historia Urbana", tome IV, 1996, no. 1-2.

Pap F., *Contribuții noi cu privire la biografia primului tipograf român* [New Contributions to the Biography of the First Romanian Printing Worker], in "Acta Musei Napocensis", 22-23, 1985-1986.

Pascu Ş., *Meșteșugurile din Transilvania până în secolul al XVI-lea* [Handicrafts from Transylvania up until the 16th Century], Bucharest 1954.

Pascu Ş., Ştefănescu Ş. et al. (eds.), *Documenta Romaniae Historica,* series C, *Transilvania (1366-1370)*, vol. 13, Bucharest 1994.

Pintescu F., *Românii din Transilvania la sfârşitul secolului XVI şi începutul secolului XVII* [Romanians from Transylvania at the end of the 16th Century and the Beginning of the 17th Century], Suceava 2004.

Pirenne H., *Medieval cities. Their origins and the revival of trade*, Princeton 1946.

Prodan D., *Iobăgia în Transilvania în sec. XVI* [Serfdom in Transylvania in the 16th Century], vol. 1, Bucharest 1967.

Id., *Supplex Libellus Valachorum*, Bucharest 1984

Răduţiu A., Gyémant L., *Autonomie şi integrare. Şcheii Braşovului între suburbiu şi oraş* [Autonomy and Integration. Şcheii Braşovului between Suburb and City], in "Historia Urbana", tom I, 1993, nr. 2.

Ştefănescu Ş., Mureşanu C. (eds.), *Istoria Românilor* [The History of Romanians], vol. IV, Bucharest 2001.

Wallerstein I., *The Modern World System: Capitalist Agriculture and the Origins of the European World-Economy in the Sixteenth Century*, New York 1974.

From Christians to Members of an Ethnic Community: Creating Borders in the City of Thessaloniki (1800-1912)

Iakovos D. Michailidis
Aristotle University of Thessaloniki

Abstract

The chapter focuses on the division of the Christian millet of the city of Thessaloniki into different and ambivalent ethnic groups during the 19th and the beginning of the 20th century. The formation and operation of the Greek and Bulgarian communities of the city, the relations between them and the policy of the Ottoman authorities are some of the related subjects analyzed. As a result of this ethnic clash, the Bulgarian community of the city declined gradually until eventually it disappeared. This was a general phenomenon, a by-product of the policy of national homogenization followed by almost all the Balkan nation states at the beginning of the 20th century.

Το άρθρο εστιάζει στις σταδιακή διαίρεση του ορθόδοξου χριστιανικού μιλίετ της πόλης της Θεσσαλονίκης σε αντιμαχόμενα εθνικά στρατόπεδα κατά τη διάρκεια του 19ου αιώνα και στα αρχές του 20ου αιώνα. Ειδικότερα, εξετάζεται η συγκρότηση και η λειτουργία της ελληνικής και της βουλγαρικής κοινότητας της πόλης, οι μεταξύ τους σχέσεις και οι αντιπαραθέσεις καθώς και η στάση που τήρησαν οι οθωμανικές αρχές. Αποτέλεσμα της σύγκρουσης των δύο εθνικών στρατοπέδων υπήρξε η σταδιακή παρακμή και η εξαφάνιση της βουλγαρικής κοινότητας της πόλης, φαινόμενο που όμως δεν αποτελεί εξαίρεση, αλλά χαρακτηρίζει εν πολλοίς την πολιτική της εθνικής ομογενοποίησης που ακολούθησαν όλα τα βαλκανικά κράτη στις αρχές του 20ου αιώνα.

Brief historical note

The city of Thessaloniki, also known as Salonica in English, was founded by the King of Macedonia, Kassandros in 316 BC, and got its name from his wife, who was Alexander the Great's sister. During the years after its foundation, Thessaloniki acquired great reputation, mainly due to its strategic location, and developed into an important political and economical hub in southeastern Europe. Galerius, who was the ruler of one of the two provinces of the Eastern Roman Empire, chose Thessaloniki in 300 AD to become the seat of his empire. During the Byzantine era the city developed into '*Symvasilevousa*' [co-reigning], a term suggesting that at that period it was ranked second following Constantinople. Thessaloniki was conquered by the Ottoman Turks in 1430. It remained under Ottoman rule for about five centuries, until 1912, when the Greek army entered the city. During these centuries the city managed to maintain its reputation, although it was hit by severe natural disasters, such as destructive earthquakes and epidemic diseases. At the same time, it became a center of attraction for thousands of new inhabitants from its hinterland, but mostly for thousands of Sephardic Jews who arrived at the city during the 15th and 16th centuries, mainly from the Iberian and Italian peninsulas, fleeing the Inquisition's persecutions.

The years of misleading cosmopolitanism

On 22 February 1908 Theodoros Askitis, an interpreter of the Greek Consulate in Thessaloniki, was assassinated while walking along one of the city's busy main roads. Askitis' assassination shocked the Greek community of Thessaloniki and his funeral turned into a protest demonstration. The results of the investigation carried out by the Ottoman authorities of the city revealed that Askitis was assassinated by Bulgarians[1]. In retaliation the Greeks killed three Bulgarians and injured another one[2].

Askitis' assassination was just one incident in the dispute between the Greeks and Bulgarians of Thessaloniki at a time when the conflict between the two countries over the acquisition of the geographic region of Macedonia had reached its peak. However, only a few decades earlier, these groups along with other ethnic groups in Thessaloniki coexisted more or less peacefully.

In the winter of 1812, the English traveller Henry Holland had made a stop in Thessaloniki as a part of his tour through Macedonia and Thessaly. According to his testimony, at the time the city's inhabitants amounted to 70,000 and it was the Ottoman Empire's third largest city in the Balkans after Constantinople and Adrianople. Holland was impressed by the busy life of the city, as well as by the commercial activities of its port. The English traveller distinguished four notable population groups, the Greeks, the Turks, the Jews and the Franks (i.e. Westerners), who lived together in harmony. The characteristic scene in a Turkish café in the city described by Holland in which "Turks, Greeks and Albanians slept, while others smoked, sang or spoke loudly", is indicative of a multinational and tolerant city. The Greeks amounted to approximately 2,000 families and most of them were involved in commerce[3]. Holland made no reference to other Christian communities in the city, which is justifiable since in the early 19th century the population in the Ottoman Empire was distinguished according to religion. Thus, the Ecumenical Patriarchate was the protector of the subjugated Orthodox Christians, regardless of ethnicity and language. Holland's report was confirmed a few decades later by Sir Henry Layard. In 1842 Layard visited the city in order to investigate the political movement that was developing among its Slav-speaking inhabitants, which some had considered to be Bulgarian, but found them stating that they were Greek[4]. Thus, by the end of the 1860s, the Christian inhabitants, Greek-, Slav- and Vlach-speaking, were loyal to the Ecumenical Patriarchate, and when asked if they were Greek or Bulgarian, the educated replied that they were Greeks, while the rest said that they were Christians.

That was the cosmopolitanism era for the city of Thessaloniki, the 'golden' era of the 19th century, when the only discernible, but not particularly strong, frontiers were religious. These frontiers separated the Muslims from the Christians, the Jews and the Armenians. The city had evolved into an important trade hub, enjoying the prosperity of its economic growth. Tens of steamboats made sure that it had a regular connection to Constantinople, Piraeus, Corfu, and Triest, while the European retailers and trade agents were taking care of the Macedonian inland product export, especially cotton, to the markets of the west[5]. Nevertheless, barriers to economic growth and social prosperity were still being created by pirates who ravaged the Thermaic Gulf. Thus, in June 1832, about seventy to eighty pirate ships seized the cargo of many of the ships of the western powers which stayed in the harbor. Only six years before, in 1826, a great fire had turned a large part of the city into ruins[6].

Creating ethnic camps

The situation started to change gradually after 1850, especially during the last quarter of the 19th century. On the one hand, the outbreak of national liberation revolutions in the Balkans, with the Greeks in the lead, gradually poisoned the relations among the inhabitants, especially between the subjugated Christians and the ruling Moslems[7]. So, in 1853 Ottoman soldiers who were passing through the city's Greek quarter caused damage to many of the houses, including the Greek and Russian Consulates[8]. This was followed by the gradual deterioration of relations within the Christian community itself, particularly after the national disillusionment of the Bulgarians, which was indicated by the symbolic move of establishing the Bulgarian Exarchate in 1870. This fact constituted the dividing line in the Macedonian Issue, since it split the Christian Orthodox millet. All Christians who followed the Bulgarian Exarchate were gradually incorporated into the Bulgarian national camp. To the contrary, all those who remained loyal to the Ecumenical Patriarchate identified themselves with the Greek side.

This gradual division of the Christian Orthodox millet of the Ottoman Macedonia into ethnic camps was the main feature of the last quarter of the 19th and early 20th century. It divided not only the different Christian language groups, but whole families too. Thus, it was a very common phenomenon that members of the same family would accede to different ethnic camps. Equally common was the phenomenon that people, families, or even whole villages would change over from one religious camp to the other, either because of necessity or due to other pressures. The English journalist Henry Brailsford who traveled in Macedonia at the beginning of the 20th century asked a peasant: "Is your village Greek ... or Bulgarian?" "Well it is Bulgarian now but four years ago it was Greek" the peasant replied[9]. Language diversity and the difficulty of attributing ethnic identities on the basis of language are clear from Victor Berard's travelling memoirs. Berard was a French traveler who visited Macedonia at the end of the 19th and the beginning of the 20th century. Two peasants, faced with they replied to one of his questions on that subject replied: "'We don't speak Greek here. We are not Greeks. We are Bulgarians', a reply given using the clearest Greek of the Greek world"[10]. Here is how one of the Greek representatives in Macedonia at the beginning of the 20th century describes the situation:

> The other day, five peasants, whom we always thought of as being on our side, came to the consulate. But last year they rose up in arms on the side of the *comitadjiis*[11]. So I tell them, you are *comitadjiis*. Of course not, they replied, but we want our freedom and so we are either on the Greek side or on the Bulgarian. This depends on which direction the wind of freedom blows from, the south or the north [...] The self serving notables were blackmailing the consulates. I remember a notable at Poroiia[12], after not having succeeded in enrolling his older son as a scholar in the Greek High School, he enrolled him at the Romanian school and created a Romanian community at Ano Poroiia. Next year, after not having succeeded in enrolling his second-born son as a scholar, he enrolled him at the Bulgarian School and created a Bulgarian community at Kato Poroiia. This constitutes a sad example of self serving attitude and liquidity of views, which luckily did not happen very often[13].

There was virtually a form of civil war among the Christian Orthodox people of the Ottoman Empire, creating civic frontiers between them[14]. Indeed, according to some of the observers, the division at the same time constituted a form of political discrimination of employment[15], since the rich and educated traders and bourgeois acceded to the Greek camp, while mainly the non educated and poor peasants constituted the Bulgarian group[16].

This split was soon detected in the city of Thessaloniki where followers of the Patriarchate and the Exarchate forged their own paths, with the former being increasingly identified with the Greeks, and the latter with the Bulgarians. According to the available statistical data, in 1863 the Slav-speaking families were no more than 500, approximately 6,000 individuals who were mainly builders and shop owners (dairymen), and they lived together with the remaining Christian families. After 1870 the number of Slav-speaking families increased with labourers from Central and Western Macedonia streaming into the city due to urbanisation. Indeed, a distinct Exarchist community began to form, which also differed from the Greek one spatially. The population increase of the Exarchist community was also accompanied by spiritual progress. Thus, in 1871 the city's first Bulgarian School was founded[17] , and in 1876 the first Exarchist church opened. This was preceded in 1862 by the opening of the first Bulgarian bookshop by

V. Mantsov[18]. Also, in 1869 a newspaper titled "Salonica" was published in four languages and circulated every Friday. In September 1880, the city's renowned Bulgarian Gymnasium was founded and was attended in the following years by many great figures of the Bulgarian nationalist movement. Lastly, the founding of the Bulgarian Commercial Agency contributed to the developing conflict with the Greek element[19].

In the early 20th century the population of Thessaloniki amounted to over 130,000 inhabitants. According to some estimates, of these, about 80,000 were Jews, 30,000 were Greeks, 20,000 were Moslems and only 1,000 were Bulgarians and generally members of the Exarchist community[20]. On the other hand, the official Bulgarian statistical data of the same period gave 10,000 Bulgarians and only 16,000 Greeks[21]. The different population figures regarding the city's Greek and Bulgarian communities are due to the different criteria used by the two statistical surveys for recording the Slav-speaking population. The Greeks used the inhabitants' national conscience as a criterion, whereas the Bulgarians used language. In this way they both interpreted, according to their own judgements, the feelings of a significant population group, that of the Slav-speaking people, who in the early 20th century were distinguished much more by their religious faith than by their ethnic choice[22]. However, it is reasonable to suggest that in the early 20th century the Bulgarian community of Thessaloniki could claim over 5,000 members, who were retailers and labourers living in separate quarters in the area of the railway station, as well as in the western and south-eastern parts of the city. Also living in the city were approximately 10,000 Western and central Europeans who were gathered in a quarter near the port and the marketplace, whereas there was also a scanty Armenian community with 474 members[23]. In the early 20th century, 86 schools of all levels, which represented 13 ethnic communities, operated in the city. Of the existing Orthodox Christian schools, 20 were Greek and had a total of 3,857 pupils, six were Bulgarian with 698 pupils, two were Romanian with 140 pupils and four were Serbian with 240 pupils[24].

Thessaloniki had a remarkable port with a mooring capacity of over 3,000 ships in 1904. It was the seat of the *vilayet* (administrative unit in the Ottoman Empire), whereas its railway links to Constantinople (Istanbul), Monastir (Bitola) and Belgrade gave the city a cosmopolitan air. In 1905 the Scottish journalist John Foster Fraser had made a stop in the city. He was impressed by the European atmosphere, the elegance of the women and the hotels along the waterfront that could be compared to those in Chamonix. The population lived in peace, they dressed in almost the same way and one had to pay particular attention to the people's characteristics in order to distinguish the Turks, the Greeks, the Armenians, the Bulgarians or the Jews. "There are three Sundays a week in Salonika" noted Fraser, "Friday for the Moslems, Saturday for the Jews and Sunday itself for the Christians. Or rather there is no Sunday at all, for there is never a day when you notice any cessation in businesses"[25]. The observations of Allen Upward, another traveller who visited Thessaloniki three years later, were more or less similar[26].

The dissolution of the non Greek Christian elements

The city of Thessaloniki constituted the conspiratorial centre for Bulgarian activity in Macedonia. Here the Internal Macedonian Revolutionary Organization (IMRO) was formed in 1893. This was an armed organisation which aimed at the autonomy of Macedonia and its final union with Bulgaria[27]. The Bulgarian revolutionary campaign reached its peak in April 1903 when Bulgarian anarchists blew up the French steamship *Guadalquivir* and planted a bomb in the Ottoman Bank. The Ottoman reaction was particularly harsh. Over 100 Bulgarians were killed during that same night, with many others tortured in the local prisons[28]. Among them were distinguished members of the city's Bulgarian community[29]. Both this and subsequent Bulgarian revolutionary movements was a source of discontent among the Greek community of Thessaloniki. In fact, in February 1904 the city's Greek inhabitants held a massive protest demonstration[30].

However, despite the noteworthy activities of the Bulgarian revolutionary organisations in the city, efforts to consolidate the Bulgarian community proved to be exceptionally difficult. The difference was not only in terms of numbers, it was also in relation to the financial strength of the city's Greek element. As a result, the Bulgarians remained in the shadow of the Greek community[31]. In fact, Bulgarian activities inevitably provoked the reaction of the Greek element. In early 1906 Athanasios Souliotis Nikolaidis, a young Greek army second lieutenant, settled in the city in order to coordinate the Greek defence. Very soon thereafter Souliotis formed the "Thessaloniki Organisation", an active, yet secret Greek network. In the beginning, the members of the Organisation changed the signs of their stores into Greek. Afterwards, members of the Organisation gathered information on the activities of their opponents and watched for suspicious activity. They often started economic struggles, mainly against the Bulgarians, since they forbade all Greeks to deal with them, resorting to violent actions such as threats, beatings and damaging property. Thus, for example, the activities of the Greek organisation led to the opening of Greek shops in Bulgarian quarters, whereas Greek construction workers from Epirus moved to the city, earning approximately the same wages as the Bulgarians. The number of Greek construction workers in the city soon quintupled. At the same time, the three sectarian grocery stores in the Greek quarter of Agia Triada were forced to close down, whereas a large building plot in the Bulgarian quarter known as Transvaal was purchased by Greeks with the financial help of the Organisation. Also, in April 1907, following the orders of the Greek Organisation, the city's Greeks attempted to cancel a festive show that was being prepared by the Bulgarian community. It is characteristic that the Greek employees of the neighbouring café went on strike on the day of the show, whereas the Ottoman owners were informed that the Greeks were displeased with the fact that the venue was offered to the Bulgarians and were threatening to boycott them[32]. Indeed, in certain cases the violation of the Organisation's orders brought about harsh punishment. For example, in June 1907 a well-known Greek real estate agent of the city was executed by the Organisation's

Execution Department for continuing to sell building plots and houses to Bulgarians. A well-known Bulgarian merchant had the same fate. He was executed by the Organisation's agents. The house of the priest of the schismatic church of Agia Triada was also burnt down and so he was forced to leave the area in the end. The Bulgarian population of Thessaloniki was practically the exclusive target of the Greek Organisation. It is indicative that during the same time the economic cooperation between the city's Greek and Jewish communities continued harmoniously[33]. Summing up the work of the Thessaloniki Organisation, the instigator Athanasios Souliotis Nikolaidis mentions in his memoirs:

> One of the main accomplishments of our Organisation was that it protected the Greek community of Macedonia from our great passion and frailty, political parties' disputes. The initiates were the ones who were setting the example. But above all, it was the participation of almost every person of the same descent that benefited the real anti-Bulgarian struggle. They were past words, they were no longer declaiming among themselves (Greek people of Thessaloniki) against the Bulgarians and the other enemies of the Nation. Instead, they were taking systematic, drastic action against them, each one according to his powers. Due to the fact that each day they were sensing the common danger and quite often they could see their struggle vindicated, they felt as if they were comrades-in-arms[34].

Political assassinations, such as those just described, became common practice throughout Macedonia and were of course also adopted in the city of Thessaloniki. "Terrorism was necessary", writes Konstantinos Mazarakis-Ainian, an officer of the Greek army, who was serving in the Greek Consulate of Thessaloniki[35]. Summing up the purpose of political assassinations were serving, the officer of the Greek army Dimitrios Kakkavos observed:

> ... every assassination of political nature had to be specifically intended, and not just to saturate blood-thirsty instincts. Instead, it had to satisfy specific causes, such as to break off transportation, punish someone who had been corrupted by money and had turned into a traitor, punish a spiritless defector, to elevate our orders' status, and finally to eliminate personal reactions of a capable and courageous opponent... It was usual practice for each political assassination to place on every assassinated person's body a letter justifying the punishment, so as not to create any confusion that the death was a result of a random accident, but it constituted the fulfillment of a specific cause, for which the victim had been chosen[36].

According to the available archival records, out of the 4,000 assassinations with political motives that were recorded in the whole of Greek Macedonia in the period between 1901 and 1912, 13 took place in the city of Thessaloniki[37]. Of these, only Askitis was Greek, whereas another one of the assassinated individuals was considered to be a Vlach traitor who was executed by the Greeks for being an instigator of the assassination of the Greek metropolitan bishop of Korytsa. The remaining eleven were Bulgarians and were probably executed in retaliation for the assassination of Askitis. They included a Bulgarian churchwarden, a doctor, a merchant and eight labourers who worked at the

Allatini brick factory. Apart from the aforementioned 13 executed individuals, there were also many unsuccessful attempted murders, such as those that took place in central parts of the city against the interpreter of the Bulgarian Commercial Agency and the inspector of the Romanian schools, as well as the injury of the Bulgarian interpreter of the Russian consulate. A regime of terror was being imposed, which the Ottoman authorities of the city could not or did not attempt to contain, considering that none of the perpetrators were ever arrested[38]. The Ottomans had every reason to incourage disputes among the Christians, sometimes helping one side and then the other, in an attempt to protect themselves from losing power. An indication of the indifference which surrounded the way the Ottoman authorities were treating the Greek-Bulgarian conflict is the fact that Askitis' assassination took place right across the building where the Ottoman police had its headquarters, without the slightest reaction on the part of the Ottoman authorities.

This third period of the confrontation among Christians in the city of Thessaloniki is characterized by the distinct constitution of ethnic camps and identities, as well as the strict spatial entrenchment of the rival ethnic groups, mainly the Greeks and the Bulgarians. They were living in separate quarters, avoiding any kind of exchange and remained in a constant state of tension.

The economic retaliation and political assassinations finally brought results that were to the advantage of the Greek side. By 1908, both in the city of Thessaloniki and in south Macedonia, Bulgarian revolutionary activity had subsided significantly, whereas that on the Greek side had significantly increased. The Young Turk Revolution in 1908 in Thessaloniki temporarily interrupted the Greek-Bulgarian dispute regarding the future of the region, however it was unable to turn back the division between the two different communities that no longer communicated spatially or economically with each other[39]. Eventually the Balkan Wars of 1912-13 and the cession of Thessaloniki to Greece in October 1912, just a few hours before the arrival of the Bulgarian army, signalled the gradual decline of the city's non-Greek communities. Right after Thessaloniki's administrative incorporation into the Greek state there was a period of assimilation of the different ethnic and religious groups into the newly-acquired territories, which at some points was accompanied by pressures on minority populations in order to make them flee the country[40]. As regards the Bulgarian community of the city, it rapidly declined since Greek-Bulgarian relations were particularly strained after 1910. Greece and Bulgaria found themselves on different sides during the Second Balkan War in 1913, and were also engaged into a harsh conflict during the First World War. This fact had very unpleasant consequences on both ethnic communities. According to the census data, in 1916 the population of Thessaloniki amounted to 165,704 inhabitants, out of which 68,205 were Greek, 61,400 were Jews, 30,000 were Moslems and only 1,800 were Bulgarians[41]. Thus, within a decade the city's Bulgarian population decreased from around 6,000 to 1,800 individuals. At the same time, the Bulgarian school closed and the building which housed it was destroyed in the following years. During the inter-war period nothing remained of the Exarchist tradition of the city.

Notes

1 Museum of the Macedonian Struggle (ed.), *Η τελευταία φάση της ένοπλης αναμέτρησης στη Μακεδονία (1907-1908). 100 έγγραφα από το Αρχείο του Υπουργείου των Εξωτερικών της Ελλάδος* [The Last Phase of the Armed Conflict in Macedonia (1907-1908). 100 documents from the Historical Archive of the Greek Foreign Ministry], Thessaloniki 1998, pp. 202-215.

2 D. Dakin, *The Greek Struggle in Macedonia 1897-1913*, Thessaloniki, 1966, p. 373, see also A. Zannas, *Αναμνήσεις* [Memoirs], in Ίδρυμα Μελετών Χερσονήσου Αίμου [Institute for Balkan Studies] (ed.), *Ο Μακεδονικός Αγώνας. Απομνημονεύματα* [The Macedonian Struggle. Memoirs], Thessaloniki 1984, p. 117.

3 H. Holland, *Ταξίδι στη Μακεδονία και Θεσσαλία (1812-1813)* [Journey in Macedonia and Thessaly], Greek trans. Giorgos Karavitis, Athens 1989, pp. 181-211.

4 M. Mazower, *Salonica. City of Ghosts. Christians, Muslims and Jews 1430-1950*, London 2004, p. 258.

5 K. Vacalopoulos, *Οικονομική λειτουργία του μακεδονικού και θρακικού χώρου στα μέσα του 19ου αιώνα στα πλαίσια του διεθνούς εμπορίου* [Economic operation in Macedonia and Thrace in the middle of the 19th century], Thessaloniki 1980; see also Emile Themopoulou, *Salonique, 1800-1875: Conjoncture Economique et Mouvement Commercial*, unpublished Ph.D Thesis, Paris 1994.

6 K. Vacalopoulos, *Πως είδαν οι Ευρωπαίοι πρόξενοι στη Θεσσαλονίκη την κατάσταση στη Μακεδονία τον περασμένο αιώνα* [How the European consuls have described the situation in Thessaloniki in the last century], in "Μακεδονικά", 1980, 20, pp. 54, 59.

7 The only distinct difference up to 1850 in the city was the contrast between the Christians and the Moslems. In fact, both during the 1821 Greek Revolution and during every other Greek revolutionary movement, the Ottoman authorities punished the city's Christian element harshly. See A. Vacalopoulos, *A History of Salonica*, Thessaloniki 1993, pp. 99-120.

8 K. Vacalopoulos, *Πως είδαν οι Ευρωπαίοι πρόξενοι στη Θεσσαλονίκη την κατάσταση στη Μακεδονία τον περασμένο αιώνα* [How the European consuls have described the situation in Thessaloniki in the last century], in "Μακεδονικά", 1980, 20, p. 60.

9 H. Brailsford, *Macedonia. Its Races and their Future*, London 1906, p.102.

10 V. Berard, *Τουρκία και ελληνισμός. Οδοιπορικό στη Μακεδονία* [Turkey and Greece. Travelling in Macedonia], Greek trans., Athens 1987, p. 141.

11 Bulgarian rebels at the beginning of the 20th century.

12 A village in Greek Macedonia

13 P. Argyropoulos, *Απομνημονεύματα* [Memoirs], in Ίδρυμα Μελετών Χερσονήσου Αίμου [Institute for Balkan Studies] (ed.), *Ο Μακεδονικός Αγώνας. Απομνημονεύματα* [The Macedonian Struggle. Memoirs], Thessaloniki 1984, pp. 27, 46.

14 V. Gounaris, *Εθνοτικές ομάδες και κομματικές παρατάξεις στη Μακεδονία των Βαλκανικών Πολέμων* [Ethnic Groups and Political Parties in Macedonia during the Balkan Wars], in *Η Ελλάδα των Βαλκανικών Πολέμων*, 1910-1914 [Greece in the Balkan Wars, 1910-1914], Athens 1993. pp. 189-202.

15 H. Vermeulen. *Greek Cultural Dominance among the Orthodox Population of Macedonia during the Last Period of Ottoman Rule*, in A. Block, H. Driessen (eds), *Cultural Dominance in the Mediterranean Area*, Nijmegen 1984, pp. 225-246.

16 J. K. Cowan, *Dance and the Body Politics in Northern Greece*, Princeton 1990, pp. 40-41.

[17] On the activities of the Bulgarian gymnasium in the city see B. Raionov, *Преди половин бек. Обществена и просвета деиност на солунските Балгари през 1881-1883 Г.* [Half a Century ago. The Civic and Educational activities of the Bulgarians of Thessaloniki], Sofia 1934.

[18] A. Ilieva, *Парвата балгарска книзарница в Солун* [The first Bulgarian gymnasium in Thessaloniki], in Πολιτιστική Εταιρεία Επιχειρηματιών Βορείου Ελλάδος [Cultural Society of Businessmen in Northern Greece] (ed.), *Θεσσαλονίκη και Φιλιππούπολη σε παράλληλους δρόμους 18ος-20ός αιώνας* [Thessaloniki and Philipoupoli in parallel roads], Thessaloniki 2000, pp. 373-387.

[19] On the establishment of the Bulgarian community in Thessaloniki, also see the article by B. Lory, *Soloun, ville slave?*, in G. Veinstein (ed.), *Salonique 1850-1918. La "ville des Juifs" et le reveil des Balkans*, Paris 1992, pp. 129-137.

[20] The data on the population composition of Macedonia comes from the Ottoman census that was carried out by the city's Ottoman governor Hilmi Pasha. See A. Chalkiopoulos, *Μακεδονία. Βιλαέτια Θεσσαλονίκης-Μοναστηρίου* [Macedonia. Vilaets of Thessaloniki and Monastir], Athens 1910, p. 1.

[21] V. Kancov, *Избрани происведениа* [Selection of Works], vol. 2, Sofia 1970, p. 440.

[22] For a comprehensive analysis over the population variety in geographical Macedonia and the Balkan irredentist visions on it see I. Koliopoulos, *Η «πέραν Ελλάς» και οι «άλλοι» Έλληνες (1800-1912)* ['Yonder' Greece and the 'Other' Greeks], Thessaloniki 2003.

[23] I. K. Hassiotis (ed.), *The Armenian Community of Salonica. History, Present Situation and Prospects*, Thessaloniki 2005, p. 24.

[24] On education in the city of Thessaloniki, see S. Ziogou-Karastergiou, *Η εκπαίδευση στη Θεσσαλονίκη: Η περίοδος της Τουρκοκρατίας* [Education in the City of Thessaloniki: The Ottoman Period], in I. Hassiotis (ed.), *Τοις αγαθοίς βασιλεύουσα. Θεσσαλονίκη. Ιστορία και πολιτισμός* [Thessaloniki. History and Civilization], vol. 2, Thessaloniki 1997, pp. 238-257.

[25] J. Foster Fraser, *Pictures from the Balkans*, London 1912, pp. 183-189.

[26] A. Upward, *The East End of Europe. The Report of an unofficial Mission to the European Provinces of Turkey on the Eve of the Revolution*, London 1908, pp. 160-162.

[27] For the establishment of IMRO see D. M. Perry, *The Politics of Terror. The Macedonian Revolutionary Movements*, 1893-1903, London 1988.

[28] Zannas, *Αναμνήσεις* cit, pp. 74-77.

[29] On the events of 1903 see Y. Megas, *Οι 'βαρκάρηδες' της Θεσσαλονίκης. Η αναρχική βουλγαρική ομάδα και οι βομβιστικές ενέργειες του 1903* [The anarchic Bulgarian group and the bomb explosions in 1903], Athens 1994.

[30] V. Georgiev, S. Trifonov, *Грущката и србската пропаганди в Македониа,краиат на XIX – нацалото на XX век* [Greek and Serbian propaganda in Macedonia, late 19th - early 20th centuries], Sofia 1995, p. 17.

[31] G. Abbott, *The Tale of a Tour in Macedonia*, London 1903, p.21.

[32] Museum of the Macedonian Struggle (ed.), *Η τελευταία φάση της ένοπλης αναμέτρησης στη Μακεδονία (1907-1908)* cit., pp. 104-105.

[33] A. Souliotis-Nikolaidis, *Απομνημονεύματα* [Memoirs], in Ίδρυμα Μελετών Χερσονήσου Αίμου [Institute for Balkan Studies] (ed.), *Ο Μακεδονικός Αγώνας. Απομνημονεύματα* [The Macedonian Struggle. Memoirs], Thessaloniki, 1984, pp. 326-330.

[34] Souliotis, Nikolaidis, *Απομνημονεύματα* cit., p. 330.

[35] K. Mazarakis-Ainian, *Ο Μακεδονικός Αγών. Αναμνήσεις*, [The Macedonian Struggle. Memoirs], in Ίδρυμα Μελετών Χερσονήσου Αίμου [Institute for Balkan Studies] (ed.), *Ο Μακεδονικός Αγώνας. Απομνημονεύματα* The Macedonian Struggle. Memoirs], Thessaloniki 1984, p. 206.

36 D. Kakkavos, *Απομνημονεύματα* [Memoirs], Thessaloniki 1972, p. 87.

37 These data come from British and Austrian diplomatic reports of the time, which have been entered into the electronic database of the Research Centre for Macedonian History and Documentation of the Thessaloniki Museum of the Macedonian Struggle.

38 Kakkavos, *Απομνημονεύματα* cit., pp. 91-93.

39 For a comprehensive analysis of the Young-Turk Revolution and for the situation that followed see D. Dakin, *The Greek Struggle in Macedonia* 1897-1913, Thessaloniki 1966, pp. 375-421.

40 The policy of assimilation based on ethnic, religious and linguistic "purity" was not only a Greek paradox. It was followed by almost all the Balkan states at the beginning of the 20th century.

41 Sp. Loukatos, *Πολιτειογραφικά Θεσσαλονίκης, Νομού και πόλης, στα μέσα της δεκαετίας του 1910, in Κέντρο Ιστορίας Θεσσαλονίκης* [Thessaloniki History Centre] (ed.), *Η Θεσσαλονίκη μετά το 1912. Συμπόσιο* [Thessaloniki after 1912. Symposium], Thessaloniki 1986, pp. 101-129.

Bibliography

Abbott G., *The Tale of a Tour in Macedonia*, London 1903.

Argyropoulos P., *Απομνημονεύματα [*Memoirs] in Ίδρυμα Μελετών Χερσονήσου Αίμου [Institute for Balkan Studies] (ed.), *Ο Μακεδονικός Αγώνας. Απομνημονεύματα* [The Macedonian Struggle. Memoirs], Thessaloniki 1984, pp. 3-60.

Brailsford H., *Macedonia. Its Races and their Future*, London 1906.

Berard V., *Τουρκία και ελληνισμός. Οδοιπορικό στη Μακεδονία* [Turkey and Greece. Travelling in Macedonia], Greek trans., Athens 1987.

Chalkiopoulos A., *Μακεδονία. Βιλαέτια Θεσσαλονίκης-Μοναστηρίου* [Macedonia. Vilaets of Thessaloniki and Monastir], Athens 1910.

Cowan K. J., *Dance and the Body Politics in Northern Greece*, Princeton 1990.

Georgiev V., Trifonov S., *Грụцката и срубската пропаганди в Македониа,краиат на XIX – нацалото на XX век* [Greek and Serbian Propaganda in Macedonia, late 19th - early 20th centuries], Sofia 1995.

Gounaris V., *Εθνοτικές ομάδες και κομματικές παρατάξεις στη Μακεδονία των Βαλκανικών Πολέμων* [Ethnic Groups and Political Parties in Macedonia during the Balkan Wars], in *Η Ελλάδα των Βαλκανικών Πολέμων,* 1910-1914 [Greece in the Balkan Wars, 1910-1914], Athens 1993. pp. 189-202.

Dakin D., *The Greek Struggle in Macedonia 1897-1913*, Thessaloniki 1966.

Foster Fraser J., *Pictures from the Balkans*, London 1912.

Hassiotis K. I. (ed.), *The Armenian Community of Salonica. History, Present Situation and Prospects*, Thessaloniki 2005.

Holland H., *Ταξίδι στη Μακεδονία και Θεσσαλία (1812-1813)*, [Journey in Macedonia and Thessaly], Greek trans. Giorgos Karavitis, Athens 1989.

Ilieva A., *Парвата балгарска книзарница в Солун* [The first Bulgarian Bookshop in Thessaloniki], in Πολιτιστική Εταιρεία Επιχειρηματιών Βορείου Ελλάδος [Cultural Society of Businessmen in Northern Greece] (ed.), *Θεσσαλονίκη και Φιλιππούπολη σε παράλληλους δρόμους 18ος-20ός αιώνας* [Thessaloniki and Philipoupoli in parallel roads], Thessaloniki 2000, pp. 373-387.

Kakkavos D., *Απομνημονεύματα* [Memoirs], in Greek, Thessaloniki 1972.

Kancov V., *Избрани происведениа* [Selection of Works], vol. 2, Sofia 1970.

Koliopoulos I., *Η «πέραν Ελλάς» και οι «άλλοι» Έλληνες (1800-1912)* ['Yonder' Greece and the 'Other' Greeks], Thessaloniki 2003.

Loukatos Sp., *Πολιτειογραφικά Θεσσαλονίκης, Νομού και πόλης, στα μέσα της δεκαετίας του 1910*, in Κέντρο Ιστορίας Θεσσαλονίκης [Thessaloniki History Centre] (ed.), *Η Θεσσαλονίκη μετά το 1912. Συμπόσιο* [Thessaloniki after 1912. Symposium], Thessaloniki 1986, pp. 101-129.

Lory B., *Soloun, ville slave?*, in Veinstein G. (ed.), *Salonique 1850-1918. La "ville des Juifs" et le reveil des Balkans*, Paris 1992, pp. 129-137.

Mazarakis-Ainian K., *Ο Μακεδονικός Αγών. Αναμνήσεις* [The Macedonian Struggle. Memoirs], in Ίδρυμα Μελετών Χερσονήσου Αίμου [Institute for Balkan Studies] (ed.), *Ο Μακεδονικός Αγώνας. Απομνημονεύματα* [The Macedonian Struggle. Memoirs], Thessaloniki 1984, pp. 167-265

Mazower M., *Salonica. City of Ghosts. Christians, Muslims and Jews 1430-1950*, London 2004.

Megas Y., *Οι 'βαρκάρηδες' της Θεσσαλονίκης. Η αναρχική βουλγαρική ομάδα και οι βομβιστικές ενέργειες του 1903* [The anarchic Bulgarian group and the bomb explosions in 1903], Athens 1994.

Museum of the Macedonian Struggle (ed.), *Η τελευταία φάση της ένοπλης αναμέτρησης στη Μακεδονία (1907-1908). 100 έγγραφα από το Αρχείο του Υπουργείου των Εξωτερικών της Ελλάδος* [The Last Phase of the Armed Conflict in Macedonia (1907-1908). 100 documents from the Historical Archive of the Greek Foreign Ministry], Thessaloniki 1998.

Perry M. D., *The Politics of Terror. The Macedonian Revolutionary Movements, 1893-1903*, London 1988.

Raionov B., *Преди половин бек. Обстествена и просвета деиност на солунските Балгари през 1881-1883 Г.* [Half a Century ago. The Civic and Educational Activities of the Bulgarians of Thessaloniki], Sofia 1934.

Souliotis-Nikolaidis A., *Απομνημονεύματα* [Memoirs], in Ίδρυμα Μελετών Χερσονήσου Αίμου [Institute for Balkan Studies] (ed.), *Ο Μακεδονικός Αγώνας. Απομνημονεύματα* [The Macedonian Struggle. Memoirs], Thessaloniki 1984, pp. 269-337

Themopoulou E., *Salonique, 1800-1875: Conjoncture Economique et Mouvement Commercial* (unpublished Ph.D thesis, Paris 1994).

Upward A., *The East End of Europe. The Report of an unofficial Mission to the European Provinces of Turkey on the Eve of the Revolution*, London 1908.

Vacalopoulos A., *A History of Salonica*, Thessaloniki 1993.

Vacalopoulos K., *Πως είδαν οι Ευρωπαίοι πρόξενοι στη Θεσσαλονίκη την κατάσταση στη Μακεδονία τον περασμένο αιώνα* [How the European consuls have described the situation in Thessaloniki in the last century], in "Μακεδονικά", 1980, 20, pp. 48-102.

Vacalopoulos K., *Οικονομική λειτουργία του μακεδονικού και θρακικού χώρου στα μέσα του 19ου αιώνα στα πλαίσια του διεθνούς εμπορίου* [Economic operation in Macedonia and Thrace in the middle of the 19th century], Thessaloniki 1980.

Vermeulen H., *Greek Cultural Dominance among the Orthodox Population of Macedonia during the Last Period of Ottoman Rule*, in Block A., Driessen H. (eds.), *Cultural Dominance in the Mediterranean Area*, Nijmegen 1984, pp. 225-246.

Zannas A., *Αναμνήσεις* [Memoirs], in Ίδρυμα Μελετών Χερσονήσου Αίμου [Institute for Balkan Studies] (ed.), *Ο Μακεδονικός Αγώνας. Απομνημονεύματα* [The Macedonian Struggle. Memoirs], Thessaloniki 1984, pp. 65-163

Ziogou-Karastergiou S., *Η εκπαίδευση στη Θεσσαλονίκη: Η περίοδος της Τουρκοκρατίας* [Education in the City of Thessaloniki: The Ottoman Period], in Hassiotis I. (ed.), *Τοις αγαθοίς βασιλεύουσα. Θεσσαλονίκη. Ιστορία και πολιτισμός* [Thessaloniki. History and Civilization], volume 2, Thessaloniki 1997, pp. 362-378.

Ethnic, Social and Mental Frontiers in Interwar Latvia: Reflections from Baltic Germans' Autobiographies

UTE HOFMANN
Chemnitz University of Technology

ABSTRACT

The present chapter deals with ethnic, social and mental frontiers in interwar Latvian society, with special focus on Riga. It analyses the extent to which past circumstances – essentially the Baltic German[1] ascendancy – impacted on relations between Baltic Germans and Latvians after the foundation of the Republic of Latvia in 1918. It is apparent that, in the aftermath of 1918, long-established ethnic and social frontiers in Baltic society, which cleaved a German upper-class from Latvian subordinates, remained. The present study, based primarily on Baltic German autobiographical literature, is an account of mental frontiers in Latvian society from the German perspective. It explores the persistence of old attitudes and perceptions – notably German paternalism, and anxiety as a minority ethnic group – in a much altered state, and assesses the impact of these ideas on relations between Baltic Germans and Latvians.

Der Aufsatz beschäftigt sich mit ethnischen, sozialen und mentalen Grenzen in der lettischen Gesellschaft der Zwischenkriegszeit, insbesondere in der Hauptstadt Riga. Es wird untersucht, inwiefern die patriarchalischen Verhältnisse der Vergangenheit die Beziehungen zwischen Deutschbalten und Letten auch noch nach der Gründung der Republik Lettland beeinflussten. Außerdem werden die Auswirkungen der Veränderungen der politischen und gesellschaftlichen Verhältnisse im Jahr 1918 analysiert. Dabei wird davon ausgegangen, dass die über Jahrhunderte dauernde Überschneidung von ethnischen und sozialen Grenzen im Baltikum eine tiefe mentale Kluft zwischen der deutschbaltischen Oberschicht und den Letten hervorgebracht hat, die während der nur zwei Jahrzehnte dauernden Zwischenkriegszeit nicht überwunden werden konnte. Da deutschbaltische Autobiographien die Quellenbasis dieses Artikels darstellen, liegt der Schwerpunkt auf der Wahrnehmung der Deutschbalten.

Aus der Untersuchung dieser Autobiographien geht hervor, dass ethnische, soziale und mentale Grenzen die lettische Gesellschaft der Zwischenkriegszeit prägten. In den Darstel-

lungen der Jahre zwischen 1918 und 1939 können vielfältige Hinweise darauf festgestellt werden, dass auf die patriarchalischen Verhältnisse zurückgehende Stereotype wie das vom unkultivierten lettischen Bauern oder das vom gütigen deutschen Herrenmenschen sowie traditionelle Verhaltensweisen fortbestanden. Dies drückt sich beispielsweise in der Seltenheit privater Kontakte, in Problemen mit der lettischen Sprache oder in Vorbehalten gegenüber binationalen Ehen aus. Diese Muster finden sich in der Mehrzahl der ausgewerteten Autobiographien, die von Autoren unterschiedlicher sozialer Herkunft sowohl während der Zwischenkriegszeit in Lettland als auch in einem größeren zeitlichen Abstand nach der Umsiedlung niedergeschrieben wurden. So kann davon ausgegangen werden, dass sie wesentliche Tendenzen des Verhältnisses zwischen Deutschbalten und Letten widerspiegeln.

The territory which became the Republic of Latvia was traditionally multi-ethnic. Since the conquest of the region by the military order the Livonian Brothers of the Sword (*Fratres militiae Christi Livoniae*) in the 13th century, Germans had settled there. In the countryside they became the masters of the native people; in the towns they formed the upper and middle classes of merchants and skilled professionals. For centuries the Germans succeeded in maintaining this privileged status. Ethnic and social frontiers in Baltic society coalesced, and the terms "peasant" and "Latvian", "master" and "German" were used interchangeably[2]. Although serfdom had been abolished in Russia's Baltic provinces in the beginning of the 19th century, this made little difference to inter-ethnic relations. But by the second half of the century, there were indications of a shift – especially in Riga, the major Baltic Sea port and dominant urban centre in the region. Until the mid-19th century, Riga, like the other Latvian towns, had been dominated by Germans[3]. But as industrialization began, more and more Latvians moved to the city, and the proportion of Germans in Riga decreased from 43 percent in 1867 to 16 percent in 1913[4]. Furthermore, Latvians began to climb the social ranks, and develop a national consciousness: 'ethnic milieus'[5] appeared in the higher reaches of Rigan society. Ethnic groupings gradually replaced class difference as the central category of social distinction; and ethnic frontiers proved much harder to transcend than class divisions[6].

When in 1918 the Republic of Latvia was founded the situation of both Latvians and Baltic Germans changed radically. The former elite became a minority without any special privileges while their former subordinates held power. Therefore, Germans needed to redefine their relationship with their fellow citizens. From the evidence of autobiographical literature it seems that Baltic Germans responded to the establishment of the Latvian Republic by reinforcing the perceptions and attitudes which typified the now obsolete German ascendancy in Latvia; these ideas continued to have an influence on the way Baltic Germans related to Latvians. While most of the evidence herein relates to Riga, some provincial material is included to provide context; the emphasis on the city also reflects the large-scale migration of rural Baltic Germans to the capital after 1918[7], which brought about an exchange of rural and urban ideas.

Historiography and sources

Historiography has displayed a lively interest in the Baltic German community. As early as the 1930s research was conducted into their relations with the Latvians. However, these early works were influenced strongly by contemporary tensions between the two groups: Latvian historians presented the Germans as cruel oppressors, whereas German historiography stressed the German 'civilizing' achievements[8]. Later studies on the interwar period have focused mainly on aspects of the minority in legal and political terms[9], and have paid less attention to interethnic relations. (In 1995 a survey of Baltic Germans on this topic was made[10], but the results were not published.) Thus far, not much use has been made of autobiographies as historical sources[11]. An exception is the Maris Saagpakk's extensive study of Baltic German literature[12], which employs methodologies from literary and textual studies but also examines cultural memory as found in autobiographies.

If autobiographies are to be used as historical sources, it is important to note their characteristics as sources. They are 'ego-documents', which make the author's self an explicit issue of writing. This can also apply to other sources like letters or diaries, but autobiographies differ in that they describe the life story of the author, or at least parts of it, in retrospect and in a coherent style. It is common to distinguish between autobiographies and memoirs. Typically, the focus of the autobiography is on personal and mental experiences, while memoirs emphasize external events and the authors' responses to them[13]. As most of the sources used here combine elements of both approaches it is thought unnecessary to distinguish between them; the term autobiography herein shall also apply to memoirs.

Usually a certain period of time elapses between the original experience and its recording on the page. The reconstruction of one's past is a very complex process which is extremely susceptible to deviation. The instability of memory is particularly problematic – for it is continually modified by current experiences. A second problem is the selectiveness of perception and memory. Humans perceive and remember only a small part of the outside world, and when they decide to write down their memories, they must select once more. In doing so the author is constrained by the need to formulate a coherent story using creative faculties – thus provoking distortions. Therefore an autobiography is not a spontaneous account, but the result of a process of selection by an author who wishes to convey a certain impression, and has carefully selected the material and the manner in which it is related. He is influenced here by the expected response of his readers, as well as by a desire to propagate a certain interpretation of events[14].

But what do that reflections mean for scholars who wish to use autobiographies as a historical source? Should autobiographies be looked at as merely fictitious texts to be analysed by literature specialists? Traditionally, autobiographies have been examined as a genre of literature; although by the early 20th century Hans Glagau began examining autobiographies as historical sources[15]. In recent decades interest in cultural and mental historical approaches has led to increased interest in ego-documents[16]. And indeed, if the characteristics of autobiographies are taken into consideration, it can be suggested that they constitute excellent sources for the study of identities and mental frontiers. Autobiographies can help us to explore the mental world of Baltic Germans after the foundation of the Republic of Latvia. They offer windows onto Baltic German attitudes towards, and relations with, the Latvian majority. Supplementing the familiar legal and political sources, autobiographies show how the already established social gulf between Latvians and Baltic Germans created a profound and enduring mental frontier. Of course, there is the problem of the representative nature of the autobiographies; but if we compare a wide temporal and social range of sources, we can discover common tendencies in terms of perceptions and of underlying mentalities. As the authors express themselves not only as individuals, but also as members of a certain social group, it is possible to suggest some general conclusions.

The thirty-one Baltic German autobiographies used for the present study depict a very heterogeneous corpus of sources. All the authors, of whom nine were women, wrote their texts in German, but there were marked social differences. One third of the autobiographies were composed by nobles, the remainder were products of the cultured middle class, or literati. Some were written by public figures like the journalist and politician Paul Schiemann, but most were private citizens. Autobiographers came from a variety of professions: politicians and public servants, pastors, writers, farmers and housewives. Two of the authors, Elisabeth Kersten and Zenta Maurina, had a mixed Latvian-German background. However, it must be conceded that all authors belonged to the upper and middle classes. This reflects the elite position which many Baltic Germans were born to. Of course, not every Baltic German was wealthy and privileged, but their perception of and relations with the Latvians cannot be taken into account in this study.

The texts were written at different times – nine before the resettlement to then German-occupied Poland in 1939. Most, however, were written later: sixteen date from after the Second World War[17]. The time when the autobiography was written is of great importance because the text reflects the author's state of mind at the time of writing – often contemporary attitudes are projected back to the past[18]. The immense political and social changes wrought during the first half of the 20th century doubtless informed the content and tone of the autobiographies. Some writers were aware of this influence. One author, for instance, remarked in the preface to his autobiography that he had considered revising his manuscript, written prior to 1945, but decided that he did not want to "endanger originality"[19]. In a foreword, written by the son of the author, the sudden end of the memoirs in 1939 is explained by the trauma of the author leaving her beloved home[20]. Attachment to a vanishing Baltic homeland seems to have motivated many Baltic Germans to produce their autobiographies. It was common for authors to claim that they were not merely recording their own lives, but documenting moribund Baltic German society in general[21]. This justified the publication of some texts which were originally intended only for members of the writer's immediate family[22]. Finally, the radical upheavals to which the Baltic Germans were exposed between 1918 and 1945 caused insecurity – which could, in some way, be managed and overcome by the self-reflective act of creating an autobiography[23].

Frontiers in Latvian society

Relations between Baltic Germans and Latvians were influenced in part by the Germans' perceptions of themselves and of Latvians. An important means of Baltic German self-definition lay in stressing their distinct ethnicity in the Latvian and Russian surroundings. Many of the autobiographies emphasise this. Chauvinism of this type was expressed in the autobiography of Herbert von Bluhmen, written after his expulsion from Latvia in the 1920s. It included observations such as: "Except for the Baltic Germans' history knows no second land, where Germans preserved doggedly their peculiarities, through the centuries to the present day, while living in the midst of strange peoples and exposed to their cravings for power"[24]. It can be assumed that the experience of expulsion intensified the importance of von Bluhmen's German identity. But such explicit stress on German ethnicity can also be found in autobiographies of authors who argued for more harmonious relations with the Latvians – for instance, in the memoirs of Paul Schiemann, also composed before the end of the Second World War[25]. But alongside their desire to be seen as a belonging to a distinct group in a 'foreign environment', the Baltic Germans developed a strong feeling of belonging to their region. They considered the Baltic region to be their home, while Germany was a distant fatherland which held little for them. Therefore Paul Schiemann stated his goal to be "staying at home [and] staying German"[26]. However, in terms of nomenclature, many Baltic Germans did not like referring to the Republic of Latvia as their home, preferring to refer to the former provinces of Livonia and Couronia[27].

With respect to the Baltic Germans' perceptions of themselves and the Latvians, the past was an important issue. The older generation of Baltic Germans found it particularly difficult to adjust to conditions in the newly-founded Latvian state. Wilhelm von Rüdiger, a Baltic German politician, was aware of this and wrote of Baltic Germans that "they have got so much from a time which they perceived as the better one [...] that their [...] wish to continue with the outdated persisted under the changed circumstances"[28]. Unsurprisingly, many stereotypes which had their roots in the period of German ascendancy may still be found in the interwar years, written many years after that era came to an end. Traditionally, the Baltic Germans had presented themselves as benevolent masters (*Herrenmenschen*) who took care of their Latvian subordinates, while the Latvians both required and accepted willingly German tutelage[29]. While the cultural achievements of Latvians were not ignored, they were normally depicted as having been inspired and facilitated by the Baltic Germans[30]. These kinds of stereotypes endured not because they were based on personal experience[31]; the stereotype of the Latvian as an uncivilized peasant could also be 'recalled' by urban Baltic Germans who had minimal contact with rural Latvians. Baltic German stereotypes regarding Latvian society did not change after the upheavals of 1918; indeed many young Baltic Germans preserved the paternalist attitudes of older generations, despite the unequivocal alteration in the relative status of German and Latvian after the First World War. A profound mental frontier existed between Latvians and Baltic Germans, which naturally influenced interaction between both groups.

Baltic German scepticism regarding Latvian society was visible in their attitudes towards the Latvian state. During the First World War they had dreamed of a German-dominated Baltic state comprising the provinces of Estonia, Couronia and Livonia[32]. Many Baltic Germans, therefore, were disappointed when separate Latvian and Estonian states came into existence. Accordingly, the autobiographies were often hostile or pessimistic towards the Latvian Republic. Some openly rejected the state's legitimacy; others were convinced that Latvians would maltreat the German minority[33]. Some were more moderate, and affirmed loyalty to the state and willingness to participate in public life[34], even though "the state itself remained strange to our hearts"[35].

This feeling of alienation from the post-1918 state extended also to the Latvian hierarchy. Helmuth Stegmann, a municipal politician in Riga, wrote in his autobiography that the Latvian elite was "different in nature" to its German counterpart[36]. The stereotype of Latvian as uncultured peasant is very evident in Stegmann's account of the Latvian upper classes: recalling a state reception, he stressed that the Latvians' behaviour was "surprisingly civilized"[37]. Similarly, Wolfgang Wachtsmuth's perception of Latvians bore the influence of the past. Writing of his relations with officials at the Ministry of Education, he asserted that the Latvians' behaviour towards him was inhibited, because of the lingering reputation of the Baltic Germans as *Herrenmenschen*[38]. Clearly, Germans perceived their relationship with Latvians as not one of equality, and the mental frontier – based on former social, political and economic differences – persisted[39].

But Wolfgang Wachtsmuth's work is not alone in attempting to relate the behaviour of Latvians to their perceptions of Baltic Germans. Another author was convinced that the Latvian intelligentsia, feeling threatened by successful Baltic Germans, began intriguing against the Germans, who responded by separating themselves from the Latvians[40]. It is not unlikely that this somewhat paranoid analysis resulted from the author's own feelings of insecurity and harassment, and was projected on a larger scale. It is especially notable that the author identifies the urban intelligentsia as responsible for the intrigues, but refrained from indicting the lower orders. This corresponds with much that was written about rural life in the autobiographies. A frequent motive was that of peasants who were reliant upon their former Baltic German masters, and happy to follow their advice and commands[41]. The implication of all this was that Baltic German-Latvian relations were amicable and harmonious when the traditional hierarchy was in place, but became destabilized and hostile when the old order was threatened.

Interaction between ethnic groups

From the evidence of the autobiographies it seems as though personal interethnic contact, beyond the professional sphere, was rare. This particularly applied in Riga and other cities, where, for instance, Baltic Germans and Latvians lived and socialised separately. Some authors refer to the preference of Baltic Germans to reside in the salubrious neighbourhood of the *Kaiserwald* (Emperor's Wood, today *Meža Parks*). In Riga there were also German hospitals, nursing homes, sports grounds and clubs and societies[42]. The most prominent Baltic German society was the so-called "*Musse*". This was described as a "time-honoured German club", where the Baltic German nobility, merchants and literati gathered[43]. Contact with Latvians was also stymied by the language difference. In general, only those who had a Latvian parent[44], or who grew up in the countryside – with Latvian nurses and frequent contact with Latvian peasants – were bilingual[45]. It was not necessary and not usual for urban Baltic Germans to know any Latvian before 1918. This changed after the foundation of the Republic of Latvia, and Latvian was made the compulsory language of state education and the bureaucracy. While young people may have adapted to these changes, their elders refer to great difficulties encountered in trying to learn Latvian. An impressive example comes from the autobiography of Wolfgang Wachtsmuth:

> When I took office in 1920 I did not understand any Latvian at all except for some colloquial words *(Küchenausdrücke),* and I had to study this new language from the beginning at the age of 44. [...] I filled a lot of booklets with words and phrases from newspapers, laws, petitions etc. and I used every free moment to memorize this vocabulary. [...] In spring I went to the house of the Latvian Provost Pavasars in Wolmar in Livonia for several months in order to study in a Latvian environment. [...] Every few months I also engaged a Latvian man from cultured circles with whom I made conversation early in the morning before I started my work[46].

The latter remarks underline how rare contact with Latvians was for people like Wachtsmuth. The persistence of a social gulf between Latvians and Baltic Germans, which language was unable to bridge fully, is exemplified in Helmuth Stegmann's autobiography. Stegmann characterised a Baltic German municipal official from Riga as having "not only a good command of the Latvian language – which was rather unusual among us – but also a naturally benevolent relationship to the Latvian people and their educated strata"[47]. This statement suggests that not only knowledge of the Latvian language, but also unprejudiced contacts with Latvians, was considered to be exceptional. Again, the use of a term such as "benevolent" with regard to his acquaintance's relations with

Latvians suggests that the author was influenced by the paternalist stereotypes which were discussed earlier.

It may be assumed that the University of Latvia in Riga, where many Baltic Germans studied, was a field of more frequent interethnic contacts. But the autobiographies indicate the reverse, and the national and mental frontiers in Latvian interwar society also existed among young people. One former student, Sven Steenberg, wrote about a "charming Latvian student" whom he befriended at the university, but he went on to state that Germans did not normally consort with their Latvian counterparts[48]. Another former student described national students' fraternities, which propagated the notion that conflict was inevitable in a "multinational state"[49]; at the same time, however, he admitted that he never personally experienced nationalist resentment at university[50]. The same pattern can be found in many autobiographies: authors perceived a general anti-German bias, although often their own experiences with Latvians were positive.

Many Baltic German autobiographies address the issue of marriage between Baltic Germans and Latvians. Wolfgang Wachtsmuth recalled a German pastor and his Latvian wife:

> The Latvian housewife gave the German parish a special character and at first we had to cope with members of the household speaking Latvian to each other. Apparently the pastor did not feel it to be strange. He was equally familiar with both languages. His bond with the country was so strong; to him the Latvians belonged so closely to the country, that a German-Latvian relationship seemed absolutely natural to him[51].

Here, the complacent pastor's ethnically-mixed household seems completely abnormal and discomfiting to Wachtsmuth – the anecdote expresses the profound mental divide between the two communities which prevented frequent and equal contact.

Many of the autobiographies share Wachtsmuth's attitudes towards the Latvians. But there are exceptions. One is the autobiography of Zenta Maurina. Maurina was of mixed descent and had no reservations towards Latvians; nationality seemed unimportant to her with regard to personal relations. She was integrated into Latvian cultural life and, though she identified herself with the Republic of Latvia, she refused to support any nationalistic efforts[52]. However she was affected by the nationalism which dominated political and social life in Latvia in the 1930s, and detractors denigrated her for her "impure blood"[53]. She recalled:

> A professor at the University of Riga wrote in an encyclopaedia that my mother was German; and doing this he hoped to prevent me reaching a Latvian audience. [...] Indeed my mother received a German upbringing and preferred speaking German to speaking Latvian. When I was a child she prayed in German with me and she always wrote the letters for her children in German. Her own mother was German, her father a German-educated Latvian. In former times I have never thought about these facts[54].

But in the climate of nationalist tension she could not ignore such questions for long. And in the interwar period ethnic frontiers were drawn by both Latvians and the Baltic Germans, making a 'middle ground' such as that occupied by Maurina increasingly untenable.

Conclusion

The analysis of Baltic German autobiographies has shown that after the changes of 1918 old stereotypes and traditional patterns of behaviour persisted and continued to influence interaction between Latvian and Baltic German. Many Baltic Germans still perceived Latvians as uncultured peasants, while they themselves remembered their former privileged position and paternal relationship with the natives. The circumstances of the past created a mental cleavage which is evident in most of the autobiographies' treatments of the interwar period. This gulf was evident in a variety of contexts – distinct housing arrangements, the lack of interest in the Latvian language, attitudes to mixed marriages and its consequences, and interethnic contact in education or professional life. The autobiographies suggest that ethnic milieus, which were identified by Hirschhausen in Riga in the pre-war time, can also be discerned in the interwar Republic of Latvia. The pre-war ethnic frontier may well have persisted as the Baltic Germans' response to their insecurity as a former elite and a minority in a newly-founded state. But we must bear in mind that the Baltic Germans had to leave Latvia in 1939; perhaps inter-ethnic relations would have improved had the communities coexisted for more than a short twenty-one-year period.

Autobiographies provide a useful source for the study of Baltic Germans *mentalités*. The large and diverse corpus of source material betrays several common features. Authors who wrote their memoirs during the interwar period, as well as authors who began their work after they had left Latvia, express a similar reservation toward the Latvians, even if there is some variation in tone[55]. It is of course, just one aspect of a greater problem, and the conclusions drawn here should be compared with other types of sources as well as evidence from both other sections of Baltic German society and the Latvians themselves.

Notes

1 There are questions over terminology here. The German minority which lived in Latvia and Estonia called themselves Balts *(Balten)*, which excluded Latvians and Estonians. Nowadays the meaning of the word has changed and Latvians, Estonians and Lithuanians are referred to as Balts. Therefore in scientific literature usually the term Baltic Germans *(Deutschbalten)* is applied. Herein the term Baltic German is used for the German minority, and Latvian is applied to the non-German majority.

2 U. von Hirschhausen, *Die Grenzen der Gemeinsamkeit. Deutsche, Letten, Russen und Juden in Riga, 1860-1914*, Göttingen 2006, p. 23.

3 See for example A. Henriksson, *The tsar's loyal Germans. The Riga German community: social change and the nationality question, 1855-1905*, New York 1983.

4 Hirschhausen, *Grenzen der Gemeinsamkeit* cit., p. 12.

5 *Ibid.*, p. 27.

6 *Ibid.*, p. 101.

7 W. Schlau, *Der Wandel in der Sozialstruktur der deutschbaltischen Volksgruppe in Lettland während der Zwischenkriegszeit*, in B. Meissner, D. Loeber, D. Henning (eds.), *Die deutsche Volksgruppe in Lettland während der Zwischenkriegszeit und aktuelle Fragen des deutsch-lettischen Verhältnisses*, Hamburg 2000, pp. 93-108.

8 I. Feldmanis, *Die lettische Historiographie*, in M. Garleff (ed.), *Zwischen Konfrontation und Kompromiss. Oldenburger Symposium: Interethnische Beziehungen in Ostmitteleuropa als historiographisches Problem der 1930er/ 1940er Jahre*, Munich 1995, p. 136-138; G. von Rauch, *Geschichte der deutschbaltischen Geschichtsschreibung*, Cologne - Vienna 1986, pp. 377, 393-394.

9 M. Garleff, *Deutschbaltische Politik zwischen den Weltkriegen. Die parlamentarische Tätigkeit der deutsch-baltischen Parteien in Lettland und Estland*, Bonn - Bad Godesberg 1976; D. Henning (ed.), *Von der Oberschicht zur Minderheit. Die deutsche Minderheit in Lettland 1917-1940*, Lüneburg 1996; G. von Pistohlkors, M. Weber (eds.), *Staatliche Einheit und nationale Vielfalt im Baltikum. Festschrift für Prof. Dr. Michael Garleff zum 65. Geburtstag*, Munich 2005.

10 C. Hasselblatt, *Erinnerungssuche. Befragungsprojekt über die interethnischen Beziehungen im Baltikum – hier: Estland und Lettland – in der Zwischenkriegszeit*, in "Nordost-Archiv" 1995, 2, pp. 635-642.

11 For exceptions see H. W. Whelan, *Adapting to Modernity. Family, Caste and Capitalism among the Baltic German Nobility*, Cologne - Vienna 1999; P. Krupnikov, *Lettland und die Letten im Spiegel deutscher und deutschbaltischer Publizistik 1895-1950*, Hannover - Döhren 1989.

12 M. Saagpakk, *Deutschbaltische Autobiographien als Dokumente des Zeit- und Selbstempfindens: Vom Ende des 19. Jh. bis zur Umsiedlung 1939*, Tallinn 2006. (http://digar.nlib.ee/otsing/sdetail.jsp?objekt=nlib-digar:1721&qtime=1172198441748, 18 April 2007). For the description of the resettlement in Baltic German autobiographies see also M. Saagpakk, *Die Umsiedlung in deutschbaltischen Autobiographien*, in "Zeitschrift für Ostmitteleuropa-Forschung", 2007, 2.

13 B. von Krusenstjern, *Was sind Selbstzeugnisse? Begriffskritische und quellenkundliche Überlegungen anhand von Beispielen aus dem 17. Jahrhundert*, in "Historische Anthropologie", 1994, 2, p. 463; W. Fuchs-Heinritz, *Biographische Forschung. Eine Einführung in Praxis und Methoden*, Wiesbaden 2005, p. 29; B. Neumann, *Identität und Rollenzwang. Zur Theorie der Autobiographie*, Frankfurt am Main 1970, pp. 6-10.

14 W. Singer, *Wahrnehmen, Erinnern, Vergessen*, in M. Kerner (ed.), *Eine Welt? – Eine Geschichte?* 43. Deutscher Historikertag in Aachen, 26 - 29 September 2000, Munich 2001, pp. 18-27; G. Rosenthal, *Erlebte und erzählte Lebensgeschichte. Gestalt und Struktur biographischer Selbstbeschreibungen*, Frankfurt am Main - New York 1995, pp. 72-80; H. P. Bahrdt, *Identität und biographisches Bewusstsein: Soziologische Überlegungen zur Funktion des Erzählens aus dem eigenen Leben für die Gewinnung und*

Reproduktion von Identität, in R. W. Brednich, H. Lixfeld, D.R. Moser, L. Röhrich (eds.), *Lebenslauf und Lebenszusammenhang. Autobiographische Materialien in der volkskundlichen Forschung.* Vorträge der Arbeitstagung der Deutschen Gesellschaft für Volkskunde in Freiburg im Breisgau, 16-18 March 1981, Freiburg im Breisgau 1982, p. 27; H. Winter, *Der Aussagewert von Selbstbiographien. Zum Status autobiographischer Urteile*, Heidelberg 1985, pp. 30-31.

15 Saagpakk, *Autobiographien* cit., p. 17.

16 See for example H. Kalinke, *Zur Geschichte und Relevanz von Selbstzeugnissen für die Alltags-, Erfahrungs- und Mentalitätsgeschichte der Deutschen in und aus dem östlichen Europa. Eine Einführung*, in H. Kalinke (ed.), *Brief, Erzählung, Tagebuch. Autobiographische Dokumente als Quellen zu Kultur und Geschichte der Deutschen in und aus dem östlichen Europa.* Referate der Tagung des Johannes-Künzig-Instituts für ostdeutsche Volkskunde, 8-9 September 1999, Freiburg 2000, p. 9.

17 For the other texts I am not able to fix the exact period of composition.

18 Saagpakk, *Autobiographien* cit., p. 32.

19 E. von Mensenkampff, *Menschen und Schicksale aus dem alten Livland*, Tilsit - Leipzig - Riga 1944, p. 7. Ernst von Mensenkampff, a noble landowner and editor of the Baltic German newspaper "Rigasche Rundschau", wrote his autobiography in the 1930s. It reveals clearly national socialist ideas.

20 C. von Stackelberg, *Verwehte Blätter. Erinnerungen aus dem alten Baltikum*, Berlin 1992, p. 10.

21 Saagpakk, *Autobiographien* cit., p. 48.

22 For example Mensenkampff, *Menschen* cit., p. 5.

23 Saagpakk, *Autobiographien* cit., p. 46.

24 H. von Bluhmen, *Meine Lebenswende: Erlebnisse und Schicksale eines Deutsch-Balten. Mit einer kulturhistorischen Betrachtung des Baltenlandes vor der Revolution*, Peine 1927, p. 169.

25 P. Schiemann, *Zwischen zwei Zeitaltern. Erinnerungen, 1903-1919*, Lüneburg 1979, p. 181.

26 *Ibid.*

27 G. von den Brincken, *Land unter. Erlebnisse aus zwei Weltkriegen, Bolschewikenzeit und Nachkriegsjahren*, Darmstadt [not dated], p. 143. Gertrud von den Brincken was a writer.

28 W. von Rüdiger, *Aus dem letzten Kapitel deutsch-baltischer Geschichte in Lettland, 1919-1939*, Hannover - Wülfel 1955, p. 14. Wilhelm von Rüdiger's autobiography was written around 1945.

29 For example see H. von Blanckenhagen, *Am Rande der Weltgeschichte. Erinnerungen aus Alt-Livland, 1913-1923*, Göttingen 1966, p. 345; Mensenkampff, *Menschen* cit., p. 122; Bluhmen, *Lebenswende* cit., p. 77.

30 For example Mensenkampff, *Menschen* cit., pp. 367, 390, 393, 408, 410.

31 H. H. Hahn, E. Hahn, *Nationale Stereotypen. Plädoyer für eine historische Stereotypenforschung*, in H. H. Hahn (ed.), *Stereotyp, Identität und Geschichte. Die Funktion von Stereotypen in gesellschaftlichen Diskursen*, Frankfurt am Main 2002, p. 22.

32 Brincken, *Land* cit., p. 20.

33 Blanckenhagen, *Rand* cit., p. 300.

34 Schiemann, *Zeitalter* cit., p. 156; W. von Rüdiger, *Aus dem letzten Kapitel deutsch-baltischer Geschichte in Lettland, 1919-1945.* Gern bei Eggenfelden 1954, p. 59.

35 Rüdiger, *Kapitel* cit., p. 59.

36 H. Stegmann, *Aus meinen Erinnerungen*, in "Baltische Hefte", 1961, 7, p. 165.

37 *Ibid.*, pp. 168-169.

[38] W. Wachtsmuth, *Wege, Umwege, Weggenossen. Lebenserinnerungen eines Balten, 1876-1950*, Munich 1954, p. 210. Wolfgang Wachtsmuth was a politician and the head of the Baltic German educational system. He wrote his autobiography between 1939 and 1945.

[39] Wachtsmuch's account is interesting in that it also discusses Latvian perceptions of Germans. Whether his conclusions can be applied more generally is an important question, but beyond the remit of the present study.

[40] Mensenkampff, *Menschen* cit., pp. 391-392.

[41] See for example Blanckenhagen, *Rande* cit., pp. 356-357, E. Christierson-Sokolowski, *Der silberne Fasan. Erinnerungen einer Deutschbaltin*, Cologne 1998, pp. 64, 146-149; E. von Fircks, *Erinnerungen. Höhen und Tiefen im Leben eines baltischen Arztes, 1905-1972*, Wedemark - Elze 1993, p. 23; S. Steenberg, *Baltische Wurzeln. Deutsch-russische Lebensräume zu Beginn des 20. Jahrhunderts*, Berlin 1993, p. 36.

[42] Stegmann, *Erinnerungen* cit., p. 104; M. von Radecki, *Mein Leben in Familie und Beruf vor dem Hintergrund des Zeitgeschehens meinen Enkeln erzählt. Teil 1. In der baltischen Heimat, 1886-1939*, Cologne 1972, pp. 163-164; Steenberg, *Wurzeln* cit., p. 33.

[43] Stegmann, *Erinnerungen* cit., p. 106. For the clubs and associations in Riga see also Hirschhausen, *Grenzen* cit.

[44] E. Kersten, *Rückblende. Erlebnisse zwischen Kurland und Kap*, Münster 1997, p. 42.

[45] B. Bielenstein, *Die Häuser aber blieben*. Riga 1998, p. 11; W. Bulmerincq, *Lebenserinnerungen des letzten deutschen Stadthauptes (Oberbürgermeister) von Riga*, Wolfenbüttel 1952, p. 13.

[46] Wachtsmuth, *Wege* cit., p. 194.

[47] Stegmann, *Erinnerungen* cit., p. 97.

[48] Steenberg, *Wurzeln* cit., p. 39.

[49] Fircks, *Erinnerungen* cit., pp. 95-96.

[50] *Ibid.*, p. 89.

[51] Wachtsmuth, *Wege* cit., p. 317-318.

[52] Z. Maurina, *Denn das Wagnis ist schön. Geschichte eines Lebens*, Memmingen 1990, pp. 158-159.

[53] Maurina, *Wagnis* cit., p. 336.

[54] *Ibid.*

[55] This is also confirmed by Saagpakk (*Autobiographien* cit., pp. 79-126). She used a different corpus of sources, which mainly includes non-published autobiographies from Estonian and German archives.

Bibliography

Autobiographies

Adolphi H., *Leben, Gedanken, Weltanschauung eines Kurländers (1841-1922)*, Riga 1923.

Adolphi R., *Erinnerungen meiner Mutter Gertrud Adolphi geb. Blumenbach. 1893 bis 1918 und 1939 bis 1945*, Lüneburg 2004.

Anderson H., *Reisender durch das Jahrhundert. Streiflichter und Zeitgeschichten aus Ost und West 1903 – 1986*, Heilbronn 1986.

Bielenstein A., *Ein glückliches Leben*, Michelstadt 2002.

Bielenstein B., *Die Häuser aber blieben*, Riga 1998.

Bielenstein W., *Kampferlebnisse eines Balten im Ringen um Glauben und Heimat,* Berlin 1939.

von Blanckenhagen H., *Am Rande der Weltgeschichte. Erinnerungen aus Alt-Livland, 1913-1923*, Göttingen 1966.

von Bluhmen H., *Meine Lebenswende: Erlebnisse und Schicksale eines Deutsch-Balten. Mit einer kulturhistorischen Betrachtung des Baltenlandes vor der Revolution*, Peine 1927.

von den Brincken G., *Land unter. Erlebnisse aus zwei Weltkriegen, Bolschewikenzeit und Nachkriegsjahren*, Darmstadt [not dated].

W. Bulmerincq, *Lebenserinnerungen des letzten deutschen Stadthauptes (Oberbürgermeister) von Riga*, Wolfenbüttel 1952.

Christierson-Sokolowski E., *Der silberne Fasan. Erinnerungen einer Deutschbaltin*, Cologne 1998.

von Fircks E., *Erinnerungen. Höhen und Tiefen im Leben eines baltischen Arztes, 1905-1972*. Wedemark - Elze 1993.

Grüner V., *"Aus meinem Leben" Erinnerungen – Aufsätze – Predigten. Herausgegeben von Ralph Ruthenberg*, Hannover - Döhren 1961.

Gurland R., *Verschleppung und Befreiung. Kurland unter der Bolschewistenherrschaft*, in E. Berg et al. (eds.), *Erlebte Geschichte. Deutschbalten im 20. Jahrhundert. Ein Lesebuch*, Lüneburg 2002, pp. 55-60.

Helmsing L., *Plaudereien aus dem Leben eines Deutsch-Balten*, Lübeck 1968.

Intelmann A., *Aufzeichnungen über das letzte Arbeitsjahr der deutschbaltischen Volksgruppe in Lettland und ihre Umsiedlung*. Bearbeitet von Jürgen von Hehn, Essen 1984.

Kersten E., *Rückblende. Erlebnisse zwischen Kurland und Kap*, Münster 1997.

Kühn L., *Erinnerungen an livländisches Landleben*, Lüneburg 1983.

Maurina Z., *Denn das Wagnis ist schön. Geschichte eines Lebens*, Memmingen 1990.

von Mensenkampff E., *Menschen und Schicksale aus dem alten Livland*, Tilsit - Leipzig - Riga 1944.

Munier-Wroblewski M., *Feste und Feiern. Jugenderinnerungen*, Hannover - Döhren 1964.

Pantenius L., *Jugenderinnerungen aus dem alten Riga*, Hannover - Döhren 1959.

von Radecki M., *Mein Leben in Familie und Beruf vor dem Hintergrund des Zeitgeschehens meinen Enkeln erzählt. Teil 1. In der baltischen Heimat, 1886-1939*, Cologne 1972.

von Rüdiger W., *Aus dem letzten Kapitel deutsch-baltischer Geschichte in Lettland, 1919-1945*, Gern bei Eggenfelden 1954.

von Rüdiger W., *Aus dem letzten Kapitel deutsch-baltischer Geschichte in Lettland, 1919-1939*. Zweiter Teil, Hannover-Wülfel 1955.

Schiemann P., *Zwischen zwei Zeitaltern. Erinnerungen, 1903-1919*, Lüneburg 1979.

von Stackelberg C., *Verwehte Blätter. Erinnerungen aus dem alten Baltikum*, Berlin 1992.

Steenberg S., *Baltische Wurzeln. Deutsch-russische Lebensräume zu Beginn des 20. Jahrhunderts*, Berlin 1993.

Stenbock-Fermor A., *Der rote Graf. Autobiographie*, 2. Auflage, Berlin 1973.

Stegmann H., *Aus meinen Erinnerungen* in "Baltische Hefte", 1961, 7, p. 156-179.

Wachtsmuth W., *Wege, Umwege, Weggenossen. Lebenserinnerungen eines Balten, 1876-1950*, Munich 1954.

Literature

Bahrdt H. P., *Identität und biographisches Bewusstsein: Soziologische Überlegungen zur Funktion des Erzählens aus dem eigenen Leben für die Gewinnung und Reproduktion von Identität*, in R. W. Brednich,

H. Lixfeld, D.R. Moser, L. Röhrich (eds.) *Lebenslauf und Lebenszusammenhang.* Autobiographische Materialien in der volkskundlichen Forschung. Vorträge der Arbeitstagung der Deutschen Gesellschaft für Volkskunde in Freiburg im Breisgau, 16-18 March 1981, Freiburg im Breisgau 1982, pp. 18-45.

Feldmanis I., *Die lettische Historiographie*, in M. Garleff (ed.), *Zwischen Konfrontation und Kompromiss. Oldenburger Symposium: Interethnische Beziehungen in Ostmitteleuropa als historiographisches Problem der 1930er/ 1940er Jahre*, Munich 1995, pp. 133-138.

Fuchs-Heinritz W., *Biographische Forschung. Eine Einführung in Praxis und Methoden*, Wiesbaden 2005.

Garleff M., *Deutschbaltische Politik zwischen den Weltkriegen. Die parlamentarische Tätigkeit der deutschbaltischen Parteien in Lettland und Estland*, Bonn - Bad Godesberg 1976.

Hahn H. H., Hahn E., *Nationale Stereotypen. Plädoyer für eine historische Stereotypenforschung*, in Hahn H. H. (ed.), *Stereotyp, Identität und Geschichte. Die Funktion von Stereotypen in gesellschaftlichen Diskursen*, Frankfurt am Main 2002.

C. Hasselblatt, Cornelius, *Erinnerungssuche. Befragungsprojekt über die interethnischen Beziehungen im Baltikum – hier: Estland und Lettland – in der Zwischenkriegszeit*, in "Nordost-Archiv", 1995, 2, pp. 635-642.

Henning D. (ed.), *Von der Oberschicht zur Minderheit. Die deutsche Minderheit in Lettland 1917-1940*, Lüneburg 1996.

Henriksson A., *The tsar's loyal Germans. The Riga German community: social change and the nationality question, 1855-1905*, New York 1983.

von Hirschhausen U., *Die Grenzen der Gemeinsamkeit. Deutsche, Letten, Russen und Juden in Riga, 1860-1914*, Göttingen 2006.

Kalinke H., *Zur Geschichte und Relevanz von Selbstzeugnissen für die Alltags-, Erfahrungs- und Mentalitätsgeschichte der Deutschen in und aus dem östlichen Europa. Eine Einführung*, in H. Kalinke (ed.), *Brief, Erzählung, Tagebuch. Autobiographische Dokumente als Quellen zu Kultur und Geschichte der Deutschen in und aus dem östlichen Europa*. Referate der Tagung des Johannes-Künzig-Instituts für ostdeutsche Volkskunde, 8-9 September 1999, Freiburg im Breisgau 2000, pp. 7-22.

Krupnikov P., *Lettland und die Letten im Spiegel deutscher und deutschbaltischer Publizistik 1895-1950*, Hannover - Döhren 1989.

von Krusenstjern B., *Was sind Selbstzeugnisse? Begriffskritische und quellenkundliche Überlegungen anhand von Beispielen aus dem 17. Jahrhundert*, in "Historische Anthropologie", 1994, 2, pp. 462-471.

Meissner B., Loeber D., Henning D. (eds.), *Die deutsche Volksgruppe in Lettland während der Zwischenkriegszeit und aktuelle Fragen des deutsch-lettischen Verhältnisses*, Hamburg 2000.

Neumann B., *Identität und Rollenzwang. Zur Theorie der Autobiographie*, Frankfurt am Main 1970.

von Pistohlkors G., M. Weber (eds.), *Staatliche Einheit und nationale Vielfalt im Baltikum. Festschrift für Prof. Dr. Michael Garleff zum 65. Geburtstag*, Munich 2005.

von Rauch G., Geschichte *der deutschbaltischen Geschichtsschreibung*, Cologne - Vienna 1986.

Rosenthal G., *Erlebte und erzählte Lebensgeschichte. Gestalt und Struktur biographischer Selbstbeschreibungen*, Frankfurt am Main - New York 1995.

Saagpakk M., *Deutschbaltische Autobiographien als Dokumente des Zeit- und Selbstempfindens: Vom Ende des 19. Jh. bis zur Umsiedlung 1939*, Tallinn 2006. (http://digar.nlib.ee/otsing/sdetail.jsp?objekt=nlib-digar:1721&qtime=1172198441748, 18 April 2007)

Saagpakk M., *Die Umsiedlung in deutschbaltischen Autobiographien*, in "Zeitschrift für Ostmitteleuropa-Forschung", 2007, 1, pp. 50-67.

Schlau, W., *Der Wandel in der Sozialstruktur der deutschbaltischen Volksgruppe in Lettland während der Zwischenkriegszeit*, in B. Meissner, D. Loeber, D. Henning (eds.), *Die deutsche Volksgruppe in Lettland während der Zwischenkriegszeit und aktuelle Fragen des deutsch-lettischen Verhältnisses*, Hamburg 2000, pp. 93-108.

Singer W., *Wahrnehmen, Erinnern, Vergessen,* in M. Kerner (ed.), *Eine Welt? – Eine Geschichte? 43.* Deutscher Historikertag in Aachen, 26 - 29 September 2000, Munich 2001, pp. 18-27.

Whelan H. W., *Adapting to Modernity. Family, Caste and Capitalism among the Baltic German Nobility*, Cologne - Vienna 1999.

Winter H., *Der Aussagewert von Selbstbiographien. Zum Status autobiographischer Urteile*, Heidelberg 1985.

Ubi bene ibi patria: Reading the City of Kiev through Polish and Czech "Spatial Stories" from the First World War Period

Olena Betlii
Kyiv-Mohyla Academy

Abstract

This chapter focuses on Kiev during the upheavals of the First World War period by analyzing Czech and Polish 'spatial stories' of the city. It examines the effect of the war on the everyday pursuits of pre-war Kievites of Czech and Polish origin and new arrivals to the city. The author ascertains whether and how their perception of Kiev was transformed during the war: from home into lost space. It is argued that Kiev played an important role in the development of the daily activities of Czechs and Poles and that, furthermore, both ethnic groups influenced the city by filling it with their own spatial practices, thereby formulating a unique identity for the city that bore special significance for its migrant communities.

Вважається, що місто гарніше за село, оскільки воно збагачено людською історією. Правдивість цієї тези можна легко підвередити на прикладі історії Києва. В даній статті увагу зосереджено на міській історії впродовж Першої світової війни та на використанні міського простору чехами і поляками. Використовуючи методологічний інструментарій Мішеля де Серто, зроблено спробу віднайти те мистецтво реакції на виклики повсякдення, яке продемонстрували згадані етнічні спільноти протягом воєнних років. У статті показано послідовність зміни використання міста – від домівки-вітчизни до втраченої території. Це відбувалося крізь призму творення свого власного простору, прочитання міста крізь наділення його об'єктів та простору значеннєвими кодами. Впродовж війни попри те, що чеська і польська спільноти значно збільшили свій кількісний та змінили свій якісний склад, сприйняття міста, його ідентичність не змінилися, однак вони щезли разом із їхніми творцями. У статті простежено просторові історії та виокремлено просторові практики, сповнені особливої пам'яті, що поділялася усіма чехами та поляками Києва. Війна змінила значення деяких об'єктів міста, готелі якого були переоблаштовані під офіси та місця політичних зібрань, публічні приміщення, цирк, стали свідками ви-

датних конгресів, монастирі та університет відкрили свої терени для формування не своїх військових підрозділів (Чеської дружини). Це лише перша спроба прочитати Київ крізь просторові історії його мешканців, прояв спокуси затримати на довше блимання вогника, який у вигляді ностальгійних спогадів дозволяє нам відчути себе в постаті тих, чиї давно зниклі кроки оживляли Київ.

Introduction

> You can meet in the streets of Prague a shabbily dressed man who is not even himself aware of his significance in the history of the great new era. He goes modestly on his way, without bothering anyone. Nor is he bothered by journalists asking for an interview. If you asked him his name he would answer you simply and unassumingly: 'I am Švejk'[1].

That is how the prominent Czech writer Jaroslav Hašek pulled an anonymous inhabitant out of the embrace of the street, introduced him and forced us to follow his steps, to read his 'spatial stories', during the 500 pages of his book. Reading this novel, one actually does what Michel de Certeau wanted all of us to do– to understand the subject in space while reading his or her own spatial stories. I consider Švejk's urban experience – 'the murmuring voice of societies' – to be a good way of demonstrating de Certeau's technique, but what can we say about Hašek in this context?

A building on Volodymyrska Street in downtown Kiev bears a plaque with the inscription: "Jaroslav Hašek, a famous Czech writer, lived here during the World War I". This is the only name that has been commemorated out of almost 50,000 Czech and Slovak people in Ukraine. A large part of this community marched through Kiev in the late winter of 1918 leaving the city for Prague via Vladivostok. However, my task here is not to write a story about Hašek, but rather to produce, or else find, de Certeau's "science of singularity"[2] – a science of the relationship which linked the everyday pursuits of the inhabitants to the particular circumstances of World War I in Kiev. Thus, my intention is to show how culture – "a system of inherited conceptions expressed in symbolic forms by means of which people communicate, perpetuate, and develop their knowledge about and attitudes toward life"[3] (Clifford Geertz) – was consumed by ordinary Czech and Polish men far from their homeland, in their new *Heimat* – a Ukrainian metropolis. This kind of approach helps avoid the pitfalls of nationally oriented studies, which still prevail in Ukrainian, Czech and Polish historiographies. The authors of *Capital Cities at War: Paris, London, Berlin 1914-1919* demonstrated that the history of World War I can be better understood if one investigates its events through urban studies, paying attention to the metropolis as the "social formation at the juncture between the national state and civil society, as defined by collectivities of many kinds"[4]. Following their approach, this chapter will not focus on the urban level of waging war but rather on the urban activities of an under-researched collection of city-dwellers, namely minority ethnic groups. Specifically this study is concerned with the Czech and

Polish indigenous population and new arrivals, who together transformed Kiev into an immigrant city by 1917.

The specific questions I will ask below, in terms of the 'science of singularity' framework, are: How did the Czechs and Poles perceive Kiev? Where did they concentrate and how did they inhabit the city space? What did their daily routes look like? Where did they start and end? Which places bound these ethnic groups together through common memories? How much did the War influence the usual traditions of city life and reformulate urban identity? In this article I attempt to answer these questions by examining them in terms of the key formula – *Ubi bene ibi patria*[5]. Research of this kind can reveal an interesting and rare phenomenon in urban history, when a city's fate depended not on the indigenous population, but on the newcomers who came to the city as refugees, rather than permanent occupants.

Kiev as *Heimat*

Polish colonization of Ukrainian territory began several centuries before the start of Czech colonization. The former can be traced back to 1569, when Ukrainian lands became an integral part of the Polish-Lithuanian Commonwealth. The latter was mainly rooted in late 19th century Pan-Slavist sympathies. Nevertheless, one should not forget that the first Czech colonists appeared in Ukraine soon after the defeat of Czech rebels in the battle of *Bila hora* [White Mountain] in the first half of the 17th century. Despite this, before World War I both ethnic communities[6] considered the land where they had settled as their motherland, their home, and a place of safety. They took root in these lands and filled them with their own memories and stories. "We were the citizens of this land, which owes everything to us", Polish colonists in Ukraine used to say (a statement echoes the discourse of colonialism worldwide)[7]. The status of Czechs and Slovaks differed slightly; it may be summarized as follows: "in the harsh conditions of the Russian Empire, most of them had lost interest in their native country and its problems, becoming thoroughly Russified"[8]. The best expression of the migrants' identification with the Ukrainian lands was conveyed by the name which both the Polish and the Czech communities used to designate Ukraine: they called it *Rus'* (referring to the medieval state Kievan Rus') and its native population, *Rusyny* (Ruthenians). The Czech colonists probably adopted the name *Rus'* from Poles[9], who wanted to emphasize their own, rather than Russian, legacy and tradition in these lands[10]. But the question is how much these attitudes were preserved within the city walls. If Ukrainian lands were perceived as a homeland, what role did Kiev play for these ethnic groups?

There are many starting points from which to answer the questions mentioned above and, in this way, to read the Czech and Polish spatial stories of Kiev. If we give the floor to a *flâneur*, we can see that the description of a city naturally begins with an edge: "I see my city picturesquely situated on the right bank of the Dnieper... I see this city immersed in the green beauty of the charmed parks that embellish the hills under the river bank..."[11]. As in this quotation, the Dnieper, which divides Kiev into two parts, was the line from which the Poles and the Czechs customarily drew their map of the city. But the river bank did not expose "an entire metropolis to view"[12], as Lake Michigan in Chicago did in Kevin Lynch's classic example of the edge, without which the city cannot be pictured[13]. Rather, it marked the developed part of the city and created a beautiful cityscape visible from the non-urbanized opposite bank of the river, where the first recreation districts began to appear at the turn of the 20th century. The river bank also had another function. It was the end of the usual path, which led a *flâneur* to the main cultural events that took place in the city and were organized in the numerous parks and districts along the Dnieper, for example, in the *Kupetski Sady* (Merchants' Gardens) or in the trade area in Podil. One could enjoy concerts, dances, talks, singing, playing cards, and flirting there. It was the most romantic part of Kiev and an area that encouraged a feeling of belonging. This kind of spatial practice neglected all differences between city-dwellers. However, these differences surfaced immediately after leaving this area. They arose when visitors returned along the routes that had led them to the river bank. Thus, at this stage we come to another possible starting point in our attempt to read the urban space, which may be narrated as follows: "Let us take a tour from the edge in summer 1914" or "Were we to follow one of the residents along her typical route to the Dnieper, the experience would be something like this"[14].

Fig. 1
View at Podil.

The task is not easy, however. Ordinary people of Czech and Polish origin left so little evidence of their city life that one may only guess at how their itineraries were organized. The sources that remain allow us to reflect on how urban space was occupied by communities in general, rather than how they articulated their social differences using the urban landscape. Indeed, in this case Kiev becomes fragmented into different parts, the histories of which can unfold "like stories held in reserve"[15]. To evoke these stories let us take a closer look at the city in general. By the beginning of World War I Kiev was one of the most pleasant cities in the Russian empire. Under the influence of the new industrial age, the city had expanded rapidly. New multistoried houses with apartments for rent were built everywhere; a regular water supply became standard across the city centre; new roads were paved; electric lights replaced the old gas lights along the streets; and tramlines connected the city centre with outlying areas. All this made Kiev increasingly attractive to businessmen, traders, and craftsmen. Also, by the end of the century it became an important educational centre. These changes caused an increase in the city's population. Part of this population growth was made up of the two ethnic groups we are interested in. Between 1897 and 1914 the Polish population grew from 35,552 to 60,000 (the total population of the city on the eve of the War was 600,000)[16]. Kiev also became attractive to the Czechs. In 1909 the young Czech community comprised as many as 3,000-3,500 members[17].

The industrial age finally defined the functions of the city districts. 'Little Paris', as people sometimes called Kiev at the time, received its newly restored and very wide street, *Khreshchatyk*, which became the main artery of the city. Its appearance was shaped by numerous hotels, stores, restaurants, cafes, and business offices. At the same time it was also the place for everyday strolling. It was beautiful, and attractive to those who had capital and wanted to start a new business in the city. So, taking into account that the Poles were the richest landlords in this part of the Russian Empire, it is not surprising that there were a large number of Polish landmarks on the *Khreshchatyk*. On this street one could find Marszak's jeweler, Fruziński's cafes and Idzikowski's bookstore and library[18]. The latter was well known in the Russian Empire and in Europe for its rich collection of music literature. In another district one could find the musical instruments store which belonged to local 'Czech king', Jindřich Jindřišek. The intellectual district was also nearby, marked by St. Volodymyr University, the Second Gymnasium, the Opera House, and the City Theatre, all of which were located along Volodymyrska Street. Although these were places which let all inhabitants enjoy the same social relations with the city, the paths that led there were quite different. On the way to the Opera House Polish inhabitants could stop by Franciszek Gołąbek's amazing Hotel François, which featured a nice restaurant with tasty deserts and famous poolrooms. In contrast, the Czech path to the opera went via the Praha hotel, which is the most famous hotel along the street. It belonged to Dr Vaclav Vondrak, one of the richest Volhynian Czechs and a deputy to the Volhynian local self-government body, the *zemstvo*. The hotel's ad-

Fig. 2
Khreshchatyk.

Fig. 3
View at St. Volodymyr University.

Fig. 4
St. Volodymyr holding a cross.

vertisements claimed: "You have not been to Kiev if you have not seen the city from the hotel's roof". The hotel was the main landmark for Czechs in Kiev.

If one continued the tour all the way to the beginning of the street, one would reach Podil, the oldest trading region, passing St. Volodymyr's hill, on top of which a figure of St. Volodymyr holding a cross was erected in 1853. This was the district most closely connected with the Poles. Normally Podil, as is typical for trading areas, had a "multiplicity of contact points"(Sennett) between ethnic groups, but once a year the area was immersed in Polish subculture. Each February many Poles from Kiev and other regions of Ukraine left their homes or homesteads to participate in the most important annual Polish event in Kiev – the Kontraktovyi Yarmarok (Contract Fair). Participation in the event could lead to a successful business deal, a good marriage proposal or a nice job offer, and guaranteed general revelry in the carnival atmosphere of non-stop balls, cards, etc. The Poles penetrated into all parts of Kiev during the fair. Hotels were overcrowded and all nearby apartments were rented[19]. The event helped unite the Polish community by bringing together Kievites of Polish origin and the Poles who lived in the provinces.

In contrast to the Poles, the Czech ethnic group in the city did not have any event which knitted their social lives together. However, there was an entire district in one of Kiev's suburbs which belonged to them. Officially, its name was Shulavka, but for the Czech inhabitants it was known as Česká Stromovka. The origins of the district are associated with the Prague born engineer Josef Křivánek, who came to Kiev as a technical assistant from the Czech plant "Broumovský a Šulc" in the early 1880s and, by 1888, became the director of Grether's plant located in Shulavka. Within ten years, the plant, which was known as the "Kiev Grether-Křivánek Machine Works and Boiler Plant" became one of the most advanced and productive machine works in Ukraine. At the end of the 1880s, another Czech, Mr. Veský, founded another factory – "Vielwerth a Dědina" – which became the largest producer of seeding machines in the region[20]. A lack of local engineers, qualified clerks and builders caused the owners to employ specialists from the Czech lands. Some of them became managers in the plants, some were workers, but regardless of their positions almost all of them dwelled in Shulavka. However, one has to remember in this context that there was another source of the growth of the Czech community in Kiev. The city became attractive to the first generation of Volhynian Czechs, who found better career opportunities in the metropolis at the beginning of the 20th century. Also, some Czechs moved to Kiev directly from Austro-Hungary for ideological reasons. These new arrivals lived in different parts of the city and some of their apartments soon became the centres of Czech intellectual life in Kiev.

What is of most interest to us is how the Poles and the Czechs constructed their urban communities through their own communication infrastructure in Kiev, or, in other words, how they inhabited the city through their own texts. On 1 February 1906 Włodzimierz Grocholski, the Vice President of the Kiev Agricultural Society, published the first edition of "Dziennik Kijowski" [Kiev Daily], which became the main media outlet of the Polish community in the city. Its motto was "the responsibility of each Pole is to care for Polish prosperity"[21] and its political priorities were close to the national democratic ones[22]. This periodical and the different Polish organizations, clubs, and charity societies, where the Poles regularly met, created a recognizable Polish culture in Kiev. It helped the Poles express their claim to the urban space of Kiev and use it to stage Polish cultural events. It also helped the Poles to read Kiev in the same way. The Czechs carried out similar practices in the city. On 17 October 1906 the first issue of the Czech newspaper "The Russian Czech" was published in Kiev by Dr. Vaclav Vondrák. Even though only a few issues were published, the role it played in Czech life was very significant. It united the Czechs and inspired them to establish closer connections through the newly founded organizations[23]. The most successful Czech project in Kiev, however, was "Čechoslovan" – the official Czech and Slovak newspaper in the Russian Empire. It was published by Věnceslav Švihovský with the financial support of Czech businessmen.

The significance of these periodicals was remarkable. Both of them stressed the identity of Kiev for their readers, showing them clear signifiers of the city's borders, landmarks, and the paths which connected them and structured city life. Through brief announce-

Fig. 5
St. Alexander's Cathedral.

ments, advertisements, and news the periodicals told their readers where to shop and what to visit. They helped the inhabitants make their own daily journeys, penetrating into different districts, passing by different landmarks, becoming *flâneurs* for a while, with the purpose of reaching places which bore significance for their ethnic groups. There were very few places that were identified with only one community. However, the main landmarks for the Poles were the two Catholic cathedrals (the old one – St. Alexander's Cathedral – in downtown Kiev, and the new one – the neo-gothic St. Nicholas' Cathedral – several miles away from the centre). The Jan Amos Komenský Charity Educational Society in Kiev located in J. Jindřišek's store in Khreshchatyk played the same role for the Czechs.

To sum up, by the beginning of World War I the Czech and Polish communities had very clear images of the metropolis. Both of them had their own infrastructure of communication, which included newspapers, stores, hotels, schools, industrial plants, and in this way they inhabited the space with their own spatial stories. As in other cities of the Russian Empire[24], this infrastructure was established by public figures, landlords, and factory owners. In so doing they organized the ordinary Czechs and Poles into new local communities in Kiev and helped them perceive Kiev as their *Heimat*.

Kiev as a rented apartment

The beginning of World War I was a turning point in the lives of the Czechs and Poles in the Russian Empire. The war became the dominant influence on the population. It was everywhere, involving each family and entering everyone's life through news and, above all, via the declarations and orders issued by the new authorities. This was a moment when all non-Russian ethnic groups were reminded by officials of their origin and citizenship regardless of their loyalty towards the empire. Those who did not apply for Russian citizenship were regarded as enemies and the government ordered them to be arrested or moved to special places under police control. There were a lot of absurd situations, mostly in Czech families, in which a husband joined the Russian army as a Russian citizen and his wife, still having Austrian citizenship, was forced to leave their home[25]. The problem of ethnicity shaped the new perception of the city dwellers. It distinguished and named outsiders. In Kiev the group that stood out was, above all, the Czech community because their native land was part of an enemy power – the Austro-Hungarian monarchy – and supplied soldiers to the army against which native Kievites had to fight. Similar situations occurred in Paris or in London, where a German waiter would suddenly become an outsider, or in Berlin, where the same would happen to British students[26].

In order to avoid mass resettlement and arrests, the Czechs had to demonstrate their loyalty to the Russian Empire. This was the first time that the Czechs were forced to change their perception of the city space because of an external influence. On 27 July 1914 they organized a meeting in downtown Kiev using the open space for their activities. Speeches were addressed to the authorities and proclaimed the willingness of the entire Czech community to apply for the Russian citizenship, as well as to establish an independent Czech state under the protection of Russia[27]. Furthermore, the government ordered the creation of a Czech unit in the Russian army on 30 July. It was called *Druzhina* and located in Kiev under the control of the Kiev headquarters[28]. The unit's flag was blessed by the clergy during a solemn meeting on Sofiivska square in Kiev on 28 September in front of the 11th-century orthodox St. Sofia's Cathedral and the monument to Bohdan Khmelnytsky, a Ukrainian hetman. Since the Middle Ages the square had been the usual place for holding great events. Thus, the meeting was not a unique or unusual use of the urban space. However, the spirit with which the Czech community used it was the first signifier of the wartime influence on the city life, when the decisive features of urban rhythms and customs were "a function of the decisions taken elsewhere"[29].

Fig. 6
St. Sofia's Cathedral.

Fig. 7
St. Michael's Monastery.

While the square became recognized as the birthplace of the Czech *Druzhina*, the other sacred place for Orthodox Christians – St. Michael's Monastery, located one mile away – opened its gates to the first volunteers to join the military unit[30]. Soon enough the Czech volunteers were joined by Czech and Slovak prisoners of war and deserters from the Austrian army. They were transported from the front line to Kiev where they faced a difficult life.

These new arrivals reformulated urban identity. They designated new landmarks, drew new edges, and imbued new routes through the city with meaning. The Czech and Slovak captives were concentrated in the Darnytsia camp located in a suburb on the opposite side of the Dnieper. Thus, the significance of the river changed for the city's inhabitants. It no longer linked the urbanized and highly industrialized area with the undeveloped but beautiful and romantic landscape. The river became a dividing line between the spatial practices used by completely different worlds, those of the prisoners of war and the city's inhabitants, rather than the connection of different practices of the same world. Moving along the bridge from the right to the left bank of the Dnieper, the deserters left normal city life, still brimming with the usual daily activities of its inhabitants, and met the challenges of the war period in poorly made barracks where they lived the stressful lives of captives.

The appearance of these newcomers in Kiev forced the local Czech community to change its role. Meetings with civilian and military authorities, in order to negotiate the deserters' destiny in Kiev, became one of the main activities of its leaders. These meetings were part of V. Vondrak's and J. Jindřišek's daily responsibilities as they tried to get the authorities to permit the captives to be drafted into the *Druzhina*[31].

The war also changed the infrastructure of communication. The Praha Hotel became the focal point of the Czech community in the city. A network of Czech organizations was also established in the Russian Empire. In August 1914 the Union of Czech Societies in Russia was founded on the initiative of the Komenský Charity Foundation; its first meeting was held in Moscow in 1915. Kiev was represented in this Union by the newly established Czech Committee for supporting war victims headed by Jiří Jindřišek. It was located on 43 Volodymyrska Street. The committee was responsible for providing former Austrian citizens with documents which confirmed their Slavic origin and allowed them to live in the Empire[32]. Thus, most of the events which occurred within the Czech community during the War period took place on Volodymyrska Street. However, this does not mean that other ethnic groups perceived the street and nearby area to be a special Czech district. The Czech spirit was to a large extent concealed within the buildings that lined the street, for example, in the Praha Hotel or in the buildings of St. Michael's Monastery, which functioned as a base for military formations.

Whereas the spatial practices of the indigenous Czech community in Kiev were influenced by two categories of countrymen, i.e., the former Austrian subjects ('war victims') and the deserters, the spatial practices of the Polish ethnic group were defined not only by the 'war victims', but also by the 'refugees'. The Regional Kiev Council of the Polish Society for Supporting War Victims was established in the city in 1915 and became a new landmark, imbued with special significance for all Polish newcomers. It represented different Polish organizations which helped refugees by providing them with housing, food, and employment[33]. Many Poles were resettled to Kiev from Congress Poland in 1915 when the Russian army left the Western provinces of the Empire after being defeated by Austrian and German forces. One of the refugees, S. Wasilewski, noted that the appropriate word for such refugees was actually "resettlers": "The mandatory evacuation organized by the authorities forced us to leave Sarny. So in September we found ourselves in the Italia Hotel on Prorizna street in Kiev"[34].

One cannot say how many Poles found themselves in the Ukrainian metropolis during the War. However, it is obvious that Kiev became the only city in the Empire where the Polish community not only maintained its activities but also developed them. According to memoirs the city came to be dominated by Polish culture[35]. It resembled February in pre-war Kiev, when Poles arrived to attend the Contract Fair. It could be also been described as a "rented apartment" (de Certeau). However, this time the opportunities were quite different from those which were offered by the Contracts Fair. Nobody could estimate for how long the city space would be borrowed by the new Polish transients. Many unknowns dictated new rules of urban usage. The growth of the Polish population resulted in the establishment of private and secondary schools, initiated by the clergy of St. Alexander's Cathedral[36]. Moreover, the refugees brought with them their newspapers, weekly periodicals, and other signifiers of their previous city life in Warsaw or in Galician towns, using which they started to influence life in Kiev. Finally, the Polish theatre was founded in Kiev in 1916. It united the Polish community within its walls, becoming a new element in the city's communication infrastructure[37].

Similar changes occurred within the Czech community in Kiev in 1916. The influence of newcomers, such as the captives, on Czech urban rhythms significantly increased. There was no part of Czech life in the city which was not transformed by their arrival. They became city dwellers and, what is more, involved the pre-war Czech community in the creation of an entirely new project – an independent Czech state. They became members of the Club of Captive Co-Workers founded in 1916 and affiliated with the Union of Czechoslovak Societies in Rus'. The club represented the interests of its members, and provided housing and food[38]. Furthermore, newcomers became members of the Czechoslovak Credit Society, which also opened on Khreshchatyk in 1916[39]. They went back and forth between the campus of St. Volodymyr University, where their new military units were trained, and their camp in Darnytsia. Not only did they settle the city, but they also articulated their existence there:

> Dear professor, the historical commission under your presidency organizes lectures for pupils in the secondary schools in Kiev. These lectures aim at the development of better understanding of current events by way of learning the history of friendly states. With this in mind, we would like to ask you to include a lecture about the history of the Czechoslovak people since the 16th century into the lecture cycle as well. We ask Pavlo Rodionovich Timoshok to deliver this lecture[40].

This letter was sent by the members of the Club, i.e., by former captives who later became responsible for the further development of the Czechoslovak military unit and the Czechoslovak life in Kiev. Their usual tactic was to find 'friends of the Czechoslovak people' who could help them either with disseminating information about their movement or with better contacts with the authorities:

> Dear Konstantin Pavlovich Belkovskii, we regard it as our duty to thank you for your efforts aimed at informing the readers of newspaper "Kievlanin" about our people. Your articles demonstrated your deep knowledge of the subject, but if necessary, we are ready to provide you with further information"[41].

This letter was sent by Vladimir Chalupa, the head of the Club and a former deserter.

Despite all the changes within the Czech and Polish communities mentioned above, their perception of Kiev was not radically altered during the first years of the War. Rather, it was supplemented by the new "underlying city form elements" (Kevin Lynch), such as a camp for captives in Darnytsia or the Polish theatre in downtown Kiev. At the same time, the significance of older landmarks for the private life of the ethnic groups only deepened. None of these changes transformed the Czech or Polish image of the city. Nevertheless, it was not the same city as it had been in June 1914. It was not a *Heimat* anymore. The uncertainties of wartime and the arrival of the new immigrants changed the attitude of the Czechs and Poles to the city. They began to believe that their well-being in Kiev was temporary. They began to lose their perception of themselves as natives of Kiev and instead began to see themselves as tenants or renters of the city space.

Kiev as a lost city

If one wants to study how a city loses its identity, one could not find a better example, than Kiev in 1917-1918. First, the city changed its status, becoming the capital city of the Ukrainian state in January 1918 and, by virtue of this, developing new spatial practices. Secondly, the city was occupied by a foreign power and became involved in civil war and revolution. Finally, it lost its population whose actions had given the city its character and identity.

The first hints of the future catastrophe appeared at the beginning of 1917, when the February Revolution drastically altered life in the entire Russian Empire. The meaning of the event for Kiev was later depicted by Mikhail Bulgakov as follows:

> But these were legendary times, times when a young, carefree generation lived in the gardens of the most beautiful city in our country. In their hearts they believed that all of life would pass in white light, quiet and peaceful, sunrises, sunsets, the Dnieper, the Khreshchatyk, sunny streets in summer, and in winter snow that was not cold or cruel, but thick and caressing... But things turned out quite differently. The legendary times were cut short and history began thunderously, abruptly. I can point out the exact moment it appeared – it was at 10:00 a.m. on March 2, 1917, when a telegram arrived in Kiev signed with two mysterious words, 'Deputy Bublikov'[42].

This indicated a change of authority in the Empire.

There is no evidence that the change of regime influenced the spatial stories of the Czechs and Poles in Kiev. The transformation did not lead them to change their perception of the city, rather it was a signal prompting them to proclaim new goals and tasks which would lead to the independence of their own states. Kiev was uniquely well suited to the pursuit of these aims, as it was located far enough from the centres of the revolution to allow a degree of freedom and normality in the city. That is why the political activities of both ethnic groups came to be based in Kiev[43]. The newly founded Polish executive committee in Rus' (*Polski Komitet Wykonawczy na Rusi*) and the Section of the Czechoslovak National Council in Russia (*Odbočka Česko-Slovenské Národní Rady v Rusku*, or OCSNR) became the main representative organs of the respective ethnic communities in Kiev.

Despite the eventful beginning to the year, in November 1917 Kiev's inhabitants continued their usual spatial practices throughout the city. However, the legendary shot fired by the cruiser *Aurora*, which signalled the beginning of the Bolshevik revolt in Petrograd on 25 October (7 November) 1917, annihilated all existing spatial practices.

The October Revolution directly affected Kiev. Newspapers wrote that the city, which had avoided the brunt of the war, faced the threat of domestic upheavals. In early November 1917 the first armed conflicts took place between the military units of the Provisional Government and the Bolsheviks in Kiev. Some Czechoslovak units were involved in the conflict. Being under the control of the Russian army headquarters (Stavka), they could not remain neutral when they received an order to help the Stavka in the clash in the Mariinski Park. The Czechoslovak leaders did not have any influence on them. They did not even know exactly what the status quo was. For example, they knew that the two Czechoslovak companies found themselves in the centre of the conflict on Mariinski Park. However, they did not know against whom those companies fought – the Bolsheviks or Ukrainians[44]. To avoid further involvement of Czechoslovak soldiers in domestic conflicts in Kiev, the Presidium of the OCSNR proclaimed strong neutrality with respect to the political situation in the former Russian Empire. They agreed to remain observers of the events in the city, rather than participants. This neutrality, however, led to their transformation into city guards later on[45].

Unlike the Czechs, the Polish ethnic group changed neither their perception of the city nor the role they played in the city life. They participated in all meetings organized by the Ukrainian authorities and had representatives in the newly established Ukrainian government. However, they could not continue their previous activities at the same rate. Life during a time of conflict dictated its own set of rules.

This became evident when Tomáš Masaryk came to Kiev, fleeing from Moscow which had fallen to the revolutionaries. In order to read Kiev through Czech spatial stories at that time, we should follow Masaryk's footsteps. He was neither an inhabitant, nor a refugee. Masaryk was a guest in the city, who visited his countrymen for his own political purposes. As a guest he became acquainted with all the places significant for the Czech community. He did not visit the Praha Hotel, probably because Dr Vondrák had lost his influence in the Czech community in April 1917 and did not support Masaryk's policies. He did, however, go to the *Hotel de France* in Khreshchatyk and Ottokar Červeny's family apartment, which became a second home for many Czechs. He visited the Ukrainian authorities and established connections with the Polish community in Kiev. The results of his movement through the city were the relocation of the OCSNR regular meetings, which were then often organized in Červeny's apartment, and that some places came to have meaning for both Czechs and Poles. As a result of his activities an anti-Habsburg movement was established, based in a circus in Kiev. A meeting of the suppressed and divided peoples of Austro-Hungary, organized in cooperation with Polish leaders, took place there on 12 December 1917 and was attended by 4,000 participants[46]. It was that "contact point" (Sennett) that allowed both ethnic groups to enter into the same relationship with the city.

At the same time Masaryk became a key figure and had a great influence on the future of the city. In early February 1918 Kiev was occupied by the Bolsheviks. Only 300 young Kiev students tried to stop the Bolsheviks' offensive and were killed near Kruty on 30 January 1918, not far from the Ukrainian capital. Ukrainian politicians sent delegates to Tomáš Masaryk and tried to use the well-disciplined Czechoslovak military units in the struggle against Bolsheviks. However, Masaryk insisted on their neutrality and did not permit the involvement of the Czechs and Slovaks in "domestic Russian affairs"[47]. Thus, the Czechs did not play the role of Roman geese. They did not attempt to save the city but it seems unlikely that they would have succeeded had they done so. The Bolshevik occupation of Kiev meant that the Czechs lost access to the city. This became evident when the Czech soldiers were forbidden to visit Kiev by the OCSNR. The reason was explained as follows: "They (Kievities) do not like us and there were occasions when our riflemen were beaten". Those Czechs who remained in Kiev, in turn, said: "I command all Czechoslovakian troops who are at the moment located in Kiev City to refrain from walking on the streets. Only in the case of necessity should individuals be sent on official assignments"[48]. Within less than a month the Ukrainian authorities came back to Kiev, but with its new allies – the German and Austro-Hungarian forces.

The Czechoslovak legion and Czech political leaders left Kiev for Vladivostok at the beginning of March. The Czechs and Slovaks who remained in the city, mostly pre-war inhabitants but also former captives who did not share Masaryk's vision, again became outsiders in the city. This time they were accused of being enemies of the Austro-Hungarian monarchy. They had to keep silent and not to show any signs of their existence in the city until the end of the war. In contrast, there was no mass exodus of Poles from the city nor did they change their routes within the city space. However, they partly reoriented their activities towards Warsaw, now that they were able to return there, and towards its main representative – the Regency Council, a creature of Germany.

This was the fourth upheaval which Kiev was to face in this short period. Bulgakov wrote:

> In that winter of 1918 the City lived a strange unnatural life which is unlikely ever to be repeated in the 20th century. Behind the stone walls every apartment was overfilled. Their normal inhabitants constantly squeezed themselves into less and less space, willy-nilly making way for new refugees crowding into the City, all of whom arrived across the arrow-like bridge from the direction of that enigmatic other city...[49].

Fig. 8
View of the bridge.

The city faced ten more upheavals. After the last one, in 1920, it was the Poles' turn to leave Kiev for good. Despite the fact that they left Kiev at different times and under different circumstances, the departure of the Polish and Czech communities transformed the image of the city for good: "Gone with the wind! Kiev stopped being a flourishing, happy, and smiling city, as I remember it from my youth. People, these wonderful Poles with strong necks and wide gestures, that set the pace in the city, were killed or died"[50].

Conclusion

There is a saying: "A city is more beautiful than a village, because it is rich with people's history". Kiev is a good illustration of this statement. Just like other cities, it was inhabited with the spatial stories of its occupants. Although wartime had a significant influence on the life of Kiev's inhabitants, the city continued to model and construct their urban life. It consisted of different elements which made the activities of the Polish and Czech communities possible. They lived their lives through familiar paths, landmarks, and edges which were established in the pre-war period. The Polish and Czech newcomers did not reformulate the local urban identity that they encountered upon their arrival. They only enriched it with new recognizable signs and meanings. The unusual circumstances of war led to old places being used in new ways. The hotels were used for everyday negotiations and offices of new organizations, the circus was turned into a hall for huge meetings, and the university and the cathedrals became the base for military units or newly founded schools.

This chapter is the first attempt to read Kiev through the 'spatial stories' of the Czech and Polish communities in the city. I am aware that important questions, such as how the urban landscape was used by different social groups within these communities, whether use of the landscape unified or divided them and how the social hierarchy of these communities operated within the city, have not been elaborated in the text. Examination of these aspects, however, needs further research and, thus, will be the subject of future publications on the issue.

According to the material analyzed in this chapter one can perceive a change in the Czech and Polish relationship with the city. Before the war they identified closely with the city rooting their lives there. During and after the conflict they began to perceive the city as a rented space and thought of returning to their native lands. Finally, after the revolution, they were forced to leave. If we follow the spatial stories of the Czechs and Poles, we can read Kiev as a unique city filled with elusive, but beautiful spatial practices which tied fond memories to the urban space. Although the city's diverse identity was lost, enough evidence remains to remind us of the footsteps of Czechs and Poles on Kiev's streets:

I would like to remind you that Kiev, thanks to its unique inhabitants, differs very much from other Russian cities... It is like a bridge between the European West and real Russia. Different nationalities, Ukrainians, Russians, Poles, Jews, Germans, Czechs and others, meeting on that bridge, created a mixture there... Different national interests of the inhabitants defined Kiev's image and gave it the character of an international city in which everybody found what they needed and what they liked... I came to Kiev only in 1909 as a Volhynian Czech who had heard about Kiev ten years earlier, and I was filled with endless respect for the metropolis of our South-Western country![51].

Notes

1 J. Hašek, *Osudy dobrého vojáka Švejka* [The Good Soldier Švejk], Bratislava 2000 [first published 1921-1923], p. 5.

2 M. de Certeau, *L'invention du quotidien*, Paris 1974 [cited from *The Practice of Everyday Life*, trans. Rendall S., Berkeley - Los Angeles 2002 , p. 9].

3 Quotation from A. Wierzbicka, *Understanding Cultures through Their Key Words: English, Polish, German, and Japanese,* New York - Oxford 1997, p. 21.

4 J. Winter, J-L. Robert, *Conclusion: towards a social history of capital cities at war,* in J. Winter, J-L. Robert (eds.), *Capital Cities at War: Paris, London, Berlin 1914-1919,* Cambridge 1997, p.549.

5 Where you feel good, there is your home (Lat.)

6 Here, the term "ethnic communities" is defined according to A. Smith and means a social network or series of networks formed by people who possessed specific cultural attributes (common name, history, culture, language, customs, traditions, religion etc.). By the end of the war the Czech and Polish groups start behaving more like national minorities, meeting one of the characteristics of a national minority suggested by Brubaker: "the demand for state recognition of this distinct ethnocultural nationality". Deeper investigation of how the Poles and Czechs in the Ukrainian lands were transformed from ethnic members into legal citizens of their future independent states is not the aim of this chapter. The issue will be elaborated in the further research. See A. Smith, *The Origins of Nations,* in G. Eley, L. Suny, *Becoming a Naitonal: A Reader,* New York - Oxford 1996, pp. 109-110; R. Brubaker, *Nationalism Reframed. Nationhood and the National Question in the New Europe,* Cambridge 1996, p. 60.

7 Д. Бовуа, *Битва за землю в Україні 1863-1914. Поляки в соціо-етнічних конфліктах* [La Bataille de la Terre en Ukraine 1863-1914. Les Polonais et les conflits socio-ethniques], trans. Z. Boryssiouk, "Критика", 1998, p. 263. This and other quotations from the Ukrainian, Russian, Polish and Czech original texts are translated by the author of the chapter.

8 J.F.N. Bradley, *The Czechoslovak Legion in Russia, 1914-1920,* New York 1991, p. 14.

9 Masaryk, the first president of the Czechoslovak Republic, would later use the name *Malorossia* (Little Russia), adopting the Russian scheme, or Ukraine, depending on the political situation.

10 It is necessary to emphasize here that the words Poles and Czechs used for the territory they inhabited were quite unique to each group and, obviously, contrasted with official Russian imperial discourse. More widely used names for the Ukraine within the empire at that time were Малороссия (Malorossia, Little Russia) or Юго-Западный край (Yugo-Zapadnyi krai, South-Western Land); both names defined the region as an integral part of the Russian Empire. Concurrently, the name Ukraine began to be used in political vocabulary. Andreas Kappeler commented that "only during the second half of the 19th and the beginning of the 20th century did the terms 'Ukraine' and 'Ukrainians', which had been used since the middle ages for particular regions, gradually become the common self-designation of the emerging nation. 'Ukraine' has served as the official name of the region only since 1917", A. Kappeler,

'Great Russians' and 'Little Russians': Russian-Ukrainian Relations and Perceptions on Historical Perspective, in The Donald W. Treadgold Papers in Russian, "East European, and Central Asian Studies", October 2003, No. 39, p. 14. See also *Nazwa geograficzna. Rozpatrywany obszar* [Geographic name. Defined region], in *Pamiętnik Kijowski*,1959, vol. I, p. 9; М. Грушевський, Хто такі українці і чого вони хочуть [Who the Ukrainians are and what they want], in Політологія: кінець XIX – перша половина XX ст. Хрестоматія, Lviv 1996, p. 180-181.

11 X. Glinka, *W cieniu Złotej bramy* [In a shadow of the Golden Gates], in *Pamiętnik Kijowski*, vol. I, 1959, p. 221.

12 But it has this function in modern Kiev.

13 See K. Lynch, *The Image of the City*, New York 1960, p. 66.

14 Here I follow R. Sennet's introduction to an imagined tour down Halstead street in Chicago around 1910. See R. Sennett, *The Uses of Disorder: Personal Identity and City Life*, New York 1971, p. 53.

15 De Certeau, *The Practice* cit., p. 108.

16 S. Nicieja, *'Polski Kijów' i jego zagłada w latach 1918-1920 w świetle wspomnień kijowian* ['Polish Kiev' and its death], in "Przegląd Wschodni", 1992/1993, vol. II, 4 (8), p. 852.

17 V. Švihovský *Kijev a kijevští Češi* [Kiev and Kievan Czechs], in *Naše zahraničí. Sborník Národní rady československé*, 1923, vol. IV, No. 4, p. 157.

18 S. Nicieja, *'Polski Kijów'* cit., p. 853; X. Glinka, *W cieniu Złotej bramy* [In a shadow of the Golden Gates], in *Pamiętnik Kijowski*, vol. I, pp. 223,234.

19 X. Glinka, *W cieniu* cit., pp. 232-235; Ернст Ф. Контракти та Контрактовий будинок у Києві, 1798-1923, [Contracts and Contract House in Kiev, 1798-1923], Kiev 1923.

20 Švihovský, *Kijev a kijevští Češi* cit., p. 157.

21 Quotation from Nicieja, *'Polski Kijów'* cit., p. 854.

22 It is common knowledge that national democrats were the most powerful group within the Polish community across Ukraine, as well as in Polish student body at the St. Volodymyr University in Kiev in which young people founded the secret organization *Polonia* in 1901. Education was another sphere to which Polish public figures paid a lot of attention. In 1904 the society *Oświata Narodowa na Rusi* [National Education in Rus'] was established by Polish businessmen.

23 Z.Rejman, *Dr. Vondrák pokrokovec – nebo reakcionář?* in "Přiloha 'Věstníku Ústředního Sdružení Čechů a Slováků z Ruska", 1930, vol. X, No. 5, p. 2; F. Kovářik, *Dr. Václav Vondrák padesátníkem, ibid.*, p. 3.

24 See the pioneering work on the issue: B. Pietrow-Ennker, G. Ulianova (eds.) *Civic Identity and the Public Sphere in Late Imperial Russia*, Moscow 2007.

25 J. Vaculík, *Dějiny volyňských Čechů* [The History of the Volhynian Czechs], Prague 1998, vol. II, p. 6.

26 Winter, *Paris, London, Berlin 1914-19* cit., pp. 14-15.

27 Archív Ministerstva Zahraničních Věci (AMZV), SA, Spolky 5, Český komitet v Moskvě, Телеграмма. Петроград 13 Богумилу Чермаку спр. В., Знаменская 19 [Archives of Ministry of Foreign Affairs in Prague, Siberian Archive, Associations, box 5, the Czech Committee in Moscow, Telegram, Petrograd 13 to Bohumil Čermák spr. V., Znamenskaia 19].

28 В. Драгомирецкий, *Чехословаки в России 1914-1920* [Czechoslovaks in Russia 1914-1920], Paris - Prague 1928, p. 14; Б. Татаров-Альберт, *Драматичні сторінки історії* [Dramatic Pages of History], in "Хроніка 2000: Чехія" [Chronicle 2000: Bohemia], Kiev 1999, vol. 29-30, t. II, p. 272-274.

29 Winter, *Paris, London, Berlin 1914-1919* cit., p. 23.

30 The *Druzhina* consisted of four companies. There were 1,012 soldiers in the unit at the beginning of October 777 of whom were of Czech origin. See F. Šteidler, *Československé zahraniční vojsko* [Czechoslovak army abroad], in Československá vlastivěda. Stát, Prague 1931, vol. V, p. 558; В. Драгомирецкий, *Чехословаки* cit., p. 18;

[31] See Н. Ходорович, *Пламенный патриот (Из воспоминаний о д-ре В. Вондраке)* in "Příloha 'Věstníku Ústředního Sdružení Čechů a Slováků z Ruska", 1930, 10, 5, p. 5.

[32] AMZV, SA. Spolky [Associations], box 13, book 2, p. 13, 17.

[33] See M. Mądzik, *Z działalności Kijowskiej Rady Okręgowej Polskich Towarzystw Pomocy Ofiarom wojny w latach I wojny światowej* [On the activities of the Regional Kiev Council of the Polish Society for Supporting war Victims during World War I], in *Pamiętnik Kijowski*, vol. VI, 'Polacy w Kijowie', Kiev 2002, pp. 184-185.

[34] S. Walewski, *C.K.O. w Winnicy na Podolu* [C.K.O. in Vinnytsia in Podole], in London 1966, vol. III, p. 149.

[35] See W. Gunther, *Polski teatr w Kijowie* [Polish theater in Kiev] in London 1966, vol. III, p. 194.

[36] The Russian authorities issued the appropriate permission in October 1915. Statistical data shows that pupils mostly consisted of newcomers, e.g. there were 79 children from Congress Poland among 150 pupils in a school founded by St. Alexander's Cathedral. See S. Sopicki, *Omówienie pracy Jana Korneckiego 'Oświata Polska na Rusi w czasie wielkiej wojny światowej'* [The discussion on Jan Kornecki's book "Polish education in Rus' during World War I"], in *Pamiętnik Kijowski*, 1959, vol. I, p. 199.

[37] At the same time Kiev became attractive to conspirators who established their own 'subculture' and had a completely different image of the city. A conspiracy network was initiated by the Polish Socialist party members in general and by Józef Piłsudski, the future head of the Polish state, in particular. Their goal was the establishment of an independent Polish Republic. In January 1915 a conspiratorial Polish military organization (*POW – Polska organizacja wojskowa*) opened a branch in Kiev. It depended on the Zhytomyr unit and was led by Józef Bromirski. By 1917 all the units of the organization in Ukraine were controlled by Kiev, which turned the city into a center of the Polish insurgent movement against the Russian empire. See M. Wrzosek, *Polski czyn zbrojny podczas Pierwszej wojny światowej: 1914-1918* [The Polish millitary action during the World War I: 1914-1918], Warsaw 1990, p. 377.

[38] AMZV, SA, Spolky, box 11, *Stanovy spolupracovníků Svazu Česko-Slovenských spolků na Rusi. Kopie. Schváleno Svazem na schůzi* [Statutes of the Club of Captive Co-Workers affiliated with the Union of Czechoslovak Societies in Rus'. Copy. Declared at the Union meeting on 26/X 1916, N. 726, 28/X 1916].

[39] V. Ambrož, *Češi a Slováci v Rusku* [Czechs and Slovaks in Russia], in *Naše zahraničí. Sborník Národní rady československé*, 1922, vol. 3, No. 3, pp. 97-100.

[40] AMZV, SA, Spolky, box 11, Его превосходительству Павлу Николаевичу Ардашеву, профессору университета св. Владимира, председателю Исторической комиссии при Киевской учебном округе, Kiev, undated.

[41] AMZV, SA, Spolky, box 11, Dopis K. Belkovskému. Odesláno 24.11.1916 [Letter to K. Belkovskii. Sent on 24 November 1916].

[42] M. Bulgakov, *The City of Kiev*, in Id., *Notes on the Cuff and Other Stories*, Ann Arbor 1991, p. 207.

[43] On 2-3 March, the first congress of Polish political parties was organized in Kiev. According to its decision the "committee of nine" was established. The committee was responsible for organization of Polish representation in *Rus'*. The delegates from more than 30 polish organizations located in Ukraine participated in its first meeting on 6 March in Kiev. The Polish executive committee in *Rus'* (*Polski Komitet Wykonawczy, or PKW*) was established by them. On 7 March J. Bartoszewicz, former editor of *Dziennik Kijowski*, was elected as its chair. Within the next three months 127 Polish Societies applied for participation in the Committee activities. See: Archiwum Akt Nowych w Warszawie (AAN), Organizacje polskie w Rosji, sygn. 37, p. 24; H. Jabłoński, *Polska autonomia narodowa na Ukrainie 1917-1918* [Polish national autonomy in Ukraine 1917-1918], Warsaw 1948, p. 36. At the same time in April Kiev became a host city for the 3rd congress of *Union of the Czech and Slovak Societies in Russia*. It was not only the most fruitful congress, but also the last one. 48 organizations and societies from

the whole Russian Empire participated at the congress, among them: the Czech Committee for war victims support of J. Jindřišek, Jan Amos Komenský Society, Voluntary Fire Units in Kvasyliv, Semyduby; the Czech Committee in Sumy; Society of Russsian-Czech-Slovak economic cooperation in Kiev, the Czechoslovakian Society in Berdychiv (factory 'Progress'); the Czechoslovak Credit Society; the Czech Society in Poltava etc: AMZV, Spolky, box. 13, *České spolky zastoupení ve Svazu česko-slovenských spolků na Rusi* [Czech association represented in the Union of Czecho-Slovak associations in Russia].

44 At that moment both the Ukrainian military units and the Bolsheviks' forces meant the same for the Czechs – as both were new political powers whose activities were directed against the Provisional Government: Vojenský historický archiv Vojenského ústředního archivu [VHA VUA - Military Historical Archive of the Central Military Archives, Prague, Czech Republic], OČSNR v Rusku – presidium [OCSNR in Russia - presidium], 1917-1918, box 6, sig. 2703. Presidium komisi. V Kyjevě 18.11.1917. Dopis I.Kudely [Presidium of the commission. Kiev 18 November 1917. Letter I. Kudely], p.3.

45 The Czechs were the only military force in Kiev, which was allowed to guard the most important urban objects by both the Ukrainian and the Bolshevik authorities. Thanks to them the dwellers had electricity and water despite military conflicts. Indeed, they were the only military authority which could guarantee safety for the electric station, spirituous fabric, water supply, warehouses. However, OCSNRR refused the Council of Landlords Society's and rectors of Kiev Polytechnic appeals to delegate the legions to guard Kiev against looters: VHA VUA, *První česko-slovenský střelecký pluk. Rozkazy* [The First Czechoslovak rifle regiment. Orders], book 11. 1917-1918. *Приказ по 1-му Чешско-Словацкому* [The order to the 1st Czechoslovak rifle regiment]; VHA VUA, *OČSNR v Rusku – presidium* [OCSNR in Russia - presidium]. 1917-1918, box 6, sig. 4093. *Presidium OČSNR, Kijev 24.01.1918. č. 3747. стрелковому «Яна Гуса» полку, № 1252. 5.02.1918* [Presidium OCSNR, Kiev 24 January 1918, c.j. 3747 to Jan Hus rifle regiment, No. 1252, 5 February 1918]; VHA VUA, *OČSNR v Rusku – presidium* [OCSNR in Russia - presidium]. 1917-1918, box 23, 1918. *Zapísy schůzí. Leden-únor. Opisy.* [Records of the meetings. January-February. Descriptions], sig. 28. *Protokol presidiální schůze konané 24.01.1918* [Minutes of the Presidium meeting held on 24 January 1918], sig. 29. *Protokol presidiální schůze konané 25.01.1918* [Minutes of the Presidium meeting held on 25 January 1918].

46 AMZV, box 6, sig. 2703. *Митинг угнетенных и расчлененных народов* [The meeting of the oppressed and divided nations], p. 2.

47 VHA VUA, *První česko-slovenský střelecký pluk. Rozkazy* [The First Czechoslovak rifle regiment. Orders], book 11. 1917-1918. *Приказ по 1-му Чешско-Словацкому* [The order to the 1st Czechoslovak rifle regiment]; VHA VUA, *OČSNR v Rusku – presidium* [OCSNR in Russia - presidium]. 1917-1918, box 6, sig. 4093. *Presidium OČSNR, Kijev 24.01.1918. č. 3747. стрелковому «Яна Гуса» полку, № 1252, 5.02.1918* [Presidium OCSNR, Kiev, 24 January 1918, c.j. 3747 to Jan Hus artillery regiment, No. 1252, 5 February 1918].

48 VHA VUA, *První česko-slovenský střelecký pluk. Rozkazy* [The First Czechoslovak rifle regiment. Orders], *book 11. 1917-1918. Приказ No. 1241; Приказ No. 1252* [Order No. 1241; Order No. 1252].

49 M. Bulgakov, *The White Guard*, trans. M. Glenny with an epilogue by Victor Nekrasov, New York - St. Louis - San Francisco 1971, pp. 56-57.

50 Glinka, *W cieniu* cit., p. 236.

51 Švihovský, *Kijev a kijevští Češi* cit., p. 153.

Bibliography

Primary sources

Unpublished:

Archiwum Akt Nowych w Warszawie (AAN) [Nation Archive, new funds, in Warsaw]

-Akta Romana Knolla
-Organizacje polskie w Rosji

Archív Ministerstva Zahraničních Věci (AMZV) [Archives of Ministry of Foreign Affairs in Prague]
-Sibiřský archív
-Korespondencja

Vojenský historický archiv Vojenského ústředního archive v Praze [Military Historical Archive of the Central Military Archives in Prague]
- OČSNR v Rusku – presidium. 1917-1918.
- První česko-slovenský střelecký pluk. Rozkazy

Published:

Ambrož V., *Češi a Slováci v Rusku* [Czechs and Slovaks in Russia], in *Naše zahraničí. Sborník Národní rady československé,* 1922, vol. 3, No 3, pp. 97-100.

Bulgakov M., *The City of Kiev,* Id., *Notes on the Cuff and Other Stories,* Ann Arbor 1991.

Bulgakov M., *The White Guard,* trans. Glenny M. with an epilogue by Victor Nekrasov, New York - St. Louis - San Francisco 1971.

Glinka X., *W cieniu Złotej bramy* [In a shadow of the Golden Gates], in *Pamiętnik Kijowski,* vol. I, London 1959, pp. 209-236.

Gunther W., *Polski teatr w Kijowie* [Polish theater in Kiev], in *Pamiętnik Kijowski,* vol. III, London 1966, p. 194-199.

Kovařík F., *Dr. Václav Vondrák padesátníkem,* in "Příloha 'Věstníku Ústředního Sdružení Čechů a Slováků z Ruska", 1930, X, 5.

Rejman Z., *Dr. Vondrák pokrokovec – nebo reakcionář?* in "Přiloha 'Věstníku Ústředního Sdružení Čechů a Slováků z Ruska", 1930, X, 5. pp. 2-3.

Švihovský V., *Kijev a kijevští Češi* [Kiev and Kievan Czechs], in *Naše zahraničí. Sborník Národní rady československé,* vol. IV, No. 4. pp.152-163.

Walewski S., *C.K.O. w Winnicy na Podolu* [C.K.O. in Vinnytsia in Podole], in *Pamiętnik Kijowski,* vol. III, London 1966, pp. 149-157.

Грушевський М., *Хто такі українці і чого вони хочуть* [*Who the Ukrainians are and what they want*], in Політологія: кінець XIX – перша половина XX ст. Хрестоматія, Lviv 1996, p. 178-189.

Перепись г. Киева 16 марта 1919 г. Ч. 1: население, Kiev 1920, tabl. II. [Census in Kiev, 16 March 1919. Part 1: population]

Ходорович Н., *Пламенный патриот (Из воспоминаний о д-ре В. Вондраке)* [Sincere Suppoter (from the memories on dr. V. Vondra)] in "Přiloha 'Věstníku Ústředního Sdružení Čechů a Slováků z Ruska", 1930, X, 5, p. 5-6.

Secondary references:

Bradley J.F.N., *The Czechoslovak Legion in Russia, 1914-1920,* New York 1991.

Certeau M. de, *The Practice of Everyday Life,* trans. Rendall S., Berkeley - Los Angeles 2002 [first published as *L'Invention du quotidien,* vol. 1, *Arts de Faire,* Paris 1974].

Hašek J., *Osudy dobrého vojáka Švejka* [The Good Soldier Švejk], Bratislava 2000 [first published in 1921-1923 in Prague].

Jabłoński H., *Polska autonomia narodowa na Ukrainie 1917-1918* [Polish national autonomy in Ukraine 1917-1918], Warsaw 1948, p. 36.

Kappeler A., *'Great Russians' and 'Little Russians': Russian-Ukrainian Relations and Perceptions on Historical Perspective,* in *The Donald W. Treadgold Papers in Russian*, "East European, and Central Asian Studies", October 2003, 39, p. 72.

Liczebność Polaków na Rusi na przełomie w. XIX i XX [The quantity of the Poles in Rus' between the 19th and 20th centuries], in *Pamiętnik Kijowski*, London 1959, t. I, pp. 86-90.

Lynch K., *The Image of the City*, New York 1960.

Mądzik M., *Z działalności Kijowskiej Rady Okręgowej Polskich Towarzystw Pomocy Ofiarom wojny w latach I wojny światowej* [From the activities of the Regional Kiev Council of the Polish Society for Supporting war Victims during World War I], in *Pamiętnik Kijowski* [Memories of Kiev], vol. VI, 'Polacy w Kijowie', Kiev 2002, pp. 177-195.

Nazwa geograficzna. Rozpatrywany obszar [Geographic name. Defined region], in *Pamiętnik Kijowski*, , vol. I, London 1959, pp. 9-10

Nicieja S., *'Polski Kijów' i jego zagłada w latach 1918-1920 w świetle wspomnień kijowian* ['Polish Kiev' and its death], in "Przegląd Wschodni", 1992/1993, II, 4 (8), pp. 851-862.

Pietrow-Ennker B., Ulianova G. (eds.), *Civic Identity and the Public Sphere in Late Imperial Russia,* Moscow 2007.

Sennett R., *The Uses of Disorder: Personal Identity and City Life,* New York, 1971,

Sopicki S., *Omówienie pracy Jana Korneckiego 'Oświata Polska na Rusi w czasie wielkiej wojny światowej'*, in *Pamiętnik Kijowski*, vol. I, London 1959, pp. 198-205.

Šteidler F., *Československé zahraniční vojsko* [Czechoslovak army abroad], in *Československá vlastivěda. Stát*, Prague 1931, vol. V, pp. 556-581.

Vaculík J., *Dějiny volyňských Čechů* [The History of the Volhynian Czechs], Prague 1998, vol. II.

Wierzbicka A., *Understanding Cultures through Their Key Words: English, Polish, German, and Japanese,* New York - Oxford 1997

Winter J., Robert J-L. (eds.), *Capital Cities at War: Paris, London, Berlin 1914-1919*, Cambridge 1997

Wrzosek M., *Polski czyn zbrojny podczas Pierwszej wojny światowej: 1914-1918* [The Polish millitary action during the First World War: 1914-1918], Warsaw 1990, p. 377.

Бовуа Д., *Битва за землю в Україні 1863-1914. Поляки в соціо-етнічних конфліктах* [La Bataille de la Terre en Ukraine 1863-1914. Les Polonais et les conflits socio-ethniques], trans. Boryssiouk Z., "Критика" 1998.

Верстюк В., Українська Центральна Рада [Ukrainian Central Rada], Kiev 1997, p. 208.

Драгомирецкий В., *Чехословаки в России 1914-1920* [Czechoslovaks in Russia 1914-1920], Paris - Prague 1928.

Луцький Ю., *Чехи на Україні (1917-1933)* [The Czechs in Ukraine (1917-1933)], in "Хроніка 2000: Чехія", [Chronicle 2000: Bohemia], Kiev 1999, vol. 29-30, t. II, p. 119.

Савченко Г., *Польські військові формування у Києві у 1917 р.*, in *Pamiętnik Kijowski*, vol. VI, Polacy w Kijowie, Kiev 2002, p. 220.

Татаров-Альберт Б., *Драматичні сторінки історії* [Dramatic Pages of History], in "Хроніка 2000: Чехія", [Chronicle 2000: Bohemia], Kiev 1999, vol. 29-30, t. II, pp. 272-284.

Illustrations from *Catalogue J*, Detroit Publishing Company, 1905: Library of Congress Prints and Photographs Division, Photochrom Collection: Fig. 1, ppmsc 03830; Fig. 2, ppmsc 03825; Fig. 3., ppmsc 03829; Fig. 4, ppmsc 03817; Fig. 5, ppmsc 03812; Fig. 6, ppmsc 03818; Fig 7., ppmsc 03823; Fig. 8, ppmsc 03819.

Kraków or Krakau? Polish Citizens' Reactions to Transformations of Urban Space by the Nazi Occupying Forces

ANNA CZOCHER
Jagiellonian University

ABSTRACT

The specific character of Krakow during occupation was to huge degree determined by the influx of German people. The authorities felt obliged to assure for the Germans the living conditions proper for someone having the status of a victor. The chapter concerns how Krakow's Polish community perceived the changes introduced by the occupiers and the Poles' reactions to the Nazi occupants' activities in the field of urban space management.

Wojna zastała Kraków w trakcie realizacji dalekosiężnego planu rozbudowy miasta. W czasie okupacji niemiecki zarząd miasta zamierzał kontynuować przedwojenny program inwestycyjny, przystosowując go do zmienionych na skutek wojny warunków polityczno-gospodarczych. Wiązało się to przede wszystkim z naczelnym zadaniem uczynienia z Krakowa czysto niemieckiego miasta, co miało się przejawiać w wyglądzie zewnętrznym i układzie strukturalnym ludności. Napływającym do Krakowa Niemcom władze chciały zapewnić odpowiednie do statusu zwycięzców warunki życia oraz uwypuklić dominującą pozycję w mieście. W tym celu stworzono całą infrastrukturę „nur für Deutsche" oraz silnie akcentowano niemieckość miasta. Polscy mieszkańcy Krakowa zasadniczo nie mieli wpływu na kierunek zachodzących zmian. Ich postawy można zatem postrzegać jako ocenę zastanej rzeczywistości bez możliwości dowolnego jej kreowania. W swoim artykule chciałbym zastanowić się nad tym, jaki był stosunek polskich mieszkańców Krakowa do działalności okupanta związanej z gospodarowaniem przestrzenią miejską. Czy miasto przekształcane przez okupanta stawało się obce dla jego rdzennych mieszkańców, w jakich kategoriach postrzegano zachodzące zmiany. Interesujące w tym kontekście jest także poszukiwanie sposobów przystosowania się lub obejścia nowych porządków w mieście.

The transformation of Krakow into a German city was not merely a question of changing names – it was also the city's external appearance and the structural make-up of its population which was about to change. The people who had theretofore inhabited the city were to be gradually replaced by German citizens. Therefore, it was the inflow of German people that to a great extent determined Krakow's unique shape as a city. Prior to September 1939 Germans constituted only a minute part of Krakow's population (less than 1%). The city was inhabited mostly by Poles (74%) and Jews (about 25%)[1]. These proportions, however, changed during the Nazi occupation. According to German data from the beginning of 1943, Krakow was inhabited by over 20,000 German soldiers and civilians, which was about 7%-8% of the entire population of the city. Poles constituted about 88% of the population, while the number of Jews who by that time had undergone mass extermination dropped to about 3%. Among the other nationalities who lived in Krakow at that time the most numerous were the Ukrainians (about 0.6%). By the late spring of 1944 the German population reached nearly 30,000 which was the highest number ever to be recorded in Krakow[2].

The foundation of Nazi policy was an ideology based on a racial doctrine. The racial policy, consistently used by the Nazis, resulted in – to put it simply – the segregation of the city's inhabitants into Germans and all those who had been allowed to aspire to "Germanness" (i.e. ethnic Germans, or *Volksdeutsche* and, to a certain extent, Ukrainians), and the rest of the population within which the people of Jewish nationality had been put into a separate category already at the beginning of the war. The division was strict and easily distinguishable even for the outside observer. An Italian war correspondent wrote:

> These are indeed [...] distinct worlds, radically separated by the law and special regulations [...]. The laws regulating that precise separation are extremely strict. Everyone has to live among his own kind: that is the central idea of the law regulating the relations among the various nationalities functioning within the borders of the Generalgouvernement. Obviously, that rule applies also to Germans who are obliged to live among their own kind[3].

Andrzej Chwalba, the author of a synthetic study on the history of Krakow under the German occupation, described that division using the concept of "inner cities", according to which Krakow at that time comprised of several separate cities: German, Polish, Jewish (up to the liquidation of the ghetto) and, in a sense, Ukrainian[4].

The separation affected the urban space management too, since the city was separated into distinct zones designed for each of the ethnic groups. Although the ultimate goal, i.e. the status quo to be introduced after the Nazis' final victory in the war, was the complete transformation of Krakow into a German city, until the war was over the city was to be divided into separate zones. In the autumn of 1939 these were to be: the German zone, the mixed (i.e. German-Polish) zone, the Polish zone and the Jewish zone. By 1942 only three zones were included in the plan: German (situated in the western part of the city), mixed (covering the city centre), and Polish (covering the remaining area)[5].

The Nazi authorities wanted to ensure that the incoming German population would live in conditions which would be fit for their status as victors. In order to provide the right living standards and emphasize Germans' dominant position in the city the entire *nur für Deusche* [For Germans only] infrastructure was created.

Thus, the best buildings and apartments in the city became part of the space reserved for the exclusive use of the German community. Apart from the buildings which had been occupied by the newly-formed Nazi administration and taken over by the German army which was stationed in the city, there was also the City Theatre, the state-of-the-art cinemas, sports halls, the best restaurants, a chain of shops, two public parks situated in the city centre and many other places which were included in the "for Germans only" design. Moreover, in the spaces where Polish and German inhabitants mixed, special seats were reserved for the latter. There were, for example, separate seats on the trams, or special benches in the Planty Park (a greenbelt surrounding the historic centre of the city).

Apart from that, some rather large-scale – considering the war conditions – construction works were undertaken in the city. It was particularly in the first years of the Nazi occupation (until 1943) that the scale of construction works was quite impressive. Major investments which had been initiated by the Polish administration before September 1939 were being completed and some new ones appeared as well. In none of the other cities in the *Generalgouvernement* did Germany build so much, nor were as many permissions for private investments issued anywhere else outside Krakow.

The decision to expand the city's administrative borders (28 May 1941) had a great impact on the German policy in the city too. The expansion of city borders went in line with the plans to create space for the new investments designed on a grand scale. On a short-term basis it gave the Nazi authorities some extra space for the inflow of German citizens, at the cost of the former inhabitants of the city who were expelled from the more elegant residential quarters. The western part of the city, which used to be considered the most attractive before the war, was now transformed into a German residential district. It was there that the occupation authorities realized their investments and built new housing estates, but their housing policy was mainly focused on the mass displacement of the people who used to live in that area.

Poles were to become the citizens of the worse sort, permanently subordinate to the master race. Therefore, although they continued to outnumber other ethnic groups in the city, their role and social status changed drastically.

In the present chapter I wish to discuss the perception of the changes introduced in the occupied city by Krakow's Polish community and to present Poles' reactions to the Nazi occupants' activities in the field of urban space management. Did the city – transformed as it was by the occupation authorities – become alien to its indigenous people? And in what categories did those people perceive the ongoing transformation? Another interesting issue in this context is the search for new solutions and new ways of adapting to (or evading) the new order. I shall deliberately omit the questions connected with occupation terror – the round-ups, the public executions, and the impediments to communication in the city which resulted from the introduction of curfew during the war. Instead, I shall concentrate only on those aspects of the occupation policy in the city which were designed to influence its character permanently. The examples which will be discussed further on do not exhaust the topic – they are merely supposed to demonstrate the direction of changes which took place in the city.

I shall not discuss the issues connected with the Jewish community here since they in fact present a totally separate topic. The policy towards the Jews which the Nazi authorities implemented from the very beginning of the occupation was radically different from the one they used towards Poles. Initially the aim of that policy was the legal and financial discrimination of the Jewish people, later, however, the objective changed into their physical extermination. Krakow's German authorities excelled in introducing anti-Jewish regulations which should be associated with the fact that Krakow, which ultimately was to become a purely German city, had to become a *Judenrein* [cleansed of Jews] city first.

The most valuable sources of information about the perception of the city by its inhabitants are all sorts of materials relating to memoirs (mostly diaries and epistolary materials, but also journals and memoirs). Unfortunately, due to the unique atmosphere which penetrated that period of Krakow's history, the people who wrote down their impressions – whether these were jotted down on the spot, or reminisced many years later – concentrated mainly on the martyrdom of the Polish nation, or on the underground activity directed against the Nazis. Apart from that, the personal testimonies contain plenty of information about the difficulties of everyday life in an occupied country – the problems with buying provisions and finding a flat. Information concerning other aspects of life, such as the writer's feelings about the city and its transformations is treated like some kind of additional, marginal remarks which the writer forgot to erase from the description of other, for him more important, issues. Thus, the scraps of information about the city are as if fished out from the ocean of texts about the difficulties of everyday life or the general mood of the occupied nation.

An additional difficulty which a researcher has to cope with while using materials relating to memoirs is the time in which they were written. Very few sources which were written regularly during the occupation period have survived. The memoirs written after the war carry the burden of the influence of the era in which they originated. There was an unwritten canon of the forms in which the occupation period could be represented in post-war Poland (beginning in the late 1940s and up to the 1980s). The canon which functioned as an element of the Eastern bloc's policy towards the Federal

Republic of Germany determined the framework for all the literature about the war and occupation – memoirs included. Therefore, the authors of the war memoirs, especially those who hoped to get their books published, tended to concentrate on their prison or labour/death camp experiences, on the fight for independence, on clandestine education, or on cultural life. Very little was written on everyday life which was merely presented in the context of the fight with the Nazi aggressors; attitudes which might be interpreted as a sign of consent to the occupation were stigmatized.

Another weakness of the diaries and memoirs describing that period is the almost non-representative nature of these sources. In most cases, the authors were members of the Krakow intelligentsia and either came from the academic or artistic circles, or represented the upper social strata of state officials and army officers.

In order to avoid a biased presentation of the issues which are at the centre of my attention here, I have decided to consult auxiliary materials. Correspondence as well as reports and circular letters issued by the RGO[6] which contained plenty of contemporary information about the general mood of the city turned out to be particularly valuable. Other auxiliary materials included periodicals – especially the classified advertisements columns (which remained unedited and uncensored by the editorial staff) and photographic material.

Reactions to the Transformations of the Urban Space Enforced by the Nazis

The authors of the memoirs narrating the story of the Nazi occupation in Krakow pay very little attention to the changes introduced by the occupying forces in the city's appearance. The majority of memoir writers fail to mention such details as construction works connected with the rearrangement of the urban space, investments, as well as renovation and rebuilding of streets (even those situated in the central parts of the city). Not only could such heavy public works not have remained unnoticed, but they must have caused temporary impediments to the traffic in the central part of Krakow[7]. The inhabitants of the city judged the investments carried out by the occupation authorities in the context of the overall Nazi policy in the city. People were usually convinced that the Nazi authorities could not have been motivated by pure good will and the investments realized in the city were associated with the plans to transform Krakow into a purely German city. Nevertheless, some of the investments and renovation works received a positive response and were said to bring order into the urban space.

> The Austrian fort at the end of Lubicz and Krakowska Streets as well as two houses at the feet of Wawel Castle have been pulled down. The arcaded colonnades running along Grodzka Street and Krakowska Street have been broken[8].
>
> The square in front of the railway station is being ordered thanks to the new, flat cobbles with which it is being paved[9].

Those citizens of Krakow who write about the investments carried out in the city estimated their size as large, especially for the war conditions. They also point out that Polish officials and architects influenced the shape of some of the investments by suggesting construction solutions which would agree with the interest of Polish Krakow[10]. The notes concerning the investments – especially those written by the opponents of the party which ruled in Poland prior to September 1939 – are also connected with the criticism of Polish pre-war municipal authorities. Therefore, in the case of those investments which raised the overall standard of the city and those which failed to be realized before the war (although, according to the critics, they could have been completed then) the public acceptance of the fact that the investments had finally been realized mixed with some grumbling voices who complained that the whole thing had to "wait until the occupation". At this point, we should also say that the occupation authorities continued to realize the general plans for the city's development which had been worked out and implemented by the pre-war Polish administration. The investment which seemed unfavourable for the city as a whole, such as the construction of a German governmental residential area, had not been realized due to the changes in the war situation which were unfavourable to Hitler's army. The use of forced labour during the realization of investment in the city remains a separate issue. The Nazis created special brigades of compulsory Construction Service, *Baudienst*, and also forced prisoners to work at construction sites which, understandingly, ignited fierce resistance among the people of Krakow[11].

On the other hand, Krakow's citizens, and especially the Krakow intelligentsia, paid particular attention to those changes whose aim was to wipe out the Polish spirit from the Krakow cityscape. On top of the list of such activities was the demolition of Krakow's monuments and commemorative plaques associated with the city's Polish history. The demolition of the monument of Mickiewicz which used to be the landmark of Krakow's Main Market Square became an event of particular importance, although it was not the first monument which had been pulled down by the Nazis[12]. If the demolition of the monument of Kościuszko which stood on Wawel Hill[13] seemed somehow justifiable to the people of Krakow in light of the fact that Wawel itself had become the headquarters of the Governor-General, and even if the demolition of the monument commemorating the battle of Grunwald[14] might have seemed an equally justifiable act, considering its strong ideological content, the demolition of the monument representing the beloved poet caused outrage among the people of Krakow and increased the hatred for the occupying force. The event itself was a breakthrough because it not only enraged the Krakow *intelligentsia*, but also ignited the rage of ordinary, uneducated people. Describing the atmosphere on that day (17 August 1940), Karolina Lanckorońska recalls that the knocking down of the monument was something unbelievable at first:

> We were [...] devastated, not so much by the very loss of that not-so-beautiful monument ("we shall make another, and a more beautiful one after the war" we thought), but rather by

> that telling demonstration of who the Germans really were. [...] Krakow, usually so peaceful, was deeply shattered – it was then that the ordinary people who initially seemed to be pretty impressed by the Germans "went berserk" for the first time[15].

The Germanisation of the urban space was also noticed by Krakow's citizens. Apparently people were particularly irritated by the vast number of German flags flapping in the city centre, especially in the Main Market Square and on the buildings occupied by the Nazi administration. The number of the flags "hanging down with the long, blood-red ribbons with the golden lining attached to them"[16] with which the city was decorated was particularly large during the celebrations of Nazi holidays and anniversaries, which made the people of Krakow feel even more bitter. They were also irritated by the plaques with Nazi propaganda scattered around the central points of the city and by the military map with the front lines marked on it which was installed in the Main Market Square during the battle of Stalingrad. Similar sentiments were aroused by the street megaphones installed in all the central points of the city which broadcast propaganda information.

The Germanisation of the name of the city, the names of its streets and of all sorts of institutions did not seem to make a major impression on the people of Krakow. Since the transformation of Krakow into a German city was to be an in-depth, large scale process, apart from the architectural changes, the new investments and renovations, it also covered the sphere of symbols and proper names associated with the city. At the beginning the Poles who worked in the municipal offices boycotted the changes in the name of the city which had been introduced by the Nazis and continued to use the old form: "the Capital Royal City of Krakow" which resulted in further bans regarding that issue introduced by the Stadthauptmann. Initially the change of the city's name from Kraków to Krakau caused an outbreak of ironic comments due to the funny associations which the pronounced form of the German word gave rise to in Polish[17]. The name did not catch on with the Polish citizens of the city anyway[18]. The German name was used by Germans and it only reached the Polish community via e.g. the German official announcements and documents (although the official documents were issued in a bilingual form, the name "Krakau" appeared in the Polish version as well). However, German periodicals published in Polish were not that consistent. Whenever official texts, such as the announcements and directives issued by the Stadthauptmann were published the German form was used, but the Polish version appeared in most articles and usually also in the majority of advertisements, and since the editors usually did not interfere with the original form of the latter we may assume that it was the Polish name – Kraków – that the people who lived in the city used in their everyday conversations.

The changes of street names did not influence the general perception of the city much. The Nazis decided to leave the original Polish names in any case and only added the German equivalent underneath. Poles continued to use the Polish street names, and only sometimes added that nowadays – i.e. under the Nazi occupation – the street also had a German name. The Polish street names with the occasional addition of their German equivalents were also used in the addresses put on the correspondence written in Polish. Official periodicals published in Polish usually used the original Polish street names as they used to be called before the war. However, there was one exception to that rule: the Polish name of the Main Market Square, *Rynek Główny*, was replaced by the German name *Adolf Hitler Platz*[19], and the new name was used quite consistently also in the advertisements and commercials of the Polish companies, which probably means that the Nazis were exceptionally determined to make that name popular and the use thereof was strictly observed. For the people of Krakow "Rynek Główny" became simply "rynek" [the market square], and it was that form which was commonly used in everyday speech.

Far more severe and difficult to evade or accept were the restrictions regarding communication within the urban space and the establishment of separate sectors in the public space to be used by Germans only which had been introduced by the Nazis. The first thing that left the people of Krakow shocked was that they were not allowed to visit Wawel Hill and, consequently, were banned from the Cathedral. But it was not only Wawel which was carefully guarded; also the building of the University of Mining and Metallurgy at No. 30 Mickiewicza Avenue which during the German occupation housed the Government of the *Generalgouvernement* was strictly controlled by the Nazis. "One was not allowed to walk down Czarnowiejska Street or Reymonta Street on the side which adjoined the buildings of the university complex which had been taken over by Germans; you had to carefully cross the street and walk on the other side of the avenue"[20]. German guards also stood at the entrance to the Potocki Palace in the Main Market Square which housed the district authorities.

Further restrictions were gradually introduced: two of the city's public parks (Jordan's Park and Krakowski Park) were closed for the Polish citizens, special *nur für Deutsche* benches appeared in the Planty greenbelt, and Poles were no longer allowed to take walks to Kościuszko's Mount because German troops were stationed there[21]. The people of Krakow felt that the new bans painfully restricted their rights to use the public space of their own city. Krakow's pride was also hurt by the directives related to racial segregation issued by the Nazis. Separate restaurants for Germans only, separate seats on the trams, separate carriages on the trains aroused even more heated emotions and had an even worse effect on the comfort of the other city dwellers. The memoirs written by Krakow's citizens give us the following images from life under the occupation:

> Their shops were full, Germans had separate trams, all the elegant coffee shops and restaurants which were beyond the reach of Poles. Buildings were adorned with their flags. [...] German melodies or official announcements were heard from the loudspeakers which hung everywhere around [...] Especially the Main Market Square was full of flags with swastikas[22]. Also those who lived in Krakow only temporarily noticed the saturation of the public sphere with elements of Germanness: I did not like that city and I guess I was afraid of it. It

was full of Germans, full of uniforms with swastikas, Nazi flags, '*nur für Deutsche*' notices, lots of German conversations in the streets – there was much more of all these things than I have seen in any other city in the *Generalgouvernement* I know"[23].

The people of Krakow did not accept the directive to expand the borders of the city issued by the Central Department of Internal Affairs of the Government of the *Generalgouvernement* on 28 May 1941 and was to be valid from 1 June of that year. Despite the fact that the directive was consistent with the urban development plan prepared by Kazimierz Dziewoński already before the war (1938), the citizens of Krakow were not pleased with it. However, it was not so much the resistance towards Nazi directives, as the character of the areas which were to be annexed to the city that was the issue here. The new annexations were mostly rural or suburban administrative units with very poor infrastructure. The citizens of Krakow feared the dispersal of investments and social aid and felt higher taxes were to be introduced[24]. Their relationship towards the newly annexed areas became apparent during the displacement of the Polish community from Krakow: the new districts were treated as suburban villages although people were frequently reminded about the fact of annexation. The letters of the Polish Welfare Committee City of Krakow[25], sent, for example, to transport companies and the inhabitants of suburban areas in 1942 during the period of mass displacement of the Polish people from the city centre clearly reflect those sentiments. The Committee called the transport companies to offer transportation services "so that to assist with the displacement of the Polish people from some districts of Krakow to other districts of the city, or to the villages situated within the administrative borders of Greater Krakow"[26]. In another letter, the Committee encourages the people to look for accommodation "outside the borders of Krakow, i.e. both in the nearby villages which have recently been annexed to the City of Krakow, and in the many towns and villages of the Krakow principality"[27].

Even the displacements within the borders of "old Krakow" were traumatic experiences for the city's citizens. These were mass displacement actions and people were usually forced to pack and move out within the short time of about two or three weeks, and in many cases that period shrunk to a mere couple of hours. The displaced people were often forced to look for a new accommodation on their own which was extremely difficult at that time since Krakow was overpopulated during the war. Moreover, the standard of the new accommodation was always lower than that of the house from which one was being expelled. Therefore, Krakow could rightly be called a city on the move, since during the entire period of Nazi occupation people were constantly forced to change accommodation. Those who used to live in the elegant western and central districts suffered not only from the feeling of homelessness, but also experienced social degradation. All over Krakow people were being thrown out of their apartments because every decent flat, and indeed, every decent place in the entire Krakow was already *nur für Deutsche*. The extremely dirty post-Jewish district which stretched from the railway station to Kazimierz was practically the only part of the city which was available for Polish people to live in[28]. At this point we must mention that also the Jewish people who lived in Krakow – both the wealthy who lived in the elegant districts, and the poor who inhabited the traditionally Jewish quarter of the city, Kazimierz – were displaced and moved into a ghetto which covered a small sector of the Podgórze quarter inhabited mostly by workers. The photographs taken by the Nazis document the peregrinations of the Poles and Jews as they walked in opposite directions: the Jews walked from Kazimierz to Podgórze, and the Poles from Podgórze to Kazimierz. The pictures in which the two processions of exiles have been captured at the point when they meet crossing the Krakow bridges are symbolic[29]. The fear of losing one's home, along with the fear of losing one's life and family was the basic malady of existence under the Nazi occupation. The feeling of injustice after one has been expelled from one's own apartment and the thirst for revenge were crucial factors which motivated people to resist the Nazi occupation.

The search for one's own space in the occupied city

The city itself was affected by the German policy in terms of its transformation in the spheres of human substance and urban space. The western part of the city became 'purely German'. The centre was German-Polish, but visually the German element prevailed. Despite the process of Germanisation of the urban public space and despite the fact that a vast number of the more stately buildings have been taken over by the German administration and transformed into apartments for the inflowing German citizens, the city centre managed to remain the centre of the Polish Krakow. A fact which certainly had an impact on that situation was the concentric spatial layout of Krakow and the concentration of the city's major offices, trade and service centres in which Poles continued to work in its central area. Moreover, before the war Krakow was a relatively small city, and therefore all of the important aspects of municipal life focused in the historic centre. The Nazi occupation changed that *status quo*, in the sense that the public space was rearranged according to the rules enforced by the occupation authorities. The people who lived under occupation shifted their activities into the space which theretofore was considered private, or semi-private. Houses became the substitute for public life[30]. They became the space of political, educational and cultural activity. In a sense, the Krakow coffee shops played a similar role; however, private houses were considered to be safer[31].

Wherever it was possible, Poles continued to use whatever was left of the public space available to them. The Planty greenbelt remained the most popular place to go for a walk. If we assume that the information included in the diaries is true, then we will have to imagine how crowded that public park must have been on a Saturday summer night[32]. The Main Market Square, despite the change of name, remained the traditional centre of trade, and the Krakow flower vendors were never removed from their stalls. It was also here that the officially approved cultural and social events took place, although we should note that their scale was extremely modest in comparison with what the cultural life used to be like before the war.

Gradually, people began to feel at home in the districts where Polish citizens used to be in the minority until the period of occupation. Poles who had been displaced from their homes in other parts of the city adapted the Kazimierz district to their own needs, which was best reflected in the number of workshops and shops, as well as numerous restaurants and cafes which were established there. Large advertisements presenting the newly-established restaurants and cafes appeared in the official press especially in the final year of the war, tempting the potential customers not only with their cuisine, but with their artistic programmes also[33].

One way of searching for one's own space in the occupied city was to ignore the order which had been introduced by the Nazis, another was the deliberate breach of bans and prohibition or the manifestation of one's discontentment. The use of the original, pre-war street names, or the humorous treatment of the Germanised form of the city's name were attempts to ignore the rules of the occupation order. The ignoring of German rules regarding the order of the public space, such as commuting in a tram carriage which had been reserved 'for Germans only', or buying in the German shops was treated as a form of anti-Nazi resistance. This kind of behaviour was typical for the young generation of Krakow's citizens who by acting in this way wanted to demonstrate their bravado and contempt for the Nazi bans. At this point we should note that although this kind of behaviour was not particularly harmful, the potential punishment could have been extremely harsh, including imprisonment and even death. Another form of active resistance against the appropriation of urban space was spreading one's own propaganda. Anti-Nazi slogans appeared on the walls and German notices were 'transformed' to give them a humorous sense[34]. An interesting example was the manifestation of people's opposition to the removal of the monument of Adam Mickiewicz from the Main Market Square. Poles simply pretended that the monument was still there and nobody walked on the spot where it used to stand – everyone just went around[35].

Managing urban space for your own needs is much easier when you know the city's topography. The indigenous inhabitants knew many secret places and passages in the city which had not been represented on any map, giving them an advantage over the occupying Nazi forces. They could just disappear among the secret streets, houses and backyards. Because the city's main streets were full of Germans, Poles often preferred to use the less popular routes, or simply used shortcuts about which only they knew. Such strategies were useful especially for those who were involved in the underground movements. The Krakow underground community even published a list of the so-called passage gates – the secret passageways between the stone houses which made it possible to quickly move from place to place without using the busy streets. The intimate knowledge of the city's topography not only made moving around the city easier, but sometimes, e.g. during round-ups, could even save lives. A woman from Krakow wrote, recalling the summer of 1944:

> My husband and I as a young married couple were returning from the house of our parents, who lived in Podgórze, to our modest rented room at Michałowskiego Street. And once again my knowledge of the old little streets and passages saved our lives. I remember it as if it happened today, how we crossed Gołębia Street, Jagiellońska Street, walked by our university [...] and saw the German helmets in the background. I guess it was my old little streets that led us safely home[36].

The establishment of special spaces which were to be used by Germans only, the appropriation of the key buildings in the city in order to emphasise the German domination, German notices in the shop windows and in the public utility places, German posters on the poster pillars – it all created the desired propaganda effect. The picture was completed by the Nazi flags and emblems and by the vast number of uniformed Germans in the streets of the city centre. The number of Germans present in the city seemed larger than it really was, and the city itself seemed completely different to the place it was before the war. Had it not been for these strategies, the seven or eight per cent of Krakow's population that Germans in fact comprised would have been dispersed in the entire mass of the rest of its inhabitants. Instead, the visualisation of domination gave rise to the opinion that

> ...in fact the number of Germans reached almost a half of Krakow's entire population. That created a cityscape which was completely different to that of Warsaw where the domination of the Polish element was never lost[37].

> The vast number of people wearing all sorts of uniforms and civilians with Hackenkreutz in their lapels was a striking sight[38].

It was, therefore, no wonder that outsiders coming to the city had the impression that Krakow was indeed becoming a German city.

The Polish citizens of Krakow had virtually no impact on the direction of changes which took place in their city. Their attitudes may, therefore, be perceived as assessments of the stagnant reality without any chances to shape it freely. Thus, the basic factor which influenced the attitudes towards the Nazi policy in the city was its direct impact on the life of the inhabitants. Compulsory changes of address and the problems which appeared as a consequence, such as lower living standards, were the changes which affected people's lives more than any other transformation introduced in the urban space by the Nazi authorities. The changes which disturbed people's private life aroused the strongest emotions and the fiercest feeling of injustice.

The administrative activities of the Nazi authorities, such as investments in the city or expansion of the city's borders, were not necessarily perceived in the context of occupation; people tended to see more of an authorities-citizen relationship here. That, in turn, resulted in an ambivalent attitude towards the actions initiated by the German administration, especially considering the fact that some of these actions turned out to be really beneficial for the city. However, the awareness that it was Germans who would benefit from the effects of all the works created dissonance. Krakow was to become a German city which justified all the investments.

Since there were no opportunities for the Poles to oppose the Nazi authorities in the field of administration, the Polish-German battle of Krakow was fought mainly in the symbolic dimension. On the one hand, there was the Germanisation of the urban space, while on the other hand there were attempts to stop it by ignoring or deliberately breaking German directives and manifestations of the Polish presence in the city by the reiteration of Polish symbols and patterns of behaviour.

Despite its external transformations, the city – seen through the eyes of its inhabitants – remains 'their own city'. The emotional attachment manifests itself even in the manner of writing about it. The city becomes anthropomorphised and is presented as someone close, someone who protects, someone you miss. Poles never lost their faith that, sooner or later, the day would come when occupation rule would end. That faith is expressed in the testimony of a woman from Krakow who during the war was a young girl: "One day I went to see Wawel[39]. I stood there and cried. There was a flag with a swastika on it flapping on Wawel Hill. And then, someone approached me, I don't know who, a stranger, and said: 'don't cry, my child, they will not last forever. Wawel is ours'"[40].

Notes

1 These are only approximate numbers. The data comes from the 1931 census in which respondents were asked about their mother tongue, and not their nationality. If we accept the linguistic criterion, then we would have to assume that Jews comprised about 21% of the entire population of the city, whereas if we look at the data concerning religion we will notice that 25.8% of Krakow's population identified themselves with Judaism. However, we must be aware that not all of the people who identified themselves with Judaism considered themselves to be Jews, just as not everyone who spoke Polish considered him/herself as a Pole. See J. Bieniarzówna, J.M. Małecki, (eds.), *Dzieje Krakowa. Kraków w latach 1918-1939*, Krakow 1997, p. 31.

2 Again, these are only approximate numbers, since various sources give very different data concerning the size of Krakow's population and its structure in terms of nationality. Moreover, the statistics did not include those who were not registered for temporal/permanent residency and those who remained in hiding. Data quoted from A. Chwalba, *Dzieje Krakowa. Kraków w latach 1939-1945*, Krakow 2002, pp. 36-37.

3 C. Malaparte, *Zima w Polsce*, "Życie Literackie" 1987, 36, pp. 2, 13.

4 Although the Ukrainian community was not a substantial group as far as sheer numbers are concerned, it managed to create a strong political, social and cultural centre in Nazi-occupied Krakow. Its strong position in the city resulted from the Nazi policy according to which Ukrainians were treated as a "privileged Slav nation".

5 Chwalba, *Dzieje Krakowa* cit., p. 70.

6 RGO – *Rada Główna Opiekuńcza* [the Central Welfare Council] – a Polish charity institution which legally operated in the Generalgouvenerment in the period of 1940-1945. Its main objective was to

bring aid to impoverished people. The scope of its social activity covered e.g. helping the poor by providing financial support and the free distribution of food, clothes and shoes. RGO also ran cheap bars for the poor, orphanages, organized occupational courses and workshops for future craftsmen and provided assistance for prisoners and those expelled.

7 A good example of such developments are the photographs representing the road works in Starowiślna Street, Dietla Avenue, Krakowska Street etc., Archives of Audio-Visual Records, catalogue numbers II 8022, II 5524, II 8015, see also K. Broński, *Ruch budowlany w Krakowie pod okupacją hitlerowska*, "Rocznik Krakowski" vol. 53, 1987, pp. 176-178.

8 J. Mikułowski-Pomorski, *Kraków w naszej pamięci*, Krakow 1991, testimony No. 60, p. 130. The abovementioned activities helped to improve the efficiency of the city traffic.

9 O. Bujwid, *Osamotnienie. Pamiętnik z lat 1932-1942*, Krakow 1990, p. 332.

10 See e.g. A. Szyszko-Bohusz, *Wawel pod okupacją niemiecką. Wspomnienia z lat 1939-1945*, "Rocznik Krakowski" 1949-1957, 31, pp. 155-174; J. Mikułowski-Pomorski, *Kraków w naszej pamięci...*, testimony No. 60, p. 130; Muzeum Historyczne Miasta Krakowa, R 761/4, Z. Żuławski, *Dokumenty chwili*, p. 49.

11 Especially the younger Poles did what they could to avoid serving in thr Baudienst by prolonging their education or getting false medical documents which declared them unfit for physical labour.

12 Adam Mickiewicz (1798-1855) – poet, the main creator of the Romantic movement in Poland and an activist of secret national organizations; from 1832 onwards Mickiewicz lived in Paris where, apart from his activity as an emigration poet, he became involved in political actions and polemical journalism.

13 During World War II Wawel Hill, i.e. the site on which the Krakow Cathedral and the Royal Castle stand was taken over by the Nazis and adapted to the needs of the Governor-General Hans Frank who appointed that place to become his headquarters. Tadeusz Kościuszko, whose monument stood on Wawel Hill, was the commander of the Polish national uprising in 1794 and a general who fought in the American War of Independence (1776-83).

14 The Grunwald Monument was created in 1910 to commemorate the 500th anniversary of the battle of Grunwald where an army led by the Polish king defeated the army of the Teutonic Knights (Order of the German House of St. Mary in Jerusalem). The monument was a symbol of anti-German resistance.

15 K. Lanckorońska, *Wspomnienia wojenne 22 X 1939 – 5 IV 1945*, Krakow 2001, pp. 73-74.

16 O. Bujwid, *Osamotnienie. Pamiętnik z lat 1932-1942*, Krakow 1990, p. 291.

17 In Polish the word "Krakau" sounds similar to a form of the verb "*krakać*" – lit. "to caw".

18 In the diaries written during the period of the occupation the people of Krakow consistently use the form "Kraków". Also in the official letters exchanged by the Polish institutions that form of the city's name was used. That was the case in the correspondence sent by the RGO (among others) and exchanged with all its branches and the Polish companies it cooperated with.

19 Rynek Główny received its new, German name – Adolf Hitler Platz – on the first anniversary of the outbreak of war, "Goniec Krakowski" 1940, No 208, p. 3.

20 S. Pigoń, *Z przędziwa pamięci. Urywki wspomnień*, Warszaw 1968, p. 251.

21 Jordan's Park and Krakowski Park were large – proportionally to the size of Krakow – parks situated in the centre of the city. After these two recreation areas had been closed, Planty became the only green area which was available for the Polish public. The statues of eminent Poles had been removed from Jordan's Park. Kościuszko's Mount (Kopiec Kościuszki) was a mount-monument built by the people of Krakow in the period of 1820-1823 in honour of Tadeusz Kościuszko. For many citizens of Krakow the

mount, as a national symbol situated among the pleasant greenery, became the destination of frequent walks and excursions.

22 Mikułowski-Pomorski, *Kraków* cit., testimony No. 3, p. 145.

23 *Ibid.*, testimony No. 102, pp. 121-122.

24 Chwalba, *Dzieje Krakowa* cit., p. 34.

25 The Committee (*Polski Komitet Opiekuńczy Kraków Miasto*) functioned as part of RGO.

26 AP Kraków, PolKO Kraków Miasto 64, letter dated 8 July, 1942, b. 395.

27 AP Kraków, PolKO Kraków Miasto 64, letter sent by Piotrowicz to the Farmers' Welfare Department (Dział Opieki nad Rolnikami) dated 2 October, 1942, p. 465.

28 K. Lanckorońska, *Wspomnienia wojenne* cit., p. 84. Before the war Kazimierz was a district very poorly equipped with public utility facilities. A pre-war daily "Nowy Dziennik" wrote on 8 July, 1939: "The streets and the pavements are a disgrace to any idea of civilization. Out of the 58 streets and squares only 3 have hard, solid surfaces. [...] Mud, dust, roads full of potholes and swamps are the usual things you will find there."

29 The pictures in the collection of State Archive in Krakow, Team of the Starost of the City of Krakow 1939-1945, catalogue number SMKr 271.

30 P. Łukasiewicz calls it the "domestication of communal life"; see P. Łukasiewicz, *Dom jako społeczne minimum – spojrzenie na okres okupacji niemieckiej*, P. Łukasiewicz, A. Siciński (eds.), *Dom we współczesnej Polsce. Szkice*, Wrocław 1992, p. 65.

31 Coffee shops were, by definition, places where everyone could come, therefore it was difficult to avoid undesirable company. They were also more exposed to round-ups and mass arrests than private flats.

32 S. Strzelichowski, *Dwa lata grudzień 1942 – październik 1944*, Wrocław 1972, p. 171. The evenings were shortened by the curfew which continued to be used throughout the entire period of the occupation. From October 25, 1939 to December 23, 1942 curfew would start at 11:00 p.m. In the summer of 1943 and 1944 curfew started at 9:00 p.m., and occasionally the time of curfew was changed to 8:00 p.m., 7:00 p.m., or even 6:00 p.m. Data quoted from T. Wroński, *Kronika okupowanego Krakowa*, Krakow 1974, p. 371.

33 "Goniec Krakowski", 1944 , see e.g. No. 278 and 295. The increase in the number of artistic programmes offered in Krakow resulted partly from the inflow of exiles who had fled from the post-Rising Warsaw.

34 One example of such activity could be the transformation of the slogan *Deutschland siegt an allen Fronten* into: *Deutschland liegt an allen Fronten*, (i.e. "Germany wins on all the fronts" changed into "Germany lies on all the fronts"). At this point we should note that in Krakow this kind of visual propaganda was performed on an incomparably lesser scale than in Warsaw.

35 Z. Stróżyk, *W Krakowie i gdzie indzie*, M. Turski (ed.), *Byli wówczas dziećmi*, Warsaw 1975, p. 224. The truthfulness of those memories is confirmed by a photograph taken in winter during the occupation period: on the snow-covered surface of the Market Square we can clearly see the footsteps of the people who went around the place where the poet's monument used to stand. The Historical Museum of the City of Krakow, Photography Department, catalogue No. Fn 9886 III.

36 J. Mikułowski- Pomorski, *Kraków* cit., testimony No. 6, p. 143.

37 S. Dobrowolski, *Memuary pacyfisty*, Krakow 1989, p. 149.

38 R. Nuszkiewicz, *Uparci*, Warsaw 1983, p. 149.

39 Wawel – the royal residence of Polish kings; a symbol of the Polish spirit and of Krakow.

40 J. Mikułowski-Pomorski, *Kraków* cit., testimony No. 82, p. 108.

Bibliography

Bieniarzówna J., Małecki J. M. (eds.), *Dzieje Krakowa. Kraków w latach 1918-1939*, Krakow 1997.

Broński K., *Ruch budowlany w Krakowie pod okupacją hitlerowska*, in "Rocznik Krakowski", 1987, 53.

Bujwid O., *Osamotnienie. Pamiętnik z lat 1932-1942*, Krakow 1990.

Chwalba A., *Dzieje Krakowa. Kraków w latach 1939-1945*, Krakow 2002.

Dobrowolski S., *Memuary pacyfisty*, Krakow 1989.

Lanckorońska K., *Wspomnienia wojenne 22 X 1939 – 5 IV 1945*, Krakow 2001.

Łukasiewicz P., *Dom jako społeczne minimum – spojrzenie na okres okupacji niemieckiej* in Łukasiewicza P., Siciński A.(eds.), *Dom we współczesnej Polsce. Szkice*, Wrocław 1992.

Malaparte C., *Zima w Polsce*, "Życie Literackie" 1987, 36.

Mikułowski-Pomorski J., *Kraków w naszej pamięci*, Krakow 1991.

Nuszkiewicz R., *Uparci*, Warsaw 1983.

Pigoń S., *Z przędziwa pamięci. Urywki wspomnień*, Warsaw 1968.

Stróżyk Z., *W Krakowie i gdzie indziej*, in *Byli wówczas dziećmi*, Turski M. (ed.), Warsaw 1975.

Strzelichowski S., *Dwa lata grudzień 1942 – październik 1944*, Wrocław 1972.

Szyszko-Bohusz A., *Wawel pod okupacją niemiecką. Wspomnienia z lat 1939-1945*, "Roczink Krakowski" 1949-1957, 31.

Wroński T. , *Kronika okupowanego Krakowa*, Krakow 1974.

Between Farm and Factory. Peasants in Urban Space in Communist Poland

Ewelina Szpak
Jagiellonian University, Krakow

Abstract

During the second half of the 19th century, industrial development in Poland led to a significant increase in migration from rural areas to the cities. This process gained a greater impetus after the Second World War, during which almost 78.9% of city dwellers died. The new communist authorities began to attract the inhabitants of overpopulated villages into the under populated towns and cities (especially in the so called "Regained Areas"). This chapter will look at three distinct groups who migrated into Polish cities in this period. The first migrants consisted mostly of young peasants and farmers who soon integrated into the city. Another group were those who lived in the surrounding villages that, soon after 1945, became incorporated into the city limits. The third group of rural migrants consisted of those for whom the city was only a working space. This study demonstrates how these three groups of rural migrants gradually became a significant element of the social sphere of the expanding cities and how they perceived the city space and themselves – their 'rusticity' and 'strangeness' in that space.

Proces migracji ludności wiejskiej do miast pojawił się w warunkach polskich na szerszą skalę wraz z rozwojem przemysłu - w II połowie XIX wieku. Przełomem był jednak koniec II wojny światowej, w wyniku której przetrzebiona została znaczna liczba mieszkańców miast. Do wyniszczonych i wyludnionych miast nowe komunistyczne władze ściągać zaczęły więc mieszkańców przeludnionych wsi. Akcji tej towarzyszyła stała, podtrzymywana jeszcze w latach 70. propaganda awansu społecznego, jaki czekać miał przybyszy ze wsi w rozwijających się i industrializujących miastach. Dla wielu napływających masowo wiejskich migrantów przebywanie w mieście i konieczność dostosowania się do nowych warunków życia stanowiła trudne zadanie, którego nie ułatwiały dodatkowo panujące wśród rdzennej społeczności miejskiej przekonania i stereotypy dotyczące osób pochodzenia wiejskiego. Sytuację pogarszała także peerelowska propaganda, kreująca niechętną kolektywizacji wieś na głównego sprawcę gospodarczych i aprowizacyjnych problemów ówczesnej Polski, podsycając tym samym szorstkie już wcześniej relacje obu grup społecznych. Metodą obrony przed społeczną deprecjacją migrantów wiejskich było zwykle „wtapianie się" w tłum przechodniów, werbalne negowanie swego pochodzenia i przejmowanie miejskiego stylu życia. Napływający masowo do miast wcześniejsi mieszkańcy wsi z biegiem lat zajmować zaczęli coraz większą przestrzeń społeczną rozrastających się miast. Przenikali powoli do większości grup ją tworzących, zasiedlali sfery mieszkalne, pojawiali się w masowo w sferach pracy oraz w przestrzeniach komunikacji miejskiej (autobusy, tramwaje, dworce, przystanki). Od lat 70. coraz śmielej wchodzili także w przestrzeń miejskiego odpoczynku (kina, kawiarnie, dancingi). Każda niemal przestrzeń miasta stawała się jednocześnie miejscem konfrontacji z wyniesionym z rodzinnej wsi zespołem norm i wartości oraz miejscem wzbogacania ich o wartości nowe. Te spotkania, jak każda interakcja, oddziaływały dwustronnie, zmieniając stopniowo każdą ze spotykających się stron.

> I do not recall when I stopped walking from Krakowskie Przedmieście via Nowy Świat to the Czytelnik publishing house on Wiejska. I enjoyed these walks. Along the royal route I would meet my close and distant acquaintances, or strangers who knew me. This was a favourable setting to develop a feeling of 'being at home'. One day I noticed that the street had changed ... Not a single familiar face, not even a nodding acquaintance. I do not know the year when the new social mass took over the cities ... It came to me that I was living in a different city. The term 'peasant clerks' came into use – the term was not so accurate in sociological terms, though it was not about the name. This was a psychophysical type omnipresent on the streets, in the shops, at the restaurants, in the offices, at the universities ... I [no longer] walked along Nowy Świat[1].

Although Kazimierz Brandys, the author of the above words, did not specify when he experienced sudden 'alienation' in the urban space, it can be concluded from his biography that it was sometime during the 1950s or 1960s[2]. These decades, as observed by the author, were a time of growing migration from rural areas into the cities. Stimulated by the propaganda of social advance and supported with the ideology of the alliance between the workers and the peasants, the mass migration had far-reaching demographic, social and cultural consequences.

The beginnings

Large scale migration of the rural population into the cities had begun in Poland due to industrial development in the second half of the 19th century. This process, however, can be more clearly discerned in the inter-war period[3]. In 1921, Poland's 632 cities had only some 6.9 million inhabitants (24% of the population), while the villages were inhabited by a population of over 20 million[4]. Among these 'cities' there were only six inhabited by more than one hundred thousand people. The majority, therefore, were small cities and towns. The latter, which were particularly common in the south-east of Poland, often resembled large villages[5]. For economic reasons, the scale of migration was not large in the 1920s and 1930s[6]. The turning point was the end of the Second World War, during which nearly 6 million Poles died, including 78.9% of the city dwellers[7]. The new communist authorities began to attract the inhabitants of overpopulated villages into the cities. This process was paralleled by a wide-scale project of "reconstructing the country", during which brigades of workers were recruited under the label of "Service for Poland", an organization consisting mainly of the rural youth[8]. The inhabitants of the overpopulated villages in south-eastern Poland were also encouraged to settle on the depopulated post-German areas in western and northern Poland. The effect of these migrations could be observed, for instance, in the social structure of Wrocław, where in 1947 as much as 48.5% of the population were rural immigrants[9].

Both of these processes were accompanied by the constant propaganda of social advance, continued even in the 1970s, which awaited the rural newcomers in the developing and industrialized cities[10]. The watchwords and the policy of the state imbibed by the rural community[11], which stimulated migration, changed the condition of Polish society radically. In 1950 the population of Poland was 25 million, including 15.2 million villagers and 9.8 million city dwellers. During the next 20 years (until 1970) the rural population remained constant, while the urban population grew to 17.2 million[12]. Therefore the entire demographic growth contributed to the population of the cities. In the years 1946-1985, migration from the villages to the cities involved nearly 6 million people (the equivalent of 40% of the urban population growth in that period). A further 2.3 million city dwellers were added due to administrative modifications (such as incorporating neighbouring villages, granting town charters to former rural settlements etc.).

The above data reveal the scale of the phenomenon of rural migration in post-War Poland[13]. Migration largely affected small and medium-sized towns, though the effects were also observable in large cities. This chapter will seek to assess whether such a powerful inflow of the rural population transformed the urban space.

If we accept the theories of Henri Lefèbvre, which assume that space is formed by society and its final configuration is an outcome of both individual and group activities[14], it can be concluded that it did. According to Lefèbvre, the first effect of socializing physical space is the manifestation of the presence of man in that space, with his everyday and festive behaviour, his power and strength, or the opposite – weakness and collapse[15]. In the case of the cities in the People's Republic of Poland, the formation of urban space, understood as above, not only involved the rural settlers. It must be taken into account that the population figures given above do not include the peasant workers or peasant clerks mentioned by K. Brandys, for whom the city was but a working space. However, through their temporary, though regular, presence they would influence the social and cultural image of the city. They were an intermediate group, suspended between two cultural spheres – the rural and the urban. Many of them would commute to the conglomerate plants and factories travelling several dozen, if not several hundred kilometres, and those whose family houses were situated much farther from their employment would stay in workers' hostels and only occasionally visit their homeland.

The new urban space, formed under the influence of the recently introduced changes, often evoked a feeling of alienation among the migrants, but also among its indigenous inhabitants. Therefore this chapter shall address the following questions: How did existing urban inhabitants tackle the changes? How did they respond to the new population in their towns and cities? How did the migrants perceive urban space? How did they perceive themselves, their 'rusticity' and 'strangeness' in that space? How did the new environment influence their sense of identity? And finally, who did they become as time progressed?

'We want to be like you' – Newcomers among city dwellers

During the late 1940s and 1950s, the most important sphere of contacts within the city for the original migrants and peasant workers was work. Like the entire urban space, the working space was usually strange and new to the migrants, and placed new demands on them. The problems with acculturation, becoming acquainted with the new methods of work and the new working rhythm, arose in particular from the fact that in many respects they were the opposite of the working methods learned and practiced on the family farms. The open space of a field, the closeness of nature and the methods and time of work determined by the time of day or year were replaced by the enclosed, crowded, dusty and noisy space of a factory. Due to everyday supervision by the strange managerial personnel, staying far from home, statutory working hours, imposed production norms, as well as the rush and almost permanent stress, typical for the city though totally unfamiliar to most of them, immigrants paid a high price for this desired advance. Emotional and physical crises would often go hand in hand with cultural shock:

> If the first stage of factory work was to be described using one word, no other term would reflect it better than 'a shock', manifested by a quasi collective headache, waking up at night. Those less resilient to the new working conditions were ordered by the doctor to find work in the open[16].

However, it was impossible for the majority of immigrants to return to their villages, where returning migrants were perceived as weak and inadequate. Shame and village ostracism were particularly strong deterrents against return[17]. According to A. Sadowski, the force of public opinion, the weight attached to assessment by the family and the neighbourhood, formed a personality type with a particularly strongly developed reflected self[18]. Obviously the thesis proposed by Sadowski is a generalization and it cannot be extended to include the entire rural community. Still, it is evident that in many everyday urban situations cultural and social deprivation could emerge. This complex, caused by an individual's rural background, resulted from the durability of the stereotypes and biases regarding the village. The significant inflow of rural migrants into the cities and the corresponding sense of threat felt by the regular city dwellers helped to consolidate such stereotypes.

> I used to work as an accountant in a large office on a very busy street ... The most difficult thing for me was not the work itself, but its environment. I could not understand many things. I was embarrassed to ask. It seemed to me that anyone who looked at me thought of me as a dumb girl from the back of nowhere. In a word – an inferiority complex, since my attire differed from that of the rest as well[19].

The conviction that urban dwellers had an unfavourable opinion of them made the newcomers develop certain defensive mechanisms. First of all, they tried to mix with the impersonal crowd of passers-by. Their solution was, therefore, to resort to imitating the behaviour, customs and lifestyle (clothes, speech) of the city dwellers and seemingly to suppress their rusticity by any means. This strategy, though, would often backfire and expose the individual to ridicule or snide remarks. Very often, especially in the case of young immigrants during the 1950s and 1960s, the unmasking factor was their colloquial speech, filled with regionalisms or vocabulary unsuitable in the urban environment[20]. It was believed that immigration led to a decline in linguistic standards, observed, for instance, among the lower rank of administrative personnel[21].

Problems with communication and a sense of inferiority hindered the new migrants from establishing good relations with their fellow workers. Although immigrants managed not to stand out in the street owing to their typically 'urban' attire, it was difficult for them to remain unnoticed among groups of workers. The immigrants were also immediately labelled with pejorative terms such as 'a country bumpkin', 'a hick', 'a stork', 'cherry-red' or 'a round-face', a term popular in the 1950s. The latter referred to a rounded figure which symbolized well-being and prosperity, and it was used with regard to peasant workers, reproached for being greedy and insatiable. The negative perception that the city dwellers had of the newcomers originated in the economic situation of the country in the 1950s. The economic policy of the state prioritized heavy industry at the expense of the food industry. The anger and frustration caused by continuous food shortages was vented by blaming the rural folk for the insufficient supplies. It was the village that was criticized instead of the inefficient economic system, while the migrating peasants often became scapegoats of the growing frustration and discontent in society. An excellent example of such an attitude are the words of a deputy manager in one of the manufacturing plants in Warsaw who commented on the difficulties with provisions in the following way: "there's no meat 'cause there's no one to feed the swine, as the swineherds have all gone to the University"[22].

The peasants were blamed for the problems of the market. In 1953 demands were made not to allow "the peasants to work in the cities, as they neglect farming and, consequently, the agricultural production is in decline"[23].

Harsh words would be addressed to the rural immigrants as well: "I would get the village by the short hair to make order ... the peasants must be forced to sell their products to state-owned shops"[24].

The situation did not improve with time. The popular opinion, held by city dwellers, that individual farmers had a direct influence on the condition of Polish economy was fuelled by government propaganda which emphasized the backwardness and benightedness of the Polish village, since the majority of farmers rejected the idea of introducing large-area collective farming. Neither the passage of time nor further rural immigration improved the image of the village in the eyes of urban communities. This phenomenon was aptly described by a prominent Polish linguist, an attentive observer of contemporary reality:

> I have been observing for years that each time some people are quarrelling in a tram, in a bus or on the street, one of the parties in the dispute uses the argument that 'you are a villager, Mister' (which can be formulated using cruder vocabulary). There are but few exceptions to this rule, especially when simple people are arguing, such that have not yet settled in and cannot adjust to the urban customs. The contempt for the village, and consequently for the peasants, one of the most significant elements of the psychology of the majority of Poles, is somewhat parallel to concealing one's social descent[25].

This observation suggests that due to the internal urge to 'penetrate into the urban environment', merge with the mass of passers-by, immigrants began to suppress their own identity. This obviously did not apply to all immigrants; it was less frequent among the peasant workers who would often identify with their family villages for their whole life and who could not adjust to the requirements of the new urban world. They were very opposed to accepting the 8-hour working day: "When I was working for 8 hours, I had the feeling of lazing about for the rest of the day, and it was a bad feeling. I could see my wife and mother-in-law working hard on the land. I cannot just lie down, I must be doing something"[26].

The peasant workers, with their particularly strong family ties, did not feel the urge to integrate with the community of city workers. Their urban space was subjectivized, limited to a few selected locations, usually the railway station, the factory and the workers' hostel for those who commuted from far away[27]. It was these workers in particular that were referred to by B. Jałowiecki in 1987: "through the character of the dwelling place and work, as well as through the method of employment, the villager always finds his or her rusticity, though he does not always meet with the city"[28].

Still, one may ask whether the villagers would have to 'meet with' the city, or whether the villager, as a regular or commuting city dweller, did not already constitute an element of the urban community? An answer to this question can be provided by observing the peasant workers in their family villages where they would often initiate innovations based on the experience and knowledge acquired in their new environment. Despite their passive contacts with the urban culture, as shown in the source texts, they did not remain uninfluenced by that culture.

Young rural migrants, usually not encumbered with the obligation to keep up a farm, had different attitudes and approaches to the city than the majority of peasant workers.

Their statements often displayed a certain ambiguity. Those who had a more reflective nature emphasized the feeling of solitude and alienation; their words indicate a tendency to underestimate themselves, the development of a 'rustic' personality, and narrow-mindedness[29]. However, many immigrants and peasant workers did not experience their rusticity and loneliness so intensely since their time was filled with work and rush, typical of urban civilization: "they are always in a hurry, absorbed, having little time for reflection. Their internal transformations usually materialize in action which does not leave them time to split hairs"[30].

Within a new space of life

Still, a characteristic feature of the majority of immigrants, often emphasized by sociologists, was their lack of concern for or practical ignorance of the important spaces in their new life[31]. The symbols of the city, its representative locations or the places of (local) commemoration often remained unseen by the new urban settlers.

The newcomers' lack of interest and their lack of understanding of city space were described by H. Radlińska in the 1930s and 1940s:

> City newcomers going about their own businesses concentrate only on themselves. They do not seek for other possibilities to learn more about the city – about the factories, laboratories, schools, etc. They do not know that the secret of city power does not lie in blatant things. They do not have any idea that the traffic is totally different in each quarter and is changeable in time and that those that are hanging around shops are mainly visitors. Not much, or rather nothing, influences newcomers. What attracts them most are the products of entertainment industry – cinemas, cafes, drinking dens. Museums, libraries, day-rooms, clubs are still inaccessible and remain unknown (...)[32].

The attitudes of newcomers towards the city space, described above, did not change much in the late 1940s and 1950s[33]. For a number of immigrants, their work spaces and workers' hostels were, for a long time, the only spaces in the city to which they had become accustomed.

As is pointed out above, the work place was the space where the most frequent contacts between the migrants and the local community occurred. In the case of those who settled in the cities for a long period, the space of social interactions expanded to other areas, such as the districts in which their dwelling places were located. In the workers' hostels, the village migrants would often occupy the same rooms or suites of rooms as their partner migrants from the same families or neighbourhood[34]. Those who were allotted a factory flat, however, were condemned to have accidental neighbours. Many considered allotment of a flat (in a block of flats) the major determinant of success in life and social advancement in the city. Due to excessive bureaucracy, the occupants had only marginal influence on their choice of home and its location within the urban space[35]. As a consequence, the residents of blocks of flats constituted heterogeneous communities. This social, cultural and professional heterogeneousness often created growing biases and misunderstandings.

As long as the space of their own dwelling units enabled the migrant families to have more freedom to release their cultural capital (the typical rustic way of arranging interiors, or assigning particular functions to certain rooms[36]), the common area for the occupants was the site of successive conflicts which stemmed from diverse customs and mentalities.

This situation is illustrated by a comment made in 1963 by a native inhabitant of Warsaw fed up with the habits of her neighbours: "People should be taught ... not to keep hens or sauerkraut on their beautiful loggias or balconies, and not to chop wood there or decorate them with dirty bedclothes..."[37].

The native city dwellers, accustomed to living in communal buildings, were also disturbed by other rural customs: "We often have to listen to loud television, raised voices, or sonorous calls; living in a homestead did not require minding other people, and now, when in the city, it is difficult to understand that noise may bother others"[38].

There are countless examples of such misconduct. As was assumed by sociologists in the 1960s, such conflicts were enhanced by the fact that the majority of rural women living in blocks of flats were not employed and stayed at home throughout the day. According to sociologists, the isolation of rural women within their flats hindered their adaptation to the urban environment. Another expression of the staunch endurance of rural habits was the rejection of urban forms of leisure, which were absent in the Polish village at the end of the 1960s and the beginning of the 1970s[39]. Due to the 'ban' on wasting time on purposeless activities, deeply rooted in the minds of rural immigrants, they would often spend their time after work cooking, fixing clothes, and rarely on reading magazines and books or more sophisticated entertainment. In the 1950s, a particularly characteristic activity for women was to put a bench in front of the block or watch the courtyard through an open window. Obviously the primitive nature of the forms of leisure observed among the immigrants in the 1950s changed with time. The changes under way in the villages in the 1960s also resulted in a gradual adoption of urban forms of leisure, while the limited access to entertainment (such as cinemas, theatres, museums, clubs etc.) was an additional incentive in the 1970s to flee from the village to the city which offered more diverse leisure activities. The immigrants of the 1970s, originating from modernized villages, thus had wider opportunities to make contact with the 'locals' in the city[40].

Everyday life in the space of the industrialized city of the Polish People's Republic showed the influence of rural culture and customs, which increased with time and as migration continued. The significant role of rural customs was particularly obvious during the traditional religious holidays, as well as family celebrations such as weddings or Holy Communion, celebrated rather lavishly, as the rural custom required[41].

Incorporated spaces - between city and village

The manifestation of rural family and holiday customs in the urban space was not only a consequence of migration. An important influence, especially in the major Polish cities, such as Krakow-Nowa Huta, Warsaw, or Wrocław, was also made by the incorporation of the surrounding villages into the city limits. The process of architectural and landscape transformation of the rural areas into urban space continued for years, and the remains of rural architecture could be seen in some cities even in the 1990s. However, incorporating former villages into the cities also implied attributing new significance to these villages. The process would take place mainly in the inhabitants' consciousness and affected both the 'urban' dwellers of the incorporating city and those living in the new social space of the city as a result of administrative decisions. For many native city dwellers, the incorporated villages would long remain strange spaces. Those forced for a variety of reasons to populate these areas often made claims such as the following: "I don't even talk to my direct neighbours. These are village people, what do they know... I don't make acquaintance with them, for why would I invite some country bumpkins into my house – they don't even know how to behave and would only run me down afterwards"[42].

The process of redefining the inhabited space was different among the rural communities entering the urban space, where the majority of the inhabitants believed that their populations had become 'better' and more valuable due to the changes. In particular, the incorporated villages were 'better' than others, situated farther from the city[43]. However, those who were forced to resettle into older areas of the city, due to administrative decisions related to the development of the incorporated space, often found the change to be unpleasant. Those rehoused into blocks of flats complained that they could not live in the new conditions. They also felt a strong attachment and identification with the abandoned space. They would often visit the places where their houses used to be, "...saying that this plot had once belonged to them or to someone they knew"[44].

Therefore, the incorporated villages built new areas at the cultural borders of the increasingly industrialized city, often perceived by many inhabitants as neither still rural nor yet urban areas. Due to the different cultures and customs clashing within these areas, they often witnessed conflicts and social misunderstandings.

Conclusions

Based on the above analysis of the problem, one can see that the peasants, the farmers, and finally the peasant workers gradually came to form a significant part of the social sphere of the expanding cities. They slowly merged with the majority of the groups constituting that social sphere, populating the dwelling spaces, appearing collectively in the working zones and utilizing the means of mass transportation (such as buses, trams and railway stations). Since the 1970s, they have also entered the sphere of urban leisure (including cinemas, coffee shops and dancehalls) with more confidence. The majority of urban spaces gradually became an area for confronting the set of standards and values taken from the family village and a place where they were enriched with new values. These new values seldom related to the values of inter-war urban culture. Traumatic experiences of individuals together with social and political consequences of the Second World War (reconstruction of social structure, sovietization of Poland) made the pre-war values of urban lifestyle strange to the newcomers. The ideological background and political discourse influenced by political shifts endorsed new values, which often twisted and caricatured the values of pre-war times[45].

The interaction of the new urban and rural values gradually transformed both parties. However, does this mean that the inflow of the rural population 'ruralized'[46] the city? Does the increasingly common appearance of rural customs and culture in the social life of the city indicate that the phenomenon of 'ruralizing' the city actually occurred in Poland? An unambiguous answer to these questions would constitute a far-reaching generalization[47]. The city's component space was already heterogeneous[48], constructed through the integration of diverse subcultures (such as the workers, the intelligentsia, the lower middle class, as well as the villagers[49]). The new cultural contents brought by the immigrants was thus one of many influences on city life. In periods of particularly high immigration the urban space (or selected sections of it) could be dominated for some time by rural culture. However, due to the staunch attempts of the newcomers to merge with the native urban population, their suppression of their own rural identity, as well as the enormous efforts made by the families of the rural immigrants to raise their children as 'burghers'[50], the impact of the immigrant culture declined gradually. Additionally, in the 1970s the starting point of the majority of the newcomers was changed. The modernization of the villages and the economic growth in the country, characteristic of the first half of the 1970s, slowly transformed relationships between the two formerly antagonistic communities, while the ongoing process of cultural adaptation of the families of earlier immigrants (which according to sociologists and psychologists continued for three generations) and the inflow of rural population into the cities, petered out in the 1980s. For these reasons and the considerable acceleration in the development of Polish cities after 1989 this rural aspect was rendered one of many influences on the social and cultural space of Polish cities by the beginning of the 21st century.

Notes

1 K. Brandys, *Miesiące 1982-1987* [The Months 1982-1987], Warsaw 1998, p. 392.

2 Kazimierz Brandys lived abroad after 1970.

3 In the first half of the 20th century the problem of the growing number of rural migrants and their cultural identity and adaptation difficulties was mentioned already by Ludwik Krzywicki and Helena

Radlińska. See for instance H. Radlińska, *Przenikanie się wsi i miasta* [Merging of the City and the Village] in: "Wiedza i Życie" 1947, no. 10, pp 896-906.

4 W. Mirowski, *Atrakcyjność miast polskich jako celu migracji* [Polish Cities as Target of Migrations], in E. Kaltenberg – Kwiatkowska (ed.), *Miasta polskie w dwusetlecie prawa o miastach* [Polish Cities on the two hundredth Anniversary of "City Law"] , Warsaw 1994, p. 110.

5 C. Brzoza, *Historia Polski 1918-1945*, [The History of Poland 1918-1945], Krakow 2006, p. 107.

6 The inability of Polish cities to absorb the large numbers of rural migrants led to increased international migration (to the United States, France, and Brazil).

7 L. Damurski, *Miasta Dolnego Śląska po II wojnie światowej (zasiedlenia, stabilizacja, integracja)* [The Lower Silesia Cities after the Second World War (settlement, stability, integration)], a doctoral thesis; See http://www.dbc.wroc.pl/Content/1350/Damurski.pdf

8 General Organization 'Service for Poland' ('Służba Polsce') – a paramilitary youth organization established on 25 February 1948. In 1949, SP had ca. 1.2 million members. The brigades worked in particular on reconstructing Warsaw and building industrial centres (such as Nowa Huta).

9 A. Sadowski, *Proces ruralizacji. Ludność miejska w mieście* [The process of ruralization. Townspeople in the town], Krakow 1994, p. 43.

10 B. Jałowiecki, *Proces urbanizacji a relacje miasto-wieś* [The process of urbanization and the relationship between the city and the countryside], Warsaw 1987, p. 23.

11 Apart from the policy of enforced industrialization, the reforms launched in 1944 are worth mentioning at this point, and in particular the agricultural reform which eliminated the class of landowners. According to Ewa Kaczyńska, "the children of the minor gentry would settle in cities on a large scale, especially in destroyed Warsaw after 1945, to gain both the influence and favour of the educated population, since they filled in the social gap left by the middle class, not so strong a group before the war, and even more exterminated by the military actions and the policy of the invaders". See E. Kaczyńska, *Pejzaż miejski z zaściankiem w tle* [An Urban Landscape with the Backwater in the background], Warsaw 1999, p. 208.

12 J. Styk., *Chłopi i wieś w perspektywie socjologicznej i historycznej,* [Peasants and village in sociological and historical perspective], Lublin 1999, p. 215.

13 It is indisputable that migration of the rural population into the cities was one of the characteristic mechanisms of 19th- and 20th-century industrialisation, resulting in the rapid expansion and development of cities. However, the specific features of post-war migrations were their unprecedented scale and ideological legitimization.

14 B. Jałowiecki, M. S. Szczepański, *Miasto i przestrzeń w perspektywie socjologicznej* [The City and the space in the sociological perspective], Warsaw 2006, pp. 161, 314-319.

15 *Ibid*, p. 161.

16 Z. Grzelak, *Przed bramą i pierwsze kroki na nowym*, [In front of the Gate and the first steps on the "new"] in D. Gałaj (ed.), *Chłoporobotnicy o sobie. Studium autobiografii* [Peasant-workers writing about themselves. The study of autobiography], Warsaw 1974, p. 40

17 B. Brzostek, *Środowisko robotnicze Warszawy w drugiej połowie lat pięćdziesiątych ze szczególnym uwzględnieniem „nowych robotników" ze wsi* [The enviroment of workers in late 1950s Warsaw with a special account of "new comers" from the countryside] in. J. Neja (ed.), *Dla władzy, obok władzy, przeciw władzy. Postawy robotników wielkich ośrodków PRL* [For Power, beside Power, against Power. Attitudes of Workers from the Polish Metropolis], Warsaw 2005, p. 64.

18 In sociology and psychology, the reflected self is the form of an individual's self-knowledge that is shaped by interpreting other people's reactions to ourselves, see A. Sadowski, *Przejawy ruralizacji mia-*

sta uprzemysłowionego (na przykładzie Białegostoku) [Aspects of ruralization in the industrialized city (Białystok case)], Białystok 1981, p. 149

19 *Drogi awansu w mieście* [Roads of Advancement in the City], in F. Jakubczak (ed.), *Młode Pokolenie Wsi Polski Ludowej* [The Young Generation of the countryside in the Polish People's Republic] ,vol. 8, Warsaw 1972. p. 109

20 Also applicable to the 1980s; according to some Polish sociolinguists, colloquial speech, 'imported' by the immigrants from the village and strongly marked with dialects, spread with time, and consequently led to a decline in linguistic standards.

21 D. Jarosz, *Pastuchy', 'okrąglaki', 'wieśniacy'. Miasto peerelowskie i jego chłopscy mieszkańcy* [A country bumpkin', 'a hick', 'a round-face', 'a stork'. Cities in the Polish People's Republic and their rural inhabitants], in "Więź", no. 5, 2007, p. 106.

22 *Ibid*, p. 106.

23 B. Brzostek., *Robotnicy Warszawy. Konflikty codzienne (1950-1954)* [Warsaw workers. Daily conflicts (1950 – 1954)], Warsaw 2002, p. 76.

24 *Ibid*, p. 76.

25 A. Głowiński, *Peereliada: komentarze do słów 1976-1981* ["Peereliada": Comments to words 1976-1981], Warsaw 1993, pp 42-43.

26 Grzelak, *Chłoporobotnicy o sobie* cit., p. 91

27 See for instance *Awans pokolenia...* [The Generation Advancement...]. p. 110; Z. Sufin, *Puławy – miasto w procesie uprzemysłowienia* [Puławy – a city in the process of industrialization], in J. Turowski (ed.), *Studia socjologiczne i urbanistyczne miast Lubelszczyzny* [Sociological and Urban Studies of Lubelszczyzna's cities], Lublin 1971, p. 144.

28 Jałowiecki, *Proces urbanizacji* cit., p. 89.

29 Grzelak, *Chłoporobotnicy o sobie* cit., p. 86.

30 *Ibid,* p. 88.

31 See for instance Kaczyńska, *Pejzaż miejski* cit., p. 18, Sadowski, *Przejawy ruralizacji* cit., 126

32 Redlińska, *Przenikanie się wsi i miasta* cit., p. 897.

33 Newcomers' lack of interest in city space was also noticeable in the 1960s and 1970s. A meaningful image of that attitude was furnished by the famous Polish director, Janusz Zaorski, in his film "Chleba naszego powszedniego" (1974).

34 B. Brzostek, *Środowisko robotnicze Warszawy w drugiej połowie lat pięćdziesiątych ze szczególnym uwzględnieniem „nowych robotników"* cit., p. 63.

35 M. Szczepański, *Przestrzeń miejska w realnym socjalizmie. Impresje socjologiczne* [The City Space in the Real Socialism Time. Sociological Impressions], in *Dla władzy, obok władzy* cit.,pp. 181-189.

36 Extreme situations also occurred, as described by some researchers: "Where the new blocks were inhabited by the families of rural origins, there were frequent problems due to incompetent use of a contemporary flat by the immigrants. It was often the case that the fittings in a flat were devastated (such as water supply and drainage, or gas heaters in bathrooms) due to incorrect use of the equipment (such as drawing water from the radiator), or using bathroom as a place to keep animals". S. Panek, E. Piasecki, *Nowa Huta. Integracja ludności w świetle badań antropologicznych* [Nowa Huta. Integration of inhabitants in light of Anthropological Research], in "Materiały i prace antropologiczne", no. 80, Wrocław 1971, p. 30

37 B. Brzostek, *Za progiem. Codzienność w przestrzeni publicznej Warszawy lat 1955-1970* [Right on one's doorstep. Everyday life in the Warsaw public space], Warsaw 2007, p. 96.

38 Kaczyńska, *Pejzaż miejski* cit., pp. 21-22.

[39] See for instance Łapińska K. *Czas wolny w świadomości społecznej mieszkańców wsi* [Leisure time in the social consciousness of villagers], in "Etnografia Polski", vol.12, 1968, pp 67-85.

[40] Due to the ongoing migration of the rural population since the 1950s, it is difficult to conclude how much the immigrants in the 1970s had to do with the native city dwellers, since at that time the 'locals' assimilated into the urban population were also the immigrants (and their families) from the 1950s.

[41] At this point it is worth recalling a fragment of *Alternatywy 4*, a popular Polish TV series which mocked contemporary reality, directed by Stanisław Bareja. In the episode called *Wesele* [A wedding], one of the occupants of a two-room flat (coming from Targówek, an infamous district of Warsaw inhabited by lower classes) arranged a wedding for his cousin to which he invited several dozen guests.

[42] Brzostek, *Za progiem* cit., p. 111.

[43] See for instance *Ibid*., p. 103.

[44] J. Turowski, P. Kryczka, *Struktury społeczne miasta „starego" i nowego miasta przemysłowego* [The Social Structure of the "old" city and the new, industrialized one], in J. Turowski (ed.), *Studia socjologiczne i urbanistyczne miast Lubelszczyzny* [Sociological and Urban Studies of Lubelszczyzna's cities], Lublin 1971, p. 152.

[45] A good example of twisted values is the shift in attitude towards commitment to the community. During Inter-war time it was connected with such fundamental values (characteristics) as initiative, enterprise, creativeness, heartfelt need and voluntariness. After 1945 the grassroots initiative became institutionalized; it became a top-down order.

[46] In Polish sociology, the term "ruralization" refers to the process of going beyond the limits of the village, the rural material products, spiritual values and the ways of conduct in combination with different forms of their consolidation in other communities. Still, it must be remembered that the same term in French sociology means the process of expansion of cities beyond the traditional urban areas, to the suburbs, where exclusive residential districts were built. See for instance Sadowski, *Proces ruralizacji* cit., p. 65.

[47] This does not mean, however, that the phenomenon of "ruralization" cannot be considered a fact in selected Polish cities, such as Białystok.

[48] For example, U. Hannerz, *Odkrywanie miasta. Antropologia obszarów miejskich* [Exploring the City. Inquiries concerning Urban Anthropology], trans. E. Klekot, Kraków 2006, p. 84.

[49] Such as the group of 'urban farmers', i.e. the city dwellers whose main source of income is farming and breeding animals on small farms scattered within the city limits. As estimated by Iwanicki, in 1960 in Polish cities there were 525,405 individual farms, i.e. 15% of the individual farms in Poland. See Z. Iwanicki, *Ludność rolnicza w miastach. Problematyka i próba typologii* [Rural population in towns. The issue and the testing typology], in "Przegląd Socjologiczny", vol. 22, no. 1, 1968, p. 43.

[50] H. Murawska, *Imigranci wiejscy w mieście* [Rural Migrants in a Town], Olsztyn 1994.

Bibliography

Drogi awansu w mieście, in Jakubczak F. (ed.), *Młode Pokolenie Wsi Polski Ludowej*, vol. 8, Warsaw 1972.

Brandys K., *Miesiące* 1982-1987, Warsaw 1998

Brzostek B., *Robotnicy Warszawy. Konflikty codzienne (1950-1954)*, Warsaw 2002

Id., *Środowisko robotnicze Warszawy w drugiej połowie lat pięćdziesiątych ze szczególnym uwzględnieniem „nowych robotników" ze wsi,* in Neja J. (ed.), *Dla władzy, obok władzy, przeciw władzy. Postawy robotników wielkich ośrodków PRL*, Warsaw 2005, pp. 58-70.

Id., *Za progiem. Codzienność w przestrzeni publicznej Warszawy lat 1955-1970*, Warsaw 2007

Głowiński A., *Peereliada: komentarze do słów 1976-1981*, Warsaw 1993

Grzelak Z, *Przed bramą i pierwsze kroki na nowym*, in Gałaj D. (ed.), *Chłoporobotnicy o sobie. Studium autobiografii*, Warsaw 1974

Hannerz U., *Odkrywanie miasta. Antropologia obszarów miejskich,* trans. Klekot E., Kraków 2006

Iwanicki Z., *Ludność rolnicza w miastach. Problematyka i próba typologii*, in "Przegląd Socjologiczny", vol. 22, no. 1, 1968, p. 34-51

Jałowiecki B., Szczepański M. S., *Miasto i przestrzeń w perspektywie socjologicznej*, Warsaw 2006

Id., *Proces urbanizacji a relacje miasto-wieś*, Warsaw 1987

Jarosz D., Pastuchy', *'okrąglaki', 'wieśniacy'. Miasto peerelowskie i jego chłopscy mieszkańcy* in "Więź", no. 5, 2007, pp. 106-116.

Kaczyńska E, *Pejzaż miejski z zaściankiem w tle*, Warsaw 1999

Łapińska K. *Czas wolny w świadomości społecznej mieszkańców wsi*, in "Etnografia Polski" vol. 12, 1968, pp. 67-85.

Mirowski W., *Atrakcyjność miast polskich jako celu migracji,* in E. Kaltenberg-Kwiatkowska (ed.), *Miasta polskie w dwusetlecie prawa o miastach*, Warsaw 1994, pp. 106-116

Murawska H., *Imigranci wiejscy w mieście*, Olsztyn 1994.

Panek S., Piasecki E., *'Nowa Huta. Integracja ludności w świetle badań antropologicznych'*, in "Materiały i prace antropologiczne", no. 80, Wrocław 1971

Radlińska H., *Przenikanie się wsi i miasta,* in "Wiedza i Życie", 1947, No. 10, pp. 896-906.

Sadowski A., *Proces ruralizacji. Ludność miejska w mieście,* Krakow 1994

Id., *Przejawy ruralizacji miasta uprzemysłowionego (na przykładzie Białegostoku),* Białystok 1981

Styk J., *Chłopi i wieś w perspektywie socjologicznej i historycznej*, Lublin 1999

Szczepański S., *Przestrzeń miejska w realnym socjalizmie. Impresje socjologiczne,* in Neja J. (ed.), *Dla władzy, obok władzy, przeciw władzy. Postawy robotników wielkich ośrodków PRL*, Warsaw 2005, pp. 181-189.

Turowski J. (ed.), *Studia socjologiczne i urbanistyczne miast Lubelszczyzny*, Lublin 1971

Creating Local and Broader Identities: Historical Monographs on Bohemian, Moravian, and Galician Towns, 1860-1900

Jaroslav Ira
Charles University in Prague

Abstract

The present chapter is an exploration of collective identities in local urban societies, as they were disclosed in late 19th-century urban historiography. It focuses on monographs dedicated to the history of towns in Bohemia, Moravia, and former Austrian Galicia, and examines the kinds of identity that these works both represented and manufactured. First, it is argued that the books primarily fostered local identity. Yet closer inspection also reveals that this kind of textual local identity was a semantically-structured and multileveled project. It exploited markers of identity that were conceived in local terms but which were also 'translocal' in many respects. Second, the chapter argues there were other identities present in the monographs; it focuses on old burgher, modern middle-class and national identities, and assesses their roles in the narratives and their textual relation to local identity.

Kapitola se zabývá identitami, jež byly reprezentovány, verbálně prosazovány a potenciálně formovány v historických monografiích českých, moravských a haličských měst, vydaných v letech 1860-1900. V první části se tvrdí, že primárně a svým celkovým významem tyto publikace konstruovaly lokální identitu. Bližší rozbor nicméně ukazuje, že běžně chápaný pojem lokální identity není schopen zcela adekvátně vyjádřit historicky specifický produkt městských monografií, jehož různorodý charakter je zčásti podmíněn také vícerozměrnou povahou města. Lokální identita jako textový konstrukt historických monografií proto osciluje mezi představou sociální identity (město jako sociální skupina), identity vázané na místo (město jako konkrétní lokalita) a identity urbánní (město jako městské prostředí). Stěžejní vazba textu a významu vždy na konkrétní lokalitu nevylučuje translokální aspekty monografií (z hlediska autorů, výstavby textu, či publika) a tedy jistou otevřenost lokální identity. Příklad autorských předmluv dále naznačuje, že lokální identita mohla spočívat nejen v uvědomělé příslušnosti k městském kolektivu a vědomí závazků z toho plynoucích (typicky obyvatelstvo), ale též, nebo výlučně, v ryze osobním vztahu jedince k městu, jejž vnímá jako pro sebe významné (cizinec či mobilní obyvatel). Historický význam města, konstruovaný monografiemi, je v obou případech prostředkem zvyšování identifikačního potenciálu města.

Druhá část ukazuje, že také některé jiné identity našly vyjádření v monografiích nebo se promítly do struktury historického vyprávění. Jejich podoby a funkce se různily. Texty evokovaly prestižní identitu dávných měšťanů, významově ovšem oproštěnou od její feudální báze, a tedy odkazující k nad-historické hodnotě lokální identity. Ukázalo se, že středostavovská identita se mohla, ale také nemusela promítat do výkladu vztahu mezi šlechtou a městy – lokální hledisko zde převážilo. Hodnotová prvořadost identity národní se naproti tomu výrazně projevila v konstrukci městských historií, a to v nejrůznějších podobách: důkazy historicky české povahy města, či naopak německého původu města i městské kultury měly sloužit v zápase mezi českým a německým nacionalismem; národní hledisko si také vynucovalo zneuznání přínosu německých měšťanů v rozvoji měst, nebo popření jejich německé etnicity; osobitý vztah dané městské minulosti k českému, resp. polskému národu, či k dějinám vlasti ovšem také posloužil jako mimořádně vhodná cesta ke konstrukci historického významu města.

It is almost a truism to say that historical representations have considerable potential to form identities[1]. When these representations take the form of the narrative history of a place 'from its origins to the present', the intention seems quite transparent. This chapter attempts to characterize identities promoted by 19th-century town monographs. The first part of the chapter will outline the basic aspects of local identity[2], with regard to 19th-century town monographs. More specifically, it will explore the parameters of local identity as revealed in the historiography, and how the 'historical significance' of a town confers a sense of identity. Finally, it asks whether local identity is understood better as a collective or a personal impulse, or something in between. The second part examines how other types of identity – including those relating to social status and nationalism – were expressed or formed in the monographs, and explores how these other identities related to local identity.

The analysis is based on a sample of forty-five historical town monographs. Here, "town monograph" refers to individual books dedicated to the comprehensive history of a specific town, but may also refer to chapters on history in a more general description of a town. Typically, these works are known as "town biographies" or "town histories", yet the monographic nature of the material is worth stressing, as it did serve to enhance the uniqueness and worthiness of the towns that the books discussed. All the books were published between 1860 and 1900. They were written in Czech (twenty), German (ten), and Polish (fifteen), and concerned Bohemian, Moravian, and Galician towns. It is hoped that the geographical and cultural range will make the generalizations drawn more plausible. Of course, more could be said about wider aspects of the books, such as their market, audience, and production. However, this is beyond the scope of the present study, which is primarily a textual analysis.

What kind of town?

Let us begin with a simple definition: local identity, when related to a town, is both the external identity of a particular town and identification with that town[3]. However, what are the characteristics of the 'town' that emerge in the 19th-century monographs? Intuitively, at least three possible meanings of the concept come to mind, when linking town and identity. A town may be understood as a territorial entity, alongside other units, such as village, district, region, or state. A town is thus basically a small-scale locality, or a place, that varies in imagination from a site with streets, quarters, and buildings, to a specific, localized point. When linked to the issue of identity, one gets an idea of personal attachment to a distinctive and meaningful place. To a certain extent, the monographs under survey emphasised the territorial aspect of towns. Town histories were part of a broader context of research into geographical units typical of the 19th century; quite normally, their authors used the words "place" and "town" indiscriminately; contemporary German urban historical works, for example, were labelled alternatively "*Stadtgeschichte*", "*Localgeschichte*", and "*Ortsgeschichte*".

It is also possible to perceive a town in terms of a collectivity, and urban communities may be seen alongside other social groups, such as nations and social classes. It is the town-as-group view that refers to the concept of collective identity that, in turn, presupposes the ideas of membership, solidarity and 'patriotism'. The monographs also represented the towns they surveyed in terms of collectivities. People came to embody the towns in which they lived. Terms like "burghers", "citizens" and "residents" were often used interchangeably with "town".

A third perspective conceives towns as spheres of a distinct environment or culture, namely *urbanity*. Regardless of what precisely the concept signifies – a legal, functional, or material 'townness' of the place, or the somewhat stronger conception of distinct civic and economic culture that fully evolved in early modern European cities[4], or the urbanized milieu of modern big cities – it places the town in terms of an urban-rural dichotomy. The identity then refers primarily to cultural patterns, specific rationality, or a kind of personality[5], which the urban condition is believed to form. The monographs did not depict urbanity explicitly: after all, many of the towns they surveyed were small and minor – towns in name alone. But they made frequent references to specific urban functions (marketplaces or junctions), institutions (craft guilds, schools), people (burghers, artisans) and trajectories (streets, city walls). Referring to their own times, authors were mostly favourable towards changes brought about by modernization, perceiving them as part of a narrative of improvement and progress, and as a precondition for a vital urban space.

It is difficult to understand adequately the kinds of identity created by the monographs if we have an overly narrow conception of towns. The books employed multiple "urban ontologies"[6] concurrently, and the very nature of the monographs added yet another one: the textual. In short, it was a rather many-faceted idea of the town – produced by and deeply interconnected with the time-specific genre of historical monographs – that was to become the object of identification.

Local collectivity and beyond?

Before exploring local identity in the monographs, let us note that "local identity" is not an unproblematic term, as it is very much rooted in territorial terms. However, it is useful in this context because territorial concerns were important aspects in the monographs. Furthermore it avoids social exclusivity. Finally, unlike the concept of urban identity, it implies the importance of individual towns (the idea that a certain town matters, and not another), which is precisely what the monographs sought to establish: this was the basic *raison d'être* of the genre.

If we accept the multidimensionality of the represented towns, it follows that the local identity, presumably promoted by the monographs, was also multidimensional. First, there was a rhetoric of collectiveness, of belonging to the town. Authors referred to 'our town', and declared in their prefaces the virtues of learning from the deeds and failures of one's ancestors. This created an illusion of a direct link between the present inhabitants and past generations of townspeople. The local public, including schoolchildren and town representatives, were the primary audience, which enhanced the pedagogic nature of the works. More significantly, when it came to the recent past, the historical narratives shifted to become memorials of collective achievements – reflecting the fact that the books were sometimes initiated and sponsored by the municipal authorities[7].

Yet the monographs by no means embodied the memory of a clearly defined 'us', especially when it came to the more distant past. It was primarily the town-as-place that linked former and present inhabitants. All the similarities notwithstanding, in this aspect the local monographs differed substantially from the national histories[8]. After all, being part of "our town", as envisioned in the monographs, did not require the same qualification as was applied to membership in the nation. This somewhat loose definition of belonging – simply having some connection to a place, by birth, or by living or working there – may have jarred the sensibilities of the longer-established town residents, who resented sharing their local identity with newcomers: the monographs cut across the native-newcomer divide.

But the town-as-place ontology had even broader implications: local identity was in fact open even to people who did not have any tangible relationship to the given town and the local society. (Indeed, the publications had many 'translocal' features. First, many authors were not natives of the towns they wrote about[9]. Second, the publications were often addressed to a wider audience: to other historians, and to the general public. Patriotic and national motivations, which were sometimes overtly declared in prefaces or elsewhere in the books, transcended local limits. The local histories were considered to be the 'building blocks' of national histories, or textual counterparts of the town-as-national monument). Returning to local identity, it appears that the spatial dimension of the town opens up the possibility of an identity that is not bound to any membership – an identity which is based on the personal relationship between an individual and the town-as-place. The individual is not a member of the town, who is required to make effective his membership and the obligations that stem from it. Rather, the town becomes a part of his personal life-story. It gets a specific meaning in his or her mind. On occasion, this identification may emerge and exert an influence on his or her behaviour and decision-making. I will demonstrate that the authors of the monographs display precisely this logic.

Historically significant places

The historical significance of a particular town (the crucial discursive product of local histories, although often at odds with the historical reality) played a dual role. From the perspective of those townspeople who felt more or less bound to a town ('I was born there and can do nothing about it; I have to live here'), it could raise their self-esteem[10]. On the other hand, for outsiders and even local people who nonetheless felt more distanced from the town, historical significance could encourage them to identify more easily with the town. Historical significance made the towns attractive. Monographs affirmed the significance of towns in different ways. They confirmed the significance of traditionally strong and strategically important towns, enhanced new industrial towns with historical glamour, asserted the past greatness of towns in decline or invented a meaningful past for obscure towns. The latter enterprises are evident in the case of the small Galician town Dobczyce, south of Krakow. The author opened with a telling description of the present town with its single new church, "only few brick houses, more houses and cottages of wood and earth [...] – that is Dobczyce". "Nowadays", he continued, "it is a poor and, except on market days, silent market-town, hardly known to anybody"[11]. However, the author maintained that "even this, nowadays so obscure a place, has vivid memories [...] It used to be the seat of the district [...], and the very ruins of the castle witness that history has not passed here without a trace"[12].

Local identity as personal relation?

We may conclude our insights into local identity by examining personal narratives that prefaced three monographs, each of them representing a different culture. The first example is the publisher's preface to the German history of the central Moravian town of Olomouc (Olmütz). It begins with a distant reminiscence:

> When I opened my bookshop in Olmütz, 37 years ago, in autumn 1844, I did not know anybody, except one officer related to me, and indeed a sort of courage was required to establish myself in an unfamiliar town. However, only few weeks later, the educated residents of Olmütz and its vicinity would meet me with so much goodwill and trust, that I could soon look forward to expanding my shop, and later consider publishing larger undertakings[13].

His entrepreneurial success ultimately "compelled" him to move to Vienna in 1870. Yet, he continues, he left Olomouc unwillingly, for he experienced "truly happy times" and "genuine family happiness" there. The publisher mentions further that, in spite of his worries, the shop in Olomouc went on flourishing, partly due to his customers' fidelity. "Hence", he concludes,

> it was but a sense of gratefulness that induced me to publish *Geschichte der königl. Hauptstadt Olmütz*, so that I could present a testimony to my respectable fellow citizens, even if a small one, of my genuine affection for this town, which had become so dear to me[14].

In relation to the textual sphere, we can possibly classify statements of this sort as relating to 'expressed' identities, even though we can doubt legitimately about the authenticity of such declarations. After all, they are public statements: these expressed identities are too *discursive* to be readily labelled as true and innermost feelings[15]. Yet, for all its possible conventionality, these and other expressions – such as, typically, the references to writing the book during one's spare time, at one's own cost, or donating profits from sales to local institutions like hospitals – did help form the cultural fabric of the epoch. Returning to the example, one can see the apparent intertwining of a personal life story with a town that becomes a personally significant place. An individual may be distanced from the town-as-group and still have meaningful bonds with the town.

The motive of gratefulness also occurs in the next example. In the preface to his monograph about Przemyśl, then an eastern Galician town, now situated in south-east Poland, a Galician priest recalls a twenty-year old past:

> From 1833 to 1845, attending schools in Przemyśl, I spent there the most pleasant youth. I experienced the care of good people there, favour and help during the hardship of school years, and in particular, through education and the motivation to scholarly work acquired in that town, I became a convinced Pole. So for such gifts, I am indebted to Przemyśl[16].

Again, the author refers to locals in terms of obligation: by gathering and publishing these pieces of history, he claims to have fulfilled his "pleasant obligation of gratefulness to Przemyśl and his residents". In fact, however, it was not a sense of duty, but affection for the town that made him write its history. The affection stemmed from a position that the town gained in his personal narrative, but there were other reasons in favour of the town besides the personal meaning: primarily its "ancientness" (*gród starożytny*) and "significance" (*znaczenie*).

The third example differs from the previous two. A secretary in the local county self-administration and an eager historian set about recording the history of the nondescript

Bohemian town of Louny, situated north-west of Prague, despite only recently settling there. But the town was already planted in his memory:

> "What a wonderful history Louny has got!", I often sighed involuntarily during my studies – enraged by the history of the Czech land, impressed by the bravery of the ancient Czechs, excited by the heroism of our forefathers, and torn by the ultimate agony of my dear homeland. I could so frequently meet the name of the city of Louny in the forefront of the most decisive events of the Czech land, reading in various chronicles and histories. Louny often came to my mind, and without knowing it any better than from history, still it fixed into my memory, so that I was most pleasantly surprised when I was later placed in Louny due to my administrative profession. Having seen at first hand my new station and impressed by a revived fervour for that royal town, I tried to seek out an extensive history of venerable Louny[17].

Actual contact with the town activated latent identification, which had evolved solely through a mediated relationship between author and town. It is also clear that the primary object of identification with the town arose from its significance in the national narrative; but it was obviously the author's national consciousness which actually imposed a meaning on it. This example suggests the question: were there other identities, beyond the local, produced by town monographs? And if so, how did they relate to local identity?

Ancient burghers, modern middle class

Enlarging on particular groupings – whether burghers, residents, 'natives' and 'foreigners', old and new elites, upper and lower classes – within towns was not a major concern of the monographs. Of course, certain groupings were unquestionably relevant, while at times the authors could not avoid their own social and political bias[18]. One such grouping which inevitably featured was the burgher class. It may be assumed that the hierarchical system which underpinned burgher status would have been at variance with the ideals of the mainly liberal authors and readers. And yet, the burghers, their interests and especially their gains and losses (liberties, privileges, penalties), were present in narratives and often made significant. Passing over the explanation that the burghers mattered and so were discussed, we may argue that burghers constituted a vehicle for establishing local identity in the distant past, in a way akin to national histories. However, as we have seen, unlike national historiography, town monographs did not emphasise continuity between historic and contemporary urban dwellers. What, then, was the link between ancient burgher and modern citizen?

Before proposing the answer, we should note that, in general, the narratives 'cleared' the burghers of their particular, socially exclusive character[19]. They became a signifier for the town *per se*, alongside other terms. We have seen that authors used the name of the town, as well as terms like "burghers", "citizens", and "residents" as equivalents, regardless of the period. German historians used "Bürger", "Bürgerthum" or "Bürgerschaft" more consistently, but rather because it could apply to both free burghers in towns and modern free citizens. The German language enabled a semantic continuity between feudal urban society and modern middle class[20] that was effectively used in the national struggle over the origin of the middle class in Bohemia. As one historian mentioned: "it is characteristic that the Czech language, despite its many new terms, has no expression for that, but generally refers to Bürger as townsman (*měsťan*), while German understands by Bürger precisely the person who possesses rights"[21].

It seems that the link between ancient burghers and contemporary residents of the town was two-pronged. First, a sense of connection between local readers and ancient burghers was possible on the basis of the territorial and urban dimensions of town identity. Readers could interpret the fortunes and actions of former residents as contributing factors to the present state of the town and its relative position within the urban network, or to the town's historical significance. Second, there was an instructive impulse at work. Histories often depicted the actions of burghers in a way which was designed to show the reader how certain decisions taken by the authorities resulted in good or evil for the town, for instance remaining loyal to the king during a rebellion, and being rewarded subsequently with privileges and a promoted status[22]. It offered lessons in patriotism and local political craft.

It was a peculiar semiotic operation, describable through the Barthesian concept of mythology[23], that enabled these relations to become active. Whatever once maintained and expressed the identity of burghers lost within the pages of the 19th-century histories its original meaning and value. But at the same time, these objects gained a new function. They became signifiers for something else: local identity.

That holds true even for the cleric and historian who utilized his town history for a moralistic critique of the new, liberal age, and in particular of the local citizens. He anticipated the disdainful reactions of liberal readers to the liberties obtained by the small west Bohemian town of Přeštice from its feudal possessors, and depicted as worthy in the book. But since his aim was not the restoration of the feudal system, but restoring the civic, moral, and religious virtues of local citizenry, his reply to potential objections centred on the town's former importance: "Even with that awful serfdom, people used to live happily here and the town held a fairly splendid position in the region." Additionally, he recalled the proud identity of former burghers: "Town-hall officers and town representatives stood in good repute and the title of 'burgher' was highly thought of by everybody"[24].

It is interesting to ask whether and how the middle class authors discussed the historical tensions between towns and nobility in town monographs – particularly as theories on 19th-century middle class have stressed the importance of a 'common enemy' in the formation of class identity[25]. Some narratives did construct a cleavage between town and nobility that could be understood as symbolic for the monographs' liberal readership. In several cases, free royal towns were represented as a crucial pillar of the kingdom, serving as a counterweight to over-mighty subjects. Occasionally, both royal and private towns were represented together with villagers as "the People", standing in opposition to aristocracy. Alternatively, a particular conflict could be portrayed as significant. The historian of Tachov (Tachau), a royal town in west Bohemia which became a private town, devoted much space to a long-lasting conflict between (German) burghers and their new (equally German) possessor in the 17th century. In the preface, however, the author presents it as part of a broader picture:

> The universal thread that runs through the Bohemian history – the struggle of aristocracy against kingdom and Bürgerthum – has endowed the history of Bohemian towns with an equal character. This discord, which carries itself from history to the present times [...] so strikes the observer, that a truthful researcher cannot shut himself away from it[26].

Yet the re/construction of discord between townspeople and nobility was not always carried out. Occasionally, the joint actions of (royal) towns and the nobility came to the fore and were interpreted as patriotic struggles against the common enemy. This is true of certain interpretations of Czech towns during the Hussite movement and the rebellions against the Habsburgs in 1547 and 1618-20. In the case of private towns, the monographs often focused on a perceived bygone 'golden age'; and many aristocrats thus became local 'heroes'. Finally, the histories often suggested the significance of private towns indirectly, by discussing those noble possessors who were important national figures.

National identities, past and present

We have already indicated on several occasions that the town monographs were permeated by nationalist and patriotic discourses[27]. In the strongly nationalist monographs, the grand narrative of the nation and its struggles sometimes dominated at the expense of the local history. In more moderate works an occasional remark or interpretation revealed the author's own national consciousness, or made reference to the greater national scheme. There were also some initial regional differences in potential. In the Czech and Polish cases, "national" was closely associated with "patriotic": local histories were interwoven with the once glorious and ultimately ill-starred histories of the Czech kingdom and the Polish Rzeczpospolita. From the German point of view, in contrast, there was no such national fatherland in which to place the local history. Yet, besides appealing to Austrian patriotism, German local historians – to the concern of their Czech counterparts – attempted to link Germans to an alternative grand narrative of Czech history.

The thesis was built on the fact that German-speaking settlers had played a decisive role in the initial development of Bohemian towns. J. Lippert, a professionally-trained historian of the towns of Litoměřice (Leitmeritz) and Trutnov (Tratenau), and who eventually became a prominent German expert in Bohemian social history, developed the most sophisticated version of this perspective. He argued that a medieval society could not progress without a mediating element, in this case the 'Bürgerthum', which served to erode the simple dichotomy of landowner and peasant. According to this thesis, Czech princes wisely invited and offered protection to German burghers in the 13th century, who arrived with knowledge of the urban system, artisan skills, and the financial means to promote an urban culture in Bohemia. Without such an influx Czechs would have had to wait another century for an indigenous 'middle class' to emerge[28].

For the most part, histories of Bohemian and Moravian towns definitely served as sites of Czech *versus* German national struggles – on a double level. On the general level, the German histories served to support the thesis that Bohemian urban culture and development was inseperable from its German elements. The historian of the north-west Bohemian spa town of Bílina (Bilin) was perhaps the most extreme exponent of the theory of the German dimension of urban development:

> The history of Bohemian towns can rightly be called the history of German element [Deutschtum] in Bohemia, since the towns, founded by the princes of the country, are almost entirely obliged to the German 'Bürgethum' – that had been planted into the country – for their development. Also most of the cultural development of Bilin has been ascribed to this circumstance[29].

On a local level, the publications often tried to prove the pure or at least essential German or Czech character of the particular town through history. Czechs and Germans thus struggled to project modern concepts of national identity onto pre-modern times. Unlike local identity discourses, national discourses created continuity based on a strong conception of the time-spanning group. The German physician and enthusiastic historian of the central Moravian town of Litovel (Littau) conducted an exhaustive survey of charters, town books, burgher names, and inscriptions on buildings and coins, to show that the town retained its predominantly German character even in the 16th century, when the Czech language began to appear in the sources, arguing that language did not always equate with national identity[30].

Czech local historians deployed several methods to answer both the demands of nationalism and the need to present historically coherent narratives of particular towns. The argument of 'German cultural advancement' was refuted by explaining German achievements in terms of the patronage of the Czech Přemyslid princes. The latter were at times condemned by the historians for placing short-term economic gain over the long-term welfare of the Czech people and nation. Přemysl Otakar II (1233-1278), the most prolific patron of royal towns, thus won an ambiguous reputation as both a great Czech king in Czech historiography, and, for German authors, the major 'Germanizer' of the Czech lands.

In Czech monographs, the Germans were not erased completely, but their role was downplayed. Lip service was paid to the German urban dimension; but their successes were often depicted as less than legitimate, reliant on medieval privileges and Habsburg Germanization policies; ultimately, it was claimed, the Germans were assimilated, defeated, or expelled. The history of the central Bohemian royal town, Čáslav, written by the skilled historian A. Sedláček, may be an illustrative case. It asserted that despite its foundation under German tutelage, the town "still nurtured the genuine national core within". Later the national make-up of the period was described thus:

> The core of the town's residents has always been Czech, and the German element in Čáslav was hardly a nationality; it was more a sort of caste. Yet it cannot be denied that German residents reigned and that the German language considerably prevailed over Czech in terms of public usage[31].

The author further minimized the role of German burghers by arguing that both 'elements' merged under the influences of Czech nationality and German customs. The Germans entered the narrative once again, during the Hussite revolution, this time as the urban "aristocracy":

> These matters [Hussite ideology] affected a rapid change in the town's mindset, easily winning adherents, against the, admittedly, impotent resistance of the town aristocracy, which suddenly surrendered in the struggle with Idea and Eagerness, lost ground, and faded away from memory[32].

Paradoxically perhaps, the Germans vanished from the towns' memory only to reemerge in history, but in an unfavourable way that resembled the situation surrounding the 'town hall struggles' between Czechs and Germans, contemporaneous with the publication of the monographs.

Complementary to these negative depictions, Germans 'disappeared' when the history narrated the overall fortunes of the town; usage of terms such as town, burghers, or residents effectively obscured the logical implication that it was precisely the German burghers who often stood behind the medieval glory of the town. To put it theoretically, the identity ascribed to the same category of people varied according to what they were supposed to signify: town and local identity, or nation and national identity.

Yet precisely the supreme position of national identity within the moral and social horizon of the period also encouraged the construction of a particular town's history within the context of the nation, or homeland, and national history. To enhance a town's prestige in these terms, the narratives had to conceptualize its past, or part of it, as either an important contribution to the nation, or at least as in some way emblematic of national history. On a general level, virtually all town histories enjoyed some value, because – the argument of several Czech and Polish local historians went – they all represented aspects and monuments of the national past. From this viewpoint, however, the towns became relegated to 'places', commonly shared by the nation; also, the urban dimension did not play any role: villages and other smaller entities were equally valuable in this way.

To get beyond this general value in the national perspective, something distinctive, if not unique, had to be found and exploited. Leaving aside exceptional cases like Prague, or Kraków, historians explored a variety of aspects to assert the individuality of their towns: from former political strength, or outstanding participation in national history, to whatever nationally relevant event that had occurred there – the birth of a famous native, an important noble possessor, or a royal visit. The historian of the western Galician town of Nowy Sącz wrote of the Polonization of the German burghers that:

> [t]his great and exceedingly important change was crowned over the course of two centuries of Polish history, in which Nowy Sącz not once played an outstanding role in nationally significant events of the foremost importance, events which ushered in the period of its greatest prosperity and significance[33].

The book continues with a story about how the recently founded royal town immediately joined the 'national' king Władysław Łokietek in the struggle against a conspiracy of Krakowian burghers and the prince of Opole in the early 14th century[34].

But as the concluding quotation from the preface to the history of the eastern Bohemian border town, Náchod, clearly illustrates, the whole edifice of a 'significant history' could often be built on less active foundations:

> I realized how often its history was narrowly and inseparably connected to the history of the entire nation in the Kingdom and its Lands. For Náchod is situated in the borderlands, through which hostile hordes have poured constantly from the east, whenever they intended to assault and eradicate this Kingdom. These rapacious hordes always directed their cruelty at Náchod first. Every stroke from abroad into the Czech kingdom always shattered firstly and most severely Náchod. Hence the history of Náchod has been a portion of the history of the Czech nation[35].

Conclusion

This chapter has argued that "local identity" best describes the potential product of the historical monographs under survey, and has attempted to sketch the basic contours of local identity. First, the subject of local identity and the potential object of identification (that is, the town), was imagined multi-dimensionally, as place, collectivity, and centre of urbanity, while being principally textual. With regard to its social scope, local identity was basically an open project, not restricted to a specific group of local or privileged people. It was critically bound with a specific locality, but never confined to a merely local relevance, origin, or purpose. Though the works harnessed ideas relating to collectivity, and often tried to provide instruction for local citizens, they were based primarily on the authors' subjective and personal relation to the towns. Asserting the historical significance of the town was a crucial means of making it a more meaningful object of identification.

Town monographs also expressed, constructed, and perhaps even helped to form other identities. The medieval burghers, for instance, were used, mutated, distorted and suppressed in the creation of certain kinds of local identity. Middle class consciousness also found its way into the local histories, although the analysis of discursive relations between towns and aristocracy revealed that this was not a unilateral process. Besides placing local histories into national stories and patriotic causes, Czechs and Germans contested the identity of towns for contemporary nationalist reasons. The exclusive nature of nationalism on the one hand, and the need to create a coherent and valuable local history on the other, led in some cases to discursive suppression (rather than erasure) of the rival ethnic group within the narrative. At any rate, local monographs utilized intensely the moral supremacy and social prevalence of national ideology for increasing the historical significance of their respective towns.

Notes

1 This chapter was written with the support of the research scheme of the Ministry of Education of the Czech Republic MSM 0021620827 /České země uprostřed Evropy v minulosti a dnes (/Czech Lands in the Middle of Europe, Past and Present), at the Faculty of Philosophy and Arts of Charles University in Prague. A version of this chapter was read at the Eighth International Conference on Urban History (Stockholm, 30.8.-2.9.2006), and is available on the CD-ROM *Urban Europe in Comparative Perspective*, (ed. L. Nilsson, Institute of Urban History, Stockholm University). Participation at the Stockholm proceedings was facilitated by a grant from the Foundation of 'Nadání Josefa, Marie a Zdeňky Hlávkových', n. 6/2/14.

2 Assigning terminology such as "local identity" to these town monographs is not unproblematic. It may be that the irreducible multidimensionality of the town concept makes it impossible to arrive at precise descriptive terminology; or terminology may not convince when separated from the medium – the monographs – that created them. However, I believe that "local identity" comes closest semantically to what these books produced.

3 For the sake of convenience the term *town* is used throughout the article, although in certain contexts *city* would be more accurate.

4 See A.C. Zijderveld, *A Theory of Urbanity: The Economic and Civic Culture of Cities*, New Brunswick - London 1998.

5 A. Haapala, *The Urban Identity: The City as a Place to Dwell*, in V. Sarapik, K. Tüür (eds.), *Koht ja Paik/ Place and Location. Studies in Environmental Aesthetics and Semiotics III* (Proceedings of the Estonian Academy of Arts 14), Tallinn 2003, p. 13-23. El. version: <http://www.eki.ee/km/place/koht_3.htm>

6 There is already a large literature in culturally-oriented urban studies, concerning the ontological and epistemological questions of what the city is, how it has been conceived and represented, and the limits of our knowledge and understanding of it. By the term "ontology" I am indirectly referring to the recent study in Polish by E. Rewers, *Post-polis. Wstęp do filozofii ponowoczesnego miasta*, Krakow 2005, in which she discusses four "critical ontologies" of the city, as they ocurred in the 20th-century philosophical thinking on cities. For an in-depth debate on ontological assumptions about cities see also A. Blum, *The Imaginative Structure of the City*, Montreal - Kingston - London - Ithaca 2003. See also the now classic works by H. Lefebvre, especially his "Right to the City" in E. Kofman, E. Lebas (eds.), *Writ-*

ings on Cities/Henri Lefebvre, Malden - Oxford - Carlton 1996, pp. 61-181 [Orig. *Le Droit à la Ville*, 1968].

7 Eight books were sponsored by the municipality, eighteen were produced at the author's expense, and nineteen were financed by other sources (such as private and religious publishers, or historical associations).

8 This echoes the distinction proposed by Hroch between nation as a group of members and region as a territory with inhabitants. M. Hroch, *Regional and National Memory: The Role of History in (Re)constructing Regional Identity*, CLIOHRES TWG 5 meeting, Bratislava, 16-17 February 2007.

9 The towns they were writing about usually served as 'temporary' places of residence, in their relatively mobile professions, since they were mostly professors, teachers, and clerics, but also local officers, cultural workers, and even lawyers or physicians. It was more the exception than the rule to write about one's native town. Many authors wrote histories of several places. Moreover, their good education allowed them to perceive local histories in a broader context. Indeed, the typical figure of a narrow-minded local antiquarian was often a myth rather than reality in 19th-century local historiography.

10 I am loosely referring here to the mechanisms described by "social identity theory" and "optimal distinctiveness theory". The latter stresses the dual need of individuals to be included and assimilated in the group, yet also to perceive themselves as distinctive – needs which are satisfied by belonging to groups that are clearly distinct from others, or that adopt explicit rules of inclusion and exclusion. R. Brown, D. Capozza, *Motivational, emotional, and cultural influences in social identity processes*, in Id. (eds.), *Social Identities: Motivational, Emotional and Cultural Influences*, Hove - New York 2006, p. 6. But in the case of towns, the sense of belonging may be inherited or assumed rather than selected. Surely, the effect of the distinctiveness mechanism is also likely to vary in individual cases, depending on to what extent the sense of belonging to a particular town is relevant for one's personal identity.

11 L. Zarewicz, *Dobczyce: Monografia historiczna*, Krakow 1878, pp. 3, 16.

12 *Ibid.*, p. 3.

13 W. Müller, *Geschichte der königlichen Hauptstadt Olmütz von den ältesten Zeiten bis zur Gegenwart*, Vienna - Olomouc 1882, *Vorwort des Herausgebers (Eduard Hölzel)*, unpaginated preface.

14 *Ibid.*

15 For problems associated with studying personal narratives, see J. Brockmeier, D. Carbaugh (eds.), *Narative and Identity: Studies in Autobiography, Self and Culture*, Amsterdam - Philadelphia 2001.

16 W. z Zaleszan (Michna), *Przemyśl i jego okolice*, Nowy Sącz 1872, p. 2.

17 R. Wunš, *Dějiny svobodného královského města Loun od počátku až do dob nejnovějších*, Prague 1868, p. i.

18 After all, many of them took active part in local, but also high politics.

19 For an excellent analysis of the construction of groups and collective actors by historical narratives, and their signifying function see A. Rigney, *The Rhetoric of Historical Representation: Three Narratives of the French Revolution*, Cambridge 2002, 2nd ed., especially chapter 3, pp. 103-136.

20 The exhaustive analysis of these semantic relations has been undertaken in R. Koselleck, K. Schreiner (eds.), *Bürgerschaft: Rezeption und Innovation der Begrifflichkeit vom Hohen Mittelalter bis ins 19. Jahrhundert*, Stuttgart 1994.

21 J. Stocklöw, *Geschichte der Stadt Tachau*, Tachau 1878, pp. 27-28.

22 F. Levý, *Dějiny královského města Rakovníka*, Rakovník 1896, p. 86.

23 R. Barthes, *Mytologie*, Prague 2004 (orig. *Mythologies*, Paris 1957).

24 V.E. Řičák, *Dějepis města Přeštic a jeho okolí*, Prague 1865, p. 107.

25 J. Kocka, *The Middle Classes in Europe*, in "The Journal of Modern History", 67, 1995, p. 788. Urban history and the making of middle class identity in Germany, France and England is explored in U. Spree,

Die Rückbesinnung auf die mittelalterliche Stadt. Die Bedeutung der Stadt als Mittel der Identitätsstiftung "mittlerer Schichten" in der deutschen, britischen und französischen Lexikographie des 18. und 19. Jahrhunderts, in Koselleck, Schreiner (eds.), *Bürgerschaft* cit., pp. 309-374. The article shows quite clearly the substantial role of relating to the urban past for middle class self-consciousness. The (idealized) history of towns served for argumentations on legitimatory, didactic, and exemplary levels. Yet, unlike 'univerzalising' and 'placeless' lexicography and political discourse, the 'individualizing' and 'place-specific' genre of local histories may, hypothetically, produce somewhat more ambiguous projections.

26 J. Stocklöw, *Geschichte der Stadt Tachau* cit., p. xi.

27 This section can discuss only a few aspects from the very complex theme of national discourses in local historiography. For the Czech texts, a detailed analysis was undertaken in my M.A. thesis, *Lokální a národní identita v dějepisectví českých měst poslední třetiny 19. století*, Prague 2005, manuscript.

28 J. Lippert, *Geschichte der Stadt Leitmeritz*, Leitmeritz 1871, pp. 25-29. To be sure, J. Lippert, a scholar and also a representative in the Austrian parliament, belonged to the category of German public men who sought sincerely for coexistence of both nationalities in Bohemia; or at least he was characterized in this way in the Czech encyclopedia by the beginning of 20th century: see "Lippert, Julius", *Ottův Slovník Naučný*, Vol. XVI, 1888-1908.

29 T. Hutter, *Die Stadt Bilin und ihre Geschichte von der ältesten Zeit bis auf unsere Tage*, Bilin 1891, p. 1.

30 J. Kux, *Geschichte der Stadt Littau von den ältesten Zeiten bis zum Jahre 1848*, Brünn 1900, pp. 82-92.

31 A. Sedláček, *Děje města Čáslavě*, Prague 1874, p. 56.

32 *Ibid.*, p. ii.

33 J. Sygański, *Nowy Sącz. Jego dzieje i pamiątki dziejowe*, Nowy Sącz 1892, p. 18.

34 *Ibid.*, p. 19-20.

35 J.K. Hraše, *Dějiny Náchoda*. Náchod 1895, p. 3.

Bibliography

Sources quoted

Hraše J.K., *Dějiny Náchoda*, Náchod 1895.

Hutter T., *Die Stadt Bilin und ihre Geschichte von der ältesten Zeit bis auf unsere Tage*, Bilin 1891.

Kux J., *Geschichte der Stadt Littau von den ältesten Zeiten bis zum Jahre 1848*, Brünn 1900.

Levý F., *Dějiny královského města Rakovníka*, Rakovník 1896.

Lippert J., *Geschichte der Stadt Leitmeritz*, Leitmeritz 1871.

Müller W., *Geschichte der königlichen Hauptstadt Olmütz von den ältesten Zeiten bis zur Gegenwart*, Vienna - Olomouc 1882.

Řičák V.E., *Dějepis města Přeštic a jeho okolí*, Prague 1865.

Sedláček A., *Děje města Čáslavě*, Prague 1874.

Stocklöw J., *Geschichte der Stadt Tachau*, Tachau 1878.

Sygański J., *Nowy Sącz. Jego dzieje i pamiątki dziejowe*, Nowy Sącz 1892.

Wunš R., *Dějiny svobodného královského města Loun od počátku až do dob nejnovějších*, Prague 1868.

z Zaleszan (Michna) W., *Przemyśl i jego okolice*, Nowy Sącz 1872.

Zarewicz L., *Dobczyce: Monografia historiczna*, Krakow 1878.

Selected literature

Applegate C., *A Nation of Provincials: The German Idea of Heimat*, Berkeley - Los Angeles - Oxford 1990.

Barthes R., *Mytologie*, Prague 2004 (orig. *Mythologies*, Paris 1957).

Blum A., *The Imaginative Structure of the City*, Montreal and Kingston - London - Ithaca 2003.

Bormann R., *Raum, Zeit, Identität: Sozialtheoretische Verortungen kultureller Prozesse*, Opladen 2001.

Brockmeier J., Carbaugh D. (eds.), *Narative and Identity: Studies in Autobiography, Self and Culture*, Amsterdam - Philadelphia 2001.

Brown R., Capozza D. (eds.), *Social Identities: Motivational, Emotional and Cultural Influences*, Hove - New York 2006.

Duncan S., *What is Locality?*, in Thrift N., Peet R. (eds.), *New Models in Geography: The Political-economy Perspective*, vol. 2, London 1989.

Friese H. (ed.), *Identities: Time, Difference, and Boundaries*, New York - Oxford 2002.

Kocka J., *The Middle Classes in Europe*, in "The Journal of Modern History", 67, 1995, pp. 783-806.

Koselleck R., Schreiner K. (eds.), *Bürgerschaft: Rezeption und Innovation der Begrifflichkeit vom Hohen Mittelalter bis ins 19. Jahrhundert*, Stuttgart 1994.

Lovell N., *Locality and Belonging*, London 1998.

Rewers E., *Post-polis: Wstęp do filozofii ponowoczesnego miasta*, Krakow 2005.

Rigney A., *The Rhetoric of Historical Representation: Three Narratives of the French Revolution*, Cambridge 2002 (2nd ed.; 1st ed. 1990).

Sarapik V., Tüür K. (eds.), *Koht ja Paik / Place and Location. Studies in Environmenal Aesthetics and Semiotics III* (Proceedings of the Estonian Academy of Arts 14), Tallinn 2003. El. version: <http://www.eki.ee/km/place/koht_3.htm>

Urbanitsch P., Stekl H. (eds.), *Kleinstadtbürgertum in der Habsburger-Monarchie 1862-1914.* (Bürgertum in der Habsburgermonarchie IX), Vienna - Cologne - Weimar 2000.

Zijderveld A.C., *A Theory of Urbanity: The Economic and Civic Culture of Cities*, New Brunswick - London 1998.

The Image of the City as a Site of Memory: Bratislava in Modern Travel Literature

Jozef Tancer
Comenius University, Bratislava

Abstract

This study deals with the image of Pressburg/Bratislava in travel literature from the end of the 18th up to the 20th centuries. The focus is on the texts of German and Austrian travellers as well as writings of local authors from the Hungarian Kingdom and later from Czechoslovakia. The analysis concentrates on three main *topoi* present in the travel literature about Bratislava in the period considered: a border town, the Pressburger, and a city of pleasure. Due to their constant appearance and ever changing meaning and function it is possible to understand these mental images as sites of memory. A topological analysis in a broader chronological setting reveals possible ideological motives for using them and enables their deconstruction, i.e. the restoration of a polysemy challenged by discourses that try to homogenize and unify the interpretation of the past.

Štúdia skúma obraz Prešporku/ Bratislavy v cestopisnej literatúre od konca 18. do konca 20. storočia. V centre pozornosti stoja texty nemeckých a rakúskych cestovateľov ako aj práce domácich uhorských, neskôr československých, resp. slovenských autorov. Analýza sa zameriava na tri dominantné topoi, ktoré sa vyskytujú v cestopisnej literatúre opisujúcej Bratislavu v sledovanom období: mesto na hranici, obyvateľ Bratislavy a mesto pôžitkov. Na základe ich konštantného výskytu pri stále meniacom sa význame a funkcii je možné chápať tieto mentálne obrazy ako miesta pamäti. Topologická analýza v širšom chronologickom rámci odhaľuje možné ideologické motívy ich používania a umožňuje ich dekonštrukciu, t. j. rekonštruovanie viacznačnosti, pre bola prekrytá diskurzmi, usilujúcimi sa o homogenizáciu a unifikáciu interpretácie dejín.

When contemporary architects, philosophers or cultural historians speak about the development of urban settlements, we hear words such as "urban palimpsest" (Andreas Huyssen), "lost legibility", or even "the fall of the city" (Bogdan Bogdanović)[1]. Descriptions such as these are an attempt to analyse critically the dynamic change of the contemporary city. Frequently, however, this change leads to irreparable damage or, at best, to the repression of historical continuity. This reality has often been very painful for inhabitants of European cities in the 20th century. The capital city of the Slovak republic, Bratislava (Pressburg/Poszony) forms such a case.

Looking at the image of Bratislava, we discover how constant it is despite the discontinuity in the city's history. This chapter will consider the problem of continuity and discontinuity in the portrayal of this city from the end of the 18th century up to the 20th century. It will concentrate on impressions conveyed in travel literature, a medium in which reflections about the phenomenon of the city occupy a central place. One can define "travel literature" in its broader meaning as fiction and nonfiction texts referring to travel: from guide books, nonfiction itineraries to travel novels[2]. Therefore this study takes into account texts which appeared as a result of a journey as well as those written for future travellers (visitors). It will analyse sources of local as well as foreign origin. The reports of German and Austrian travellers will provide an outsiders' view: the authors from the Hungarian Kingdom and later from Czechoslovakia and Slovakia will give the inside perspective.

The study consists of three parts. In the first part I will briefly explain the notion of the image of the city as I try to make use of it. Later on, I will present three main *topoi* travel literature exploits when depicting Bratislava. In the last section I will suggest a way to analyze the various forms of the city-image referring to the theory of the sites of memory.

The Image of the City

Kevin Lynch, an American expert in urban studies, sees the image of a city as the result of a long study of many different elements and their reciprocal relations, on which basis we may construct a complex picture of the city[3]. To consider these elements is of great importance for all who strive for perfect understanding. Although the perception of a city depends on several subjective factors, Lynch considers the urban image to contain an objective component: the generalized images inhabitants have of their city, created through the perception of basic structural elements such as path, edge, district, node and landmark[4]. We may, by analogy with this urban concept, speak of a city's image, transmitted through travel literature that is also determined by a certain perception or observation strategies. This picture of course often draws from the partial experiences of individual travel authors, and often reveals more about the observer than about the object of observation. Nevertheless, this subjectivity is not the only influence on travellers or the specific circumstances of their voyages. Mental 'snapshots', captured in travel descriptions, obey general formal rules which determine their content: above all the practical rules of travel and the 'poetic' rules of describing itineraries, both objects of the *ars apodemica*.

Apodemic manuals give travellers a precise catalogue of phenomena to observe on their trips: climactic conditions, the lifestyle of the population, their character, etc. These recommendations structure the vision of travellers by directing their analysis to certain preconceived subjects. Objects of observation are, to some extent, no longer selected subjectively. Though the travel possibilities as well as the goals of travel changed between the 16th and 18th centuries, apodemic advice from this period established a certain pattern of observation that enjoyed a lengthy afterlife[5].

This is confirmed when comparing the texts describing Bratislava from the last three centuries. We find considerable commonalities, despite differences in time and cultural context, as if the texts had simply ignored the changes to the face of the city. Descriptions of the city's character produce the same images over and over again. This phenomenon cannot be explained through stable continuous urban development. The city of Bratislava over the last three centuries has undergone profound transformation. The recurring images survive despite the tempestuous chaos engendered by various political regimes that have sought to form the image of the city according to their own principles.

The explanation is to be found in the specific methods of characterization used to create descriptive images of a city. Also, it arises from the suitability of cities as sites of memory. To be recognized as such, the city requires a formal unity of expression. This memorial function requires that images of the city contain not only visual stability, but also semantic elasticity, a flexibility of meaning that allows memory to be reinterpreted.

The First Urban Image: A Border Town

Travelling is an activity that confronts a person with foreign cultures. Mental images of others also shape images of the self. The encounter with foreigners is one of the basic experiences of a traveller, as well as a main theme of travel descriptions, even though this is not always made explicit. The contrast between the known and the unknown appears in many images that take this dichotomy. One of them is the image of the border. The border can both divide and unite. In travel literature, Pressburg is often described as a border town. This portrayal is mediated through several different images with many different meanings. Here it is the division between the known and the unknown world, there is that between the Occident and the Orient, and in other places it is a region in which different cultures meet and influence each other ("crossroads of cultures"), or even a place of transit or expansion. These images reflect not only the objective geographic location of the city, but also the political and cultural projections and goals which unite Pressburg with different historical epochs. The mental map is overlapping with the geographical one[6].

Terra incognita

After decades of war with the Ottomans, Hungary had become largely unknown to Western Europe. The estate uprisings and epidemics of the 17th and early 18th centuries did little to make the country attractive for travellers. Nor was there an appropriate infrastructure to guarantee a safe journey: no well-built roads, no network of hotels, no reliable postal service. Even in 1835, A. Schmidl's travel book for the Kingdom of Hungary advised the reader against travelling in Hungary unarmed[7]. The Hungarian ethnographer and lawyer Johann Csaplovics lamented, in his 1829 *Gemälde von Ungern*, that such images

> created certain prejudices that, even if all reasonable people today acknowledge them as unfounded, continue to perpetuate themselves. People consider Hungary's climate unhealthy, its people half-barbarians, and therefore the country itself as unsafe for foreigners, indeed one believes that there is still a certain antipathy against foreigners[8].

While educated Hungarians became famous for their work in both the 18th and the 19th century, it did not lie in their power to reduce these unfounded slanders against their country, nor its reputation as an unknown land, an image repeated continually in travel literature from the 16th century on.

Occident and Orient

A further attribute that corresponded to the image of a *terra incognita* was the oriental character of the country. Even in the Ancient world, the dichotomy Occident-Orient contained a political subtext, contrasting the political thoughtfulness of the Greek *polis* with oriental despotism. In the Middle Ages, this conflict was intensified with confessional struggles between Christendom and Islam. Images of the Orient became linked with images of fear and danger; the Orient as "other" became a symbol of that enmity[9]. The oriental image of Hungary dates back to the Ottoman expansion, which made a deep impression on the modern history of Hungary. The presence of Islam and the Ottomans in Hungary over almost two hundred years made the country appear strange to Western European eyes, a non-European place with a backward civilization. Europe stopped at Vienna. Exactly there the Bavarian doctor Anton Quitzman began his *German letters about the Orient*: "I chose Vienna because it is the border of Europe, on whose walls the violence of the Oriental flood repeatedly broke; I chose Vienna, because it has a certain similarity with the Orient, namely that one can write the most fantastic things about them without study, and still be believed"[10]. If Vienna was for Quitzman the last place of European culture, then Pressburg was the first place that lay abroad in a foreign space. His first letter from Pressburg starts with the following words: "Dear Friend! Herewith you receive my first letter from a foreign land! [*aus der Fremde; J.T.*]"[11].

Crossroad of cultures

One variant of the dichotomy between Occident-Orient offers Pressburg as the mediator between two worlds, as a crossroad of cultures. Pressburg "serves as the middle section between East and West, not only in spiritual, but also in a political and material sense"[12], wrote Thomas Szekcö, a teacher at the Pressburg Lutheran gymnasium in an 1865 description of the city's cultural diversity. From the perspective of 19th-century national cultures seeking homogeneity, he saw the mediative role of Pressburg as a great obstacle for the development of a single national identity. The city's location on the border meant that the city had "the fate of all transition points and places, since the role of transmitting cultures normally works to its own disadvantage, because among the influence of so many different elements a self-sufficient, individual or even civic character can not develop, which for example has stamped Debrecen as a properly Magyar city, Munich as a southern German, or Berlin as a northern German city"[13].

Pressburg as a Gate

The position of Pressburg on the border also led to an image of the city as a gate, which political regimes have used for their own purposes in the 20th century. This image rests on the geographic description of the pass between the Devín rocks and the Hainburg hills, the *porta hungarica*. Even in the 19th century, the city was described as guarding this gate, even though the gate itself had been open to all possible tribes, peoples, and armies. The metaphor referred primarily to the city's geographic location at the crossroads of various historical migrations, but in the first Czechoslovak republic one saw the city as a geopolitical gate, "which opens the way to the world, to international contacts with all peoples that lie on the banks of the Danube"[14]. For the Slovak Republic, the satellite state of the German Reich (1939-1945), Bratislava was also a gate, but not one linking political and economic partners, but simply the "German gate to the south-east"[15] which serves to fulfill "the historical mission"[16] of the city. Pressburg, the "European necessity in the Danube basin"[17], was seen as "an important base for the propagation of cultural values"[18]. The image of the gate was associated neither with cultural exchange nor with partnership between neighbours. Instead, the gate metaphor justified the claims to territory or to a sphere of influence, and hopes to expand them.

Even after the Second World War, the image of the border was a favourite trope in descriptions of the city. Even though the Iron Curtain (itself an example of a dichotomy image) had shut the Pressburg gate, the city was still described as a region "in which the Eastern and Western parts of Europe stretch out hands to each other"[19]. In actual fact, hands could only be extended decades later.

The Second Urban Image: the Pressburger

Images of the city rest not only on its geographic and political location, on its panorama or other 'static' elements. They also contained dynamic images of the city: the inhabitants. The specific image of the city depends on the specific character of its population. This relationship is firmly established in all descriptions of the city from the earliest travellers to the most recent attempts to create a historical image of Pressburg. So in 1933 we read, for example, in the work of Emil Portisch, author of the first popular history of the city, "when we say, for example, this is a Berliner, that is a Praguer, this is a Viennese, this should mean more than describe the city of residence [...] this characterizes a certain species of humanity!"[20] What images of the city's inhabitants can be found in traveler's accounts?

In the 18th and 19th centuries, the image of Pressburgers contained considerable ethnic diversity, which reflects not only the composition of its population but also its position as a border town. The character of Pressburgers was seen as a combination of typical Austrian-Viennese characteristics and typical Hungarian-Magyar characteristics. Viennese light-heartedness and liveliness was mixed with Hungarian seriousness and patriotism. The city doctor Paul Kolbány described the Pressburger in 1811 as follows: "The Pressburger is direct and open-hearted to foreigners and strangers, if one speaks to him politely [...] he accepts foreigners with hospitality and friendliness. [...] He loves his king, loves his fatherland, has great national pride, which is justified by the history of his fatherland, the constitution and its freedom"[21]. Pride was one of the most striking characteristics of Hungarians, even for authors who did not think highly of describing national characteristics. "I know that it is a very useless activity to try and describe a nation because one will find so many exceptions", wrote the Hungarian savant Karl Gottlieb Windisch. "But there are certain main features which are more common among one nation than among others [...] one ascribes to the Hungarians a certain pride, and I will not contradict"[22]. Depending on their stance, we find authors with a variety of attitudes toward this characteristic. Some criticized it as the source of all hatred and contempt for everything foreign[23], others linked it to the fatherland discourse, which had positive connotations in the 18th century, such as for example Friedrich Nicolai, who described Hungarian national pride as the "mother of many noble sentiments and deeds"[24].

While many authors found evidence of Germanophobia in Pressburg, above all in the expressions of Magyar national pride, the colourful ethnic composition of the population left most with the impression of a friendly and tolerant atmosphere. Multilingualism, cultivated in many of the city's families, was the basis for common, peaceful understanding. The multilingualism of the inhabitants enabled a certain identity game, as illustrated by an anecdote from Saxon preacher Heinrich Pröhle from 1849.

After smoking was forbidden next to guard posts, the following scenes supposedly took place:

> The first post calls to the passing smoker in German, who blows a cloud of smoke in his face, he shrugs his shoulder, doesn't understand German, and continues. The next calls to him in Hungarian, he shakes his head, and doesn't understand Hungarian. Then a Slovak calls to the passerby to take the pipe from his mouth, but he gives a pitying look, doesn't understand Slovak, and continues on his way. So in a few days the police rule, probably introduced by the Hungarian chancellery in Vienna, was scattered to the winds by the opposition of smokers[25].

The political regimes of the 20th century have deeply transformed the face of Pressburg and its inhabitants. Under the Czechoslovak Republic, the city was noticeably Slovakized. The wartime Slovak state had decimated the city's Jewish population; the post-war regime eliminated the remaining Germans and a part of the Hungarians in the name of struggle against class enemies. The original multi-ethnicism became the target of ideological criticism. The old multi-ethnic images of the city were replaced by internationalism, but an internationalism that was only cultivated within the context of the Eastern block and the friendly regimes. "...[T]oday no inhabitant of Bratislava would be surprised to be addressed [in Slovak] by a black student from Africa, a brown Bulgarian or broad-backed Korean"[26].

The opening of borders in 1989 returned the lost diversity to the city in the form of Western tourists, and memories of old Pressburg were revived. The former civic culture was juxtaposed with the systematic proletarianization of the post-war period. This was particularly the case among those unable to bear the strident Slovak nationalism of the post-communist period. Though historians and ethnologists warned against transforming the Pressburg of the interwar period, or even of the period before the transformations of 1918-1919, into a multi-ethnic paradise, many idyllic images appeared in public spaces showing the old Pressburg as a place where all ethnic groups met together peacefully in coffee houses and wine cellars. The old Pressburger became a modern urban hero. The local press in Bratislava began a heated "Battle of Frogs and Mice" over who has the right to call themselves genuine Pressburgers. To be a 'spotless' Pressburger, was it necessary to have parents from the city, or did one need grandparents from both sides? Old Pressburg guides were consulted nostalgically, and were reprinted in new uncritical editions to cultivate the Pressburg myths. Milan Lasica summarized the situation pithily in the introduction to one of these reprints: "To be an old Pressburger today is something like claiming to come from Atlantis. We all know that Atlantis existed, but nobody can remember it"[27].

The Third Urban Image: A City of Pleasure

The most recent literature on Pressburg markets the city as the place where "the Danube and wine come together"[28]. This metaphor encapsulates the next *topos* in travel literature: Pressburg as a city of pleasure. This *topos* does not depend on anything specifically local. The flip side of seeing Hungary as a *terra incognita* was the Hungarian conviction about the country's exclusiveness: *extra Hungariam non est vita*. From another perspective, one can see the phenomenon of pleasure as part of the oriental image of Hungary, which was mentioned above. The Orient was known in Europe primarily for its luxury commodities, and associated with fabulous riches and uninhibited pursuit of pleasure. The exotic strangeness of the Orient simultaneously attracted and alienated Europeans.

The exclusive lifestyle was also demonstrated by the wealthier segments of Hungarian society. Matthias Bel described the extravagant public meals in the streets of Pressburg and passed on a pun that appears to capture the Pressburg attitude toward culinary affairs: instead of the official Latin name *Posonium*, the city was known jokingly as *Opsonium* [dessert][29]. The comparatively low cost of fruit and wine contributed to the city's reputation as a paradise for gourmets. Many foreign travelers mentioned the dangers of cheap alcohol. According to one eye-witness, for example, German traveller Heinrich Sander spent his trip to Pressburg in a drunken haze with an upset stomach. His reports are remarkably sober in light of such conditions[30].

The pleasure-seeking nature of Pressburgers struck many as unchecked hedonism. They resembled above all the Viennese, whose joy in eating and drinking was a favourite theme of travel writers. Kolbány, the physician mentioned above, concluded that "in no respect are the Pressburger and the Viennese more frequently condemned than for their excesses as in eating, and he seems to have earned the reproach, since the consumption is really quite high here"[31]. He did, however, defend the Pressburgers from the comments of the unpopular critic Nicolai: "Our love of eating is not, however, nearly so horrible or exaggerated as Mr. Nicolai would like to convince the world it is"[32].

Travel literature did not at all attempt to distract Pressburgers away from their pleasure-seeking nature. At the beginning of the 19th century, thanks to technological developments, entirely new travel desires appeared. The more and more frequent Danube steamboat travellers discovered natural landscapes, sunsets, and panoramas. These were also linked to the character of Pressburg: "While the beautiful region invites pleasure, it goes without saying that it clears the mind and lends one the proper feeling. These are the true characteristics of Pressburg's inhabitants, whose profession is frequently to enjoy the landscape"[33].

In harmony with this attitude, many authors pointed to the Pressburger habit of promenading in city parks and gardens, as well as taking excursions in the immediate vicinity. While this depiction of sensual pleasures is only one of the themes in travel literature of the 18th and early 19th centuries, it moved to the center of travel accounts in the second half of the 19th century. This change was linked to the development of mass tourism, which brought forth new elements in travel strategies. The intellectual pleasures of a foreign culture, cultivated in the century of Enlightenment, dissolved in sensual pleasures of various kinds.

With the spread of mass tourism directed toward consumption and relaxation, a new sort of travel companion stepped onstage: the city guide. The first work of this kind, from the pen of Ludwig Deutschinger, appeared in Pressburg in 1873[34]. Its composition emphasized above all the possibilities for relaxation and entertainment offered by the city. From this perspective it is characteristic that the reader was first given information about accommodation and dining, and about local cultural events, and only afterwards about the city's history and sights. There was a detailed list of Pressburg restaurants, coffee houses, wine cellars and beer houses, and Pressburg specialties, such as nut or poppy seed pastries, were praised.

A visit to Pressburg brothels, located on the so-called Castle grounds, also belonged to the city's attractions. Of course, official city guides passed over these establishments in silence, but the curiosity of travellers nevertheless rested on these spaces. What sort of reputation must Pressburg have had for Thomas Mann to allow the main character of his Doctor Faustus to be infected with syphilis precisely in Pressburg?

Modern travel guides hardly diverge from their historical predecessors. Contemporary tourism has at its core the same form as it had at the end of the 19th century, though the palette of consumer experiences becomes continually more monotonous under the influence of globalization. Local specialties such as nut or poppy seed pastries are rarely served in Pressburg coffee houses and pastry shops. The city has become a popular goal for day travelers from nearby Vienna, and one can see the most important sights in a standard two-hour tour. The city's popularity as a city of pleasure has also not diminished, as is shown by the city's new nicknames among Austrian travellers: "Gratislava" (from *Gratis*, "free," a reference to low prices), "Fressburg" (from *fressen*, "to eat like a pig") and "Partyslava."

Images of the City as Sites of Memory

Having given a brief overview of three *topoi* discussed in the travel literature on Pressburg – the city as a border town, the character of its inhabitants, and the sensual pleasures the city had to offer – the chronological presentation of material shows a certain consistency in the choice of images used to present the city. The repeated use of certain images reinforces patterns of thought and expression that can retroactively be read as sites of memory. They show a certain continuity of form (the use of identical signifiers), but this continuity shows significant semantic shifts on closer examination. Though the literal meaning of commonly-used expressions remains constant, their connotations evolve with the changing political context.

It is helpful to look at the concept of *topos* not only as a fixed cliché (Ernst Curtius), but to return to its original rhetorical function as a mechanism for proofs and arguments when preparing a public speech (*inventio*). This perspective looks not at the frequency of images, but rather at the motive for their use: how they are instrumentalized. This opens up the functional character of sites of memory, and makes possible their deconstruction, i.e. the restoration of a polysemy shaken by homogenizing power discourses.

This can be illustrated with the example of the gate metaphor discussed above. The nationalism of the 19th century instrumentalized this image in the attempt to eliminate everything foreign from one's own culture. The first Czechoslovak republic used the image to show its openness to other cultures. In the ideology of the wartime Slovak state, the gate metaphor indicated the aggressive policy of National Socialism. Individual ideologues reached for images passed down through history. The process uses the moment of discontinuity as well as of continuity. When assigning a traditional image a new meaning new accents become possible (discontinuity). Choosing a well-known image gives the new outlook the appearance of historical legitimacy (continuity). Sites of memory are the object of current struggle no less than material sites in the public space.

The discontinuous moment of instrumentalization becomes visible where the reinterpreted image diverges from the empirically verifiable reality of history. Let us consider another example from recent history. One of the first Pressburg guides to appear in German after the fall of Communism was published in Bremen by Temmen Press in 1991. The guide begins with an essay by the Slovak author Anton Hykisch, known in Slovakia mostly for his historical novels. Hykisch's essay, *A City with Contradictions*, sought to problematize the black and white picture of Slovak Bratislava. After forty years in the Eastern Bloc, he placed the city back in Central Europe with the aid of cultural coordinates. He alluded to the architectonic image of the city with comparisons to Vienna, Budapest and Krakow, recalling traces of a multi-ethnic past. With these comparisons he pushed the city even closer to Western Europe by ascertaining a similarity between Pressburg Castle and the Tower of London.

Hykisch described the typical atmosphere of Pressburg with a place that no foreigner would visit: the great fruit and vegetable market on Miletičova Street:

> here you can find many stalls with fruit and vegetables from the rich southern plains ... here too gather the Slovaks. Good beer is not only drawn in great quantities, but also wine from the region. The scent of spiced sausages (klobásky) fills the air, which the locals eat with very spicy pepperoni soaked in vinegar. Instead of hamburgers and hotdogs, people eat large portions of fried pork ("Gypsy style"), or slurp goulash. A colorful gypsy girl speaks to you, offers you smuggled gold or to read your palm, and probably both are an illusion. Maybe

> you will also be perplexed by the lack of hygiene. The service in the pub is homey, familiar, perhaps a bit vulgar. The world is different here, and even smells different[35].

One cannot deny the sensual qualities of this description, but its description of objective reality does not seem to be as illusory as the palm-reading of the colorful gypsy girl. This picture of the market recalls Matthias Bel's descriptions of dinners on Pressburg streets, or of Turkish bazaars swimming with colours, scents, voices and speculators. And so it is no surprise that, immediately after this description, Hykisch situates Pressburg exactly where the city had previously been placed, despite the protests of Hungarian scholars: the Orient, or more precisely, on the frontier of the Orient, which began somewhere between Bratislava and Vienna. This cultural-historical location offered Hykisch the flexible metaphor of a gate: "Bratislava and the rest of Slovakia are the gate to south-east Europe, to Hungary, to the Balkans, and to the orient"[36].

What did Hykisch achieve with these inherited images? The historical continuity, destroyed by the Second World War and the post-War Communist regime, is recreated in the imagination. Instead of a critical contemplation of the present (which perhaps should not be expected from a tourist guide), we find a pleasant, sentimental illusion which draws its images from the rich reservoir of *topoi* taken from existing travel literature. Hykisch's essay, like the rest of today's nostalgic literature about Pressburg, reflects a longing for the past more than a reflection of the present-day city which the visitor would encounter while strolling through Bratislava.

It strikes me as noteworthy that in his description Hykisch – as a native of the city – adopts for himself a foreign perspective. This can be explained by remembering that the intended public for this guide is a German reader. Using a well-known *topos* makes the unknown and exotic somehow familiar, so that the city suddenly seems to be an intimate stranger, something semi-exotic. This example also illustrates the semantic shift that certain *topoi* undergo in the long-term perspective in connection with the development of modern tourism. While Hungarian scholars of the 18th and 19th centuries were annoyed that the oriental reputation of the country scared foreign visitors away, it is precisely this reputation that is now used to entice tourists.

Stylizing Pressburg as an oriental city also pushes into the background the city's history as a socialist metropolis, which often alienates western tourists. Hykisch's essay does not say anything direct about this period in the city's history. He only alludes to the socialist era with images of suburbs lacking in fantasy, and even these are not assigned to any specific time.

Sites of memory do not exist per se; they are constructed by carriers of memory. These images of the city tell not only about the development of the city, but also about the history of its inhabitants and last but not least about the investigators of the city images. As these themes coalesce, so the analytical consideration of city images becomes part of the places of memory, at their new level of meaning.

Notes

1 A. Huyssen, *Prítomnosť minulého. Urbánne palimpsesty a politika pamäti,* Bratislava 2005. B. Bogdanović, *Mesto a démoni,* Martin 2002. For more sources related to the *topos* of the "end of the city" see M. Schroer, *Räume, Orte, Grenzen,* Frankfurt a.M. 2006, pp. 227-231.

2 See G. von Wilpert, *Sachwörterbuch der Literatur,* Stuttgart 1989, p. 759-760.

3 K. Lynch, *The Image of the City,* Cambridge 1960. For this study the Czech translation was used: K. Lynch, *Obraz města. The Image of the City,* Prague 2004.

4 *Ibid*., p. 47.

5 Cf. J. Stagl, *Die Methodisierung des Reisens im 16. Jahrhundert,* in P. J. Brenner (ed.), *Der Reisebericht. Die Entwicklung einer Gattung in der deutschen Literatur,* Frankfurt a. M. 1989, pp. 140-177; W. E. Stewart, *Die Reisebeschreibung und ihre Theorie im Deutschland des 18. Jahrhunderts,* Bonn 1978.

6 For the problem of a settlement's border position from the perspective of the cultural memory research see G. Kiliánová, *Identita a pamäť. Devín/ Theben/ Dévény ako pamätné miesto,* Bratislava 2005.

7 A. Schmidl, *Reisehandbuch durch das Königreich Ungarn mit den Nebenländern und Dalmatien, nach Serbien, Bukarest und Constantinopel,* Vienna 1835, pp. 7-8.

8 J. von Csaplovics, *Gemälde von Ungern,* Pest 1829, vol. 1. p. 5.

9 See the article *Orient* in P. Dinzelbacher (ed.), *Europäische Mentalitätsgeschichte,* Stuttgart 1993 as well as the classical study in this field E. W. Said, *Orientalism,* New York 1978.

10 E.A. Quitzmann, *Reisebriefe aus Ungarn, dem Banat, Siebenbürgen, den Donaufürstenthümern, der Europäischen Türkei und Griechenland,* Stuttgart 1850, p. 54. We can find the oriental image of Bratislava already in 16th-century documents. A significant example is preserved in graphic art – see the analysis of the Leyden sketchbook in L. Klusáková, *Cestou do Cařihradu. Osmanská města v 16. století viděná křesťanskými očima*, Prague 2003, pp. 142-145.

11 *Ibid*., p. 48.

12 *Presburg und seine Umgebungen,* Pressburg 1865, p. 86.

13 *Ibid.*

14 V. Šrobár, *Poznámky o presídlení prvej slovenskej vlády do Bratislavy dňa 4. II. 1919,* in *Pamätný spis Bratislavy, hlavného mesta Slovenska 1919-1934,* Bratislava 1934, p. 13.

15 Quotation from F. Karmasin, *Preßburg in der neuen Slowakei. Geschichte, Kultur, Wirtschaft. Mit 32 Bildtafeln in Kupfertiefdruck und einem Stadtführer,* Pressburg 1940, p. 7.

16 *Ibid.*

17 *Bratislava. Hlavné mesto Slovenska. Pressburg. Hauptstadt der Slowakei,* Basel 1943, p. 9.

18 *Ibid.*

19 L. Šášky, *Bratislava,* Bratislava 1967, p. 31.

20 E. Portisch, *Geschichte der Stadt Pressburg - Bratislava. Volkstümliche Darstellung in 2 Bänden,* Pressburg – Bratislava 1933, p. 3.

21 P. von Kolbány, *Bemerkungen über den ansteckenden Typhus, der im Jahre 1809/10 in Preßburg herrschte,* Pressburg 1811, p. 142.

22 K.G. von Windisch, *Politisch-geographisch- und historische Beschreibung des Königreichs Hungarn,* Pressburg 1772, p. 9.

23 J.W. Fischer, *Reisen durch Oesterreich, Ungarn, Steyermark, Venedig, Böhmen und Mähren in den Jahren 1801 und 1802,* Vienna 1803, p. 35.

[24] F. Nicolai, *Beschreibung einer Reise durch Deutschland und die Schweiz, im Jahre 1781. Nebst Bemerkungen über Gelehrsamkeit, Industrie, Religion und Sitten,* Berlin - Stettin 1785, vol. VI, p. 357.

[25] H. Pröhle, *Schilderungen aus dem Volksleben in Ungarn, Böhmen, Mähren, Oberösterreich, Tyrol und Wien,* Vienna 1849, p. 56.

[26] Šášky, *Bratislava* cit, p. 13.

[27] M. Lasica, *Byť starým Prešpurákom...,* in K. Benyovszky, *Prechádzka starým Prešporkom,* Bratislava 2001, p. 5.

[28] V. Tomčík, *Bratislavské dni a noci,* Bratislava 2006, p. 6.

[29] *Bratislava Mateja Bela,* Bratislava 1984, p. 42.

[30] See J. Tancer, *Die Innensicht der Außensicht. Pressburg in den deutschsprachigen Reiseberichten des 18. Jahrhunderts,* in E. Frimmová, E. Klecker (eds.), *Itineraria Posoniensia,* Bratislava 2005, pp. 294-303.

[31] Kolbány, *Bemerkungen* cit., p. 126.

[32] *Ibid.*

[33] E. M. Arndt, *Reisen durch einen Theil Teutschlands, Ungarns, Italiens und Frankreichs,* Leipzig 1804, vol. 2, part 1, p. 289.

[34] L. Deutschinger, *Führer durch Pressburg und seine Umgebungen. Mit besonderer Berücksichtigung von Hainburg, Theben und Ballenstein,* Pressburg 1873.

[35] S. Holubanská, Z. Guldanová, A. Hykisch, *Bratislava/ Preßburg. Die Stadt an der Donau. Ein illustriertes Reisehandbuch,* Bremen 1991, p. 6.

[36] *Ibid.*, pp. 6-7.

Bibliography

Arndt E.M., *Reisen durch einen Theil Teutschlands, Ungarns, Italiens und Frankreichs,* vol. 2, Leipzig 1804.

Bogdanović B., *Mesto a démoni,* Martin 2002.

Bratislava. Hlavné mesto Slovenska. Pressburg. Hauptstadt der Slowakei, Basel 1943.

Bratislava Mateja Bela, Bratislava 1984.

Csaplovics J. von, *Gemälde von Ungern,* 2 vol., Pest 1829.

Deutschinger L., *Führer durch Pressburg und seine Umgebungen. Mit besonderer Berücksichtigung von Hainburg, Theben und Ballenstein,* Pressburg 1873.

Dinzelbacher P. (ed.), *Europäische Mentalitätsgeschichte,* Stuttgart 1993.

Fischer J.W., *Reisen durch Oesterreich, Ungarn, Steyermark, Venedig, Böhmen und Mähren in den Jahren 1801 und 1802,* Vienna 1803.

Holubanská S., Guldanová Z., Hykisch A., *Bratislava/ Preßburg. Die Stadt an der Donau. Ein illustriertes Reisehandbuch,* Bremen 1991.

Huyssen A., *Prítomnosť minulého. Urbánne palimpsesty a politika pamäti,* Bratislava 2005.

Kiliánová G., *Identita a pamäť. Devín/ Theben/ Dévény ako pamätné miesto,* Bratislava 2005.

Klusáková L., *Cestou do Cařihradu. Osmanská města v 16. století viděná křesťanskými očima,* Prague 2003.

Kolbány P., *Bemerkungen über den ansteckenden Typhus, der im Jahre 1809/10 in Preßburg herrschte,* Pressburg 1811.

Lasica M., *Byť starým Prešpurákom...,* in Karl Benyovszky, *Prechádzka starým Prešporkom,* Bratislava 2001.

Lynch K., *The Image of the City*, Cambridge 1960.

Id., *Obraz města. The Image of the City*, Prague 2004.

Nicolai F., *Beschreibung einer Reise durch Deutschland und die Schweiz, im Jahre 1781. Nebst Bemerkungen über Gelehrsamkeit, Industrie, Religion und Sitten*, vol. VI, Berlin - Stettin 1785.

Portisch E., *Geschichte der Stadt Pressburg - Bratislava. Volkstümliche Darstellung in 2 Bänden*, Pressburg (Bratislava) 1933.

Presburg und seine Umgebungen, Pressburg 1865.

Preßburg in der neuen Slowakei. Geschichte, Kultur, Wirtschaft. Mit 32 Bildtafeln in Kupfertiefdruck und einem Stadtführer, Pressburg (Bratislava) 1940.

Pröhle H., *Schilderungen aus dem Volksleben in Ungarn, Böhmen, Mähren, Oberösterreich, Tyrol und Wien*, Vienna 1849.

Quitzmann E. A., *Reisebriefe aus Ungarn, dem Banat, Siebenbürgen, den Donaufürstenthümern, der Europäischen Türkei und Griechenland*, Stuttgart 1850.

Said E. W., *Orientalism*, New York 1978.

Schmidl A., *Reisehandbuch durch das Königreich Ungarn mit den Nebenländern und Dalmatien, nach Serbien, Bukarest und Constantinopel*, Vienna 1835.

Schroer M., *Räume, Orte, Grenzen*, Frankfurt am Main 2006.

Stagl J, *Die Methodisierung des Reisens im 16. Jahrhundert*, in P. J. Brenner (ed.), *Der Reisebericht. Die Entwicklung einer Gattung in der deutschen Literatur*, Frankfurt am Main 1989, pp. 140-177.

Stewart W. E., *Die Reisebeschreibung und ihre Theorie im Deutschland des 18. Jahrhunderts*, Bonn 1978.

Šášky L., *Bratislava*, Bratislava 1967.

Šrobár V., *Poznámky o presídlení prvej slovenskej vlády do Bratislavy dňa 4. II. 1919*, in *Pamätný spis Bratislavy, hlavného mesta Slovenska 1919-1934*, Bratislava 1934.

Tancer J., *Die Innensicht der Außensicht. Pressburg in den deutschsprachigen Reiseberichten des 18. Jahrhunderts*, in E. Frimmová, E. Klecker (eds.), *Itineraria Posoniensia*, Bratislava 2005.

Tomčík V., *Bratislavské dni a noci*, Bratislava 2006.

Wilpert G. von, *Sachwörterbuch der Literatur*, Stuttgart 1989.

Windisch K. G. von, *Politisch-geographisch- und historische Beschreibung des Königreichs Hungarn*, Pressburg (Bratislava) 1772.

Marking the City
Place-Making and the Aesthetics of Urban Spaces

Ruth Wallach
University of Southern California

Abstract

Two examples of public art in transit locations, the temporary *Books of Groningen*, curated by Daniel Libeskind in the provincial Dutch capital of Groningen, and the Los Angeles County Metropolitan Transportation Authority's permanent Metro Art works at the Metro Rail stations, are analyzed as emblematic of place making public art projects. The chapter argues that despite the differences in their settings and aesthetics, the projects exemplify a unified, strategic vision of the city as a formal public place, and counteract the notions of the urban milieu as a fragmented, tactical, and unmappable space.

Public spaces in urban areas comprised of streets, squares, and transportation networks, have been symbolically defined in a variety of ways, as sites of daily ritual and public performativity, as spaces of economic production, and as sites of state control and of political activities. The visual and aesthetic demarcation of public spaces is important in the shaping of urban environments and their uses by members of the public. In one of the most noted European examples of strategic urban development, the Popes of the 16th and 17th centuries reasserted the increasingly marginalized political and religious power of the Papacy by remapping and redesigning baroque Rome to appear equal to, if not greater than, the Rome of antiquity. The 'new' Papal Rome necessitated longer and wider streets that ensured vistas and spacious squares dominated by monumental structures. Among these structures were resituated ancient Roman columns and newly designed fountains, which were part of a program to visually reorganize public space. The idea of newly re-marking urban public spaces persisted and, furthermore, urban markings came to encompass a variety of types of monuments. When, in the 1980s, the Dutch city of Groningen decided to commemorate the millennium of its foundation, it turned to a noted European architect, Daniel Libeskind, to devise a temporary program for marking the boundaries of the city. Libeskind's project, entitled *The Books of Groningen*, created nine discreet markings, mostly columnar or monumental in nature. The markings commemorated not just the history of the city, but also its historic boundaries, which appeared to function as psychological demarcations of the urban boundaries from all else. Like baroque Rome's columns, most of the Books of Groningen were located at or near transportation routes. In the last decade of the 20th century, at around the time of the Books of Groningen project, the county of Los Angeles invested in a public art program for the city's newly built Metro Rail system. The programme did not seek monumentality, yet these public art works contextualized the modern, fragmented city within a cohesive economic and social urban narrative. Both projects typify attempts to construct contemporary cities as physically unified places for consumption by a generically defined middle class.

This chapter discusses two different art in public places projects that mark liminal urban spaces of transportation through public art installations, thus defining and contextualizing what lies within and around as *city*. One of the projects re-marks the boundaries of the north-eastern Dutch city of Groningen, through a program of contemporary monuments placed along highways, canals, and railways, to commemorate the city's millennium. The other re-inscribes the disparate histories of Los Angeles into a geographically centralized narrative through permanent public art installations at the metro stations. In Groningen, the city used art to commemorate temporarily its medieval boundaries and to circumscribe a specific physical and economic geography for public consumption; in Los Angeles, the Metropolitan Transportation Authority (Metro) symbolically marked the city's new metro system for public use in a city that lacks a history of public space. Public art is often perceived as a tool of gentrification, however its place within urban development is more complex. Although the geography and the ideas represented in these two case studies are vastly different, both re-define the urban environment through symbolic and aesthetic means in order to conceive of the city as a unified, memorable and physically comprehensible place.

The idea that the city is an aesthetic and memorial form is not new. Neither is the practice of reshaping city spaces for political and economic purposes through public works and through visual reorganization or erasure of existing place-makers. Baroque Rome offers a notable, although not unique, example of harnessing political and aesthetic practices in a centralized urban redesign. In *Design of Cities* Edmund Bacon discusses Pope Sixtus V's efforts in the 16th century to recreate Rome as a premier city in Christendom by unifying city spaces through orderly points punctuated by Egyptian obelisks and columns. His ideas were expanded in the following century. Richard Krautheimer, in *The Rome of Alexander VII, 1655-1667,* extensively describes the re-conceptualization of baroque Rome with its historical accretion of narrow streets and irregular spaces by Pope Alexander VII in terms of "[l]ong straight streets and regular open squares, clearly outlined...the basic elements of an ideal of urban beauty"[1]. The image of the new, visually more regulated Rome provided the decorum and dignity due to a major city where public behavior could be ritually stage-set as if in a theatre[2]. The Popes were sensitive to the negative effect of the city's impractical layout, and sought to position the Eternal City as equal to other international urban centres not only politically but also aesthetically. Similar to these and other examples of redesigning cities through transportation axes, the two projects I examine mark urban transportation routes within a cohesive aesthetic framework despite the fact that they come from two very different practices of design for public spaces. Unlike earlier historic examples, the two projects are rooted in contemporary democratic processes, so that the city is symbolically patterned into a comprehensible urban place for consumption by all its citizens.

While reasons for reshaping cities on an aesthetic level are varied and complex, urban socio-economic redevelopment is often a major (although not an exclusive) driving force behind beautification and public art programmes. Various projects for the redevelopment of urban centres in Southern California, François Mitterand's *Grands Travaux* in Paris, or many cities' massive rebuilding projects to accommodate the Olympic Games are just a few examples of recent large-scale publicly financed urban-works programmes which also include major aesthetic components. The inclusion of art and design within urban redevelopment ties individualized artistic capital to the practical needs of the civic power structures to visually frame public spaces, thus creating a powerful symbolic symbiosis. Public art commissions are also part of the emblematic language that contextualizes urban space as place, a piece of the puzzle that maps the urban experience for members of the public at large.

In the 19th century, the French poet Charles Baudelaire iconically romanticized Paris and its streets by filtering the urban experience through the eyes of an aesthete. In his famous 1860s essay, *Le peintre de la vie moderne* [The Painter of Modern Life], Baudelaire enunciated the aesthetic sensibilities of his time. His descriptions of modernity and of the artist-spectator of city life were influential in subsequent theorizing of the urban setting in the history of art and architecture. Baudelaire's city is a concentration of public spectacle, where public space is defined by the street full of cafés and other anchors of commercialized leisure, such as arcades, parks, and department stores, where habitués observe or join at will the fast-paced life well into the gas-lit evenings. Baudelaire's modern painter is a *flâneur*, the man of the crowd who rapidly records scenes of the bourgeois "pageant of fashion"[3], a pageant which, as Walter Benjamin observed, was inextricably intertwined with the political force of the capitalist market place[4].

The concept of the city and its arteries as seen through the aesthetic eye has been complicated in the 20th century by the distinction between the notions of public *space* and public *place*. Place-making in the built and the urban environment, particularly within the contexts of pervasive transportation and communication networks, is a quotidian act of negotiating personal and social relations, and of mapping the city through symbolic and ritualistic patterns. Michel de Certeau, analyzing the spaces of everyday life, wrote: "In modern Athens, the vehicles of mass transportation are called metaphorai. To go to work or come home, one takes a 'metaphor' – a bus or a train"[5]. Within the metaphoric context, the city is an immense "texturology....The act of walking is to the urban system what the speech act is to language or to the statement uttered"[6]. Certeau's overlay of metaphor upon the urban networks of transportation underscores the city as both a physical and an abstracted concept. Just as a written text is a system of signs, so too the street, transformed by the walker or driver into practiced space, becomes heterotopic, infused with geographic and social meanings that amplify or displace each other, and that are continuously re-mapped by both the individual and the power apparatuses. The processes of urban social mapping are multi-layered, allowing for a variety of real, imaginary, and aesthetic readings, some of which are contradictory[7].

Marc Augé argues that contemporary post-industrial societies are more about space than about place. *Space* is an abstract term, malleable in its plasticity to a variety of physical and temporal organizational principles, and is particularly useful for mobile societies. Augé calls the spaces of supermodernity *non-places*, a term he applies particularly to spaces inhabited by transit, commerce, and leisure activities[8]. Furthermore, according to Augé, non-places are defined through the transmission of information and image, and he constructs non-places as essentially banal[9].

Augé's non-places are heterotopic, layering space with a multiplicity of usage, hyper-stacking of information, and over-simulation of the real. Yet despite his dispassionate definition of the spaces of transit as non-places, Augé elsewhere personalizes a quintessential urban transportation experience composed of his daily routine of riding in the Paris metro. In this account, the metro emerges as a physical manifestation, a place for the repository of personal memories, as well as of historic and geographic collective memories, where the name of each station references particular places and events within the national history of France. The collective historic memory is thus commingled with individual memories and rituals of daily commuting, adding a meaningful narrative to public transportation.

Such commemoration concretizes the city as a distinctive and legible geographic environment[10] at a time when the concept of the *city* has been deconstructed as a *place* and reconstructed as a *space*. The urban historian Paul Virilio argues that the physical dimension of contemporary cities has been dissolved, and that space is merely an extension of the technological and the economic functions of the marketplace, as for example when he says that "the way one gains access to the city is no longer through a gate, an arch of triumph, but rather through an electronic audiencing system whose users are not so much inhabitants or privileged residents as they are interlocutors in permanent transit"[11]. The idea of urban physical boundaries is important, yet for Virilio that idea is exemplified less by surface than by interface, as when he asks: "Does a greater metropolis still have a façade?"[12] The answer is, ultimately, no. The contemporary city is mechanistic, a node in the networks, an agglomeration of communication lines, in which time and space become irrelevant. Architecture is no longer an organizing principle for urban space, because it is de-centred by other technologies and replaced, as Virilio notes, by a "monumental wait for service in front of machinery"[13]. If in the past cities may have had geographic and ethnographic identities, contemporary cities lack a unifying fabric, and are spatially unmappable and cognitively incomprehensible.

In response to this conundrum, public art partly functions to map artificially places and sites, in recognition that an urban environment is "not just a physical manifestation, but one that is constituted through social, economic, and political processes"[14]. Site specificity injects public art into contemporary urban discourse on the ideology of place/space. Such discourse provides little analysis of the public itself, except to warn that it is not a unified and uncontested totality. Within the spaces of social interactions, the public is a network. It is possibly democratic and pluralistic, but it is not necessarily benevolent. The public inhabits a complex realm comprised of political, urban, and commercial spaces, and of popular entertainment. It generates a variety of meanings, including aesthetic, for anything within its space. The contemporary public may lack the ability to coalesce around common symbols, presenting challenges to attempts at a unifying expression. For the purpose of urban place-making, following Habermas, the term *public* appears to connote the bourgeoisie, encompassing the lower and the middle classes, as a defining and legitimizing social arrangement. Habermas articulates a powerful concept of the public sphere, one that is focused on civil institution and rational public debate. He argues that the public sphere is in principle all-inclusive, at least in the realms of civic and economic discourse[15]. Nevertheless, and possibly because Habermas' institutionalized public sphere has its limitations, the contemporary bourgeoisie is understood as being a fairly porous category, and purposely so, in order to invoke a different public at different times. Thus, members of the urban middle class can be locals or tourists, they move through public space (streets, sidewalks, plazas, lobbies, transportation lines) on their way somewhere (work, leisure, home, etc.), or to linger. Members of the middle-class public are also, in a broad sense, performative, as they continuously incorporate and enact socially constructed identities through language, gestures, and other social conventions[16]. The spectrum for the public's performativity is wide, but there are edges, and these edges are continuously re-defined through economy and geography. Civic organizations, such as those commissioning public art, construe the urban public realm in rational terms, and attempt to bridge meaningfully the strategic needs of civil society and the tactical needs of private individuals. To that purpose, public art agencies map out the symbolic context for the preservation and propagation of urban collective memory by giving it a tangible mode of visual expression. As a symbolic device, public art plays a role in the selective production of spatial language, urban memory, and social experiences, and it is part of the political, social, and mythic texturology of city development.

The two examples I examine below mark urban spaces of transit through public art installations, thus making them part of urban place-making narratives. There is considerable contrast between these projects. They occur in two very different cities – Groningen is a medium sized, relatively homogenous, Dutch city of about 180,000 residents with an old centre originally surrounded by walls, and Los Angeles is a sprawling modern metropolis of seemingly independent neighborhoods, suburbs, and exurbs, encompassing a city of almost 4 million within a county of 10 million ethnically diverse residents. The intellectual and aesthetic foundations for these markers are different, as well. Yet despite their considerable difference, both projects speak of the city as a potentially unified work of aesthetic production, capable of infusing the public realm with symbolic meaning. Both projects are emblematic of many similar projects throughout the world.

Although the *Books of Groningen* project memorializes a former medieval town securing its distinctiveness from its surroundings, it accommodates postmodern ideas of art displaced from gallery space into public space, ostensibly in order to hold up an aesthetic and critical mirror to monolithic public (i.e., bourgeois) taste. The Los Angeles Metro Art projects are much more populist in nature. They map this enormous city as user-friendly by making the Metro Rail system a pleasant transit space for all. In this case, art provides a context for a unified public activity, as well as a textual and textured excursion through the various histories within the city. Both projects are strongly rooted in an orthodox conception of urban environments as defined by grand public places and major public works, and by receptive and culturally homogenized citizenry. Both projects are metaphoric. They narrate space through design practices, albeit using different idioms, and offer distinct examples concerned with reversing the instability of the public's mental construct of cities as places.

The city of Groningen, a provincial capital, and a node in Dutch foreign trade with its northern neighbors since the Middle Ages[17], conceived of the city marking project as part of an effort to commemorate a millennium since its first mention in medieval annals in the year 1040. The city began developing a large urban re-design program in the 1980s, and invited the architect Daniel Libeskind to create a plan for a curated commemorative temporary art project called in Dutch *Stadsmarkering Groningen*, the purpose of which was to re-mark the boundaries of the city in time and space. Libeskind's proposal, submitted to the City Council, came in the physical form of a book made of aluminum plates held together with nuts and bolts, and henceforth became popularly known as the *Books of Groningen*. The proposal described the city as a semeiotic system, both physical and symbolic, arranged in a complex matrix of abstract ideas which incorporated the names of ancient Greek muses of the arts, color schemes, generic places within the city, and units of time, to create what may be called an urban cosmology.

The *Books of Groningen* connected nine access routes into the city, starting from the south and moving clockwise, each marked by a monument named after a letter of the

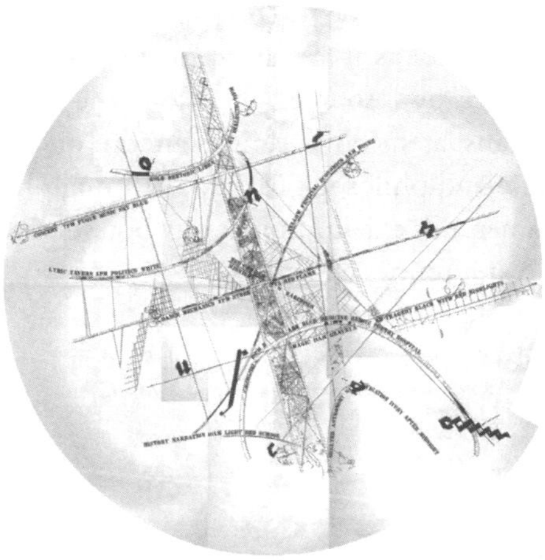

Fig. 1
Daniel Libeskind, "Cosmology of the City," *Books of Groningen*, 1992.

city's ancient name, Cruoninga. The proposal was interpreted by several invited "creative all-round intellectuals"[18] with international reputations in a variety of disciplines. The group consisted of ten men, including three architects, a playwright, a dance choreographer, an architectural historian, two visual artists, an economist, and an urban theorist, who responded to Libeskind's overall project idea with varying degrees of literalness. The markers, inaugurated in December 1990, are located along a 60 kilometre-long peripheral line that circles the city, a distance a little over 37 miles. The markers are accessible by car, foot, and bicycle. The brief descriptions of the markers below are intended to give the reader a sense of the participants' definition of the city[19]. The architectural historian Kurt Forster created a marker titled *Gate Tower Clio* for the letter C, commemorating the city's prominence in the natural gas industry and in agriculture. Forster designed a tower bearing seven flame-shaped weather vanes to represent the days of the week. Each day at 10:40 in the morning and evening (an allusion to the first mention of the city in medieval annals composed in the year 1040), blue neon digits on top of the pylon lit up for one minute. Forster's stated purpose was to mark elements of the city's history. Forster also alluded to the more general historic purpose of a public column, when he wrote "As a *column* at the entrance to a town famous for shipbuilding, the electric pylon becomes a modern *columna rostrata*, a commemorative marker studded with flames in allusion to the bronze prows of captured ships in antiquity"[20].

The economist Akira Asada designed a monumental three-page book-form as a marker for the letter R. Page one, symbolizing the foundation of the city, was built of stone, like a medieval wall, with video monitors imbedded in it. Referring to the modern city as a node on global communications networks, page two was a glass box with an LED panel, which could be used to display information related to economic activities of the city. Page three was made of iron, with the letter R inlaid upon it. This page also acted as a bridge over water, lying across a canal, and functioned as access to "the living dialectic of pages one and two"[21], old and new technologies, philosophies, and economic theories. The base of the marker was inlaid with transparent film bearing random quotes from famous European and Japanese economic and philosophical texts. Through his installation, Asada claimed international commerce as a definition of city boundaries: "The exchange of commodities begins where communities end"[22].

Fig. 2
Akira Asada and Shiro Takatani, "Book R", *Books of Groningen*, 1992.

The architect Daniel Libeskind's marker for the letter U is titled *A Walk Along the Boundary*. It is a billboard displaying a collage of images from movies and art history, supported by a grove of metal poles pointing in different directions. The effect is that of an informational puzzle simultaneously marking everywhere and nowhere. Libeskind drew the concept for his marker from Gustave Flaubert's controversial unfinished novel of 1880, *Bouvard et Pécuchet*. This episodic, proto-semeiotic novel, and particularly its last chapter, the "Dictionary of Accepted Ideas," captured Flaubert's misanthropic indictment of bourgeois social and intellectual wisdom of his times. Libeskind used Flaubert to express his own pessimism with the mechanistic vulgarity of contemporary urban space.

The marker for the letter O is designed by the performance artist Thom Puckey. It is an enormous brick chimney from which protrudes a tree-like sculpture made of copper, its branches shaped like flames or tentacles. This is in part a reference to the history of the old brick-laying method of construction, once important to the development of Groningen and other old cities. It is also a commentary on the radical changes in the 20th century, when industrial age, brick-and-mortar economies were displaced by information age economies.

The marker for the first letter N in Cruoninga is designed by the architect Gunnar Daan. The marker is an architectural mesh positioned above a bicycle path near a canal. In his own description of the marker Daan asks "what remains [of architecture] if the roof, the window, the doors, the carpet, the sink, and the light switches have disappeared? What remains is geometry, size, and proportion, rhythm, structure, a catalogue of types"[23]. Daan directly links his marker to a definition of a city, which echoes Habermas' description of 18th-century public space, although not necessarily of Groningen per se: "The drawings of streets and stoa in the nets might initiate ideas about the city – vaguely associated with politics or the café life"[24].

The marker for the letter I, entitled *Brüchstück für Luigi Nono* (*A Fragment for Luigi Nono*) and designed by the playwright Heiner Müller, is a tall black stele with an epitaph to the 20th-century Italian composer, located next to six tombstones that together feature a relief of a world map. Marked in red on the map are locations of contemporary wars. Hidden microphones play a musical composition by Nono, which incorporates the sounds of children and women screaming, and which memorializes the atrocities of the Auschwitz death camp.

The marker for the second letter N is a piece of land art designed by the choreographer William Forsythe, conceptually encompassing the geography and history of the maritime merchant class in Holland. It consists of a 400-metre canal (approximately 1300

Fig. 3
William Forsythe, "Book N", *Books of Groningen*, 1992.

feet) with a bar laid across it. On one side of the canal are young trees, pulled down into a semi-arc by wires attached to the bar, creating a forced canopy over the canal.

The architect John Hejduk's marker for the letter G is called *The Tower of Cards/The Tower of Letters/The Joker's Perch*. It consists of a slender tower of cards symbolizing time, a second tower bearing a wheel of fortune on which a joker sits, and a third tower spelling the name of the city. This work references time and movement[25], and explicitly relates to Libeskind's kabalistic interest in numerology.

The marker for the final letter A, titled *Architektron Urania*, is designed by the artist/architect team of Leonhard Lapin and Enn Laansoo. It is a double helix tower, symbolic of life, and meant to serve as a navigational beacon. The top is capped by a cover functioning as a border between heaven and earth, which is supposed to feature a cosmic navigational instrument to represent enlightenment[26].

In the city centre is a marker called *Narcissus*, designed by the urban theorist Paul Virilio. *Narcissus* is a well located at the base of a church tower. Positioned in the centre of the city, it is also the centre of inertia[27], although the other markers do not radiate from it. It is a tomb, a time capsule, an antithesis to the technological networks of control that underscore Virilio's thoughts on contemporary urban development.

City identity and its historic context play out differently in the Los Angeles Metro Art works. The Metro Art programme has commissioned over 250 artists for a wide variety of original art projects throughout the Los Angeles county public transportation system. "Artists are selected through a peer review process with community input; all works are created especially for their transit-related sites"[28]. Close to 80 public art works have been installed in the stations of the four Metro Rail lines, which were constructed since the mid-1990s, and at least several dozen more are in the plans for the expanding rail routes. These projects evolved as an integral part of the city's rail system, and some were the result of collaborations between artists and metro station architects. They function as place-making symbols for a city that is attempting to redefine its urban form.

While the permanent public art works in the Metro Rail stations are too numerous to describe here, the intellectual sources for many of them are specific histories of Los Angeles and its communities[29]. Visually, they fall into several general categories. Some stations feature tile murals, and on some occasions, members of local communities, where the stations are located, have participated in the process of mural creation. An example is the mural composition on the Metro Blue Line's Slauson station created by the muralists East Los Streetscapers. The work is called *South Central Suite*, and its various elements explore the social history of the neighbourhood around the station, as well as the history of the larger geographic area, from prehistoric times to the 20th century. On the street level the large ceramic and concrete panels "celebrate the values that are shared by the people who live and work in the station area: love and family, church and school, work ethic and community service"[30]. At the platform level, the smaller porcelain-enameled steel murals survey the area's geologic and historic periods, spanning the continental drift, prehistoric life, the first human being, Native American cultures, Mexican ranchos, urbanization, etc[31].

Fig. 4
East Los Streetscapers, "South Central Suite", 1995. Slauson Station, Metro Blue Line, Los Angeles.

Some stations feature sculptural works, such as Therman Statom's *Into the Light* at Westlake/MacArthur Park station on the Metro Red Line. In this work, massive sculptures in various media depicting a house, a ladder, a leaf, a cone, and a diamond shape float in ethereal light suspended from the station's skylight, and change in perspective as commuters pass underneath them. This gargantuan rendition of ordinary objects represents "positive forces" creating shadow patterns on the floor "as the glass and metal pieces collect and refract the changing natural light filtering through the skylight above"[32].

Fig. 5
Therman Statom, "Into the Light", 1993. Westlake/MacArthur Park Station, Metro Red Line, Los Angeles.

A different example of a sculptural composition is Stephen Antonakos' *Neons for Pershing Square* on the Metro Red Line station at Pershing Square in the centre of Los Angeles. This work commemorates the first neon sign in the United States, which was installed near this location in 1924. The neon sculptures are suspended from the station's high ceiling, bringing about an aesthetic experience: "not only the columns [of the station], the ceiling and the walls, but the space all around them is brought into the experience of the art"[33].

Some of the sculptural works are functional, such as Horace Washington's *A Tribute to Industry* at the Vernon station on the Metro Blue Line, where sculptural seating pays tribute to this industrial area's century-old garment and manufacturing economies[34], while enhancing the narrow sliver of the open-air station. Other Metro Rail stations feature installations where a larger story is told through compounded and complex artistic design. One of several historically complex narratives is Margaret Garcia's Universal City station on the Metro Red Line. Today, Universal City is famous for its studio lot amusement park and for Jon Jerde's simulated townscape in the City Walk shopping mall. However, the site of the station is adjacent to Campo de Cahuenga, where in 1847 Mexico relinquished control of California, which joined the United States in 1850. The artwork at the station provides a complex experience for any viewer interested not just in the history of the place but also in the ways in which histories are written, mixing text with images of people and objects. Garcia originally named her work *The Trees of Califas*, using an old Spanish name for California, saying that the "station is situated on a sacred site, sacred because of its history, our history"[35]. The escalator level gives view to a bilingual timeline highlighting many important dates and events related to the area. The station's supporting columns are clad in handmade colourful tiles offering a detailed visual and textual record of the events leading to the pivotal point when Mexico relinquished territorial control. The text on the tile panels provides a broader view on the 19th-century history of the political relations and skirmishes between the United States and Mexico in the Southwest. Echoing Dolores Hayden's emphasis on mining urban landscapes to nurture citizens' public memory in order to resurrect the contested social and political history of city spaces[36], the artist writes: "The history of this station is so important and so overlooked, for the indigenous peoples, the Gabrielino-Tongva tribes, the Mexican settlers – half of whom were of African descent – and for the United States immigrants who came and settled here"[37]. Kate Diamond, the architect who worked with Garcia on designing the station, concurred with this sentiment when she wrote "our goal was more than just design of a wonderful, functional subway station that would serve the transit-going public. Our mission was to make this important California history visible again"[38].

The somewhat detailed description of the two projects is intended to serve as a backbone for analyzing the nature of the public places that they demarcate. The Groningen markers represent the city as a nexus of aesthetic, political, and ecological ideas. Art as symbolic representation of complex issues entered the public space of roadways, with only some evidence of public reaction to the placement of the markers and to the aesthetic ideas expressed in them. Almost all the projects had to be altered from the way they were originally conceived. Some changes had to do with safety, others with cost.

Most of these markers do not serve a practical function, and as such emerge from an architectural tradition of symbolic monuments, particularly those which announce the city, such as memorial archways (for example, the Arc de Triomphe) or obelisks (e.g., the Washington monument). Yet unlike most traditional monuments, they lack inscription or any overt reference to place or history. They are abstractions. If the markers speak mostly to the "artists" of the project and to the curators and audience of the subsequent Groninger Museum show and its catalogue, they pose a question about the place of arcane and idiosyncratic ideas and objects outside of the walls of academia and museums. In his proposal, Daniel Libeskind imprints on the blank canvas of the city the Art (or is it Architecture?) which corresponds to his interests, overriding the public's presumed interests in expressive city places, which may or may not be the same as his. There is little publicness about these projects with the exception of their placement within public spaces.

The markers of Groningen also have more contemporary vernacular counterparts, particularly roadside billboards and signs. In the book *Learning from Las Vegas*, the architect Robert Venturi and his co-authors write about the roadside mini-mall strip (a non-place in Augé's terms, emblematic of the American urban environment and also common in Europe) as heir to historic monumental landscapes such as the gardens in Versailles. Accordingly, the mini-mall parking lot that divides high-speed highway and low, sparse buildings produces no enclosure and little direction....To move through this landscape is to move over vast expansive texture, the megatexture of the commercial landscape....But it is the highway signs through their sculptural forms or pictorial silhouettes, their particular positions in space, their infected shapes, and their graphic meaning, which identify and unify the megatexture.... Symbol dominates space[39].

Similarly, the *Books of Groningen* are designed to dominate the flat landscape of Holland, a testament to the designers' complex ideas about aesthetics, the flow of city spaces, personal politics, notions about nature, etc., while at the same time symbolically encompassing and defining the city for ritualized, marketed consumption. The markers may speak to an individual member of the public, but if they do not, that does not matter, as legibility is not necessarily an important component of the works. The project's design solicited little public discussion, and the markers themselves did not elicit public dialogue, as they represented the designers' individualistic statements. In such a monological conception, the public's opinion was almost irrelevant, specific histories were immaterial, neighbourhoods and communities subsumed in a synoptic vision of the city as geographically, intellectually and culturally homogenized. At the same time, they inserted the private contemplation of the museum into the horizontal public space of the countryside, producing a cultural cross-contamination. The markers' deeper meaning was obscured without a curatorial description; nevertheless, they were eye catching because of their unusual visibility above ground. It was unlikely that a habitual driver or walker would experience all ten markers within the same trip, so their monumentality was individualized. Given that the original impetus for the project was to temporarily commemorate the millennial anniversary of the city, the monumental *Books* fulfilled this function, albeit in a rather orthodox way, reminiscent of the connected nodal points of baroque Rome. According to a local architect, the *Books* were a "typical example of a theatrical approach"[40] to space, providing "calculated entertainment value. The city as an intoxicating amusement park[41]. There was a general feeling that the markers could not possibly have succeeded in any deeper sense: 'Identity is most of the time nothing more than a set of prejudices'"[42]. Because these markers were difficult to read without curatorial intervention, their effect as urban place-makers was ambiguous and difficult to articulate beyond the initial surprise and fascination.

The Los Angeles Metro Rail works are emblematic of Metro Art in many American and European cities. City governments are looking to curb urban sprawl by investing into public transportation networks, better station design, and a better overall experience for the habitual commuter and the occasional tourist. Yet despite a strong commitment to a more congenial urban experience for the public, what constitutes good urban experience or how the public is defined are concepts that are not clearly articulated by the sponsoring agencies. Those involved in public art processes rarely discuss how members of the public map urban spaces of flows, such as the metro, or how they read and reproduce their interactions with that space. The interstice between the theorized urban space and the purportedly pluralistic practice of public art is fraught with the politics of power. On an official level, significant for civic policy and for funding, the role of public art in contemporary society is to beautify cities so as to make their consumption more pleasing, comfortable, and safe. Rosalyn Deutsche critiques public art's reductivist approach to fulfilling "supposedly essential human and social needs....Just as function is limited to utilitarianism, social activity is constricted to narrow problem solving so that the provision of useful objects automatically collapses into a social good"[43]. Public art's function for social and public benefit, she argues, feeds into the hegemonic discourse on urban integration, so that art "prescribes places in the city for people to sit, to stand, to play, to eat, to read, even to dream. Building on this foundation, the new art claims to unify a whole sequence of divided spheres"[44]. Following Deutsche, from the perspective of city planning, public art becomes part of urban improvement projects and serves as an index of urban sophistication[45]. Typically, public art commissions require a certain amount of community input, a concept that is difficult to embrace intellectually (what is the community?) and practically (where does community input begin and end?). In the case of Metro Art, such commissions are further problematized by the transit setting. Public art in transit locations is important in urban mitigation processes that include building new or improving existing public transportation systems, or it is used for the purpose of changing the perception of a skeptical public toward public transit. While this scepticism arises from a variety of historic economic and urban development conditions, it is in part aesthetic. Older public transportation systems, such as early 20th-century metro in Paris or New York, are now romanticized for their *Gesamtkunstwerk*, the fusing of art and architecture to beautify the functional engineering design of subway stations. Because contemporary architecture is largely unadorned and because public places are framed by cheap prefabricated materials, public art to some extent fills the void left by lack of ornamentation. It also functions in mitigating the impersonal effects of generic urbanization on the social fabric of public spaces. Creating a sense of inhabited and habitable places in urban transportation nodes is an important theme in the implementation of public art, particularly in a large modern metropolis like Los Angeles, which is multi-centred and suburbanized. The metropolis is struggling to get beyond the legacy of car culture, which formed the basis for its modernist urban architecture, unconnected to its geographic surroundings or to city history. Furthermore, the Metro Art programme in Los Angeles responds to the needs of Metro planners to create both pleasant and inspiring public spaces within the stations. In order to inspire commuters, many of the artists choose to memorialize strands of the city's local histories, geographies and communities. Yet the mining of urban histories is complex, particularly in Los Angeles with its history of romanticizing the Other (specifically its Mexican past), while simultaneously erasing the Other's traces in the process. For example, Margaret Garcia's interpretation of the history of Campo de Cahuenga, briefly highlighted earlier, was challenged by a local historic preservation group. The theatrical subterranean space of the Universal City Metro Rail station became literally the theatre of a debate over which histories were important to be written within its confines and made available to the commuter public.

Art projects in transportation nodes speak of the artists' understanding of the city's history and mythology, and as such they can be analyzed by art historians and critics, but how do they speak to the public's interactions with the city as a place? Nicolai Ouroussoff, the former architectural critic of the "*Los Angeles Times*", writes that subways are symbols of "egalitarian values, places where the varied faces of the city confront one another on equal terms"[46]. Can this be assumed about transportation overall? Generally, art critics and public art planners appear to take quite a few things for granted: for example, that the spaces of transportation form a level playing field, or that public art is in direct opposition to museum Art, the latter somehow inaccessible or inappropriate for a public environment, or that art has a normative, universal definition, or that art is a defined economic and cultural good. The last assumption is certainly echoed in the Groningen project. There is also a presumption that the Los Angeles Metro Art projects, through the public bureaucratic selection process, are inherently comprehensible to members of the publics and do not require curatorial intervention.

Such debates leave out those on whose behalf they are waged; however, this does not diminish the public-ness of both projects in the sense that Habermas further defined the public as the site for opinion and debate based on shared normative but potentially unstated values. Yet what is the norm against which to judge the context created by public art in transit and transitory locations? If Metro Art works create a pleasing, educational, and informational environment, as public art administrators imply they should, are they didactic and patronizing of the public? And what is at stake for cities that pride themselves on being cultural meccas, if the public for the projects is made up of commuters who read them on a quotidian basis in a state of distraction?

I originally became interested in these projects because of their intellectual and aesthetic symbolic contrast. Despite this, they shared in common an attempt to counteract the heterotopic notion of the city in the Foucauldian sense of "heterotopia", as a place and space without coherent language, without unifying syntax, unmappable[47]. Art was an instrument used to define urban space as public, however that public was conceived. The notions of marking the city as a series of interconnected public spaces, as well as a center of concentrated human activities, span across historic periods and cultures. The former idea, defining the city as a centred and logical physical and historic space is important particularly in the case of Los Angeles. The latter, describing the city as a palimpsest of cultural and memorial symbols plays a greater role in Groningen. Both projects conceptualize the cities as centered public (as opposed to private or corporate) realms, spatially united and centralized as discursive sites[48]. Art becomes a tool, an invocation of the city, something that lets the public not just look at the environment but see it and situate within it, and be a part of the intellectual and economic urban milieu. "[A]rt brings in tourists and deep-pocketed sophisticates. World-class cities have buildings designed by famous architects, controversial public art pieces and passels of van Goghs. World-class cities in turn attract large companies, community investment and good international press. Art, in short, is good business"[49]. City business, that is.

Notes

1 R. Krautheimer, *The Rome of Alexander VII, 1655-1667*, Princeton 1985.

2 *Ibid.*, pp. 114-115.

3 C. Baudelaire, *The Painter of Modern Life and Other Essays*, London 1995.

4 W. Benjamin, *The Writer of Modern Life: Essays on Charles Baudelaire*, Cambridge-Mass 2006.

5 M. Certeau, *The Practice of Everyday Life*, Berkeley 1984.

6 *Ibid.*, pp. 92, 98.

7 M. Foucault, *Other Spaces: The Principles of Heterotopia*, in "Lotus International", 1986, 48/49, pp. 9-17. Michel Foucault's concept of heterotopia is a space of deviance and otherness, which offers an alternative to totalizing institutional social power structures, whether utopian or dystopian.

8 M. Augé, *Non-Places: Introduction to an Anthropology of Supermodernity*, London 1995,

9 *Ibid.*, p. 96. Parentheses in the original.

[10] K. Lynch, *The Image of the City*, Cambridge-Mass 1965.

[11] P. Virilio, *The Overexposed City*, in "Zone", 1986, 1/2, pp. 15-31.

[12] *Ibid.*, p. 17.

[13] *Ibid.*, p. 19.

[14] M. Kwon, *One Place After Another: Site-specific Art and Locational Identity*, Cambridge-Mass 2002.

[15] J. Habermas, *The Structural Transformation of the Public Sphere: An Inquiry into a Category of Bourgeois Society*, Cambridge-Mass 1991.

[16] J. Butler, *Performative Acts and Gender Constitution*, in S. Case (ed.), *Performing Feminisms: Feminist Critical Theory and Theatre*, Baltimore 1990, pp. 270-282.

[17] G. Burke, *The Making of Dutch Towns: A Study in Urban Development from the Tenth to the Seventeenth Centuries*, London 1956.

[18] V. Grassmuck, *A Combinatorial Cosmology of the Contemporary City*, in "Intercommunication" 1992, 2, http://waste.informatik.hu-berlin.de/Grassmuck/Texts/Groningen.html.

[19] The markers are also described on the following web site, http://skye.fol.nl/citymark.html.

[20] K. Forster, *Book C*, in A. Papadakis (ed.), *Marking the City Boundaries: Groningen*, London 1992, pp. 29-33. Italics in the original.

[21] A. Asada, *Book R*, in A. Papadakis (ed.), *Marking the City Boundaries: Groningen*, London 1992, pp. 35-39.

[22] *Ibid.*, p. 35. Parentheses in the original.

[23] G. Daan, *Book N*, in A. Papadakis (ed.), *Marking the City Boundaries: Groningen*, London 1992, pp. 53-57.

[24] *Ibid*, cit., p. 53.

[25] J. Hejduk, *Book G*, in A. Papadakis (ed.), *Marking the City Boundaries: Groningen*, London 1992, pp. 67-71.

[26] L. Lapin, E. Laansoo, *Book A*, in A. Papadakis (ed.), *Marking the City Boundaries: Groningen*, London 1992, pp. 73-77.

[27] P. Virilio, *Principle*, in A. Papadakis (ed.), *Marking the City Boundaries: Groningen*, London 1992, pp. 78-85.

[28] *Metro Art*, http://www.metro.net/about_us/metroart/default.htm.

[29] The majority are described on the Metro's Metro Art web site, http://www.metro.net/art.

[30] *Ibid.*

[31] *Ibid.*

[32] *Ibid.*

[33] *Ibid.*

[34] *Ibid.*

[35] K. Maese, *MTA Art Transports Passengers Into Another World*, in "Downtown News", 19 June 2000, pp. 1, 5.

[36] D. Hayden, *The Power of Place Urban Landscapes as Public History*, Cambridge-Mass 1995.

[37] *Metro Art*, cit.

[38] *Ibid.*

[39] R. Venturi, D. Scott Brown, S. Izenour, *Learning from Las Vegas: The Forgotten Symbolism of Architectural Form*, Cambridge-Mass 1977.

[40] Harm Tilman, quoted in Grassmuck, *A Combinatorial Cosmology* cit.

41 Syntax in the original.

42 Geert Bekaert, quoted in Grassmuck, *A Combinatorial Cosmology* cit.

43 R. Deutsche, *Evictions: Art and Spatial Politics*, Cambridge-Mass 1996.

44 *Ibid*., p. 65.

45 D. Sotero, *New Metro Art Projects Enhance Rapid Bus Experience*, in "Metro Report", 7 April 2004.

46 N. Ouroussoff, *The Red Line: Architecture as Afterthought*, in "Los Angeles Times", 25 June 2000.

47 S. Leong, *Readings of the Attenuated Landscape*, in M. Bell and S. Leong (eds.), *Slow Space*, New York 1998, pp. 186-213.

48 E. Charlesworth (ed.), *City Edge: Case Studies in Contemporary Urbanism*, Amsterdam 2005,.

49 J. Steinhauer, *The Arts Administration*, in "New York Times", 23 October 2005.

Bibliography

Augé M., *Non-places: Introduction to an Anthropology of Supermodernity*, London 1995.

Baudelaire C., *The Painter of Modern Life and Other Essays*, London 1995.

Benjamin W., *The Writer of Modern Life: Essays on Charles Baudelaire*, Cambridge-Mass 2006.

Burke G., *The Making of Dutch Towns: A Study in Urban Development from the Tenth to the Seventeenth Centuries*, London 1956.

Butler, J., *Performative Acts and Gender Constitution: An Essay in Phenomenology and Feminist Theory*, in S. Case (ed.), *Performing Feminisms: Feminist Critical Theory and Theatre*, Baltimore 1990, pp. 270-282.

Certeau M., *The Practice of Everyday Life*, Berkeley 1984 (original edition, *L'Invention du quotidien*, Paris, 1974).

Charlesworth E., (ed.), *City Edge: Case Studies in Contemporary Urbanism*, Amsterdam 2005.

Deutsche R., *Evictions: Art and Spatial Politics*, Cambridge-Mass 1996.

Foucault M., *Other Spaces: The Principles of Heterotopia*, in "Lotus International", 1986, 48/49, pp. 9-17.

Grassmuck V., *A Combinatorial Cosmology of the Contemporary City; 'The Books of Groningen-Marking the City'*, in "*Intercommunication*", 1992, 2, http://waste.informatik.hu-berlin.de/Grassmuck/Texts/Groningen.html.

Habermas J., *The Structural Transformation of the Public Sphere: An Inquiry into a Category of Bourgeois Society*, Cambridge-Mass 1991.

Hayden D., *The Power of Place: Urban Landscapes as Public History*, Cambridge-Mass 1995.

Krautheimer R., *The Rome of Alexander VII, 1655-1667*, Princeton 1985.

Kwon, M., *One Place After Another: Site-specific Art and Locational Identity*, Cambridge 2002.

Leong S., *Readings of the Attenuated Landscape*, in M. Bell and S. Leong (eds.), *Slow Space*, New York 1998, pp. 186-213.

Los Angeles Metropolitan Transportation Authority, *Metroart*, http://www.metro.net/art.

Lynch K., *The Image of the City*, Cambridge-Mass 1965.

Maese K., *MTA Art Transports Passengers Into Another World*, "Downtown News", 19 June 2000.

Ouroussoff N., *Architecture Review: The Red Line: Architecture as Afterthought*, in "Los Angeles Times", 25 June 2000.

Papadakis A. (ed.), *Marking the City Boundaries: Groningen,* London 1992.

Sotero D., *New Metro Art Projects Enhance Rapid Bus Experience*, in "Metro Report", 7 April 2004.

Steinhauer J., *The Arts Administration*, in "New York Times", 23 October 2005.

Venturi R., Scott Brown D., Izenour S., *Learning from Las Vegas: The Forgotten Symbolism of Architectural Form*, Cambridge-Mass 1977.

Virilio P., *The Overexposed City*, in "Zone", 1986, 1/2, pp. 15-31.

Between Urban and Rural Culture: Public Use of History and Cultural Heritage in Building Collective Identities (1990-2007)

Luďa Klusáková
Charles University in Prague

Abstract

This chapter will assess the strategies of revival used by small provincial and rural towns and their results, as well as their motivation and context. It explores these strategies on the basis of three case studies: Gers in Gascony in the south west of France, Třebíčsko in Vysočina in the Czech Republic, and Dukla in Šariš in Slovakia, bringing Western and East Central Europe into comparative perspective. These towns, which are mostly a significant distance from capital cities, large urban centres, motorways and railway corridors, have focused on marketing their natural environment and historical heritage. As part of a strategy of revival, the small towns have attempted to construct an identity supported by historical examples that locate them within larger – regional, national and supranational – identities. They have discovered the power of history to brand them and, with the help of national and international lists of cultural heritage (UNESCO), they have attempted to display their historical and cultural heritage as a marketable value. In this context, the chapter contributes to the discussion of interconnections between local (urban), regional and national (and supranational) identities.

Kapitola studuje strategie obnovy vypracované malými provinčními venkovskými městy a jejich výsledky. Na třech příkladech – Gers v Gaskoňsku v jihozápadní Francii, Třebíčsku na Vysočině v České republice a Poddukelském regionu v Šariši na Slovensku sleduje v komparativní perspektivě revitalizaci vnitřní periferie v západní a východní střední Evropě. Současně se snahou oživit města a jejich venkovské regiony posilují vytváření kolektivní identity, kterou podporují příklady z historie a poukazují na příslušnost k větším regionálním, národním i nadnárodním identitám. Objevují moc historie při etiketizaci a marketingu a s pomocí národních a mezinárodních seznamů památek a kulturního dědictví (UNESCO) se pokoušejí těchto hodnot ekonomicky využít. Stať zkoumá strategie, které vybrané regiony použily, a klade si otázku, jaká byla jejich motivace a v jakých souvislostech se tak stávalo. Tato problematika obsahuje také otázky vnímání našeho a cizího prostoru, kdy sledovaná hranice prochází mezi městským a venkovským prostředím, mezi centrem a periferiemi. Autorka se opírá o koncept renesance venkova ve formulaci B. Kaysera. Kapitola nejprve definuje a představuje vybrané regiony a města, která je reprezentují, následně porovnává jejich revitalizační strategie a způsob využívání historie. Periferní regiony a malá města využívají výhod informační společnosti a inovativně vytvářejí revitalizační strategie, které nemusí nutně vznikat jako kopie vzoru hlavního města. Nicméně jejich využití historie, památek i umění v marketingu nese společné dobové rysy, na něž v této knize upozornila také Ruth Wallach. Potřeba identifikace s větším regionem, s národní komunitou, případně s nadnárodní, e.i. evropskou kulturou je v těchto procesech zjevná, ale není novým rysem, jak vyplývá z kapitoly Jaroslava Iry. Přičemž potřeba identifikace nemá jen kulturní, ale rovněž sociální obsah a nemůže stavět na stereotypu neschopnosti a bezmoci. Naopak přestože jsou periferní a venkovské, tyto komunity vstupují do procesu revitalizace jako aktivní občanské iniciativy, které přispívají k rozvoji společenského života a mají dobré znalosti své kultury a historie.

This chapter can be read in various ways. It can be seen as a contribution to the analysis of how regions are constructed, and consequently marketed for tourism[1]. Alternatively, it can be read as an analysis of the way in which communities perceive what is 'theirs' and what is 'alien' and also of the use of borders in public discourse. The chapter will focus on a type of border which has been discussed with great interest by historians, sociologists, anthropologists, and geographers; that which divides urban and rural space. This form of border was once physical and visible, but in recent times it is more likely to be symbolic, expressed by cultural values, modes of life and expansion of technologies and new amenities. It is, however, still possible to locate the border between urban and rural areas. This chapter will analyse such borders in small towns on the peripheries of large cities, and in geographically peripheral regions that are at a considerable distance from any significant urban area. During the last twenty years there has been quite a bit of research into the strategies used to revive rural villages and towns[2]. These strategies have enhanced their social and economic life and also increased their identification with their local region. These processes were first analysed in Western Europe; however quite similar tendencies can also be detected in other parts of the continent.

The use of history in strategies of revival raises the question of whether there is an interaction between the historical importance of places and public evaluation of their historical value. It also encourages us to assess the role and power of memory embodied in historical monuments, particularly those registered on the List of World Cultural Heritage of UNESCO, in the self-presentation of cities, places and regions. This chapter will make use of case studies to assess these questions in comparative perspective. Three historically and culturally defined regions, comparable in size, location and geographic conditions, were chosen for analysis: Gascony in the south-west of France, concentrating on its core department of Gers; Moravia, in the eastern part of the Czech Republic, particularly Vysočina in the Czech-Moravian Highlands; and Šariš in the north-east of Slovakia, focusing on the recently defined Dukla region on the Polish-Slovak-Ukrainian border. These regions faced a variety of shared and unique problems and employed comparable strategies to overcome them.

Administrative regions in France, the Czech Republic and Slovakia mostly do not follow the borders of historical provinces or cultural regions. Moravia is approximately the size of historical Gascony. Both regions split into many geographic and cultural (folkloric) regions and micro regions. One of the administrative districts of Moravia is Vysočina, which is mostly identified with the folkloric region Horácko and is about the same size as the department of Gers in Gascony. Vysočina and Gers can both be divided into several *pays*, which have specific folkloric features. Similarly, the administrative region of Prešovský kraj in the north east of Slovakia stretches across the historical districts (*župa*) of Spiš, Šariš and Zemplín. When traditional culture and regions are discussed, the names of these historical districts, from the times of Hungarian rule, are used. Also, the names of these regions are invariably used in literature designed to promote the area to tourists[3]. New Prešovský kraj is larger than Gers, but old Šariš is comparable in size. The label "Dukla region" has recently appeared as part of the revival strategy of the town and district of Svidník, which is historically part of Šariš[4]. This region would be comparable with one of the *cantons* of Gers, or with associations of *communes* like Porte de Gascogne[5]. While in Gers we may perceive the chief city, Auch, as the prime keeper of Gascon identity, we may identify several areas that perform that role in Vysočina and Šariš.

Gascony, the Czech-Moravian Highlands and, to an even greater extent, Šariš in north-eastern Slovakia can be defined as internal peripheries of their countries, as border regions which are dependent on distant cores. All three, in an attempt to improve their social and economic situation, have chosen to use their history, the beauty of the landscape, and the absence of industry in the countryside as a magnet to attract the new industry of mass tourism. All three regions contain local monuments listed on the UNESCO list of world cultural heritage. By observing and analysing local attitudes to these monuments and the memories they represent, we can assess how these regions make use of local memory and history. All three regions struggled with problems which they tried to turn to their advantage. The chapter is based on longitudinal observation, repeated visits and analysis of regional historiography and regional journals, all of which motivated the application of a comparative perspective. Local media, regional administration and self-government, as well as regional and national academic communities participated in the debate over which strategies should be used to make small towns and regions attractive. These strategies influenced the dynamics of collective memory and aspects of local and regional identity. The chapter will first describe the three chosen regions and their small towns, and then discuss and compare their strategies for revival.

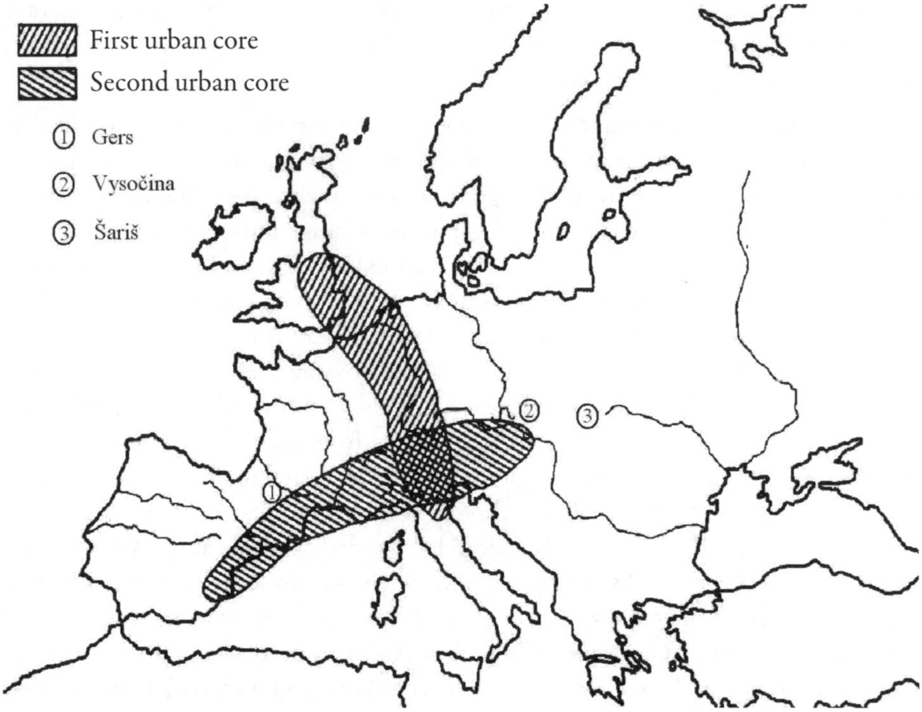

Fig. 1
Gers, Vysočina, and Šariš on the map of Europe

What regional borders?

Today, Gascony is a culturally defined region in the south-west of France. It has no officially or administratively defined borders. The idea of Gascony relies on the memory of its past as one of the historical provinces of France[6]. In several departments north of the Pyrenees, roughly between Bordeaux and Toulouse, we can find various indications of a sense of belonging to this entity. One of these departments, Gers, identifies itself as the very heart of Gascony, as its true modern descendant. Being Gascon is perceived as a very positive attribute and a significant emphasis is placed on the Gascon character of the region. The current positive nature of Gascon identity is especially interesting, because, since early modernity being a Gascon, behaving like a Gascon, or producing *Gasconnade*, had a slightly negative, or at least not a serious, connotation. Indeed when, in 1978, Robert Escarpit, professor of the sociology of literature and president of the University Bordeaux III, suggested changing the University's name to *Université de Gas-*

cogne, his proposal was rejected by the academic council, because such a name would not sound serious enough[7]. In 1990 this university finally was named after Michel de Montaigne, who, born in Périgord, identified himself as Gascon.

Gascony is not an administrative unit; it does not function or exist in the same sense as an official region, which has defined borders and regional government. Nor does it function as one of various euro-regions or micro-regions, created by and sustained by governmental projects.

Fig. 2
The location of Gascony and Gers on the map of France

Instead, Gascony is defined by the historical influence of its language. Although it has practically disappeared from usage and is today only visible in toponymy, the history of the language, as with all Occitan languages (dialects), has not been forgotten. Despite the dominance of the *langue d'oil* over the whole territory of the *langue d'oc*, there are still discernible regional accents and spoken dialects, as well as deep cultural differences[8]. The region is further defined by the local styles of rural and urban settlement; being dominated by the remnants of medieval fortified villages and small towns. The origins of these towns are often preserved in their names, which contain words like *sauveté, castelnau, bastide, villefranche*. Gascony is a hilly country, which is bordered in the south by the Pyrenees and in the north by the Massif-Central, in the west it reaches the Atlantic and in the east it is delimited by the flow of the river Garonne. Historically, Gascony existed as an entity only for a brief period in the middle ages. Since this time it has been part of the *grand-gouvernement de Guyenne-et-Gascogne*, which borders Languedoc and Foix in the east, Spain in the south, and Guyenne in the north[9]. It has always been part of several administrative units, but the idea of creating a Greater Gascony as an administrative entity, with its centre in Auch, proved to be a failure[10].

After the revolutionary reorganisation, which dissolved the borders of the old provinces and created new departments, Auch became the centre of the department of Gers, which took its name from the local river. The departments of Hautes-Pyrénées, Landes, Pyrénées-Atlantiques, Haute-Garonne, Lot-et-Garonne, and Tarn-et-Garonne were also created in the region. These departments, with geographically descriptive names, hid, and began to dissolve, the old *Gascogne*. Two hundred years later, however, due to the 1982 law of decentralisation, it appears that we can observe the revival of regionalism, and the rebirth of Gascony and Gascon identity.

Fig. 3
Vysočina and Třebíčsko on the map of Czech Republic

Today, Moravia is culturally defined as part of the Czech Republic. Several administrative units, called *kraj* in both Czech and Slovak, are identified as Moravian. Those within the heartland of the region, are considered to be more Moravian than the others, especially by outsiders. Moravia is currently split into several administrative units, and does not function as a single body, although in the past it did. Unlike Gascony, Moravia has always had recognised borders and official administrative status; in the middle ages it was a markgravate, ruled by the son of the king of Bohemia. During Habsburg rule it became administratively linked directly to Vienna and its autonomy gradually vanished. In historical terms it can be said that it was a land with a certain autonomy lying between the Bohemia, Silesia, Upper Hungary and Lower Austria. Today, northern Moravia has practically integrated the residual part of Silesia. There is also a strong Moravian identity, although it is based almost entirely on culture. As is the case in Gascony, Moravia can be seen as a linguistic region, defined by spoken dialects and accent. Today, however, the dominant language is Czech. Toponymy demonstrates regional belonging, especially to strangers, by the addition of the adjective 'Moravian' to local place names: Moravský Krumlov, Moravské Budějovice, Moravská Třebová. Other adjectives perform a similar function but are less obvious to outsiders: *Uherský* (Hungarian) and *Slezský* (Silesian). The mountainous parts of the region and its plains and valleys exhibit differing forms of rural and urban settlement, especially in the south-eastern part of Moravia. There is nothing in Moravia as unique as the region of the *bastides* in France. The medieval colonisation towns, which are common in Moravia, also appear in most of central and east-central Europe. In a similar manner to Gascony, Moravia is split into numerous folkloric regions and micro-regions. For example, Vysočina, Horácko and Třebíčsko all signify ethnographically defined *pays*. Geographically, Moravia is made up of two huge valleys bordered by mountains in the north (Jeseníky), east (Beskydy, Bílé Karpaty) and west (Českomoravská Vysočina), and delimited by the Dyje and Morava rivers in the south.

Fig. 4
Prešovský kraj, Šariš and Dukla region on the map of Slovakia

Along the north east of the Slovak border with Poland lies the second largest administrative region in Slovakia – Prešovský kraj, which comprises several cultural or ethnographic regions[11]. These regions are often named after territorial units, or *župa,* from the period of Hungarian rule, such as Spiš (Zips), Šariš (Saros) and Zemplín. All these labels are also linked to particular cultures, dialects, ethnicities, and histories. Šariš, which is the central region, is rather mountainous and not evenly developed. It is situated in the eastern part of the Carpathian belt. The provincial capital, Prešov, is eccentrically located in its south. The discourse that presents Dukla as a region is a new phenomenon[12]. It is the result of the effort to build a collective identity for the inhabitants of Svidník and the surrounding region and to give that region a more attractive name. This, in effect, loosens its borders. It does not, however, weaken the influence of the culture of Šariš.

The general setting of these three regions is similar – they are mountainous border regions, which in the case of Gers and Dukla, has led to meetings and exchanges with many 'Others'. In the case of Gers or Gascony this interaction stems from the inflow of Iberic or Spanish influences and inspirations across Pyrenees and the acceptance of sizeable economic and political immigration from Spain. There was also considerable Italian immigration after the First World War, as well as the *Pieds noirs – les rapatriés –* from Algiers and other former French African colonies, who settled mainly in the south. Traces of Huguenot, and Sephardic influences also remain, as the legacy of a difficult past. The area is also influenced by the Roman tradition of written law, and northern French efforts to integrate the south into French culture[13]. The Dukla region is a crossroads and a melting pot with a variety of influences. These include Polish, Ukrainian, Ruthenian (Trans Carpathian), Hungarian and German ethnic influences. The north east of Slovakia is also on the border of Catholicism and Orthodoxy, which motivated the emergence of the Greek-Catholic confession. There were also some Protestant and Jewish communities. The strongest influences are Roman-Catholic, Greek-Catholic, Orthodox, Slovak and Ruthenian. The influence of the border in both compared cases – north east Slovakia and Gascony – thus creates a particularly interesting and diverse culture, displayed in language, music and cuisine. The Moravian example is less complicated. The hills and forests of the Czech-Moravian Highlands separated Bohemia from Moravia in middle ages. In modern times it became a region of interaction, which was not perceived, especially on the Czech side, to be culturally part of deep Moravia, and as a matter of fact it is not so folkloric and picturesque as southern or eastern Moravia. All three regions were also affected by emigration of the local population, heading either to their capital cities, or further away, often to America. As has been discussed in the case of Gascony, all these regions suffered from negative connotations associated with their regional identities, and particularly with rural identity.

Perceiving peripherality

The three regions are on the periphery geographically and also metaphorically. Gascony was always very far from Paris, it was also on the border, and neighbours were often enemies. A region is created by the definition of its borders and centres. Gascony is a region of small towns, which balance between the dominance of two provincial capitals – Toulouse and Bordeaux. The departmental city, which presents itself as the chief city of Gascons, Auch, is a small town by French standards. Gers has one of the lowest densities of population and settlement in France; it also has a comparatively ageing population[14]. Even today there are no large motorways or railway corridors crossing the region. The area did not experience modern industrialisation; agriculture was the dominant economic sector throughout the 20th century and food production remains the only industry[15].

The Dukla region has remained a geographical periphery until this day. It was one of the forgotten and backward corners of Austria-Hungary, which suffered during the wars of the nineteenth century, and was extremely damaged by the First and even more so by the Second World War. Until the mid-20th century it was totally rural. Although post-war reconstruction brought in some industries, schools, hospitals and other social and cultural amenities, the region lacked infrastructure, and the social and economic conditions here were worse than in the rest of the country until the mid-1970s. In the mid-1990s it was classified as a deprived region, with below average levels of education, and high unemployment[16]. Regional building industries broke down and agriculture declined. The local administrative centres, Svidník and Bardejov, lacked entrepreneurial motivation and foreign investment. The provincial centre, Prešov, fared only slightly better. However, Bardejov had the best prospects thanks to the wealth of its historical heritage and the proximity of the spa town of Bardejovské kúpele[17]. The economic transformation after the political and economic structural changes in 1990 had a visible impact on settlement, the countryside, and demography. It led to economic migration to the larger cities (Prešov, Košice, Bratislava), and abroad, especially the Czech Republic (Prague and Brno). Before and between the wars, migration overseas was the typical reaction to the economic problems of families in this region, and it reappeared in the 1990s[18].

The Czech-Moravian border was thoroughly isolated from the centre until modern times, when the imperial road network and later railways connected it with Prague and Vienna, the Bohemian and imperial capital cities. Vienna was, however, easier to access, and the labour market there was larger and more attractive for labour migration than that of Prague, until the end of the Austro-Hungarian empire. The Czech-Moravian border was always a friendly one. The region is divided into several administrative districts and in the recent administrative reframing of the republic, an administrative region (*kraj*), Vysočina, was created and Jihlava was made its chief city. This was due to Jihlava's role as the regional centre during the 18th and 19th centuries. In social and economic terms the Czech-Moravian border was a social periphery which attracted industrialisation before the Second World War and particularly during the communist regime. Although the region does not touch the Austrian border, it is close enough to be influenced by its proximity. Thus the region profited from the opening of borders after 1989. However, the economic changes of the last decade of the 20th century led to difficulties in the region, including the collapse of traditional enterprises and unemployment[19]. This explains the high expectations and the effort put into the development of UNESCO and festival tourism[20].

Public use of history

The three regions have developed strategies for the improvement of similar situations, within a comparable space of time. Changes began in Gascony after the 1982 law of decentralisation created the present day regions in France as *collectivités territoriales*. The transformations in the present regions of east central Europe started in the 1990s. All three regions attempted to turn weakness to their advantage. The lack of industry or the process of de-industrialisation in these regions created the chance to take advantage of a new economic opportunity, tourism. To get on the tourist map a region needs a good strategy. History has an important role in the strategies of these three regions, which is to brand them, in order to give the region a particular image. This is quite common, as the historicity of places is highly valued not only by occidental culture, but also by global tourism, and therefore a place without a known history is handicapped in the market for investments or any other kind of economic activities, and even more so for tourism. This, of course, is not particularly revealing. What is more interesting is the question of the agents in this process. Who are the carriers of the idea of regionalism and who invents these strategies? What kind of history and memory was, and is, used in order to encode the identity of the town and its region, and how was this done?

One commonly used and very prestigious way of profiting from a rich cultural history, which needs a large investment of time, and professional preparation, is inclusion on the UNESCO world list of cultural heritage. Visits to UNESCO sites have proven to be quite fashionable amongst tourists. The three regions that this chapter is studying in comparative perspective have made use of this strategy.

In the heart of Gascony, in the department of Gers we can identify four sites which have proven their particular qualities and have been registered on the UNESCO list. The first is the pilgrim's road to Compostela; the second, the Roman bridge in Artigue. The other two locations are, in fact, stopping points on the route, namely the cathedral in Auch, and the Collegiate Church in La Romieu[21].

In Moravia, there are seven monuments registered by UNESCO, and three of them are on the Czech-Moravian border: the city and castle of Telč on the Czech side, and Zelená hora (church) near Žďár, and Třebíč (the church and the Jewish city and cemetery) on the Moravian side[22].

In the case of north-eastern Slovakia, the historical centre of the town of Bardejov, with its Jewish historical heritage, has been listed by UNESCO[23]. In 2002 the wooden churches of the Carpathian regions of Slovakia were proposed for evaluation, these include a number of important Greek-Catholic and Orthodox churches[24]. Last to be registered was the Primeval Beech Forest which stretches across the borders of Ukraine and Slovakia[25]. Also, in the Dukla region, there is a very important *lieu de mémoire*, which has not been put forward to be registered on this prestigious list. However, it may have an even greater influence on regional identity: this is the mountain pass, the site of battles during the First and Second World War and, today, the location of large Second World War cemeteries and memorials on both the Polish and Slovak sides of the border. It is the place that gives the region its name, and contributes greatly to its identity.

This leads us to the question of the impact of these official UNESCO sites on regional identity, and the nature of other historically, culturally or geographically defined components of that identity. How is this choice made? Who is behind it and how does it happen? We can search for answers predominantly in the regional press, in self-presentations and in guides produced by authors who are interested in the region, write with empathy, but are often outsiders. The author, in her analysis, also relies on 'observation' which provided her with closer insight and comparable evidence[26].

The case of Gers in Gascony

The most intensive declarative identification with the Gascon culture and mode of life is present in Auch, the departmental town of Gers, which has declared itself the capital and heart of Gascony. The *Maison de Gascogne* hosts exhibitions and sales of regional products, which are all labelled with 'stickers' confirming that they are really, truly and only *gascon*. History is a very strong component of this image, it is cumulative, and everything is included, even difficult and bloody conflicts. The presentation of history is factual and consensual. However it has several highlights, and some very positively presented heroes: *le bon roi Henry*, *le brave d'Artagnan* and all the cohorts of *cadets de Gascogne* in his shadow, and the *intendant* Etigny, who is particularly present in Auch. Both d'Artagnan and Etigny have statues in the town. The two sites of architectural heritage – the cathedral in Auch and the collegiate church in La Romieu are objects of pride and care. Both are also stops on the *Route Jacquaire* which crosses the department, and has many stops here. The pilgrim route to Santiago de Compostela is publicised with an effort to present the pilgrimage as the lived experience of history, and as the opportunity for healthy hiking in well preserved landscapes[27]. The role of history as part of identity is accompanied by the image of nature unspoiled by industry and the defects of modern civilisation, and by openness to new technologies (cyberspace). Last, but not least, we discover the image of the region as a place where it is a pleasure to live and settle down, and not only to visit[28]. During the summer months the principal journal of the French South, *La Dépêche du Midi,* publishes a special issue highlighting all places of interest and all events in the region, and distributes this offprint free of charge. This last argument, "the region, where it is a pleasure to live" is heavily publicised in the journal, on the regional websites and supported by the programme of events. These events are the main public effort to display how to live in the region and how to share the experience of regional identity. Bernard Kayser, quoting Alain Lefebvre, called this trend a '*festivalomanie*', which is the symbiosis between culture and economic interests through tourism. The cultural events are meant to attract the visiting public as well as local elites, who wish to present their locality and region as interesting enough to justify their decision to settle there. The festivals come in various shapes and sizes, and experience varying degrees of success. The festivals of Gers are thought to be especially successful; four of them are particularly effective in attracting paying visitors. These events have a contemporary content and, as they have already been running for several years, the organizers believe that they have founded a new tradition. The most successful festivals in Gers include the festival of Jazz in Marciac, that of Country Music in Mirande and the races for trucks and motorcars in Nogaro. Only Pentecôtavic – a fiesta held on Pentecost – and corridas in Vic-Fézensac and in several other communities stem from regional culture. The same town also hosts a new tradition, the Tempo Latino, a festival of music of Latin and Afro-American origin, like salsa. In Gers, and Gascony as a whole, the role of the local initiatives of the villages and small towns in the regeneration of the region through tourism, has been of interest to researchers for about twenty years[29]. These small towns, full of remarkable architecture and rich in history, are charming *bastides*, but they attract far more visitors during a festival, which, although commercial, offers an opportunity for visitors to learn more about the history and culture of the region[30]. In Gers it is believed that these festivals prove the potential of *tourisme événementiel.* The festivals are no longer limited to the capital city or large important towns, such as Prague, Cannes, Avignon or Karlovy Vary. By holding them in an unknown locality, the events become effective tools in the local economy, and put the whole region on the map. The success of the Jazz festival in Marciac prompted the creation of a Country festival in Mirande in 1993. In consequence the neighbouring communities decided to create a consortium, *Coeur d'Astarac en Gascogne*, situated in the *département* of Gers, which aims to encourage cooperation and increase the regional benefit of festival tourism[31]. In the consortium there are only two communities which have more than thousand inhabitants and so the character of a small town, Mirande and Miélan. The Mayor of Mirande is the head of the consortium and the two towns have the strongest vote. Together they collect a special regional tax, and both have profited from the effect of festival tourism, which is clear from the growing numbers of paying visitors. Mirande is essential to these activities, and has benefited greatly from festival related events. In this context it would be interesting to compare Mirande's role in Gascon festival strategies with that of Třebíč, Bardejov and Svidník in their regions.

Festival tourism is only one part of the complex regional tourist policies of Gers. The other initiatives of this economic sector include: spas, agrotourism, family tourism, arts and historical monuments, sports and gastronomy. Although Gers has no direct access to the seashore, it offers a variety of landscapes, and tourist activities. The national network of *gîtes de France* has responded to the need for a sufficient number of beds for tourists. Although studies of this region do highlight an insufficient infrastructure, this does not appear to be as urgent when compared with insufficiencies of non-western regions.

The case of Třebíč in the Czech-Moravian Highlands

Although three sites in the Czech-Moravian Highlands (Českomoravská Vysočina) have been registered by UNESCO – Zelená Hora, Telč and Třebíč, each of which individually offers a particular image of the region – this chapter will focus on the last one. The cemetery in Zelená Hora, near the town of Žďár nad Sázavou, is decorated by an exquisite church in a Baroque/gothic style. Žďár is largely known as the site of old engineering industries, which does not particularly improve the image of the town. It is, however, surrounded by beautiful landscapes, which are protected and registered as a natural park – reservation Žďárské vrchy. The second monument, the town of Telč, is on the edge of Vysočina and opens onto the pond region of South Bohemia. Telč is a protected urban complex and castle, which was already registered on the list of urban reservations of the former Czechoslovak state[32]. The third, Třebíč, in the heart of the region, is a town with a long history. Although the town was once home to many drapers, Třebíč has been labelled as a town of cobblers due to its important leather and shoe production, which emerged in the mid-18th century, and made Třebíč the largest producer of leather in Moravia[33]. In 1931, Tomáš Baťa bought the shoe manufacturers from the local tanner and shoemaker Budishowsky and built a modern factory in Borovina, where he also constructed one of his famous settlements for workers. The descendant of the factory finally closed in 1999[34]. There was also a large engineering plant, which still exists; industries that used sophisticated textile knitting machines, which have disappeared; and a nuclear power station in Dukovany, which is not far from Třebíč. The role of this industrial heritage in the public image of the town is now overshadowed by the town's successful entry into the UNESCO club.

Třebíč has discovered that there is evidence of a historical coexistence of Christian and Jewish communities in the town and that the town was actually multi-cultural. This was not a forgotten past, but it was not fully known. The town has an old centre around the market square, and a castle with a remarkable church on the hill above the river Jihlava. There were also quite a few 20th century constructions, although these are no longer perceived to be aesthetically pleasing. There are many such towns in the country, some better preserved, with more refined architecture or nicer castles. Třebíč, however, is quite original, because the town adopted an unexpected strategy, and competed for registration in the UNESCO list with a part of its past which was rediscovered, reconstructed and reintegrated into the town's identity as its unique and most marketable quality. Surprisingly, this rediscovered past has contributed significantly to a stronger local identity.

As in many Moravian towns, Jewish merchants and artisans have settled in the town of Třebíč since the middle ages[35]. The Jewish community resided in a rural settlement below the castle, separated from the Christian town by the river. This area became a Ghetto between 1723 and 1849, until the full emancipation of the Jewish community in 1850 transformed the settlement into an urban district. From this time Jews could move out of the Ghetto into other parts of the town, which they did, and some bought houses in the best places around the square. The old Jewish town was left to the town's poor. The holocaust and Nazi persecution, however, resulted in a total disappearance of the Třebíč Jews. The Jewish district slowly became dilapidated, and in the last decade of the 20th century it was inhabited by the Roma community. The old Jewish town consisted of small houses, around two streets which followed the river. Across the hill, not visible from the town's square, was the Jewish cemetery. As the cemetery was the property of the Jewish Community, and there were no more Jews in town, it was no longer used. It deteriorated so much that its total reconstruction and removal was planned by the town authorities. However, a former grammar school professor, Bohumír Pavlík, who grew up near this cemetery, found it extremely regrettable that this cultural treasure, and the memories it evoked, would soon disappear, and so he initiated its historical renovation. He began his work alone, but then he sought the assistance of the grammar school students and volunteers in the town; later help arrived from across the republic and eventually from all over the world. Gradually the cemetery wall was restored, the tombs recovered and cleaned. This public initiative, carried out by volunteers, changed the destiny of the cemetery. Some funding was received from the ministry of culture, and step by step the heritage was rediscovered, restored and re-appreciated[36]. This also helped the revalorisation of the former Jewish town and its reconstruction became a town priority. The function of the district was changed: it is now primarily residential, with developing tertiary functions. There are also small offices, small businesses, galleries and restaurants. The large local factory, the Subak tannery, was refurbished as a town social housing project; in one of the former synagogues a museum and cultural centre was established, which organises various events; the area is also home to a festival of Jewish culture. The Jewish town, cemetery and the Roman Catholic Church, which is architecturally influenced by French Burgundy, obtained registration on the UNESCO list. The main agent of this successful story was the old professor, who had begun its successful reconstruction in 1983. Without him and the student volunteers, the acceptance of Třebíč onto this prestigous list in 2003 would not have been possible. This success story has had a very positive effect on Třebíč, and it also influences the town's neighbourhood. The reconstruction of the old Jewish town was facilitated by a creative and innovative approach and the support of various civic initiatives. In quite a short time it became acknowledged as the major component of the town´s identity, overshadowing all others.

The case of Bardejov, Svidnik and the Dukla region

The two towns of Bardejov and Svidnik are located in north-eastern Slovakia, not far from one another. The story of Bardejov is a variation on that of Třebíč combined with that of Telč. Bardejov has one of the best preserved historical centres among the medieval towns of Slovakia, largely due to the fact that the region was not touched by the first wave of industrialisation in the 19th century. Near to the town are spas that take advantage of the mineral springs which have long attracted many important visitors. The heritage site that led to the town's inclusion on the UNESCO list is a recently discovered suburban Jewish settlement, where the *mikve* [ritual bath] was found and reconstructed. Thus Bardejov, which already enjoyed the charm typical of old merchant towns, obtained the extra advantage of membership in the UNESCO club, which is generally perceived to be of great benefit to the region. However, the identity of the region near the Dukla pass has been influenced by a totally different story. It is a story of poverty, war, destruction, painful losses, and post-war reconstruction. These are the memories that influence the identity of Svidník, which, although its known history goes back almost seven hundred years, has no built heritage. Svidník is a completely new, modern town; nevertheless its history is creating its identity. The town and its surrounding area is a *lieu de mémoire par excellence.* It is not only that the area is replete with war memorials and cemeteries; the act of repeated commemoration sustains the memory, and unites the town community. The agents of this memory are the local government, the town hall, history museums and the schools. The community preserves the memory of war, and the stories of reconstruction. It has its favourite heroes, and it keeps their stories alive. The division of Czechoslovakia into the Czech and Slovak states, raised a very contentious question: to whom will the memory of Dukla now belong? Will it be nationalized, and become only Slovak, or will it also remain a Czech *lieu de mémoire*? Some actors were indifferent: however, for some it was a politically problematic continuity of the previous regime. The representatives and inhabitants of the town and region of Svidník, believed that this place of memory could be reinterpreted. By a coincidence of interests the town hall representatives on the Polish side of the border, in the town of Dukla and the Consulate general of the Czech Republic in Polish Katowice, both began to develop the image of the war memorials as places of interaction between four or even five memories – Slovak, Polish, Czech, Ukrainian and Russian. After fourteen years of systematic work, this form of commemoration is accepted as a tradition. It is built on the common interpretation of the battle of Dukla, as the most important mountain battle of the Second World War. All victorious powers have their great battles; in this part of Europe, we have Dukla. The commemoration has an established ritual which starts on the Polish side, in the war cemetery in Dukla, where Czechoslovak, Soviet and Polish combatants are buried. It continues at the memorial cross, which was donated by Pope John Paul II, and then at two other war graves of Czechoslovak soldiers. The commemoration at Dukla is opened by a military ritual in which military units and individuals are called to stand to order, to which it is replied that those who were called fell on the field of honour. This ceremony, performed by a regional regiment dressed in a special uniform, is a very emotional act, intended to invoke empathy and patriotic feeling amongst local students, who participate with veterans and other guests in the commemoration. The ceremonies honouring the dead that take place here, at the cross and the other two graves, are accompanied by the prayers of Catholic, Orthodox, and Greek Catholic clergymen. The next day the commemorations continue on the Slovak side of the border, where the presence of the president of the republic provides the gravity of an official state act. This memorial helps to maintain the historical consciousness of a border town that is losing population through economic migration, and trying to find new forms of economic development, due to the decline of the farming and textile industries. The area also benefits from the varied ideas and values that have been created by its place on a cultural crossroad. A similar situation prevails on the Polish side of the border, which is one of the most peripheral and remote regions in the country. Poland has few highland regions, due to this the mountainous landscape of the south is a popular attraction for urban tourists. This has led to the emergence of a better infrastructure for tourism, and the appearance of the region in popular tourist guidebooks. Due to the fact that Slovakia is mostly mountainous, and has many traditional resorts, Svidník has to make much more effort to get onto the tourist map. It has beautiful landscapes, interesting rural wooden architecture and excellent local cuisine, but it lacks infrastructure, marketable beds and hotels.

Strategies for the revival of the region

When Bernard Kayser analysed the situation in the rural regions of Western Europe, particularly in France, and questioned who was behind the strategies for *renaissance rurale*, he defined its preconditions and the framework in which it functioned. First, he concluded that the process of rebirth in rural regions varies from place to place, and takes the form of a social movement. It is driven by the will of those who live in the region, and the willingness of decision makers at various social levels to take this movement into account. Kayser argues that *renaissance* is not the usual process in every rural region. On the contrary we find all phases from rebirth to decline: from *renaissance* through *décadence* to *désertification*. The social movement of regional rebirth appears only in regions having favourable conditions, and it has been encouraged by the reversal of the values of urban society. Rural culture, which was formerly despised by modern urban society, came to be admired. Similarly, an idealised image of rural landscapes emerged, comprised of idealised villages embellished with flowers and free of the noises and smells of everyday life. This image of the rural world also integrates the small provincial burghs and towns and their societies. The flight from the towns and the rejuvenation of rural landscapes are two sides of the same coin. In this context, some authors use a newly created term, rurbanisation. This concept, however, is more associated with urban-rural peripheries, while the study of the renaissance of the rural landscape focuses more on regions that are distant from urban centres, in the *campagne profonde*[37].

Fig. 5
Initiatives of valorisation of the historical heritage: Lombez in Gers.

The renaissance of agricultural regions, according to Kayser, is the result of various initiatives and releases the hidden potential of the rural world, which is based on social structures, on monuments, buildings of historical importance and institutional networks at a regional and local level. He highlights the inventive new capacities of rural societies and positive approaches to the implementation of innovations, be they economic, social, technological or cultural. Kayser, himself based in Toulouse in provincial France, believes this innovative rural movement has an important influence on society, as it deconstructs the border between the dominant, urban world, and the dependent rural periphery. It may seem to some (like Yves Lacoste) to be an overuse of the term periphery, which is also an important concept describing the organisational trends of both modern and post-modern society: however, in this context it seems hardly imaginable that one could find a more pertinent term[38].

Furthermore, the innovative spirit in rural and small urban societies was facilitated by their reframing or restructuring. B. Kayser points to a synergy of indigenous rural settlement and new social groups which settled or resettled in the rural environment. These social groups include a variety of professions from artisans, workers, and employees up to managers, entrepreneurs, intellectuals or artists.

What has been presented in these case studies, confirms the conclusion previously made by B. Kayser: *'la symbiose entre la culture et l'économie passe essentiellement par le tourisme. L'action culturelle est destinée a constituer un pôle d'attraction pour un public extérieur tout en satisfaisant les aspirations des élites locales'*[39]. The innovations that are successful are those that animate the place and its society, propose the residents and visitors to live through the experience and do not only promote the individual locality, but its entire region.

The project to revive rural regions in France was supported by the *politique culturelle* of the French republic and of regional governments as an answer to the critical conditions of deeply rural regions. We have to bear in mind that these policies emerged after the law of decentralisation introduced by the Mitterand government in 1982. In Slovakia (and Poland) and in the Czech Republic efforts to regenerate rural regions appeared as a reaction to economic changes after 1990. The projects were stimulated by unemployment and economic migration from such regions on one hand, and by various projects offered to the regions by the EU and consequently by the state governments on the other.

In both Western and East-Central Europe, rural regions have recently become more appreciated by urban societies. There has been a renaissance in their cultural life and more activities have been developed. In Gers, in Gascony, and in the Czech-Moravian Highlands it is pertinent to speak of a tendency to return to the countryside, or to flee the town for the sake of the *périurbain,* or rurban, small towns and villages. All these regions have seen extensive cooperation between all interested parties, including the original inhabitants, those who returned and resettled, those who chose to move from the city to the rural region and those who organized public life in that region. Together they have discovered the principles of creativity and an appreciation of innovation. They have rejuvenated regional cultural life, a process which has been concentrated in small towns and burghs.

In France, the process has been more the result of redistribution and diffusion of surplus, rather than the result of crisis. Social geographers evaluate the situation as part of the continual growth of state revenue, although slow and with problems, which permits attempts to reach spatial balance in support of regional culture. Gers is a successful example, although the picture is far from ideal. France is, of course, a special case. It is large and has a significant number of regions with distinct cultural identities, but the rebirth of regionalism is not exclusive to France, or to the 'old' countries of the European Union.

The three case studies that have been presented in this chapter, demonstrate that we have to reconsider the relationship between urban and rural space and the character of the frontier between them. In modern society this frontier had negative connotations. These are now dissolving, as the infrastructure permitting comfortable life in rural conditions seems more developed.

Regional identity is very important for the self-esteem of local societies. It has been demonstrated in the case studies that it is the result of the systematic efforts of local elites and volunteers from elsewhere, who may or may not be professional historians or art historians. The local, the regional, and the national cannot be separated. Local identity loses much of its importance without the regional perspective and the importance of a region is justified through its role within a national or supranational context.

There also appears to be a crisis in the perception of novelty and in the presentation of innovation. There is a belief that the repeated, the old and the traditional have a better chance of being accepted. Urban society increasingly values historicity and many are questioning, contesting and even rejecting the aesthetic and technical value of most recent (20th century) investments. In the information age, when increased travel opportunities and internet communication have transformed access to information, it is no longer easy to trace how the ideas that inspired the renewal of rural space emerged. On the other hand it is very interesting to analyse how these changes were produced, who decided to implement them and how the structures of civic society were involved.

Although sociologists and historians have recognised the contribution of smaller towns towards various innovations, in public discourse small towns were, until recently, perceived as the home of conservative societies fond of traditions and resistant to change. Bernard Kayser has pointed to a new paradigm of *renaissance rurale,* which he characterises as a revolution in values. Kayser mainly draws on sociological research and appreciates the new inventive capacity of the *monde rural*, which is not only the village and hamlet, but also the small town. He emphasises the novelty of its ability to *valoriser les innovations*, whether economic, social, technological or cultural[40]. Kayser has also analysed the changes in the nature of the border between urban and rural spaces and societies. He believes that, at the end of the 20th century, it can be characterised more as a cultural frontier than as a physical border; fluid and more permeable. Rural and urban landscapes intertwine, and rural and urban settlements are often difficult to discern, especially in western countries. In Western Europe we can see a simultaneous convergence and penetration of rural and urban regions; this process, however, does not occur with the same intensity and dynamics in East Central-Europe.

Conclusion

The border between the urban and rural in East-Central Europe can be explained more often in terms of culture, than in terms of economics, finances, or technologies. The difference between urban and rural was, and perhaps still is, most clearly perceived by the absence of urban comfort and amenities, like sidewalks and street lights, let alone various urban services. The lack of these symbols of urban settlement in rural areas is largely the result of the decisions of local government. During the 1990s, the redefinition of urban space in East-Central Europe created new internal borders between districts. Following the attempted gentrification of dilapidated quarters, significant changes were made to urban areas. Over the last fifteen years, the rediscovery of urban spaces and their redefinition has had a significant impact on large cities, especially capitals. The policies and choices of small towns were partially inspired by those of the capitals. These ideas were swiftly adopted due to the advantages of modern communications technology. Memory and historical heritage helped to intensify a feeling of collective memory central to the strategies of regional revival used by planners and investors, as well as by civic bodies. Ruth Wallach has demonstrated in the preceding chapter that art in a city is important business in contemporary societies[41]. This exploration of the strategies of small towns and provincial regions suggests that, in small towns, history has a marketable value, and can become part of business. Artistic monuments and historical heritage are used as instruments to motivate identification and consequently for labelling urban space to facilitate its usage and understanding[42]. The strategies of small towns and provincial regions also demonstrate a need to identify with larger units, which may be imagined national or even supranational communities. This is testified by street names, museums and monuments commemorating not local, but national history. This is an important factor in the struggle for a collective identity which has both a cultural and a social content. This tendency is not a novelty, as is demonstrated by the analysis carried out by Jaroslav Ira[43].

Fig. 6
Square next to the war memorial in Barran, Gers, named after patriotic association *Le Souvenir français* created in 1887 in Alsace Lorraine during German occupation. Members are supposed to care for war graves and memorials. (Photograph by the author, 2007)

Creating a collective identity for a region requires a good knowledge of the regional history and culture. As we have seen in the examples presented, rather than proclaiming that as peripheries they are helpless victims of modernisation, strong, active civic bodies can elaborate appropriate strategies to contribute to the social and economic life of their region.

Only thus are they able to find support from national and international bodies, and succeed in putting themselves 'on the map', according to their desires and those of their citizens.

Notes

1 This chapter was written with the support of the research scheme of the Ministry of Education of the Czech Republic MSM 0021620827 *České země uprostřed Evropy v minulosti a dnes* [Czech Lands in the Middle of Europe, Past and Present], held by the Faculty of Philosophy and Arts of Charles University in Prague. Maps used in the article were compiled by the autor; the map of urban cores in Fig. 1 is based on P. Hohenbergh - L. Hollen Lees, *The Making of Urban Europe, 1000-1994*, Cambridge 1996, p. 371.

2 B. Kayser, *La renaissance rurale. Sociologie des campagnes du monde occidental*, Paris 1990, p. 316.

3 Z. Beňušková (ed.), *Tradičná kultúra regionov Slovenska. Prehlad charakteristických znakov* [Traditional culture of regions of Slovakia. An overview of characteristic features], Bratislava 2005, p. 241.

4 Basic statistics of the chosen regions: Gers - 6291 km2, 174,587 inhabitants; Auch - 21838 inhabitants (1999); Vysočina - 6795 km2, 511,645 inhabitants; Třebíč - 38882 inhabitants (2007); Prešovský kraj - 8993 km2, 789968 inhabitants; Svidník - 12384 inhabitants (2005); Bardejov -33374 inhabitants (2005).

5 http://www.paysportesdegascogne.com/pays/t_present.php (visited on 1 January 2008).

6 G. Sourbadère, *La Terre et les Hommes en Gascogne*, Auch 2001, pp. 9-19.

7 R. Escarpit, *Comment peut-on être gascon?* in R. Escarpit (ed): *La Gascogne. Pays, nation, région?*, Paris 1982, pp. 9-10.

8 E. Le Roy Ladurie, *Histoire de France des régions. La périphérie française, des origines à nos jours*, Paris 2001, p. 272 ff..

9 *Novempopulanie* or *Aquitanie IIIe* of the Gallo-Roman period took its name from the *Vascons*, the peoples that crossed the Pyrenées from the south, seeking refuge from the Visigoths. It became the duchy of Gascony in 768, in 1036 it came under the control of the family of Poitiers-et-Aquitaine. In 1137 it was united to the French crown through the marriage of Aliénor d'Aquitaine to Louis VII, but through her second marriage with Henry II Plantagenet (1152) Gascony was under English rule until 1453, when it was re-united with France by Charles VII.

10 The idea of creating a province, which would integrate all regions of Gascony was a project of the *intendant* Mégret d'Etigny. Auch used to be the seat of a *generalité* and *intendant* between 1716-1789.

11 *Regióny Slovenska. Regions of Slovakia*, Statistical Office of the Slovak Republic, Bratislava 2004, pp. 46 -49.

12 P. Gojdič, *Svidník*, Svidník 1996 (multilingual booklet); regional journal published since 2001, "*Podduklianske Novinky*" has also its website www.ke.telecom.sk\podduklianskenovinky .

13 F. Braudel, *The Identity of France I. History and Environment*, New York 1990, esp. p. 85 ff.

[14] It is estimated that about 30% of the population is over 60 years of age, which explains the relatively low level of unemployment. According to the *Dictionnaire national des communes de France*, Edition conforme au recensement de 1990, Albin Michel/Berger-Levrault 1991, Gers had 174 587 inhabitants, at a density of 27.75 per km^2. The situation was similar in Ariège (27.84), Lot (29.88) and Aveyron (30.88).

[15] P. Deboflе, P. L. Feral, *Le Gers a deux cents ans (1790-1990). 200ème anniversaire de la création du département*, Auch 1990; P. L. Feral (ed.), *Pays du Gers. Coeur de la Gascogne I- II*, Pau 1988-1990.

[16] 18.5%, while the average for Slovakia was 13.1%, according to V. Krivý, V. Feglová, D. Balko, *Slovensko a jeho regióny: sociokultúrne súvislosti volebného správania* [Slovakia and its regions: social and cultural context of electoral behaviour], Bratislava 1996, p. 318.

[17] *Ibid.*, p. 317-320.

[18] It was estimated that from 45 000 inhabitants of Dukla region (Svidník and its district) 7.7% migrated to work abroad, i.e. Czech republic, USA and UK., *ibid.*, p. 324.

[19] According to the Czech statistic office by 1995 average unemployment was 13.1%; by the end of 2004 unemployment in the Vysočina region varied from 5.01 - 14.0%, while in the district of Třebíč it was 11-14.0%. http://www.czso.cz/xj/edicniplan.nsf/t/C3004347E5/$File/k38.jpg (2 January 2008).

[20] R. Zejda, *Třebíčsko. Turisticko-vlastivědný průvodce obcemi a jejich okolím* [Třebíč- region. Tourist and educational guide through communities and their surroundings], Tišnov 2001, esp. pp. 144-159.

[21] The route to Santiago de Compostella in France was registered in 1998; this included the Cathedral St. Marie in Auch and the Colegiate church in La Romieu; http://whc.UNESCO.org/en/list/868/multiple=1&unique_number=1019 (9 January 2008).

[22] The historic centre of Telč was registered in 1992; the Pilgrimage Church of St. John of Nepomuk at Zelená Hora (Žďár) in 1994; the Jewish quarter and St. Procopius basilica in Třebíč were registered in 2003. http://whc.UNESCO.org/en/statesparties/cz (9 December 2007).

[23] Bardejov was registered in 2000. http://whc.UNESCO.org/en/statesparties/sk (8 December 2007).

[24] http://whc.UNESCO.org/en/tentativelists/1730/ (8 December 2007).

[25] http://whc.UNESCO.org/en/list/1133 (8 December 2007).

[26] The author has visited the compared regions many times in various ways, but her observations were not carried out using an ethnological method.

[27] P. Huchet, Y. Boëlle, *Sur les chemins de Compostelle*, Rennes 1999.

[28] J.-F. Aramendy, T. Casel, C. David, P. Labaume, L. Laffitte, M. Larribe, P.Pieux, *Paysages de Midi-Pyrenées*, Toulouse 2000.

[29] See Kayser, *La renaissance rurale* cit., p. 255-6; G. Alirol, *Preface* to G. Tautil (ed.), *Chemins d'Occitanie. Espace, territoire, identité, démocratie (politique occitane, 1974-2000)* Paris/Montréal (Canada) 1997, p. 11-14; these efforts are also documented in the recent work of A. Theulle. *Les manifestations culturelles, facteur de développement local? L'exemple du festival de country de la ville de Mirande (Gers) et son incidence pour la communauté de communes du 'Coeur d'Astarac en Gascogne'*, Mémoire de maitrise d'aménagement du territoire, Université Paul Valéry, Montpellier, Juin 2004, p. 124.

[30] B. Cursente, G. Loubès, *Villages gersois, II - Les bastides*, Collection 'Gascogne Insolite', Publication Chambre d'Agriculture du Gers, Auch 1991; J. Dubourg: *Histoire des bastides de Midi-Pyrénées*, Luçon 1997.

[31] Communauté de communes 'Coeur d'Astarac en Gascogne' - 16 communities, 7110 inhabitants. The consortium was created in 1999 by 5 communities: Mirande, Miélan, Laas, Monclar sur l'Osse, Saint-Maur. Later it grew: by 1 January 2004 it had accepted a further six, and by 2004 it had 16 members : Armous, Cau, Bars, Bassoues, Castelnau d'Angles, Laas, Lamazère; Marseillan; Mascaras; Miélan,

Mirande; Monclar sur l'Osse, Montesaquiou, Mouches, Pouylebon, St Christaud and St Maur Soules. http://www.coeur-dastarac.fr/coeur-dastarac/coeur-dastarac/accueil.htm (11 January 2008)

[32] *Paměť měst. Městské památkové rezervace v českých zemích* [Memory of cities. Urban heritage reservations in the Czech Lands], Prague 1975, p. 336.

[33] J. Janák, *Třebíč. Dějiny města II* [Třebíč. History of the town, II], Brno 1981, passim.

[34] The former factory is now waiting to be turned into a residential district. http://www.trebicsky-zpravodaj.cz/borovinska-tovarna-z-pohledu-blizke-budoucnosti_85.html (1 September 2007).

[35] J. Klenovský, *Jewish monuments of Třebíč*, Brno 2004, passim; R. Fišer, *Třebíč. Osudy židovských domů* [Třebíč. The destinies of Jewish houses], Třebíč 2005, pp. 21-29.

[36] The cemetery was registered on the national list of historical monuments and landmarks in 2002 (Klenovský, *Jewish monuments* cit., p. 66.)

[37] Kayser, *La renaissance rurale* cit., pp. 28-30.

[38] Y. Lacoste, *De la géopolitique aux paysages. Dictionnaire de la géographie*, Paris 2003, pp. 293-294.

[39] Kayser, *La renaissance rurale* cit., pp. 255-6, citing A. Lefebvre in *Aujourd'hui, la culture du monde rural*, Toulouse 1987.

[40] B. Kayser, *La renaissance rurale* cit., passim.

[41] R. Wallach, *Marking the City. Place-making and the Aesthetics of Urban Spaces*, in this volume, pp. 281-298.

[42] K. Lynch, *The Image of the City*, New York 1960; on the contribution of the UNESCO list to the instrumentalisation of heritage see T. Vahtikari, *Urban Interpretations of World Heritage. Re-defining the City* in M. Niemi, V. Vuolanto (eds.), *Reclaiming the City. Innovation, Culture, Experience*, Helsinki 2003, pp. 63 - 79; This issue is explored in this volume by J. Tancer, *The Image of the City as a Site of Memory: Bratislava in Modern Travel Literature*, pp. 267-280.

[43] J. Ira, *Creating Local and Broader Identities: Historical Monographs on Bohemian, Moravian, and Galician Towns, 1860-1900*, in this volume, pp. 251-266.

Bibliography

Braudel F., *Identité de France I. Histoire et environement*, Paris 1986 [*The Identity of France I. History and Environment*, New York 1988].

Illner M., *Regional Development in the Czech Republic Before and After the Accession. Some Speculative Scenarios*, in "Informationen zur Raumentwicklung", Nov.-Dec. 2001, pp. 751-756.

Illner M., Andrle A., *The Regional Aspect of Post-Communist Transformation in the Czech Republic*, in "Czech Sociological Review", 2, 1994, p. 107-127.

Id., *The Terrain of Local Politics in the Czech Republic*, in "*Centre for Central and Eastern European Studies, Working Paper No. 14, Rural Transition Series*", pp. 1-14, http://www.liv.ac.uk/history/centres/cehome.htm.

Hughes J., Sasse G., Gordon C., *The Regional Deficit in Eastward Enlargement of the European Union: Top Down Policies and Bottom Up Reactions*, "Working Paper" 29/01, first published in 2001 by the ESRC "One Europe or Several?" Programme, Sussex European Institute, University of Sussex, http://www.one-europe.ac.uk, p. 55.

Kayser B., *La renaissance rurale. Sociologie des campagnes du monde occidental*, Paris 1990.

Kolb B. M., *Tourism Marketing for Cities and Towns. Using Branding and Events to Attract Tourists,* Elsevier, Oxford 2006.

Le Roy Ladurie E., *Histoire de France des régions. La périphérie française, des origines à nos jours,* Paris 2001.

Lipták L., *Changes of Changes. Society and Politics in Slovakia in the 20th Century,* Bratislava 2002.

Rugg D. S., *Eastern Europe*, London 1985.

Vahtikari T., *Urban Interpretations of World Heritage. Re-defining the City* in Niemi M., Vuolanto V. (eds.), *Reclaiming the City. Innovation, Culture, Experience*, Studia Fennica Historica 6, Helsinki 2003, pp. 63-79.

Conclusion: Frontiers and Identities on Urban, Regional and National Scales

Luďa Klusáková, Laure Teulières

The focus of this volume has been on urban perspectives in the exploration of various spatial scales of interaction concerning frontiers and identities. Its nineteen chapters highlight the importance of the European city and its distinctive features in the shaping of European societies. In this context, a major theme is the notion of "cities and their regions". This denotes, in the first place, the hinterland of the town or city, but secondly also the wider region to which the city, with its hinterland, belongs. This is invariably an important interaction, and it is a major focus of almost all the book's chapters. It includes both the expansion of the administrative town border into suburban territories, and the incorporation of surrounding villages within the city limits. The frequent tendency towards the social and/or ethnic domination of the countryside by the city should also be pointed out. Within this context, the reader may note also various points of comparison in regard to long-lasting socio-ethnic divisions which arise from this urban versus rural cleavage. In Ireland, for instance, the particular methods of maintaining the 'Englishness' of the town set it apart from its hinterland where concurrently a sort of 'gaelicisation' of society operated. Another instance which is explored is the ethnic/national relationships between Latvians and Germans, which also find an echo in the relations (and the tensions) between Romanians and Hungarians in Transylvania. Such troubled relationships powerfully influenced urban social life. Many chapters explore them. There is also a particular emphasis here on the relationship between chronology, social and historical context, since the authors are mostly historians with anthropological interests or sociologists with historical training. And since the volume's time span is very long, from the middle ages to the present, the types of situations analysed are necessarily very varied.

We may imagine Europe's multiple cultural identities as a flower garden, in which the cities constituted a particular flower, lovingly tended by the gardeners – in essence the custodians of the city's identity, who might range from the town hall, to urban dwellers, or even authors writing about the city. Urban societies mirror the problems of national societies, and reflect more general Europe-wide themes. Even just focusing on the connecting themes of major importance as they were defined in the previous volume, viz. (1) Civility and Savagery; (2) Construction and Deconstruction of Borders and

Frontiers; (3) Challenging Identities (most often by mobility or migrations); and (4) Construction of Images and Stereotypes, we may say that they have reappeared in full measure in this third volume in the analyses of the problem at a lower – urban and regional – level.

The link between the present analysis of urban and regional perspectives on frontiers and identities, which consequently draw in the national perspective, and these four emblematic themes was not deliberately planned. It has come about naturally. It is a spontaneous outcome of the exchange of ideas and the results of research. The connecting themes illustrated and developed the very diverse – sometimes obvious, sometimes quite sophisticated and hidden – connections to the larger and smaller issues of discourse in the social sciences at present, and underlined the constructed aspect of both, the frontier and identity as a result of construction and imagination, and of contest and conquest. The lesson which was already formulated in the volume *Imagining Frontiers – Contesting Identities*, that frontiers and identities are formulated, constructed, challenged and deconstructed on various different levels, and in various dimensions – in local societies, in the framework of relations between urban and regional social networks, but also at inter-regional, national and transnational levels – is further explored in the present book. These various levels and planes of identification and modes of construction of frontiers point to more general methodological questions, as well as to particular concepts and sources of a problematic nature.

Several important issues emerged in the chapters, and these have been discussed from various points of view. First, there are the internal, physical and administrative borders, established by city administration, by lords, by the state, by local rules, which promote very strong senses of identity. The link to the paradigm of civility and savagery, one of the second-year connecting themes, is very clear in the discussions by William Aird of gendered spaces in Durham and by Kieran Hoare of Irish towns. On the one hand, the state exploited towns for its own purposes, but on the other, there is little or no difference between gender prejudices and the discourse of savagery. Another connecting theme explores landmarks and cityscape as key elements of identity. Town walls not only create new physical but also symbolic borders, as is shown by Bram Vannieuwenhuyze in the example of medieval Brussels or Frédéric Moret for the suburbs of 19th-century Paris. Significant monuments also contribute to the shaping of urban identities. They sometimes even help in the preservation of memory in a repressive context: the Adam Mickiewicz monument destroyed by the Nazis played this role for the Polish people of Krakow. Various other chapters in the volume also highlight the extent to which architecture and monuments help to define and characterize urban spaces and identities. This process is epitomized by the way in which public art projects help to define place, as Ruth Wallach shows by the examples of Groningen and Los Angeles.

The chapters in this book have focused on the analysis of the processes of identification, which are supported by the construction of physical or symbolic barriers, from local, urban, regional, or national perspectives. In most instances, it has seemed preferable to explore this process in comparative perspective. In those cases where a direct comparison is problematic, parallel histories suggest lessons of a comparative nature. The comparative approach is present first in the general strategy of the research group, in the questioning common to the team, and second in the particular method of systematic analysis by the authors of the several chapters. Although the nineteen chapters display the problematic in vast range across and beyond Europe, the lacunae in themes and periods are also very evident. These reflect the limited size of the volume, and the particular interests of members of the research group. In terms of their regional scope, the limited range of members' interests obviously leaves the volume unbalanced, but intensive collaboration year on year promotes a more coherent and cohesive presentation of results. These gaps are less pronounced if the other volumes in the series are considered: cross-checking is facilitated by the index which also points up cross-references.

The peculiar, fluid and interconnected relations and tensions between and among religions and ethnicities, or between mentalities and politics, can hardly be separated from one another. They represent the strongest theme, the most obvious tensions, relations, and conflicts which are staged in the urban pageant. These tensions set people on the road: they initiate exile, and they motivate migration. These strong tensions and even conflicts were reflected in memoirs, and various personal documents, but also in judicial documents and those of religious communities, and in the periodical press of the modern and contemporary era. The reciprocal images of 'others' also point to the question of integration, tolerance or discrimination against alterity, the themes to which the third transversal theme volume is devoted.

The reflections and constructions of local and regional identities point on the one hand to diversity in the treatment of the various locations and dimensions of regions, on the other they all treat the city as a text and as a region as well. The imaginative side of identification, and the use of mental or cognitive mapping to explore it has appeared already in the previous volume, along with the comparative approach: in the present book, it can be followed like a 'thread of Ariadna' through more or less all chapters. However, the analysis of urban spaces and societies draws attention to the dichotomy of public and private in physical and social space, and this appears in the present volume as a new and important theme in the discussion of the research group.

Let us reflect for a moment on the overall profile of our volume. We see that it rests very firmly on the methodological pillars of the new urban history, mental mapping and identity theory, social interactions and interethnic relations. The book shows how collaboration within and beyond the group, in this case with urban historians, has prompted a fruitful treatment of the urban theme through the prism of frontiers and identities. The book is distinctively urban, and the reaction of urban historians to it may perhaps open an interesting debate on frontiers and identities in urban spaces and societies.

The urban or the city-specific is here the factor which prompts the construction of barriers, or intensifies the identification of its inhabitants. The city is the 'stage' for frontiers and identities that really makes a difference. The city is clearly not just about the spatial scales but also about the peculiar environment, the city is an 'agent' which – hopefully we can agree on this – alters or gives new meanings or functions to frontiers and identities. For example, the chapters written by Ewelina Szpak and Anna Czocher have much to say about these points. In commentaries on the chapters, Elena Mannová raised the question of whether we can speak about the identity of the city. For her, the citizens have an identity, while the city has an image. The question is whether this difference encapsulates the theoretical approach, or whether it exists objectively. For many authors, such as for Olena Betlii, the spatial usage of the town engraves spatial stories into the palimpsest of the town, which can be read like a text. It has its image, but it also has its unmistakable identity. Jaroslav Ira again underlines the quite different sources of inspiration and hierarchy of importance depending on the chosen optics: Michel de Certeau, Kevin Lynch, Walter Benjamin (in urban perspective), versus Celia Applegate, Anthony D. Smith (in the flow between nation-region-city/locality) and with Larry Wolff and Frederik Barth (when frontiers, boundaries are in the ascendant), which make a difference in focus and in some cases in understanding or usage of particular terms. While Laurent Gaissad or Ruth Wallach explicitly refer to Foucault's notion of 'heterotopia', many of the authors in this volume tackle the question of frontiers and identity by insisting on discontinuity, porosity, and fluidity. They think it out within a framework of acculturation processes.

We may conclude that precisely the interaction between these urban and regional entities and/or dimensions is one of the most crucial and most fully developed themes of the volume and that, in very interesting ways, it raises basic questions about the definition and use of the notion of region in various dimensions and contexts. Region is the most frequently used notion in both urban and national contexts, and also within civilisational discourse. Is there a difference in understanding the region in regard to city-and-region relations as opposed to region-and-nation relations? And of course we should not forget city-nation relations. What are the rules for determining the borders of regions? They are optional, changeable, and instrumentalised as well. The citizens and other inhabitants of cities or regions can move in and out. Identification with a region can be multiple. One individual may have strong identity feelings with respect to several regions. In contrast, it is not that easy to move in and out where a national community or a state is concerned. Even nowadays it is not always possible to be a citizen of two states or effectively to have two national identities. The transition from one national/state community to another is not usually possible on the basis of mere personal decision. Large European cities of the 21st century are declared to be multicultural. In the early modern period, this multiculturality was defined mostly by language and religion, and was controlled by law (as Blanka Szeghyová and Markéta Rubešová show), while the concept of culture is now often used as synonym for civilisation. These problems of contemporary cities also raise the question of whether civilisational identity can be shared? Is it possible to multiply or readily to change one's religious identity? Perhaps in the 21st century all is possible, but in European societies in historical perspective, religious identity was unique, as Miroslav Hroch has claimed in our discussions. Also there is a basic difference in the way an individual becomes a member of regional community as opposed to a member of a national community.

The nation-building processes – so original to European conditions – have codified the rules of national identification, of the inclusion and exclusion from the national community, and they obviously differ strikingly from those of the town or region. The state and the nation claim that they are indispensable for stable social identification, while processes of urban (or local) and regional identification are optional. Thus the rise of national representation as a predominant process of identification has opened up a gap with respect to the earlier periods of time considered in the book. This phenomenon, as it has impacted deeply on urban and regional identities and helped in part to reshape them, has constituted a core problematic for historians, and not just because the chronology and rhythms of evolution are dissimilar in European space and history. How has the study of the relationship between the regional and national perspective, respectively the state and its regions, evolved in contemporary historiography and in the past? This is one of the main questions prompted by this conclusion. It also underlines, finally, the need for more comparative studies between European regions. These questions and suggestions, stemming from chapters of the present book, are already being addressed in the discussions surrounding the genesis of the fourth volume of the series, which will be devoted to frontiers and identities in the wider dimension of regions and states.

Notes on Contributors

William M. Aird

William M. Aird lectures on Medieval History at Cardiff University, Wales. He was awarded a PhD by Edinburgh University in 1991. With a particular interest in the history of the Normans in the 11th and 12th centuries, he is the author of *St. Cuthbert and the Normans. The Church of Durham, 1071-1153* (Woodbridge, 1998) and *Duke Robert Curthose of Normandy, 1087-1134* (Woodbridge, forthcoming). His current research concerns the medieval *Life of St Margaret of Scotland*.

Olena Betlii

Olena Betlii is Lecturer in EU foreign policy at the Diplomatic academy of Ukraine and Lecturer in History at the National University of "Kyiv-Mohyla academy" in Kiev, Ukraine, where she took her PhD. Her research interests cover mental mapping, regional identity, and otherness discourse issues with a particular interest in the development or construction of Central Europe's symbolic map and identity politics in terms of EU enlargement. Her bibliography contains fourteen articles on this topic.

Anna Czocher

Anna Czocher graduated from the Jagiellonian University is currently the department head at the Krakow branch of the Archives of the Institute of National Remembrance and she is a PhD student at the Faculty of History of the Jagiellonian University. She is completing a doctoral thesis entitled *Everyday Life in occupied Krakow in the years 1939-1945*, focusing on the history of the customs of the Polish inhabitants of the city (family life, leisure time, celebrations).

Laurent Gaissad

Laurent Gaissad completed a PhD in sociology and social sciences (University of Toulouse le Mirail, France, 2006), and presently holds a two-year post-doctoral fellowship at the Fonds de la Recherche Scientifique (FNRS / Université Libre de Bruxelles, Belgium) in a comparative history research program dedicated to "Norms, gender and sexuality" (19-20th centuries). His surveys on sex in public space (men-to-men and sex work), and his publications in various fields (socio-anthropology, urban history and geography, public health), lead him to work at present on the dialectics of exposure / secrecy in urban and rural contexts. Formerly teaching assistant in sociology and anthropology (urban studies and inter-cultural relations) in Toulouse, he is also a member of FRAMESPA (CNRS / University of Toulouse le Mirail).

Kieran Hoare

Kieran Hoare received his MA in Irish History in University College Cork, Ireland in 1993, with the thesis "The Earldom and Supremacy of Desmond: the case study of a lordship, 1329-1583". He is currently a doctoral student at National University of Ireland, Galway, Ireland. His areas of interest relate to the development of an urban oligarchy in Irish towns in the 15th and 16th centuries, their interaction with Tudor state formation and their hinterlands, as well as the operation of municipal government within the towns themselves.

Ute Hofmann

Ute Hofmann has studied Modern History, Sociology and Applied Linguistics at Chemnitz University of Technology. She graduated in 2006 and is now working on her doctoral thesis about the political engagement of the Bohemian nobility during the 1860s.

Jaroslav Ira

Jaroslav Ira graduated in 2005 with a degree in history and political science at Charles University in Prague. At present, he is a postgraduate student of general history at the same institution. He specializes in the modern history of East-Central Europe concentrating in particular on the formation of territorial, urban, and political identities as displayed in the chapter of this book, and on theoretical and methodological problems of historiography, urban studies, and the study of texts.

Dobrochna Kałwa

Dobrochna Kałwa is an Assistant Professor in the Institute of History (Jagiellonian University, Cracow). The main fields of her research interest are gender history, the history of feminism in Poland, oral history, the memory of communism and the history of everyday life in modern Poland. Among her publications are *An active woman in interwar Poland. Dilemma of women's movement*, and *Customs in Poland. From the Middle Ages to the Present* (as co-author).

Barbara Klich-Kluczewska

Barbara Klich-Kluczewska is Assistant Professor at the Institute of History, Jagiellonian University in Kraków. Her research interests cover the social and urban history of the post-war Poland; the history of everyday life and the history of customs in the 19th and 20th centuries, and the methodology of private life and alternative sources. She is the author of *Przez dziurke od klucza. Życie prywatne w Krakowie w latach 1945-1989* [Through the Keyhole. Private Life in Cracow 1945-1989]. Her current projects concern taboo as a mental border in the societies of Poland and Czechoslovakia in the 1960s and 1970s.

Luďa Klusáková

Luďa Klusáková is Associate Professor of History (1988) at the Faculty of Philosophy & Arts, Charles University in Prague, Czech Republic. Since 2000, she has been responsible for the Seminar of General and Comparative History. She took her scientific degree from the same university in 1981 for her comparative research on the modernization of European urban networks. Her publications include *The Road to Constantinople: The Sixteenth-Century Ottoman Towns Through Christian Eyes* (2002; and 2004 in Czech), as well as many articles on problems of urban innovations, modernity and backwardness. Recently, she was the editor of *"We" and "the Others": European Societies in Search of Identity, Studies in Comparative History (Studia Historica LIV, AUC Philosophica et Historica 3/2000, Prague 2004), and co-editor of "Meeting the Other" Studies in Comparative History* (*Studia Historica LVI, AUC, Philosophica et Historica 2/2003, Prague 2007).* Her current interest is represented by the chapter in this book.

Iakovos Michailidis

Iakovos Michailidis is an Assistant Professor in Contemporary and Modern History at the Department of History & Archaeology (Aristotle University of Thessaloniki, Greece). His research interests focus on population movements in South East Europe, the position of minorities and the intervention of the Great Powers. Among his recent publications are *The War of Statistics: Slav-Speaking Emigrants and Refugees from Greece (1912-1930)* and *Greek – Yugoslav Relations (1944-1949)* (in two volumes).

Frédéric Moret

Frédéric Moret completed a thesis in history (University Paris 7) in 1994 and is Maître de Conférences and Director of the Humanity and Social Sciences Department of the University Paris-Est Marne la Vallée. His first interests focused on the urban conceptions developed by the utopian socialists and he published on this subject *Les Socialistes et la Ville Grande-Bretagne, France. 1820-1850* (ENS éditions, 1999). At present, he works on different aspects of urban history in the first half of the 19th century : the impact of the building of the fortifications of Paris on the development of the metropolis, but also the municipal reform of 1835 in Great Britain. He coordinates a research project of his laboratory (Analyse Comparée des Pouvoirs, University Paris-Est Marne la Vallée) on the petitions sent to the French parliamentary assemblies from 1815 to 1940, supported by the French National Research Agency (ANR).

Florin Pintescu

Florin Pintescu is currently Associate Professor at the Ştefan cel Mare University of Suceava (Romania) where he teaches European Mediaeval History, Theory of International Relations, Geopolitics and Geostrategy. He received his Ph.D. from the Alexandru Ioan Cuza University of Iaşi (Romania) in 2003. His main research interests are European mediaeval military history, Geopolitics and Geostrategy.

Markéta P. Rubešová

Markéta P. Rubešová received her MA degree in General History and Hebrew Studies at Charles University, Prague, Czech Republic in 2007, with a thesis entitled 'The Ottoman State and Society as Reflected in Rabbinic Literature of the 16th - 18th Centuries'. She is currently a doctoral student at Charles University, Prague. Her research interests include Jewish history under Christianity and under Islam in a comparative perspective, the individual and society in the historical process, Jewish emancipation and 'assimilation', especially the question of continuity and change in the sphere of the individual and collective identities.

Blanka Szeghyová

Blanka Szeghyová studied history and archive studies, English and Latin languages at the Comenius University in Bratislava, Slovakia. In 2004 she completed her PhD. in history with a dissertation on *Judiciary and Judicial Practice in the Pentapolitana towns in the 16th Century* and in 2005 edited a book of conference proceedings *The Role of Magic in the Past.* At present, she is a junior researcher at the Historical Institute of the Slovak Academy of Sciences. Her research interests include crime and punishment, the history of mentalities and urban history in the early modern period.

Ewelina Szpak

Ewelina Szpak is a PhD student in her fourth year at the Institute of History, Jagiellonian University, Krakow. In 2004, she graduated from the History Department of the Jagiellonian University with her Master's thesis entitled *Everyday Life of the inhabitants of State Farms during the Communist Period*, which was published in 2005. The main fields of her research interests are oral and rural history, the history of mentalities and everyday life. Her current project concerns mental changes under communism in Polish rural societies.

Jozef Tancer

Jozef Tancer is an Assistant Professor in German Literature at the Department of German, Dutch and Scandinavian Studies, Comenius University in Bratislava. He received his Ph.D. degree in 2005 with a dissertation on the German press and literature in 18th-century Bratislava (published in 2008 as *In the Shadows of Vienna. German Press and Literature in the 18th century Bratislava,* Bremen, edition lumière). His research focuses on German culture in the Hungarian Kingdom, especially on the German historical press and travel literature. He has co-edited books of conference proceedings: *German Language and Culture in the Pressburg Region* (2002) and *German Language and Culture in the Zips Region* (2007).

Laure Teulières

Laure Teulières completed a PhD in history and in 2007 was elected *maître de conférence* at the History department of the Université de Toulouse – le Mirail. Specializing in migration history and cultural history, her most notable publications include *Immigrés d'Italie et paysans de France, 1920-1944* (Toulouse 2002), and she recently coordinated thematic papers such as "In memory of migrations" (*Diasporas. Histoire et sociétés*, 2005), "Images of migrations" (*Migrance*, 2007), and "Heritage and immigration" (*Les Cahiers de Framespa*, 2007). A member of the Laboratory FRAMESPA (CNRS / University of Toulouse in France), she works at present on issues of migrant memories and collective identities in France and in transnational perspective. She is also a member of the editorial committee for the scientific review «Diasporas. Histoire et sociétés».

Bram Vannieuwenhuyze

Bram Vannieuwenhuyze is a PhD student at Ghent University (Belgium). He has written a Masters thesis on the civil services of the medieval town of Brussels (1229-1477). Currently, he is completing his PhD thesis on the urban development of medieval and early modern Brussels, which will be defended at Ghent University in Spring 2008. In the future, he plans to conduct a comparative study on medieval toponomy and its relationship with urban society, topography and development.

Ruth Wallach

Ruth Wallach holds a Masters in Library Science from the University of California in Los Angeles (UCLA) and a Masters in Public Art Studies from the University of Southern California (USC). She is currently Head of the Architecture and Fine Arts Library at USC. In addition to disciplinary areas within academic librarianship, her research also focuses on public art within the contemporary urban context.

Index

Publications of the CLIOHRES Network of Excellence

Thematic Work Group 1, "States, Legislation, Institutions"

1. *Public Power in Europe: Studies in Historical Transformation*, James S. Amelang, Siegfried Beer eds., 2006;
2. *Communities in European History: Representations, Jurisdictions, Conflicts*, Juan Pan-Montojo, Frederik Pedersen eds., 2007;
3. *Making, Using and Resisting the Law in European History*, Günther Lottes, Eero Medijainen, Jón Viðar Sigurðsson eds., 2008.

Thematic Work Group 2, "Power and Culture"

1. *Power and Culture: Hegemony, Interaction and Dissent*, Ausma Cimdiņa, Jonathan Osmond eds., 2006;
2. *Power and Culture. Identity, Ideology, Representation*, Jonathan Osmond, Ausma Cimdiņa eds., 2007;
3. *Power and Culture: New Perspectives on Spatiality in European History*, Pieter François, Taina Syrjämaa, Henri Terho eds., 2008.

Thematic Work Group 3, "Religion and Philosophy"

1. *Religion, Ritual and Mythology. Aspects of Identity Formation in Europe*, Joaquim Carvalho ed., 2006;
2. *Religion and Power in Europe: Conflict and Convergence*, Joaquim Carvalho ed., 2007;
3. *Bridging the Gaps: Sources, Methodology and Approaches to Religion in Europe*, Joaquim Carvalho ed., 2008.

Thematic Work Group 4, "Work, Gender and Society"

1. *Professions and Social Identity. New European Historical Research on Work, Gender and Society*, Berteke Waaldijk ed., 2006;
2. *Reciprocity and Redistribution: Work and Welfare Reconsidered*, Gro Hagemann ed., 2007;
3. *Rhetorics of Work*, Dimitra Lampropoulou, Carla Salvaterra, Yannis Yannitsiotis eds., 2008.

Thematic Work Group 5, "Frontiers and Identities"

1. *Frontiers and Identities: Exploring the Research Area*, Lud'a Klusáková, Steven G. Ellis eds., 2006;
2. *Imagining Frontiers. Contesting Identities*, Steven G. Ellis, Lud'a Klusáková eds., 2007;
3. *Frontiers and Identities: Cities in Regions and Nations*, Lud'a Klusáková, Laure Teulières eds., 2008.

Thematic Work Group 6, "Europe and the World"

1. *Europe and the World in European Historiography*, Csaba Lévai ed., 2006;
2. *Sights and Insights: Interactive Images of Europe and the Wider World*, Mary N. Harris ed., 2007;
3. *Europe and its Empires*, Mary N. Harris, Csaba Lévai eds., 2008.

Transversal Themes

1. *Citizenship in Historical Perspective*, Steven G. Ellis, Guðmundur Hálfdanarson, Ann Katherine Isaacs eds., 2006.
2. *Immigration and Emigration in Historical Perspective*, Ann Katherine Isaacs ed., 2007.
3. *Discrimination and Tolerance in Historical Perspective*, Guðmundur Hálfdanarson ed., 2008.

Doctoral Dissertations

1. Florencia Peyrou, *La Comunidad de Ciudadanos. El Discurso Democrático-Republicano en España, 1840-1868* (2006);
2. Marta Smagacz, *Revitalisation of Urban Space. Social changes in Kraków's Kazimierz and the Ticinese District of Milan* (2007);
3. Andreas Gémes, *Austria and the 1956 Hungarian Revolution. Between Solidarity and Neutrality* (2008).
4. Vitaly V. Tichonov, *A Historian of the "Old School". Boris Ivanovich Syromyatnikov's Scientific Biography* (2008).

Under the aegis of CLIOHRES.net

www.cliohres.net

Printed in May 2008
by Industrie Grafiche Pacini Editore S.p.A.
on behalf of Edizioni PLUS - Pisa University Press